MW00700806

THE CAMBRIDGE EDITION OF THE
COMPLETE FICTION OF
HENRY JAMES

THE CAMBRIDGE EDITION OF THE
COMPLETE FICTION OF

HENRY JAMES

GENERAL EDITORS
Michael Anesko, *Pennsylvania State University*
Tamara L. Follini, *University of Cambridge*
Philip Horne, *University College London*
Adrian Poole, *University of Cambridge*

ADVISORY BOARD
† Martha Banta, *University of California, Los Angeles*
Ian F. A. Bell, *Keele University*
Gert Buelens, *Universiteit Gent*
Susan M. Griffin, *University of Louisville*
Julie Rivkin, *Connecticut College*
John Carlos Rowe, *University of Southern California*
Ruth Bernard Yeazell, *Yale University*
Greg Zacharias, *Creighton University*

THE CAMBRIDGE EDITION OF THE

COMPLETE FICTION OF

HENRY JAMES

HENRY JAMES

The Aspern Papers and Other Tales
1884–1888

EDITED BY

ROSELLA MAMOLI ZORZI
AND
SIMONE FRANCESCATO

CAMBRIDGE
UNIVERSITY PRESS

CAMBRIDGE
UNIVERSITY PRESS

University Printing House, Cambridge CB2 8BS, United Kingdom

One Liberty Plaza, 20th Floor, New York, NY 10006, USA

477 Williamstown Road, Port Melbourne, VIC 3207, Australia

314–321, 3rd Floor, Plot 3, Splendor Forum, Jasola District Centre,
New Delhi – 110025, India

103 Penang Road, #05–06/07, Visioncrest Commercial, Singapore 238467

Cambridge University Press is part of the University of Cambridge.

It furthers the University's mission by disseminating knowledge in the pursuit of
education, learning, and research at the highest international levels of excellence.

www.cambridge.org
Information on this title: www.cambridge.org/9781107029644
DOI: 10.1017/9781139342438

© Cambridge University Press 2022

This publication is in copyright. Subject to statutory exception
and to the provisions of relevant collective licensing agreements,
no reproduction of any part may take place without the written
permission of Cambridge University Press.

First published 2022

Printed in the United Kingdom by TJ Books Limited, Padstow Cornwall

A catalogue record for this publication is available from the British Library.

Library of Congress Cataloging-in-Publication Data
Names: James, Henry, 1843–1916, author. | Mamoli Zorzi, Rosella, 1940-author. |
Francescato, Simone, 1973– author.
Title: The Aspern papers and other tales, 1884–1888 / Henry James ; edited
by Rosella Mamoli Zorzi and Simone Francescato.
Description: Cambridge, United Kingdom ; New York, NY : Cambridge
University Press, 2022. | Series: The Cambridge edition of the complete
fiction of Henry James | Includes bibliographical references.
Identifiers: LCCN 2021038913 (print) | LCCN 2021038914 (ebook) | ISBN
9781107029644 (hardback) | ISBN 9781139342438 (ebook)
Subjects: BISAC: LITERARY CRITICISM / European / English, Irish, Scottish,
Welsh | LCGFT: Short stories. | Literary criticism.
Classification: LCC PS2112 .M36 2022 (print) | LCC PS2112 (ebook) | DDC
813/.4–dc23
LC record available at https://lccn.loc.gov/2021038913
LC ebook record available at https://lccn.loc.gov/2021038914

ISBN 978-1-107-02964-4 Hardback

Cambridge University Press has no responsibility for the persistence or accuracy of
URLs for external or third-party internet websites referred to in this publication
and does not guarantee that any content on such websites is, or will remain,
accurate or appropriate.

CONTENTS

The Aspern Papers and Other Tales 1884–1888

CONTENTS

ILLUSTRATIONS

ACKNOWLEDGEMENTS

The present volume of the Cambridge Edition of the *Complete Fiction of Henry James* aims at providing new textual data for a chronological selection of James's short stories, some of which have received considerable scholarly attention over the years. As such, it is necessarily indebted to the important work of many Jamesian critics of the past and the present, to whom the editors' gratitude goes. This volume would never have reached completion without the unstinting generosity and tireless support of our Volume Editor, Adrian Poole, whose innumerable corrections, suggestions, and identifications of allusions were essential. We are deeply grateful to our General Editors, Philip Horne and Tamara Follini, for carefully revising our many drafts and files and also for suggesting significant changes, and also thank Philip for allowing us to use his ongoing work on James's *Notebooks*. We would like to extend our thanks to our General Editor in the United States, Michael Anesko, for his careful and generous corrections, and to Pierre Walker and Greg Zacharias, not only for their important work on James's correspondence but also for sending us unpublished letters regarding the tales here presented. Gratitude goes to Oliver Herford for supplying the texts to the Prefaces to the *New York Edition*, and to Sarah Wadsworth for allowing us to use her unpublished findings on one of the tales.

Our gratitude goes to the Center for Henry James Studies at Creighton University (Omaha, NE), to Susan Halpert and the staff at the Houghton Library of Harvard University, to Cambridge University Library, to the British Library, and to Anna Benedetti and the staff at the Library of Ca' Foscari University of Venice, for providing us with essential material.

ABBREVIATIONS

The Tales

AP	'The Aspern Papers'
GR	'Georgina's Reasons'
L	'The Liar'
LP	'Louisa Pallant'
MT	'Mrs. Temperly'
MW	'The Modern Warning'
NEW	'A New England Winter'
P	'Pandora'
PD	'The Path of Duty'

The following are sources where the tales (abbreviated in square brackets) appear.

AB	*The Author of Beltraffio* (Boston: James R. Osgood & Co., 1884) [P, GR, PD]
AM	*Atlantic Monthly* [AP]
AP	*The Aspern Papers; Louisa Pallant; The Modern Warning* (London and New York: Macmillan, 1888) [AP, LP, MW]
C	*Century Magazine* [L, NEW]
DMOS	*Daisy Miller and Other Stories*, ed. Jean Gooder (Oxford: Oxford University Press, 1985) [P]
EIM	*English Illustrated Magazine* [PD]
HNM	*Harper's New Monthly Magazine* [LP, MW]
HW	*Harper's Weekly* [MT]
LoA	*Library of America*

LonL	*A London Life*, 2 vols. (London and New York: Macmillan, 1889) [L, MT]
NYE	*The New York Edition of the Novels and Tales of Henry James* (New York: Charles Scribner's Sons, 1907–9), vol. XII [AP, L], vol. XIII [LP], vol. XVIII [P]
NYS	*New York Sun* [P, GR]
Poole	*The Aspern Papers and Other Stories*, ed. Adrian Poole, new edition (Oxford and New York: Oxford University Press, 2013)
SR1	*Stories Revived*, vol. I (London: Macmillan & Co., 1885) [P, PD]
SR2	*Stories Revived*, vol. II (London: Macmillan & Co., 1885) [GR]
TTC	*Tales of Three Cities* (London: Macmillan & Co., 1884) [NEW]
TTC2	*Tales of Three Cities* (Boston: James R. Osgood & Co., 1884) [NEW]

Other Works by Henry James

Amb	*The Ambassadors*, ed. Nicola Bradbury, *CFHJ* 18 (Cambridge: Cambridge University Press, 2015)
CFHJ	The Cambridge Edition of the *Complete Fiction of Henry James*
CLHJ	*The Complete Letters of Henry James*, ed. Pierre A. Walker and Greg W. Zacharias; Michael Anesko and Greg W. Zacharias (Lincoln, NE: University of Nebraska Press, 2006–) (NB: Quotations from this source will appear as clear text; i.e., evidence of HJ's cancellations and insertions will not appear unless warranted by their context.)
DM	*Daisy Miller: A Study*, 2 vols. (London: Macmillan & Co., 1879)

CN	*The Complete Notebooks of Henry James,* ed. Leon Edel and Lyall H. Powers (New York and Oxford: Oxford University Press, 1987)
CTW1	*Collected Travel Writings: Great Britain and America: English Hours, The American Scene, Other Travels,* ed. Richard Howard (New York: Library of America, 1993)
CTW2	*Collected Travel Writings: The Continent: A Little Tour in France, Italian Hours, Other Travels,* ed. Richard Howard (New York: Library of America, 1993)
CWAD1	*The Complete Writings of Henry James on Art and Drama,* vol. 1, *Art,* ed. Peter Collister (Cambridge: Cambridge University Press, 2016)
CWAD2	*The Complete Writings of Henry James on Art and Drama,* vol. 2, *Drama,* ed. Peter Collister (Cambridge: Cambridge University Press, 2016)
EL	*Essays in London and Elsewhere* (New York: Harper & Brothers, 1893)
H	*Hawthorne* (London: Macmillan & Co., 1879)
HJL	*Henry James Letters,* ed. Leon Edel, 4 vols. (Cambridge, MA: Harvard University Press, 1974–84; London: Macmillan, 1974–84)
LC1	*Literary Criticism: Essays on Literature, American Writers, English Writers,* ed. Leon Edel and Mark Wilson (New York: Library of America, 1984)
LC2	*Literary Criticism: French Writers, Other European Writers, The Prefaces to the New York Edition,* ed. Leon Edel and Mark Wilson (New York: Library of America, 1984)
LL	*Henry James: A Life in Letters,* ed. Philip Horne (Harmondsworth: Penguin, 1999; New York: Viking Press, 1999)
LPB	*Letters from the Palazzo Barbaro,* ed. Rosella Mamoli Zorzi (London: Pushkin Press, 1998)

NC2	Henry James. *Nouvelles completes 1877–1888 II*, ed. Évelyne Labbé (Paris: Éditions de la Pléiade, 2003)
NSBMY	*Notes of a Son and Brother and The Middle Years: A Critical Edition*, ed. Peter Collister (Charlottesville, VA: University of Virginia Press, 2011)
PE	*The Painter's Eye: Notes and Essays on the Pictorial Arts*, ed. John L. Sweeney (Cambridge, MA: Harvard University Press, 1956)
PoL	*The Portrait of a Lady*, ed. Michael Anesko, *CFHJ* 7 (Cambridge: Cambridge University Press, 2016)
PP	*Partial Portraits* (London and New York: Macmillan & Co., 1888)
PPL	*Portraits of Places* (London and New York: Macmillan & Co., 1883)
PS	*Parisian Sketches: Letters to the New York Tribune 1875–1876*, edited and introduced by Leon Edel and Ilse Dusoir Lind (London: Rupert Hart-Davis, 1958)
S1864–1874	*Henry James: Complete Stories 1864–1874*, ed. Jean Strouse (New York: Library of America, 1999)
S1874–1884	*Henry James: Complete Stories 1874–1884*, ed. William L. Vance (New York: Library of America, 1999)
S1884–1891	*Henry James: Complete Stories 1884–1891*, ed. Edward W. Said (New York: Library of America, 1999)
S1892–1898	*Henry James: Complete Stories 1892–1898*, ed. John Hollander and David Bromwich (New York: Library of America, 1996)
S1898–1910	*Henry James: Complete Stories 1898–1910*, ed. Denis Donoghue (New York: Library of America, 1996)
SBOC	*A Small Boy and Others: A Critical Edition*, ed. Peter Collister (Charlottesville, VA: University of Virginia Press, 2011)
TS	*Transatlantic Sketches* (Boston, MA: James R. Osgood & Co., 1875)

WD	*The Wings of the Dove* (London: Archibald Constable & Co., 1902)
WWS	*William Wetmore Story and His Friends*, 2 vols. (Boston: Houghton Mifflin, 1903)

Other Works

Appleton's 1879	*Appleton's Dictionary of New York and its Vicinity* (New York: D. Appleton & Co., 1879)
HJE	Robert L. Gale, *A Henry James Encyclopedia* (New York: Greenwood Press, 1989)
Murray's 1868	*Handbook for Travellers in Southern Italy* (London: John Murray, 1868)
Murray's 1877	*Handbook for Travellers in Northern Italy* (London: John Murray, 1877)

GENERAL EDITORS' PREFACE

The Cambridge Edition of the *Complete Fiction of Henry James* (hereafter *CFHJ*) has been undertaken in the belief that there is a need for a full scholarly, informative, historical edition of his work, presenting the texts in carefully checked, accurate form, with detailed annotation and extensive introductions. James's texts exist in a number of forms, including manuscripts (though most are lost), serial texts, and volumes of various sorts, often incorporating significant amounts of revision, most conspicuously the so-called *New York Edition* (hereafter *NYE*) published by Charles Scribner's Sons in New York and Macmillan & Co. in London (1907–9). Besides these there are also pirated editions, unfinished works published posthumously, and other questionable forms. The *CFHJ* takes account of these complexities, within the framework of a textual policy which aims to be clear, orderly, and consistent.

This edition aims to represent James's fictional career as it evolves, with a fresh and expanded sense of its changing contexts and an informed sense of his developing style, technique, and concerns. Consequently it does not attempt to base its choices on the principle of the 'last lifetime edition', which in the case of Henry James is monumentally embodied in the twenty-four volumes of the *NYE*, the author's selection of nine longer novels (six of them in two volumes) and fifty-eight shorter novels and tales, and including eighteen specially composed Prefaces. The *CFHJ*, as a general rule, adopts rather the text of the first published book edition of a work, unless the intrinsic particularities and the publishing history of that work require an alternative choice, on the ground that emphasis on the first context in which it was written and read will permit an unprecedented fullness of attention to the transformations in James's writing over five decades, as well as the rich literary and social contexts of their original publication.

There are inevitably cases where determining 'the first published book edition' requires some care. If, for instance, James expresses a preference for the text of one particular early book edition over another, or if the first edition to be published is demonstrably inferior to a later impression or edition, or if authorial supervision of a particular early edition or impression can be established, then a case can be made for choosing a text other than the first published book edition. Volume Editors have exercised their judgment accordingly. They have made a full collation of authoritative versions including serial as well as volume publication in Britain and America, and specify which version serves as their copy text.

The *CFHJ*'s Introductions aim to be full and authoritative, detailing the histories of composition, publication (in magazine and book form), reception, and authorial revision, and making economical reference to subsequent adaptation and transformation into other forms, including drama, film, and opera. Editors have refrained from offering emphatic interpretations or mounting critical arguments of their own, though it is hoped the material they present will inform and stimulate new readings. Particular attention has been given to the social, political, and cultural contexts of James's period, and especially those of the countries in which a specific work is set; details of James's personal exposure to relevant people and events, of the magazines and publishing houses where he published (editors, policies, politics, etc.), have provided valuable material. Introductions conclude with a Bibliography in support of the information supplied and the aspects of the text's production emphasized in the Introduction, including a list of contemporary reviews.

Each volume contains, in addition to a Chronology of James's life and literary career, a volume-specific Chronology incorporating dates of composition, negotiation with publishers and editors, dispatch of instalments, stages of printing, and initial reception history, as well as relevant comments by or to James appearing in letters or other forms.

Fullness and helpfulness of annotation is one of the main aims of the *CFHJ*. As James's world recedes into the past, more and more of its features need explanation to readers: both the physical, geographical, and historical world of places and people, and the cultural world of beliefs, values, conventions, social practices, and points of reference – to operas, plays, books, paintings; and indeed certain linguistic explanations have become increasingly necessary (especially regarding the presence of slang or linguistic innovation, both English and American). For such explanations, James's correspondence, criticism, and other writings have been drawn on as a prime source of helpful comment, conveying his own experience and attitudes in a way that richly illuminates his fictional texts. Newspapers and magazines of the period, travel guides, the work of other writers, also contribute, filling out the picture of the implied worlds beyond the text. Furthermore, the *CFHJ* sets out to provide the fullest possible details of James's allusions to poetry, the Bible, and the plays of Shakespeare, as well as other literary and culturally significant works – offering suggestive but concise plot summaries when appropriate or quotation of the passages drawn on, so that the act of allusion is brought to life and the reader can trace something of James's allusive processes. Editors have abstained, on the other hand, from purely interpretative notes, speculation, and personal comments: the notes always concern a point of information, even if that point has a critical bearing.

Appendices include sources and relevant contextual documents, including correspondence, entries from the Prefaces to the *NYE* and from the Notebooks, where appropriate. For the novels revised and published in the *NYE*, the whole Preface is printed in an Appendix; for tales revised and published in the *NYE*, the relevant extract from the Preface is reproduced. The Prefaces and Notebooks have also been collected in newly edited volumes of their own.

*

Most of James's fiction exists in a number of different textual states, most notably in the difference between initial publication (in periodical and volume form) and the revised versions of the novels and tales prepared near the end of his career for the *NYE*. (In the case of three late tales – 'Fordham Castle', 'Julia Bride', and 'The Jolly Corner' – first book publication was in the *NYE*.) Works excluded by James from the *NYE* were incorporated in the edition posthumously published in thirty-five volumes by Macmillan in 1921–3, but these were of course published without authorial revision. The textual differences affecting those works that *are* included in the *NYE* are predictably most extensive in the case of early works such as *Roderick Hudson* (1875), *The American* (1877), 'Daisy Miller' (1879), and *The Portrait of a Lady* (1881).

Readers may see for themselves the full extent of James's revisions, along with all other variants, both preceding and succeeding the texts printed here, in the lists of Textual Variants. These are normally presented in the following form. Each volume includes a comprehensive list of all sub-stantive variants in the line of textual transmission leading up to copy text ('Textual Variants I'), preceded by a brief commentary in which edi-tors address this stage of the textual history, drawing attention to the main features of the changes and dealing with questions such as house style. Variations in punctuation within a sentence (usually by the insertion or removal of commas, or changes in the use of colons and semi-colons) have not normally been considered substantive. Over end-of-sentence punctua-tion, however, particularly in the matter of changing full stops to exclama-tions or vice versa, Volume Editors have exercised their judgment. A second section ('Textual Variants II') offers a comprehensive list of all substantive variants subsequent to copy text, and a brief commentary which summa-rizes the main issues raised by the changes made. The length of lists of vari-ants and commentary inevitably varies greatly from case to case. In certain cases, for reasons explained in the volume concerned, there is a single list of 'Textual Variants'.

*

The *Complete Fiction of Henry James* consists of twenty-two novels (vols. 1–22), 113 tales (vols. 23–32), and two supplementary volumes (vols. 33 and 34) devoted respectively to the Prefaces that James wrote for the *NYE* and to his Notebooks. They appear in this edition in the order in which they were first published. The distinction between 'novels' and 'tales' is some-times a crude one: between long fictions such as *The Portrait of a Lady* and *The Golden Bowl* and short ones such as 'Benvolio' and 'The Beldonald Holbein' there lie many shorter novels and longer tales, and it is hard to categorize with confidence well-known works such as *Washington Square* and *The Sacred Fount*, 'The Aspern Papers' and 'The Turn of the Screw'. We have deemed to be 'novels' those fictions which when they first took volume form were published as independent entities (with the single exception of *In the Cage*, which despite its relative brevity first appeared as a slim vol-ume) and those to be 'tales' all which were not. The former include some of James's lesser-known works, such as *Watch and Ward, Confidence, The Other House, The Outcry* and the two unfinished at the time of his death, *The Sense of the Past* and *The Ivory Tower*.

The division of James's tales into ten volumes has been ordered chronologically on the basis of first publication, according to the following principles:

1) The determining date of a story's publication is that of the first appearance of any part of it (as some straddle three issues of a magazine). Thus, for example, 'A London Life' (June–September 1888, *Scribner's Magazine*) before 'The Lesson of the Master' (July–August 1888, *Universal Review*).

2) Where two tales have the same start date, the priority is determined by which completes its publication earlier. Thus, for example, 'The Modern Warning' (originally entitled 'Two Countries', June 1888, *Harper's New Monthly Magazine*) precedes 'A London Life' (June–September 1888, *Scribner's Magazine*).

3) Where two tales have the same start date and the same date of completion (often only taking one issue), the priority is determined by alphabetical order (of tale title). Thus, for example, 'De Grey: A Romance' (July 1868, *Atlantic Monthly*) precedes 'Osborne's Revenge' (July 1868, *Galaxy*).

4) Because it cannot usually be determined exactly *when* a magazine dated only 'June' actually appeared, 'June' is treated as preceding any particular date in June, including '1 June'. Thus 'The Private Life' (April 1892, *Atlantic Monthly*) precedes 'The Real Thing' (16 April 1892, *Black and White*); and principle 4 overrides principle 2, so that 'The Author of "Beltraffio"' (June–July 1884, *English Illustrated Magazine*) precedes 'Pandora' (1 and 8 June 1884, *New York Sun*).

5) Where tales have not been published in periodicals before being collected in book form, the precise date of book publication counts as first publication and determines their place in the order.

6) Where tales have not been published in periodicals before being collected in book form, and several tales appear in the same book, the order of tales in the book determines our ordering (even when their order of composition is known to have been different), as it is closer to the order in which original readers would preponderantly have read them.

7) In the single case where only a fragment of a tale survives and therefore was not published within James's lifetime, 'Hugh Merrow', the tale has been placed provisionally in accordance with the date of the only extant *Notebooks* entry, 11 September 1900.

*

Emendations have been made sparingly and only to clearly erroneous readings. Where there is only one version of a work and it requires emendation, the original (erroneous) reading has been recorded in the List of Emendations. Where a later or earlier text has a reading that shows the copy text to be in error, this reading has been incorporated and the copy text's reading recorded in the apparatus. The fact that a later or earlier text has a reading that seems preferable to that of the copy text has not in itself provided sufficient grounds for emendation, although like all other variants, it has been recorded in the list of Textual Variants. Unusual and inconsistent spellings have not been altered, and only annotated in exceptional cases. Misprints and slipped letters have been corrected, and the corrections noted. Contractions have not been expanded, superscript has not been converted, and spelling and punctuation have not normally been changed.

James's writings were of course published on both sides of the Atlantic, and there are corresponding differences in spelling between British and American texts, in volume and serial form: 'colour/color', 'recognise/recognize', 'marvellous/marvelous', and so on. These differences have been preserved when they occur in the textual variants, but they have not been systematically recorded, being deemed to be matters of accident rather than substance. The form taken by inverted commas (single or double) also varies between texts, as does their placement (before or after commas, full stops, etc.); being judged matters of accident, these have been regularized. Double quotation marks have been adopted for all the James texts published in this edition. When the text of the *NYE* is cited in the Introduction, Notes, or textual apparatus, its distinctive typography has not been retained, and this also applies to the texts of the tales first published in the *NYE* and of the Prefaces: the contractions rendered there as, for example, 'is n't' and 'did n't' have here been partially normalized as single words, 'isn't' and 'didn't'. Editorial ellipses have been enclosed in square brackets but authorial ellipses have not.

The punctuation of the copy text adopted has also been preserved. There are considerable differences of punctuation between the different forms in which a particular work of James's appears. It is often hard to distinguish with certainty those which can be accounted for by differences in the house styles of particular publishers, British and American, and those which are matters of authorial choice. Whatever the agency behind such differences, there is a case for recognizing the difference of sense made by the presence or absence of a comma, by the change of an exclamation to a full stop, and so on. Nevertheless, the scale of such differences is too great to make a comprehensive record feasible within the limits of a print edition. Volume editors have therefore exercised their judgment over the most helpful way to inform readers of the nature of such differences.

References to money pose particular difficulties for modern readers, not only because the sums concerned have to be multiplied by an apparently ever-inflating figure to produce approximate modern equivalents, but because the quantity and quality of what could be bought and done with these sums (especially involving property or real estate) has also changed radically – and will very possibly continue to do so during the lifetime of this edition. We do however know that throughout James's own life the pound sterling was equal to $4.85, and certain other figures can be established, such as that in 1875 the US dollar was equivalent to 5.19 French francs. For the calculation of particular sums in James's writings, volume editors have supplied readers with as much reliable information as they can command at the date of publication for this edition, but as time goes on readers will inevitably have to make adjustments.

Translations have been provided for all foreign words and phrases that appear in the text. Those which are common and uncontroversial (such as *piazza* and *table d'hôte*) are collected in a glossary at the end; those judged to be less than obvious in meaning, or dependent for their meaning on the specific context, are explained in an endnote.

The General Editors warmly acknowledge the gracious permission of Bay James, custodian of the James Estate, for the publication of material still in copyright; and the generous cooperation of Greg Zacharias and his associates at the Center for Henry James Studies at Creighton University in Omaha, Nebraska, home of an indispensable parallel project, *The Complete Letters of Henry James*, published by the University of Nebraska Press. We thank David Supino for offering his sage advice whenever it was sought. Finally, we are deeply grateful for the guidance and support provided by our editors at Cambridge University Press, Linda Bree and Bethany Thomas, and Senior Content Managers Victoria Parrin and Sharon McCann.

GENERAL CHRONOLOGY OF JAMES'S LIFE AND WRITINGS

Compiled by Philip Horne

1843   Henry James is born on 15 April 1843 at 21 Washington Place in New York City, second of the five children of Henry James (1811–82), speculative theologian and social thinker, and his wife Mary Walsh Robertson James (1810–82). Siblings: William (1842–1910), psychologist, philosopher, Harvard professor; Garth Wilkinson ('Wilky', 1845–83); Robertson ('Bob', 1846–1910); Alice (1848–92), diarist.

1843–5 Taken to Paris and London by his parents; earliest memory (from age 2) is of the Place Vendôme in Paris.

1845–7 Returns to United States. Childhood in Albany.

1847–55 Family settles in New York City; taught by tutors and in private schools.

1855–8 Family travels in Europe: Geneva, London, Paris, Boulogne-sur-mer.

1858   Jameses reside in Newport, Rhode Island.

1859–60 James family travels: HJ at scientific school, then the Academy (later the University) in Geneva. Summer 1860: HJ learns German in Bonn.

1860–2 James family returns to Newport in September 1860. HJ makes friends with future critic Thomas Sargent Perry and artist John La Farge, fellow students at William Morris Hunt's art academy. From 1860 HJ 'was continually writing stories, mainly of a romantic kind' (Perry). In 1861 HJ injures his back helping extinguish a fire in Newport. Along with William James, exempted from service in Civil War, in which younger brothers fight, and Wilky is seriously wounded.

1862   Enters Harvard Law School for a term. Begins to send stories to magazines.

1864   February: first short story of HJ's 113, 'A Tragedy of Error',
        published anonymously in *Continental Monthly*. May: Jameses
        move to 13 Ashburton Place, Boston. October: first of HJ's many
        reviews, of Nassau W. Senior's *Essays on Fiction*, published
        unsigned in *North American Review*.

1865   March: first signed tale, 'The Story of a Year', appears in *Atlantic
        Monthly*. HJ appears also as a critic in first number of the *Nation*
        (New York).

1866–8 Summer 1866: becomes friends with William Dean Howells,
        novelist, critic, and influential editor. November 1866: James
        family moves to 20 Quincy Street, beside Harvard Yard.
        November 1867: meets Charles Dickens at home of James
        T. Fields, and 'tremble[s] ... in every limb' (*Notes of a Son
        and Brother*). HJ continues reviewing and writing stories in
        Cambridge.

1869–70 On 27 February 1869 lands at Liverpool. Travels in England,
        meeting John Ruskin, William Morris, Charles Darwin, and
        George Eliot; also in Switzerland and Italy. 1870: death of his
        much-loved cousin Minny Temple.

1870–2 May 1870: reluctantly returns to Cambridge. August–
        December 1871: publishes first novel, *Watch and Ward*, in the
        Atlantic Monthly; January–March 1872, publishes art reviews in
        Atlantic.

1872–4 May 1872: HJ accompanies invalid sister Alice and aunt
        Catherine Walsh, 'Aunt Kate', to Europe. Writes travel pieces for
        the *Nation*. October 1872–September 1874: periods (without
        family) in Paris, Rome, Switzerland, Homburg, Italy again.
        Spring 1874: begins first long novel, *Roderick Hudson*, in
        Florence. September 1874: returns to the US.

1875   First three books published: *A Passionate Pilgrim, and Other
        Tales* (January); *Transatlantic Sketches* (April); *Roderick Hudson*
        (November). Six months in New York City (111 East 25th Street),
        then three in Cambridge.

1875–6   11 November 1875: arrives at 29 rue de Luxembourg as Paris
          correspondent for *New York Tribune*. Begins *The American*.
          Meets Gustave Flaubert, Ivan Turgenev, Edmond de
          Goncourt, Alphonse Daudet, Guy de Maupassant, and Émile
          Zola.

1876–7   December 1876: moves to London, taking rooms at 3 Bolton
          Street, off Piccadilly. Visits to Paris, Florence, and Rome. May 1877:
          The American published in Boston.

1878   February: *French Poets and Novelists* published, first collection
          of essays, first book published in London. May: revised version
          of *Watch and Ward* published in book form in Boston. June–
          July: 'Daisy Miller' appears in *Cornhill Magazine* and is quickly
          pirated by two American periodicals, establishing reputation
          in Britain and America. September: *The Europeans* published.
          Meets William Ewart Gladstone, Alfred Lord Tennyson, and
          Robert Browning.

1879   June: first English edition of *Roderick Hudson*, revised;
          October: *The Madonna of the Future and Other Tales*;
          December: *Confidence* (novel); *Hawthorne* (critical
          biography).

1880   April: *The Diary of a Man of Fifty and A Bundle of Letters*;
          late winter 1880: travels to Italy; meets Constance Fenimore
          Woolson in Florence. December 1880: *Washington Square*.

1881–3   October 1881: returns to US; travels between Cambridge,
          New York, and Washington, DC. November 1881: *The Portrait
          of a Lady*. January 1882: death of mother. May: returns to
          England till father dies in December 1882. February 1883:
          The Siege of London, The Pension Beaurepas, and *The Point of
          View*; summer 1883: returns to London and will not return
          to US for twenty-one years. November 1883: Macmillan
          publish fourteen-volume collected edition of HJ's fiction.
          September 1883: *Daisy Miller: A Comedy*; December 1883:
          Portraits of Places (travel essays). November 1883: death of
          Wilky James.

1884   Sister Alice joins HJ in London, living nearby. September 1884: *A Little Tour in France* published; also HJ's important artistic statement 'The Art of Fiction'. October 1884: *Tales of Three Cities*. Becomes friends with Robert Louis Stevenson and Edmund Gosse. Writes to his friend Grace Norton: 'I shall never marry ... I am both happy enough and miserable enough, as it is.'

1885–6   Writes two serial novels: *The Bostonians* (*Century*, February 1885–February 1886); *The Princess Casamassima* (*Atlantic*, September 1885–October 1886). February 1885: collection of tales, *The Author of Beltraffio [&c.]*; May 1885: *Stories Revived*, in 3 vols.

1886–7   February 1886: *The Bostonians* published. 6 March: moves to flat, 34 De Vere Gardens, in Kensington, West London. October 1886: *The Princess Casamassima* published. December 1886–July 1887: visits Florence and Venice. Continues friendship with American novelist Constance Fenimore Woolson.

1888   *The Reverberator*, *The Aspern Papers [&c.]* and *Partial Portraits* all published.

1888–90   1889: Collection of tales, *A London Life [&c.]*, published. 1890: *The Tragic Muse*. Temporarily abandons the novel form in favour of playwriting.

1890–1   Dramatizes *The American*, which has a short run in 1891. December: young friend and (informal) agent Wolcott Balestier dies of typhoid in Dresden.

1892   February: story collection *The Real Thing and Other Tales* published. March: death of Alice James in London.

1893   Volumes of tales published: March, *The Real Thing*; June, *The Private Life [&c.]*; September, *The Wheel of Time [&c.]*; also, June, *Picture and Text* (essays on illustration) and *Essays in London and Elsewhere* (critical and memorial essays).

1894   Deaths of Constance Fenimore Woolson (January) and Robert Louis Stevenson (December).

1895   5 January: premiere of *Guy Domville*, greeted by boos and
        applause. James abandons playwriting for years. Visits
        Ireland. Volumes of tales published: May, *Terminations*; June,
        Embarrassments. Takes up cycling.

1896–7 *The Other House* (1896), *The Spoils of Poynton* (1897), *What
        Maisie Knew* (1897). February 1897: starts dictating due to
        wrist problems. September 1897: takes lease on Lamb House,
        Rye.

1898   May: has signed up with literary agent James Brand Pinker,
        who will act for him for the rest of his life. June: moves to Lamb
        House. August: *In the Cage* published. October: 'The Turn of the
        Screw' published (in *The Two Magics*); proves his most popular
        work since 'Daisy Miller'. Kent and Sussex neighbours include
        Stephen Crane, Joseph Conrad, H. G. Wells and Ford Madox
        Hueffer (Ford).

1899   April: *The Awkward Age* published. August: buys the freehold of
        Lamb House.

1900   May: shaves off his beard. August: *The Soft Side* (tales).
        Friendship with Edith Wharton develops. Begins *The Sense of
        the Past*, but leaves it unfinished.

1901   February: *The Sacred Fount*.

1902–3 August 1902: *The Wings of the Dove* published. February
        1903: *The Better Sort* (tales) published. September 1903: *The
        Ambassadors* published (completed mid-1901, before *The Wings
        of the Dove*, but delayed by serialization); also *William Wetmore
        Story and his Friends* (biography).

1904–5 August 1904: sails to US for first time in twenty-one years.
        November: *The Golden Bowl* published. Visits New England,
        New York, Philadelphia, Washington, the South, St Louis,
        Chicago, Los Angeles, and San Francisco. Lectures on 'The
        Lesson of Balzac' and 'The Question of Our Speech'. Meets
        President Theodore Roosevelt. Elected to American Academy of
        Arts and Letters.

1905   July: writes early chapters of *The American Scene*; simultaneously begins revising works for *New York Edition of the Novels and Tales of Henry James*. October: *English Hours* (travel essays) published.

1906–8   Selects, arranges, prefaces, and has illustrations made for *New York Edition* (published 1907–9, 24 vols.). January 1907: *The American Scene* published. August 1907: hires new amanuensis, Theodora Bosanquet. 1908: *The High Bid* (play) produced at Edinburgh.

1909–11   October 1909: *Italian Hours* (travel essays) published. Health problems, aggravated by failure of the *New York Edition*. Death of Robertson ('Bob') James. Travels to US. William James dies 26 August 1910. October 1910: *The Finer Grain* (tales). Returns to England August 1911. October: *The Outcry* (play converted into novel) published.

1911   In autumn, begins work on autobiography.

1912   June: honorary doctorate at Oxford. October: takes flat at 21 Carlyle Mansions, Cheyne Walk, Chelsea; suffers from shingles.

1913   March: *A Small Boy and Others* (first autobiographical book) published. Portrait painted by John Singer Sargent for seventieth birthday on 15 April.

1914   March: *Notes of a Son and Brother* (second autobiographical book) published. (The fragment of a third, *The Middle Years*, appears posthumously in 1917.) When World War One breaks out, becomes passionately engaged with the British cause, working with Belgian refugees and later wounded soldiers. October: *Notes on Novelists* published. Begins *The Ivory Tower*; resumes work on *The Sense of the Past*, but is unable to complete either novel.

1915   Honorary president of the American Volunteer Motor Ambulance Corps. July: quarrels with H. G. Wells about purpose of art, declaring 'It is art that *makes* life, makes interest, makes importance'; becomes a British citizen in protest against US neutrality, describing the decision to his nephew Harry (Henry James III) as 'a simple act and offering of allegiance and devotion' after his forty-year domicile. Writes essays about the war (collected in *Within the Rim*, 1919) and Preface to *Letters from America* (1916) by his dead friend Rupert Brooke. On 2 December suffers a stroke. First volumes of Uniform Edition of Tales by Martin Secker, published in 14 vols. 1915–20.

1916   Awarded the Order of Merit. Dies on 28 February. Funeral in Chelsea Old Church; ashes smuggled back to America by sister-in-law and buried in the family plot in Cambridge, Massachusetts.

INTRODUCTION

This volume* presents nine tales by Henry James that were written and published between 1884 and 1888, after James had achieved success with 'Daisy Miller' (1878) and *The Portrait of a Lady* (1881), two works centred on the so-called 'international theme' – the confrontation between American and European ethics and mores. Most of these tales belong to the period when James was writing *The Bostonians* and *The Princess Casamassima* (both published in 1886), the two novels where James more overtly dealt with contemporary political issues, feminism, and social protest.

The tales were written after James had definitively opted to live in England. In his early thirties he had established himself in London, taking rooms at 3 Bolton Street in December 1876, after spending a year in Paris, where he had arrived as correspondent for the *New York Tribune* on 11 November 1875. These 'apprenticeship' years were extremely important for James, and left indelible traces on him. In Paris he met the Russian expatriate writer Ivan Turgenev, who introduced him to Gustave Flaubert. He also became acquainted with Edmond de Goncourt, Alphonse Daudet, Guy de Maupassant, and Émile Zola, the heirs of Balzac, representatives of French literary realism and its new developments in naturalism. James's admiration for their commitment to formal and stylistic ideals was tempered by his distaste for their choice of subjects drawn from 'low life' and their eagerness to represent physical, mental, and spiritual degradation.

In the French capital he was also exposed to theories of painting and writing that invoked new concepts both of 'realism' and of 'impressionism'. On a previous trip to Europe in 1874, James had witnessed the public debate surrounding impressionism raised by a series of so-called Salons des Refusés.

---

* Although this edition is the result of the close collaboration of the two editors, for the purposes of scholarly responsibility we declare that Rosella Mamoli Zorzi is responsible for the contents relating to 'A New England Winter', 'Mrs. Temperly', 'Louisa Pallant', 'The Aspern Papers', and 'The Modern Warning', and Simone Francescato is responsible for 'Pandora', 'Georgina's Reasons', 'The Path of Duty' and 'The Liar'.

The first such salon had taken place in 1863 in response to the rejection by the official Paris Salon of paintings by artists including Édouard Manet, Camille Pissarro, and James McNeill Whistler, and continued with further 'alternative' salons in 1874, 1875, and 1886. James was initially not in favour of the new movement. However, he later grew to admire it, in particular thanks to his friend and fellow American, the painter John Singer Sargent.[1] Echoes of this period and these experiences can be found in the French background of the painter Florimond in the story 'A New England Winter' and in the portraits painted for the Paris house in 'Mrs. Temperly'.

Between 1877 and 1881, from London, James made three visits to the Continent. His 1877 trip took him first to Paris in September and then to Florence and Rome in October and November. In the meantime, in May 1877 his novel *The American* had been published in book form in Boston. In 1880 he was in Rome again, where he saw the American sculptor William Wetmore Story (of whom he would eventually, reluctantly, write a biography that expresses much of James's divided feelings about the life of the expatriate artist, *William Wetmore Story and his Friends* (1903)). He met the writer Constance Fenimore Woolson in Florence, a friendship that would develop until Woolson's tragic early death in 1894. In 1881 he travelled via Marseilles to San Remo, Genoa, Milan, and Venice, where he struggled to finish his third and most ambitious full-length novel of his early career, *The Portrait of a Lady*, published later that year in November.

Eager to revisit his homeland after a five-year absence, James had set off for America the month before, in October 1881. He saw his family in Cambridge, and visited New York and Washington, where he spent time with Henry Adams and his wife, Marian 'Clover' Hooper. He had to leave the capital suddenly, however, when his mother died on 29 January 1882, the beginning of a more permanent severance from his American origins and such roots as the vagrant lifestyle of his family had encouraged him to acquire. Though he returned to London in May, and made a tour of France in the summer, he sailed back to the United States in December of the same year, arriving just too late to see his father alive. The death of

---

[1] Viola Hopkins Winner, *Henry James and the Visual Arts* (Charlottesville, VA: University of Virginia Press, 1970), pp. 50–1. For James's revision of his views on the impressionists, see also Peter Brooks, *Henry James Goes to Paris* (Princeton, NJ: Princeton University Press, 2007), pp. 30–2.

Henry James Senior marked the end of his youth and early manhood; in April 1883 he would be forty years old. After several months in Boston and Washington, Henry James – no longer 'Junior' – returned to London in the summer of 1883: he was to remain absent from his native land for the next twenty-one years.

Back in England, James learnt of his brother Garth ('Wilky') Wilkinson's death (15 November 1883). This new loss was added to that of both of his parents, who had died within the year 1882. However, before learning of Wilky's death, James expressed 'an earnest wish to hear that Wilky has laid down forever the burden of all his troubles. All the last news of him is a record of unmitigated suffering, & he was long-ago ready to go' (Letter to Elizabeth ('Lizzie') Boott, 14 October 1883, *CLHJ 1883–1884* 1:243). As much tenderness as James felt towards Wilky – who had been as a young boy his 'extremely easy yokefellow and playfellow' (*SBOC* 22) and had lived with him recently in Boston – he could only wish his suffering would cease. In the letter to Lizzie Boott, James's sympathy focused on Wilky's sad return from the American Civil War, a tragic reminder of which was a sketch of his wounded brother in his possession done by their elder sibling William; later he inserted it in *Notes of a Son and Brother* (1914), where he remembered Wilky's happy, sociable character. James's moving tribute to his brother there suggests that Wilky never recovered, physically or emotionally, from the war.[2]

The phase of James's career covered by the tales in this volume was thus marked at its start by a sharply enforced rupture of his personal connection with the land of his birth. By the same token it threw him back all the more powerfully on the literary connections he had already forged in Europe, both in London and Paris. In February the following year, 1884, James spent a month in the French capital, seeing his old friends Daudet, Zola, and Edmond de Goncourt. About them he wrote to his friend and fellow novelist, W. D. Howells: 'They do the only kind of work, to-day, that I respect; & in spite of their ferocious pessimism & their handling of unclean things, they are at least serious and honest' (*LL* 153). Turgenev had also commanded his

---

[2] James was much closer to Wilky than he was to his youngest brother, Robertson ('Bob'), another, albeit less obvious, victim of the Civil War, who lived on until 1910. Wilky never really recovered, and after failing in a Florida enterprise and other ventures, he suffered from rheumatism and a heart condition. This is why James thought his condition so desperate.

respect, without such attendant discomfort, but the Russian writer had died the previous September. This was yet another close personal loss, deeply felt by James, as he wrote to Grace Norton on 23 February 1884: 'I greatly miss Turgenieff, & see how much his presence here has been for me in all these last visits of mine to Paris' (*CLHJ 1883–1884* 2:42). Turgenev's friendship in 1875 had been one of the great joys of James's Parisian life. Before meeting him, James had written a highly appreciative essay on the Russian writer in the *North American Review* of April 1874. When Turgenev died, James wrote a long essay published in the January 1884 issue of the *Atlantic Monthly*, underlining his greatness both as a writer and as a man, 'the most touching of writers, the most lovable of men' (*LC2* 1007); in James's memory many places in Paris were linked with the *déjeuners* they had shared. One of James's most important critical reflections on the novel, his essay on 'The Art of Fiction' (September 1884), while generally indebted to the literary climate of Paris and the circle of Flaubert and the Goncourts, singled out the Russian writer as a master and model of inspiration.

This essay gave coherent expression to James's long-lasting interest in the aesthetic parallels between the art of fiction and the art of painting. He had long been a keen observer of the visual arts, and of artists. On 23 February 1884, for example, James renewed an acquaintance with John Singer Sargent that had begun in the autumn of 1882. Sargent's portrait *Madame X* (Madame Gautreau), shown at the Paris Salon of 1884, had caused a commotion that may have contributed to the artist's moving to England, on James's advice. On 2 June 1884 James wrote to his old friend Lizzie Boott about Sargent: 'I saw & shall probably see again a great deal of him; I was able, I think, to make things pleasant & easy for him. I like him extremely (he is more intelligent about artistic things than all the painters here rolled together) & in short we are excellent friends' (*CLHJ 1883–1884* 2:135). In 1885 James was to spend time in the artistic colony in the English countryside at Broadway, in the Cotswolds, where such painters as Sargent, Frank Millet, Edwin A. Abbey, and others gathered in the summer to paint *en plein air*, as James described them in articles later collected in *Picture and Text* (1893).[3]

---

[3] The articles were published between 1886 and 1891, mainly in *Harper's Weekly* and *Harper's New Monthly*. See *The Complete Writings of Henry James on Art and Drama*, vol. 1, *Art*, ed. Peter Collister (Cambridge: Cambridge University Press, 2016), pp. 404–93.

In September 1884 James published *A Little Tour in France,* a collection of essays about the French *provinces,* through which he had rambled in September and October 1882. He described to Isabella Stewart Gardner from Paris how he had spent six weeks 'wandering about the provinces— Touraine, Anjou, Poitiers, Gascony, Provence, Burgundy'. Then he had proceeded to see the castles of the Loire and 'a hundred more castles & ruins, as well as cathedrals, old walled towns, Roman remains & curiosities of every sort' (*CLHJ 1880–1883* 2:228). The tour had provided a blessed respite from a year of grief, in the interim between the death of his mother the previous January and the death of his father the following December.

In November 1884 James's ailing sister Alice joined him in England. He went to meet her at Liverpool, finding her exhausted from the voyage, and accompanied her to London, where she took lodgings at 40 Clarges Street, near to his own in Bolton Street. Early in 1885, in desperate pursuit of better health, Alice moved to the seaside resort of Bournemouth on the south coast, where she was joined by Katharine Loring (1849–1943) and her sister Louisa. From this time, Katharine would be Alice's devoted companion until her death in 1892. Meanwhile brother Henry was busily engaged on *The Bostonians,* which started serial publication in the *Century* in February 1885. When James went to visit Alice in Bournemouth at the end of April, he spent a good deal of time with another invalid, Robert Louis Stevenson, with whom he developed a close friendship. They had first met back in 1879, but were prompted to closer engagement by James's essay 'The Art of Fiction' and Stevenson's reaction to it, 'A Humble Remonstrance' (December 1884), where he had taken issue with the older writer, declaring that 'No art – to use the daring phrase of Mr James – can successfully "compete with life"'.[4] A friendly correspondence had ensued along with an invitation to visit, and James spent many evenings with the Stevensons in Bournemouth. In 1888 he would publish a long and laudatory essay on the author of *Treasure Island, Kidnapped,* and *The Strange Case of Dr Jekyll and Mr Hyde,* and in 1900, after Stevenson's early death in 1894, thousands of miles away in Western Samoa, a long review of his correspondence – in effect another

[4] *R. L. Stevenson on Fiction: An Anthology of Literary and Critical Essays,* ed. Glenda Norquay (Edinburgh: Edinburgh University Press, 1999), p. 93.

portrait of his friend. James and Stevenson were both friends of Sargent's, and one wonders if the wish to write a 'literary portrait', apparently no longer fashionable, expressed at the beginning of James's 1888 essay, might be linked to Sargent's portrait of Stevenson (1885) that he admired ('Sargent's little picture of him, shuffling about in his room & pulling his moustache. It is very queer & charming').[5]

On 2 May 1885 James was shocked to read in *The Times* that his Boston publisher, James R. Osgood, had gone bankrupt. Since signing a contract with Osgood two years previously for a full-length novel and three short stories, he had been looking forward to the largest financial returns his work had achieved so far: $4,000 for the novel and $2,000 for the tales, on delivery of the completed manuscripts.[6] Osgood's collapse left James in such difficulties that he had to borrow $1,000 from his brother William. When Benjamin Ticknor took over Osgood & Co., James wrote to him at the end of June, negotiating a new contract to supersede what had turned out to be the 'insanely unprofitable' one with Osgood (*LL* 177). He retained for himself the rights of *The Bostonians* in Britain and successfully demanded that the rights for America should revert to him in five years' time. But the experience had been deeply demoralizing, and it sapped the confidence with which he was settling down to his next full-length novel, *The Princess Casamassima*.[7]

Returning to London for a few days in June, James found a cottage on Hampstead Heath for his sister Alice and Katharine Loring. He went to Dover in August to make progress with *The Princess Casamassima*, which

[5] Fred Kaplan, *Henry James: The Imagination of Genius. A Biography* (New York: William Morrow, 1992), p. 310. In fact Sargent painted three portraits of Stevenson: the first (December 1884) was later destroyed, possibly by Stevenson's wife, Fanny; the second (August 1885), representing Stevenson 'shuffling about' while his wife sits in an armchair, with an open door between them, is now at the Crystal Bridges Museum (Bentonville, Arkansas); the third (1887), of Stevenson sitting and smoking in a straw armchair, is now at the Taft Museum (Cincinnati, Ohio). See *John Singer Sargent*, eds. Elaine Kilmurray and Richard Ormond (London: Tate Gallery Publishing, 1998), p. 120, and *Sargent: Portraits of Artists and Friends*, ed. Richard Ormond and Elaine Kilmurray (London: National Portrait Gallery, 2015), pp. 108–11.
[6] Michael Anesko, *'Friction with the Market': Henry James and the Profession of Authorship* (New York: Oxford University Press, 1986), p. 84.
[7] See the *CFHJ* edition of *The Bostonians*, edited by Daniel Karlin (2019), pp. cxvii–cxxii. See the *CFHJ* edition of *The Princess Casamassima*, edited by Adrian Poole (2021).

would begin serial publication in the *Atlantic* the following month, then on to Paris for eight weeks, while Alice and Katharine moved to 7 Bolton Row, five minutes away from his own lodgings in Bolton Street. Yet after nine years there, he was himself ready to move.

Coming back from Paris at the beginning of November 1885, James started looking for a new apartment. The following month he wrote to Grace Norton that he had found it in Kensington, at 34 De Vere Gardens, where he would move the following March, and which would remain his London base for the next ten years or so, until leaving for Lamb House in Rye. The year of 1886 was largely taken up with *The Princess Casamassima*, which finished serialization in October and was promptly issued in book form; the much delayed *Bostonians* had appeared as a volume in February.[8] James was acutely disappointed by the lack of success of these two novels – a significant decline from the acclaim enjoyed by 'Daisy Miller' (1878), *The Portrait of a Lady* (1881), and other fictions just a few years earlier – and the scanty pecuniary returns were a measure of his failure to sustain, let alone to extend, the popularity for which he strove.

With *The Princess* finally published, James was ready to reward himself with a trip to the Continent. On 3 December 1886 he left England, stopping in Milan and Pisa and arriving in Florence five days later. His apartment and servants were taken over by Alice. He spent December at Bellosguardo, the delightful hilltop south of the Arno, in the Villa Brichieri, rented by his close friend, the novelist Constance Fenimore Woolson, who was staying nearby at the Villa Castellani. When Woolson moved into the Villa Brichieri in January, James moved down to the city, to the Hôtel du Sud. His essay on Woolson was published in *Harper's Weekly*, on 12 February. Ten days later he left for Venice to stay with Katharine de Kay Bronson, an American lady who had been living there since 1875 with her daughter Edith. The Bronson couple were old friends from Newport. James was given hospitality in the Gothic Palazzo Giustinian Recanati,[9] adjoining Mrs Bronson's Casa Alvisi on the Grand Canal, in front of the Salute Church. This was a sort of wing

---

[8] *The Bostonians* was published on 16 February 1886 in Britain; *The Princess Casamassima* on 22 October 1886 in Britain and on 2 November 1886 in the United States.

[9] Documented in contemporary photographs; now totally transformed into a plain twentieth-century building.

for Mrs Bronson's many guests, who included the poet Robert Browning and and his sister Sarianna. During that month James caught a cold and thought his jaundice had been caused by the 'pestilent if romantic emanations' of the city,[10] alluding to a current nineteenth-century view of Venice.

By 12 April he was back in Florence, staying again at the Villa Brichieri, but sharing it this time, on different floors, with Constance Fenimore Woolson. Here he began 'The Aspern Papers', based on a story he had heard three months before, shortly after arriving in Florence (see below). Although in his Preface to the tale, written many years later, James linked the story to Claire Claremont, former mistress of Lord Byron, both his Florentine and Venetian hostesses may also have provided inspiration for the women at the centre of the story. On 25 May he left for Venice again, staying this time with Daniel Sargent Curtis and Ariana Wormeley Curtis at the magnificent Palazzo Barbaro, where he was to return more than once, celebrating it finally as Milly Theale's Palazzo Leporelli in *The Wings of the Dove* (1902). Meanwhile he was finishing 'The Aspern Papers', announcing it to his editor Aldrich as 'brilliant, & of a thrilling interest' (12 June 1887, *HJL* 3:185). Though he sent the whole manuscript by 21 June, it was not published until the following year in the *Atlantic Monthly* (March–May 1888), in three parts (not two, as James had wished). It was to become one of James's most popular tales.

During his second Venetian stay in 1887, the Curtises' salon was frequented also by the writer Paul Bourget, for whom James had written a letter of introduction. Bourget was a friend of Luigi Gualdo (1844–98), an Italian writer who also wrote in French and lived in Paris, and who liked talking about possible subjects for stories or novels with his friends and acquaintances. James seems to have met him in Venice,[11] and he may have heard Gualdo's story of the portrait of an imaginary child, about which he was to enquire some years later, writing to Bourget.[12]

---

[10] Letter to Mrs Edmund Gosse, 14 April 1887, *Selected Letters of Henry James to Edmund Gosse 1882–1915: A Literary Friendship*, ed. Rayburn S. Moore (Baton Rouge, LA: Louisiana University Press, 1988), p. 45.

[11] See Daniela Sannino, *Portrait de l'artiste en passeur: Luigi Gualdo mediatore e critico letterario tra Italia e Francia* (Napoli: Università degli Studi di Napoli Federico II, 2009), p. 398, note 418.

[12] On 22 September 1895 James thought about 'Gualdo's charming little subject of *The Child*' (*CN* 131) and again in 1900; he even wrote to Bourget to find out if Gualdo had ever written and published the story. Bourget replied that Gualdo had not, and James made a note on 11

On 1 July 1887 James travelled back to England, passing at a leisurely pace through Vicenza, Mantua, Cremona, Brescia, Bergamo, and Stresa, where he spent a week with his aged friend, the actress Fanny Kemble. James had already visited Brescia in September 1869, at the suggestion of Charles Eliot Norton (*CLHJ 1855–1872* 2:97–8), on his way to Venice; he had been fascinated there by a beautiful Greek bronze statue representing Victory in the museum, and about which he had written to his mother (*CLHJ 1855–1872* 2:97). Stresa, a tourist destination on Lake Maggiore, would be used as a partial setting in 'Louisa Pallant' (first published in February 1888) and later in *The Wings of the Dove* (1902).

By 21 July he was back in London. The same month he wrote to Grace Norton that he had started a new novel, which would 'be called [probably] *The Tragic Muse*' (*HJL* 3:198), on which he was to work for the next three years. It was published in the *Atlantic Monthly*, January 1889–May 1890. The novel was centred on an actress and the world of the stage. James's interest in the theatre intensified; he published an essay titled 'The Acting in Mr. Irving's *Faust*' (December 1887) while he was writing the novel. Following on from *The Tragic Muse* (1890), James would for several years try his hand at writing for the theatre himself, leading up to the West End performance of his play *Guy Domville* in January 1895. The lack of success of this experience left him deeply bruised, but it helped to develop what he called the 'scenic method' that distinguished the fiction writing to which he returned.

James had been revitalized by the time he had spent on the Continent in the first half of 1887. But his resurgent confidence was checked by the pace at which his editors moved, or failed to. He complained that the 'things' he had written while abroad were being 'buried in the bosom of the *Century*, *Harper*, *Atlantic* etc., who keep them, annoyingly, for what they suppose to be the mystic hour' (*HJL* 3:197–8). Of all the stories James had sent out, only one appeared in 1887 – 'Cousin Maria', published by *Harper's Weekly* with illustrations by C. S. Reinhart in August (reprinted in 1889 in *A London Life*

September 1900 that the subject was 'quite *disponible*' (*CN* 192). Gualdo's hint was the 'germ' for the unfinished 'Hugh Merrow' and for 'Maud-Evelyn' (1900). In fact Gualdo *had* published his 'Una creazione' on this subject as far back as 1877, in the August and September issues of *Fanfulla*: the painter in this story is called Gustavo Zorne, and one wonders whether the name was suggested to Gualdo by that of the Swedish painter Anders Zorn (1860–1920).

under the revised title of 'Mrs. Temperly'). Several essays were published, however, among them one on John Singer Sargent in the October number of *Harper's New Monthly Magazine*. Though Sargent himself had left for America, James went to the painters' colony in Broadway for a couple of days in October 1887 (*HJL* 3:200), repeating a visit he had enjoyed now for three years in succession. In December there appeared in *Macmillan's Magazine* his review essay about a memoir of Emerson. In the same month James participated in the ongoing debate on international copyright by writing a letter to the American Copyright League.

At the beginning of 1888 James felt that his situation had deteriorated badly, since the publication of *The Bostonians* and *The Princess Casamassima* '[had] reduced the desire, and the demand, for my productions to zero', although he still hoped that all his 'buried prose [would] kick off its various tombstones at once' (letter to W. D. Howells, 2 January 1888, *HJL* 3:209). An afternoon at the theatre with Frederic Leighton two days later (*HJL* 3:211) must have reminded him of the enormous success of the painter as compared with his own as a writer. In 1884 James had been struck by the 'worldly prosperity and success' of John Everett Millais and Leighton, and contrasted 'the great rewards of the successful painter, here, and his glory and honour generally, with the so much more modest emoluments of the man of letters'. James added: 'Leighton in particular overwhelms me—his sumptuosity, his personal beauty, his cleverness, his gorgeous house, his universal attainments, his portraits of duchesses, his musical parties, his perfect French and Italian—and German—his general air of being above all human dangers and difficulties!' (letter to Grace Norton, 28 March 1884, *CLHJ 1883–1884* 2:83–4).[13]

The gloom induced by his own dangers and difficulties was alleviated as his buried works began to kick off their tombstones. In February his short novel *The Reverberator* started its six-month serial run in *Macmillan's* and 'Louisa Pallant' appeared in *Harper's New Monthly*, while the following month saw 'The Aspern Papers' begin to appear in the *Atlantic*, followed by 'The Liar' (May–June), 'Two Countries' (June, later retitled 'The Modern Warning'), 'A London Life' (June–September), 'The Lesson of the

---

[13] The editors thank Greg Zacharias for advance access to the text of this letter.

Master' (July and August), and 'The Patagonia' (August–September), in various magazines on both side of the Atlantic, not to mention essays on Maupassant, Stevenson, Loti, the Goncourts, and 'London'. The year 1888 also saw the publication in volume form of *Partial Portraits* (May), *The Reverberator* (June), and 'The Aspern Papers' (with 'Louisa Pallant' and 'The Modern Warning') in September. Altogether, this was a year for James of remarkable revival. His friend and fellow writer W. D. Howells noted as much – that in 1888 James was presenting 'simultaneously some of the best work' of his life in the form of the short story:

With 'The Aspern Papers' in *The Atlantic*, 'The Liar' in *The Century*, 'A London Life' in *Scribner's* and 'Louisa Pallant' and 'Two Countries' in *Harper's* […] the effect was like an artist's exhibition. One turned from one masterpiece to another, making his comparisons, and delighted to find that the stories helped rather than hurt one another, and their accidental massing enhanced his pleasure in them.[14]

James's London life continued in his spacious De Vere Gardens flat. He visited Alice, now settled with Katharine in Leamington, passing 'several hours with her every month', as he wrote to Grace Norton (*HJL* 3:217); saw his old friends Mrs Kemble and Edmund Gosse; and went to the Royal Academy to see 'two great portraits', *Mrs Marquand* and *Mrs Boit*, sent over by Sargent. He was busy writing *The Tragic Muse* and also many letters, including those mourning the premature death in March of his old friend Lizzie Boott Duveneck (as she had become on her recent marriage to fellow artist Frank Duveneck). In October and November James travelled to the Continent for a brief holiday in Geneva – where he saw Woolson – and to Genoa, Monte Carlo, and Paris, to be back in London at the end of the year.

*

The 'germs' for most of the tales in this volume were recorded in James's *Notebooks*: the writer often considered 'a situation' and a 'subject' interesting and likely to develop into a story. For 'Pandora' James wrote that

---

[14] Michael Anesko, *Letters, Fictions, Lives: Henry James and William Dean Howells* (New York: Oxford University Press, 1997), p. 268. William Dean Howells, 'Editor's Study' [stories reprinted in *The Aspern Papers* and *A London Life*], *Harper's Monthly 77* (October 1888), 799–804; 800.

he wanted to explore further the subject of the 'self-made girl', as he had previously done in 'Daisy Miller'. Very often the 'germ' of the tale was a story or anecdote that someone had told him at dinner or tea; this is true for the origin of 'Georgina's Reasons', 'The Path of Duty', and 'The Aspern Papers'. Sometimes the idea for a story seems to have come to James from reading a book, as in the case of 'The Modern Warning'. For the other tales in this volume there is no 'germ' recorded in the *Notebooks*: 'Cousin Maria' (which became 'Mrs. Temperly') is mentioned only as a possible alternative to 'Louisa Pallant' for *Harper's Weekly* (*CN* 35).

In some of these nine stories James went back to the 'international theme' that had made 'Daisy Miller' a success. If 'Pandora', after a brief episode on board a ship from England, is entirely set in the United States, the presence of a puzzled German observer, Count Vogelstein, has the effect of presenting the American 'self-made girl' from a European perspective, though she is also a new phenomenon to the habitués of Washington society. In 'Georgina's Reasons' the theme emerges towards the end, through a Neapolitan setting in which two American sisters form a sharp contrast with the title character. All these tales from 'Daisy Miller' onwards feature prominent contrasts between different 'types' of American, especially American women, some of whom are comparatively 'Europeanized' and some of whom are distinctly not. In 'A New England Winter' the cold, 'Puritan' Boston stands out against the artistic atmosphere of Paris, through the figure of the impressionist painter, Florimond Daintry, and his mother's preoccupations. In 'The Path of Duty' the focus is on British hypocrisy – seen through the eyes of an American woman: in his 1876 letters James often wrote about his negative impressions of English mores and of the Tories,[15] much as he appreciated London as a place where he could write. In 'Cousin Maria' (later 'Mrs. Temperly'), the Paris where an American woman takes her daughters to give them the best the Old World can offer (including a husband for at least one of them) is a world of manners much more refined than in America, even if not so sincere. 'Louisa Pallant' focuses on the corruption present in an American

---

[15] On the other hand, the 'Liberal' Reform Club was much appreciated by James, who found in its members a social network useful to advance his professional career. See Greg Zacharias, 'Liberal London, Home, and Henry James's Letters from the Later 1870s', *Henry James Review*, 35.2 (2014), 127–40.

woman who has lived most of her life in Europe: she is no longer a naive and innocent heroine. At least two of the three main American characters in 'The Aspern Papers' are similarly corrupted, both the critic who tries to get hold of the eponymous papers and the very old woman living in Venice, a city recognized as a symbol of European deception and intrigue. In 'Two Countries' (later 'The Modern Warning') British tradition and conservatism are opposed to American democracy, defended by two hyper-patriotic characters. The theme of the marriage of an American girl to a British lord had been treated very differently by James in 'An International Episode' (1878), where the American Bessie Alden, with whom Lord Lambeth has fallen in love, finally refuses him, as Isabel Archer in *The Portrait of a Lady* (1881) refuses the marriage offered to her by Lord Warburton, in a choice of personal freedom over wealth and status.

In some of these tales James seems to confront the technological developments of the age, while in others the focus is on the inward presence of 'conscience'. The new 'age of newspapers and telegrams and photographs and interviewers' (*AP* 6) is one of the themes of 'The Aspern Papers', as it had been in the novella *The Reverberator*, published very shortly beforehand. James was becoming increasingly interested around this time in the erosion of 'the private life' and the means taken to protect personal privacy from the threat of exposure to publicity. Technological advances are associated with the emergence of a more independent type of young woman, as in 'Pandora', where 'the rise in prices, the telephone, the discovery of dynamite, the Chassepôt rifle, the socialistic spirit' are among 'the complications of modern life' (*SR1* 89) – which include the possibilities of marrying a new kind of American girl.

Several of these tales test the possibilities of one of James's favourite narrative devices, the 'unreliable observer' (most notably in 'Pandora', 'Louisa Pallant', 'The Liar') who sometimes coincides with the homodiegetic, first-person narrator ('The Aspern Papers'). In 'The Path of Duty' James also experiments with a written and self-contradictory document providing a frame to the tale: the unnamed American woman who is the author of the memoir writes 'it out for you' (*S1884–1891* 123) – that is, for *another* unnamed American – only to declare a few paragraphs later, to the reader's bafflement, that she will never 'betray' the characters of the story by sending or sharing this writing: 'after I have written out my reminiscences for your delectation, I shall simply keep them for my own' (*S1884–1891* 124).

This type of framing device, descending from the tradition of the discovered manuscript, was used in different ways by James: in the early tale 'A Light Man' (1869) ('I resume these old notes' (*S1864–74* 399)), 'The Solution' (1889) ('Oh yes, you may write it down' (*S1884–91* 664)), 'Sir Edmund Orme' (1891) ('I found these pages' (*S1884–91* 851)), 'The Visits' (1892) ('One of the listeners had taken many notes' (*S1892–98* 147)), 'Glasses' (1896) ('Yes indeed, I say to myself, pen in hand' (*S1892–98* 525)), 'The Way it Came' (1896) ('These pages evidently date from years ago' (*S1892–98* 609)), and most successfully in 'The Turn of the Screw' (1898). In these stories James not only recovers a long-standing literary device, he alters it by questioning the reliability of the manuscript's author.

James's interest in female attire and house decoration is evident in several of the stories here, such as the description of Rachel Torrance's clothes and ornaments and the Daintrys' very different Boston interiors in 'A New England Winter', the elegant Parisian Parc Monceau house in 'Mrs. Temperly', the wealthy abode on New York's Fifth Avenue of the bigamist's second marriage in 'Georgina's Reasons', and the fictional British country house of Stayes in 'The Liar', not to mention the unadorned and dilapidated palace of the Bordereau ladies in 'The Aspern Papers'. James still relies on the representation of a certain material environment as a tool for characterization, a realist tenet earlier practised by Balzac.

Of course there are echoes of James's own experiences of different localities in America and Europe: for example, the contrast between Boston and New York, which are seen respectively as America's intellectual and business capitals, their different 'mentality' being embodied by specific characters, such as the Theory sisters and Georgina Gressie in 'Georgina's Reasons', or Miss Daintry and Rachel Torrance in 'A New England Winter'. There is the contrast between London and Paris, the latter of which is ever-present in James as an appealing alternative to the British capital. There are the classic Grand Tour destinations of Florence, Genoa, Naples, and Venice. We also find some less usual settings such as Washington DC, the spa town of Homburg in Germany, and the beautiful Italian town of Stresa on Lake Maggiore. These were all places James had visited, and many of them fictionalize familiar touristic destinations of the period, as well as the routes leading to them. We find the trip from Washington to Mount Vernon in 'Pandora', the visit to the Royal Bourbon Museum,

Posillipo, and Pompeii near Naples in 'Georgina's Reasons', the observation of spa town rules in Homburg ('Louisa Pallant'), and the familiar descent into Italy along the Simplon road through the many tourist towns on the banks of Lake Como ('The Modern Warning') and Lake Maggiore (again 'Louisa Pallant') on the way to Milan. These routes and attractions were all widely advertised and promoted in popular guidebooks such as Murray's and Baedeker's.

'Pandora'

In a long notebook entry dated 29 January 1884 (see Appendix A), James expressed his determination to return to the figure of the young American woman, previously epitomized in his highly successful 'Daisy Miller' (1878). The play he derived from it, 'Daisy Miller: A Comedy' had been published in the *Atlantic Monthly*. James planned to make a concise story, involving a hero, 'a foreign secretary of Legation—German—inquiring & conscientious', and a heroine coming from a 'humble social background' who makes a position 'for herself—&, indirectly, indirectly, for her family' in the American capital. The story was to be set in New York and in Washington in particular. In a letter to Isabella Stewart Gardner from Washington DC (23 January 1882), James wrote of his observation of local women in a way that called for a comparison with the heroine of this story: 'There are also some charming girls—not rosebuds, e.g. Miss Bayard and Miss Frelinghuysen, who are happy specimens of the *finished* American girl—the American Girl who has profited by the sort of social education that Washington gives' (*CLHJ 1880–1883* 2:90). About a year later, in another entry during his American stay after his parents' death, James referred to this 'specimen' as the 'self-made girl' ('a very good subject for a short story. Very modern, very local; much might be done') (17 May 1883, *CN* 22). In his Preface to the volume of the *NYE* (xviii) that includes 'Daisy Miller' and 'Pandora' (Appendix B), we find a longer reflection on the figure of the 'self-made girl' as well as on the character who was to become Pandora. Apparently James found inspiration in 'a young lady present at a certain pleasure-party, but present in rather perceptibly unsupported and unguaranteed fashion, as without other connexions, without more operative "backers", than a proposer possibly half-hearted and a slightly sceptical seconder'. This young lady was presented to James as

an interesting representative of a new social and local variety, the "self-made", or at least self-making, girl, whose sign was that—given some measurably amusing appeal in her to more or less ironic curiosity or to a certain complacency of patron-age—she was anywhere made welcome enough if she only came, like one of the dismembered charges of Little Bo-Peep, leaving her "tail" behind her. (*LC2* 1271–3)

James's choice of the protagonist's name, Pandora, is particularly elusive and has puzzled critics. According to Hesiod's version of the Greek myth, Pandora ('all gifts') was the first woman created by the gods. Out of curi-osity, she opened a jar given to her by Zeus, thus releasing all the evils of humanity, leaving only hope inside. This mythical figure had many liter-ary and iconographic versions in the nineteenth century, from Goethe to Dante Gabriel Rossetti.[16] A possible connection with Goethe's unfinished play *Pandora* (1810) is strengthened by the fact that Goethe figures as one of the authors read by the female protagonist in the story. Adeline Tintner also mentions, as possible sources of inspiration for James, six paintings of the mythical Pandora displayed in London in 1883, among them a blonde *femme fatale* by Rossetti. Jean Gooder argues that the name might also refer to the doll-sized mannequins then used in the couturiers of Paris.[17] As for

---

[16] Their possible connections with James's tale are explored by Adeline Tintner in *The Pop World of Henry James: From Fairy Tales to Science Fiction* (Ann Arbor, MI: UMI Research Press, 1989), pp. 111–22. Tintner argues that 'the mention of Goethe perhaps is there to suggest that German aspect of the legend in the person of Count Vogelstein, whose "curiosity" about Pandora exposes him to the demon of unrequited love. Goethe's *Pandora* expresses the love of an older man for a young girl who leaves him. Count Vogelstein, like Goethe, is an Epimetheus figure' (p. 112). She also adds: 'Pandora, by the time James wrote his legend, was embedded in two traditions, that followed by Hawthorne and Longfellow, where a chest is opened by a curious girl who lets loose evil, and that followed by Calderon and Goethe, where a girl favoured by the Gods is presented with a chest whose contents, Science and Art, are also gifts to the world' (*ibid.*).

[17] 'A "Pandora" was the name given to the doll-sized figures used especially by Parisian fashion houses to model outfits for their customers. These dolls, complete to every accessory, were exported for display. [...] There is a temptingly apt irony, for a tale figuring Henry Adams, in the anticipation of the "manikin" of *The Education of Henry Adams* (1918).' *Daisy Miller and Other Stories*, ed. Jean Gooder (Oxford: Oxford University Press, 1985), p. 277.

real women who may have inspired James's heroine, Sarah Wadsworth has proposed that this character could be based on Alice Mason (1838–1913), whom James befriended in Rome in the 1870s. By the time James was taking notes for the story, Mason, whose life was marked by gossip and scandal and whose personality resembled that of James's heroine, had started to cruise the Mediterranean on board a chartered steam yacht called *Pandora*.[18]

The male protagonist of the story, the Prussian diplomat Otto Vogelstein, stands out as one of the only two German reflectors in James's *oeuvre* to observe and criticize American culture, the other being Dr Staub in the epistolary story 'A Bundle of Letters' (1878).[19] Both these two characters somehow reflect James's reservations about Germany and the German character, which one finds in his letters and travel essays. Although Vogelstein strongly recalls the American expatriate Winterbourne in 'Daisy Miller', interestingly, at the early stages of their acquaintance, Daisy actually compares her young compatriot to a German:

She asked him if he was a "real American"; she shouldn't have taken him for one; he seemed more like a German—this was said after a little hesitation—especially when he spoke. Winterbourne, laughing, answered that he had met Germans who spoke like Americans; but that he had not, so far as he remembered, met an American who spoke like a German. (*DMOS* 11)

Pierre Walker has noticed that the only German diplomat mentioned in James's letters from 1875 to 1880 was Baron Friedrich von Holstein

---

[18] Sarah Wadsworth, 'The Real Thing: Henry James and the Material World', unpublished conference paper, University of Aberdeen, 16–19 July 2014.

[19] See Evelyn Hovanec, *Henry James and Germany* (Amsterdam: Rodopi, 1979), p. 113. The character of Vogelstein echoes observations on the German character in James's travel essays. In 'Homburg Reformed' (1873) James wrote: 'The success of the Fatherland one sees reflected more or less vividly in all true German faces, and the relation between the face and the success seems demonstrated by a logic so unerring as to make envy vain. It is not the German success I envy, but the powerful German temperament and the comprehensive German brain. With these advantages one needn't be restless; one can afford to give a good deal of time to sitting out under the trees over pipes and beer and discussion tinged with metaphysics. But success of course is most forcibly embodied in the soldiers and officers who now form so large a proportion of every German group' (*CTW*2 641). James did not favour Germany, especially in comparison with France and Italy. In his essay 'Venice: An Early Impression' (1873) he wrote: 'Germany is ugly, […] Munich is a nightmare, Heidelberg a disappointment (in spite of its charming castle) and even Nuremberg not a joy forever' (*CTW*2 345).

(1837–1909), whom James met when he was living in Paris in 1875–6.[20] His name appears in two letters of 1876 (14 March to William and 24, 25 May to Alice). In the first James writes:

I have seen something of late of one Baron Holstein, German secrétaire d'am-bassade—one of the most acute & intelligent men I have ever met. We occasion-ally dine together—he being the only detached male that I know (he is by the way the gentleman whose attentions to Mrs. Sumner—he was then secretary in Washington—were the prime cause of the explosion of the Hon Charles, & the consequent separation.) (*CLHJ 1872–1876* 3:81)

Holstein served as member of the legation in Washington between 1866 and 1867, and his relation to the above-mentioned Alice Mason, then newly married to Senator Charles Sumner, led to Holstein's withdrawal and to the separation (and later divorce) of the couple.[21]

Another possible source for the name Pandora can be traced back to the American celebrity Blanche Roosevelt Tucker-Macchetta (1853–98), singer, actress, and writer, whom James saw in London in 1886 and who elicited scathing comments from the American writer. In a letter to Francis Boott dated 15 August of that year, he wrote: 'I have but just escaped from the jaws of Blanche Roosevelt, who used to sing in opera—didn't she?—& who is now here married to a Milanese, trying to be literary & assaulting me (with compliments) on my productions' (*CLHJ 1884–1886* 2:153). Roosevelt made an opera out of Henry Wadsworth Longfellow's Hesiod-based poem 'The Masque of Pandora' (1875) with music composed by Alfred Cellier (1844–91), which was performed unsuccessfully on 10 January 1881 at the Boston Theater, featuring Roosevelt in the role of Pandora. In the introduction to her own book on Longfellow (*The Home Life of Henry W. Longfellow* (New York: C. W. Carleton & Co., 1882)), Roosevelt refers to a letter by the poet, showing that he had grown used to addressing her as 'Pandora' (21). Longfellow's collection also contained a poem titled 'Charles Sumner', dedi-cated to the recently deceased senator (who had died in 1874).

---

[20] We are indebted to Pierre Walker for generously suggesting this connection.

[21] Born in Boston in 1838, Alice Mason married William Sturgis Hooper in 1857. He died in 1863 and three years later she married Sumner; they separated shortly thereafter and divorced in 1873.

As the 29 January 1884 notebook entry shows, 'Pandora' was to feature Washington alongside New York as a primary setting. James had visited Washington in 1882 (and again in 1883) and participated in the social life of the city, thanks to his friends Henry and 'Clover' Adams.[22] In a letter to Sir John Clark from Washington DC, dated 8 January 1882, James wrote:

I find here our good little friends the Adamses, whose extremely agreeable house may be said to be one of the features of Washington. They receive a great deal & in their native air they bloom, expand, emit a genial fragrance. They don't pretend to conceal (as why should they?) their preference of America to Europe, & they rather rub it into me, as they think it a wholesome discipline for my demoralized spirit. One excellent reason for their liking Washington better than London is that they are, vulgarly speaking, "someone" here, & that they are nothing in your complicated Kingdom. (*CLHJ 1880–1882* 2: 65–66)[23]

In the story James included a literary rendition of the Adamses as Mr and Mrs Bonnycastle ('I might even *do* Henry Adams and his wife', he noted on 29 January 1884).[24] The name Bonnycastle may echo that of the Hardcastles in *She Stoops to Conquer*, a play frequently performed in James's childhood in New York (*SBOC* 91) and, at the same time, it may allude to the Adamses' 'extremely agreeable house'.

'Pandora' is one of the first stories James decided to publish in a popular newspaper. Embittered by the mediocre profits from Macmillan's (see

[22] Henry Adams (1838–1918), the famous historian, was a descendant of two presidents of the United States. His autobiography, *The Education of Henry Adams* (1907), is one of the great texts of American intellectual history. He was also the author of *Democracy* (1880), a novel on Washington's political life. After Marian 'Clover' Adams (1843–85) took her own life, a fine funerary monument by Augustus Saint-Gaudens, the Adams Memorial (1891), was erected, which James went to see in 1905. See also 'The Modern Warning' for analogies regarding her suicide.

[23] On the rendition of the Adamses in the story, see Robert L. Gale, '"Pandora" and Her President', *Studies in Short Fiction*, 1 (Spring 1964), 222–5; George Monteiro, 'Washington Friends and National Reviewers: Henry James's "Pandora"', *Research Studies*, 43.1 (March 1975), 38–44.

[24] Marian Adams was fictionalized in another short story, 'The Point of View' (1882); for her reaction to it see *The Letters of Mrs. Henry Adams, 1865–1883*, ed. Ward Thoron (Boston, MA: Little, Brown, 1936), p. 403. In her biography of Marian Adams, Natalie Dykstra refers to her Washington salon as 'a gilded cage, which "left out on the whole more people than it took in", as Henry James described it in his short story "Pandora"' (*Clover Adams: A Gilded and Heartbreaking Life* (Boston, MA: Houghton Mifflin, 2012), p. 125).

the letter to Frederick Macmillan, 29 January 1884, *CLHJ 1883–1884* 2: 4, 5), in January 1884 he agreed to sell two stories ('Pandora' and 'Georgina's Reasons') to Charles A. Dana (1819–97), then owner and editor (1868–97) of the *New York Sun* (see Textual Introduction). Dana was gathering material from various American authors for a syndicated publication (the 'coordinated publication of fiction in multiple newspapers').[25] Such authors included Bret Harte, W. D. Howells, and Mark Twain. Critics have debated the reasons why James decided to publish in popular newspapers in spite of his well-known contempt for them. However, in a letter to William (10 October 1883), James had given another reason for his possibility of publishing in the *Sun*: 'To be so well paid as that is to have leisure to work carefully, artistically, and according to one's taste and that's the real and only seduction of the thing to me' (*CLHJ 1883–1884* 1:237–8), adding that 'one would be supplying a very large general public with artistic work'.[26]

Further evidence for James's desire both to earn more and to reach a wider audience can be found in three letters addressed respectively to his sister Alice, to Thomas Bailey Aldrich (editor of the *Atlantic Monthly*), and to his friend Thomas Sergeant Perry:

I am writing a couple of short tales—as a trial, to begin with—for Dana & the Sun! The die is cast—but I don't in the least repent of it—as I see no shame in offering my productions to the widest public, & in their being "brought home", as it were, to the great American people. I have lately finished two nouvelles for Osgood & the Century: one to be published in three & one in two instalments. After this I am to do one in six, on the same contract, & that will finish this business. It will have had its advantages, but it will not have been (owing to my want of greediness in making my bargain) supremely lucrative. I am, however, trusting to the Dana business to more than make up for that. (letter to Alice James, 5 February 1884, *CLHJ 1883–1884* 2:10)[27]

And three or four short tales, from my teeming hand, are to appear (this is a profound secret)—have been, in a word, secured, *à prix d'or* in—*je vois* [sic] *le donne en mille*—the New York Sunday Sun!! This last fact, I repeat, is really as yet *a complete*

---

[25] Charles Johanningsmeier, 'Henry James's Dalliance with the Newspaper World', *Henry James Review*, 19.1 (1998), 38.

[26] According to Johanningsmeier the possibility of reaching a wider audience and earning more money probably prevailed over James's reluctance to circulate his works in the *New York Sun*, a minor venue, though still a respectable one (*ibid.*, 40).

[27] The editors thank Greg Zacharias for advance access to the text of this letter.

& sacred secret. Please bury it in oblivion & burn my letter. I mention it, with the preceding items, simply to denote that by July 1865 [*sic*] I expect to have described as be[ing] in the enjoyment of a popularity which will require me to ask $500 a number for the successive instalments of *The Princess Casamassima* [...]. (letter to Aldrich, 3 February 1884, from Paris, *CLHJ 1883–1884* 2:22)

I am engaged to write (that is, to publish two ~~novels~~ "serials" next year—one of six months', the other of a year's duration. So I have work cut out, & so have you, if you read me. These are to be the best things I have done, & the former a remorseless exploitation of Boston. Look out, in Marlborough St; I am especially hard on the far end. Lately I have been doing some short things which you will see in due time—in the Century, & eke three or four in (horresco referens!) the New York Sunday *Sun*! This last item by the way, is for the present, till the things appear, a profound secret. That journal has bribed me with gold—it is a case of gold pure & simple; & moreover the reasons against my ~~offering~~ exposing myself in it do not seem to me serious. Meanwhile, tace. (letter to T. S. Perry, 6 March 1884; *CLHJ 1883–1884* 2:55)

Sarah Wadsworth has recently advanced another explanation for James's willingness to appear in the *Sun*, linked to the particular subject of 'Pandora'. According to her, 'James's story contains, redeems, and disseminates the narrative of the "self-made girl" in the very forum in which her prototype was subjected to public scrutiny, insinuation, and outright condemnation.'[28]

As the dates of these letters suggest, James most likely composed the stories for the *Sun* in the months immediately before their June 1884 publication.[29] 'Pandora' obtained mixed reviews. The negative ones deemed it unimpressive ('traverses much the same ground that Mr. James has passed over in several "international sketches"' (*Christian Union*)), downright bad ('a complete failure' (*New York Tribune*)), or simply compared it unfavourably to James's earlier work ('In "Pandora" we are introduced to a highly disagreeable "Daisy Miller", a trifle more honest, but not less provincial' (*Independent*)).[30] Those that were positive mostly praised James's characterization of the two protagonists and his ability to sketch Washington society. One reviewer in the *Daily Tribune* wrote: 'Nothing could well be more genial

---

[28] Unpublished conference paper, University of Aberdeen, July 2014.
[29] See Johanningsmeier, 'Henry James's Dalliance', 39.
[30] For details of the reviews of these tales see below.

and delightfully humorous than the story of "Pandora" [...] The distinctness with which the character of Pandora is brought out, and its perfectly
consistent development, are above all praise. Washington society has never
been touched by so able a pen. Count Vogelstein is infinitely diverting.' With
regard to the description of the capital, in the *Boston Daily Advertiser* we
read: 'A subsequent journey to Washington enables Mr. James to turn a seeing eye upon that capital, and, as always, he finds fresh and adequate forms
of expression for what he sees.' The *Literary World* even concluded that
'Pandora' was 'by far the cleverest thing in [what was] decidedly a miscella-
neous collection [*The Author of Beltraffio* (1885)] '. Some reviewers proudly
advertised it as a work that made amends for the unpatriotic portrait of
the American woman James had offered in 'Daisy Miller'. In the twentieth
century the story was praised by as illustrious a reader as Ezra Pound, who
particularly admired James's skilled satirical portrait of a German diplomat: '*Pandora*, of the best. Let it pass as a sop to America's virginal charm; as
counter-weight to *Daisy Miller*, or to the lady of *The Portrait*.'[31]

Many critics have interpreted this story in the light of 'Daisy Miller',
inspired by James's reference to his famous work in the text (it is the
book Vogelstein reads on board the transatlantic steamer). The nature of
Pandora's aggressive social climbing has been a recurrent topic in criticism, which has related it to the promotion of her family and Mr Bellamy,
her 'passive' fiancé,[32] and to the reaction of those who surround her (Mrs
Dangerfield, the Bonnycastles, and, obviously, Count Vogelstein). Peter
Buitenhuis has pointed out that the story exemplifies James's full aware-
ness that reality is often perceived through 'literary schemata' (Vogelstein
identifying Pandora with the Daisy Miller of his book), praising also the
indirectness through which glimpses of Washington's social and political
life are offered to the reader.[33] Comparing it to 'Daisy Miller', Evelyne Labbé
underlines the stronger presence of realistic, sociological details, provided
by the observation of a systematic reflector (Vogelstein) and the worldly Mr
Bonnycastle (*NC2* 1473).

[31] Ezra Pound, 'A Shake Down', *The Little Review*, 5 (August 1918), 25.
[32] Adeline R. Tintner, *The Book World of Henry James: Appropriating the Classics* (Ann Arbor, MI: UMI Research Press, 1987), p. 266.
[33] Peter Buitenhuis, *The Grasping Imagination: The American Writings of Henry James* (Toronto: University of Toronto Press, 1970), pp. 122–6.

'Georgina's Reasons'

This was the second story James wrote for Dana's newspaper, along with 'Pandora', in the first half of 1884. The earliest 'germ' for it can be found in an extended notebook entry dated 26 March 1884 (see Appendix A), where James mentions being struck by a 'very incredible' story told to him by his friend, the famous British actress Fanny Kemble (1809–93), about 'a young girl, in one of the far Western cities of America, who formed an attachment to a young US officer quartered in the town and of whose attentions to her her family wholly disapproved'. James was particularly impressed by the situation of 'two persons secretly married, and one of whom (the husband, naturally) is tied by a promise to be silent, yet wishes to break this marriage in order to recover his freedom – to marry again, to beget legitimate children. The interest of the other is that the marriage never be known – her honour, her safety concerned, &c.'. Although James found the anecdote 'singularly crude & incoherent', he basically left all the details he had thus received unvaried for the final draft of the story (*CN* 26–7).

In a letter dated 24 December 1886, written by James to his friend John Hay, the American statesman and writer (1838–1905), further information emerges concerning the inspiration for the story and James's disappointment about the final outcome:

Let me add that it wasn't King[34] who told me the tale of "Georgina's Reasons." He has told me many—but for that ugly narrative I am not indebted to him. It was imparted to me by my dear old friend Fanny Kemble, to whom it had been told by her brother-in-law, Edward Sartoris, who had it from his queer little daughter-in-law Nelly Grant—endowed for that occasion only, it would appear, with the favor of articulate speech. She gave it (as I understood the matter) as something that had befallen—or been transacted by—a girl she personally knew in some American—*western*—town. It struck me as a *theme*, & I pulled it about a little, put it in New York, Naples, &c (pour donner le change) & made frankly, I think, a very bad & unsuccessful story of it. (*CLHJ 1884–1886* 2: 275)[35]

---

[34] A dear friend of James and Hay, Clarence King (1842–1901) was an American pioneering geologist and art critic; influenced by the works of John Ruskin, he was a co-founder of the Society for the Advancement of Truth in Art (1863), an American group similar to the English Pre-Raphaelite Brotherhood.

[35] See also George Monteiro, *Henry James and John Hay: The Record of a Friendship* (Providence, RI: Brown University Press, 1965), pp. 100–1.

Meanwhile a real-life model for the character of Mildred Theory, the ailing and intelligent sister of Kate, the woman Captain Benyon would like to marry, may be found in James's own sister Alice, whose first nervous crisis had occurred as early as 1868.

'Georgina's Reasons' is an odd item in the Jamesian catalogue as it features an unprecedented version of the young American woman abroad, and seems partly inspired by the Victorian sensation stories, involving bigamy, exemplified by Mary Elizabeth Braddon's best-selling novels *Lady Audley's Secret* (1862) and *Aurora Floyd* (1863), which James had reviewed in his twenties (*LC1* 741–6).[36] Some of the newspapers that reprinted the story thus blatantly advertised it for its sensational content. Like 'Pandora', this story was published in the *New York Sun* (20, 27 July and 3 August 1884) and concomitantly in nine other American newspapers (see Textual Introduction). One of these, the *Chicago Tribune*, featured the following headline: 'GEORGINA'S REASONS! / Henry James's Latest Story / A woman who commits bigamy and enforces silence on her husband! Two other lives made miserable by her heartless action!'[37]

The contemporary reviews were mainly negative, insisting on the disturbing, embarrassing subject and lack of verisimilitude. Most of them openly sided with the male protagonist, Raymond Benyon, and were very harsh on the title character. In the *Boston Daily Advertiser* we read:

"Georgiana's [sic] Reasons" is a disagreeable and almost impossible story. Georgina's beauty does not save her from being a hateful woman whose reasons are sure to have been unworthy. Captain Benyon, who begins by loving and ends by hating her, is a fine fellow, but neither he nor the lovely Miss Theory and her sister can save "Georgiana's [sic] Reasons" from being essentially unpleasant.

In the *Chicago Daily Tribune*: '"Georgina's Reasons" is the indecent history of an atrocious crime. Its exceeding cleverness cannot atone for the baseness of its subject. The evil woman represented is too horrible to contemplate: the good women are failures; and the reader turns with relief to the silly woman, Mrs. Percival.' Or again: '"Georgina's Reasons" is unpleasant in subject and

---

[36] Tintner, *Pop World of Henry James*, pp. 159–64; Donatella Izzo, *Portraying the Lady: Technologies of Gender in the Short Stories of Henry James* (Lincoln, NE: University of Nebraska Press, 2001), pp. 192–212); Roslyn Jolly, 'Henry James in Mid-Career: "Georgina's Reasons" and the Possibilities of Style', *Style*, 47.3 (2013), 345–8.

[37] Leon Edel, *Henry James: The Middle Years 1884–1894* (London: Rupert Hart-Davis, 1963), pp. 56–7.

almost unwholesome in tone' (*Christian Union*). An anonymous reviewer even came to describe the female protagonist as a 'moral monster' (*Independent*). In judging the story 'the most disagreeable' included in the collection headed by *The Author of Beltraffio* (1885), a reviewer in the *New York Times* wrote:

such a subject as that which forms the theme of 'Georgina's Reasons' is not in Mr. James's province. The heroine, though she may be married, is a wanton of the basest type. Her degradation comes, as Mr. James rather laboriously explains it, not from any outburst of passion but from curiosity. His ingenuity in the construction of a character such as Georgina's is apparently all he cares for. The bond of marriage in this story, uncertain though Mr. James has made it, is a mistake in an artistic sense, and it seems as if artistic perfection is what Mr. James most craves for. Had Georgina's child been born without the best suspicion of legitimacy it would have been better for the dramatic effect of the story. Altogether, the subject is very *risqué* and uncomfortable.

Some reviews remarked upon James's failure in imitating the current French literary fashion. The critic of the *Literary World* commented:

As for *Georgina's Reasons* and *The Path of Duty*—such productions are common in French literature of a certain class, but they are rather new to English fiction. If the sexual relations in their baser aspect must form the theme of the novelist, one would prefer the free, bold treatment of a Fielding to the morbid vein of analysis that Mr. James has assumed. It is hard to see how such writing can be profitable either to author or reader.

The reviewer concluded that the story was 'simply a study in depravity, as revolting as it could well be'. *Lippincott's Magazine* also dismissed James's story as a failed attempt at exploring the violation of the moral code, and as a poor imitation of the French school of *'l'art pour l'art'*. The *Critic* associated the tale specifically with the degenerate products of French literature.

James himself retrospectively provided a negative judgement on this tale in two letters, in the aforementioned one to John Hay ('a bad and unsuccessful story') and in one to F. W. H. Myers[38] dated 13 November 1894:

Of *Georgina's Reasons* I mainly remember that I thought them pretty bad at the time—I mean thought the tale a feeble one, and that impression has remained with

---

[38] Frederick William Henry Myers (1843–1901) was one of the founders of the Society for Psychical Research (1882), and his work influenced William James. Henry James made his acquaintance in 1879 (see *NC2* 1482, note 6).

me. I daresay it is one of the worst I was ever guilty of. I have been looking for it this a.m.—to appreciate your remarks better, but I find that I seem to be without the volume that contains it. The thing is dim to me; what they did, and what they should have done; there only sticks to me rather definitely the memory of the limited anecdote (told me by a friend, a lady, as something told to *her*—and having happened in some American western town) in which I originally saw the adumbration of a story. In general, moreover, I think that after one has done, *tant bien que mal*, a thing of that sort, one becomes intensely irresponsible about it—getting away from it as from a kind of relinquished execution or terminated connection. That, at least, is the feeble way *I* feel. One saw it, one did it, with all the vividness that was in one at the time; but the act accomplished, and the spasm over, one can't *relive* that experience, one can only thirst for another with different material. So it is that I, at least, can never lift my finger to defend or to explain. There they are, poor things, and *why* they were I did once seem to know; but I have always consentingly forgotten. So moreover it is that when the ingenuous ask which of one's "things" one likes best, I am filled [with] a secret horror at being supposed to "like" any of them. I loathe them all! What I "like" is the art—more than I can say; and the works have only a temporary tolerance—reflected from that. None the less I am inconsequent enough to like immensely those who also tolerate.   (*HJL* 3:488–9)

The character of Georgina Gressie resurfaces in a poem titled 'Henry James' by R. L. Stevenson (collected in *Underwoods*, 1887), where she is alluded to in unflattering terms as 'that far different she / Gressie, the trivial sphinx' (*HJL* 3:207, footnote 2). More recent critics have generally concentrated on understanding the extent of James's participation in the sensation genre (see footnote 37 above). The main interpretational issue regards identification of the 'reasons' behind Georgina's behaviour. According to some, the story could be read as a pioneering fictional account of a woman's insanity.[39] Others have identified, behind the writer's conscious imitation of the sensation genre, an underlying subversion of the gender roles spread by this very genre: Georgina's behaviour, thus, could never find a proper explanation or justification in a male-oriented society.[40] Jolly reads the whole tale as 'a story that invokes a range of genres without committing exclusively to any

[39] Tintner, *Pop World of Henry James*, pp. 162–4, but also Jolly, 'Henry James in Mid-Career', 351–4.
[40] Izzo, *Portraying the Lady*, p. 201.

one of them', thereby illuminating 'some of the stylistic choices and challenges James faced as an author in the mid-1880s'.[41] Many commentators have also noticed the secondary characters, pointing out the similarities, of the names if nothing more, between Kate and Mildred Theory in this story and Kate Croy and Milly Theale in *The Wings of the Dove*. Mildred Theory also offers some similarities with the invalid Rose Muniment in *The Princess Casamassima*, another fictional character partly inspired by Alice James. In 1975 a film adaptation of the story for German TV was made by director Volker Schlöndorff, who, according to Moeller and Lellis, had 'deliberately turned a detached, third-person narrative into a subjective, first-person drama'.[42]

'A New England Winter'

The first idea James had for 'A New England Winter' was recorded in his *Notebooks* on 18 January 1881:

Mrs. T., living in America (say at Newport,) has a son, young, unmarried, clever and selfish, who persists in living in Europe, and whom she therefore sees only at long intervals. He prefers European life, & takes his filial duties very lightly. She goes out to see him from time to time, but dares not fix herself permanently near him, for fear of boring him. At last however he comes home, to pay a short visit, and all her desire is to induce him to remain with her for some months. She has reason to believe that he will grow very tired of her quiet house; & in order to enhance its attraction she invites a young girl—a distant relative, from another part of the country, to stay with her. (*CN* 17: for the full version of this note, see Appendix A)

The story was first published in the 1884 August and September issues of *Century* magazine, then collected in *Tales of Three Cities* in the same year

---

[41] Jolly, 'Henry James in Mid-Career', 345.
[42] Hans-Bernhard Moeller and George Lellis, *Volker Schlöndorff's Cinema: Adaptation, Politics, and the 'Movie-Appropriate'* (Carbondale, IL: Southern Illinois University Press, 2002), p. 121. 'In portraying a man's desire to possess an unresponsive woman, Schlöndorff employs [the] mechanism of voyeurism, of a male gaze directed at an idealized woman, to create a visual analogue to the character's internal state. In giving a story of female resistance an uncomprehending male point of view, he strengthens the woman's mystery and power.' See Volker Schlöndorff, dir., *Georgina's Gründe: Nach der Erzählung 'Georgina's Reasons' von Henry James*, camera Sven Nykvist, film, 63 mins, Bavaria on behalf of WDR/ORTF, broadcast première 27 April 1975, ARD Television.

(see Textual Introduction). It developed in more complex ways than the notebook outline suggests. James inserted two more characters, those of Miss Daintry and Mrs Mesh, and he gave Rachel Torrance, the 'distant relative, from another part of the country', an especially lively characterization, while moderating some of the son's cleverness. More importantly, the initial hypothesis of a Newport setting gave way to a very accurate description of both the topography and the social mores of Boston, a city which James had already used in less detailed ways in *The Europeans* (1878) and was to portray more fully in *The Bostonians*. Moreover, in the *Notebooks* there is no hint of the son being a painter, and an impressionist, a topic that becomes important in a story where both impressionism and naturalism are explicitly referred to, even if mostly in ironic terms.

The conclusion to the note (see Appendix A) shows James imagining more than one possibility for the denouement. He thinks first of the son's advances being rejected, and of his return to Europe 'in disgust and dudgeon [...], while the mother is left lamenting!' Then he imagines an alternative 'happy ending', perhaps aimed at the magazine readers, in which the girl surrenders to the young man's passion and they marry. Both possibilities leave the mother alone, and the separation from her son complete. In the event, the finished story provides an outcome more merciful to the mother, who travels to Europe with her son. James's notebook entry had suggested the presence of another woman with whom the son is entangled in Europe, as so many American young men are in his fiction – Florimond, he envisioned, has 'a connection with some woman abroad' – but she is never mentioned in the finished work.

James played out the confrontation between America and Europe by contrasting Boston and Paris. However, the description of Boston is strongly detailed and has a variety of characteristics, while Paris as such remains hazily in the background. Boston appears as the 'cold' city of the Puritan tradition, symbolically represented by the abundant snow, but it also has more nuanced characteristics and is described in some detail in the walks of Mrs Daintry and her son Florimond. Mrs Daintry walks from the Back Bay to Beacon Hill, from the new filled-in marshy area south of the Charles River to the old Boston neighbourhood, even now the most elegant part of the city; important historical landmarks of the city are explicitly mentioned, such as the Public Garden and Boston Common, or the most elegant and exclusive literary club, the Athenæum, where Mrs Daintry borrows her books; the State House golden dome built by Charles Bulfinch; the gallery of Doll & Richards, where painters such as Winslow Homer, Lizzie Boott, John La Farge, Émile Lambinet, and Childe Hassam exhibited in the 1880s and 1890s. John Appleton Brown (1844–1902), mentioned in the story as exhibiting at Doll's, was a minor American impressionist whose work was in fact shown there, and James wrote on his paintings twice, in 1872 and 1875.[43]

If the story takes place mainly on Beacon Hill and in the new areas of the Back Bay, other parts of the city are carefully described, such as for example the busy suburbs along Washington Street, to the south-west, where Florimond, the young 'impressionist', wanders in slushy streets crowded with thronging pedestrians, obstructed by horse-cars, bordered with strange, 'promiscuous' shops, which seem at once 'violent and indifferent'. Particularly in the description of this area, James offers lively passages in a realistic style while also documenting the new Boston of horse-cars, railways, and the telegraph in addition to the Harvard spaces in Cambridge.

James's depiction of the (not particularly gifted) painter Florimond makes him a (weak) representative of impressionism, of which, as mentioned above, James was initially not in favour. This character is one among the many fictional painters who appear in James's stories, from Mr Locksley in the early 'A Landscape Painter' (1866) to Walter Puddick in 'Mora Montravers' (1909). Florimond, however, although he has lived in Paris for six years, does not seem to belong to the bohemian milieu there, even if he asserts that he misses the 'studio talk', the connection with 'naturalists (in art and literature)' when he is in Boston: his neat appearance makes him belong more to the tradition of Boston than to that of Paris. We also find a character described in Orientalizing terms, the 'Smyrniote'-looking Rachel Torrance, from Brooklyn, an outsider who, with her black hair, coins in her coiffure and seamless clothes, seems to represent a dramatic alternative to the restrained Bostonian spinster, Miss Daintry, but also to the good if excessively motherly Mrs Daintry, who gives in to the 'new' as regards her home, but keeps an attentive eye on the heirlooms her sister-in-law has inherited.

[43]   Adeline R. Tintner, *The Museum World of Henry James* (Ann Arbor, MI: UMI Research Press, 1986), p. 107.

James had first imagined the story being told 'as a journal of the mother', perhaps desiring to experiment once again with the diary form he had deployed a year earlier in 'The Impressions of a Cousin' (1883), but he abandoned this for a traditional omniscient narrator who addresses the reader, although in some parts, especially the beginning, the story is presented from Mrs Daintry's point of view. This decision points to what Buitenhuis underlines as 'a major change' in James's technique in 'A New England Winter', proposing that the story is 'in part an attempt to make a series of impressionistic verbal paintings of Boston'.[44] James wrote to Howells from Paris on 21 February 1884 about this tale: 'It is not very good—on the contrary; but it will perhaps seem to you to put into form a certain impression of Boston' (*CLHJ 1883–1884* 2:29). Howells would no doubt have been very sensitive to James's efforts; in the novel he published a year later, *The Rise of Silas Lapham*, he too would use Boston as the setting for the novel's action, and choose the Back Bay as the setting for the grandiose house of the newly rich protagonist.

On 2 January 1884 James jotted down several names in his *Notebooks* that feature in some of his immediately subsequent fictions, notably 'Daintry' and 'Florimond', which he would use in this tale, but also 'Benyon' in 'Georgina's Reasons', 'Vandeleur' and 'Ambrose' in 'The Path of Duty', 'Ambient' in 'The Author of Beltraffio', and 'Mathias' and 'Chancellor' in *The Bostonians* (*CN* 23). Most of them came from the London *Times* of that date. However, the name of Florimond seems to link this story with Longfellow, and other references to the popular American poet are present in the text. Mrs Daintry is said to have chosen this name for her son because 'every one was reading old ballads in Boston' when the 'rosy babe' was born. In 1841 Longfellow had published his *Ballads and Other Poems*, and in 1876–9 he published an anthology in thirty-one volumes, *Poems of Places*, with a section on Scottish ballads. The ballad of Florimond, 'who slew the dragon by the sea', does not appear here, however, but in the anonymous *Complaynt of Scotland* (1548), reprinted in 1872 by the Early English Text Society. A very well-known poem by Longfellow, 'The Children's Hour' (1860), is explicitly quoted in James's tale to contrast the absence of Mrs Mesh's children in their

---

[44] Buitenhuis, *Grasping Imagination*, pp. 133, 137.

mother's life with the affectionate three girls in the poem who rush downstairs to embrace their father. These references to Longfellow might lead one to surmise that Mrs Daintry's servant, Beatrice, might be connected to the protagonist of *Evangeline* (1847), as they both come from Nova Scotia.

In spite of James's reservations about this tale, Howells responded appreciatively: 'The study pleases me throughout; the mother with her struggles—herculean struggles—with such shadowy problems; the son with the sincere Europeanism of an inalienable, wholly uninspired American. As for the vehicle, it is delicious.'[45] Favourable reviews praised the description of Boston (*Boston Daily Advertiser* and the *Hartford Daily Courant*),[46] although the story was judged unpatriotic by the *Literary World*. The *Boston Daily Advertiser* also appreciated the character of Rachel Torrance, 'a beautiful and rather unusual girl'. In general, however, reviews were not particularly enthusiastic: the *Athenæum* judged 'Lady Barberina' a better story, and the *New York Daily Graphic* simply associated it with 'Lady Barberina' (1884); the *Chicago Tribune* considered the story 'a little dull and very incomplete'. The story has been discussed by Buitenhuis (1970) and by Tintner (1986);[47] the latter sees the figure of Mrs Mesh as partly suggested by Isabella Stewart Gardner, the great future collector and founder of the museum in Boston that bears her name, who lived at the time on Beacon Street (in close proximity to Mrs Mesh, whose home is round the corner on Arlington Street) and whom James saw with some frequency in the first eight months of 1883.

'The Path of Duty'

According to a notebook entry dated 29 January 1884 (see Appendix A), the germ for 'The Path of Duty' derived from a story mentioned to James by Gertrude Tennant (1819–1918), art patron and renowned hostess of a London literary salon. The story was about a young Lord Stafford, son of the Duke of Sutherland, who had been in love with Lady Grosvenor for years before she married Lord Grosvenor. The young man, pressured by his family, engages to marry the daughter of Lord Rosslyn, but shortly

---

[45] Anesko, *Letters, Fictions, Lives*, p. 247.
[46] See Contemporary Reception, for specific dates.
[47] Buitenhuis, *Grasping Imagination*, pp. 136–9; Tintner, *Museum World*, pp. 199–205.

afterwards Lord Grosvenor dies and his wife, Lady G., becomes free. Should young Lord S. hold to his promise of marriage or find a way out of it, and present himself in due course to Lady G.? What would Lady G. do if he did so? James was fascinated by this story 'capable of several different turns, according to the character of the actors' (*CN* 23), but he discarded the possibility of the young girl consenting in advance to her potential husband having a secret affair with the older woman. As James reasoned, they did things differently across the Channel: 'If I were a Frenchman & a naturalist, this is probably the treatment I shld. adopt,' James observed. (For a full version of this note, see Appendix A.)

There were at least three possible points of view, James noted, and it was easy to imagine more than one issue, 'though only one is rigidly honourable' – the path of duty that would provide the tale's title. It was what lay behind or beyond the English proprieties that intrigued him, the possibility of a dangerous liaison between lovers who have officially renounced it, and the plight of the 'poor little bride' supposed to have got what she wanted. It was a situation at the heart of some of his greatest long fictions, from *The Portrait of a Lady* to *The Golden Bowl* (1904). James could see that 'the note on which this particular story would close', a 'noble renunciation', would be an arrangement 'congenial to the characteristic manner of H.J.— I shall probably try it'. James also added that perhaps it would help to have the story told by someone outside the triangle, observing at fairly close quarters, to a visitor from a much greater distance, an American, say. In the event the tale does indeed feature a highly characterized first-person narrator, an American woman in whom the triumphantly virtuous lovers confide. With comparable virtue, she refuses to share the written memoir of their story with anyone – except of course with us, the readers (see above).

The story appeared in the December 1884 issue of the *English Illustrated Magazine* (see Textual Introduction). It was received rather unenthusiastically by contemporary reviewers, who paired it with 'Georgina's Reasons' for the presence of the disturbing themes so dear to contemporary French writers: 'In "The Path of Duty", Mr James exhibits a maze of moral entanglement with an art which is distinctly of the modern French school' (*Chicago Daily Tribune*). While commenting on the whole collection in which it appeared in February the following year (*The Author of Beltraffio*, 1885), an anonymous reviewer for the Boston *Literary World* dismissed this story as 'the least successful and least interesting of the number'. Some reviews insisted on its obscurity and ineffectiveness: '"The Path of Duty" is tortuous and involved, and when uncoiled the strand you hold escapes you entirely' (*New York Times*); '"The Path of Duty" is over a ground scarcely debatable, from beginning to end' (*The Independent*).

Critics have placed this tale with other works specifically related to England and its social manners, such as the long stories 'The Siege of London' (1883), 'Lady Barberina' (1884), and 'A London Life' (1888).[48] Comparisons have been made between it and *The Golden Bowl*, specifically between the characters of Joscelind and Maggie Verver, and between the couple Tester–Vandeleur and Prince Amerigo–Charlotte Stant.[49] A central problem, as for 'The Liar', has been that of establishing the reliability of the anonymous narrator, the American lady living in London, who is Ambrose Tester's confidante.[50]

'Mrs. Temperly'

There is no sign of a 'germ' in James's *Notebooks* for this story, but only a reference of 12 January 1887 where James suggests he might replace it with 'Louisa Pallant' if *Harper's* editor Schuyler should not like it. However *Harper's* did accept it, and on 5 February 1887, having just heard that they were going to publish his story, then entitled 'Cousin Maria', James wrote to John Foord (1842–1922), editor at *Harper's Weekly*, from Florence, asking to have the proofs, unless it were too late, as the story had been sent 'in MS, & not in type-copy', and experience had taught him 'that in this case the printed text is apt to be terribly impure'. James promised to send it back 'with the minimum of delay'. He also said that the story was written 'in an attempt to supply Harper's Weekly" [*sic*] with a tale of the proper length

---

[48] John L. Kimmey, 'James's London Tales of the 1880s', *Henry James Review*, 8.1 (Fall 1986), 37–46.

[49] Marius Bewley, *The Complex Fate: Hawthorne, Henry James and Some Other American Writers* (London: Chatto & Windus, 1952), pp. 88, 95; Ora Segal, *The Lucid Reflector: The Observer in Henry James's Fiction* (New Haven, CT: Yale University Press, 1969), pp. 177–9.

[50] Bewley, *Complex Fate*; Edmund Wilson, 'The Ambiguity of Henry James', in Gerald Willen (ed.), *A Casebook on Henry James's 'The Turn of the Screw'* (New York: Thomas Y. Crowell, 1960), pp. 115–53.

for one of its "holiday numbers". It proved too long—very short things are difficult for me to do'.[51]

The problem of length was a familiar one to James, and 'Cousin Maria' was in fact issued in three instalments in *Harper's Weekly* (6–20 August 1887), with 'ugly big drawings', as James thought them,[52] by Charles S. Reinhart (1844–96), the American illustrator (see Textual Introduction). In spite of James's negative observation, however, recent archival work by Amy Tucker has shown that James did not dislike *all* the drawings Reinhart did of his work, and was especially opposed to the way they were reproduced in magazines. After Reinhart's illustrations for 'Cousin Maria', 'Louisa Pallant', and 'Two Countries' had been published, James wrote to the artist that he wanted to buy his drawings (though not those for 'Cousin Maria', which he did not like). About the other illustrations he wrote to Reinhart in 'a state of thunderous excitement' on 27 July 1888, underlining how Reinhart's work 'to be fully appreciated [...] must be seen as it comes from your hand', losing a lot 'in the way it's interpreted for publication'.[53] No doubt, as Tucker has shown, the mere bloated scale of the drawings in the magazine was excessive and deprived James of the authorial control he always wished to keep over his published work. James was to write approvingly on Reinhart in his essay 'Our Artists in Europe' (*Harper's New Monthly*, June 1889) and in an article in *Harper's Weekly* (14 June 1890), revised for publication in *Picture and Text* (1893).

Much like the earlier 'The Siege of London' (1883), 'Mrs. Temperly' develops a variant of the international theme in which an American woman attempts to gain a place in upper-class European society. In the latter story a lady from California seems to conquer with ease a French milieu. It deals with the love of a young American painter for a young American woman, Dora Temperly, whose mother is trying to arrange life for her and her other two daughters, Effie and Tishy, by finding a husband for at least the first in

---

[51] Unpublished letter of Henry James to John Foord, 5 February 1887, Morgan.1 MS (Koch Collection) 34 DVG. Courtesy of Philip Horne.

[52] Letter of 22 January 1889, *The Correspondence of Henry James and the House of Macmillan, 1877–1914*, ed. Rayburn S. Moore (London: Macmillan, 1993), p. 149.

[53] Amy Tucker, *The Illustration of the Master: Henry James and the Magazine Revolution* (Stanford, CA: Stanford University Press, 2010), p. 156.

Paris. The story begins in a big hotel in New York on the eve of the family's departure, while the rest is set in Paris. Dora, the girl loved by the painter, Raymond Bestwick, is totally subject to her mother's will and destined to be the duenna, even if too young to be such, in the society where a rich French nobleman is found for one of her sisters.

This lightly satirical rendering of the hunt for husbands on the part of mothers, a theme developed differently soon after in 'Louisa Pallant', is perhaps at its best in the description of the French interiors which Mrs Temperly manages to arrange and use for her receptions. Her success is ensured by the elegant residence she has taken up in a fashionable area of Paris, near the Parc Monceau, and by the presence in her rooms of the splendid Madame de Brives, a marquise, who opens all doors to the best society in Paris, brings in refined gentlemen as well as a secretary of a foreign embassy, and provides a husband for one of the girls, Effie.

There are several references to art in the story, starting with the figure of Dora, who can be perceived as 'angular', 'like a figure on the predella of an early Italian painting' – 'angular' was an adjective James used throughout his life to describe the figures in this type of painting, even in his autobiography (*SBOC* 208). Various 'valuable specimens of contemporary French art' have been chosen by Mrs Temperly to adorn her walls, among them a portrait by Jules Bastien-Lepage (1848–84), known for his landscapes with peasants and for his portraits, among them one of the famous actress Sarah Bernhardt. In 1876 James wrote on Bastien-Lepage's portrait of the Minister of Education Henry Alexandre-Wallon, praising the painting as 'a very fine portrait in a secondary manner' (*PS* 119). Six years later he praised the painter's skill in his portrait of Joan of Arc (*CWAD1* 341). A bust of Effie ('the work of one of the sculptors who are the pride of contemporary French art') clinches her social success, while no portraits of any kind are ordered for Dora or the other sister, the dwarfish Tishy. (This name will be used again by James in *The Awkward Age* (1899)). Raymond is said to see Dora as 'the Cinderella of the house', suggesting a comparison with the famous fairy tale.[54]

The *New York Times* totally disparaged the story, writing: "'Mrs. Temperly", we defy the most appreciative of readers to understand at all. You have a

---

[54] Tintner, *Pop World of Henry James*, pp. 30–6.

picture of a good American hotel and a well fitted-up Parisian salon, and through them flit Mrs. Temperly, the vacuous Dora, and the dissatisfied Raymond. Of all sketches it is the most sketchy. It leaves no more trace behind it than would a drop of ether.' On the other hand, despite finding it 'very slight', the *Boston Daily Advertiser* appreciated it as 'a delightful study of a very interesting type of American womankind'.

'Louisa Pallant'

The germ for this story was recorded by James in his *Notebooks* on 12 January 1887 (see Appendix A), on the same day as those for 'The Marriages' (1891) and 'The Aspern Papers': 'The idea of a worldly mother & a worldly daughter—the latter of whom has been trained up so perfectly by the former that she excels & surpasses her, & the mother, who has some principle of goodness still left in her composition, is appalled at her own work.' He imagines the story being told by an elderly American for whom the mother was once an object of romantic attachment, and who is now responsible for a wealthy young nephew, whom he fears the women are out to 'bag' (*CN* 34–5). The story takes up the theme of 'Mrs. Temperly', a mother's quest for a great marriage for her daughter(s). Here, however, the focus is on the interior crisis of Mrs Pallant, who realizes her daughter has learnt her lesson too well and become 'so hard, so cruelly ambitious' (CN 34).

The story was first published in *Harper's New Monthly Magazine*, February 1888, with illustrations by Charles S. Reinhart (see Textual Introduction). It also found a place in volume XIII of the *New York Edition*, headed by *The Reverberator*, along with three much earlier tales which all first appeared in the 1870s, 'Madame de Mauves' (1874), 'A Passionate Pilgrim' (1871), and 'The Madonna of the Future' (1873). In the Preface, 'Louisa Pallant', partly set in Homburg, is presented together with 'Madame de Mauves' (see Appendix B), a story in which the title character's 'widowed mamma' is described as 'fonder of Homburg and Nice than of letting out tucks in the frocks of a vigorously growing daughter' (Ch. 2).

James kept the first-person narrator envisaged in the *Notebooks* and the very words he had started to imagine for the beginning of the story (see Appendix A). He developed it along the lines laid down, abandoning the name of

Mrs Grift (close to the maiden name of his friend Robert Louis Stevenson's wife – Fanny van de Grift) for Mrs Pallant, a name intriguingly echoing Pallanza, a town on Lago Maggiore where the second part of the story is set, and choosing Bad Homburg, for the first part, over the other possible venues of Switzerland and Florence that he had toyed with. The choice of settings seems derived from a John Murray guidebook. Bad Homburg, a German spa town famous until recently for its gambling (banned in 1872), had featured in the earlier tale 'Eugene Pickering' (1874). Mrs Pallant, who refused the narrator twenty years earlier in favour of a rich man, is now spending time there with her daughter Linda. She is trying on the one hand to economize – ironically her marriage for money has left her poor – and on the other to find a rich young man for her daughter. From Bad Homburg the tale ends up in Baveno and Stresa on Lago Maggiore. Part of this itinerary, the St Gotthard route, had been exploited by James in another early story, 'At Isella' (1871), where the narrator explicitly peruses his 'Murray's North Italy' (S1864–74 612).

When she sees that her former suitor's nephew is captivated by her all too perfect daughter, Louisa Pallant seems to have a crisis of honesty, and warns the young man off. We are not told what she says to young Archer Pringle, and when James's friend Laura Wagnière asked him about this he replied:

I don't think I know! Your curiosity is communicative and makes me wish immensely I did.

But that isn't part of the story—what Mrs. Pallant said to the young man. It was something pretty bad of course to make him give up. But the particular thing is a secondary affair whether it were true or whether it were false. The primary affair is that she told him something, no matter what—which *did* make him give up. The primary affair is also the nature and the behaviour of the lovely and inscrutable Linda. (10 March 1888, *HJL* 3:225)

James expanded further in this letter, on his having 'no light on what she said', dealing with the hypotheses apparently suggested by Mrs Wagnière.

The collision between American sincerity and acquired European falsity is a familiar one, but here it takes a complex form, as Mrs Pallant is appalled to recognize in her daughter a corrupt image of her own self, and makes reparation, as it seems, for the way in which she has brought her up. The narrator might in fact be unreliable as he was 'wounded' and left alone by Linda's mother's early refusal, a theme also developed by James in 'The Diary of a Man of Fifty'.[55]

In his 'Editor's Study' (*Harper's Monthly*, 77 (October 1888)), Howells praised the story, finding it 'an unmixed pleasure if you delight in a well-taken point of view', and appreciating the characterization of the 'imagined narrator'. 'Just for attitude, just for light, firm touch, the piece is simply unsurpassed outside the same author's work.'[56] Howells noticed that James left it to the reader to decide whether the attitude of the mother towards her daughter was justified, just as he left the reader to decide if Lady Chasemore's suicide was justified and justifiable in 'Two Countries' (later 'The Modern Warning'). In the *Detroit Free Press* 'Louisa Pallant', with 'The Aspern Papers' and 'The Modern Warning', was judged as a group of 'interesting tales by that popular author, Henry James', written in 'Mr. James's own graceful style', while *The Athenæum* considered it 'a trivial tale'. Thirty years later in the *Little Review* (1918), Ezra Pound pronounced this story 'a study in the maternal or abysmal relation, good James'.[57]

'The Aspern Papers'

'The Aspern Papers' is one of James's most successful and popular stories. Its origin is described at length in James's *Notebooks*, Florence, 12 January 1887:

Hamilton (V.L.'s brother) told me a curious thing of Capt. Silsbee—the Boston art-critic & Shelley-worshipper; that is of a curious adventure of his. Miss Claremont, Byron's ci-devant [former] mistress (the mother of Allegra) was living, until lately, here in Florence, at a great age, 80 or thereabouts, & with her lived her niece, a younger Miss Claremont—of about 50. Silsbee knew that they had interesting papers—letters of Shelley's and Byron's—he had known it for a long time & cherished the idea of getting hold of them. To this end he laid the plan of going to lodge with the Miss Claremonts' [sic]—hoping that the old lady [,] in view of her great age & failing condition, would die while he was there, so that he might then

55 Philip L. Nicoloff, 'At the Bottom of Things in Henry James's "Louisa Pallant"', *Studies in Short Fiction*, 7.3 (Summer 1970), 409–20.
56 Anesko, *Letters, Fictions, Lives*, p. 268.
57 Pound, 'Shake Down', 29.

put his hand upon the documents, which she hugged close in life. He carried out this scheme—& things *se passèrent* [happened] as he had expected. The old woman *did* die—& then he approached the younger one—the old maid of 50—on the subject of his desires. Her answer was—"I will give you all the letters if you marry me!" H. says that Silsbee *court encore* [is still running away].   (*CN* 33–4)

James goes on to describe a fortuitous visit by the Countess Gamba, whose husband was a nephew of Teresa Guiccioli, Byron's lover. The Guiccioli family refused to show Byron's letters to anyone – the countess herself had actually burned one of them. (This notebook entry appears in full in Appendix A.)

One can see that the plot of the story was all there in this entry, even if embryonically. James has an unnamed first-person narrator tell the story of his hunt for the American poet Jeffrey Aspern's papers, kept by two women, Juliana Bordereau, the old lady who had had an affair in her youth with the poet, and her unmarried niece, Tita, living in a dilapidated old palace in Venice, where the empty central *sala* is recognizably similar to those painted by John Singer Sargent. The choice of a first-person narrator is essential to the story, whether one agrees with defining him as an 'unreliable narrator', as Wayne C. Booth does, untruthful in his telling and immoral in the actions he narrates, or whether one agrees with Philip Horne, who underlines the 'distance in time between the narrator and his past self', allowing us to 'recognize that his present re-presentation of his past thoughts and actions may express different intentions and a new process of judgement'.[58]

As described at the start of this section, James spent over six months from December 1886 to the end of June 1887 in Florence and Venice, moving between them, but he wrote most of this tale in April and May, on Bellosguardo, looking down on Florence. The story was ready by 12 June 1887, when he wrote to his editor Thomas Bailey Aldrich shortly after arriving back in Venice:

I send you herewith (in another parcel,) the first half of the type-copy of a story—without having sounded you first on the subject. You may see in this a subtle device

---

[58] Philip Horne, *Henry James and Revision: The New York Edition* (Oxford: Clarendon Press, 1990), p. 269. See also Wayne C. Booth *The Rhetoric of Fiction* (Chicago: University of Chicago Press, 1961), pp. 354–63; and Susanne Kappeler, *Writing and Reading in Henry James* (London: Macmillan, 1980), pp. 14–21.

to entrap you [...] If you don't dislike it—& I don't see why you should, as it is brilliant, & of a thrilling interest—I should be very glad that you should print it early. If you do I will give you another of the same—or of a somewhat smaller length. This thing ("The Aspern Papers") makes 2 parts of the maximum size—that of the longest instalments of the *Princess*. I think it would suffer a grave injury from being cut otherwise. [...] The second half is in London, being type-copied, & I am expecting it within *a week*. The moment it comes it will follow its mate.

(LL 189–90)

A 'portion of the *2d* part' arrived from the copyist before he had finished the letter so James sent this off too. He was keen to receive payment in advance: 'I blush to own it, but I am in want of money' (*LL* 190). On 21 June he sent the 'remainder and end' of the tale, again from Venice (*HJL* 3:189).

'The Aspern Papers' was originally published in the *Atlantic Monthly*, in March–May 1888, in three parts (see Textual Introduction). The volume of the *New York Edition* (1908) which included other tales[59] had a frontispiece, 'Juliana's Court', which referred to 'The Aspern Papers'. In his correspondence with the photographer Alvin Langdon Coburn (1882–1966), James had recommended that he capture an image of the Palazzo Cappello for this frontispiece – the palace that he admitted having had in mind while composing the tale,[60] telling Coburn that he had already written to the occupant, Constance Fletcher (6 December 1906, *HJL* 4:428). However, as in the case of the Palazzo Barbaro for the *Wings of the Dove*, James did not insist. If the views he suggested did not 'yield satisfaction', Coburn could photograph some other *riva* or palace ('do it at a venture'), the gist being to find 'a symbolized and generalized Venice' (*HJL* 4:427–8). The photographer should 'judge for yourself, face to face with the object, how much, on the spot, it seems to lend itself to a picture' (*HJL* 4:426). Coburn seemed to fulfil James's wish to have a 'representative, or symbolic, scene or object', a wish he had expressed in his letter to his agent, J. B. Pinker: the photogra-

---

[59] Vol. XII included 'The Turn of the Screw', 'The Liar', and 'The Two Faces'.

[60] In a letter to Jane von Glehn (née Emmet; later Emmet de Glehn) of 1913, James also mentioned the Palazzo Cappello where Constance Fletcher and her mother had lived: 'Constance Fletcher & her place in Venice. "Yes, of course I thought of that old palace-garden in the Aspern Papers – & it was her extraordinary mother who spoke of the place to me as so "comme il faut."' Unpublished letter of Jane von Glehn to Roger Quilter, copying HJ's to her, 22 September 1913, BL Add. MS 70597, fols. 41–4. Courtesy of Philip Horne.

pher presented the image of a small ornamental tree beside a modest door-way, which became the frontispiece for the *New York Edition* of 'The Aspern Papers'.[61]

The subject of the preservation or accessibility of the letters of a great poet or novelist was always fascinating to James, who on occasion can be seen to relish the cultural enrichment that comes with the possibility of reading an author's letters, but sometimes seems more in sympathy with the instinct for privacy destroyed by 'the investigative "curiosity" of modern culture'.[62] It is well known that James burnt letters in his possession on several occasions. However, we can exemplify his ambivalence on this subject by quoting from his review of Balzac's *Correspondance* in 1876, where he admits to being thankful for the volume in spite of his 'bad conscience': 'it is always a question whether we have a right to investigate a man's life for the sake of anything but his official utterance—his results' (*LC2* 69).

This review was written more than ten years before 'The Aspern Papers', and James in the meantime had become more and more sensitive to the excessive publicity given to private lives by modern journalists. He strongly disapproved of Julian Hawthorne's 'blackguardly betrayal' of confidence in an article on his father's old friend James Russell Lowell in 1886,[63] and the following year he expressed his views on Mary Mercy McClellan's 'inconceivable letter about the Venetian society whose hospitality she had been enjoying'. McClennan's article, published in the New York *World*, was a sign, James wrote (17 November 1887), of 'the invasion, the impudence and shamelessness, of the newspaper and the interviewer, the devouring *publicity* of life, the extinction of all sense between public and private' (*CN* 40).

[61] Anesko, '*Friction with the Market*', p. 154.

[62] Richard Salmon, *Henry James and the Culture of Publicity* (Cambridge: Cambridge University Press, 1997), p. 91.

[63] Gary Scharnhorst, 'The Aspern Papers and the Ethics of Literary Biography', *Modern Fiction Studies*, 36.2 (Summer 1990), 211–17; 215. In a rich discussion on the subject, Declan Kiely also mentions James's 'uneasiness with the practice of setting before the public texts culled from unpublished papers whose author never intended them to see the light of day' regarding Julian Hawthorne's 1872 publication of his father's *French and Italian Notebooks*; see '"Pardon My Too Many Words": Henry James Manuscripts and Letters at the Morgan Library & Museum', in Colm Tóibín, Marc Simpson, and Declan Kiely (eds.), *Henry James and American Painting* (University Park: Pennsylvania State University Press and the Morgan Library and Museum, 2017), p. 101.

This episode was the starting point for his novel *The Reverberator* (published in *Macmillan's* from February to July 1888).[64] Other comments on the publication of letters by great writers such as Flaubert or George Sand, as well as Balzac, underline James's anxious position as regards the 'ironies of the traffic between the private and public aspects of writing'.[65] The question of the right to burn or publish the papers of a famous person would be again the subject of an 1892 story, 'Sir Dominick Ferrand'.

James discusses the change in attitudes towards the subject of the rights to privacy and the desire for knowledge, especially where an artist is concerned, in the 1908 Preface to the *New York Edition* of 'The Aspern Papers'. He connects these issues with the idea of 'a palpable imaginable *visitable* past', represented in this case by Miss Claremont, the old, old lady, who had in her youth been an intimate of Byron and Shelley, and had lived until very recently without James being at all aware of her:

The Italian side of the legend closely clung; if only because the so possible terms of my Juliana's life in the Italy of other days could make conceivable for her the fortunate privacy, the long uninvaded and uninterviewed state on which I represent her situation as founded. Yes, a surviving unexploited unparagraphed Juliana was up to a quarter of a century since still supposeable—as much so as any such buried treasure, any such grave unprofaned, would defy probability now. And then the case had the air of the past just in the degree in which that air, I confess, most appeals to me—when the region over which it hangs is far enough away without being too far.

I delight in a palpable imaginable *visitable* past—in the nearer distances and the clearer mysteries, the marks and signs of a world we may reach over to as by making a long arm we grasp an object at the other end of our own table. The table is the one, the common expanse, and where we lean, so stretching, we find it firm and continuous. That, to my imagination, is the past fragrant of all, or of almost all, the poetry of the thing outlived and lost and gone, and yet in which the precious element of closeness, telling so of connexions but tasting so of differences, remains appreciable. (*LC2* 1177)

---

[64] See Richard Salmon's introduction to the *CFHJ* edition of the novel (2018), pp. xxvii–xxxv.

[65] Adrian Poole, introduction to *The Aspern Papers and Other Stories*, ed. Adrian Poole (Oxford and New York: Oxford University Press, 1983), p. viii.

Wayne C. Booth underlined the discrepancy between the early notebook entry and the interest in the '*visitable* past' expressed in the Preface, suggesting that the narrator's descriptions of Venice have a different tone from the rest of his narration, more James's than the fictional character's.[66] Millicent Bell has further argued that James's focus on the *visitable* past is self-contradictory, as the Romantic past of Aspern and Juliana is *not* in fact retrieved: the papers are never actually 'palpable', they only exist in the surmise of the narrator or the reported voice of Tita. A void is at the centre of the story, the impossibility of reconstructing the very past which is called for in the Preface. This is a failure that, for J. Hillis Miller, is at the heart of the narrative making 'The Aspern Papers' 'a story about the impossibility of knowing and possessing the historical past through narrative'.[67]

The anecdote from which the story grew was heard in Florence, as mentioned above. If one wonders why James should have transposed the setting from Florence to Venice, various explanations can be found, including the one offered by James in the Preface: 'Delicacy had demanded, I felt, that my appropriation of the Florentine legend should purge it, first of all, of references too obvious; so that, to begin with, I shifted the scene of the adventure. Juliana, as I saw her, was thinkable only in Byronic and more or less immediately post-Byronic Italy' (*LC2* 1179).

If 'delicacy' as regards the real persons of the anecdote is to be considered, the reference to 'Byronic' Italy is telling. The legend of Byron's excesses in Venice was still alive in James's time, fostered as it had been by Byron himself.[68] Byron's legend fitted perfectly with the image of Venice as the place of beauty and dissolution, as the city of intrigue and conspiracy. Both these elements may have worked on James's imagination, suggesting the change of setting to a city which he was visiting at the time. James was well aware of the 'black legend' of Venice, made even more popular in the *Histoire de la République de Venise* (1819) by the French historian Daru. As late as 1903, in *William Wetmore Story and His Friends*, James was quoting darkly romantic

---

[66] Booth, *Rhetoric of Fiction*, pp. 359–60.

[67] J. Hillis Miller, *Literature as Conduct: Speech Acts in Henry James* (New York: Fordham University Press, 2005), p. 19.

[68] In the first book edition of 'The Aspern Papers', James added the name of Casanova, which again is associated with the eroticism and moral corruption of Venice. See variants in the present volume.

passages from Story's letters: 'before me the dagger of the cloaked bravo or of the jealous husband gleams, and I hear the splash of the body as it falls into the dark canal' (*WWS* 1: 194). James distanced himself from Story's view, but the number of references to 'the black legend' present in the book shows he was very much aware of this tradition, which went back to Elizabethan times, together with the myth of the city's sensuous beauty.[69] It is not a coincidence that James should set the story of Juliana's passion in the city celebrated for its erotic power. Venice's 'accretions of history' have been underlined.[70]

The descriptions of Venice in the tale may be usefully compared with those in the several essays that James devoted to it (see *CTW2* 287–364). James's great art gave new life to the hackneyed representation of Venice: the city is not only the background to a story of deceit and intrigue; it becomes the mirror of the labyrinthine psychology of both the narrator and his antagonist, Juliana Bordereau, whose moves are no less clever, ambiguous, and deceitful than those of the narrator. If the unnamed narrator is devious and lying – he presents himself with a fake *carte de visite* and a false name – his antagonist, Juliana, is an equally subtle character, who manages to extract huge sums from him but keeps him at a distance while continuing to solicit his interest, not least by dangling in front of him the portrait of the poet. Her duplicity is underlined by the 'horrible green shade' that covers her once beautiful eyes, like a mask.

Several sources have been indicated for this 'green shade'. Edel suggested James's great-aunt Wyckoff as a possible source for the figure of the ancient Juliana, connecting her presence in New York to the 'visitable past'.[71] In *A Small Boy and Others*, James remembers an old Russian Countess Gerebsoff reclining on a chaise longue 'under a mushroom hat with a green veil' (*SBOC* 223). In his 1876 review of Balzac's *Correspondance*, he explicitly translated and quoted Balzac's description of his visit to Ludwig Tieck (1773–1853): 'He had an old countess, his contemporary in spectacles, almost an octogenarian—a

---

[69] Tony Tanner, *Venice Desired* (Cambridge, MA: Harvard University Press, 1992), pp. 157–209.

[70] Anthony Curtis, *The Turn of the Screw and The Aspern Papers* (Harmondsworth: Penguin, 1984), p. 12; Rosella Mamoli Zorzi, '*The Aspern Papers*: From Florence to an Intertextual City, Venice', in Dennis Tredy, Annick Duperray, and Adrian Harding (eds.), *Henry James's Europe* (Cambridge: OpenBook Publishers, 2011), pp. 103–11.

[71] Leon Edel, '*The Aspern Papers*: Great-Aunt Wyckoff and Juliana Bordereau', *Modern Language Notes* (June 1952), 392–5.

mummy with a green eye-shade, whom I supposed to be a domestic divinity' (*LC2* 86).[72] It may further have been inspired by the veil worn by the protagonist of Hawthorne's story 'The Minister's Black Veil' (1836), or by the veil worn by Venetian '*spose non sposate*' (unmarried brides, i.e. spinsters), represented in Cesare Vecellio's *Habiti antichi* (1598), as Anthony Marasco has suggested.[73] The 'green shade' has also been seen in relation to Andrew Marvell's poem 'The Garden' (1681), generally relevant to the garden of 'The Aspern Papers', a space where the relationship between the narrator and Tita develops, but also a place where the narrator can only live alone, as in Marvell's poem.[74] Joshua Parker has suggested to the editors of this volume that the 'green shade' may be identified with the green eyeshade or visor worn by bank accountants, which would echo Juliana's greed for and handling of money.

More generally, Philip Horne was the first to notice a possible source for the tale in the novel *The Italians* (1875) by Frances Elliot reviewed by James in 1875 (*LC1* 1011–13). Horne writes:

It is thrilling to find fore-echoes of *The Aspern Papers* in a review of *The Italians* (1875) by Frances Elliot ('a mistress of the art of disappointing one'), where a count besieges a marchesa and her niece; the marchesa 'falls asleep, one night, burning all papers,' starting a fire from which the count 'turns up' to save the ladies; and once betrothed he has a crucial 'sudden disaffection' from the niece.[75]

---

[72] The latter part of this sentence in the original is 'quasi octogénaire, une momie à garde-vue vert, qui m'a paru être une divinité domestique': Honoré de Balzac, *Correspondance 1819–1850* (Paris: Calmann Lévy, 1876), vol. II, p. 51. Sarah Chambré's welcome indication of a source in *Le Père Goriot* ('La vieille demoiselle Michonneau gardait sur ses yeux fatigués un crasseux abat-jour en taffetas vert [...] qui aurait effarouché l'ange de la Pitié', p. 59) reinforces the possibility of a Balzac source. Balzac had used a 'garde-vue en taffetas vert' previously in his novella *Ferragus* (*La Comédie humaine*, vol. IX, *Scènes de la vie parisienne, Tome I* (Paris: Imprimerie de E. Martinet, 1843), p. 73).

[73] Anthony Marasco, 'Venice and the Veil: A Note on the Motives of Juliana Bordereau in *The Aspern Papers*', in Francesca Bisutti and Pia Masiero (eds.), *A Rosella: Saggi in onore di Rosella Mamoli Zorzi* (Venice: Supernova, 2012), pp. 149–58.

[74] Jeanne Campbell Reesman, '"The Deepest Depths of the Artificial": Attacking Women and Reality in "The Aspern Papers"', in Joseph Dewey and Brooke Horvath (eds.), '*The Finer Thread, The Tighter Weave*': *Essays on the Short Fiction of Henry James* (West Lafayette, IN: Purdue University Press, 2001), pp. 42–68; Horne, *Henry James and Revision*, p. 283; Adrian Poole, *The Aspern Papers and Other Stories*, ed. Adrian Poole, new edition (Oxford and New York: Oxford University Press, 2013), p. 241.

[75] Philip Horne, 'Independent Beauty', *Journal of American Studies*, 21.1 (April 1987), 87–93; 90.

As for the actual plot of the story, Pushkin's 'Queen of Spades' (1834) has seemed to a number of critics a plausible possibility for a source: in Pushkin's story the protagonist in the depths of night sneaks into the old lady's quarters and tries to steal her secret; confronts her – and she collapses – and he is baffled and defeated.[76] In Pushkin's story the object of desire is money and at the end it turns into a ghost tale.

Much discussion has also centred on the figure of the American poet, Jeffrey Aspern, for whom Edgar Allan Poe, Nathaniel Hawthorne, and Walt Whitman have been proposed as models. As for the living characters in the tale, the character of Mrs Prest is known to be based on Mrs Bronson, famous for her generosity and help to poor Venetians as well as to poor American artists such as Whistler. James's complex friendship with Constance Fenimore Woolson – which included their living together in the same house on Bellosguardo, even if on different floors, unbeknownst to friends and family – may have contributed to the characterization of the spinster Miss Tita. James's dismay and despair on hearing of Miss Woolson's probable suicide in 1894 seem full of a sense of guilt, as if Constance had expected more than friendship from him.[77] As for the marginal figure of the narrator's friend and Aspern 'fellow worshipper', John Cumnor, the Victorian reader would have associated the name with Matthew Arnold's Oxford poem *The Scholar Gipsy* (1853), with its references to the Cumnor hills and its celebration of 'the elusive figure of the poet who will come no more'.[78]

The very house that inspired the fictional abode of the Misses Bordereau was clearly identified by Henry James to the photographer Alvin L. Coburn as the Palazzo Soranzo Cappello on the Rio Marin, in the letter quoted above. Constance Fletcher, the novelist, with her mother and Eugene

---

[76] See Neil Cornwell, 'Pushkin and Henry James: Secrets, Papers and Figures', in *Two Hundred Years of Pushkin*, eds. Robert Read and Joe Andrews (Amsterdam and New York: Rodopi, 2004), vol. 3, pp. 193–210; and Joseph S. O'Leary, 'Pushkin in "The Aspern Papers"', *The Henry James E-Journal*, 2 (2000); and Angus Wrenn, 'Henry James (1843–1916): Henry James's Europe', in Michael Bell (ed.), *Cambridge Companion to European Novelists* (Cambridge: Cambridge University Press, 2012), p. 311.

[77] Edel, *Middle Years*, pp. 224–7; Lyndall Gordon, *A Private Life of Henry James: Two Women and His Art* (London: Chatto & Windus, 1998), pp. 276–80. 'The shattered dream of Constance Fenimore Woolson', in *Two Lovers of Venice. Byron and Constance Fenimore Woolson*, ed. Carlo Campana, Gregory Dowling, Rosella Mamoli Zorzi (Venice: Supernova, 2014), p. 52.

[78] Poole, Introduction to *The Aspern Papers* (2013), p. xv.

Benson, the American painter, probably lived there already in 1887: Benson went to say goodbye to James at the end of James's first 1887 Venice visit.[79] The Palazzo Cappello, like all Venetian palaces in the course of the nineteenth century, surely had some of the same dilapidated qualities that were present in what James described as the 'ghostly old villa' of Bellosguardo,[80] in Florence, where he wrote the story.

As for the names of the Misses Bordereau, the French meaning of *bordereau*, an account register, a bill, 'even an invoice',[81] could point to Juliana's greed for money. Bordereau, seen as a 'memorandum [...] a list of documents', hints at the objectified view of Juliana, seen by the narrator only as the keeper of the papers.[82] The name of 'Tita' was changed to 'Tina' in the *New York Edition*: James may have changed it, feeling it was 'somewhat incongruous' if it brought to mind the imperial power of Titus, the Roman Emperor. But it might also be so because Tita in Venice is mostly a man's name, such as Giovanni Battista Falcieri (known as 'Tita') (1798–1874), the personal servant of Lord Byron, present at his death in Missolonghi in 1824. James may have been conscious of this. The suggestion has been made that James may have taken the name from Constance Fenimore Woolson's character in *Anne* (1880–2).[83] The character of Tita in Woolson's novel refers to a very young and somewhat wild girl, whose name comes from 'Petite'. James may have wanted to clarify the incongruity of her name in the *New York Edition*: Tita/Tina was neither tiny nor petite – she was tall.

James pronounced his novella 'brilliant' from the start, and on receiving the first printed volumes from his publisher he declared the book 'charmingly pretty'. On 13 October 1888 he wrote to Frederick Macmillan from Geneva – he was now writing *The Tragic Muse* and visiting Constance Fenimore Woolson – that 'if the public would only show some practical agreement in

[79] Edel, *Middle Years*, p. 213.
[80] Letter to R. L. Stevenson, 19 December 1886, *CLHJ 1884–1886* 2:267. The editors thank Greg Zacharias for advance access to the text of this letter.
[81] Rod Mengham, 'Wall to Wall: Figuring "The Aspern Papers"', in N. H. Reeve (ed.), *Henry James: The Shorter Fiction* (London: Macmillan, 1997), pp. 41–59; 41.
[82] George Monteiro, 'The "Bordereau" of The Aspern Papers', *Quarterly Journal of Short Articles, Notes and Reviews*, 22.1 (Winter 2009), 33–5; 33.
[83] Jeannine Hayat, 'Fiction ou réalité: Les biographies de Constance Fenimore Woolson', *Revue LISA e-journal* (1 January 2005), 12; Gordon, *Private Life*, pp. 208–20.

this estimate there would be no wormwood mingled with my honey'.[84] The quality of 'The Aspern Papers' was at least partly recognized the following month by a review in the *New York Sun* (11 November 1888): it was 'one of Mr. James's finest achievements'. Although 'insignificant in plot and of moderate quality in respect of the characters', it was judged 'a masterly study of human nature and emotions'. Other reviews insisted on the 'scanty materials', acknowledging the skill of the writer in the 'admirable psychical analysis' (*New York Tribune*); *Life* underlined the 'skill' of the author and so did the *Literary World*, considering James's 'master hand' in treating such a 'slight' incident. The *Sun* reviewer also underlined the 'special charm' given to the story by its Venetian setting, judged a 'slight Venetian pastoral' by the *Critic*, although treated with great vitality. The *Saturday Review* similarly emphasized the charm of the story for 'Lovers of Venice'. The *London Daily Telegraph* commented on the 'subtle fun' which would 'fail [...] to be appreciated' by its readers. Most of the reviews dealt with the title story rather than with the other tales in the volume, with the exception of the *Academy*, which treated at length 'The Modern Warning'. As mentioned above, W. D. Howells in *Harper's Monthly* hailed 'The Aspern Papers', along with other stories ('The Liar', 'A London Life', 'Louisa Pallant', 'Two Countries' ['The Modern Warning']) as masterpieces in 'an artist's exhibition'.[85] Ezra Pound however considered it 'inferior' without giving any reason for his judgement.[86]

The popularity of 'The Aspern Papers' has generated a number of etchings, and adaptations for stage, film, and opera. Edward Piper's lithographs were reprinted in a special edition of *The Aspern Papers* (1990) in memory of the artist (1938–90). In 1993 Peter Milton created a portfolio of eighteen reproductions of drawings made for *The Aspern Papers*, basing his etchings on a visit to the Palazzo Capello in Rio Marin, in Venice. Michael Redgrave first staged *The Aspern Papers: A Comedy of Letters* in 1959 at the Queen's Theatre, London. (It is notable that the anonymous narrator is given a name – with James's initials and his first name: 'Henry Jarvis'.) Two years later it was translated by Marguerite Duras and Robert Antelme and staged by Raymond Rouleau at the Théâtre des Mathurins in Paris. The following

[84] *Correspondence of Henry James and the House of Macmillan*, ed. Moore, p. 148.
[85] Anesko, *Letters, Fictions, Lives*, p. 268.
[86] Pound, 'Shake Down', 29.

year the Redgrave version transferred successfully to Broadway, since when it has enjoyed several revivals, including one in 1984 when Redgrave's daughter Vanessa won an Olivier award as best actress for her portrayal of Miss Tina. Another stage version by Martin Zuckerman was produced off Broadway in 2008. *The Golden Age*, a play by A. R. Gurney vaguely inspired by *The Aspern Papers*, was performed in New York in 1984 with an Upper East Side setting.[87]

The film and television productions based on this novella are helpfully listed by J. Sarah Koch in 'A Henry James Filmography'.[88] There have been four movies: *The Lost Moment* of 1947, written by Leonardo Bercovici and directed by Martin Gabel; *Les Papiers d'Aspern* of 1981, directed in Portugal and co-written with Michael Graham by the French-based Argentinian film-maker Eduardo De Gregorio; *Els Papels de Aspern* of 1991, directed and co-written with Manuel Valls by the Catalan director Jordi Cadena; and *The Aspern Papers* directed by Mariana Hellmund in 2010, set in Venezuela. The latest movie has been collaboratively produced by James Ivory, Charles S. Cohen, Joely Richardson, Francois Sarkozy, Film House Germany's Christian Angermayer and Klemens Hallmann, and Summerstorm's Gabriela Bacher. Ivory's presence is important because he explicitly and publicly said that he had always hoped he could film *The Aspern Papers* in Venice.[89] He was not the director in this case, but the executive producer; the director was a first-time French film-maker, Julien Landais, and the film project was announced to much acclaim at the Cannes Festival in May 2016. Part of the appeal was undoubtedly the fact that Vanessa Redgrave (who had played Olive Chancellor in Ivory's *The Bostonians*, 1984) starred as Juliana.[90] The film was based on a script adapted from the 2002 stage play

[87] A. R. Gurney, *The Golden Age: A Play in Two Acts* (New York: Dramatists Play Service, 1984). We thank Philip Horne for this information.

[88] In Susan Griffin (ed.), *Henry James Goes to the Movies* (Lexington, KT: University of Kentucky Press, 2002), pp. 340–1.

[89] Interview for 'Incroci di Civiltà' at the Teatro Goldoni, Venice, 2015. Rosella Mamoli Zorzi, 'The Aspern Papers: Again and Yet Again?', in *Reading Henry James in the Twenty-First Century*, ed. Dennis Tredy, Annick Duperray and Adrian Harding (Newcastle upon Tyne: Cambridge Scholars Publishing, 2019), pp. 105–15.

[90] One should note that the Redgrave family's list of Henry James adaptations extends to 'The Turn of the Screw' as well. Only two years after his stage success with 'The Aspern Papers',

by Jean Pavans,[91] one of the most important French translators of James's works, whose *Les Papiers de Aspern* had been staged by Jacques Lassalle that year at the Théâtre Vidy-Lausanne, in a co-production with the Comédie-Francaise. The actors included Françoise Seigner (Juliana), Catherine Hiegel (Tita), and Jean-Damien Barbin (Morton). It was staged again in 2003 and 2004 at the Théâtre du Vieux-Colombier. The play was also performed at the Comédie Française and staged by Jacques Lassalle in 2002. The movie, based on an English translation of Pavans' play, was presented at the Venice Film Festival in 2017.

There have been eight television productions, including the filming of Dominick Argento's important opera, *The Aspern Papers*, that premièred in Dallas in November 1988 and was revived twenty-five years later in 2013. In this opera, Aspern is a composer and the setting is moved to Lake Como.

Michael Halliwell has written on Argento's opera as well as on Philip Hagemann's (US 1988) and Redgrave's 1959 stage versions.[92] Italian composer Salvatore Sciarrino created a *Two-Act Singspiel* (1978), with a libretto by Giorgio Marini and Sciarrino, out of fragments of the text, and British composer Michael Hurd produced an opera in 1995 (in Australia). There is a novel based on 'The Aspern Papers': Emma Tennant's *Felony: The Private History of 'The Aspern Papers'* (2002), where James becomes a character writing *The Aspern Papers* and showing it to Constance Fenimore Woolson. In John Drury's long poem, *Burning the Aspern Papers* (2003), the author imagines Tina reading Aspern's poems to Juliana just before burning them, and comparing her own relationship with the narrator to Juliana's with Aspern.

Michael Redgrave played the role of the Uncle in Jack Clayton's 1961 film adaptation *The Innocents*; his daughter Lynn Redgrave later played the role of the governess for the 1974 American television adaptation, *The Turn of the Screw*, by Dan Curtis.

[91] Jean Pavans translated James's works for the La Différence editions from 1990 onwards; he has also translated works by Wharton, Stein, and Pinter. Among his recent works are *Le Musée Intérieur de Henry James* (2016). Pavans wrote a libretto based on *The Beast in the Jungle* for composer Arnaut Petit in 2011. His recent translation of Shelley's *La Révolte de l'Islam* (2016) is also relevant to the film version of *The Aspern Papers*.

[92] Michael Halliwell, *Opera and the Novel: The Case of Henry James*, ed. Walter Bernhart (Amsterdam: Rodopi, 2005), pp. 368–413, 413–25, and 425–6.

'The Liar'

'The Liar' is set entirely in England and explores the complex triangle between a painter, a mythomaniac colonel, and his wife. The story is also about the revealing power of portraits, a theme for which James seems to go back to Hawthorne and which he addresses on several other occasions, such as 'The Story of a Masterpiece' (1868), 'Travelling Companions' (1870), 'The Sweetheart of M. Briseux' (1873), 'The Real Thing' (1893), and 'The Beldonald Holbein' (1901), but also in novels like *The Tragic Muse, The Wings of the Dove,* and *The Sense of the Past.* The origin of 'The Liar' has two different versions. The first is a notebook entry dated 19 June 1884, where James traces a story outline inspired by Alphonse Daudet's novel *Numa Roumestan* (1881) that he highly esteemed and discussed extensively in two essays in the *Atlantic Monthly,* in 1882, and in the *Century Magazine,* in 1883 (later reprinted in *Partial Portraits,* 1888).[93] In this entry James considers the possibility of writing a 'very short' tale about a pure and intelligent woman married to an attractive man, but a 'tremendous, though harmless, liar'. The main event would be the woman becoming a liar herself in order to protect him. Another version of the story's origin is provided by James in the Preface to volume XII of the *New York Edition,* where he mentions having found inspiration in getting acquainted with a 'most unbridled colloquial romancer' and his 'magnificent' wife during a London dinner (*LC2* 1189–90). F. O. Matthiessen and Kenneth Murdock explain the disparity between these two versions by arguing that James probably forgot the earlier notebook entry with the passing of time, thus relying more on the later 'personal' experience.[94] As Philip Horne suggested to us, the Colonel in the story also reminds one of a passage from a letter written by James during his 1870 stay in the Malvern water-cure establishment: 'There, socially, with my friend Jameson are the swells—including that tremendous old liar Major Jones who is forever whopping about his tigers in India & his

---

[93] On the same date as the notebook entry, James wrote a letter to Daudet thanking him for having sent a copy of his last novel *Sapho.* He appreciated the book although he thought that the male protagonist, whom he misnamed Jean Gauvin (instead of 'Gaussin'), was lacking definition.

[94] F. O. Matthiessen and Kenneth Murdock. *The Notebooks of Henry James* (Chicago: University of Chicago Press, 1981), p. 62.

salmon in Norway & his wild goats in Chinese Tartary—a good specimen I suppose of a very common English figure' (to Alice James, 27 February 1870, *CLHJ 1855–1872* 2:308).

As for other possible literary influences, Robert J. Kane postulated James's debt to Hawthorne's 'The Prophetic Pictures' (from *Twice-Told Tales*, 1837).[95] No real-life models have been convincingly suggested for the characters in the story. Very little help can be found in a letter James wrote on 13 October 1896, in reply to a man called Anton Capadose who complained about the use of his name in the story. James explained:

"Capadose" must be in one of my old note-books. I have a dim recollection of having found it originally in the first columns of *The Times*, where I find almost all the names I store up for my puppets. It was picturesque and rare and so I took possession of it [...] my romancing Colonel was a charming man, in spite of his little weakness.   (*HJL* 4:39)

'The Liar' was first published in the *Century Magazine* in May and June 1888 (see Textual Introduction), and was generally praised in the contemporary reviews. It was one of the tales that W. D. Howells described as 'masterpieces' in his review in *Harper's Monthly* (October 1888), as cited above.[96] In the *Literary World* an anonymous critic wrote:

Of the stories contained in this volume [*A London Life*], "The Liar" is by far the best. It is a study in the perversities, not in the great tragedy-compelling faults of human nature, and the clever and lightly cynical delineation fits the theme perfectly—the drama does not overstep the line of the most conventional immobility of behavior. The gratuitous fictions of Colonel Capadose, his betrayal by a too faithful portrait, the sudden dismay and unshaken fidelity of his wife, are points skilfully taken and marvelously sustained.

A positive critique also came from the *Boston Daily Advertiser*:

In "The Liar", however, Mr. James is at his best; his art at his finest. This is a delightfully acute study of a modern Münchausen and the vulgarizing effect which marriage with him had upon a perfectly truthful woman. We need say nothing of the analysis of character, but we may note that the plot is admirably contrived to help it

---

[95]   Robert J. Kane, 'Hawthorne's "The Prophetic Pictures" and James's "The Liar"', *Modern Language Notes*, 65 (April 1950), 257–8.

[96]   Anesko, *Fictions, Stories, Lives*, p. 268.

forward, and that through its means, the psychological problem attains an almost dramatic interest.

The reviewer in the *New York Times* appeared to appreciate the tale's conceit, albeit in an equivocal way:

"The Liar" is rather a story of art than anything else. Is it possible for a man to paint a picture so powerfully that every stroke of the brush tells that it is the portrait of a liar? That was what the clever Mr. Lyon, the artist, did. To keep his hand in he made his sitter get off all kinds of bouncers [lies]. The bigger the lie the more perfect becomes the work. "The Liar" is one of Mr. James's eccentricities.

The *Critic* lamented the fact that a good writer like James was wasting his energies devoting them to dangerous subjects: 'In "The Liar" Mr James utterly spoils the effect of the story by following the example of Corneille in "Le Menteur" and prefixing a title that "leaves nothing to be desired"—with a vengeance. Lessing has a story of a raven trying to breed eagles; but, verily, here is an eagle with a nestful of ravens.' Neither was Robert Timsol in *Lippincott's Monthly Magazine* impressed by the tale; he wrote:

"The Liar" is an exquisite character-sketch, and bearable, since nobody is killed and nothing badly broken,—for there was not much to break. Mr. James would be a genius if he could be touched by a coal from the altar: almost any altar would do, if it had warmth upon it. But he is past his first youth, and perhaps no longer open to the softening influences which might make it possible for his admirers to regard him as a being of like passions with themselves.

Yet praise came from twentieth-century critics and writers, including Ezra Pound, who wrote in 1918: '"The Liar" is superb in its way, perhaps the best of the allegories, of the plots invented purely to be an exposition of impression. It is magnificent in its presentation of the people, both the old man and the Liar, who is masterly'.[97]

The majority of scholars tend to associate this story with other works by James that are similarly focused, as earlier pointed out, on the revealing power of portraits and on a triangle of relations, in particular the early tale 'The Story of A Masterpiece'.[98] Many years later, in the course of dictating

[97]   Pound, 'Shake Down', p. 29.

[98]   Edna Kenton, 'Some Bibliographical Notes on Henry James', *Hound & Horn* (April–May 1934), 535–40, 535; Segal, *Lucid Reflector*, p. 101; Winner, *Henry James and the Visual Arts*, p. 94;

notes on his unfinished novel, *The Sense of the Past*, James recalled 'The Liar'
as he wrote 'I don't want to repeat what I have done at least a couple of
times, I seem to remember, and notably in The Liar—the "discovery," or the
tell-tale representation of an element in the sitter written clear by the artist's projection of it on canvas' (*CN* 530).[99] However, the question that has
puzzled critics is the identification of the real liar in the story. Early readers
of the story ultimately saw Capadose as the culprit. A turning point in criticism was Marius Bewley's reading in 1952, the first to question the reliability
of the main reflector Oliver Lyon. Bewley proposed that Lyon could be as
big a liar as the mythomaniac Capadose.[100] Wayne C. Booth followed and
expanded this argument, explaining that James made his central reflector
unaware of his own hidden motives as a disappointed lover. For Booth, a
few unequivocal intrusions by a reliable narrator in the text would 'underline the difference between Lyon's picture of himself and the true picture'.[101]

'The Modern Warning'

James entered the 'germ' for this story in his *Notebook* on 9 July 1884: 'This
idea has been suggested to me by reading Sir Lepel Griffin's book about
America. Type of the conservative, fastidious, exclusive Englishman (in
public life, clever, &c,), who hates the U.S.A. & thinks them a contamination to England, a source of *funeste* warning, &c, & an odious country
socially' (*CN* 29) (see Appendix A). James then goes on to outline the plot,
in which the patriotic American girl falls in love with and marries the man
who hates the United States, while questioning whether he need supply his
heroine with a brother as well as the possibility of her suicide. The book
that James had read was *The Great Republic, A Criticism of America*, by
Sir Lepel Griffin (1838–1908), a British administrator and diplomat in the
Indian Civil Service for almost thirty years. Griffin's book was the result of
a three-week visit to the United States and it caused controversy when it

and more extensively Daniel T. O'Hara, '"*Monstrous Levity*": Between Realism and Vision in
Two of Henry James's Artist Tales', *Henry James Review*, 28.3 (2007), 242–8.
[99] See Christina E. Albers, *A Reader's Guide to the Short Stories of Henry James* (New York: G. K.
Hall, 1997), p. 471.
[100] Bewley, *Complex Fate*, pp. 84–7.
[101] Booth, *Rhetoric of Fiction*, p. 351.

came out in 1884. The *Spectator* reviewed it in December that year, recognizing the necessity to counter the usual praise of America in recent books but declaring that 'The voice of criticism [...] must proceed from accurate knowledge and impartial view. Of these two indispensable qualifications, Sir Lepel Griffin possesses neither the one nor the other.' Sir Lepel Griffin had presented the United States as

the apotheosis of Philistinism, the perplexity and despair of statesmen, the Mecca to which turns every religious or social charlatan, where the only god worshipped is Mammon, and the highest education is the share-list; where political life is shunned by an honest man as the plague; where to enrich jobbers, and monopolists, and contractors, a nation has emancipated its slaves and enslaved its freemen; where the people is gorged and drunk with materialism, and where wealth has become a curse, instead of a blessing.[102]

In spite of James's explicit mention of Griffin's volume, one may also think of James Bryce's *American Commonwealth* (1888), the only book whose popularity bore comparison with Alexis de Tocqueville's classic *Democracy in America* (1835 and 1840). Bryce (1838–1922) visited the United States in 1870, 1881, and 1883. He was a professor of jurisprudence at Oxford, a Liberal politician, and later British ambassador to the United States (1907–13), and was well known to James from 1877 onwards, his first years of residence in London. In 1879 James described Bryce to his brother William, perhaps prematurely, as 'a distinctly able fellow' (*CLHJ 1878–1880* 1:126). One cannot help noticing that 'Bryce' rhymes with 'Grice'. In both Lepel's book and Bryce's James found sources for a story published with the title 'Two Countries' in *Harper's New Monthly Magazine* in June 1888, with illustrations by Charles S. Reinhart, which would become 'The Modern Warning' in a collection published by Macmillan in September of the same year. (See Textual Introduction).

In this tale James developed again his 'international theme', creating the characters of the deeply patriotic American young woman, the conservative and aristocratic British politician, and that of the American brother,[103]

---

[102] Quoted in George Monteiro, 'Americanism in Henry James' "A Modern Warning"', *American Literary Realism*, 43.2 (Winter 2011), 169–70.

[103] On the possible interpretation of marriage as a metaphor for political relations between nations, see Mary Burke, 'The Marriage Plot and the Plot against the Union: Irish Home Rule

as sketched in the *Notebook* entry. The story begins at Cadenabbia, where Macarthy Grice joins his mother and sister Agatha. Agatha's excursion on the lake with Sir Rufus Chasemore, who is courting her, anticipates the betrayal of her country and of her brother.[104] James added a book by Sir Rufus to his sketch of the story as we find it in the *Notebooks*. This book, *The Modern Warning*, is written after a brief visit to the United States, during which his prejudices about Agatha's country are only confirmed.

The end of the story is melodramatic and was perceived as such by contemporary reviewers. James eventually used the possibility of suicide as he did also in 'The Patagonia' (1888). One is tempted to connect Agatha's sudden suicide by poison with the suicide of Marian 'Clover' Hooper Adams, in Washington on 6 December 1885.[105] Clover and her husband Henry Adams were close friends of James, who spent much time with them in Washington in 1882 (see above). That capital is central to this story, as it is after his visit to Washington that Sir Rufus tells his wife that he wants to write a book on America. The political world of Washington has matched his negative judgement of the country. Leon Edel also speculates that Lady Chasemore's suicide may owe something to that of Clover Adams ('the tale itself, with its sharp words between Americans and English—its dialogue between the civilizations of the Old and New World—contains echoes of Henry James's talks with Mrs Adams.'), although he concedes that Agatha Grice herself owes nothing to James's incisive and argumentative friend.[106] Kaplan suggests that the suicide of a friend of Paul Bourget's in Rome may have influenced James.[107]

James added another strand to the international theme of America versus England by giving the Grices an Irish origin, kept alive by Macarthy's name. Sir Rufus also has Irish antecedents, his grandmother is Irish, but this is not enough to bridge the gulf between them. The different Irish strands have

and Endangered Alliances in Henry James's "The Modern Warning"', *Irish Studies Review*, 23.2 (2015), 184–93.

[104] Virginia C. Fowler, *Henry James's American Girl: The Embroidery on the Canvas* (Madison, WI: University of Wisconsin Press, 1984), p. 48.

[105] See Monteiro, 'Americanism in Henry James', p. 173.

[106] Edel, *Middle Years*, p. 104.

[107] Kaplan, *Henry James*, p. 320.

been thoroughly analysed by Denis Flannery.[108] Alice James, whose diary shows a keen interest in Ireland and the burning issue of Home Rule, appreciated the story.

The possibilities of misinterpreting James's representation of America and Britain by partisan readers on either side of the Atlantic were endless, it seems. James himself thought the international theme of the tale might be found 'overdone, threadbare' in his *Notebook* entry. Yet he could scarcely have anticipated the interpretation of the story as a celebration of America in a savage response by the *Scottish Review* (13 April 1889): 'In *The Modern Warning* we find the American Eagle screeching anew, and disposed to wave aloft the Star Spangled Banner, while he dances on the faded worn-out Union Jack, and we feel inclined to say, "My dear bird, do not screech so loud. Nobody denies the glories of the Great American nation! And at any rate be logical. If Great Britain is the home of a worn-out despised nation, be not so exuberantly exultant over every American girl who contrives to get herself chosen as a wife by a son of that degenerate race."'[109]

Howells included 'A Modern Warning' in his praise of the 1888 collection of stories published by Macmillan. The conclusion of the story with a suicide was however generally criticized: it was 'unworthy of Mr. James' (*Saturday Review*); 'Mr James neither need nor should have ended it by the suicide of the luckless Agatha, distracted between wifely and sisterly love. Tragedy interspersed with comedy is good literature; comedy ending in tragedy, though unfortunately only too true to life, is not good literature, or very rarely so' (*Academy*); 'in the name of all probability we must protest against Mr. James's needless slaughter of Lady Chasemore [...] her suicide comes upon the reader with a shock of surprise which immediately turns to indignation at the author for perpetrating such wanton murder!' (*Literary World*). *The Athenæum* found 'the realistic sketch of Mr. Macarthy Grice, an American chauvinist', 'amusing', although it underlined that 'the tragedy of the conclusion' was 'out of harmony with the comedy of the opening of the story'. On 18 November 1888 William James wrote to Henry after receiving the book edition, commenting favourably on 'The Aspern Papers' but

[108] Denis Flannery, 'Irish Strands and the Imperial Eye: Henry James's "The Modern Warning"', *Henry James Review*, 31.1 (2010), 39–45.

[109] Kevin J. Hayes (ed.), *Henry James: The Contemporary Reviews* (Cambridge: Cambridge University Press, 1996), p. 217.

noticing that 'The suicide of the American bride in the modern warning [sic] was rather abrupt, a piece of wanton tragedy as it seems. I am eager for all the other stories.'[110] Not so Alice James, who wrote to William: 'The best for its data is "*The Modern Warning,*" wh. will be considered *unnatural* by the bourgeois. I feel as if *I* were the heroine.'[111] This appreciation is perhaps linked to Alice's opinions and theories on suicide as an act of independence, as described in her *Diary* on 5 August 1889.[112] Ezra Pound did notice that 'The Modern Warning' had been excluded from James's 'collected edition'.[113]

∗

The nine tales gathered in this volume, spanning the mid to the late 1880s, undoubtedly exemplify James's steadfast interest in – as well as mastery of – the art of short fiction, in a transitional period which saw him exposed to the suggestions of naturalism and impressionism. He was also reworking subject matter and motifs already explored in the previous decades, such as the international theme that had made him famous at the end of the 1870s.

In these tales James also dealt with contemporary issues, primarily with the ever-growing publicity of private lives, especially as it regarded writers and artists. Although he experienced periods of frustration, as when publication of his work was delayed, or when his American publisher went bankrupt, James succeeded in producing, and experimenting with, new forms of writing that were to foreshadow the great novels and stories of the beginning of the new century.

Contemporary Reception

This is a selection of contemporary reviews from the time of the stories' publication up until James's death in 1916. Many reviews are reprinted, as noted, in Roger Gard (ed.), *Henry James: the Critical Heritage* (London: Routledge &

[110] *The Correspondence of William James*, vol. 2, *William and Henry, 1885–1896*, ed. Ignas K. Skrupskelis, Elizabeth M. Berkeley *et al.* (Charlottesville, VA: University of Virginia Press, 1992), p. 99.

[111] *The Death and Letters of Alice James: Selected Correspondence*, ed. Ruth B. Yeazell (Berkeley, CA: University of California Press, 1981), p. 149.

[112] *The Diary of Alice James*, ed. Leon Edel (New York: Dodd, Mead, 1964), p. 52.

[113] Pound, 'Shake Down', 29.

Kegan Paul, 1968) and Kevin J. Hayes (ed.), *Henry James: The Contemporary Reviews* (Cambridge: Cambridge University Press, 1996); hereafter, Gard and Hayes, respectively. For abbreviations within square brackets, see p. xii.

New York Tribune (9 July 1884), 6. [NEW, P]

Literary World [Boston] 15 (September 1884), 308–9. [NEW]

Hartford Daily Courant (25 October 1884), 1. [NEW]

Nation [New York] 39 (November 1884), 442. [*TTC*]

New York Daily Graphic (6 November 1884), 31. [NEW]

Athenæum [London] 2981 (13 December 1884), 797. [NEW]

Boston Daily Advertiser (13 December 1884), 2. [NEW]

Chicago Daily Tribune (31 January 1885), 9. [NEW]

Springfield (Mass.) Republican (8 February 1885), 4. [P]

New York Times (15 February 1885), 4. [GR, P, PD]

Public Ledger and Daily Transcript [Philadelphia] (18 February 1885), 2. [P]

New York Daily Graphic (20 February 1885), 819. [P]

Boston Daily Advertiser (24 February 1885), 3. [GR, P]

Christian Union [New York] (26 February 1885), 21. [GR, P]

Literary World [Boston] 16 (21 March 1885), 102. [GR, P, PD]

Lippincott's Magazine [Philadelphia] (April 1885), 424. [GR]

Chicago Daily Tribune (4 April 1885), 9. [GR, P, PD]

Independent [New York] 37 (9 April 1885), 11. [GR, P, PD]

Critic [New York] 3 (2 May 1885), 206–7. [GR]

Pall Mall Gazette [London] (28 May 1885), 5. [GR, P]

Athenæum [London] 3007 (13 June 1885), 756. [SR]

Cambridge Review [Cambridge, UK] 10 (1888–9), 126–7. [AP]

Harper's Monthly 77 (October 1888), 799–804. [AP, L, LP, MT, MW]

Saturday Review [London], 66 (3 November 1888), 527. [AP, LP, MW]

Academy [London] 862 (10 November 1888), 302. [AP, LP, MW]

New York Sun (11 November 1888), 4. [AP]

New York Tribune (13 November 1888), 8. [AP, LP, MW]

Boston Evening Journal (16 November 1888), 2. [AP]

Athenæum [London] 3186 (17 November 1888), 660. [AP, LP]

Boston Herald (19 November 1888), 3. [AP]

Epoch [New York] 4 (23 November 1888), 290–1. [AP]

Chicago Inter-Ocean (24 November 1888), 11. [AP]

Churchman [Hartford, CT] 58 (24 November 1888), 643, in Hayes 217. [AP]

Life [New York] 12 (29 November 1888), 302–3; in Hayes 213–14. [AP, LP, MW]

Literary World [London] 38 (30 November 1888), 445–6. [AP]

Graphic [London] 39 (1 December 1888), 586. [AP]

Detroit Free Press (8 December 1888), 3. [LP, AP, MW]

Literary World [Boston] 19 (8 December 1888), 451. [AP, MW]

Boston Daily Advertiser (10 December 1888), 5. [AP]

New York Times (16 December 1888), 19. [AP]

Indianapolis Journal (17 December 1888), 3. [AP]

Hartford Daily Courant (18 December 1888), 2. [AP]

Christian Union [New York] (20 December 1888), 737. [AP]

Daily Telegraph [London] (25 December 1888), 7. [AP]

Critic [New York] 12 (9 February 1889), 61–2. [AP, LP, MW]

Universal Review [London] 3 (March 1889), 427–8. [AP]

Scottish Review [Paisley and London] 13 (April 1889), 448. [AP, LP, MW]

Nation [New York] 48 (25 April 1889), 353. [AP]

Athenæum [London] 3211 (11 May 1889), 598–9. [MT]

Boston Daily Advertiser (14 May 1889), 5. [MT, L]

Literary World [Boston] 20.11 (25 May 1889), 178. [L]

Blackwood's Edinburgh Magazine 145.884 (June 1889), 809. [L]

American 18.462 (15 June 1889), 138. [L]

Boston Evening Transcript (15 June 1889), 6. [MT]

Critic [New York] 12 (6 July 1889), 3. [L]

Epoch [New York] 5 (19 July 1889), 389. [L]

Nation [New York] 49 (25 July 1889), 77. [MT]

Harper's New Monthly Magazine [New York] 79 (August 1889), 477–8. [MT]

New York Times (12 August 1889), 3. [L, MT]

Spectator [London] 43 (17 August 1889), 213. [L]

Lippincott's Monthly Magazine [Philadelphia] (September 1889), 433–4. [L]

Little Review [Chicago] 5 (August 1918), 9–39. [AP, L, LP, P]

TEXTUAL INTRODUCTION

Choice of Copy Text

This volume presents nine stories by Henry James written and published between 1884 and 1888. All had a first magazine publication – eight of them in the American magazines the *New York Sun, Century Magazine, Harper's Weekly* and *Harper's Monthly Magazine,* and *Atlantic Monthly*; one, 'The Path of Duty', in an English magazine, the *English Illustrated Magazine* – and all were followed by English and American volume editions.

The copy text for this volume presents the first book edition of each story. For the first four tales – 'Pandora', 'Georgina's Reasons', 'A New England Winter', and 'The Path of Duty' – we have used as copy texts the first British volume editions published by Macmillan, rather than the earlier American editions published by James R. Osgood, as the former display a greater number of revisions by James.[1] With the exception of 'A New England Winter', published by Macmillan just two months after the Osgood edition, the British editions of these four tales appeared several months after the American edition, and so James had more time to revise them. For the remaining five tales – 'Mrs. Temperly', 'Louisa Pallant', 'The Aspern Papers', 'The Liar', and 'The Modern Warning' – we have used as copy texts the editions published in London and New York by Macmillan of *The Aspern Papers* (2 vols., 1888) for 'The Aspern Papers', 'Louisa Pallant', and 'The Modern Warning', and of *A London Life* (2 vols., 1889) for 'The Liar' and 'Mrs. Temperly'.

History of Publication

'Pandora' was first published in the *New York Sun* on 1 and 8 June 1884, and was printed at the same time in nine other American newspapers, according to Dana's project (see Introduction).[2] The story was later

---

[1] See *S1874–1884*, p. 928.

[2] Charles Johanningsmeier, 'Henry James's Dalliance with the Newspaper World', *Henry James Review*, 19.1 (1998), 37, note 2. The other nine newspapers were the *San Francisco Chronicle, St*

collected in the American volume *The Author of Beltraffio* (Boston: James R. Osgood, February 1885) and in the first volume of the British *Stories Revived* (London: Macmillan, 15 May 1885). Vandersee showed that James made two separate revisions of the magazine text, one for the Osgood (twenty changes) and another for the Macmillan editions (forty changes).[3] James further revised the Osgood version for inclusion in volume XVIII of the *New York Edition* (1909), where 'Daisy Miller' opened the volume, followed by 'Pandora', 'The Patagonia', 'The Marriages', 'The Real Thing', 'Brooksmith', 'The Beldonald Holbein', 'The Story in It', 'Flickerbridge', and 'Mrs. Medwin'.

'Georgina's Reasons' was published in the *New York Sun* (20 and 27 July, and 3 August 1884) and concomitantly in nine other American newspapers. It was reprinted the following year in *The Author of Beltraffio* (Boston: James R. Osgood, February 1885) and in the second volume of *Stories Revived* (London: Macmillan, 15 May 1885), but it was not included in the *New York Edition*.

'A New England Winter' was published in the August and September issues of *Century Magazine* in 1884 (vol. 28, nos. 4 and 5), and then collected in *Tales of Three Cities* (Boston: James R. Osgood, 17 October 1884; London: Macmillan, 18 November 1884). The order of the stories was changed in the British edition, where 'Lady Barberina' opened the volume, perhaps in order to make the book more appealing to British readers. On 14 March 1884 James wrote to Benjamin Ticknor, a partner in Osgood's, that he preferred the book not to be called '"Impressions" &c; and I think "*Tales of Three Cities*" will do very well' (*LL* 147). It was not included in the *New York Edition*, in spite of the original plan to include it.[4]

'The Path of Duty' appeared in the December 1884 issue of the *English Illustrated Magazine*, a newly established monthly publication by Macmillan (October 1883 – August 1913). Oddly, the tale featured no accompanying

Louis Globe-Democrat, Chicago Tribune, New Orleans' Times-Democrat, Savannah Morning News, Syracuse Daily Standard, Cincinnati Enquirer, Philadelphia's Time, and the Springfield Republican.

3 For details on these revisions see Charles Vandersee, 'James's "Pandora": The Mixed Consequences of Revision', *Studies in Bibliography*, 21 (1968), 93–108.
4 Michael Anesko, '*Friction with the Market': Henry James and the Profession of Authorship* (New York: Oxford University Press, 1986), p. 148.

illustration. The story was also published in *The Author of Beltraffio* (Boston: Osgood, February 1885) and in the first volume of *Stories Revived* (London: Macmillan, 15 May 1885). It was not reprinted in the *New York Edition*.

'Mrs. Temperly', under the title 'Cousin Maria', was published in three instalments in *Harper's Weekly* (6, 13, and 20 August 1887), with 'ugly big drawings'[5] by Charles S. Reinhart (1844–96), the American illustrator. On 5 July 1888 James wrote to Macmillan proposing the publication of three volumes, the third of which was to include 'The Lesson of the Master', 'The Patagonia', and 'Mrs. Temperley' (the new title for 'Cousin Maria'), trying to make some money out of the existing material. The story was then published as 'Mrs. Temperly' (without the e) in volume II of *A London Life*, containing 'A London Life', 'The Patagonia', 'The Liar', 'Mrs. Temperly' (2 vols., London: Macmillan, April 1889). It was not included in the *New York Edition*.

'Louisa Pallant' was first published in vol. 76 of *Harper's New Monthly Magazine*, with illustrations by Charles S. Reinhart (February 1888), then revised and reprinted in September the same year in volume II of *The Aspern Papers; Louisa Pallant; The Modern Warning*. It was revised and reprinted as the last story in volume XIII of the *New York Edition* (1908), following 'The Reverberator', 'Madame de Mauves', 'A Passionate Pilgrim', and 'The Madonna of the Future'. On 18 March 1908 James wrote to Scribner's that he was not sending the Preface to vol. XII in view of the fact that that volume was now to 'terminate with "The Author of Beltraffio" and "Louisa Pallant"' (*LL* 346). The Preface and the revised 'Louisa Pallant' were then sent to Scribner's on 23 April (*LL* 347). 'The Author of Beltraffio' instead went into vol. XV (*LL* 349). According to James (Preface, *LoA* 1192), the order of the stories in this volume was determined by their length rather than by their date.

'The Aspern Papers' was published in vol. 61 of the *Atlantic Monthly* in three parts (not in two, as James had wished), in March, April, and May (1888, issues 365–7). On 24 May 1888 James wrote to Macmillan that he would like to see the volume edition 'take a forward step' (*Correspondence of HJ and Macmillan*, p. 140), asking him, 'will you take them [AP] in hand & will you let me know the idea you may have about them?' (*ibid.*), again

---

[5] Henry James to Macmillan, of 22 January 1889, *The Correspondence of Henry James and the House of Macmillan, 1877–1914*, ed. Rayburn S. Moore (London: Macmillan, 1993), p. 149.

underlining his need to have some money. Macmillan offered an advance of £200 for three books (the other two being *A London Life* and *The Lesson of the Master*) on 6 July 1888. The novella was revised and reprinted in September 1888 in the two-volume edition of *The Aspern Papers; Louisa Pallant; The Modern Warning* (London and New York: Macmillan). It was very amply revised for publication in the *New York Edition*, vol. XII (1908), where it opened the volume, followed by 'The Turn of the Screw', 'The Liar', and 'The Two Faces'.

'The Liar' was first published in the *Century Magazine* in May and June 1888. It was later included in vol. II of *A London Life* (London and New York, April 1889; along with the eponymous story, 'The Patagonia', and 'Mrs. Temperly'). As James wrote to his publisher, he hoped that this collection, issued in two volumes by Macmillan in April 1889, could bring him some money (*Correspondence of HJ and Macmillan*, p. 140). The two-volume collection was later reprinted in a single volume in New York in the week of 29 April 1889. After a second London edition in one volume, the collection was reprinted by Heinemann & Balestier in 1891, as vol. XXX in the English Library, Leipzig. The story was extensively revised for inclusion in vol. XII of the *New York Edition* (1908).

'The Modern Warning', with the title 'Two Countries', was published in vol. 77 of *Harper's New Monthly Magazine* in June 1888, with illustrations by Charles S. Reinhart, and reprinted in September of the same year with the new title in vol. II of the Macmillan volume, *The Aspern Papers; Louisa Pallant; The Modern Warning*.

Of these nine stories, only four were selected, revised, and discussed in James's Prefaces for the *New York Edition*: 'Pandora' (vol. XVIII, 1909), 'Louisa Pallant' (vol. XIII, 1908), 'The Aspern Papers' (vol. XII, 1908), and 'The Liar' (vol. XII, 1908). Both 'The Path of Duty' and 'A New England Winter' were included in the original plan;[6] the latter was 'later excised for want of space'.[7] The reasons for James's selection or rejection of his own works for the *New York Edition* are complex, but one can reasonably believe

---

[6] 'The Path of Duty' would appear in vol. XVII (26 February 1908), 'A New England Winter' in vol. XIV (26 February 1908): see Anesko, *'Friction with the Market'*, pp. 159, 155.

[7] See Michael Anesko, *Monopolizing the Master: Henry James and the Politics of Modern Literary Scholarship* (Stanford, CA: Stanford University Press, 2012), p. 13.

that the five omitted stories were considered by James less important. There may have been other motives: James's supposed plan to have twenty-three volumes in imitation of Balzac's *Comédie Humaine* (although initially there were to be but sixteen);[8] his realization after using fifteen volumes for his novels that he had too many stories, so that he had to leave out the 'Scenes of American Life';[9] the excessive quantity of material, but certainly also the preoccupation with the market,[10] also in relationship with the current *de luxe* editions; a specific selection based on what Martha Banta calls an 'aesthetics of refusal'.[11]

The question of James's revisions and their results is highly debated.[12] It can be said that, in general, a more positive view of the revisions has prevailed in the recent past, although already in the nineteen forties critics such as Matthiessen were in favour.[13] Essential in illuminating the deep reasons for James's revising is Horne's *Henry James and Revision* (1990): revisions are part of the renewal of a writer's 'creative intimacy', the way they may save themselves from 'the limbo of disconnection' (p. 99). A specific chapter of Horne's book is devoted to 'The Aspern Papers' (ch. 8, pp. 265–88).

---

[8] Anesko, 'Friction with the Market', p. 145.
[9] Leon Edel, *Henry James*, vol. 5, *The Master* (Philadelphia, PA: J. B. Lippincott, 1972), pp. 322–3.
[10] Anesko, 'Friction with the Market', p. 145ff.
[11] Martha Banta, 'The Excluded Seven: Practice of Omission, Aesthetics of Refusal', in David McWhirter (ed.), *Henry James's New York Edition: The Construction of Authorship* (Stanford, CA: Stanford University Press, 1995), pp. 240–60. On James's relationship with his 'old' works, see Philip Horne, *Henry James and Revision: The New York Edition* (Oxford: Clarendon Press, 1990), p. 78.
[12] See Hershel Parker, *Flawed Texts and Verbal Icons: Literary Authority in American Fiction* (Evanston, IL: Northwestern University Press, 1984), pp. 85–114; and David McWhirter, *Henry James's New York Edition: The Construction of Authorship* (Stanford, CA: Stanford University Press, 1995).
[13] See F. O. Matthiessen, *Henry James: The Major Phase* (London: Oxford University Press, 1946).

CHRONOLOGY OF COMPOSITION
AND PRODUCTION

1881

18 January: Notebook entry for 'A New England Winter' (see Appendix A).

March: James travels from France to Italy, stopping in Genoa (partial setting for 'Georgina's Reasons') for a day before proceeding to Milan and Venice, where he is a guest of Katharine De Kay Bronson and stays in a wing of the Casa Alvisi on the Grand Canal.

October: James returns to the United States, where his travels to Boston and Cambridge may have provided further impressions for 'A New England Winter', and those to New York and Washington DC respectively for 'Georgina's Reasons' and 'Pandora'.

November: *The Portrait of a Lady* published in three volumes by Macmillan.

1882

January: James enjoys Washington, and stays with his friends Henry and 'Clover' Adams. Meets President Chester A. Arthur and Oscar Wilde, who had just begun an American tour. Receives news of his mother's illness and leaves for Boston, but arrives too late to see her alive. Turns 'Daisy Miller' into a play.

May: Returns to England.

September: Leaves for Paris and starts a long tour of provincial towns in France, impressions of which will be recorded in various essays published in the *Atlantic Monthly* in 1883–4 and later as a book, *A Little Tour in France*, in September 1884.

November: 'Venice' published in *Century Magazine* 25: 3–23.

December: Receives news of his father's illness. James leaves Europe too late to see him alive (Henry James Sr had died on the 18th).

1883

17 May: In his notebooks James observes that the 'self-made girl' would make 'a very good subject for a short story' (*CN* 22).

Summer: Returns to London from the United States, which he will not revisit for the next twenty-one years.

3 September: *Daisy Miller: A Comedy in Three Acts* published in Boston by James R. Osgood.

13 November: Macmillan publishes fourteen-volume collected edition of James's fiction.

15 November: Death of brother Garth Wilkinson ('Wilkie') James.

18 December: Macmillan publishes *Portraits of Places.*

1884

2 January: Notebook entry for the names Daintry and Florimond ('A New England Winter') and Vandeleur and Ambrose ('The Path of Duty'). In the same month James publishes essays 'Ivan Turgénieff' (*Atlantic Monthly*, 42–55) and 'Matthew Arnold' (*English Illustrated Magazine*, 241–6).

29 January: The American edition of *Portrait of Places* published (Boston: James R. Osgood). Writing to Macmillan, James laments that his royalties are 'virtually *nil*' (*HJL* 3:22). In a notebook entry James wants to go back to the figure of the young American girl abroad, adding 'I might even *do* Henry Adams and his wife'. He also pens another entry containing the 'germ' of 'The Path of Duty' (see Appendix A). In the same month James agrees to sell two of his stories ('Pandora' and 'Georgina's Reasons') to Charles Dana's *New York Sun* (see Introduction).

2 February: James goes to Paris for a month.

5 February: Letter to sister Alice: 'I am writing a couple of short tales—as a trial, to begin with—for Dana & the Sun!' (see Introduction).

23 February: Mentions in a letter to Grace Norton having renewed friendship with John Singer Sargent.

26 March: Notebook entry containing the 'germ' for 'Georgina's Reasons' (see Appendix A).

May: Begins serialization of 'Lady Barberina' and 'The Author of Beltraffio' (June) respectively in *Century Magazine* and the *English Illustrated Magazine*.

1 and 8 June: 'Pandora' appears in the *English Illustrated Magazine*.

19 June: Notebook entry for 'The Liar' (see Appendix A).

9 July: Notebook entry for 'The Modern Warning' (see Appendix A).

20, 27 July and 3 August: 'Georgina's Reasons' appears in the *New York Sun*. James will comment negatively on this story on 24 October 1886 and 13 November 1894 (see Introduction).

August–September: 'A New England Winter' published in *Century Magazine*.

August: Begins writing *The Bostonians*, to start serialization in the *Century* in February 1885 (and conclude February 1886). James goes to Dover.

September: Publishes *A Little Tour in France* (Boston: James R. Osgood) and one of his most appreciated artistic statements, 'The Art of Fiction' (*Longman's Magazine*, 502–21).

17 October: Publishes *Tales of Three Cities* (Boston: James R. Osgood): the volume includes 'The Impressions of a Cousin', 'Lady Barberina', and 'A New England Winter'; it is published in London by Macmillan (18 November), with the stories in a different order (see Textual Introduction).

December: 'The Path of Duty' published in the *English Illustrated Magazine*.

1885

January: James writes that he is 'revamping and almost rewriting various old and early (short) tales, which I have dug out of dusty periodicals and half a dozen of which are to be published, with three or four recent ones (Beltraffio etc.) in three volumes by Macmillan to be republished later in America' (*HJL* 3:65–6).

February: *The Author of Beltraffio* published by James R. Osgood; it includes 'Pandora', 'Georgina's Reasons', 'The Path of Duty', and 'Four Meetings'.

18 April: In reply to Osgood, who has repeatedly complained about his handwriting, James writes that he has hired a typist (*CLHJ 1884–1886* 1:156).

5 May: Writes to Frederick Macmillan that he is worried about the bankruptcy of his American publisher James R. Osgood (*CLHJ 1884–1886* 1:168). The three-volume *Stories Revived* (London: Macmillan) comes out on 15 May and includes fourteen tales, among them 'The Author of Beltraffio', 'Pandora', 'The Path of Duty', and 'Georgina's Reasons'. Begins writing *The Princess Casamassima*, to start serialization in the *Atlantic Monthly* in September (and concluding October 1886).

1886

16 February: *The Bostonians* published in three volumes by Macmillan in London and on 19 March by Macmillan in New York.

19 June: The essay 'William Dean Howells' appears in *Harper's Weekly* (394–5).

22 October: *The Princess Casamassima* published in 3 volumes (London and New York: Macmillan).

8 December 1886: Arrives in Florence and stays in Bellosguardo at the Villa Brichieri, rented to him by Constance Fenimore Woolson while she lives nearby at the Villa Castellani until the end of the year.

24 December: Letter to John Hay in which James explains the origin of 'Georgina's Reasons.'

1887

1 January: Moves to the Hotel du Sud in Florence on New Year's Day, when Constance Fenimore Woolson moves to the Villa Brichieri.

12 January: Notebook entry for 'germ' of 'The Aspern Papers' (see Introduction and Appendix A).

21 January: Notebook entry for 'Louisa Pallant' (see Appendix A).

12 February: Publishes 'Miss Constance Fenimore Woolson' in *Harper's Weekly* (114–15).

22 February: Travels to Venice, where he is a guest of Katharine de Kay Bronson. Catches cold and is ill with jaundice. Returns to Florence.

11 April: Back in Bellosguardo at the Villa Brichieri, where he lives with Constance Fenimore Woolson, but on a different floor. Here he writes 'The Aspern Papers' in April and May.

2 May: Sends long-delayed article on Robert Louis Stevenson to Robert Underwood Johnson, an editor of *Century Magazine*.

25 May: Leaves for Venice again, where he is a guest of Daniel Sargent Curtis and Ariana Wormeley Curtis at the Palazzo Barbaro.

12 June: Sends to publisher 'first half of the type-copy' of 'The Aspern Papers' while the second half is 'in London, being type-copied'.

21 June: Sends final part of 'The Aspern Papers' from the Palazzo Barbaro.

1 July: Leaves Venice and travels to Vicenza, Mantua, Cremona, Brescia, Bergamo, Stresa (a location used in 'Louisa Pallant') and Switzerland, then to London.

23 July: Writes to Grace Norton: 'I wrote a good many (short) things while I was abroad—but they are buried in the bosom of the *Century*, *Harper*, *Atlantic* etc., who *keep* them, annoyingly, for what they suppose to be the mystic hour. *Pazienza* (that sounds conceited), and they will come' (*HJL* 3:197–8).

6–20 August: 'Cousin Maria' (later 'Mrs. Temperly') published in *Harper's Weekly*, with 'ugly big drawings' by C. S. Reinhart (see note 52 to the Introduction).

October: *Harper's New Monthly Magazine* publishes 'John S. Sargent'.

December: Writes to Stevenson, regretting that his essay on him is not yet out, like other work which 'the beastly periodicals hold' back (*HJL* 3:206); at the beginning of the new year he will lament to Howells that demand for his work is reduced 'to zero' (*HJL* 3:209).

1888

2 January: Letter to Howells in which James hopes that all his 'buried prose [will] kick off its various tombstones at once' (see Introduction).

February: Various long-awaited publications: 'Louisa Pallant' published in *Harper's New Monthly Magazine* illustrated by C. S. Reinhart, and 'The Reverberator' (*Macmillan's Magazine*).

March–May: 'The Aspern Papers' published in *Atlantic Monthly*.

8 May: *Partial Portraits* (London and New York: Macmillan).

May–June: 'The Liar' published in *Century Magazine*.

June: *The Reverberator* in two volumes by Macmillan; 'The Modern Warning' in *Harper's New Monthly Magazine* with the title 'Two Countries'.

September: *The Aspern Papers, Louisa Pallant, The Modern Warning* published in two volumes by Macmillan.

13 October: Letter to Macmillan about 'The Aspern Papers': 'The book is charmingly pretty [...] & if the public would only show some practical agreement in this estimate there would be no wormwood mingled with my honey' (Anesko, *'Friction with the Market'*, p. 122). Arrives in Geneva, where he continues to write *The Tragic Muse*, started in the summer of 1887, and sees Constance Fenimore Woolson. He proceeds to Genoa and Monte Carlo in November, spending December in Paris, then joining sister Alice in Leamington, Warwickshire, for a week just after Christmas.

1889

January: *The Tragic Muse* begins serialization in *Atlantic Monthly*.

April: *A London Life* published; it includes 'The Liar' and 'Mrs. Temperly'.

BIBLIOGRAPHY

The Bibliography serves the volume as a whole. It does not aim for comprehensive coverage of everything that has been written on the nine tales in this volume; rather, it is limited to works that are explicitly cited in the editorial matter, or, if not cited, works that contribute information and evidence directly relevant to the history of the texts' genesis, composition, reception and afterlife. The titles of some secondary and related works are followed by abbreviations in square brackets that indicate the tale(s) to which they refer.

The Aspern Papers and Other Tales

'Pandora', *New York Sun*, 1 June 1884, 1–2; 8 June 1884, 1–2. (US)
  The Author of Beltraffio; Pandora; Georgina's Reasons; The Path of Duty; Four Meetings (Boston, MA: James R. Osgood & Co., 1885), pp. 81–156.
  Stories Revived, vol. I, comprising 'The Author of Beltraffio', 'Pandora', 'The Path of Duty', 'A Day of Days', and 'A Light Man' (London: Macmillan & Co., 1885), pp. 71–143.
  New York Edition of the Novels and Tales of Henry James (New York: Scribner's, 1909), vol. XVIII, pp. 95–168.
'Georgina's Reasons', *New York Sun*, 20 July 1884, 1–2; 27 July 1884, 1–2; 3 August 1884, 1–2. (US)
  The Author of Beltraffio; Pandora; Georgina's Reasons; The Path of Duty; Four Meetings (Boston, MA: James R. Osgood & Co., 1885), pp. 159–257.
  Stories Revived, vol. II, comprising 'Georgina's Reasons', 'A Passionate Pilgrim', 'A Landscape-Painter', and 'Rose-Agathe' (London: Macmillan & Co., 1885), pp. 1–95.
'A New England Winter', *Century Magazine*, 28.4 (August 1884), 573–587; 28.5 (September 1884), 733–43. (US)
  Tales of Three Cities, comprising 'The Impressions of a Cousin', 'Lady Barberina', and 'A New England Winter' (Boston, MA: James R. Osgood & Co., 1884), pp. 269–359.

Tales of Three Cities, comprising 'Lady Barberina', 'A New England Winter', and 'The Impressions of a Cousin' (London: Macmillan & Co., 1884), pp. 129–208.

'The Path of Duty', *English Illustrated Magazine*, 2.15 (December 1884), 240–56. (UK)

The Author of Beltraffio; Pandora; Georgina's Reasons; The Path of Duty; Four Meetings (Boston, MA: James R. Osgood & Co., 1885), pp. 261–317.

Stories Revived, vol. I, comprising 'The Author of Beltraffio', 'Pandora', 'The Path of Duty', 'A Day of Days', and 'A Light Man' (London: Macmillan & Co., 1885), pp. 71–198.

'Mrs. Temperly', published as 'Cousin Maria' in *Harper's Weekly*, vol. 31, 6 August 1887, 557–8; 13 August 1887, 577–8; and 20 August 1887, 593–4. (US)

A London Life; The Patagonia; The Liar; Mrs. Temperly, vol. II (London and New York: Macmillan & Co., 1889), pp. 279–361.

'Louisa Pallant', published as 'Louisa Pallant: A Story' in *Harper's New Monthly Magazine*, 76.453 (February 1888), 336–55. (US)

The Aspern Papers; Louisa Pallant; The Modern Warning, vol. II (London and New York: Macmillan & Co., 1888), pp. 3–96.

The Novels and Tales of Henry James (New York: Scribner's, 1908), vol. XIII, pp. 495–550.

'The Aspern Papers', *Atlantic Monthly*, 61 (March 1888), 296–315; (April 1888), 461–82; and (May 1888), 577–94. (US)

The Aspern Papers; Louisa Pallant; The Modern Warning, vol. I (London and New York: Macmillan & Co., 1888), pp. 1–239.

The Novels and Tales of Henry James (New York: Scribner's, 1908), vol. XII, pp. 3–143.

'The Liar', *Century Magazine*, 36 (May 1888), 123–35; (June 1888), 213–23. (US)

A London Life; The Patagonia; The Liar; Mrs. Temperly, vol. II (London and New York: Macmillan & Co., 1889), pp. 147–275.

The Novels and Tales of Henry James (New York: Scribner's, 1908), vol. XII, pp. 313–88.

'The Modern Warning', published as 'Two Countries' in *Harper's New Monthly Magazine*, 77 (June 1888), 83–116. (US)

The Aspern Papers; Louisa Pallant; The Modern Warning, vol. II (London and New York: Macmillan & Co., 1888), pp. 99–258.

Archival Sources Consulted

Theodora Bosanquet, Diary, 25 December 1909; Houghton Library, bMS Eng 1213.1 Box 1

Henry James to John Foord, 5 February 1887, Morgan.1 MS (Koch Collection) 34 DVG (courtesy of Philip Horne).

Henry James to Jane von Glehn [1913], LH MS copy: LH MS copy (in letter of Jane von Glehn to Roger Quilter of Mon[day] 22 [September 1913] from Lago di Garda), British Library, Add. MS 70597, fols. 41–4.

Sarah Wadsworth, '"Pandora" and the Popular Press', unpublished conference paper, University of Aberdeen Conference 2014: 'The Real Thing. Henry James and the Material World.'

Other Works by Henry James, His Family and Friends

The Ambassadors, ed. Nicola Bradbury (Cambridge: Cambridge University Press, 2015).

The American (Boston, MA: James R. Osgood and Co., 1877).

The Aspern Papers and Other Stories, ed. Adrian Poole (Oxford and New York: Oxford University Press, 1983; new edition 2013).

The Bostonians, ed. Daniel Karlin (Cambridge: Cambridge University Press, 2019).

Il carteggio Aspern, Introduction by Sergio Perosa, translation and notes by Gilberto Sacerdoti (Venice: Marsilio, 1991).

Collected Travel Writings: Great Britain and America: English Hours, The American Scene, Other Travels, ed. Richard Howard (New York: Library of America, 1993).

Collected Travel Writings: The Continent: A Little Tour in France, Italian Hours, Other Travels, ed. Richard Howard (New York: Library of America, 1993).

The Complete Letters of Henry James 1855–1872, 2 vols., ed. Pierre A. Walker and Greg W. Zacharias, with an introduction by Alfred Habegger (Lincoln, NE: University of Nebraska Press, 2006).

The Complete Letters of Henry James 1872–1876, 3 vols., ed. Pierre A. Walker and Greg W. Zacharias, with an introduction by Millicent Bell (Lincoln, NE: University of Nebraska Press, 2008).

The Complete Letters of Henry James 1876–1878, 2 vols., ed. Pierrre A.Walker and Greg W. Zacharias, with an introduction by Martha Banta (Lincoln, NE: University of Nebraska Press, 2012, 2013).

The Complete Letters of Henry James 1878–1880, 2 vols., ed. Pierrre A.Walker and Greg W. Zacharias, with an introduction by Michael Anesko (Lincoln, NE: University of Nebraska Press, 2014, 2015).

The Complete Letters of Henry James 1880–1883, 2 vols., ed. Michael Anesko and Greg W. Zacharias, associate editor Katie Sommer. With an introduction by Susan M. Griffin (Lincoln, NE: University of Nebraska Press, 2016, 2017).

The Complete Letters of Henry James 1883–1884, 2 vols., ed. Michael Anesko and Greg W. Zacharias, associate editor Katie Sommer. With an introduction by Kathleen Lawrence (Lincoln, NE: University of Nebraska Press, 2018, 2019).

The Complete Letters of Henry James 1884–1886, 2 vols., ed. Michael Anesko and Greg W. Zacharias, associate editor Katie Sommer. With an introduction by Adrian Poole (Lincoln, NE: University of Nebraska Press, 2020, 2021).

The Complete Notebooks, ed. Leon Edel and Lyall H. Powers (New York: Oxford University Press, 1987).

The Complete Plays of Henry James, ed. Leon Edel (Philadelphia, PA: Lippincott, 1949).

The Complete Writings of Henry James on Art and Drama, 2 vols., ed. Peter Collister (Cambridge: Cambridge University Press, 2016).

The Correspondence of Henry James and Henry Adams, 1877–1914, ed. and with an introduction by George Monteiro (Baton Rouge, LA: Louisiana University Press, 1992).

The Correspondence of Henry James and the House of Macmillan, 1877–1914, ed. Rayburn S. Moore (London: Macmillan, 1993).

The Correspondence of William James, ed. Ignas K. Skrupskelis, Elizabeth M. Berkeley *et al.*, 12 vols. (Charlottesville, VA: University of Virginia Press, 1992–4).

Daisy Miller and Other Stories, ed. Jean Gooder (Oxford: Oxford University Press, 1985).

The Death and Letters of Alice James: Selected Correspondence, ed. Ruth B. Yeazell (Berkeley, CA: University of California Press, 1981).

The Diary of Alice James, ed. Leon Edel (New York: Dodd, Mead, 1964).

English Hours, with an introduction by Leon Edel (New York: Oxford University Press, 1981).

Essays in London and Elsewhere (New York: Harpers & Brothers, 1893).

The Europeans, ed. Susan Griffin (Cambridge: Cambridge University Press, 2015).

The Golden Bowl (New York: Charles Scribner's Sons, 1904; London: Methuen & Co., 1905).

Hawthorne (London: Macmillan & Co., 1879).

Henry James: Complete Stories 1864–1874, ed. Jean Strouse (New York: Library of America, 1999).

Henry James: Complete Stories 1874–1884, ed. William L. Vance (New York: Library of America, 1999).

Henry James: Complete Stories 1884–1891, ed. Edward W. Said (New York: Library of America, 1999).

Henry James: Complete Stories 1892–1898, ed. John Hollander and David Bromwich (New York: Library of America, 1996).

Henry James: Complete Stories 1898–1910, ed. Denis Donoghue (New York: Library of America, 1996).

Henry James on Culture, Collected Essays on Politics and the American Social Scene, ed. Pierre A. Walker (Lincoln, NE: University of Nebraska Press, 2004).

Henry James Letters, ed. Leon Edel, 4 vols. (Cambridge, MA: Belknap Press of Harvard University Press, 1974–84).

Henry James. Letters from the Palazzo Barbaro, ed. Rosella Mamoli Zorzi (London: Pushkin Press, 1998).

Henry James. Letters to Isabella Stewart Gardner, ed. Rosella Mamoli Zorzi (London: Pushkin Press, 2009).

Henry James: A Life in Letters, ed. Philip Horne (Harmondsworth: Allen Lane, 1999; New York: Viking, 1999).

Henry James. Nouvelles completes 1877–1888 II, ed. Évelyne Labbé (Paris: Éditions de la Pléiade, 2003).

Henry James, Su letti di asfodelo. Lettere a Caroline Fitzgerald (Letters to Caroline Fitzgerald), ed. Rosella Mamoli Zorzi and Gottardo Pallastrelli (Milan: Archinto, 2018).

'The Late James Payn', in *Autobiographies*, ed. Philip Horne (New York: Library of America, 2016).

Letter to Mrs. Frances Carruth Prindle, 1 August 1901, in 'Letters and Comment', *Yale Review*, n.s. 1 (October 1923), 207–8.

The Letters of Henry James, selected and edited by Percy Lubbock, 2 vols. (London: Macmillan, 1920).

A London Life and the Reverberator, ed. Philip Horne (Oxford and New York: Oxford University Press, 1989).

The Other House (London: Macmillan, 1896).

The Painter's Eye: Notes and Essays on the Pictorial Arts, ed. John L. Sweeney (Cambridge, MA: Harvard University Press, 1956)

Parisian Sketches, Letters to the New York Tribune 1875–1876, ed. and with an introduction by Leon Edel and Isle Dusoir Lind (London: Rupert Hart-Davis, 1958).

The Portrait of a Lady, ed. Michael Anesko (Cambridge: Cambridge University Press, 2016).

Portraits of Places (London: Macmillan & Co., 1883).

The Princess Casamassima, ed. Adrian Poole (Cambridge: Cambridge University Press, 2020).

The Reverberator, ed. Richard Salmon (Cambridge: Cambridge University Press, 2018).

Roderick Hudson (Boston, MA: James R. Osgood, 1875).

Selected Letters of Henry James, ed. and with an introduction by Leon Edel (London: Rupert Hart-Davis, 1956).

Selected Letters of Henry James to Edmund Gosse 1882–1915. A Literary Friendship, ed. Rayburn S. Moore (Baton Rouge, LA: Louisiana State University Press, 1988).

The Tragic Muse, 3 vols (London: Macmillan & Co., 1890).

Travelling in Italy with Henry James, ed. and with an introduction by Fred Kaplan (London: Hodder & Stoughton, 1994), pp. 41–59.

The Turn of the Screw and The Aspern Papers, ed. and with an introduction by Anthony Curtis (Harmondsworth: Penguin, 1984).

Washington Square, 2 vols. (London: Macmillan & Co., 1881).

William James: Writings 1902–1910, ed. Bruce Kuklick (New York: Library of America, 1987).

William Wetmore Story and His Friends, 2 vols. (Edinburgh and London: William Blackwood & Sons, 1903; Boston: Houghton, Mifflin & Co., 1903).

The Wings of the Dove, 2 vols. (New York: Charles Scribner's Sons, 1902).

Secondary and Related Works

Adams, Marian, *The Letters of Mrs. Henry Adams, 1865–1883*, ed. Ward Thoron (Boston, MA: Little, Brown, 1936).

Albers, Christina E., *A Reader's Guide to the Short Stories of Henry James* (New York: G. K. Hall, 1997).

Anesko, Michael, *'Friction with the Market': Henry James and the Profession of Authorship* (New York: Oxford University Press, 1986). [AP, MW]

Letters, Fictions, Lives: Henry James and William Dean Howells (New York: Oxford University Press, 1997). [NEW, MT, LP, AP, L]

Monopolizing the Master: Henry James and the Politics of Modern Literary Scholarship (Stanford, CA: Stanford University Press, 2012). [NEW, AP, PD]

Aziz, Maqbool (ed.), *The Tales of Henry James*, 3 vols. (Oxford: Clarendon Press, 1978–84).

Baedeker's Guide to Northern Italy (Leipzig: K. Baedeker, 1886).

Baedeker's Italy: Handbook for Travellers: Third Part, Southern Italy, Sicily etc. (Leipzig: K. Baedeker, 1867).

Baedeker's Paris and Its Environs (Leipzig: K. Baedeker, 1878).

Baedeker's Switzerland: Handbook for Travellers (Leipzig: K. Baedeker, 1879).

Balzac, Honoré de, *Le Cousin Pons*, ed. André Lorant (Paris: Gallimard, 1973).

Banta, Martha, 'The Excluded Seven: Practice of Omission, Aesthetics of Refusal', in David McWhirter (ed.), *Henry James's New York Edition: The Construction of Authorship* (Stanford, CA: Stanford University Press, 1995), pp. 240–60.

Basch, Norma, *Framing American Divorce: From the Revolutionary Generation to the Victorians* (Berkeley and Los Angeles: University of California Press, 1999).

Beach, Joseph Warren, *The Method of Henry James* (Philadelphia: Albert Saifer, 1918; reprinted 1954). [L]

Bell, Millicent, *Meaning in Henry James* (Cambridge, MA: Harvard University Press, 1991). [AP]

Bewley, Marius, *The Complex Fate: Hawthorne, Henry James and Some Other American Writers*, with an introduction and two interpolations by F. R. Leavis (London: Chatto & Windus, 1952). [PD, L]

Blackburn, Simon, *The Oxford Dictionary of Philosophy* (Oxford: Oxford University Press, 2005).

Booth, Wayne C., *The Rhetoric of Fiction* (Chicago: University of Chicago Press, 1961). [L]

Bradbury, Nicola, *An Annotated Critical Bibliography of Henry James* (New York: St Martin's Press, 1987).

Bradley, John (ed.), *Henry James and Homo-Erotic Desire*, with an introduction by Sheldon N. Novick (London: Palgrave Macmillan, 1999).

  Henry James on Stage and Screen (New York: Palgrave Macmillan, 2000).

Brewer's Dictionary of Phrase and Fable, 19th edn, ed. Susie Dent (London: Chambers Harrap, 2012).

Brooks, Peter, *Henry James Goes to Paris* (Princeton, NJ: Princeton University Press, 2007).

Brooks, Van Wyck, *The Dream of Arcadia: American Writers and Artists in Italy, 1760–1915* (New York: E. P. Dutton, 1958).

Buitenhuis, Peter, *The Grasping Imagination: The American Writings of Henry James* (Toronto: University of Toronto Press, 1970). [P, NEW, MW]

Buonomo, Leonardo, 'Echoes of the Heart: Henry James's Evocation of Edgar Allan Poe in "The Aspern Papers"', *Humanities* 10.1 (2021), 1–12. [AP]

Burk, Kathleen, *Old World, New World: The Story of England and America* (London: Little, Brown, 2007).

Burke, Mary, 'The Marriage Plot and the Plot against the Union: Irish Home Rule and Endangered Alliances in Henry James's "The Modern Warning"', *Irish Studies Review*, 23.2 (2015), 184–93. [MW]

Cargill, Oscar, *The Novels of Henry James* (New York: Macmillan, 1961). [GR]

Charteris, Evan, *John Sargent* (London: William Heinemann, 1927). [AP]

Church, Joseph, 'Writing and the Dispossession of Woman in "The Aspern Papers"', *American Imago* 47 (1990), 23–42. [AP]

Collister, Peter, '"As an Artist and as a Bachelor": The Sexual Dynamics of "The Liar"', *Henry James Review*, 34 (Winter 2013), 64–82. [L]

Cornwell, Neil, 'Pushkin and Henry James: Secrets, Papers and Figures', in Robert Read and Joe Andrews (eds.), *Two Hundred Years of Pushkin* (Amsterdam and New York: Rodopi, 2004), vol. 3, pp. 193–210. [AP]

Crowley, John W., 'The Wiles of a Witless Woman: Tina in *The Aspern Papers*', *Emerson Society Quarterly*, 22 (1976), 159–68. [AP]

Curl, James Stevens, *A Dictionary of Architecture and Landscape Architecture* (Oxford: Oxford University Press, 2007).

Curtis, L. P., *Anglo-Saxons and Celts: A Study of Anti-Irish Prejudice in Victorian England* (New York: New York University Press, 1968).

Dakers, Caroline, *The Holland Park Circle: Artists and Victorian Society* (New Haven, CT: Yale University Press, 1999).

Despotopoulou, Anna. '"Terrible Traps to Memory": National Monuments, Collective Memory, and Women in Henry James', *Modern Fiction Studies*, 63.3 (2017), 429–51. [P]

Dowling, Gregory, 'Raking It Up: John Drury's *Burning The Aspern Papers*', in Melanie H. Ross and Greg Zacharias (eds.), *Tracing Henry James* (Newcastle upon Tyne: Cambridge Scholars, 2008), pp. 237–54. [AP]

Dykstra, Natalie, *Clover Adams: A Gilded and Heartbreaking Life* (Boston, MA: Houghton Mifflin, 2012). [P]

Edel, Leon, '*The Aspern Papers*: Great Aunt Wyckoff and Juliana Bordereau', *Modern Language Notes*, 67.6 (June 1952), 392–5. [AP]

Henry James, 5 vols. (Philadelphia: J. B. Lippincott, 1953–72).

Henry James: The Conquest of London, 1870–1883 (London: Rupert Hart-Davis, 1962).

Henry James: The Middle Years 1884–1894 (London: Rupert Hart-Davis, 1963).

Edel, Leon, and Dan H. Laurence, *A Bibliography of Henry James* (London: Rupert Hart-Davis, 1957), 3rd edn, revised with the assistance of James Rambeau (Oxford: Clarendon Press, 1985).

Esposizione Nazionale Artistica Venezia (Venice: Stabilimento dell'Emporio, 1887).

Favaro, Tiziana (ed.), *Palazzo Soranzo-Cappello, storia, restauro e recupero funzionale* (Venice: Soprintendenza per i Beni Architettonici, 2005). [AP]

The First One Hundred Years of the Boston Athenæum from 1807 to 1907 (Boston, MA: Boston Athenæum, 1907).

Flannery, Denis, *Henry James: A Certain Illusion* (Aldershot: Ashgate Publishing, 2000). [AP]

'Irish Strands and the Imperial Eye: Henry James's "The Modern Warning"', *Henry James Review*, 31 (2010), 39–45. [MW]

Follini, Tamara L., 'James, Ruskin, and the Stones of Venice', in Melanie H. Ross and Greg Zacharias (eds.), *Tracing Henry James* (Newcastle upon Tyne: Cambridge Scholars, 2008), pp. 124–36. [AP]

Fowler, Virginia C., *Henry James's American Girl: The Embroidery on the Canvas* (Madison, WI: University of Wisconsin Press, 1984). [MW]

Freedman, Jonathan L., *Professions of Taste: Henry James, British Aestheticism and Commodity Culture* (Palo Alto, CA: Stanford University Press, 1990).

Freedman, Jonathan L. (ed.), *The Cambridge Companion to Henry James* (Cambridge: Cambridge University Press, 1998). [AP]

Funston, Judith E., *Henry James, 1975–1987, a Reference Guide* (Boston, MA: G. K. Hall, 1991).

'James's Portrait of the Artist as Liar', *Studies in Short Fiction*, 26 (1989), 431–8. [L]

Gale, Robert L., *The Caught Image: Figurative Language in the Fiction of Henry James* (Chapel Hill, NC: University of North Carolina Press, 1964 [1954]). [GR, PD]

A Henry James Encyclopedia (Westport, CN: Greenwood Press, 1989).

'"Pandora" and Her President', *Studies in Short Fiction*, 1 (Spring 1964), 222–5. [P]

Gard, Roger (ed.), *Henry James: The Critical Heritage* (London: Routledge & Kegan Paul, 1968).

Gargano, James W., '"The Aspern Papers" The Untold Story', *Studies in Short Fiction* 10 (1973), 1–10. [AP]

Geismar, Maxwell, *Henry James and the Jacobites* (Boston, MA: Houghton Mifflin, 1963). [P, GR, PD, L]

Gere, Charlotte, *Artistic Circles: Design and Decoration in the Aesthetic Movement* (London: V&A Publishing, 2010).

Giorcelli, Cristina, *Henry James e l'Italia* (Rome: Edizioni di Storia e Letteratura, 1968).

Gordon, Lyndall, *A Private Life of Henry James: Two Women and His Art* (London: Chatto & Windus, 1998).

Griffin, Susan (ed.), *Henry James Goes to the Movies* (Lexington, KT: University of Kentucky Press, 2002). [GR, AP]

Habegger, Alfred, *Henry James and the 'Woman Business'* (Cambridge: Cambridge University Press, 1989). [GR]

Harbert, Earl N., *The Force So Much Closer Home: Henry Adams and the Adams Family* (New York: New York University Press, 1977). [P]

Halliwell, Michael, *Opera and the Novel: The Case of Henry James*, ed. Walter Bernhart (Amsterdam: Rodopi, 2005). [AP]

Harden, Edgar F., *A Henry James Chronology* (London: Palgrave Macmillan, 2005).

Harding, Constance, 'The Identity of Miss Tina in *The Aspern Papers*', *Studies in the Humanities*, 5 (1976), 28–31. [AP]

Harlow, Virginia, *Thomas Sergeant Perry: A Biography* (Durham, NC: Duke University Press, 1950).

Hayat, Jeannine, 'Fiction ou réalité: Les biographies de Constance Fenimore Woolson', *Revue LISA e-journal* (1 January 2005), www2.newpaltz .edu/~hathawar/ejournal2.html

Hayes, Kevin J. (ed.), *Henry James: The Contemporary Reviews* (Cambridge: Cambridge University Press, 1996).

Heffernan, Julián Jiménez, '"On the Outer Edge": The Temptation of Bohemia in Henry James', *Studies in American Fiction*, 44.1 (2017), 53–86.

Hewish, Andrew. 'Cryptic Relations in Henry James's "The Aspern Papers"', *Henry James Review*, 37.3 (2016), 254–60. [AP]

Hiner, Susan, 'Fan Fashion in Balzac's *Le Cousin Pons*', *Romance Studies*, 25.3 (July 2007), 175–87.

Honour, Hugh, and John Fleming, *The Venetian Hours of Henry James, Whistler and Sargent* (London: Walker Books, 1991). [AP]

Horn, Pamela, *Children's Work and Welfare, 1780–1890* (Cambridge: Cambridge University Press, 1995). [PD]

Horne, Philip, *Henry James and Revision: The New York Edition* (Oxford: Clarendon Press, 1990). [AP]

'Henry James: Varieties of Cinematic Experience', in John R. Bradley (ed.), *Henry James on Stage and Screen* (New York: Palgrave Macmillan, 2000), pp. 35–55.

'Independent Beauty', *Journal of American Studies*, 21.1 (April 1987), 87–93.

'Sense of the West', *Times Literary Supplement*, 19 September 2018.

Hotten, John Camden, *The Slang Dictionary* (London: Chatto & Windus, 1874).

Hovanec, Evelyn A., *Henry James and Germany* (Amsterdam: Rodopi 1974). [P]

Hunting, Constance, 'The Identity of Miss Tina', *Studies in the Humanities*, 5.2 (1976), 28–31. [AP]

Izzo, Donatella, *Portraying the Lady: Technologies of Gender in the Short Stories of Henry James* (Lincoln, NE: University of Nebraska Press, 2001). [GR]

Jeffares, Bo, *The Artist in Nineteenth Century English Fiction* (Atlantic Highlands, NJ: Humanities Press, 1979).

Jemsem-Osinski, B., 'The Key to the Palpable Past: A Study of Miss Tina in *The Aspern Papers*', *Henry James Review*, 3.1 (1981), 4–10. [AP]

Johanningsmeier, Charles, 'Henry James's Dalliance with the Newspaper World', *Henry James Review*, 19.1 (1998), 36–52. [P, GR]

Johnstone, Violette, 'February Fashions: Paris', *Woman's World* (London, Paris, New York, and Melbourne), 1.4 (February 1888).

Jolly, Roslyn, 'Henry James in Mid-Career: "Georgina's Reasons" and the Possibilities of Style', *Style*, 47.3 (2013), 343–63. [GR]

Jones, Granville H., 'Henry James's "Georgina's Reasons": The Underside of *Washington Square*', *Studies in Short Fiction*, 11.2 (1974), 189–94. [GR]

Kane, Robert J., 'Hawthorne's "The Prophetic Pictures" and James's "The Liar"', *Modern Language Notes*, 65 (April 1950), 257–8. [L]

Kaplan, Fred, *Henry James: The Imagination of Genius. A Biography* (New York: William Morrow, 1992).

Kappeler, Susanne, *Writing and Reading in Henry James* (London: Macmillan, 1980). [AP]

Kennedy, Gerald, 'James and Edgar Allan Poe. A Speculation' 6 (1973), *Poe Studies*, 17–18.

Kenton, Edna, 'Some Bibliographical Notes on Henry James', *Hound & Horn* (April–May 1934), 535–40. [L]

Kiely, Declan, '"Pardon My Too Many Words": Henry James Manuscripts and Letters at the Morgan Library & Museum', in Colm Tóibín, Marc Simpson, and Declan Kiely (eds.), *Henry James and American Painting* (University Park: Pennsylvania State University Press and the Morgan Library and Museum, 2017), pp. 99–133.

Kilmurray, Elaine, and Richard Ormond (eds.), *John Singer Sargent* (London: Tate Gallery Publishing, 1998).

Kimmey, John L., 'James's London Tales of the 1880s', *Henry James Review*, 8.1 (Fall 1986), 37–46.

Knowles, Elisabeth, *The Oxford Dictionary of Phrase and Fable* (Oxford: Oxford University Press, 2006).

Leyden, John. *The Complaint of Scotland Written in 1548* (Edinburgh: A. Constable, 1801).

Lewis, R. W. B., *The Jameses: A Family Narrative* (New York: Farrar, Straus & Giroux, 1991).

MacDonald, Bonney, *Henry James's Italian Hours: Revelatory and Resistant Impressions* (Ann Arbor, MI: UMI Research Press, 1989).

Mamoli Zorzi, Rosella, '"A Knock-down Insolence of Talent": Sargent, James, and Venice', in W. Adelson *et al.* (eds.), *Sargent's Venice* (New Haven, CT: Yale University Press, 2006), pp. 140–59.

'"A studio was a place to learn to see": Henry James, the London 'Picture Sundays' and the Artists' Studios", in *American Phantasmagoria. Modes of Representation in US Culture*, ed. Rosella Mamoli Zorzi and Simone Francescato (Venice: Supernova, 2017), pp. 139–72.

'The Aspern Papers: Again, and Yet Again?', in *Reading Henry James in the Twenty-First Century*, ed. Dennis Tready, Annick Duperray and Adrian Harding (Newcastle upon Tyne: Cambridge Scholars, 2019), pp. 105–15.

'The Aspern Papers: From Florence to an Intertextual City, Venice', in Dennis Tredy, Annick Duperray, and Adrian Harding (eds.), *Henry James's Europe* (Cambridge: OpenBook Publishers, 2011), pp. 103–11. [AP]

'"Foresti' in Venice in the Second Half of the 19th Century: Their Passion for Paintings, Brocades, *and* Glass", *Atti, Study Days on Venetian Glass*, 174.1 (Venice: Istituto Veneto di Scienze, Lettere ed Arti, 2015–16).

'Henry James and Italy', in Greg W. Zacharias (ed.), *A Companion to Henry James* (Chichester: Wiley-Blackwell: 2008), pp. 434–55.

Ralph Curtis, un pittore americano a Venezia (Venice: Supernova, 2019)

'The Shattered Dream of Constance Fenimore Woolson', in *Two Lovers of Venice: Byron and Constance Fenimore Woolson*, ed. Carlo Campana, Gregory Dowling and Rosella Mamoli Zorzi (Venice: Supernova, 2014), pp. 37–72.

'Silence and Voices in James's Venice' in *Linguae, Rivista di lingue e culture moderne*, 1, 2020, pp. 91-102.

'Il sogno americano nel Campidoglio', in *Il sogno delle Americhe. Promesse e tradimenti*, ed. Francesca Bisutti De Riz, Patrizio Rigobon and Bernard Vincent (Padua: Studio Editoriale Gordini, 2007), pp. 175–85.

'Su letti di asfodelo' *Lettere a Caroline Fitzgerald*, ed. Rosella Mamoli Zorzi and Gottardo Pallastrelli (Milan: Archinto, 2018).

Mamoli Zorzi, Rosella (ed.), *Robert Browning a Venezia* (Venice: Fondazione Querini Stampalia, 1989).

Marasco, Anthony Louis, 'Venice and the Veil: A Note on the Motives of Juliana Bordereau in *The Aspern Papers*', in Francesca Bisutti and Pia Masiero (eds.), *A Rosella: Saggi in onore di Rosella Mamoli Zorzi* (Venice: Supernova, 2012), pp. 149–58. [AP]

Matthiessen, F. O. (ed.), *The American Novels and Stories of Henry James* (New York: Alfred Knopf, 1947). [P, NEW]

Maves, Carl, *Sensuous Pessimism: Italy in the Work of Henry James* (Bloomington, IN: Indiana University Press, 1973). [GR]

McCauley, Elizabeth Anne, Alan Chong, Rosella Mamoli Zorzi, and Richard Lingner, *Gondola Days: Isabella Stewart Gardner and the Palazzo Barbaro Circle* (Easthampton, MA: Antique Collectors' Club, 2004).

McWhirter, David, *Henry James's New York Edition: The Construction of Authorship* (Stanford, CA: Stanford University Press, 1995).

McWhirter, David (ed.), *Henry James in Context* (Cambridge: Cambridge University Press, 2010).

Mengham, Rod, 'Wall to Wall: Figuring "The Aspern Papers"', in N. H. Reeve (ed.), *Henry James: The Shorter Fiction* (London: Macmillan, 1997), pp. 41–59. [AP]

Midgley, R. L., *Boston Sights: or, Handbook for Visitors* (Boston: A . Williams & Co., 1865).

Miller, J. Hillis, *Literature as Conduct: Speech Acts in Henry James* (New York: Fordham University Press, 2005).

Moeller, Hans-Bernard, and George Lellis, *Volker Schlöndorff's Cinema: Adaptation, Politics, and the 'Movie-Appropriate'* (Carbondale, IL: Southern Illinois University Press, 2002). [GR]

Monteiro, George, 'Americanism in Henry James' "A Modern Warning"', *American Literary Realism*, 43.2 (Winter 2011), 169–74. [MW]

'The "Bordereau" of "The Aspern Papers"', *Quarterly Journal of Short Articles, Notes and Reviews*, 22.1 (Winter 2009), 33–5. [AP]

Henry James and John Hay: The Record of a Friendship (Providence, RI: Brown University Press, 1965). [P, GR]

'New Christians and "The Liar"', in *Reading Henry James: A Critical Perspective on Selected Works* (Jefferson, NC: McFarland, 2016).

'Washington Friends and National Reviewers: Henry James's "Pandora"', *Research Studies*, 43.1 (March 1975), 38–44. [P]

Murray's Handbook for Travellers to Northern Italy (London: John Murray, 1869, 1874, 1877).

Murray's Handbook for Travellers to Southern Italy (London: John Murray, 1868).

Nicoloff, Philip L., 'At the Bottom of Things in Henry James's "Louisa Pallant"', *Studies in Short Fiction*, 7.3 (Summer 1970), 409–20.

Novick, Sheldon M., *Henry James: The Young Master* (New York: Random House, 1996).

O'Hara, Daniel T., '"Monstrous Levity": Between Realism and Vision in Two of Henry James's Artist Tales', *Henry James Review*, 28.3 (Fall 2007), 242–8.

O'Leary, Joseph S., 'Pushkin in "The Aspern Papers"', *Henry James E-Journal*, 2 (2000), www2.newpaltz.edu/~hathawar/ejournal2.html.

Ormond, Richard, and Elaine Kilmurray, *Sargent: Portraits of Artists and Friends* (London: National Portrait Gallery, 2015).

Parker, Hershel, *Flawed Texts and Verbal Icons: Literary Authority in American Fiction* (Evanston, IL: Northwestern University Press, 1984).

Peck, Thurston, *What Is Good English? and Other Essays* (New York: Dodd, Mead, 1899).

Pemble, John, *Venice Rediscovered* (Oxford: Clarendon Press, 1995).

Person, Leland S., Jr., 'Eroticism and Creativity in "The Aspern Papers"', *Literature and Psychology*, 32 (Spring 1996), 259–62. [AP]

Poole, Adrian, *Shakespeare and the Victorians* (London: Arden Shakespeare, 2003)

Pound, Ezra, 'A Shake Down', *The Little Review*, 5 (August 1918), 9–39.

Putt, S. Gorley, *Henry James: A Reader's Guide* (Ithaca, NY: Cornell University Press, 1966). [P, GR, PD, L]

Reesman, Jeanne Campbell, '"The Deepest Depths of the Artificial": Attacking Women and Reality in "The Aspern Papers"', in Joseph

Dewey and Brooke Horvath (eds.), 'The Finer Thread, The Tighter Weave': Essays on the Short Fiction of Henry James (West Lafayette, IN: Purdue University Press, 2001), pp. 42–68. [AP]

Rivkin, Julie, 'Speaking with the Dead: Ethics and Representation in "The Aspern Papers"', Henry James Review, 10 (Spring 1989), 284–307. [AP]

Ross, Melanie, and Greg W. Zacharias (eds.), Tracing Henry James (Newcastle upon Tyne: Cambridge Scholars, 2008).

Rowe, John Carlos, The Other Henry James (Durham, NC: Duke University Press, 1998). [AP]

Ryan, Michael, Literary Theory: A Practical Introduction (Oxford: Basil Blackwell, 1999). [AP]

Salmon, Richard, Henry James & the Culture of Publicity (Cambridge: Cambridge University Press, 1997). [AP]

Sannino, Daniela, 'Portrait de l'artiste en passeur: Luigi Gualdo mediatore e critico letterario tra Italia e Francia', PhD thesis, University of Naples Federico II, 2009.

Shalub, Patrick B. Jersey City (Charleston SC: Arcadia Publishing, 1995).

Scharnhorst, Gary, '"The Aspern Papers" and the Ethics of Literary Biography', Modern Fiction Studies, 36.2 (Summer 1990), 211–17. [AP]

Sedgwick, Eve Kosofsky, Epistemology of the Closet (Berkeley, CA: University of California Press, 1990).

Segal, Ora, The Lucid Reflector: The Observer in Henry James's Fiction (New Haven, CT: Yale University Press, 1969).

Shaloub, Patrick B., Jersey City (Charleston, SC: Arcadia Publishing, 1995).

Smith, Janet Adam (ed.), Henry James and Robert Louis Stevenson (London: Rupert Hart-Davis, 1948). [GR]

Smith, Logan Pearsall, Saved from the Salvage, with a memoir of the author by Cyril Connolly (Edinburgh: Triagara Press, 1982). [AP]

Soria, Regina, Dictionary of Nineteenth-Century American Artists in Italy, 1760–1914 (Rutherford, NJ: Farleigh Dickinson University Press, 1982).

Stevenson, Robert L., R. L. Stevenson on Fiction: An Anthology of Literary and Critical Essays, ed. Glenda Norquay (Edinburgh: Edinburgh University Press, 1999).

Stocking, Marion Kingston, 'Miss Tina and Miss Plin', in Donald H. Reiman et al. (eds.), The Evidence of Imagination: Studies of Interactions *between Life and Art in English Romantic Literature* (New York: New York University Press, 1978), pp. 372–84. [AP]

Supino, David J., *Henry James: A Bibliographical Catalogue of a Collection of Editions to 1921*, 2nd edn (Liverpool: Liverpool University Press, 2014).

Tanner, Tony, *Venice Desired* (Cambridge, MA: Harvard University Press, 1992).

Tintner, Adeline R., *The Book World of Henry James: Appropriating the Classics* (Ann Arbor, MI: UMI Research Press, 1987). [P, GR]

The Cosmopolitan World of Henry James: An Intertextual Study (Baton Rouge, LA: Louisiana University Press, 2000).

Henry James and the Lust of the Eyes (Baton Rouge, LA: Louisiana State University Press, 1993).

'Henry James and Miss Braddon: "Georgina's Reasons" and the Victorian Sensation Novel', *Essays in Literature*, 10.1 (1983), 119–24. [GR]

The Museum World of Henry James (Ann Arbor, MI: UMI Research Press, 1986). [P, L]

The Pop World of Henry James: From Fairy Tales to Science Fiction (Ann Arbor, MI: UMI Research Press, 1989), 159–66; revised from Tintner, 'James and Miss Braddon'. [P, GR]

Tóibín, Colm, 'Henry James in Ireland: A Footnote', *Henry James Review*, 30.3 (Fall 2009), 211–22; reprinted in Susan Griffin (ed.), *All a Novelist Needs: Colm Tóibín on Henry James* (Baltimore, MD: Johns Hopkins University Press, 2010). [MW]

Tóibín, Colm, Marc Simpson, Declan Kiely, *Henry James and American Painting* (University Park, Penn.: The Pennsylvania State University Press, 2017).

Tredy, Dennis, Annick Duperray, and Adrian Harding (eds.), *Henry James's Europe: Heritage and Transfer* (Cambridge: OpenBook Publishing, 2011).

Tucker, Amy, *The Illustration of the Master: Henry James and the Magazine Revolution* (Stanford, CA: Stanford University Press, 2010).

Tuttleton, James W., and Agostino Lombardo (eds.), *The Sweetest Impression of Life: The James Family and Italy* (New York: New York University Press, 1990).

Vandersee, Charles, 'James's "Pandora": The Mixed Consequences of Revision', *Studies in Bibliography*, 21 (1968), 93–108. [P, GR]

Veeder, William, 'The Aspern Portrait', *Henry James Review*, 20 (Winter 1999), 22–4. [AP]

Walker, Pierre (ed.), *Henry James on Culture: Collected Essays on Politics and the American Social Scene* (Lincoln, NE: University of Nebraska Press, 2004).

Waller, Nicole, 'A Garden in the Middle of the Sea: Henry James's Aspern Papers and Transnational Studies', *Journal of Transnational Studies*, 3.2 (2011), 245–59. [AP]

Walmeir, Joseph J., 'Miss Tina Did It: A Fresh Look at "The Aspern Papers"', *Centennial Review*, 26 (Summer 1982), 256–67. [AP]

Wharton, Edith, *A Backward Glance* (New York: Appleton, 1934).

Wharton, Edith, *Novellas and Other Writings*, ed. Cynthia Wolff (New York: Library of America, 1990).

Whitehill, Walter Muir, *Boston: A Topographical History* (Cambridge, MA: Belknap Press of Harvard University Press, 1959).

Wilson, Edmund, 'The Ambiguity of Henry James', in Gerald Willen (ed.), *A Casebook on Henry James's "The Turn of the Screw"* (New York: Thomas Y. Crowell, 1960), pp. 115–53. [PD]

Winner, Viola Hopkins, *Henry James and the Visual Arts* (Charlottesville, VA: University of Virginia Press, 1970). [L]

Woolf, Virginia, 'The Old Order', in *The Essays of Virginia Woolf*, vol. 2, *1912–1918*, ed. Andrew McNeillie (New York: Harcourt Brace Jovanovich, 1986), pp. 167–76. [P]

Wrenn, Angus, 'Henry James (1843–1916): Henry James's Europe', in Michael Bell (ed.), *Cambridge Companion to European Novelists* (Cambridge: Cambridge University Press, 2012), pp. 310–26.

Henry James and the Second Empire (London: Legenda, 2009). [GR, AP]

Wright, Nathalia, *American Novelists in Italy: The Discoverers, Allston to James* (Philadelphia, PA: University of Pennsylvania Press, 1965). [L]

Yeazell, Ruth Bernard (ed.), *The Death and Letters of Alice James* (Berkeley, CA: University of California Press, 1981).

Yilmaz, Şuhnaz, *Turkish-American Relations, 1800–1952: Between the Stars, Stripes and the Crescent* (London: Routledge, 2015).

Zacharias, Greg W. (ed.), *A Companion to Henry James* (Chichester: Wiley-Blackwell, 2008). [AP]

'Liberal London, Home, and Henry James's Letters from the Later 1870s', *Henry James Review*, 35.2 (2014), 127–40.

Palazzo Soranzo Cappello, Rio Marin, Venice.
Photograph courtesy of the Archivio
Carlo Montanaro, Venice.

Verrocchio's Colleoni. Photograph courtesy of the Archivio Carlo
Montanaro, Venice.

THE ASPERN PAPERS AND OTHER TALES
1884–1888

Pandora

I

It has long been the custom of the North German Lloyd steamers,[1] which convey passengers from Bremen to New York, to anchor for several hours in the pleasant port of Southampton, where their human cargo receives many additions. An intelligent young German, Count Otto Vogelstein, hardly knew, a few years ago, whether to condemn this custom or approve it. He leaned over the bulwarks of the *Donau* as the American passengers crossed the plank—the travellers who embark at Southampton are mainly of that nationality—and curiously, indifferently, vaguely, through the smoke of his cigar, saw them absorbed in the huge capacity of the ship, where he had the agreeable consciousness that his own nest was comfortably made. To watch from a point of vantage the struggles of later comers—of the uninformed, the unprovided, the bewildered—is an occupation not devoid of sweetness, and there was nothing to mitigate the complacency with which our young friend gave himself up to it; nothing, that is, save a natural benevolence which had not yet been extinguished by the consciousness of official greatness. For Count Vogelstein was official, as I think you would have seen from the straightness of his back, the lustre of his light, elegant spectacles, and something discreet and diplomatic in the curve of his moustache, which looked as if it might well contribute to the principal function, as cynics say, of the lips—the concealment of thought. He had been appointed to the secretaryship of the German legation at Washington,[2] and in these first days of the autumn he was going to take possession of his post. He was a model character for such a purpose—serious, civil, ceremonious, stiff, inquisitive, stuffed with knowledge, and convinced that at present the German empire[3] is the country in the world most highly evolved. He was quite aware, however, of the claims of the United States, and that this portion of the globe presented an enormous field for study. The process of inquiry had already begun, in spite of his having as yet spoken to none of his fellow-passengers; for Vogelstein inquired not only with his tongue—he inquired with his eyes (that is, with his spectacles), with his ears, with his nose, with his palate, with all his senses and organs.

He was an excellent young man, and his only fault was that he had not a high sense of humour. He had enough, however, to suspect this deficiency, and he was aware that he was about to visit a highly humorous people. This suspicion gave him a certain mistrust of what might be said of him; and if circumspection is the essence of diplomacy, our young aspirant promised well. His mind contained several millions of facts, packed too closely together for the light breeze of the imagination to draw through the mass. He was impatient to report himself to his superior in Washington, and the loss of time in an English port could only incommode him, inasmuch as the study of English institutions was no part of his mission. But, on the other hand, the day was charming; the blue sea, in Southampton Water, pricked all over with light, had no movement but that of its infinite shimmer. And he was by no means sure that he should be happy in the United States, where doubtless he should find himself soon enough disembarked. He knew that this was not an important question and that happiness was an unscientific term, which he was ashamed to use even in the silence of his thoughts. But lost in the inconsiderate crowd, and feeling himself neither in his own country nor in that to which he was in a manner accredited, he was reduced to his mere personality; so that, for the moment, to fill himself out, he tried to have an opinion on the subject of this delay to which the German steamer was subjected in English waters. It appeared to him that it might be proved to be considerably greater than the occasion demanded.

Count Vogelstein was still young enough in diplomacy to think it necessary to have opinions. He had a good many, indeed, which had been formed without difficulty; they had been received ready-made from a line of ancestors who knew what they liked. This was, of course—and he would have admitted it—an unscientific way of furnishing one's mind. Our young man was a stiff conservative, a Junker of Junkers;[4] he thought modern democracy a temporary phase, and expected to find many arguments against it in the United States. In regard to these things, it was a pleasure to him to feel that, with his complete training, he had been taught thoroughly to appreciate the nature of evidence. The ship was heavily laden with German emigrants,[5] whose mission in the United States differed considerably from Count Otto's. They hung over the bulwarks, densely grouped; they, leaned forward on their elbows for hours, with their shoulders on a level with their ears; the men in furred caps, smoking long-bowled pipes, the women with babies hidden in their shawls. Some were yellow Germans and some were black,[6] and all of them looked greasy and matted with the sea-damp. They were destined to swell the current of western democracy, and Count Vogelstein doubtless said to himself that they would not improve its quality. Their numbers, however, were striking, and I know not what he thought of the nature of this evidence.

The passengers who came on board at Southampton were not of the greasy class; they were for the most part American families who had been spending the summer, or a longer period, in Europe. They had a great deal of luggage, innumerable bags and rugs and hampers and sea-chairs, and were composed largely of ladies of various ages, a little pale with anticipation, wrapped in striped shawls and crowned with very high hats and feathers. They darted to and fro across the gangway, looking for each other and for their scattered parcels; they separated and reunited, they exclaimed and declared, they eyed with dismay the occupants of the steerage, who seemed numerous enough to sink the vessel, and their voices sounded faint and far as they rose to Vogelstein's ear over the tarred sides of the ship. He observed that in the new contingent there were many young girls, and he remembered what a lady in Dresden[7] had once said to him—that America was a country of girls. He wondered whether he should like that, and reflected that it would be a question to study, like everything else. He had known in Dresden an American family, in which there were three daughters who used to skate with the officers; and some of the ladies now coming on board seemed to him of that same habit, except that in the Dresden days feathers were not worn quite so high.

At last the ship began to creak and slowly budge, and the delay at Southampton came to an end. The gangway was removed, and the vessel indulged in the awkward evolutions which were to detach her from the land. Count Vogelstein had finished his cigar, and he spent a long time in walking up and down the upper deck. The charming English coast passed before him, and he felt that this was the last of the old world. The American coast also might be pretty—he hardly knew what one would expect of an American coast; but he was sure it would be different. Differences, however, were half the charm of travel. As yet, indeed, there were very few on the steamer. Most of his fellow-passengers appeared to be of the same persuasion, and that persuasion the least to be mistaken. They were Jews and commercial,[8] to a man. And by this time they had lighted their cigars and put on all manner of seafaring caps, some of them with big ear-lappets, which somehow had the effect of bringing out their peculiar facial type. At last the new voyagers began to emerge from below and to look about them, vaguely, with that suspicious expression of face which is to be perceived in the newly embarked, and which, as directed to the receding land, resembles that of a person who begins to perceive that he is the victim of a trick. Earth and ocean, in such glances, are made the subject of a general objection, and many travellers, in these circumstances, have an air at once duped and superior, which seems to say that they could easily go ashore if they would.

It still wanted two hours of dinner, and, by the time Vogelstein's long legs had measured three or four miles on the deck, he was ready to settle himself in his sea-chair and draw from his pocket a Tauchnitz novel[9] by an American author whose pages, he had been assured, would help to prepare him. On the back of his chair his name was painted in rather large letters, this being a pre-caution taken at the recommendation of a friend, who had told him that on the American steamers the passengers—especially the ladies—thought nothing of pilfering one's little comforts. His friend had even said that in his place he would have his coronet painted. This cynical adviser had added that the Americans are greatly impressed by a coronet. I know not whether it was scepticism or modesty, but Count Vogelstein had omitted this ensign of his rank; the precious piece of furniture which, on the Atlantic voyage, is depended upon to remain steady among general concussions, was emblazoned simply with his title and name. It happened, however, that the blazonry was huge; the back of the chair was covered with enormous German characters.[10] This time there can be no doubt; it was modesty that caused the secretary of the legation, in placing himself, to turn this portion of his seat outward, away from the eyes of his companions—to present it to the balustrade of the deck. The ship was passing the Needles—the beautiful outermost point of the Isle of Wight.[11] Certain tall white cones of rock rose out of the purple sea; they flushed in the afternoon light, and their vague rosiness gave them a kind of human expression, in face of the cold expanse towards which the ship was turned; they seemed to say farewell, to be the last note of a peopled world. Vogelstein saw them very comfortably from his place, and after a while he turned his eyes to the other quarter, where the sky and sea, between them, managed to make so poor an opposition. Even his American novelist was more amusing than that, and he prepared to return to this author.

In the great curve which it described, however, his glance was arrested by the figure of a young lady who had just ascended to the deck, and who paused at the mouth of the companion-way. In itself this was not an extraordinary phenomenon; but what attracted Vogelstein's attention was the fact that the young person appeared to have fixed her eyes on him. She was slim, brightly dressed, and rather pretty. Vogelstein remembered in a moment that he had noticed her among the people on the wharf at Southampton. She very soon saw that he was looking at her; whereupon she began to move along the deck with a step which seemed to indicate that she was coming straight towards him. Vogelstein had time to wonder whether she could be one of the girls he had known at Dresden; but he presently reflected that they would now be much older than this. It was true they came straight towards one, like that. This young lady, however, was no longer looking at him, and though she passed near him it was now tolerably clear that she had come upstairs simply to take a general survey. She was a quick, handsome, competent girl, and she wished to see what one could think of the ship, of the weather, of the appearance of England from such a position as that; possibly even of one's fellow-passengers. She satisfied herself promptly on these points, and then she looked about, while she walked, as if she were in search of a missing object; so that Vogelstein presently saw this was what she really had come up for. She passed near him again, and this time she almost stopped, with her eyes bent upon him attentively. He thought her conduct remarkable, even after he had perceived that it was not at his face, with its yellow moustache, she was looking, but at the chair on which he was seated. Then those words of his friend came back to him,—the speech about the people, especially the ladies, on the American steamers taking to themselves one's little belongings. Especially the ladies, he might well say; for here was one who apparently wished to pull from under him the very chair he was sitting on. He was afraid she would ask him for it, so he pretended to read, without meeting her eye. He was conscious that she hovered near him, and he was curious to see what she would do. It seemed to him strange that such a nice-looking girl (for her appearance was really charming) should endeavour by acts so flagrant to attract the attention of a secretary of legation. At last it became evident to him that she was trying to look round a corner, as it were, trying to see what was written on the back of his chair. "She wants to find out my name; she wants to see who I am!" This reflection passed through his mind, and caused him to raise his eyes. They rested on her own—which for an appreciable moment she did not withdraw. The latter were brilliant and expressive, and surmounted a delicate aquiline nose, which, though pretty, was perhaps just a trifle too hawk-like. It was the oddest coincidence in the world; the story Vogelstein had taken up treated of a flighty, forward little American girl, who plants herself in front of a young man in the garden of an hotel.[12] Was not the conduct of this young lady a testimony to the truthfulness of the tale, and was not Vogelstein himself in the position of the young man in the garden? That young man ended by speaking to his invader (as she might be called), and after a very short hesitation Vogelstein followed his example. "If she wants to know who I am, she is welcome," he said to himself; and he got out of the chair, seized it by the back, and, turning it round, exhibited the superscription to the girl. She coloured slightly, but she smiled and read his name, while Vogelstein raised his hat.

"I am much obliged to you. That's all right," she remarked, as if the discovery had made her very happy.

It seemed to him indeed all right that he should be Count Otto Vogelstein; this appeared even a rather flippant mode of disposing of the fact. By way of rejoinder, he asked her if she desired his seat.

"I am much obliged to you; of course not. I thought you had one of our chairs, and I didn't like to ask you. It looks exactly like one of ours; not so much now as when you sit in it. Please sit down again. I don't want to trouble you. We have lost one of ours, and I have been looking for it everywhere. They look so much alike; you can't tell till you see the back. Of course I see there will be no mistake about yours," the young lady went on, with a frank smile. "But we have such a small name—you can scarcely see it," she added, with the same friendly intention. "Our name is Day. If you see that on anything, I should be so obliged if you would tell me. It isn't for myself, it's for my mother; she is so dependent on her chair, and that one I am looking for pulls out so beautifully. Now that you sit down again and hide the lower part, it does look just like ours. Well, it must be somewhere. You must excuse me; I am much obliged to you."

This was a long and even confidential speech for a young woman, presumably unmarried, to make to a perfect stranger; but Miss Day acquitted
herself of it with perfect simplicity and self-possession. She held up her head
and stepped away, and Vogelstein could see that the foot she pressed upon
the clean, smooth deck was slender and shapely. He watched her disappear
through the trap by which she had ascended, and he felt more than ever like
the young man in his American tale.[13] The girl in the present case was older
and not so pretty, as he could easily judge, for the image of her smiling eyes
and speaking lips still hovered before him. He went back to his book with
the feeling that it would give him some information about her. This was
rather illogical, but it indicated a certain amount of curiosity on the part of
Count Vogelstein. The girl in the book had a mother, it appeared, and so had
this young lady; the former had also a brother, and he now remembered that
he had noticed a young man on the wharf—a young man in a high hat and
a white overcoat—who seemed united to Miss Day by this natural tie. And
there was some one else too, as he gradually recollected, an older man, also
in a high hat, but in a black overcoat—in black altogether—who completed
the group, and who was presumably the head of the family. These reflections
would indicate that Count Vogelstein read his volume of Tauchnitz rather
interruptedly. Moreover, they represented a considerable waste of time; for
was he not to be afloat in an oblong box, for ten days, with such people, and
could it be doubted that he should see a great deal of them?

It may as well be said without delay that he did see a great deal of them.
I have depicted with some precision the circumstances under which
he made the acquaintance of Miss Day, because the event had a certain
importance for this candid Teuton;[14] but I must pass briefly over the incidents that immediately followed it. He wondered what it was open to him,
after such an introduction, to do with regard to her, and he determined
he would push through his American tale and discover what the hero did.
But in a very short time he perceived that Miss Day had nothing in common with the heroine of that work, save a certain local quality and the
fact that the male sex was not terrible to her. Her local quality, indeed, he
took rather on trust than apprehended for himself. She was a native of a
small town in the interior of the American continent; and a lady from New
York, who was on the ship, and with whom he had a good deal of conversation, assured him Miss Day was exceedingly provincial.[15] How this lady

9

ascertained the fact did not appear, for Vogelstein observed that she held no communication with the girl. It is true that she threw some light on her processes by remarking to him that certain Americans could tell immediately who other Americans were, leaving him to judge whether or no she herself belonged to the discriminating class. She was a Mrs. Dangerfield, a handsome, confidential, insinuating woman, and Vogelstein's talk with her took a turn that was almost philosophic. She convinced him, rather effectually, that even in a great democracy there are human differences, and that American life was full of social distinctions, of delicate shades, which foreigners are often too stupid to perceive. Did he suppose that every one knew every one else, in the biggest country in the world, and that one was not as free to choose one's company there as in the most monarchical communities? She laughed these ideas to scorn, as Vogelstein tucked her beautiful furred coverlet (they reclined together a great deal in their elongated chairs) well over her feet. How free an American lady was to choose her company she abundantly proved by not knowing any one on the steamer but Count Otto.

He could see for himself that Mr. and Mrs. Day had not her peculiar stamp. They were fat, plain, serious people, who sat side by side on the deck for hours, looking straight before them. Mrs. Day had a white face, large cheeks, and small eyes; her forehead was surrounded with a multitude of little tight black curls, and her lips and cheeks moved as if she had always a lozenge in her mouth. She wore entwined about her head an article which Mrs. Dangerfield spoke of as a "nuby"[16]—a knitted pink scarf which covered her coiffure and encircled her neck, leaving among its convolutions a hole for her perfectly expressionless face. Her hands were folded on her stomach, and in her still, swathed figure her little bead-like eyes, which occasionally changed their direction, alone represented life. Her husband had a stiff gray beard on his chin, and a bare, spacious upper lip, to which constant shaving had imparted a kind of hard glaze. His eyebrows were thick and his nostrils wide, and when he was uncovered, in the saloon, it was visible that his grizzled hair was dense and perpendicular. He might have looked rather grim and truculent, if it had not been for the mild, familiar, accommodating gaze with which his large, light-coloured pupils—the leisurely eyes of a silent man—appeared to consider surrounding objects. He was evidently more friendly than fierce,

10

but he was more diffident than friendly. He liked to look at you, but he would not have pretended to understand you much nor to classify you, and would have been sorry that it should put you under an obligation. He and his wife spoke sometimes, but they seldom talked, and there was something passive and patient about them, as if they were victims of a spell. The spell, however, was evidently pleasant; it was the fascination of prosperity, the confidence of security, which sometimes makes people arrogant, but which had had such a different effect upon this simple, satisfied pair, in which further development of every kind appeared to have been arrested.

Mrs. Dangerfield told Count Vogelstein that every morning, after breakfast, the hour at which he wrote his journal, in his cabin, the old couple were guided upstairs and installed in their customary corner by Pandora.[17] This she had learned to be the name of their elder daughter, and she was immensely amused by her discovery. "Pandora"—that was in the highest degree typical; it placed them in the social scale, if other evidence had been wanting; you could tell that a girl was from the interior—the mysterious interior about which Vogelstein's imagination was now quite excited—when she had such a name as that. This young lady managed the whole family, even a little the small beflounced sister, who, with bold, pretty, innocent eyes, a torrent of fair, silky hair, a crimson fez,[18] such as is worn by male Turks, very much askew on top of it, and a way of galloping and straddling about the ship in any company she could pick up (she had long, thin legs, very short skirts, and stockings of every tint), was going home, in elaborate French clothes, to resume an interrupted education. Pandora overlooked and directed her relatives; Vogelstein could see that for himself, could see that she was very active and decided, that she had in a high degree the sentiment of responsibility, and settled most of the questions that could come up for a family from the interior. The voyage was remarkably fine, and day after day it was possible to sit there under the salt sky and feel one's self rounding the great curves of the globe. The long deck made a white spot in the sharp black circle of the ocean and in the intense sea-light, while the shadow of the smoke-steamers trembled on the familiar floor, the shoes of fellow-passengers, distinctive now, and in some cases irritating, passed and repassed, accompanied, in the air so tremendously "open," that rendered all voices weak and most remarks rather flat, by fragments of opinion on the run of the ship. Vogelstein by this time had finished his little American story, and now definitely judged that Pandora Day was not at all like the heroine. She was of quite another type; much more serious and preoccupied, and not at all keen, as he had supposed, about making the acquaintance of gentlemen. Her speaking to him that first after-noon had been, he was bound to believe, an incident without importance for herself, in spite of her having followed it up the next day by the remark, thrown at him as she passed, with a smile that was almost familiar, "It's all right, sir. I have found that old chair!" After this she had not spoken to him again, and had scarcely looked at him. She read a great deal, and almost always French books, in fresh yellow paper;[19] not the lighter forms of that literature, but a volume of Sainte-Beuve, of Renan, or at the most, in the way of dissipation, of Alfred de Musset.[20] She took frequent exercise, and almost always walked alone, not, apparently, having made many friends on the ship, and being without the resource of her parents, who, as has been related, never budged out of the cosy corner in which she planted them for the day.

Her brother was always in the smoking-room, where Vogelstein observed him, in very tight clothes, his neck encircled with a collar like a palisade. He had a sharp little face, which was not disagreeable; he smoked enormous cigars, and began his drinking early in the day; but his appearance gave no sign of these excesses. As regards euchre[21] and poker and the other distractions of the place, he was guilty of none. He evidently understood such games in perfection, for he used to watch the players, and even at moments impartially advise them; but Vogelstein never saw the cards in his hand. He was referred to as regards disputed points, and his opinion carried the day. He took little part in the conversation, usually much relaxed, that prevailed in the smoking-room, but from time to time he made, in his soft, flat, youthful voice, a remark which everyone paused to listen to, and which was greeted with roars of laughter. Vogelstein, well as he knew English, could rarely catch the joke; but he could see, at least, that these were the most transcendent flights of American humour. The young man, in his way, was very remarkable, for, as Vogelstein heard some one say once, after the laughter had subsided, he was only nineteen. If his sister did not resemble the dreadful little girl in the tale I have so often mentioned, there was, for Vogelstein, at least an analogy between young Mr. Day and a certain small brother—a candy-loving Madison, Hamilton, or Jefferson[22]—who, in the Tauchnitz volume, was attributed to that unfortunate maid. This was what the little Madison would have grown up to at nineteen, and the improvement was greater than might have been expected.

The days were long, but the voyage was short, and it had almost come to an end before Count Vogelstein yielded to an attraction peculiar in its nature and finally irresistible, and, in spite of Mrs. Dangerfield's warnings, sought an opportunity for a little continuous talk with Miss Pandora Day. To mention this sentiment without mentioning sundry other impressions of his voyage, with which it had nothing to do, is perhaps to violate proportion and give a false idea; but to pass it by would be still more unjust. The Germans, as we know, are a transcendental people,[23] and there was at last a vague fascination for Vogelstein in this quick, bright, silent girl, who could smile and turn vocal in an instant, who imparted a sort of originality to the filial character, and whose profile was delicate as she bent it over a volume which she cut as she read, or presented it, in absent-minded attitudes, at the side of the ship, to the horizon they had left behind. But he felt it to be a pity, as regards a possible acquaintance with her, that her parents should be heavy little burghers,[24] that her brother should not correspond to Vogelstein's conception of a young man of the upper class, and that her sister should be a Daisy Miller *en herbe*. Repeatedly warned by Mrs. Dangerfield, the young diplomatist was doubly careful as to the relations he might form at the beginning of his sojourn in the United States. Mrs. Dangerfield reminded him, and he had made the observation himself, in other capitals, that the first year, and even the second, is the time for prudence. One is ignorant of proportions and values; one is exposed, lonely, thankful for attention; and one may give one's self away to people who afterwards prove a great encumbrance. Mrs. Dangerfield struck a note which resounded in Vogelstein's imagination. She assured him that if he didn't "look out" he would be falling in love with some American girl with an impossible family. In America, when one fell in love with a girl, there was nothing to be done but marry her, and what should he say, for instance, to finding himself a near relation of Mr. and Mrs. P. W. Day? (These were the initials inscribed on the back of the two chairs of that couple.) Vogelstein felt the peril, for he could immediately think of a dozen men he knew who had married American girls. There appeared now to be a constant danger of marrying the American girl; it was something one had to reckon with, like the rise in prices, the telephone, the discovery of dynamite, the Chassepôt rifle, the socialistic spirit;[25] it was one of the complications of modern life.

It would doubtless be too much to say that Vogelstein was afraid of falling in love with Pandora Day, a young woman who was not strikingly beautiful, and with whom he had talked, in all, but ten minutes. But, as I say, he went so far as to wish that the human belongings of a girl whose independence appeared to have no taint either of fastness, as they said in England, or of subversive opinion, and whose nose was so very well bred, should not be a little more distinguished. There was something almost comical in her attitude toward these belongings; she appeared to regard them as a care, but not as an interest; it was as if they had been entrusted to her honour and she had engaged to convey them safe to a certain point; she was detached and inadvertent; then, suddenly, she remembered, repented, and came back to tuck her parents into their blankets, to alter the position of her mother's umbrella, to tell them something about the run of the ship. These little offices were usually performed deftly, rapidly, with the minimum of words, and when their daughter came near them, Mr. and Mrs. Day closed their eyes placidly, like a pair of household dogs that expect to be scratched. One morning she brought up the captain to present to them. She appeared to have a private and independent acquaintance with this officer, and the introduction to her parents had the air of a sudden inspiration. It was not so much an introduction as an exhibition, as if she were saying to him, "This is what they look like; see how comfortable I make them. Aren't they rather queer little people? But they leave me perfectly free. Oh, I can assure you of that. Besides, you must see it for yourself." Mr. and Mrs. Day looked up at the captain with very little change of countenance; then looked at each other in the same way. He saluted and bent towards them a moment; but Pandora shook her head, she seemed to be answering for them; she made little gestures as if she were explaining to the captain some of their peculiarities, as, for instance, that they wouldn't speak. They closed their eyes at last; she appeared to have a kind of mesmeric influence[26] on them, and Miss Day walked away with the commander of the ship, who treated her with evident consideration, bowing very low, in spite of his supreme position, when, presently after, they separated. Vogelstein could see that she was capable of making an impression; and the moral of our episode is that in spite of Mrs. Dangerfield, in spite of the resolutions of his prudence, in spite of the meagreness of the conversation that had passed between them, in spite of Mr. and Mrs. Day and the young man in the smoking-room, she had fixed his attention.

It was the evening after the scene with the captain that he joined her, awkwardly, abruptly, irresistibly, on the deck, where she was pacing to and fro alone, the evening being mild and brilliant and the stars remarkably fine. There were scattered talkers and smokers, and couples, unrecognisable, that moved quickly through the gloom. The vessel dipped, with long, regular pulsations; vague and spectral, under the stars, with its swaying pinnacles spotted here and there with lights, it seemed to rush through the darkness faster than by day. Vogelstein had come up to walk, and as the girl brushed past him he distinguished Pandora's face (with Mrs. Dangerfield he always spoke of her as Pandora) under the veil that seemed intended to protect it from the sea-damp. He stopped, turned, hurried after her, threw away his cigar, and asked her if she would do him the honour to accept his arm. She declined his arm, but accepted his company, and he walked with her for an hour. They had a great deal of talk, and he remembered afterwards some of the things she said. There was now a certainty of the ship getting into dock the next morning but one, and this prospect afforded an obvious topic. Some of Miss Day's expressions struck him as singular; but, of course, as he knew, his knowledge of English was not nice enough to give him a perfect measure.

"I am not in a hurry to arrive; I am very happy here," she said. "I'm afraid I shall have such a time putting my people through."

"Putting them through?"

"Through the custom-house. We have made so many purchases. Well, I have written to a friend to come down, and perhaps he can help us. He's very well acquainted with the head. Once I'm chalked,[27] I don't care. I feel like a kind of black-board by this time, any way. We found them awful in Germany."

Vogelstein wondered whether the friend she had written to was her lover, and if she were betrothed to him, especially when she alluded to him again as "that gentleman that is coming down". He asked her about her travels, her impressions, whether she had been long in Europe, and what she liked best; and she told him that they had gone abroad, she and her family, for a little fresh experience. Though he found her very intelligent he suspected she gave this as a reason because he was a German and she had heard that Germans were fond of culture. He wondered what form of culture Mr. and Mrs. Day had brought back from Italy, Greece, and Palestine (they had travelled for two years and been everywhere), especially when their daughter said, "I wanted father and mother to see the best things. I kept them three hours on the Acropolis. I guess they won't forget that!" Perhaps it was of Pheidias and Pericles[28] they were thinking, Vogelstein reflected, as they sat ruminating in their rugs. Pandora remarked also that she wanted to show her little sister everything while she was young; remarkable sights made so much more impression when the mind was fresh; she had read something of that sort in Goethe, somewhere.[29] She had wanted to come herself when she was her sister's age; but her father was in business then, and they couldn't leave Utica.[30] Vogelstein thought of the little sister frisking over the Parthenon and the Mount of Olives,[31] and sharing for two years, the years of the schoolroom, this extraordinary odyssey of her parents, and wondered whether Goethe's dictum[32] had been justified in this case. He asked Pandora if Utica were the seat of her family; if it were a pleasant place; if it would be an interesting city for him, as a stranger, to see. His companion replied frankly that it was horrid, but added that all the same she would ask him to "come and visit us at our home," if it were not that they should probably soon leave it.

"Ah! You are going to live elsewhere?"

"Well, I am working for New York. I flatter myself I have loosened them while we have been away. They won't find Utica the same; that was my idea. I want a big place, and, of course, Utica——" And the girl broke off with a little sigh.

"I suppose Utica is small?" Vogelstein suggested.

"Well, no, it's middle-sized. I hate anything middling", said Pandora Day. She gave a light, dry laugh, tossing back her head a little as she made this declaration. And looking at her askance, in the dusk, as she trod the deck that vaguely swayed, he thought there was something in her air and port that carried out such a spirit.

"What is her social position?" he inquired of Mrs. Dangerfield the next day. "I can't make it out at all, it is so contradictory. She strikes me as having so much cultivation and so much spirit. Her appearance, too, is very neat. Yet her parents are little burghers. That is easily seen."

16

"Oh, social position!" Mrs. Dangerfield exclaimed, nodding two or three times, rather portentously. "What big expressions you use! Do you think everybody in the world has a social position? That is reserved for an infinitely small minority of mankind. You can't have a social position at Utica, any more than you can have an opera-box. Pandora hasn't got any; where should she have found it? Poor girl, it isn't fair of you to ask such questions as that."

"Well," said Vogelstein, "if she is of the lower class, that seems to be very— very——" And he paused a moment, as he often paused in speaking English, looking for his word.

"Very what, Count Vogelstein?"

"Very significant, very representative."

"Oh, dear, she isn't of the lower class," Mrs. Dangerfield murmured, helplessly.

"What is she, then?"

"Well, I'm bound to admit that since I was at home last she is a novelty. A girl like that, with such people—it's a new type."

"I like novelties," said Count Vogelstein, smiling, with an air of considerable resolution. He could not, however, be satisfied with an explanation that only begged the question; and when they disembarked in New York, he felt, even amid the confusion of wharf and the heaps of disembowelled baggage, a certain acuteness of regret at the idea that Pandora and her family were about to vanish into the unknown. He had a consolation, however: it was apparent that for some reason or other—illness or absence from town—the gentleman to whom she had written had not, as she said, come down. Vogelstein was glad—he couldn't have told you why—that this sympathetic person had failed her; even though without him Pandora had to engage single-handed with the United States custom-house. Vogelstein's first impression of the western world was received on the landing-place of the German steamers, at Jersey City[33]—a huge wooden shed, covering a wooden wharf which resounded under the feet, palisaded with rough-hewn, slanting piles, and bestrewn with masses of heterogeneous luggage. At one end, towards the town, was a row of tall, painted palings, behind which he could distinguish a press of hackney-coachmen, brandishing their whips and awaiting their victims, while their voices rose, incessant, with a sharp, strange sound, at once fierce and familiar. The whole place, behind the fence, appeared to bristle and resound. Out there was America, Vogelstein said to himself, and he looked towards it with a sense that he ought to muster resolution. On the wharf people were rushing about amid their trunks, pulling their things together, trying to unite their scattered parcels. They were heated and angry, or else quite bewildered and discouraged. The few that had succeeded in collecting their battered boxes had an air of flushed indifference to the efforts of their neighbours, not even looking at people with whom they had been intimate on the steamer. A detachment of the officers of the customs was in attendance, and energetic passengers were engaged in attempts to draw them towards their luggage or to drag heavy pieces towards them. These functionaries were good-natured and taciturn, except when occasionally they remarked to a passenger whose open trunk stared up at them, imploring, that they were afraid the voyage had had a good deal of sameness. They had a friendly, leisurely, speculative way of performing their office, and if they perceived a victim's name written on the portmanteau, they addressed him by it, in a tone of old acquaintance. Vogelstein found, however, that if they were familiar, they were not indiscreet. He had heard that in America all public functionaries were the same, that there was not a different *tenue*, as they said in France, for different positions; and he wondered whether at Washington the President and ministers, whom he expected to see, would be like that.

He was diverted from these speculations by the sight of Mr. and Mrs. Day, who were seated side by side upon a trunk, encompassed, apparently, by the accumulations of their tour. Their faces expressed more consciousness of surrounding objects than he had hitherto perceived, and there was an air of placid expansion in the mysterious couple which suggested that this consciousness was agreeable. Mr. and Mrs. Day, as they would have said, were glad to get back. At a little distance, on the edge of the dock, Vogelstein remarked their son, who had found a place where, between the sides of two big ships, he could see the ferry-boats pass; the large, pyramidal, low-laden ferry-boats of American waters. He stood there, patient and considering, with his small neat foot on a coil of rope, his back to everything that had been disembarked, his neck elongated in its polished cylinder, while the fragrance of his big cigar mingled with the odour of the rotting piles, and his little sister, beside him, hugged a huge post and tried to see how far she could crane over the water without falling in. Vogelstein's servant, an Englishman (he had taken him for practice in the language), had gone in pursuit of an examiner; he had got his things together and was waiting to be released, fully expecting that for a person of his importance the ceremony would be brief. Before it began he said a word to young Mr. Day, taking off his hat at the same time to the little girl, whom he had not yet greeted, and who dodged his salute by swinging herself boldly outwards, to the dangerous side of the pier. She was not much "formed" yet, but she was evidently as light as a feather.

"I see you are kept waiting, like me. It is very tiresome," Count Vogelstein said.

The young man answered without looking behind him.

"As soon as we begin we shall go straight. My sister has written to a gentleman to come down."

"I have looked for Miss Day to bid her good-bye," Vogelstein went on; "but I don't see her."

"I guess she has gone to meet that gentleman; he's a great friend of hers."

"I presume he's her lover!" the little girl broke out. "She was always writing to him, in Europe."

Her brother puffed his cigar in silence for a moment. "That was only for this. I'll tell on you," he presently added.

But the younger Miss Day gave no heed to his announcement; she addressed herself to Vogelstein. "This is New York; I like it better than Utica."

Vogelstein had no time to reply, for his servant had arrived with one of the emissaries of the customs; but as he turned away he wondered, in the light of the child's preference, about the towns of the interior. He was very well treated. The officer who took him in hand, and who had a large straw hat and a diamond breastpin, was quite a man of the world, and in reply to the formal declarations of the Count only said, "Well, I guess it's all right; I guess I'll just pass you;" and he distributed, freely, a dozen chalk-marks.[34] The servant had unlocked and unbuckled various pieces, and while he was closing them the officer stood there wiping his forehead and conversing with Vogelstein. "First visit to our country, Count? —quite alone—no ladies? Of course the ladies are what we are after." It was in this manner he expressed himself, while the young diplomatist wondered what he was waiting for, and whether he ought to slip something into his palm. But Vogelstein's visitor left him only a moment in suspense; he presently turned away, with the remark, very quietly uttered, that he hoped the Count would make quite a stay; upon which the young man saw how wrong he should have been to offer him a tip. It was simply the American manner, and it was very amicable, after all. Vogelstein's servant had secured a porter, with a truck, and he was about to leave the place when he saw Pandora Day dart out of the crowd and address herself, with much eagerness, to the functionary who had just liberated him. She had an open letter in her hand, which she gave him to read, and he cast his eyes over it, deliberately, stroking his beard. Then she led him away to where her parents sat upon their luggage. Vogelstein sent off his servant with the porter, and followed Pandora, to whom he really wished to say a word in farewell. The last thing they had said to each other on the ship was that they should meet again on shore. It seemed improbable, however, that the meeting would occur anywhere but just here on the dock; inasmuch as Pandora was decidedly not in society, where Vogelstein would be, of course, and as, if Utica was not—he had her sharp little sister's word for it—as agreeable as what was about him there, he would be hanged if he would go to Utica. He overtook Pandora quickly; she was in the act of introducing the customs-officer to her parents, quite in the same manner in which she had introduced the captain of the steamer. Mr. and Mrs. Day got up and shook hands with him, and they evidently all prepared to have a little talk. "I should like to introduce you to my brother and sister," he heard the girl say; and he saw her look about her for these appendages. He caught her eye as she did so, and advanced, with his hand outstretched, reflecting the while that evidently the Americans, whom he had always heard described as silent and practical, were not unversed in certain social arts. They dawdled and chattered like so many Neapolitans.

"Good-bye, Count Vogelstein," said Pandora, who was a little flushed with her various exertions, but did not look the worse for it. "I hope you'll have a splendid time, and appreciate our country."

"I hope you'll get through all right," Vogelstein answered, smiling and feeling himself already more idiomatic.

"That gentleman is sick that I wrote to," she rejoined; "isn't it too bad? But he sent me down a letter to a friend of his, one of the examiners, and I guess we won't have any trouble. Mr. Lansing, let me make you acquainted with Count Vogelstein," she went on, presenting to her fellow-passenger the wearer of the straw hat and the breast-pin, who shook hands with the young

German as if he had never seen him before. Vogelstein's heart rose for an instant to his throat. He thanked his stars that he had not offered a tip to the friend of a gentleman who had often been mentioned to him, and who had been described by a member of Pandora's family as her lover.

"It's a case of ladies this time," Mr. Lansing remarked to Vogelstein, with a smile which seemed to confess, surreptitiously, and as if neither party could be eager, to recognition.

"Well, Mr. Bellamy says you'll do anything for *him*," Pandora said, smiling very sweetly at Mr. Lansing. "We haven't got much; we have been gone only two years."

Mr. Lansing scratched his head a little, behind, with a movement which sent his straw hat forward in the direction of his nose. "I don't know as I would do anything for him that I wouldn't do for you," he responded, returning the smile of the girl. "I guess you had better open that one." And he gave a little affectionate kick to one of the trunks.

"Oh, mother, isn't he lovely! It's only your sea-things," Pandora cried, stooping over the coffer instantly, with the key in her hand.

"I don't know as I like showing them," Mrs. Day murmured, modestly.

Vogelstein made his German salutation to the company in general, and to Pandora he offered an audible good-bye, which she returned in a bright, friendly voice, but without looking round, as she fumbled at the lock of her trunk.

"We'll try another, if you like," said Mr. Lansing, laughing.

"Oh no, it has got to be this one! Good-bye, Count Vogelstein. I hope you'll judge us correctly!"

The young man went his way and passed the barrier of the dock. Here he was met by his servant, with a face of consternation which led him to ask whether a cab were not forthcoming.

"They call 'em 'acks 'ere, sir," said the man, "and they're beyond everything. He wants thirty shillings to take you to the inn."[35]

Vogelstein hesitated a moment. "Couldn't you find a German?"

"By the way he talks he *is* a German!" said the man; and in a moment Count Vogelstein began his career in America by discussing the tariff of hackney-coaches in the language of the fatherland.

II

Vogelstein went wherever he was asked, on principle, partly to study American society, and partly because, in Washington, pastimes seemed to him not so numerous that one could afford to neglect occasions. Of course, at the end of two winters he had a good many of various kinds, and his study of American society had yielded considerable fruit. When, however, in April, during the second year of his residence, he presented himself at a large party given by Mrs. Bonnycastle,[36] and of which it was believed that it would be the last serious affair of the season, his being there (and still more his looking very fresh and talkative) was not the consequence of a rule of conduct. He went to Mrs. Bonnycastle's simply because he liked the lady, whose receptions were the pleasantest in Washington, and because if he didn't go there he didn't know what he should do. That absence of alter-natives had become rather familiar to him in Washington—there were a great many things he did because if he didn't do them he didn't know what he should do. It must be added that in this case, even if there had been an alternative, he would still have decided to go to Mrs. Bonnycastle's. If her house was not the pleasantest there, it was at least difficult to say which was pleasanter; and the complaint sometimes made of it that it was too limited, that it left out, on the whole, more people than it took in, applied with much less force when it was thrown open for a general party. Towards the end of the social year, in those soft, scented days of the Washington spring,[37] when the air began to show a southern glow, and the little squares and circles (to which the wide, empty avenues converged according to a plan so ingenious, yet so bewildering[38]) to flush with pink blossom and to make one wish to sit on benches—at this period of expansion and condo-nation Mrs. Bonnycastle, who during the winter had been a good deal on the defensive, relaxed her vigilance a little, became humorously inconsist-ent, vernally reckless, as it were, and ceased to calculate the consequences of an hospitality which a reference to the back-files—or even to the morning's issue—of newspapers might easily show to be a mistake. But Washington

life, to Vogelstein's apprehension, was paved with mistakes; he felt himself
to be in a society which was founded on necessary lapses. Little addicted as
he was to the sportive view of existence, he had said to himself, at an early
stage of his sojourn, that the only way to enjoy the United States would
be to burn one's standards and warm one's self at the blaze. Such were the
reflections of a theoretic Teuton, who now walked for the most part amid
the ashes of his prejudices. Mrs. Bonnycastle had endeavoured more than
once to explain to him the principles on which she received certain people
and ignored certain others; but it was with difficulty that he entered into her
discriminations. She perceived differences where he only saw resemblances,
and both the merits and defects of a good many members of Washington
society, as that society was interpreted to him by Mrs. Bonnycastle, he was
often at a loss to understand. Fortunately she had a fund of good humour
which, as I have intimated, was apt to come uppermost with the April blos-
soms, and which made the people she did not invite to her house almost as
amusing to her as those she did. Her husband was not in politics, though
politics were much in him; but the couple had taken upon themselves
the responsibilities of an active patriotism; they thought it right to live in
America, differing therein from a great many of their acquaintance, who
only thought it expensive. They had that burdensome heritage of foreign
reminiscence with which so many Americans are saddled; but they carried
it more easily than most of their country-people, and you knew they had
lived in Europe only by their present exultation, never in the least by their
regrets. Their regrets, that is, were only for their ever having lived there, as
Mrs. Bonnycastle once told the wife of a foreign minister. They solved all
their problems successfully, including those of knowing none of the people
they did not wish to, and of finding plenty of occupation in a society supposed to be meagrely provided with resources for persons of leisure. When,
as the warm weather approached, they opened both the wings of their door,
it was because they thought it would entertain them, and not because they
were conscious of a pressure. Alfred Bonnycastle,[39] all winter indeed, chafed
a little at the definiteness of some of his wife's reserves; he thought that,
for Washington, their society was really a little too good. Vogelstein still
remembered the puzzled feeling (it had cleared up somewhat now) with
which, more than a year before, he had heard Mr. Bonnycastle exclaim one
evening, after a dinner in his own house, when every guest but the German

secretary, who often sat late with the pair, had departed, "Hang it, there is only a month left; let us have some fun—let us invite the President!"

This was Mrs. Bonnycastle's carnival, and on the occasion to which I began my little chapter by referring, the President had not only been invited but had signified his intention of being present. I hasten to add that this was not the same functionary to whom Alfred Bonnycastle's irreverent allusion had been made. The White House had received a new tenant[40] (the old one, then, was just leaving it), and Otto Vogelstein had had the advantage, during the first eighteen months of his stay in America, of seeing an electoral campaign, a presidential inauguration, and a distribution of spoils.[41] He had been bewildered, during those first weeks, by finding that in the national capital, in the houses that he supposed to be the best, the head of the State was not a coveted guest; for this could be the only explanation of Mr. Bonnycastle's whimsical proposal to invite him, as it were, in carnival. His successor went out a good deal, for a President.

The legislative session was over, but this made little difference in the aspect of Mrs. Bonnycastle's rooms, which, even at the height of the congressional season,[42] could not be said to overflow with the representatives of the people. They were garnished with an occasional senator, whose movements and utterances often appeared to be regarded with a mixture of alarm and indulgence, as if they would be disappointing if they were not rather odd, and yet might be dangerous if they were not carefully watched. Vogelstein had grown to have a kindness for these conscript fathers of invisible families, who had something of the toga[43] in the voluminous folds of their conversation, but were otherwise rather bare and bald, with stony wrinkles in their faces, like busts and statues of ancient law-givers. There seemed to him something chill and exposed in their being at once so exalted and so naked; there were lonesome glances in their eyes, sometimes, as if in the social world their legislative consciousness longed for the warmth of a few comfortable laws ready-made. Members of the House were very rare, and when Washington was new to Vogelstein he used sometimes to mistake them, in the hall and on the staircases where he met them, for the functionaries engaged for the evening to usher in guests and wait at supper. It was only a little later that he perceived these functionaries were almost always impressive, and had a complexion which served as a livery. At present, however, such misleading figures were much less to be

24

encountered than during the months of winter, and, indeed, they never were to be encountered at Mrs. Bonnycastle's. At present the social vistas of Washington, like the vast fresh flatness of the lettered and numbered streets,[44] which at this season seemed to Vogelstein more spacious and vague than ever, suggested but a paucity of political phenomena. Count Otto, that evening, knew every one, or almost every one. There were very often inquiring strangers, expecting great things, from New York and Boston, and to them, in the friendly Washington way, the young German was promptly introduced. It was a society in which familiarity reigned,[45] and in which people were liable to meet three times a day, so that their ultimate essence became a matter of importance.

"I have got three new girls," Mrs. Bonnycastle said. "You must talk to them all."

"All at once?" Vogelstein asked, reversing in imagination a position which was not unknown to him. He had often, in Washington, been discoursed to at the same moment by several virginal voices.

"Oh no; you must have something different for each; you can't get off that way. Haven't you discovered that the American girl expects something especially adapted to herself? It's very well in Europe to have a few phrases that will do for any girl. The American girl isn't any girl; she's a remarkable individual in a remarkable genus. But you must keep the best this evening for Miss Day."

"For Miss Day!" Vogelstein exclaimed, staring. "Do you mean Pandora?"

Mrs. Bonnycastle stared a moment, in return; then laughed very hard. "One would think you had been looking for her over the globe! So you know her already, and you call her by her pet name?"

"Oh no, I don't know her; that is, I haven't seen her, nor thought of her, from that day to this. We came to America in the same ship."

"Isn't she an American, then?"

"Oh yes; she lives at Utica, in the interior."

"In the interior of Utica? You can't mean my young woman then, who lives in New York, where she is a great beauty and a great success, and has been immensely admired this winter."

"After all," said Vogelstein, reflecting and a little disappointed, "the name is not so uncommon; it is perhaps another. But has she rather strange eyes, a little yellow, but very pretty, and a nose a little arched?"

"I can't tell you all that; I haven't seen her. She is staying with Mrs. Steuben.[46] She only came a day or two ago, and Mrs. Steuben is to bring her. When she wrote to me to ask leave she told me what I tell you. They haven't come yet."

Vogelstein felt a quick hope that the subject of this correspondence might indeed be the young lady he had parted from on the dock at New York, but the indications seemed to point the other way, and he had no wish to cherish an illusion. It did not seem to him probable that the energetic girl who had introduced him to Mr. Lansing would have the entrée of the best house in Washington; besides, Mrs. Bonnycastle's guest was described as a beauty and as belonging to the brilliant city.

"What is the social position of Mrs. Steuben?" it occurred to him to ask in a moment, as he meditated. He had an earnest, artless, literal way of uttering such a question as that; you could see from it that he was very thorough.

Mrs. Bonnycastle broke into mocking laughter. "I am sure I don't know! What is your own?" And she left him, to turn to her other guests, to several of whom she repeated his question. Could they tell her what was the social position of Mrs. Steuben? There was Count Vogelstein, who wanted to know. He instantly became aware, of course, that he ought not to have made such an inquiry. Was not the lady's place in the scale sufficiently indicated by Mrs. Bonnycastle's acquaintance with her? Still, there were fine degrees, and he felt a little unduly snubbed. It was perfectly true, as he told his hostess, that, with the quick wave of new impressions that had rolled over him after his arrival in America, the image of Pandora was almost completely effaced; he had seen a great many things which were quite as remarkable in their way as the daughter of the Days. But at the touch of the idea that he might see her again at any moment she became as vivid in his mind as if they had parted but the day before; he remembered the exact shade of the eyes he had described to Mrs. Bonnycastle as yellow; the tone of her voice when, at the last, she expressed the hope that he would judge America correctly. Had he judged it correctly? If he were to meet her again she doubtless would try to ascertain. It would be going much too far to say that the idea of such an ordeal was terrible to Otto Vogelstein; but it may at least be said that the thought of meeting Pandora Day made him nervous. The fact is certainly singular, but I shall not take upon myself to explain it; there are some things that even the most philosophic historian is not bound to account for.

He wandered into another room, and there, at the end of five minutes, he was introduced by Mrs. Bonnycastle to one of the young ladies of whom she had spoken. This was a very intelligent girl, who came from Boston, showing much acquaintance with Spielhagen's novels.[47] "Do you like them?" Vogelstein asked, rather vaguely, not taking much interest in the matter, as he read works of fiction only in case of a sea-voyage. The young lady from Boston looked pensive and concentrated; then she answered that she liked some of them, but that there were others she did not like, and she enumerated the works that came under each of these heads. Spielhagen is a voluminous writer, and such a catalogue took some time; at the end of it, moreover, Vogelstein's question was not answered, for he could not have told you whether she liked Spielhagen or not. On the next topic, however, there was no doubt about her feelings. They talked about Washington as people talk only in the place itself, revolving about the subject in widening and narrowing circles, perching successively on its many branches, considering it from every point of view. Vogelstein had been long enough in America to discover that, after half a century of social neglect, Washington had become the fashion,[48] possessed the great advantage of being a new resource in conversation. This was especially the case in the months of spring, when the inhabitants of the commercial cities came so far southward to escape that boisterous interlude. They were all agreed that Washington was fascinating, and none of them were better prepared to talk it over than the Bostonians. Vogelstein originally had been rather out of step with them; he had not seized their point of view, had not known with what they compared this object of their infatuation. But now he knew everything; he had settled down to the pace; there was not a possible phase of the discussion which could find him at a loss. There was a kind of Hegelian element in it; in the light of these considerations the American capital took on the semblance of a monstrous, mystical *Werden*.[49] But they fatigued Vogelstein a little, and it was his preference, as a general thing, not to engage the same evening with more than one new-comer, one visitor in the freshness of initiation. This was why Mrs. Bonnycastle's expression of a wish to introduce him to three young ladies had startled him a little; he saw a certain process, in which he flattered himself that he had become proficient, but which was after all tolerably exhausting, repeated for each of the damsels. After separating from his bright Bostonian he rather evaded Mrs. Bonnycastle, and contented himself with the conversation of old friends, pitched, for the most part, in a lower and more sceptical key.

At last he heard it mentioned that the President had arrived, had been some half-an-hour in the house, and he went in search of the illustrious guest, whose whereabouts at Washington parties was not indicated by a cluster of courtiers. He made it a point, whenever he found himself in company with the President, to pay him his respects; and he had not been discouraged by the fact that there was no association of ideas in the eye of the great man as he put out his hand, presidentially, and said, "Happy to see you, sir." Vogelstein felt himself taken for a mere constituent, possibly for an office-seeker; and he used to reflect at such moments that the monarchical form had its merits: it provided a line of heredity for the faculty of quick recognition. He had now some difficulty in finding the chief magistrate, and ended by learning that he was in the tearoom, a small apartment devoted to light refection, near the entrance of the house. Here Vogelstein presently perceived him, seated on a sofa, in conversation with a lady. There were a number of people about the table, eating, drinking, talking; and the couple on the sofa, which was not near it, but against the wall, in a kind of recess, looked a little withdrawn, as if they had sought seclusion and were disposed to profit by the diverted attention of the others. The President leaned back; his gloved hands, resting on either knee, made large white spots. He looked eminent, but he looked relaxed, and the lady beside him was making him laugh. Vogelstein caught her voice as he approached—he heard her say, "Well, now, remember; I consider it a promise." She was very prettily dressed, in rose-colour; her hands were clasped in her lap, and her eyes were attached to the presidential profile.

"Well, madam, in that case it's about the fiftieth promise I have given to-day."

It was just as he heard these words, uttered by her companion in reply, that Vogelstein checked himself, turned away, and pretended to be looking for a cup of tea. It was not customary to disturb the President, even simply to shake hands, when he was sitting on a sofa with a lady, and Vogelstein felt it in this case to be less possible than ever to break the rule, for the lady on the sofa was none other than Pandora Day. He had recognised her without her appearing to see him, and even in his momentary look he had perceived that she was now a person to be reckoned with. She had an air of elation,

of success; she looked brilliant in her rose-coloured dress; she was extracting promises from the ruler of fifty millions[50] of people. What an odd place
to meet her, Vogelstein thought, and how little one could tell, after all, in
America, who people were! He didn't wish to speak to her yet; he wished to
wait a little, and learn more; but, meanwhile, there was something attractive in the thought that she was just behind him, a few yards off, that if he
should turn he might see her again. It was she whom Mrs. Bonnycastle had
meant; it was she who was so much admired in New York. Her face was the
same, yet Vogelstein had seen in a moment that she was vaguely prettier; he
had recognised the arch of her nose, which suggested ambition. He took
two ices, which he did not want, in order not to go away. He remembered
her *entourage* on the steamer: her father and mother, the silent burghers, so
little "of the world," her infant sister, so much of it, her humorous brother,
with his tall hat and his influence in the smoking-room. He remembered
Mrs. Dangerfield's warnings—yet her perplexities too, and the letter from
Mr. Bellamy, and the introduction to Mr. Lansing, and the way Pandora had
stooped down on the dirty dock, laughing and talking, mistress of the situation, to open her trunk for the customs. He was pretty sure that she had paid
no duties that day; that had been the purpose, of course, of Mr. Bellamy's
letter. Was she still in correspondence with this gentleman, and had he
recovered from his sickness? All this passed through Vogelstein's mind,
and he saw that it was quite in Pandora's line to be mistress of the situation, for there was nothing, evidently, on the present occasion that could call
itself her master. He drank his tea, and as he put down his cup he heard the
President, behind him, say, "Well, I guess my wife will wonder why I don't
come home."

"Why didn't you bring her with you?" Pandora asked.

"Well, she doesn't go out much. Then she has got her sister staying with
her—Mrs. Runkle, from Natchez.[51] She's a good deal of an invalid, and my
wife doesn't like to leave her."

"She must be a very kind woman," Pandora remarked, sympathetically.

"Well, I guess she isn't spoiled yet."

"I should like very much to come and see her," said Pandora.

"Do come round. Couldn't you come some night?" the President
responded.

"Well, I will come some time. And I shall remind you of your promise."

"All right. There's nothing like keeping it up. Well," said the President, "I must bid good-bye to these kind folks."

Vogelstein heard him rise from the sofa, with his companion, and he gave the pair time to pass out of the room before him, which they did with a certain impressive deliberation, people making way for the ruler of fifty millions and looking with a certain curiosity at the striking pink person at his side. When, after a few moments, Vogelstein followed them across the hall, into one of the other rooms, he saw the hostess accompany the President to the door, and two foreign ministers and a judge of the Supreme Court address themselves to Pandora Day. He resisted the impulse to join this circle; if he spoke to her at all he wished to speak to her alone. She continued, nevertheless, to occupy him, and when Mrs. Bonnycastle came back from the hall he immediately approached her with an appeal. "I wish you would tell me something more about that girl—that one, opposite, in pink?"

"The lovely Day—that is what they call her, I believe? I wanted you to talk with her."

"I find she is the one I have met. But she seems to be so different here. I can't make it out."

There was something in his expression which provoked Mrs. Bonnycastle to mirth. "How we do puzzle you Europeans; you look quite bewildered!"

"I am sorry I look so; I try to hide it. But, of course, we are very simple. Let me ask, then, a simple question. Are her parents also in society?"

"Parents in society! D'où tombez-vous? Did you ever hear of a girl—in rose-colour—whose parents were in society?"

"Is she, then, all alone?" Count Vogelstein inquired, with a strain of melancholy in his voice.

Mrs. Bonnycastle stared at him a moment, with her laughter in her face. "You are too pathetic. Don't you know what she is? I supposed, of course, you knew."

"It's exactly what I am asking you."

"Why, she's the new type. It has only come up lately. They have had articles about it in the papers. That's the reason I told Mrs. Steuben to bring her."

"The new type? What new type, Mrs. Bonnycastle?" said Vogelstein, pleadingly, and conscious that all types in America were new.

Her laughter checked her reply for a moment, and by the time she had recovered herself the young lady from Boston, with whom Vogelstein had been talking, stood there to take leave. This, for an American type, was an old one, he was sure; and the process of parting between the guest and her hostess had an ancient elaboration. Vogelstein waited a little; then he turned away and walked up to Pandora Day, whose group of interlocutors had now been reinforced by a gentleman that had held an important place in the cabinet of the late occupant of the presidential chair. Vogelstein had asked Mrs. Bonnycastle if she were "all alone;" but there was nothing in Pandora's present situation that suggested isolation. She was not sufficiently alone for Vogelstein's taste; but he was impatient, and he hoped she would give him a few words to himself. She recognised him without a moment's hesitation, and with the sweetest smile, a smile that matched the tone in which she said, "I was watching you; I wondered whether you were not going to speak to me."

"Miss Day was watching him," one of the foreign ministers exclaimed, "and we flattered ourselves that her attention was all with us!"

"I mean before," said the girl, "while I was talking with the President."

At this the gentlemen began to laugh, and one of them remarked that that was the way the absent were sacrificed, even the great; while another said that he hoped Vogelstein was duly flattered.

"Oh, I was watching the President too," said Pandora. "I have got to watch *him*. He has promised me something."

"It must be the mission to England," the judge of the Supreme Court suggested. "A good position for a lady; they have got a lady at the head, over there."[52]

"I wish they would send you to my country," one of the foreign ministers suggested. "I would immediately get recalled."

"Why, perhaps in your country I wouldn't speak to you! It's only because you are here," the girl returned, with a gay familiarity which with her was evidently but one of the arts of defence. "You'll see what mission it is when it comes out. But I will speak to Count Vogelstein anywhere," she went on. "He is an older friend than any one here. I have known him in difficult days."

"Oh yes, on the ocean," said the young man, smiling. "On the watery waste,[53] in the tempest!"

"Oh, I don't mean that so much; we had a beautiful voyage, and there wasn't any tempest. I mean when I was living in Utica. That's a watery waste, if you like, and a tempest there would have been a pleasant variety."

"Your parents seemed to me so peaceful!" Vogelstein exclaimed, with a vague wish to say something sympathetic.

"Oh, you haven't seen them on shore. At Utica they were very lively. But that is no longer our home. Don't you remember I told you I was working for New York? Well, I worked—I had to work hard. But we have moved."

"And I hope they are happy," said Vogelstein.

"My father and mother? Oh, they will be, in time, I must give them time. They are very young yet; they have years before them. And you have been always in Washington?" Pandora continued. "I suppose you have found out everything about everything."

"Oh no; there are some things I can't find out."

"Come and see me, and perhaps I can help you. I am very different from what I was on the ship. I have advanced a great deal since then."

"Oh, how was Miss Day on the ship?" asked the cabinet minister of the last administration.

"She was delightful, of course," said Vogelstein.

"He is very flattering; I didn't open my mouth!" Pandora cried. "Here comes Mrs. Steuben to take me to some other place. I believe it's a literary party, near the Capitol. Everything seems so separate in Washington. Mrs. Steuben is going to read a poem. I wish she would read it here; wouldn't it do as well?"

This lady, arriving, signified to Pandora the necessity of their moving on. But Miss Day's companions had various things to say to her before giving her up. She had an answer for each of them, and it was brought home to Vogelstein, as he listened, that, as she said, she had advanced a great deal. Daughter of small burghers as she was, she was really brilliant. Vogelstein turned away a little, and, while Mrs. Steuben waited, asked her a question. He had made her, half an hour before, the subject of that inquiry to which Mrs. Bonnycastle returned so ambiguous an answer; but this was not because he had not some direct acquaintance with Mrs. Steuben, as well as a general idea of the esteem in which she was held. He had met her in various places, and he had been at her house. She was the widow of a commodore[54]—a handsome, mild, soft, swaying woman, whom every one liked, with glossy bands of black hair and a little ringlet depending behind each ear. Some one had said that she looked like the Queen in *Hamlet*.[55] She had written verses which were admired in the South, wore a full-length portrait of the commodore on her bosom, and spoke with the accent of Savannah.[56] She had about her a positive odour of Washington. It had certainly been very crude in Vogelstein to question Mrs. Bonnycastle about her social position.

"Do kindly tell me," he said, lowering his voice, "what is the type to which that young lady belongs. Mrs. Bonnycastle tells me it's a new one." Mrs. Steuben for a moment fixed her liquid eyes upon the secretary of legation. She always seemed to be translating the prose of your speech into the finer rhythms with which her own mind was familiar. "Do you think anything is really new?" she asked. "I am very fond of the old; you know that is a weakness of we Southerners." The poor lady, it will be observed, had another weakness as well.[57] "What we often take to be the new is simply the old under some novel form. Were there not remarkable natures in the past? If you doubt it you should visit the South, where the past still lingers."

Vogelstein had been struck before this with Mrs. Steuben's pronunciation of the word by which her native latitudes were designated: transcribing it from her lips, you would have written it (as the nearest approach) the Sooth. But, at present, he scarcely observed this peculiarity; he was wondering, rather, how a woman could be at once so copious and so unsatisfactory. What did he care about the past, or even about the Sooth? He was afraid of starting her again. He looked at her, discouraged and helpless, as bewildered almost as Mrs. Bonnycastle had found him half an hour before; looked also at the commodore, who, on her bosom, seemed to breathe again with his widow's respirations. "Call it an old type, then, if you like," he said in a moment. "All I want to know is *what* type it is! It seems impossible to find out."

"You can find out by the newspapers. They have had articles about it. They write about everything now. But it isn't true about Miss Day. It is one of the first families. Her great-grandfather was in the Revolution."[58]

Pandora by this time had given her attention again to Mrs. Steuben. She seemed to signify that she was ready to move on. "Wasn't your great-grand-father in the Revolution?" Mrs. Steuben asked. "I am telling Count Vogelstein about him."

"Why are you asking about my ancestors?" the girl demanded, smiling, of the young German. "Is that the thing that you said just now that you can't find out? Well, if Mrs. Steuben will only be quiet you never will."

Mrs. Steuben shook her head, rather dreamily. "Well, it's no trouble for a Southerner to be quiet. There's a kind of languor in our blood. Besides, we have to be, to-day. But I have got to show some energy to-night. I have got to get you to the end of Pennsylvania Avenue."[59]

Pandora gave her hand to Count Vogelstein, and asked him if he thought they should meet again. He answered that in Washington people were always meeting, and that at any rate he should not fail to come and see her. Hereupon, just as the two ladies were detaching themselves, Mrs. Steuben remarked that if Count Vogelstein and Miss Day wished to meet again the picnic would be a good chance—the picnic that she was getting up for the following Thursday. It was to consist of about twenty bright people, and they would go down the Potomac to Mount Vernon.[60] Vogelstein answered that, if Mrs. Steuben thought him bright enough, he should be delighted to join the party; and he was told the hour for which the tryst was taken.

He remained at Mrs. Bonnycastle's after every one had gone, and then he informed this lady of his reason for waiting. Would she have mercy on him and let him know, in a single word, before he went to rest—for without it rest would be impossible—what was this famous type to which Pandora Day belonged?

"Gracious, you don't mean to say you have not found out that type yet!" Mrs. Bonnycastle exclaimed, with a return of her hilarity. "What have you been doing all the evening? You Germans may be thorough, but you certainly are not quick!"

It was Alfred Bonnycastle who at last took pity on him. "My dear Vogelstein, she is the latest, freshest fruit of our great American evolution. She is the self-made girl!"[61]

Vogelstein gazed a moment. "The fruit of the great American Revolution? Yes, Mrs. Steuben told me her great-grandfather——" But the rest of his sentence was lost in the explosion of Mrs. Bonnycastle's mirth. He bravely continued his interrogation, however, and, desiring his host's definition to be defined, inquired what the self-made girl might be.

"Sit down, and we'll tell you all about it," Mrs. Bonnycastle said. "I like talking this way after a party's over. You can smoke, if you like, and Alfred will open another window. Well, to begin with, the self-made girl is a new feature. That, however, you know. In the second place, she isn't self-made at all. We all help to make her, we take such an interest in her."

"That's only after she is made!" Alfred Bonnycastle broke in. "But it's Vogelstein that takes an interest. What on earth has started you up so on the subject of Miss Day?"

Vogelstein explained, as well as he could, that it was merely the accident of his having crossed the ocean in the steamer with her; but he felt the inadequacy of this account of the matter, felt it more than his hosts, who could know neither how little actual contact he had had with her on the ship, how much he had been affected by Mrs. Dangerfield's warnings, nor how much observation at the same time he had lavished on her. He sat there half an hour, and the warm, dead stillness of the Washington night—nowhere are the nights so silent—came in at the open windows, mingled with a soft, sweet, earthy smell—the smell of growing things. Before he went away he had heard all about the self-made girl, and there was something in the picture that almost inspired him. She was possible, doubtless, only in America; American life had smoothed the way for her. She was not fast nor emancipated nor crude nor loud, and there was not in her, of necessity at least, a grain of the stuff of which the adventuress is made. She was simply very successful, and her success was entirely personal. She had not been born with the silver spoon[62] of social opportunity; she had grasped it by honest exertion. You knew her by many different signs, but chiefly, infallibly, by the appearance of her parents. It was her parents that told the story; you always saw that her parents could never have made her. Her attitude with regard to them might vary, in innumerable ways; the great fact on her own side being that she had lifted herself from a lower social plane, done it all herself, and done it by the simple lever of her personality. In this view, of course, it was to be expected that she should leave the authors of her being in the shade. Sometimes she had them in her wake, lost in the bubbles and the foam that showed where she had passed; sometimes, as Alfred Bonnycastle said, she let them slide; sometimes she kept them in close confinement; sometimes she exhibited them to the public in discreet glimpses, in prearranged attitudes. But the general characteristic of the self-made girl was that, though it was frequently understood that she was privately devoted to her kindred, she never attempted to impose them on society, and it was striking that she was much better than they. They were almost always solemn and portentous, and they were for the most part of a deathly respectability. She was not necessarily snobbish, unless it was snobbish to want the best. She didn't cringe, she didn't make herself smaller than she was; on the contrary, she took a stand of her own, and attracted things to herself. Naturally, she was possible only in America, only in a country where certain competitions were absent. The natural history of this interesting creature was at last completely exhibited to Vogelstein, who, as he sat there in the animated stillness, with the fragrant wreath of the western world in his nostrils, was convinced of what he had already suspected, that conversation in the United States is much more psychological than elsewhere. Another thing, as he learned, that you knew the self-made girl by was her culture, which was perhaps a little too obvious. She had usually got into society more or less by reading, and her conversation was apt to be garnished with literary allusions, even with sudden quotations. Vogelstein had not had time to observe this element in a developed form in Pandora Day; but Alfred Bonnycastle said that he wouldn't trust her to keep it under in a *tête-à-tête*. It was needless to say that these young persons had always been to Europe; that was usually the first thing they did. By this means they sometimes got into society in foreign lands before they did so at home; it was to be added, on the other hand, that this resource was less and less valuable; for Europe, in the United States, had less and less prestige, and people in the latter country now kept a watch on that roundabout road. All this applied perfectly to Pandora Day—the journey to Europe, the culture (as exemplified in the books she read on the ship), the effacement of the family. The only thing that was exceptional was the rapidity with which she had advanced; for the jump she had taken since he left her in the hands of Mr. Lansing struck Vogelstein, even after he had made all allowance for the abnormal homogeneity of American society, as really considerable. It took all her cleverness to account for it. When she moved her family from Utica, the battle appeared virtually to have been gained.

Vogelstein called on her the next day, and Mrs. Steuben's blackamoor[63] informed him, in the communicative manner of his race, that the ladies had gone out to pay some visits and look at the Capitol.[64] Pandora apparently had not hitherto examined this monument, and the young man wished he had known the evening before of her omission, so that he might have offered to be her initiator. There is too obvious a connection for me to attempt to conceal it between his regret and the fact that in leaving Mrs. Steuben's door he reminded himself that he wanted a good walk, and took his way along Pennsylvania Avenue. His walk had become fairly good by the time he reached the great white edifice which unfolds its repeated colonnades and uplifts its isolated dome at the end of a long vista of saloons and tobacco-shops. He slowly climbed the great steps, hesitating a little, and wondering why he had come there. The superficial reason was obvious enough, but there was a real one behind it which seemed to Vogelstein rather wanting in the solidity that should characterise the motives of an emissary of Prince Bismarck.[65] The superficial reason was a belief that Mrs. Steuben would pay her visit first—it was probably only a question of leaving cards—and bring her young friend to the Capitol at the hour when the yellow afternoon light gives a tone to the blankness of its marble walls. The Capitol was a splendid building, but it was rather wanting in tone. Vogelstein's curiosity about Pandora Day had been much more quickened than checked by the revelations made to him in Mrs. Bonnycastle's drawing-room. It was a relief to see the young lady classified; but he had a desire, of which he had not been conscious before, to judge really to the end how well a girl could make herself. His calculations had been just, and he had wandered about the rotunda[66] for only ten minutes, looking again at the paintings, commemorative of national history, which occupy its panels, and at the simulated sculptures, so touchingly characteristic of early American taste, which adorn its upper reaches, when the charming women he had hoped for presented themselves in charge of a licensed guide. He went to meet them, and did not conceal from them that he had marked them for his own. The encounter was happy on both sides, and he accompanied them through the queer and endless interior, through labyrinths of white, bare passages, into legislative and judicial halls. He thought it a hideous place; he had seen it all before, and he asked himself what he was doing *dans cette galère*. In the lower House there were certain bedaubed walls, in the basest style of imitation, which made him feel faintly sick; there was a lobby adorned with artless prints and photographs of eminent congressmen, which was too serious for a joke and too comical for anything else.

But Pandora was greatly interested; she thought the Capitol very fine; it was easy to criticise the details, but as a whole it was the most impressive building she had ever seen. She was very good company; she had constantly something to say, but she never insisted too much; it was impossible to be less heavy, to drag less, in the business of walking behind a cicerone. Vogelstein could see, too, that she wished to improve her mind; she looked at the historical pictures, at the uncanny statues of local worthies, presented by the different States[67]—they were of different sizes, as if they had been "numbered," in a shop—she asked questions of the conductor, and in the chamber of the Senate requested him to show her the chairs of the gentlemen from New York. She sat down in one of them, though Mrs. Steuben told her *that* senator (she mistook the chair, dropping into another State) was a horrid old thing. Throughout the hour that he spent with her Vogelstein seemed to see how it was that she had made herself. They walked about afterwards on the magnificent terrace that surrounds the Capitol,[68] the great marble table on which it stands, and made vague remarks (Pandora's were the most definite) about the yellow sheen of the Potomac, the hazy hills of Virginia, the far-gleaming pediment of Arlington,[69] the raw, confused-looking country. Washington was beneath them, bristling and geometrical; the long lines of its avenues seemed to stretch into national futures. Pandora asked Vogelstein if he had ever been to Athens, and, on his replying in the affirmative, inquired whether the eminence on which they stood did not give him an idea of the Acropolis in its prime. Vogelstein deferred the answer to this question to their next meeting; he was glad (in spite of the question) to make pretexts for seeing her again.

He did so on the morrow; Mrs. Steuben's picnic was still three days distant. He called on Pandora a second time, and he met her every evening in the Washington world. It took very little of this to remind him that he was forgetting both Mrs. Dangerfield's warnings and the admonitions—long familiar to him—of his own conscience. Was he in peril of love? Was he to be sacrificed on the altar of the American girl—an altar at which those other poor fellows had poured out some of the bluest blood in Germany, and at which he had declared himself that he would never seriously worship? He decided that he was not in real danger; that he had taken his precautions too well. It was true that a young person who had succeeded so well for herself might be a great help to her husband; but Vogelstein, on the whole, preferred that his success should be his own; it would not be agreeable to him to have the air of being pushed by his wife. Such a wife as that would wish to push him; and he could hardly admit to himself that this was what fate had in reserve for him—to be propelled in his career by a young lady who would perhaps attempt to talk to the Kaiser as he had heard her the other night talk to the President. Would she consent to relinquish relations with her family, or would she wish still to borrow plastic relief from that domestic background? That her family was so impossible was to a certain extent an advantage; for if they had been a little better the question of a rupture would have been less easy. Vogelstein turned over these ideas in spite of his security, or perhaps, indeed, because of it. The security made them speculative and disinterested. They haunted him during the excursion to Mount Vernon, which took place according to traditions long established.

Mrs. Steuben's picnickers assembled on the steamer, and were set afloat on the big brown stream which had already seemed to Vogelstein to have too much bosom and too little bank. Here and there, however, he became aware of a shore where there was something to look at, even though he was conscious at the same time that he had of old lost great opportunities of idyllic talk in not sitting beside Pandora Day on the deck of the North German Lloyd. The two turned round together to contemplate Alexandria,[70] which for Pandora, as she declared, was a revelation of old Virginia. She told Vogelstein that she was always hearing about it during the civil war, years before. Little girl as she had been at the time, she remembered all the names that were on people's lips during those years of reiteration. This historic spot had a certain picturesqueness of decay, a reference to older things, to a dramatic past. The past of Alexandria appeared in the vista of three or four short streets, sloping up a hill and bordered with old brick warehouses, erected for merchandise that had ceased to come or go. It looked hot and blank and sleepy, down to the shabby waterside where tattered darkies dangled their bare feet from the edge of the rotting wharves. Pandora was even more interested in Mount Vernon (when at last its wooded bluff began to command the river) than she had been in the Capitol; and after they had disembarked and ascended to the celebrated mansion she insisted on going into every room it contained. She declared that it had the finest situation in the world, and that it was a shame they didn't give it to the President for his villeggiatura. Most of her companions had seen the house often, and were now coupling themselves, in the grounds, according to their sympathies, so that it was easy for Vogelstein to offer the benefit of his own experience to the most inquisitive member of the party. They were not to lunch for another hour, and in the interval Vogelstein wandered about with Pandora. The breath of the Potomac, on the boat, had been a little harsh, but on the softly-curving lawn, beneath the clustered trees, with the river relegated to a mere shining presence far below and in the distance, the day gave out nothing but its mildness, and the whole scene became noble and genial.

Vogelstein could joke a little on great occasions, and the present one was worthy of his humour. He maintained to his companion that the shallow, painted mansion looked like a false house, a "fly,"[71] a structure of daubed canvas, on the stage; but she answered him so well with certain economical palaces she had seen in Germany, where, as she said, there was nothing but china stoves and stuffed birds, that he was obliged to admit the home of Washington was after all really *gemüthlich*.[72] What he found so, in fact, was the soft texture of the day, his personal situation, the sweetness of his suspense. For suspense had decidedly become his portion; he was under a charm which made him feel that he was watching his own life and that his susceptibilities were beyond his control. It hung over him that things might take a turn, from one hour to the other, which would make them very different from what they had been yet; and his heart certainly beat a little faster as he wondered what that turn might be. Why did he come to picnics on fragrant April days with American girls who might lead him too far? Would not such girls be glad to marry a Pomeranian[73] count? And would they, after all, talk that way to the Kaiser? If he were to marry one of them he should have to give her some lessons. In their little tour of the house Vogelstein and his companion had had a great many fellow-visitors, who had also arrived by the steamer and who had hitherto not left them an ideal privacy. But the others gradually dispersed; they circled about a kind of showman, who was the authorised guide, a big, slow, genial, familiar man, with a large beard, and a humorous, edifying, patronising tone, which had immense success when he stopped here and there to make his points, to pass his eyes over his listening flock, then fix them quite above it with a meditative look, and bring out some ancient pleasantry as if it were a sudden inspiration. He made a cheerful thing even of a visit to the tomb of the *pater patriæ*. It is enshrined in a kind of grotto in the grounds, and Vogelstein remarked to Pandora that he was a good man for the place, but that he was too familiar.

"Oh, he would have been familiar with Washington," said the girl, with the bright dryness with which she often uttered amusing things.

Vogelstein looked at her a moment, and it came over him, as he smiled, that she herself probably would not have been abashed even by the hero with whom history has taken fewest liberties. "You look as if you could hardly believe that," Pandora went on. "You Germans are always in such awe of great people." And it occurred to Vogelstein that perhaps, after all, Washington would have liked her manner, which was wonderfully fresh and natural. The man with the beard was an ideal cicerone for American shrines; he played upon the curiosity of his little band with the touch of a master, and drew them away to see the classic ice-house[74] where the old lady had been found weeping in the belief that it was Washington's grave. While this monument was under inspection Vogelstein and Pandora had the house to themselves, and they spent some time on a pretty terrace, upon which certain windows of the second floor opened—a little roofless verandah, which overhung in a manner, obliquely, all the magnificence of the view—the immense sweep of the river, the artistic plantations, the last-century garden, with its big box-hedges and remains of old espaliers. They lingered here for nearly half an hour, and it was in this spot that Vogelstein enjoyed the only approach to intimate conversation that fate had in store for him with a young woman in whom he had been unable to persuade himself that he was not interested. It is not necessary, and it is not possible, that I should reproduce this colloquy; but I may mention that it began—as they leaned against the parapet of the terrace and heard the fraternising voice of the showman wafted up to them from a distance—with his saying to her, rather abruptly, that he couldn't make out why they hadn't had more talk together when they crossed the ocean.

"Well, I can, if you can't," said Pandora. "I would have talked if you had spoken to me. I spoke to you first."

"Yes, I remember that," Vogelstein replied, rather awkwardly.

"You listened too much to Mrs. Dangerfield."

"To Mrs. Dangerfield?"

"That woman you were always sitting with; she told you not to speak to me. I have seen her in New York; she speaks to me now herself. She recommended you to have nothing to do with me."

"Oh, how can you say such dreadful things?" the young man murmured, blushing very red.

"You know you can't deny it. You were not attracted by my family. They are charming people when you know them. I don't have a better time anywhere than I have at home," the girl went on, loyally. "But what does it matter? My family are very happy. They are getting quite used to New York. Mrs. Dangerfield is a vulgar wretch; next winter she will call on me."

"You are unlike any girl I have ever seen; I don't understand you," said poor Vogelstein, with the colour still in his face.

"Well, you never will understand me, probably; but what difference does it make?"

Vogelstein attempted to tell her what difference it made, but I have not space to follow him here. It is known that when the German mind attempts to explain things it does not always reduce them to simplicity, and Pandora was first mystified, then amused, by some of her companion's revelations. At last I think she was a little frightened, for she remarked irrelevantly, with some decision, that lunch would be ready and they ought to join Mrs. Steuben. He walked slowly, on purpose, as they left the house together, for he had a vague feeling that he was losing her.

"And shall you be in Washington many days yet?" he asked her as they went.

"It will all depend. I am expecting some news. What I shall do will be influenced by that."

The way she talked about expecting news made him feel, somehow, that she had a career, that she was active and independent, so that he could scarcely hope to stop her as she passed. It was certainly true that he had never seen any girl like her. It would have occurred to him that the news she was expecting might have reference to the favour she had asked of the President, if he had not already made up his mind, in the calm of meditation, after that talk with the Bonnycastles, that this favour must be a pleasantry. What she had said to him had a discouraging, a somewhat chilling, effect; nevertheless it was not without a certain ardour that he asked of her whether, so long as she stayed in Washington, he might not come and see her.

"You may come as often as you like," she answered, "but you won't care for it long."

"You try to torment me," said Vogelstein.

She hesitated a moment. "I mean that I may have some of my family."

"I shall be delighted to see them once more."

She hesitated again. "There are some you have never seen."

In the afternoon, returning to Washington on the steamer, Count Vogelstein received a warning. It came from Mrs. Bonnycastle, and constituted, oddly enough, the second occasion on which an officious female friend had, on the deck of a vessel, advised him on the subject of Pandora Day.

"There is one thing we forgot to tell you, the other night, about the self-made girl," Mrs. Bonnycastle said. "It is never safe to fix your affections upon her, because she has almost always got an impediment somewhere in the background."

Vogelstein looked at her askance, but he smiled and said, "I should understand your information—for which I am so much obliged—a little better if I knew what you mean by an impediment."

"Oh, I mean she is always engaged to some young man who belongs to her earlier phase."

"Her earlier phase?"

"The time before she had made herself—when she lived at home. A young man from Utica, say. They usually have to wait; he is probably in a store. It's a long engagement."

"Do you mean a betrothal—to be married?"

"I don't mean anything German and transcendental. I mean that peculiarly American institution, a precocious engagement; to be married, of course."

Vogelstein very properly reflected that it was no use his having entered the diplomatic career if he were not able to bear himself as if this interesting generalisation had no particular message for him. He did Mrs. Bonnycastle, moreover, the justice to believe that she would not have taken up the subject so casually if she had suspected that she should make him wince. The whole thing was one of her jokes, and the notification, moreover, was really friendly. "I see, I see," he said in a moment. "The self-made girl has, of course, always had a past. Yes, and the young man in the store—from Utica—is part of her past."

"You express it perfectly," said Mrs. Bonnycastle. "I couldn't say it better myself."

"But, with her present, with her future, I suppose it's all over. How do you say it in America? She lets him slide."

"We don't say it at all!" Mrs. Bonnycastle cried. "She does nothing of the sort; for what do you take her? She sticks to him; that, at least, is what we expect her to do," Mrs. Bonnycastle added, more thoughtfully. "As I tell you, the type is new. We haven't yet had time for complete observations."

"Oh, of course, I hope she sticks to him," Vogelstein declared simply, and with his German accent more apparent, as it always was when he was slightly agitated.

For the rest of the trip he was rather restless. He wandered about the boat, talking little with the returning revellers. Towards the last, as they drew near Washington, and the white dome of the Capitol hung aloft before them, looking as simple as a suspended snowball, he found himself, on the deck, in proximity to Mrs. Steuben. He reproached himself with having rather neglected her during an entertainment for which he was indebted to her bounty, and he sought to repair his omission by a little friendly talk. But the only thing he could think of to say to her was to ask her by chance whether Miss Day were, to her knowledge, engaged.

Mrs. Steuben turned her Southern eyes upon him with a look of almost romantic compassion. "To my knowledge? Why, of course I would know! I should think you would know too. Didn't you know she was engaged? Why, she has been engaged since she was sixteen."

Vogelstein stared at the dome of the Capitol. "To a gentleman from Utica?"

"Yes, a native of her place. She is expecting him soon."

"Oh, I am so glad to hear it," said Vogelstein, who decidedly, for his career, had promise. "And is she going to marry him?"

"Why, what do people get engaged for? I presume they will marry before long."

"But why have they never done so, in so many years?"

"Well, at first she was too young, and then she thought her family ought to see Europe—of course they could see it better with her—and they spent some time there. And then Mr. Bellamy had some business difficulties which made him feel as if he didn't want to marry just then. But he has given up business, and I presume he feels more free. Of course it's rather long, but all the while they have been engaged. It's a true, true love," said Mrs. Steuben, who had a little flute-like way of sounding the adjective.

"Is his name Mr. Bellamy?" Vogelstein asked, with his haunting reminiscence. "D. F. Bellamy, eh? And has he been in a store?"

"I don't know what kind of business it was; it was some kind of business in Utica. I think he had a branch in New York. He is one of the leading gentlemen of Utica, and very highly educated. He is a good deal older than Miss

Day. He is a very fine man. He stands very high in Utica. I don't know why you look as if you doubted it."

Vogelstein assured Mrs. Steuben that he doubted nothing, and indeed what she told him struck him as all the more credible, as it seemed to him eminently strange. Bellamy had been the name of the gentleman who, a year and a half before, was to have met Pandora on the arrival of the German steamer; it was in Bellamy's name that she had addressed herself with such effusion to Bellamy's friend, the man in the straw hat, who was to fumble in her mother's old clothes. This was a fact which seemed to Vogelstein to finish the picture of her contradictions; it wanted at present no touch to be complete. Yet even as it hung there before him it continued to fascinate him, and he stared at it, detached from surrounding things and feeling a little as if he had been pitched out of an over-turned vehicle, till the boat bumped against one of the outstanding piles of the wharf at which Mrs. Steuben's party was to disembark. There was some delay in getting the steamer adjusted to the dock, during which the passengers stood watching the process, over the side and extracting what entertainment they might from the appearance of the various persons collected to receive it. There were darkies and loafers and hackmen, and also individuals with tufts on their chins, toothpicks in their mouths, their hands in their pockets, rumination in their jaws, and diamond-pins in their shirt-fronts, who looked as if they had sauntered over from Pennsylvania Avenue to while away half an hour, forsaking for that interval their various postures of inclination in the porticos of the hotels and the doorways of the saloons.

"Oh, I am so glad! How sweet of you to come down!" It was a voice close to Vogelstein's shoulder that spoke these words, and the young secretary of legation had no need to turn to see from whom it proceeded. It had been in his ears the greater part of the day, though, as he now perceived, without the fullest richness of expression of which it was capable. Still less was he obliged to turn to discover to whom it was addressed, for the few simple words I have quoted had been flung across the narrowing interval of water, and a gentleman who had stepped to the edge of the dock without Vogelstein's observing him tossed back an immediate reply.

"I got here by the three o'clock train. They told me in K Street[75] where you were, and I thought I would come down and meet you."

45

"Charming attention!" said Pandora Day, with her friendly laugh; and for some moments she and her interlocutor appeared to continue the conversation only with their eyes. Meanwhile Vogelstein's, also, were not idle. He looked at Pandora's visitor from head to foot, and he was aware that she was quite unconscious of his own nearness. The gentleman before him was tall, good-looking, well-dressed; evidently he would stand well not only at Utica, but, judging from the way he had planted himself on the dock, in any position which circumstances might compel him to take up. He was about forty years old; he had a black moustache and a business-like eye. He waved a gloved hand at Pandora, as if, when she exclaimed, "Gracious, ain't they long!" to urge her to be patient. She was patient for a minute, and then she asked him if he had any news. He looked at her an instant in silence, smiling, after which he drew from his pocket a large letter with an official seal, and shook it jocosely above his head. This was discreetly, covertly done. No one appeared to observe the little interview but Vogelstein. The boat was now touching the wharf, and the space between the pair was inconsiderable.

"Department of State?" Pandora asked, dropping her voice.

"That's what they call it."

"Well, what country?"

"What's your opinion of the Dutch?" the gentleman asked, for an answer.

"Oh, gracious!" cried Pandora.

"Well, are you going to wait for the return trip?" said the gentleman.

Vogelstein turned away, and presently Mrs. Steuben and her companions disembarked together. When this lady entered a carriage with Pandora, the gentleman who had spoken to the girl followed them; the others scattered, and Vogelstein, declining with thanks a "lift" from Mrs. Bonnycastle, walked home alone, in some intensity of meditation. Two days later he saw in a newspaper an announcement that the President had offered the post of Minister to Holland to D. F. Bellamy, of Utica; and in the course of a month he heard from Mrs. Steuben that Pandora's long engagement had terminated at the nuptial altar. He communicated this news to Mrs. Bonnycastle, who had not heard it, with the remark that there was now ground for a new induction as to the self-made girl.

Georgina's Reasons

I

She was certainly a singular girl, and if he felt at the end that he didn't know her nor understand her, it is not surprising that he should have felt it at the beginning. But he felt at the beginning what he did not feel at the end, that her singularity took the form of a charm which—once circumstances had made them so intimate—it was impossible to resist or conjure away. He had a strange impression (it amounted at times to a positive distress, and shot through the sense of pleasure, morally speaking, with the acuteness of a sudden twinge of neuralgia) that it would be better for each of them that they should break off short and never see each other again. In later years he called this feeling a foreboding, and remembered two or three occasions when he had been on the point of expressing it to Georgina.[76] Of course, in fact, he never expressed it; there were plenty of good reasons for that. Happy love is not disposed to assume disagreeable duties; and Raymond Benyon's[77] love was happy, in spite of grave presentiments, in spite of the singularity of his mistress and the insufferable rudeness of her parents. She was a tall, fair girl, with a beautiful cold eye, and a smile of which the perfect sweetness, proceeding from the lips, was full of compensation; she had auburn hair, of a hue that could be qualified as nothing less than gorgeous, and she seemed to move through life with a stately grace, as she would have walked through an old-fashioned minuet. Gentlemen connected with the navy have the advantage of seeing many types of women; they are able to compare the ladies of New York with those of Valparaiso, and those of Halifax with those of the Cape of Good Hope.[78] Raymond Benyon had had these opportunities, and, being fond of women, he had learned his lesson; he was in a position to appreciate Georgina Gressie's[79] fine points. She looked like a duchess—I don't mean that in foreign ports Benyon had associated with duchesses—and she took everything so seriously. That was flattering for the young man, who was only a lieutenant, detailed for duty at the Brooklyn navy-yard,[80] without a penny in the world but his pay; with a set of plain, numerous, seafaring, God-fearing relations in New Hampshire,[81] a considerable appearance of talent, a feverish, disguised ambition, and a slight impediment in his speech.[82] He was a spare, tough young man; his dark hair was straight and fine, and his face, a trifle pale, smooth and carefully drawn. He stammered a little, blushing when he did so, at long intervals. I scarcely know how he appeared on shipboard, but on shore, in his civilian's garb, which was of the neatest, he had as little as possible an aroma of winds and waves. He was neither salt nor brown nor red nor particularly "hearty." He never twitched up his trousers, nor, so far as one could see, did he, with his modest, attentive manner, carry himself as a person accustomed to command. Of course, as a subaltern, he had more to do in the way of obeying. He looked as if he followed some sedentary calling, and was indeed supposed to be decidedly intellectual. He was a lamb with women, to whose charms he was, as I have hinted, susceptible; but with men he was different, and, I believe, as much of a wolf as was necessary. He had a manner of adoring the handsome, insolent queen of his affections (I will explain in a moment why I call her insolent); indeed, he looked up to her literally, as well as sentimentally, for she was the least bit the taller of the two.

He had met her the summer before on the piazza of an hotel at Fort Hamilton, to which, with a brother-officer, in a dusty buggy, he had driven over from Brooklyn[83] to spend a tremendously hot Sunday—the kind of day when the navy-yard was loathsome; and the acquaintance had been renewed by his calling in Twelfth Street[84] on New Year's day—a considerable time to wait for a pretext, but which proved the impression had not been transitory. The acquaintance ripened, thanks to a zealous cultivation (on his part) of occasions which Providence, it must be confessed, placed at his disposal none too liberally; so that now Georgina took up all his thoughts and a considerable part of his time. He was in love with her, beyond a doubt; but he could not flatter himself that she was smitten with him, though she seemed willing (what was so strange) to quarrel with her family about him. He didn't see how she could really care for him—she was marked out by nature for so much greater a fortune; and he used to say to her, "Ah, you don't—there's no use talking, you don't—really care for me at all!" To which she answered, "Really? You are very particular. It seems to me it's real enough if I let you touch one of my finger-tips!" That was one of her ways of being insolent.

Another was simply her manner of looking at him, or at other people, when they spoke to her, with her hard, divine blue eye—looking quietly, amusedly, with the air of considering, wholly from her own point of view, what they might have said, and then turning her head or her back, while, without taking the trouble to answer them, she broke into a short, liquid, irrelevant laugh. This may seem to contradict what I said just now about her taking the young lieutenant in the navy seriously. What I mean is that she appeared to take him more seriously than she took anything else. She said to him once, "At any rate you have the merit of not being a shop-keeper;" and it was by this epithet she was pleased to designate most of the young men who at that time flourished in the best society of New York. Even if she had rather a free way of expressing general indifference, a young lady is supposed to be serious enough when she consents to marry you. For the rest, as regards a certain haughtiness that might be observed in Georgina Gressie, my story will probably throw sufficient light upon it. She remarked to Benyon once that it was none of his business why she liked him, but that, to please herself, she didn't mind telling him she thought the great Napoleon, before he was celebrated, before he had command of the army of Italy, must have looked something like him; and she sketched in a few words the sort of figure she imagined the incipient Bonaparte to have been—short, lean, pale, poor, intellectual, and with a tremendous future under his hat. Benyon asked himself whether he had a tremendous future, and what in the world Georgina expected of him in the coming years. He was flattered at the comparison, he was ambitious enough not to be frightened at it, and he guessed that she perceived a certain analogy between herself and the Empress Josephine.[85] She would make a very good empress—that was true; Georgina was remarkably imperial. This may not at first seem to make it more clear why she should take into her favour an aspirant who, on the face of the matter, was not original, and whose Corsica was a flat New England seaport; but it afterwards became plain that he owed his brief happiness—it was very brief—to her father's opposition; her father's and her mother's, and even her uncles' and her aunts'. In those days, in New York, the different members of a family took an interest in its alliances; and the house of Gressie looked askance at an engagement between the most beautiful of its daughters and a young man who was not in a paying business. Georgina declared that they were meddlesome and vulgar; she could sacrifice her own people, in that way,

49

without a scruple; and Benyon's position improved from the moment that Mr. Gressie—ill-advised Mr. Gressie—ordered the girl to have nothing to do with him. Georgina was imperial in this—that she wouldn't put up with an order. When, in the house in Twelfth Street, it began to be talked about that she had better be sent to Europe with some eligible friend, Mrs. Portico for instance, who was always planning to go and who wanted as a companion some young mind, fresh from manuals and extracts, to serve as a fountain of history and geography— when this scheme for getting Georgina out of the way began to be aired, she immediately said to Raymond Benyon, "Oh yes, I'll marry you!" She said it in such an off-hand way that, deeply as he desired her, he was almost tempted to answer, "But, my dear, have you really thought about it?"

This little drama went on, in New York, in the ancient days, when Twelfth Street had but lately ceased to be suburban,[86] when the squares had wooden palings, which were not often painted, when there were poplars in important thorough-fares and pigs in the lateral ways, when the theatres were miles distant from Madison Square, and the battered rotunda of Castle Garden[87] echoed with expensive vocal music, when "the park" meant the grass-plats of the City Hall,[88] and the Bloomingdale Road was an eligible drive, when Hoboken, of a summer afternoon, was a genteel resort, and the handsomest house in town was on the corner of Fifth Avenue and Fifteenth Street.[89] This will strike the modern reader, I fear, as rather a primitive epoch; but I am not sure that the strength of human passions is in proportion to the elongation of a city. Several of them, at any rate, the most robust and most familiar—love, ambition, jealousy, resentment, greed—subsisted in considerable force in the little circle at which we have glanced, where a view by no means favourable was taken of Raymond Benyon's attentions to Miss Gressie. Unanimity was a family trait among these people (Georgina was an exception), especially in regard to the important concerns of life, such as marriages and closing scenes. The Gressies hung together; they were accustomed to do well for themselves and for each other. They did everything well: got themselves born well (they thought it excellent to be born a Gressie), lived well, married well, died well, and managed to be well spoken of afterwards. In deference to this last-mentioned habit, I must be careful what I say of them. They took an interest in each other's concerns, an interest that could never be regarded as of a meddlesome nature, inasmuch as they all thought alike about all their affairs, and interference took the happy form of congratulation and encouragement. These affairs were invariably lucky, and, as a general thing, no Gressie had anything to do but feel that another Gressie had been almost as shrewd and decided as he himself would have been. The great exception to that, as I have said, was this case of Georgina, who struck such a false note, a note that startled them all, when she told her father that she should like to unite herself to a young man engaged in the least paying business that any Gressie had ever heard of. Her two sisters had married into the most flourishing firms, and it was not to be thought of that—with twenty cousins growing up around her—she should put down the standard of success. Her mother had told her a fortnight before this that she must request Mr. Benyon to cease coming to the house; for hitherto his suit had been of the most public and resolute character. He had been conveyed up-town, from the Brooklyn ferry,[90] in the "stage," on certain evenings, had asked for Miss Georgina at the door of the house in Twelfth Street, and had sat with her in the front parlour if her parents happened to occupy the back, or in the back if the family had disposed itself in the front. Georgina, in her way, was a dutiful girl, and she immediately repeated her mother's admonition to Benyon. He was not surprised, for, though he was aware that he had not, as yet, a great knowledge of society, he flattered himself he could tell when and where a polite young man was not wanted. There were houses in Brooklyn where such an animal was much appreciated, and there the signs were quite different.

They had been discouraging, except on Georgina's part, from the first of his calling in Twelfth Street. Mr. and Mrs. Gressie used to look at each other in silence when he came in, and indulge in strange perpendicular salutations, without any shaking of hands. People did that at Portsmouth, N.H.,[91] when they were glad to see you; but in New York there was more luxuriance, and gesture had a different value. He had never, in Twelfth Street, been asked to "take anything," though the house had a delightful suggestion, a positive aroma, of sideboards, as if there were mahogany "cellarettes"[92] under every table. The old people, moreover, had repeatedly expressed surprise at the quantity of leisure that officers in the navy seemed to enjoy. The only way in which they had not made themselves offensive was by always remaining in the other room; though at times even this detachment, to which he owed some delightful moments, presented itself to Benyon as a form of disapprobation. Of course, after Mrs. Gressie's message, his visits were practically at an end: he wouldn't give the girl up, but he wouldn't be beholden to her father for the opportunity to converse with her. Nothing was left for the tender couple—there was a curious mutual mistrust in their tenderness—but to meet in the squares, or in the topmost streets, or in the side-most avenues, on the spring afternoons. It was especially during this phase of their relations that Georgina struck Benyon as imperial. Her whole person seemed to exhale a tranquil, happy consciousness of having broken a law. She never told him how she arranged the matter at home, how she found it possible always to keep the appointments (to meet him out of the house) that she so boldly made, in what degree she dissimulated to her parents, and how much, in regard to their continued acquaintance, the old people suspected and accepted. If Mr. and Mrs. Gressie had forbidden him the house, it was not, apparently, because they wished her to walk with him in the Tenth Avenue or to sit at his side under the blossoming lilacs in Stuyvesant Square.[93] He didn't believe that she told lies in Twelfth Street; he thought she was too imperial to lie; and he wondered what she said to her mother when, at the end of nearly a whole afternoon of vague peregrination with her lover, this rustling, bristling matron asked her where she had been. Georgina was capable of simply telling the truth; and yet if she simply told the truth it was a wonder that she had not been still more simply packed off to Europe. Benyon's ignorance of her pretexts is a proof that this rather oddly-mated couple never arrived at perfect intimacy, in spite of a fact which remains to be related. He thought of this afterwards, and thought how strange it was that he had not felt more at liberty to ask her what she did for him, and how she did it, and how much she suffered for him. She would probably not have admitted that she suffered at all, and she had no wish to pose for a martyr.

Benyon remembered this, as I say, in the after years, when he tried to explain to himself certain things which simply puzzled him; it came back to him with the vision, already faded, of shabby cross-streets, straggling toward rivers, with red sunsets, seen through a haze of dust, at the end; a vista through which the figures of a young man and a girl slowly receded and disappeared, strolling side by side, with the relaxed pace of desultory talk, but more closely linked as they passed into the distance, linked by its at last appearing safe to them—in the Tenth Avenue—that the young lady should take his arm. They were always approaching that inferior thorough-fare; but he could scarcely have told you, in those days, what else they were approaching. He had nothing in the world but his pay, and he felt that this was rather a "mean" income to offer Miss Gressie. Therefore he didn't put it forward; what he offered, instead, was the expression—crude often, and almost boyishly extravagant—of a delighted admiration of her beauty, the tenderest tones of his voice, the softest assurances of his eye, and the most insinuating pressure of her hand at those moments when she consented to place it in his arm. All this was an eloquence which, if necessary, might have been condensed into a single sentence; but those few words were scarcely needed when it was as plain that he expected, in general, she would marry him, as it was indefinite that he counted upon her for living on a few hundred a year. If she had been a different girl he might have asked her to wait, might have talked to her of the coming of better days, of his prospective promotion, of its being wiser, perhaps, that he should leave the navy and look about for a more lucrative career. With Georgina it was difficult to go into such questions; she had no taste whatever for detail. She was delightful as a woman to love, because when a young man is in love he discovers that; but she could not be called helpful, for she never suggested anything. That is, she never had done so till the day she really proposed—for that was the form it took—to become his wife without more delay. "Oh yes, I will marry you:" these words, which I quoted a little way back, were not so much the answer to something he had said at the moment as the light conclusion of a report she had just made (for the first time) of her actual situation in her father's house.

"I AM afraid I shall have to see less of you," she had begun by saying. "They watch me so much."

"It is very little already," he answered. "What is once or twice a week?"

"That's easy for you to say. You are your own master, but you don't know what I go through."

"Do they make it very bad for you, dearest? Do they make scenes?" Benyon asked.

"No, of course not. Don't you know us enough to know how we behave? No scenes; that would be a relief. However, I never make them myself, and I never will—that's one comfort for you, for the future, if you want to know. Father and mother keep very quiet, looking at me as if I were one of the lost, with little hard, piercing eyes, like gimlets. To me they scarcely say anything, but they talk it all over with each other, and try and decide what is to be done. It's my belief that my father has written to the people in Washington—what do you call it?—the Department—to have you moved away from Brooklyn—to have you sent to sea."

"I guess that won't do much good. They want me in Brooklyn; they don't want me at sea."

"Well, they are capable of going to Europe for a year, on purpose to take me," Georgina said.

"How can they take you if you won't go? And if you should go, what good would it do if you were only to find me here when you came back, just the same as you left me?"

"Oh, well!" said Georgina, with her lovely smile, "of course they think that absence would cure me of——cure me of ——" And she paused, with a kind of cynical modesty, not saying exactly of what.

"Cure you of what, darling? Say it, please say it," the young man murmured, drawing her hand surreptitiously into his arm.

"Of my absurd infatuation!"

"And would it, dearest?"

"Yes, very likely. But I don't mean to try. I shall not go to Europe—not when I don't want to. But it's better I should see less of you—even that I should appear—a little—to give you up."

"A little? What do you call a little?"

Georgina said nothing for a moment. "Well, that, for instance, you shouldn't hold my hand quite so tight!" And she disengaged this conscious member from the pressure of his arm.

"What good will that do?" Benyon asked.

"It will make them think it's all over—that we have agreed to part."

"And as we have done nothing of the kind, how will that help us?"

They had stopped at the crossing of a street; a heavy dray was lumbering slowly past them. Georgina, as she stood there, turned her face to her lover and rested her eyes for some moments on his own. At last, "Nothing will help us; I don't think we are very happy," she answered, while her strange, ironical, inconsequent smile played about her beautiful lips.

"I don't understand how you see things. I thought you were going to say you would marry me," Benyon rejoined, standing there still, though the dray had passed.

"Oh yes, I will marry you!" And she moved away across the street. That was the way she had said it, and it was very characteristic of her. When he saw that she really meant it, he wished they were somewhere else—he hardly knew where the proper place would be—so that he might take her in his arms. Nevertheless, before they separated that day he had said to her he hoped she remembered they would be very poor, reminding her how great a change she would find it. She answered that she shouldn't mind, and presently she said that if this was all that prevented them the sooner they were married the better. The next time he saw her she was quite of the same opinion; but he found, to his surprise, it was now her conviction that she had better not leave her father's house. The ceremony should take place secretly, of course; but they would wait awhile to let their union be known.

"What good will it do us, then?" Raymond Benyon asked.

Georgina coloured. "Well, if you don't know, I can't tell you!"

Then it seemed to him that he did know. Yet, at the same time, he could not see why, once the knot was tied, secrecy should be required. When he asked what especial event they were to wait for, and what should give them the signal to appear as man and wife, she answered that her parents would probably forgive her if they were to discover, not too abruptly, after six months, that she had taken the great step. Benyon supposed that she had ceased to care whether they forgave her or not; but he had already perceived that the nature of women is a queer mosaic. He had believed her capable of marrying him out of bravado, but the pleasure of defiance was absent if the marriage was kept to themselves. It now appeared that she was not especially anxious to defy; she was disposed rather to manage and temporise. "Leave it to me; leave it to me. You are only a blundering man," Georgina said. "I shall know much better than you the right moment for saying, 'Well, you may as well make the best of it, because we have already done it!'"

That might very well be, but Benyon didn't quite understand, and he was awkwardly anxious (for a lover) till it came over him afresh that there was one thing at any rate in his favour, which was simply that the finest girl he had ever seen was ready to throw herself into his arms. When he said to her, "There is one thing I hate in this plan of yours—that, for ever so few weeks, so few days, your father should support my wife"—when he made this homely remark, with a little flush of sincerity in his face, she gave him a specimen of that unanswerable laugh of hers, and declared that it would serve Mr. Gressie right for being so barbarous and so horrid. It was Benyon's view that from the moment she disobeyed her father she ought to cease to avail herself of his protection; but I am bound to add that he was not particularly surprised at finding this a kind of honour in which her feminine nature was little versed. To make her his wife first—at the earliest moment—whenever she would, and trust to fortune and the new influence he should have, to give him, as soon thereafter as possible, complete possession of her: this finally presented itself to the young officer as the course most worthy of a lover and a gentleman. He would be only a pedant who would take nothing because he could not get everything at once. They wandered further than usual this afternoon, and the dusk was thick by the time he brought her back to her father's door. It was not his habit to come so near it, but to-day they had so much to talk about that he actually stood with her for ten minutes at the foot of the steps. He was keeping her hand in his, and she let it rest there while she said—by way of a remark that should sum up all their reasons and reconcile their differences—

"There's one great thing it will do, you know: it will make me safe."

"Safe from what?"

"From marrying any one else."

"Ah, my girl, if you were to do that——!" Benyon exclaimed; but he didn't mention the other branch of the contingency. Instead of this, he looked aloft at the blind face of the house (there were only dim lights in two or three windows, and no apparent eyes) and up and down the empty street, vague in the friendly twilight; after which he drew Georgina Gressie to his breast and gave her a long, passionate kiss. Yes, decidedly, he felt they had better be married. She had run quickly up the steps, and while she stood there, with her hand on the bell, she almost hissed at him, under her breath, "Go away, go away; Amanda's coming!" Amanda was the parlour-maid; and it was in those terms that the Twelfth Street Juliet dismissed her Brooklyn Romeo.[94] As he wandered back into the Fifth Avenue, where the evening air was conscious of a vernal fragrance from the shrubs in the little precinct of the pretty Gothic church[95] ornamenting that pleasant part of the street, he was too absorbed in the impression of the delightful contact from which the girl had violently released herself to reflect that the great reason she had mentioned a moment before was a reason for their marrying, of course, but not in the least a reason for their not making it public. But, as I said in the opening lines of this chapter, if he did not understand his mistress's motives at the end, he cannot be expected to have understood them at the beginning.

Mrs. Portico, as we know, was always talking about going to Europe; but she had not yet—I mean a year after the incident I have just related—put her hand upon a youthful cicerone. Petticoats, of course, were required; it was necessary that her companion should be of the sex which sinks most naturally upon benches, in galleries and cathedrals, and pauses most frequently upon staircases that ascend to celebrated views. She was a widow with a good fortune and several sons, all of whom were in Wall Street,[96] and none of them capable of the relaxed pace at which she expected to take her foreign tour. They were all in a state of tension; they went through life standing. She was a short, broad, high-coloured woman, with a loud voice and superabundant black hair, arranged in a way peculiar to herself, with so many combs and bands that it had the appearance of a national coiffure. There was an impression in New York, about 1845,[97] that the style was Danish; someone had said something about having seen it in Schleswig-Holstein.[98] Mrs. Portico had a bold, humorous, slightly flamboyant look; people who saw her for the first time received an impression that her late husband had married the daughter of a bar-keeper or the proprietress of a menagerie. Her high, hoarse, good-natured voice seemed to connect her in some way with public life; it was not pretty enough to suggest that she might have been an actress. These ideas quickly passed away, however, even if you were not sufficiently initiated to know—as all the Gressies, for instance, knew so well—that her origin, so far from being enveloped in mystery, was almost the sort of thing she might have boasted of. But, in spite of the high pitch of her appearance she didn't boast of anything; she was a genial, easy, comical, irreverent person, with a large charity, a democratic, fraternising turn of mind, and a contempt for many worldly standards, which she expressed not in the least in general axioms (for she had a mortal horror of philosophy), but in violent ejaculations on particular occasions. She had not a grain of moral timidity, and she fronted a delicate social problem as sturdily as she would have barred the way of a gentleman she might have met in her vestibule with the plate-chest. The only thing which prevented her being a bore in orthodox circles was that she was incapable of discussion. She never lost her temper, but she lost her vocabulary, and ended quickly by praying that heaven would give her an opportunity to act out what she believed. She was an old friend of Mr. and Mrs. Gressie, who esteemed her for the antiquity of her lineage and the frequency of her subscriptions, and to whom she rendered the service of making them feel liberal—like people too sure of their own position to be frightened. She was their indulgence, their dissipation, their point of contact with dangerous heresies; so long as they continued to see her they could not be accused of being narrow-minded—a matter as to which they were perhaps vaguely conscious of the necessity of taking their precautions. Mrs. Portico never asked herself whether she liked the Gressies; she had no disposition for morbid analysis, she accepted transmitted associations, and found, somehow, that her acquaintance with these people helped her to relieve herself. She was always making scenes in their drawing-room, scenes half indignant, half jocose, like all her manifestations, to which it must be confessed that they adapted themselves beautifully. They never "met" her, in the language of controversy; but always collected to watch her, with smiles and comfortable platitudes, as if they envied her superior richness of temperament. She took an interest in Georgina, who seemed to her different from the others, with suggestions about her of being likely not to marry so unrefreshingly as her sisters had done, and of a high, bold standard of duty. Her sisters had married from duty, but Mrs. Portico would rather have chopped off one of her large plump hands than behave herself so well as that. She had, in her daughterless condition, a certain ideal of a girl who should be beautiful and romantic, with wistful eyes, and a little persecuted, so that she, Mrs. Portico, might get her out of her troubles. She looked to Georgina, to a considerable degree, to give actuality to this vision; but she had really never understood Georgina at all. She ought to have been shrewd, but she lacked this refinement, and she never understood anything until after many disappointments and vexations. It was difficult to startle her, but she was much startled by a communication that this young lady made her one fine spring morning. With her florid appearance and her speculative mind, she was probably the most innocent woman in New York.

Georgina came very early, earlier even than visits were paid in New York thirty years ago; and instantly, without any preface, looking her straight in the face, told Mrs. Portico that she was in great trouble and must appeal to her for assistance. Georgina had in her aspect no symptom of distress; she was as fresh and beautiful as the April day itself; she held up her head and smiled, with a sort of familiar challenge, looking like a young woman who would naturally be on good terms with fortune. It was not in the least in the tone of a person making a confession or relating a misadventure that she presently said, "Well, you must know, to begin with—of course, it will surprise you—that I am married."

"Married, Georgina Gressie!" Mrs. Portico repeated, in her most resonant tones.

Georgina got up, walked with her majestic step across the room, and closed the door. Then she stood there, her back pressed against the mahogany panels, indicating only by the distance she had placed between herself and her hostess the consciousness of an irregular position. "I am not Georgina Gressie—I am Georgina Benyon; and it has become plain, within a short time, that the natural consequence will take place."

Mrs. Portico was altogether bewildered. "The natural consequence?" she exclaimed, staring.

"Of one's being married, of course; I suppose you know what that is. No one must know anything about it. I want you to take me to Europe."

Mrs. Portico now slowly rose from her place and approached her visitor, looking at her from head to foot as she did so, as if to measure the truth of her remarkable announcement. She rested her hands on Georgina's shoulders a moment, gazing into her blooming face, and then she drew her closer and kissed her. In this way the girl was conducted back to the sofa, where, in a conversation of extreme intimacy, she opened Mrs. Portico's eyes wider than they had ever been opened before. She was Raymond Benyon's wife; they had been married a year, but no one knew anything about it. She had kept it from every one, and she meant to go on keeping it. The ceremony had taken place in a little Episcopal church at Haarlem,[99] one Sunday afternoon, after the service. There was no one in that dusty suburb who knew them; the clergyman, vexed at being detained, and wanting to go home to tea, had made no trouble; he tied the knot before they could turn round. It was ridiculous how easy it had been. Raymond had told him frankly that it must all be under the rose,[100] as the young lady's family disapproved of what she was doing. But she was of legal age, and perfectly free; he could see that for himself. The parson had given a grunt as he looked at her over his spectacles; it was not very complimentary, it seemed to say that she was indeed no chicken. Of course she looked old for a girl; but she was not a girl now, was she? Raymond had certified his own identity as an officer in the United States navy (he had papers, besides his uniform, which he wore), and introduced the clergyman to a friend he had brought with him, who was also in the navy, a venerable paymaster. It was he who gave Georgina away, as it were; he was a dear old man, a regular grandmother, and perfectly safe. He had been married three times himself, and the first time in the same way. After the ceremony she went back to her father's; but she saw Mr. Benyon the next day. After that she saw him—for a little while—pretty often. He was always begging her to come to him altogether; she must do him that justice. But she wouldn't—she wouldn't now—perhaps she wouldn't ever. She had her reasons, which seemed to her very good but were very difficult to explain. She would tell Mrs. Portico in plenty of time what they were. But that was not the question now, whether they were good or bad; the question was for her to get away from the country for several months—far away from any one who had ever known her. She should like to go to some little place in Spain or Italy, where she should be out of the world until everything was over.

Mrs. Portico's heart gave a jump as this serene, handsome, domestic girl, sitting there with a hand in hers and pouring forth her extraordinary tale, spoke of everything being over. There was a glossy coldness in it, an unnatural lightness, which suggested—poor Mrs. Portico scarcely knew what. If Georgina was to become a mother it was to be supposed she would remain a mother. She said there was a beautiful place in Italy—Genoa[101]— of which Raymond had often spoken, and where he had been more than once, he admired it so much; couldn't they go there and be quiet for a little while? She was asking a great favour, that she knew very well; but if Mrs. Portico wouldn't take her she would find some one who would. They had talked of such a journey so often; and, certainly, if Mrs. Portico had been willing before, she ought to be much more willing now. The girl declared that she *would* do something, go somewhere, keep, in one way or another, her situation unperceived. There was no use talking to her about telling;

she would rather die than tell. No doubt it seemed strange, but she knew what she was about. No one had guessed anything yet—she had succeeded perfectly in doing what she wished—and her father and mother believed—as Mrs. Portico had believed, hadn't she?—that, any time the last year, Raymond Benyon was less to her than he had been before. Well, so he was; yes, he was. He had gone away—he was off, goodness knew where—in the Pacific; she was alone, and now she would remain alone. The family believed it was all over, with his going back to his ship, and other things, and they were right; for it was over, or it would be soon.

V

Mrs. Portico, by this time, had grown almost afraid of her young friend; she had so little fear, she had even, as it were, so little shame. If the good lady had been accustomed to analysing things a little more, she would have said she had so little conscience. She looked at Georgina with dilated eyes—her visitor was so much the calmer of the two—and exclaimed, and murmured, and sank back, and sprang forward, and wiped her forehead with her pocket-handkerchief. There were things she didn't understand; that they should all have been so deceived, that they should have thought Georgina was giving her lover up (they flattered themselves she was discouraged or had grown tired of him) when she was really only making it impossible she should belong to any one else. And with this, her inconsequence, her capriciousness, her absence of motive, the way she contradicted herself, her apparent belief that she could hush up such a situation for ever! There was nothing shameful in having married poor Mr. Benyon, even in a little church at Haarlem, and being given away by a paymaster; it was much more shameful to be in such a state without being prepared to make the proper explanations. And she must have seen very little of her husband; she must have given him up, so far as meeting him went, almost as soon as she had taken him. Had not Mrs. Gressie herself told Mrs. Portico, in the preceding October it must have been, that there now would be no need of sending Georgina away, inasmuch as the affair with the little navy-man—a project in every way so unsuitable—had quite blown over?

"After our marriage I saw him less—I saw him a great deal less," Georgina explained; but her explanation only appeared to make the mystery more dense.

"I don't see, in that case, what on earth you married him for!"

"We had to be more careful; I wished to appear to have given him up. Of course we were really more intimate; I saw him differently," Georgina said, smiling.

"I should think so! I can't for the life of me see why you weren't discovered."

"All I can say is we weren't. No doubt it's remarkable. We managed very well—that is, I managed; he didn't want to manage at all. And then father and mother are incredibly stupid!"

Mrs. Portico exhaled a comprehensive moan, feeling glad, on the whole, that she hadn't a daughter, while Georgina went on to furnish a few more details. Raymond Benyon, in the summer, had been ordered from Brooklyn to Charlestown, near Boston,[102] where, as Mrs. Portico perhaps knew, there was another navy-yard, in which there was a temporary press of work, requiring more oversight. He had remained there several months, during which he had written to her urgently to come to him, and during which, as well, he had received notice that he was to rejoin his ship a little later. Before doing so, he came back to Brooklyn for a few weeks, to wind up his work there, and then she had seen him—well, pretty often. That was the best time of all the year that had elapsed since their marriage. It was a wonder at home that nothing had then been guessed, because she had really been reckless, and Benyon had even tried to force on a disclosure. But they were dense, that was very certain. He had besought her again and again to put an end to their false position,[103] but she didn't want it any more than she had wanted it before. They had had rather a bad parting; in fact, for a pair of lovers, it was a very queer parting indeed. He didn't know, now, the thing she had come to tell Mrs. Portico. She had not written to him. He was on a very long cruise. It might be two years before he returned to the United States. "I don't care how long he stays away," Georgina said, very simply.

"You haven't mentioned why you married him. Perhaps you don't remember!" Mrs. Portico broke out, with her masculine laugh.

"Oh yes; I loved him."

"And you have got over that?"

Georgina hesitated a moment. "Why, no, Mrs. Portico, of course I haven't. Raymond's a splendid fellow."

"Then why don't you live with him? You don't explain that."

"What would be the use when he's always away? How can one live with a man who spends half his life in the South Seas?[104] If he wasn't in the navy it would be different; but to go through everything—I mean everything that making our marriage known would bring upon me: the scolding and the exposure and the ridicule, the scenes at home—to go through it all just for the idea, and yet to be alone here, just as I was before, without my husband after all, with none of the good of him"—and here Georgina looked at her hostess as if with the certitude that such an enumeration of inconveniences would touch her effectually—"really, Mrs. Portico, I am bound to say I don't think that would be worth while; I haven't the courage for it."

"I never thought you were a coward," said Mrs. Portico.

"Well, I am not, if you will give me time. I am very patient."

"I never thought that either."

"Marrying changes one," said Georgina, still smiling.

"It certainly seems to have had a very odd effect upon you. Why don't you make him leave the navy and arrange your life comfortably, like every one else?"

"I wouldn't for the world interfere with his prospects—with his promotion. That is sure to come for him, and to come immediately, he has such talents. He is devoted to his profession; it would ruin him to leave it."

"My dear young woman, you are a living wonder!" Mrs. Portico exclaimed, looking at her companion as if she had been in a glass case.

"So poor Raymond says," Georgina answered, smiling more than ever.

"Certainly, I should have been very sorry to marry a navy-man; but if I had married him I would stick to him, in the face of all the scoldings in the universe!"

"I don't know what your parents may have been; I know what mine are," Georgina replied, with some dignity. "When he's a captain we shall come out of hiding."

"And what shall you do meanwhile? What will you do with your children? Where will you hide them? What will you do with this one?"

Georgina rested her eyes on her lap for a minute; then, raising them, she met those of Mrs. Portico. "Somewhere in Europe," she said, in her sweet tone.

"Georgina Gressie, you're a monster!" the elder lady cried.

"I know what I am about, and you will help me," the girl went on.

"I will go and tell your father and mother the whole story—that's what I will do!"

"I am not in the least afraid of that—not in the least. You will help me; I assure you that you will."

"Do you mean I will support the child?"

Georgina broke into a laugh. "I do believe you would, if I were to ask you! But I won't go so far as that; I have something of my own. All I want you to do is to be with me."

"At Genoa; yes, you have got it all fixed! You say Mr. Benyon is so fond of the place. That's all very well; but how will he like his baby being deposited there?"

"He won't like it at all. You see I tell you the whole truth," said Georgina, gently.

"Much obliged; it's a pity you keep it all for me! It is in his power, then, to make you behave properly. *He* can publish your marriage, if you won't; and if he does you will have to acknowledge your child."

"Publish, Mrs. Portico? How little you know my Raymond! He will never break a promise; he will go through fire first."

"And what have you got him to promise?"

"Never to insist on a disclosure against my will; never to claim me openly as his wife till I think it is time; never to let any one know what has passed between us if I choose to keep it still a secret—to keep it for years—to keep it for ever. Never do anything in the matter himself, but to leave it to me. For this he has given me his solemn word of honour, and I know what that means!"

Mrs. Portico, on the sofa, fairly bounced.

"You do know what you are about! And Mr. Benyon strikes me as more demented even than yourself. I never heard of a man putting his head into such a noose. What good can it do him?"

"What good? The good it did him was that it gratified me. At the time he took it he would have made any promise under the sun. It was a condition I exacted just at the very last, before the marriage took place. There was nothing at that moment he would have refused me; there was nothing I couldn't have made him do. He was in love to that degree—but I don't want to boast," said Georgina, with quiet grandeur. "He wanted—he wanted——" she added; but then she paused.

"He doesn't seem to have wanted much!" Mrs. Portico cried, in a tone which made Georgina turn to the window, as if it might have reached the street. Her hostess noticed the movement and went on, "Oh, my dear, if I ever do tell your story I will tell it so that people will hear it!"

"You never will tell it. What I mean is that Raymond wanted the sanction—of the affair at the church—because he saw that I would never do without it. Therefore, for him, the sooner we had it the better, and, to hurry it on, he was ready to take any pledge."

"You have got it pat enough," said Mrs. Portico, in homely phrase. "I don't know what you mean by sanctions, or what you wanted of 'em."

Georgina got up, holding rather higher than before that beautiful head which, in spite of the embarrassments of this interview, had not yet perceptibly abated its elevation. "Would you have liked me to—to not marry?"

Mrs. Portico rose also, and, flushed with the agitation of unwonted knowledge—it was as if she had discovered a skeleton in her favourite cupboard—faced her young friend for a moment. Then her conflicting sentiments resolved themselves into an abrupt question, implying, for Mrs. Portico, much subtlety: "Georgina Gressie, were you really in love with him?"

The question suddenly dissipated the girl's strange, studied, wilful coldness; she broke out, with a quick flash of passion—a passion that, for the moment, was predominately anger, "Why else, in heaven's name, should I have done what I have done? Why else should I have married him? What under the sun had I to gain?"

A certain quiver in Georgina's voice, a light in her eye which seemed to Mrs. Portico more spontaneous, more human, as she uttered these words, caused them to affect her hostess rather less painfully than anything she had yet said. She took the girl's hand and emitted indefinite admonitory sounds. "Help me, my dear old friend, help me," Georgina continued, in a low, pleading tone; and in a moment Mrs. Portico saw that the tears were in her eyes.

"You are a precious mixture, my child!" she exclaimed. "Go straight home to your own mother and tell her everything; that is your best help."

"You are kinder than my mother. You mustn't judge her by yourself."

"What can she do to you? How can she hurt you? We are not living in pagan times," said Mrs. Portico, who was seldom so historical. "Besides, you have no reason to speak of your mother—to think of her even—so! She would have liked you to marry a man of some property; but she has always been a good mother to you."

At this rebuke Georgina suddenly kindled again; she was, indeed, as Mrs. Portico had said, a precious mixture. Conscious, evidently, that she could not satisfactorily justify her present stiffness, she wheeled round upon a grievance which absolved her from self-defence. "Why, then, did he make that promise, if he loved me? No man who really loved me would have made it, and no man that was a man as I understand being a man! He might have seen that I only did it to test him—to see if he wanted to take advantage of being left free himself. It is a proof that he doesn't love me—not as he ought to have done; and in such a case as that a woman isn't bound to make sacrifices!"

Mrs. Portico was not a person of a nimble intellect; her mind moved vigorously, but heavily; yet she sometimes made happy guesses. She saw that Georgina's emotions were partly real and partly fictitious, that, as regards this last matter especially, she was trying to "get up" a resentment, in order to excuse herself. The pretext was absurd, and the good lady was struck with its being heartless on the part of her young visitor to reproach poor Benyon with a concession on which she had insisted, and which could only be a proof of his devotion, inasmuch as he left her free while he bound himself. Altogether, Mrs. Portico was shocked and dismayed at such a want of simplicity in the behaviour of a young person whom she had hitherto believed to be as candid as she was stylish, and her appreciation of this discovery expressed itself in the uncompromising remark, "You strike me as a very bad girl, my dear; you strike me as a very bad girl!"

VI

It will doubtless seem to the reader very singular that, in spite of this reflection, which appeared to sum up her judgment of the matter, Mrs. Portico should in the course of a very few days have consented to everything that Georgina asked of her. I have thought it well to narrate at length the first conversation that took place between them, but I shall not trace further the successive phases of the girl's appeal, or the steps by which—in the face of a hundred robust and salutary convictions—the loud, kind, sharp, simple, sceptical, credulous woman took under her protection a damsel whose obstinacy she could not speak of without getting red with anger. It was the simple fact of Georgina's personal condition that moved her; this young lady's greatest eloquence was the seriousness of her predicament. She might be bad, and she had a splendid, careless, insolent, fair-faced way of admitting it, which at moments, incoherently, inconsistently, irresistibly, transmuted the cynical confession into tears of weakness; but Mrs. Portico had known her from her rosiest years, and when Georgina declared that she couldn't go home, that she wished to be with her and not with her mother, that she couldn't expose herself—she absolutely couldn't—and that she must remain with her and her only till the day they should sail, the poor lady was forced to make that day a reality. She was over-mastered, she was cajoled, she was, to a certain extent, fascinated. She had to accept Georgina's rigidity (she had none of her own to oppose to it—she was only violent, she was not continuous), and once she did this it was plain, after all, that to take her young friend to Europe was to help her, and to leave her alone was not to help her. Georgina literally frightened Mrs. Portico into compliance. She was evidently capable of strange things if thrown upon her own devices. So, from one day to another, Mrs. Portico announced that she was really at last about to sail for foreign lands (her doctor having told her that if she didn't look out she would get too old to enjoy them), and that she had invited that robust Miss Gressie, who could stand so long on her feet, to accompany her. There was joy in the house of Gressie at this announcement, for, though the danger was over, it was a great general advantage to Georgina to go, and the Gressies were always elated at the prospect of an advantage. There was a danger that she might meet Mr. Benyon on the other side of the world; but it didn't seem likely that Mrs. Portico would lend herself to a plot of that kind. If she had taken it into her head to favour their love-affair she would have done it openly, and Georgina would have been married by this time. Her arrangements were made as quickly as her decision had been—or rather had appeared—slow; for this concerned those mercurial young men down town. Georgina was perpetually at her house; it was understood in Twelfth Street that she was talking over her future travels with her kind friend. Talk there was, of course, to a considerable degree; but after it was settled they should start nothing more was said about the motive of the journey. Nothing was said, that is, till the night before they sailed; then a few plain words passed between them. Georgina had already taken leave of her relations in Twelfth Street, and was to sleep at Mrs. Portico's in order to go down to the ship at an early hour. The two ladies were sitting together in the firelight, silent with the consciousness of corded luggage, when the elder one suddenly remarked to her companion that she seemed to be taking a great deal upon herself in assuming that Raymond Benyon wouldn't force her hand. He might choose to acknowledge his child, if she didn't; there were promises and promises, and many people would consider they had been let off when circumstances were so altered. She would have to reckon with Mr. Benyon more than she thought.

"I know what I am about," Georgina answered. "There is only one promise for him. I don't know what you mean by circumstances being altered."

"Everything seems to me to be altered," poor Mrs. Portico murmured, rather tragically.

"Well, he isn't, and he never will! I am sure of him, as sure as that I sit here. Do you think I would have looked at him if I hadn't known he was a man of his word?"

"You have chosen him well, my dear," said Mrs. Portico, who by this time was reduced to a kind of bewildered acquiescence.

"Of course I have chosen him well. In such a matter as this he will be perfectly splendid." Then suddenly, "Perfectly splendid, that's why I cared for him," she repeated, with a flash of incongruous passion.

This seemed to Mrs. Portico audacious to the point of being sublime; but she had given up trying to understand anything that the girl might say or do. She understood less and less after they had disembarked in England and begun to travel southward; and she understood least of all when, in the middle of the winter, the event came off with which in imagination she had tried to familiarise herself, but which, when it occurred, seemed to her beyond measure strange and dreadful. It took place at Genoa; for Georgina had made up her mind that there would be more privacy in a big town than in a little; and she wrote to America that both Mrs. Portico and she had fallen in love with the place and would spend two or three months there. At that time people in the United States knew much less than to-day about the comparative attractions of foreign cities; and it was not thought surprising that absent New Yorkers should wish to linger in a seaport where they might find apartments, according to Georgina's report, in a palace painted in fresco by Vandyke and Titian.[105] Georgina, in her letters, omitted, it will be seen, no detail that could give colour to Mrs. Portico's long stay at Genoa. In such a palace—where the travellers hired twenty gilded rooms for the most insignificant sum—a remarkably fine boy came into the world. Nothing could have been more successful and comfortable than this transaction—Mrs. Portico was almost appalled at the facility and felicity of it. She was by this time in a pretty bad way; and—what had never happened to her before in her life—she suffered from chronic depression of spirits. She hated to have to lie, and now she was lying all the time. Everything she wrote home, everything that had been said or done in connection with their stay in Genoa, was a lie. The way they remained indoors to avoid meeting chance compatriots was a lie. Compatriots in Genoa, at that period, were very rare; but nothing could exceed the business-like completeness of Georgina's precautions. Her nerve, her self-possession, her apparent want of feeling, excited on Mrs. Portico's part a kind of gloomy suspense; a morbid anxiety to see how far her companion would go took possession of the excellent woman who, a few months before, hated to fix her mind on disagreeable things. Georgina went very far indeed; she did everything in her power to dissimulate the origin of her child. The record of his birth was made under a false name, and he was baptized at the nearest church by a Catholic priest. A magnificent contadina was brought to light by the doctor in a village in the hills, and this big, brown, barbarous creature, who, to do her justice, was full of handsome, familiar smiles and coarse tenderness, was constituted nurse to Raymond Benyon's son. She nursed him for a fortnight under the mother's eye, and she was then sent back to her village with the baby in her arms and sundry gold coin knotted into a corner of her pocket-handkerchief. Mr. Gressie had given his daughter a liberal letter of credit on a London banker, and she was able, for the present, to make abundant provision for the little one. She called Mrs. Portico's attention to the fact that she spent none of her money on futilities; she kept it all for her small pensioner in the Genoese hills. Mrs. Portico beheld these strange doings with a stupefaction that occasionally broke into passionate protest; then she relapsed into a brooding sense of having now been an accomplice so far that she must be an accomplice to the end.

VII

The two ladies went down to Rome—Georgina was in wonderful trim—
to finish the season, and here Mrs. Portico became convinced that she
intended to abandon her offspring. She had not driven into the country to
see the nursling before leaving Genoa; she had said that she couldn't bear
to see it in such a place and among such people. Mrs. Portico, it must be
added, had felt the force of this plea, felt it as regards a plan of her own,
given up after being hotly entertained for a few hours, of devoting a day, by
herself, to a visit to the big contadina. It seemed to her that if she should
see the child in the sordid hands to which Georgina had consigned it, she
would become still more of a participant than she was already. This young
woman's blooming hardness, after they got to Rome, acted upon her like a
kind of Medusa-mask.[106] She had seen a horrible thing, she had been mixed
up with it, and her motherly heart had received a mortal chill. It became
more clear to her every day that, though Georgina would continue to send
the infant money in considerable quantities, she had dispossessed herself of
it for ever. Together with this induction a fixed idea settled in her mind—
the project of taking the baby herself, of making him her own, of arranging
that matter with the father. The countenance she had given Georgina up to
this point was an effective pledge that she would not expose her; but she
could adopt the poor little mortal without exposing her, she could say that
he was a lovely baby—he was lovely, fortunately—whom she had picked
up in a wretched village in Italy, a village that had been devastated by brigands.[107] She could pretend—she could pretend; oh, yes, of course, she could
pretend! Everything was imposture now, and she could go on to lie as she
had begun. The falsity of the whole business sickened her; it made her so
yellow that she scarcely knew herself in her glass. None the less, to rescue the
child, even if she had to become false still, would be in some measure an
atonement for the treachery to which she had already surrendered herself.
She began to hate Georgina, who had dragged her into such an abyss, and
if it had not been for two considerations she would have insisted on their

separating. One was the deference she owed to Mr. and Mrs. Gressie, who had reposed such a trust in her; the other was that she must keep hold of the mother till she had got possession of the infant. Meanwhile, in this forced communion, her detestation of her companion increased; Georgina came to appear to her a creature of clay and iron.[108] She was exceedingly afraid of her, and it seemed to her now a wonder of wonders that she should ever have trusted her enough to come so far. Georgina showed no consciousness of the change in Mrs. Portico, though there was, indeed, at present, not even a pretence of confidence between the two. Miss Gressie—that was another lie to which Mrs. Portico had to lend herself—was bent on enjoying Europe, and was especially delighted with Rome. She certainly had the courage of her undertaking, and she confessed to Mrs. Portico that she had left Raymond Benyon, and meant to continue to leave him, in ignorance of what had taken place at Genoa. There was a certain confidence, it must be said, in that. He was now in Chinese waters,[109] and she probably should not see him for years. Mrs. Portico took counsel with herself, and the result of her cogitation was that she wrote to Mr. Benyon that a charming little boy had been born to him, and that Georgina had put him to nurse with Italian peasants; but that, if he would kindly consent to it, she, Mrs. Portico, would bring him up much better than that. She knew not how to address her letter, and Georgina, even if she should know, which was doubtful, would never tell her; so she sent the missive to the care of the Secretary of the Navy,[110] at Washington, with an earnest request that it might immediately be forwarded. Such was Mrs. Portico's last effort in this strange business of Georgina's. I relate rather a complicated fact in a very few words when I say that the poor lady's anxieties, indignations, repentances, preyed upon her until they fairly broke her down. Various persons whom she knew in Rome notified her that the air of the Seven Hills was plainly unfavourable to her; and she had made up her mind to return to her native land when she found that, in her depressed condition, malarial fever[111] had laid its hand upon her. She was unable to move, and the matter was settled for her in the course of an illness which, happily, was not prolonged. I have said that she was not obstinate, and the resistance she made on the present occasion was not worthy even of her spasmodic energy. Brain-fever made its appearance, and she died at the end of three weeks, during which Georgina's attentions to her patient and protectress had been unremitting. There were other

Americans in Rome who, after this sad event, extended to the bereaved young lady every comfort and hospitality. She had no lack of opportunities for returning under a proper escort to New York. She selected, you may be sure, the best, and re-entered her father's house, where she took to plain dressing; for she sent all her pocket-money, with the utmost secrecy, to the little boy in the Genoese hills.

VIII

"Why should he come if he doesn't like you? He is under no obligation, and he has his ship to look after. Why should he sit for an hour at a time, and why should he be so pleasant?"

"Do you think he is very pleasant?" Kate Theory[112] asked, turning away her face from her sister. It was important that Mildred should not see how little the expression of that charming countenance corresponded with the inquiry.

This precaution was useless, however, for in a moment Mildred said, from the delicately draped couch on which she lay at the open window, "Kate Theory, don't be affected."

"Perhaps it's for you he comes. I don't see why he shouldn't; you are far more attractive than I, and you have a great deal more to say. How can he help seeing that you are the cleverest of the clever? You can talk to him of everything: of the dates of the different eruptions,[113] of the statues and bronzes in the museum,[114] which you have never seen, *poverina*, but which you know more about than he does, than any one does. What was it you began on last time? Oh yes, you poured forth floods about Magna Graecia.[115] And then—and then——"

But with this Kate Theory paused; she felt it wouldn't do to speak the words that had risen to her lips. That her sister was as beautiful as a saint, and as delicate and refined as an angel—she had been on the point of saying something of that sort. But Mildred's beauty and delicacy were the fairness of mortal disease,[116] and to praise her for her refinement was just to remind her that she had the tenuity of a consumptive. So, after she had checked herself, the younger girl—she was younger only by a year or two—simply kissed her tenderly and settled the knot of the lace handkerchief that was tied over her head. Mildred knew what she had been going to say, knew why she had stopped. Mildred knew everything, without ever leaving her room, or leaving, at least, that little *salon* of their own, at the pension, which she had made so pretty by simply lying there, at the window that had the view of the bay and of Vesuvius, and telling Kate how to arrange and how to rearrange everything. Since it began to be plain that Mildred must spend her small remnant of years altogether in warm climates, the lot of the two sisters had been cast in the ungarnished hostelries of southern Europe. Their little sitting-room was sure to be very ugly, and Mildred was never happy till it was remodelled. Her sister fell to work, as a matter of course, the first day, and changed the place of all the tables, sofas, chairs, till every combination had been tried and the invalid thought at last that there was a little effect.

Kate Theory had a taste of her own, and her ideas were not always the same as her sister's; but she did whatever Mildred liked, and if the poor girl had told her to put the door-mat on the dining-table, or the clock under the sofa, she would have obeyed without a murmur. Her own ideas, her personal tastes, had been folded up and put away, like garments out of season, in drawers and trunks, with camphor and lavender. They were not, as a general thing, for southern wear, however indispensable to comfort in the climate of New England, where poor Mildred had lost her health. Kate Theory, ever since this event, had lived for her companion, and it was almost an inconvenience for her to think that she was attractive to Captain Benyon. It was as if she had shut up her house and was not in a position to entertain. So long as Mildred should live, her own life was suspended; if there should be any time afterwards, perhaps she would take it up again; but for the present, in answer to any knock at her door, she could only call down from one of her dusty windows that she was not at home. Was it really in these terms she should have to dismiss Captain Benyon? If Mildred said it was for her he came she must perhaps take upon herself such a duty; for, as we have seen, Mildred knew everything, and she must therefore be right. She knew about the statues in the museum, about the excavations at Pompeii,[117] about the antique splendour of Magna Graecia. She always had some instructive volume on the table beside her sofa, and she had strength enough to hold the book for half-an-hour at a time. That was about the only strength she had now. The Neapolitan winter had been remarkably soft,[118] but after the first month or two she had been obliged to give up her little walks in the garden. It lay beneath her window like a single enormous bouquet; as early as May, that year, the flowers were so dense. None of them, however, had a colour so intense as the splendid blue of the bay, which filled up all the rest of the view. It would have looked painted if you had not been able to see the little movement of the waves. Mildred Theory watched them by the hour, and the breathing crest of the volcano, on the other side of Naples, and the great sea-vision of Capri,[119] on the horizon, changing its tint while her eyes rested there, and wondered what would become of her sister after she was gone. Now that Percival[120] was married—he was their only brother, and from one day to the other was to come down to Naples to show them his new wife, as yet a complete stranger, or revealed only in the few letters she had written them during her wedding-tour—now that Percival was to be quite taken up, poor Kate's situation would be much more grave. Mildred felt that she should be able to judge better after she should have seen her sister-in-law how much of a home Kate might expect to find with the pair; but even if Agnes should prove—well, more satisfactory than her letters, it was a wretched prospect for Kate—this living as a mere appendage to happier people. Maiden-aunts were very well, but being a maiden-aunt was only a last resource, and Kate's first resources had not even been tried.

Meanwhile the latter young lady wondered as well, wondered in what book Mildred had read that Captain Benyon was in love with her. She admired him, she thought, but he didn't seem a man that would fall in love with one like that. She could see that he was on his guard: he wouldn't throw himself away. He thought too much of himself, or at any rate he took too good care of himself, in the manner of a man to whom something had happened which had given him a lesson. Of course what had happened was that his heart was buried somewhere, in some woman's grave; he had loved some beautiful girl—much more beautiful, Kate was sure, than she, who thought herself meagre and dusky—and the maiden had died, and his capacity to love had died with her. He loved her memory; that was the only thing he would care for now. He was quiet, gentle, clever, humorous, and very kind in his manner; but if any one save Mildred had said to her that if he came three times a week to Posilippo,[121] it was for anything but to pass his time (he had told them he didn't know another lady in Naples), she would have felt that this was simply the kind of thing—usually so idiotic—that people always thought it necessary to say. It was very easy for him to come; he had the big ship's boat, with nothing else to do; and what could be more delightful than to be rowed across the bay, under a bright awning, by four brown sailors with *Louisiana*[122] in blue letters on their immaculate white shirts and in gilt letters on their fluttering hat-ribbons? The boat came to the steps of the garden of the pension, where the orange-trees hung over and made

79

vague yellow balls shine back out of the water. Kate Theory knew all about that, for Captain Benyon had persuaded her to take a turn in the boat, and if they had only had another lady to go with them he could have conveyed her to the ship and shown her all over it. It looked beautiful, just a little way off, with the American flag hanging loose in the Italian air. They would have another lady when Agnes should arrive; then Percival would remain with Mildred while they took this excursion. Mildred had stayed alone the day she went in the boat; she had insisted on it, and, of course it was really Mildred who had persuaded her; though now that Kate came to think of it, Captain Benyon had, in his quiet, waiting way—he turned out to be waiting long after you thought he had let a thing pass—said a good deal about the pleasure it would give him. Of course, everything would give pleasure to a man who was so bored. He was keeping the *Louisiana* at Naples, week after week, simply because these were the commodore's orders. There was no work to be done there, and his time was on his hands; but of course the com-modore, who had gone to Constantinople[123] with the two other ships, had to be obeyed to the letter, however mysterious his motives. It made no dif-ference that he was a fantastic, grumbling, arbitrary old commodore; only a good while afterwards it occurred to Kate Theory that, for a reserved, cor-rect man, Captain Benyon had given her a considerable proof of confidence in speaking to her in these terms of his superior officer. If he looked at all hot when he arrived at the pension she offered him a glass of cold "orangeade."[124] Mildred thought this an unpleasant drink—she called it messy; but Kate adored it and Captain Benyon always accepted it.

The day I speak of, to change the subject, she called her sister's attention to the extraordinary sharpness of a zigzaging cloud-shadow on the tinted slope of Vesuvius; but Mildred remarked in answer only that she wished her sister would marry the Captain. It was in this familiar way that constant meditation led Miss Theory to speak of him; it shows how constantly she thought of him, for, in general, no one was more ceremonious than she, and the failure of her health had not caused her to relax any form that it was possible to keep up. There was a kind of slim erectness even in the way she lay on her sofa; and she always received the doctor as if he were calling for the first time.

"I had better wait till he asks me," Kate Theory said. "Dear Milly, if I were to do some of the things you wish me to do, I should shock you very much."

"I wish he would marry you, then. You know there is very little time, if I wish to see it."

"You will never see it, Mildred. I don't see why you should take so for granted that I would accept him."

"You will never meet a man who has so few disagreeable qualities. He is probably not very well off. I don't know what is the pay of a captain in the navy——"

"It's a relief to find there is something you don't know," Kate Theory broke in.

"But when I am gone," her sister went on, calmly, "when I am gone there will be plenty for both of you."

The younger girl, at this, was silent for a moment; then she exclaimed, "Mildred, you may be out of health, but I don't see why you should be dreadful!"

"You know that since we have been leading this life we have seen no one we liked better," said Milly. When she spoke of the life they were leading— there was always a soft resignation of regret and contempt in the allusion— she meant the southern winters, the foreign climates, the vain experiments, the lonely waitings, the wasted hours, the interminable rains, the bad food, the pottering, humbugging doctors, the damp pensions, the chance encounters, the fitful apparitions of fellow-travellers.

"Why shouldn't you speak for yourself alone? I am glad you like him, Mildred."

"If you don't like him, why do you give him orangeade?"

At this inquiry Kate began to laugh, and her sister continued—

"Of course you are glad I like him, my dear. If I didn't like him, and you did, it wouldn't be satisfactory at all. I can imagine nothing more miserable; I shouldn't die in any sort of comfort."

Kate Theory usually checked this sort of allusion—she was always too late—with a kiss; but on this occasion she added that it was a long time since Mildred had tormented her so much as she had done to-day. "You will make me hate him," she added.

"Well, that proves you don't already," Milly rejoined; and it happened that almost at this moment they saw, in the golden afternoon, Captain Benyon's boat approaching the steps at the end of the garden. He came that day, and he came two days later, and he came yet once again after an interval equally brief, before Percival Theory arrived with Mrs. Theory from Rome. He seemed anxious to crowd into these few days, as he would have said, a good deal of intercourse with the two remarkably nice girls—or nice women, he hardly knew which to call them—whom in the course of a long, idle, rather tedious detention at Naples, he had discovered in the lovely suburb of Posilippo. It was the American consul[125] who had put him into relation with them. The sisters had had to sign in the consul's presence some law-papers, transmitted to them by the man of business who looked after their little property in America, and the kindly functionary, taking advantage of the pretext (Captain Benyon happened to come into the consulate as he was starting, indulgently, to wait upon the ladies) to bring together "two parties" who, as he said, ought to appreciate each other, proposed to his fellow-officer in the service of the United States that he should go with him as witness of the little ceremony. He might, of course, take his clerk, but the Captain would do much better; and he represented to Benyon that the Miss Theorys (singular name, wasn't it?) suffered, he was sure, from a lack of society; also that one of them was very sick, that they were real pleasant and extraordinarily refined, and that the sight of a compatriot literally draped, as it were, in the national banner would cheer them up more than most anything, and give them a sense of protection. They had talked to the consul about Benyon's ship, which they could see from their windows, in the distance, at its anchorage. They were the only American ladies then at Naples—the only residents, at least—and the Captain wouldn't be doing the polite thing unless he went to pay them his respects. Benyon felt afresh how little it was in his line to call upon strange women; he was not in the habit of hunting up female acquaintance, or of looking out for the particular emotions which the sex only can inspire. He had his reasons for this abstention, and he seldom relaxed it; but the consul appealed to him on rather strong grounds. And he suffered himself to be persuaded. He was far from regretting, during the first weeks at least, an act which was distinctly inconsistent with his great rule—that of never exposing himself to the danger of becoming entangled with an unmarried woman. He had been obliged to make this rule, and had adhered to it with some success. He was fond of women, but he was forced to restrict himself to superficial sentiments. There was no use tumbling into situations from which the only possible issue was a retreat. The step he had taken with regard to poor Miss Theory and her delightful little sister was an exception on which at first he could only congratulate himself. That had been a happy idea of the ruminating old consul; it made Captain Benyon forgive him his hat, his boots, his shirt-front—a costume which might be considered representative, and the effect of which was to make the observer turn with rapture to a half-naked lazzarone. On either side the acquaintance had helped the time to pass, and the hours he spent at the little pension at Posilippo left a sweet, and by no means innutritive, taste behind.

As the weeks went by his exception had grown to look a good deal like a rule; but he was able to remind himself that the path of retreat was always open to him. Moreover, if he should fall in love with the younger girl there would be no great harm, for Kate Theory was in love with her sister, and it would matter very little to her whether he advanced or retreated. She was very attractive, or rather she was very attracting. Small, pale, attentive without rigidity, full of pretty curves and quick movements, she looked as if the habit of watching and serving had taken complete possession of her, and was literally a little sister of charity. Her thick black hair was pushed behind her ears, as if to help her to listen, and her clear brown eyes had the smile of a person too full of tact to carry a sad face to a sick-bed. She spoke in an encouraging voice, and had soothing and unselfish habits. She was very pretty, producing a cheerful effect of contrasted black and white, and dressed herself daintily, so that Mildred might have something agreeable to look at. Benyon very soon perceived that there was a fund of good service in her. Her sister had it all now; but poor Miss Theory was fading fast, and then what would become of this precious little force? The answer to such a question that seemed most to the point was that it was none of his business. He was not sick—at least not physically—and he was not looking out for a nurse. Such a companion might be a luxury, but was not, as yet, a necessity. The welcome of the two ladies, at first, had been simple, and he scarcely knew what to call it but sweet; a bright, gentle, jocular friendliness remained the tone of their intercourse. They evidently liked him to come; they liked to see his big transatlantic ship hover about those gleaming coasts of exile. The fact of Miss Mildred being always stretched on her couch—in his successive visits to foreign waters Benyon had not unlearned (as why should he?) the pleasant American habit of using the lady's personal name[126]—made their intimacy seem greater, their differences less; it was as if his hostesses had taken him into their confidence and he had been—as the consul would have said—of the same party. Knocking about the salt parts of the globe, with a few feet square on a rolling frigate for his only home, the pretty flower-decked sitting-room of the quiet American sisters became, more than anything he had hitherto known, his interior. He had dreamed once of having an interior, but the dream had vanished in lurid smoke, and no such vision had come to him again. He had a feeling that the end of this was drawing nigh; he was sure that the advent of the strange brother, whose wife was certain to be disagreeable, would make a difference. That is why, as I have said, he came as often as possible the last week, after he had learned the day on which Percival Theory would arrive. The limits of the exception had been reached.

He had been new to the young ladies at Posilippo, and there was no reason why they should say to each other that he was a very different man from the ingenuous youth who, ten years before, used to wander with Georgina Gressie down vistas of plank-fences brushed over with advertisements of quack medicines.[127] It was natural he should be, and we, who know him, would have found that he had traversed the whole scale of alteration. There was nothing ingenuous in him now; he had the look of experience, of having been seasoned and hardened by the years. His face, his complexion, were the same; still smooth-shaven and slim, he always passed, at first, for a decidedly youthful mariner. But his expression was old, and his talk was older still—the talk of a man who had seen much of the world (as indeed he had to-day) and judged most things for himself, with a humorous scepticism which, whatever concessions it might make, superficially, for the sake of not offending, for instance, two remarkably nice American women who had kept most of their illusions, left you with the conviction that the next minute it would go quickly back to its own stand-point. There was a curious contradiction in him; he struck you as serious, and yet he could not be said to take things seriously. This was what made Kate Theory feel so sure that he had lost the object of his affections; and she said to herself that it must have been under circumstances of peculiar sadness, for that was, after all, a frequent accident, and was not usually thought, in itself, a sufficient stroke to make a man a cynic. This reflection, it may be added, was, on the young lady's part, just the least bit acrimonious. Captain Benyon was not a cynic in any sense in which he might have shocked an innocent mind; he kept his cynicism to himself, and was a very clever, courteous, attentive gentleman. If he was melancholy, you knew it chiefly by his jokes, for they were usually at his own expense; and if he was indifferent, it was all the more to his credit that he should have exerted himself to entertain his countrywomen.

X

The last time he called before the arrival of the expected brother he found Miss Theory alone, and sitting up, for a wonder, at her window. Kate had driven into Naples to give orders at the hotel for the reception of the travellers, who required accommodation more spacious than the villa at Posilippo (where the two sisters had the best rooms) could offer them; and the sick girl had taken advantage of her absence, and of the pretext afforded by a day of delicious warmth, to transfer herself for the first time in six months to an arm-chair. She was practising, as she said, for the long carriage-journey to the north, where, in a quiet corner they knew of, on the Lago Maggiore,[128] her summer was to be spent. Raymond Benyon remarked to her that she had evidently turned the corner and was going to get well, and this gave her a chance to say various things that were in her mind. She had various things on her mind, poor Mildred Theory, so caged and rest-less, and yet so resigned and patient as she was; with a clear, quick spirit, in the most perfect health, ever reaching forward, to the end of its tense little chain, from her wasted and suffering body; and, in the course of the perfect summer afternoon, as she sat there, exhilarated by the success of her effort to get up and by her comfortable opportunity, she took her friendly visitor into the confidence of most of her anxieties. She told him, very promptly and positively, that she was not going to get well at all, that she had proba-bly not more than a twelvemonth yet to live, and that he would oblige her very much by not forcing her to waste any more breath in contradicting him on that head. Of course she couldn't talk much; therefore she wished to say to him only things that he would not hear from any one else. Such for instance was her present secret—Katie's and hers—the secret of their fearing so much that they shouldn't like Percival's wife, who was not from Boston but from New York.[129] Naturally, that by itself would be nothing, but from what they had heard of her set—this subject had been explored by their correspondents—they were rather nervous, nervous to the point of not being in the least reassured by the fact that the young lady would

86

bring Percival a fortune. The fortune was a matter of course, for that was just what they had heard about Agnes's circle—that the stamp of money was on all their thoughts and doings. They were very rich and very new and very splashing, and evidently had very little in common with the two Miss Theorys, who, moreover, if the truth must be told (and this was a great secret), did not care much for the letters their sister-in-law had hitherto addressed them. She had been at a French boarding-school in New York, and yet (and this was the greatest secret of all) she wrote to them that she had performed a part of the journey through France in a "diligance"!¹³⁰ Of course, they would see the next day; Miss Mildred was sure she should know in a moment whether Agnes would like them. She could never have told him all this if her sister had been there, and Captain Benyon must promise never to tell Kate how she had chattered. Kate thought always that they must hide everything, and that even if Agnes should be a dreadful disappointment they must never let any one guess it. And yet Kate was just the one who would suffer, in the coming years, after she herself had gone. Their brother had been everything to them, but now it would all be different. Of course it was not to be expected that he should have remained a bachelor for their sake: she only wished he had waited till she was dead and Kate was married. One of these events, it was true, was much less sure than the other; Kate might never marry, much as she wished she would. She was quite morbidly unselfish, and didn't think she had a right to have anything of her own—not even a husband.

Miss Mildred talked a good while about Kate, and it never occurred to her that she might bore Captain Benyon. She didn't, in point of fact; he had none of the trouble of wondering why this poor, sick, worried lady was trying to push her sister down his throat. Their peculiar situation made everything natural, and the tone she took with him now seemed only what their pleasant relations for the last three months led up to. Moreover, he had an excellent reason for not being bored: the fact, namely, that, after all, with regard to her sister, Miss Mildred appeared to him to keep back more than she uttered. She didn't tell him the great thing—she had nothing to say as to what that charming girl thought of Raymond Benyon. The effect of their interview, indeed, was to make him shrink from knowing, and he felt that the right thing for him would be to get back into his boat, which was waiting at the garden-steps, before Kate Theory should return from Naples. It came over him, as he sat there, that he was far too interested in knowing what this young lady thought of him. She might think what she pleased; it could make no difference to him. The best opinion in the world—if it looked out at him from her tender eyes—would not make him a whit more free or more happy. Women of that sort were not for him, women whom one could not see familiarly without falling in love with them, and whom it was no use to fall in love with unless one was ready to marry them. The light of the summer-afternoon, and of Miss Mildred's pure spirit, seemed suddenly to flood the whole subject. He saw that he was in danger, and he had long since made up his mind that from this particular peril it was not only necessary but honourable to flee. He took leave of his hostess before her sister reappeared, and had the courage even to say to her that he should not come back often after that; they would be so much occupied by their brother and his wife! As he moved across the glassy bay, to the rhythm of the oars, he wished either that the sisters would leave Naples or that his confounded commodore would send for him.

When Kate returned from her errand, ten minutes later, Milly told her of the Captain's visit, and added that she had never seen anything so sudden as the way he left her. "He wouldn't wait for you, my dear, and he said he thought it more than likely that he should never see us again. It is as if he thought you were going to die too!"

"Is his ship called away?" Kate Theory asked.

"He didn't tell me so; he said we should be so busy with Percival and Agnes."

"He has got tired of us; that is all. There is nothing wonderful in that; I knew he would."

Mildred said nothing for a moment; she was watching her sister, who was very attentively arranging some flowers. "Yes, of course, we are very dull, and he is like everybody else."

"I thought you thought he was so wonderful," said Kate—"and so fond of us."

"So he is; I am surer of that than ever. That's why he went away so abruptly."

Kate looked at her sister now. "I don't understand."

"Neither do I, *cara*. But you will, one of these days."

"How, if he never comes back?"

"Oh, he will—after a while—when I am gone. Then he will explain; that, at least, is clear to me."

"My poor precious, as if I cared!" Kate Theory exclaimed, smiling as she distributed her flowers. She carried them to the window, to place them near her sister, and here she paused a moment, her eye caught by an object, far out in the bay, with which she was not unfamiliar. Mildred noticed its momentary look, and followed its direction.

"It's the Captain's gig going back to the ship," Milly said. "It's so still one can almost hear the oars."

Kate Theory turned away, with a sudden, strange violence, a movement and exclamation which, the very next minute, as she became conscious of what she had said—and, still more, of what she felt—smote her own heart (as it flushed her face) with surprise and with the force of a revelation. "I wish it would sink him to the bottom of the sea!"

Her sister stared, then caught her by the dress, as she passed from her, drawing her back with a weak hand. "Oh, my darling dear!" And she drew Kate down and down toward her, so that the girl had nothing for it but to sink on her knees and bury her face in Mildred's lap. If that ingenious invalid did not know everything now, she knew a great deal.

Mrs. Percival proved very pretty; it is more gracious to begin with this dec-laration, instead of saying, in the first place, that she proved very vapid. It took a long day to arrive at the end of her silliness, and the two ladies at Posilippo, even after a week had passed, suspected that they had only skirted its edges. Kate Theory had not spent half an hour in her company before she gave a little private sigh of relief; she felt that a situation which had promised to be embarrassing was now quite clear, was even of a primitive simplicity. She would spend with her sister-in-law, in the coming time, one week in the year; that was all that would be mortally possible. It was a bless-ing that one could see exactly what she was, for in that way the question set-tled itself. It would have been much more tiresome if Agnes had been a little less obvious; then one would have had to hesitate and consider and weigh one thing against another. She was pretty and silly, as distinctly as an orange is yellow and round; and Kate Theory would as soon have thought of look-ing to her to give interest to the future as she would have thought of look-ing to an orange to impart solidity to the prospect of dinner. Mrs. Percival travelled in the hope of meeting her American acquaintance, or of making acquaintance with such Americans as she did meet, and for the purpose of buying mementos for her relations. She was perpetually adding to her store of articles in tortoise-shell, in mother-of-pearl, in olive-wood, in ivory, in filigree, in tartan lacquer,[131] in mosaic; and she had a collection of Roman scarfs and Venetian beads which she looked over exhaustively every night before she went to bed. Her conversation bore mainly upon the manner in which she intended to dispose of these accumulations. She was constantly changing about, among each other, the persons to whom they were respec-tively to be offered. At Rome one of the first things she said to her hus-band after entering the Coliseum[132] had been, "I guess I will give the ivory work-box to Bessie and the Roman pearls to Aunt Harriet!" She was always hanging over the travellers' book at the hotel; she had it brought up to her, with a cup of chocolate, as soon as she arrived. She searched its pages for the magical name of New York, and she indulged in infinite conjecture as to who the people were—the name was sometimes only a partial cue—who had inscribed it there. What she most missed in Europe, and what she most enjoyed, was the New Yorkers; when she met them she talked about the people in their native city who had "moved" and the streets they had moved to. "Oh yes, the Drapers are going up town, to Twenty-fourth Street, and the Vanderdeckens are going to be in Twenty-third Street,[133] right back of them. My uncle, Mr. Henry Platt,[134] thinks of building round there." Mrs. Percival Theory was capable of repeating statements like these thirty times over—of lingering on them for hours. She talked largely of herself, of her uncles and aunts, of her clothes—past, present and future. These articles, in especial, filled her horizon; she considered them with a complacency which might have led you to suppose that she had invented the custom of draping the human form. Her main point of contact with Naples was the purchase of coral;[135] and all the while she was there the word "set"— she used it as if every one would understand—fell with its little flat, common sound upon the ears of her sisters-in-law, who had no sets of anything. She cared little for pictures and mountains; Alps and Apennines[136] were not productive of New Yorkers, and it was difficult to take an interest in Madonnas who flour-ished at periods when apparently there were no fashions, or at any rate no trimmings.

I speak here not only of the impression she made upon her husband's anxious sisters, but of the judgment passed on her (he went so far as that, though it was not obvious how it mattered to him) by Raymond Benyon. And this brings me at a jump (I confess it's a very small one) to the fact that he did, after all, go back to Posilippo. He stayed away for nine days, and at the end of this time Percival Theory called upon him to thank him for the civility he had shown his kinswomen. He went to this gentleman's hotel, to return his visit, and there he found Miss Kate, in her brother's sitting-room. She had come in by appointment from the villa, and was going with the others to look at the royal palace,[137] which she had not yet had an oppor-tunity to inspect. It was proposed (not by Kate), and presently arranged, that Captain Benyon should go with them; and he accordingly walked over marble floors for half an hour, exchanging conscious commonplaces with the woman he loved. For this truth had rounded itself during those nine days of absence; he discovered that there was nothing particularly sweet in his life when once Kate Theory had been excluded from it. He had stayed away to keep himself from falling in love with her; but this expedient was in itself illuminating, for he perceived that, according to the vulgar adage, he was locking the stable-door after the horse had been stolen. As he paced the deck of his ship and looked toward Posilippo his tenderness crystallised; the thick, smoky flame of a sentiment that knew itself forbidden, and was angry at the knowledge, now danced upon the fuel of his good resolutions. The latter, it must be said, resisted, declined to be consumed. He determined that he would see Kate Theory again, for a time just sufficient to bid her good-bye and to add a little explanation. He thought of his explanation very lovingly, but it may not strike the reader as a happy inspiration. To part from her dryly, abruptly, without an allusion to what he might have said if every-thing had been different—that would be wisdom, of course, that would be virtue, that would be the line of a practical man, of a man who kept himself well in hand. But it would be virtue terribly unrewarded—it would be virtue too austere even for a person who flattered himself that he had taught him-self stoicism. The minor luxury tempted him irresistibly, since the larger—that of happy love—was denied him; the luxury of letting the girl know that it would not be an accident—oh, not at all—that they should never meet again. She might easily think it was, and thinking it was would doubtless do her no harm. But this wouldn't give him his pleasure—the platonic sat-isfaction of expressing to her at the same time his belief that they might have made each other happy and the necessity of his renunciation. That, probably, wouldn't hurt her either, for she had given him no proof whatever that she cared for him. The nearest approach to it was the way she walked beside him now, sweet and silent, without the least reference to his not hav-ing come back to the villa. The place was cool and dusky, the blinds were drawn to keep out the light and noise, and the little party wandered through the high saloons, where precious marbles and the gleam of gilding and satin made reflections in the rich dimness. Here and there the cicerone, in slip-pers, with Neapolitan familiarity, threw open a shutter to show off a picture or a tapestry. He strolled in front with Percival Theory and his wife, while this lady, drooping silently from her husband's arm as they passed, felt the stuff of the curtains and the sofas. When he caught her in these experiments the cicerone, in expressive deprecation, clasped his hands and lifted his eye-brows; whereupon Mrs. Theory exclaimed to her husband, "Oh, bother his

92

old king!" It was not striking to Captain Benyon why Percival Theory had married the niece of Mr. Henry Platt. He was less interesting than his sisters—a smooth, cool, correct young man, who frequently took out a pencil and did a little arithmetic on the back of a letter. He sometimes, in spite of his correctness, chewed a toothpick, and he missed the American papers, which he used to ask for in the most unlikely places. He was a Bostonian converted to New York; a very special type.[138]

"Is it settled when you leave Naples?" Benyon asked of Kate Theory.

"I think so; on the twenty-fourth. My brother has been very kind; he has lent us his carriage, which is a large one, so that Mildred can lie down. He and Agnes will take another; but of course we shall travel together."

"I wish to heaven I were going with you!" Captain Benyon said. He had given her the opportunity to respond, but she did not take it; she merely remarked, with a vague laugh, that of course he couldn't take his ship over the Apennines. "Yes, there is always my ship," he went on. "I am afraid that in future it will carry me far away from you."

They were alone in one of the royal apartments;[139] their companions had passed, in advance of them, into the adjoining room. Benyon and his fellow-visitor had paused beneath one of the immense chandeliers of glass, which in the clear, coloured gloom, through which one felt the strong outer light of Italy beating in, suspended its twinkling drops from the decorated vault. They looked round them confusedly, made shy for the moment by Benyon's having struck a note more serious than any that had hitherto sounded between them, looked at the sparse furniture, draped in white overalls, at the scagliola floor,[140] in which the great cluster of crystal pendants seemed to shine again.

"You are master of your ship—can't you sail it as you like?" Kate Theory asked, with a smile.

"I am not master of anything. There is not a man in the world less free. I am a slave. I am a victim."

She looked at him with kind eyes; something in his voice suddenly made her put away all thought of the defensive airs that a girl, in certain situations, is expected to assume. She perceived that he wanted to make her understand something, and now her only wish was to help him to say it. "You are not happy," she murmured simply, her voice dying away in a kind of wonderment at this reality.

The gentle touch of her words—it was as if her hand had stroked his cheek—seemed to him the sweetest thing he had ever known. "No, I am not happy, because I am not free. If I were—if I were, I would give up my ship, I would give up everything, to follow you. I can't explain; that is part of the hardness of it. I only want you to know it, that if certain things were different, if everything was different, I might tell you that I believe I should have a right to speak to you. Perhaps some day it will change; but probably then it will be too late. Meanwhile, I have no right of any kind. I don't want to trouble you, and I don't ask of you—anything! It is only to have spoken just once. I don't make you understand, of course. I am afraid I seem to you rather a brute, perhaps even a humbug. Don't think of it now; don't try to understand. But some day, in the future, remember what I have said to you, and how we stood here, in this strange old place, alone! Perhaps it will give you a little pleasure."

Kate Theory began by listening to him with visible eagerness; but in a moment she turned away her eyes. "I am very sorry for you," she said, gravely.

"Then you do understand enough?"

"I shall think of what you have said—in the future."

Benyon's lips formed the beginning of a word of tenderness, which he instantly suppressed; and in a different tone, with a bitter smile and a sad shake of the head, raising his arms a moment and letting them fall, he rejoined, "It won't hurt any one, your remembering this!"

"I don't know whom you mean." And the girl, abruptly, began to walk to the end of the room. He made no attempt to tell her whom he meant, and they proceeded together in silence till they overtook their companions.

XII

There were several pictures in the neighbouring room, and Percival Theory and his wife had stopped to look at one of them, of which the cicerone announced the title and the authorship as Benyon came up. It was a modern portrait of a Bourbon princess,[141] a woman young, fair, handsome, covered with jewels. Mrs. Percival appeared to be more struck with it than with anything the palace had yet offered to her sight, while her sister-in-law walked to the window, which the custodian had opened, to look out into the garden. Benyon noticed this; he was conscious that he had given the girl something to reflect upon, and his ears burned a little as he stood beside Mrs. Percival and looked up, mechanically, at the royal lady. He already repented a little of what he had said; for, after all, what was the use? And he hoped the others wouldn't observe that he had been making love.

"Gracious, Percival! Do you see who she looks like?"[142] Mrs. Theory said to her husband.

"She looks like a lady who has a big bill at Tiffany's,"[143] this gentleman answered.

"She looks like my sister-in-law; the eyes, the mouth, the way the hair's done—the whole thing."

"Which do you mean? You have got about a dozen."

"Why, Georgina, of course—Georgina Roy. She's awfully like."

"Do you call her your sister-in-law?" Percival Theory asked. "You must want very much to claim her."

"Well, she's handsome enough. You have got to invent some new name, then. Captain Benyon, what do you call your brother-in-law's second wife?" Mrs. Percival continued, turning to her neighbour, who still stood staring at the portrait. At first he had looked without seeing; then sight, and hearing as well, became quick. They were suddenly peopled with thrilling recognitions. The Bourbon princess—the eyes, the mouth, the way the hair was done, these things took on an identity, and the gaze of the painted face seemed to fasten itself to his own. But who in the world was Georgina Roy, and what was this talk about sisters-in-law? He turned to the little lady at

95

his side a countenance unexpectedly puzzled by the problem she had lightly presented to him.

"Your brother-in-law's second wife? That's rather complicated."

"Well, of course, he needn't have married again," said Mrs. Percival, with a small sigh.

"Whom did he marry?" asked Benyon, staring. Percival Theory had turned away. "Oh, if you are going into her relationships," he murmured, and joined his sister at the brilliant window, through which, from the distance, the many-voiced uproar of Naples came in.

"He married first my sister Cora,¹⁴⁴ and she died five years ago. Then he married *her*;" and Mrs. Percival nodded at the princess.

Benyon's eyes went back to the portrait; he could see what she meant—it stared out at him. "Her? Georgina?"

"Georgina Gressie! Gracious, do you know her?"

It was very distinct—that answer of Mrs. Percival's, and the question that followed it as well. But he had the resource of the picture; he could look at it, seem to take it very seriously, though it danced up and down before him. He felt that he was turning red, then he felt that he was turning pale. "The brazen impudence!" That was the way he could speak to himself now of the woman he had once loved, and whom he afterwards hated, till this had died out too. Then the wonder of it was lost in the quickly growing sense that it would make a difference for him—a great difference. Exactly what, he didn't see yet; only a difference that swelled and swelled as he thought of it, and caught up, in its expansion, the girl who stood behind him so quietly, looking into the Italian garden.

The custodian drew Mrs. Percival away to show her another princess, before Benyon answered her last inquiry. This gave him time to recover from his first impulse, which had been to answer it with a negative; he saw in a moment that an admission of his acquaintance with Mrs. Roy (Mrs. Roy!—it was prodigious!) was necessarily helping him to learn more. Besides, it needn't be compromising. Very likely Mrs. Percival would hear one day that he had once wanted to marry her. So, when he joined his companions a minute later he remarked that he had known Miss Gressie years before, and had even admired her considerably, but had lost sight of her entirely in later days. She had been a great beauty, and it was a wonder that she had not married earlier. Five years ago, was it? No, it was only two. He had been going to say that in so long a time it would have been singular he should not have heard of it. He had been away from New York for ages; but one always heard of marriages and deaths. This was a proof, though two years was rather long. He led Mrs. Percival insidiously into a further room, in advance of the others, to whom the cicerone returned. She was delighted to talk about her "connections," and she supplied him with every detail. He could trust himself now; his self-possession was complete, or, so far as it was wanting, the fault was that of a sudden gaiety which he could not, on the spot, have accounted for. Of course it was not very flattering to them—Mrs. Percival's own people—that poor Cora's husband should have consoled himself; but men always did it (talk of widows !) and he had chosen a girl who was—well, very fine-looking, and the sort of successor to Cora that they needn't be ashamed of. She had been awfully admired, and no one had understood why she had waited so long to marry. She had had some affair as a girl—an engagement to an officer in the army—and the man had jilted her, or they had quarrelled, or something or other. She was almost an old maid—well, she was thirty, or very nearly—but she had done something good now. She was handsomer than ever, and tremendously striking. William Roy had one of the biggest incomes in the city, and he was quite affectionate. He had been intensely fond of Cora—he often spoke of her still, at least to her own relations; and her portrait, the last time Mrs. Percival was in his house (it was at a party, after his marriage to Miss Gressie), was still in the front parlour. Perhaps by this time he had had it moved to the back; but she was sure he would keep it somewhere, anyway. Poor Cora had had no children; but Georgina was making that all right; she had a beautiful boy. Mrs. Percival had what she would have called quite a pleasant chat with Captain Benyon about Mrs. Roy. Perhaps *he* was the officer—she never thought of that! He was sure he had never jilted her? And he had never quarrelled with a lady? Well, he must be different from most men.

He certainly had the air of being so before he parted that afternoon with Kate Theory. This young lady, at least, was free to think him wanting in that consistency which is supposed to be a distinctively masculine virtue. An hour before he had taken an eternal farewell of her; and now he was alluding to future meetings, to future visits, proposing that, with her sister-in-law, she should appoint an early day for coming to see the *Louisiana,* She had supposed she understood him, but it would appear now that she had not understood him at all. His manner had changed too. More and more off his guard, Raymond Benyon was not aware how much more hopeful an expression it gave him, his irresistible sense that somehow or other this extraordinary proceeding of his wife's would set him free. Kate Theory felt rather weary and mystified, all the more for knowing that henceforth Captain Benyon's variations would be the most important thing in life for her.

XIII

That officer, on his ship in the bay, lingered very late on the deck that night—lingered there, indeed, under the warm southern sky, in which the stars glittered with a hot, red light, until the early dawn began to show. He smoked cigar after cigar; he walked up and down by the hour; he was agitated by a thousand reflections; he repeated to himself that it made a difference—an immense difference; but the pink light had deepened in the east before he had discovered in what the change consisted. By that time he saw it clearly—it consisted in Georgina's being in his power now, in place of his being in hers. He laughed as he sat alone in the darkness at the thought of what she had done. It had occurred to him more than once that she would do it; he believed her capable of anything; but the accomplished fact had a freshness of comicality. He thought of William Roy, of his big income, of his being "quite affectionate," of his blooming son and heir, of his having found such a worthy successor to poor Mrs. Cora. He wondered whether Georgina had mentioned to him that she had a husband living, but was strongly of the belief that she had not. Why should she, after all? She had neglected to mention it to so many others. He had thought he knew her, in so many years, that he had nothing more to learn about her, but this ripe stroke revived his sense of her audacity. Of course it was what she had been waiting for, and if she had not done it sooner it was because she had hoped he would be lost at sea in one of his long cruises and relieve her of the necessity of a crime. How she must hate him to-day for not having been lost, for being alive, for continuing to put her in the wrong! Much as she hated him, however, his own loathing was at least a match for hers. She had done him the foulest of wrongs—she had ravaged his life. That he should ever detest in this degree a woman whom he had once loved as he loved her he would not have thought possible in his innocent younger years. But neither would he have thought it possible then that a woman should be such a cold-blooded devil as she had been. His love had perished in his rage, his blinding, impotent rage, at finding that he had been duped and measuring

99

his impotence. When he learned, years before, from Mrs. Portico, what she had done with her baby, of whose entrance into life she herself had given him no intimation, he felt that he was face to face with a full revelation of her nature. Before that it had puzzled him, it had mocked him; his relations with her were bewildering, stupefying. But when, after obtaining, with difficulty and delay, a leave of absence from Government, and betaking himself to Italy to look for the child and assume possession of it, he had encountered absolute failure and defeat, then the case presented itself to him more simply. He perceived that he had mated himself with a creature who just happened to be a monster, a human exception altogether. That was what he couldn't pardon—her conduct about the child; never, never, never! To him she might have done what she chose—dropped him, pushed him out into eternal cold, with his hands fast tied—and he would have accepted it, excused her almost, admitted that it had been his business to mind better what he was about. But she had tortured him through the poor little irrecoverable son whom he had never seen, through the heart and the human vitals that she had not herself and that he had to have, poor wretch, for both of them.

All his effort, for years, had been to forget those horrible months, and he had cut himself off from them so that they seemed at times to belong to the life of another person. But to-night he lived them over again; he retraced the different gradations of darkness through which he had passed, from the moment, so soon after his extraordinary marriage, when it came over him that she already repented and meant, if possible, to elude all her obligations. This was the moment when he saw why she had reserved herself—in the strange vow she extracted from him—an open door for retreat; the moment, too, when her having had such an inspiration (in the midst of her momentary good faith, if good faith it had ever been) struck him as a proof of her essential depravity. What he had tried to forget came back to him: the child that was not his child produced for him when he fell upon that squalid nest of peasants in the Genoese country, and then the confessions, retractations, contradictions, lies, terrors, threats, and general bottomless, baffling mendacity and idiocy of every one in the place. The child was gone; that had been the only definite thing. The woman who had taken it to nurse had a dozen different stories, her husband had as many, and every one in the village had a hundred more. Georgina had been sending money—she had managed, apparently, to send a good deal—and the whole country seemed to have been living on it and making merry. At one moment, the baby had died and received a most expensive burial; at another, he had been entrusted (for more healthy air, Santissima Madonna!) to the woman's cousin, in another village. According to a version which for a day or two Benyon had inclined to think the least false, he had been taken by the cousin (for his beauty's sake) to Genoa, when she went for the first time in her life to the town to see her daughter in service there, and had been confided for a few hours to a third woman, who was to keep him while the cousin walked about the streets, but who, having no child of her own, took such a fancy to him that she refused to give him up, and a few days later left the place (she was a Pisana) never to be heard of more. The cousin had forgotten her name—it had happened six months before. Benyon spent a year looking up and down Italy for his child, and inspecting hundreds of swaddled infants, inscrutable candidates for recognition. Of course he could only get further and further from real knowledge, and his search was arrested by the conviction that it was making him mad. He set his teeth and made up his mind, or tried to, that the baby had died in the hands of its nurse. This was, after all, much the likeliest supposition, and the woman had maintained it, in the hope of being rewarded for her candour, quite as often as she had asseverated that it was still somewhere, alive, in the hope of being remunerated for her good news. It may be imagined with what sentiments toward his wife Benyon had emerged from this episode. To-night his memory went further back—back to the beginning and to the days when he had had to ask himself, with all the crudity of his first surprise, what in the name of perversity she had wished to do with him. The answer to this speculation was so old, it had dropped so out of the line of recurrence, that it was now almost new again. Moreover, it was only approximate, for, as I have already said, he could comprehend such baseness as little at the end as at the beginning. She had found herself on a slope which her nature forced her to descend to the bottom. She did him the honour of wishing to enjoy his society, and she did herself the honour of thinking that their intimacy, however brief, must have a certain consecration. She felt that with him, after his promise (he would have made any promise to lead her on), she was secure, secure as she had proved to be, secure as she must think herself. That security had helped her to ask herself, after the first flush of passion was over, and her native, her twice-inherited worldliness had had time to open its eyes again, why she should keep faith with a man whose deficiencies (as a husband before the world—another affair) had been so scientifically exposed to her by her parents. So she had simply determined *not* to keep faith; and her determination, at least, she did keep.

By the time Benyon turned in he had satisfied himself, as I say, that Georgina was now in his power; and this seemed to him such an improvement in his situation that he allowed himself, for the next ten days, a license which made Kate Theory almost as happy as it made her sister, though she pretended to understand it far less. Mildred sank to her rest, or rose to fuller comprehensions, within the year, in the Isle of Wight;[145] and Captain Benyon, who had never written so many letters as since they left Naples, sailed westward about the same time as the sweet survivor. For the *Louisiana* at last was ordered home.

XIV

CERTAINLY, I will see you if you come, and you may appoint any day or hour you like. I should have seen you with pleasure any time these last years. Why should we not be friends, as we used to be? Perhaps we shall be yet. I say "perhaps" only, on purpose, because your note is rather vague about your state of mind. Don't come with any idea about making me nervous or uncomfortable. I am not nervous by nature, thank heaven, and I won't, I positively won't (do you hear, dear Captain Benyon?) be uncomfortable. I have been so (it served me right) for years and years; but I am very happy now. To remain so is the very definite intention of yours ever

> Georgina Roy.

This was the answer Benyon received to a short letter that he despatched to Mrs. Roy after his return to America. It was not till he had been there some weeks that he wrote to her. He had been occupied in various ways: he had had to look after his ship; he had had to report at Washington; he had spent a fortnight with his mother at Portsmouth, N.H.; and he had paid a visit to Kate Theory in Boston. She herself was paying visits; she was staying with various relatives and friends. She had more colour—it was very delicately rosy—than she had had of old, in spite of her black dress; and the effect of her looking at him seemed to him to make her eyes grow still prettier. Though sisterless now, she was not without duties, and Benyon could easily see that life would press hard on her unless some one should interfere. Every one regarded her as just the person to do certain things. Every one thought she could do everything, because she had nothing else to do. She used to read to the blind, and, more onerously, to the deaf. She looked after other people's children while the parents attended anti-slavery conventions.[146]

She was coming to New York, later, to spend a week at her brother's, but beyond this she had no idea what she should do. Benyon felt it to be awkward that he should not be able just now to tell her; and this had much to do with his coming to the point, for he accused himself of having rather hung fire. Coming to the point, for Benyon, meant writing a note to Mrs. Roy (as he must call her), in which he asked whether she would see him if he should present himself. The missive was short; it contained, in addition to what I have hinted, little more than the remark that he had something of importance to say to her. Her reply, which we have just read, was prompt. Benyon designated an hour, and rang the doorbell of her big modern house, whose polished windows seemed to shine defiance at him.

As he stood on the steps, looking up and down the straight vista of the Fifth Avenue, he perceived that he was trembling a little, that he was nervous, if she were not. He was ashamed of his agitation, and he pulled himself vigorously together. Afterwards he saw that what had made him nervous was not any doubt of the goodness of his cause, but his revived sense (as he drew near her) of his wife's hardness, her capacity for insolence. He might only break himself against that, and the prospect made him feel helpless. She kept him waiting for a long time after he had been introduced; and as he walked up and down her drawing-room, an immense, florid, expensive apartment, covered with blue satin, gilding, mirrors and bad frescoes, it came over him as a certainty that her delay was calculated. She wished to annoy him, to weary him; she was as ungenerous as she was unscrupulous. It never occurred to him that, in spite of the bold words of her note, she, too, might be in a tremor, and if any one in their secret had suggested that she was afraid to meet him, he would have laughed at this idea. This was of bad omen for the success of his errand; for it showed that he recognised the ground of her presumption—his having the superstition of old promises. By the time she appeared he was flushed, very angry. She closed the door behind her, and stood there looking at him, with the width of the room between them.

The first emotion her presence excited was a quick sense of the strange fact that, after all these years of loneliness, such a magnificent person should be his wife. For she was magnificent, in the maturity of her beauty, her head erect, her complexion splendid, her auburn tresses undimmed, a certain plenitude in her very glance. He saw in a moment that she wished to seem to him beautiful, she had endeavoured to dress herself to the best effect. Perhaps, after all, it was only for this she had delayed; she wished to give herself every possible touch. For some moments they said nothing; they had not stood face to face for nearly ten years, and they met now as adversaries. No two persons could possibly be more interested in taking each other's measure. It scarcely belonged to Georgina, however, to have too much the air of timidity, and after a moment, satisfied, apparently, that she was not to receive a broadside, she advanced, slowly, rubbing her jewelled hands and smiling. He wondered why she should smile, what thought was in her mind. His impressions followed each other with extraordinary quickness of pulse, and now he saw, in addition to what he had already perceived, that she was waiting to take her cue: she had determined on no definite line. There was nothing definite about her but her courage; the rest would depend upon him. As for her courage, it seemed to glow in the beauty which grew greater as she came nearer, with her eyes on his and her fixed smile; to be expressed in the very perfume that accompanied her steps. By this time he had got a still further impression, and it was the strangest of all. She was ready for anything, she was capable of anything, she wished to surprise him with her beauty, to remind him that it belonged, after all, at the bottom of everything, to him. She was ready to bribe him, if bribing should be necessary. She had carried on an intrigue before she was twenty; it would be more, rather than less, easy for her now that she was thirty. All this and more was in her cold, living eyes, as, in the prolonged silence, they engaged themselves with his; but I must not dwell upon it, for reasons extraneous to the remarkable fact. She was a truly amazing creature.

"Raymond!" she said, in a low voice—a voice which might represent either a vague greeting or an appeal.

He took no heed of the exclamation, but asked her why she had deliberately kept him waiting, as if she had not made a fool enough of him already. She couldn't suppose it was for his pleasure he had come into the house.

She hesitated a moment, still with her smile. "I must tell you I have a son, the dearest little boy. His nurse happened to be engaged for the moment, and I had to watch him. I am more devoted to him than you might suppose."

He fell back from her a few steps. "I wonder if you are insane," he murmured.

"To allude to my child? Why do you ask me such questions then? I tell you the simple truth. I take every care of this one. I am older and wiser. The other one was a complete mistake; he had no right to exist."

"Why didn't you kill him then with your own hands, instead of that torture?"

"Why didn't I kill myself? That question would be more to the point. You are looking wonderfully well," she broke off, in another tone; "hadn't we better sit down?"

"I didn't come here for the advantage of conversation," Benyon answered. And he was going on, but she interrupted him.

"You came to say something dreadful, very likely; though I hoped you would see it was better not. But just tell me this, before you begin. Are you successful, are you happy? It has been so provoking, not knowing more about you."

There was something in the manner in which this was said that caused him to break into a loud laugh; whereupon she added—

"Your laugh is just what it used to be. How it comes back to me! You *have* improved in appearance," she continued.

She had seated herself, though he remained standing; and she leaned back in a low, deep chair, looking up at him, with her arms folded. He stood near her and over her, as it were, dropping his baffled eyes on her, with his hand resting on the corner of the chimney-piece. "Has it never occurred to you that I may deem myself absolved from the promise I made you before I married you?"

"Very often, of course. But I have instantly dismissed the idea. How can you be 'absolved'? One promises, or one doesn't. I attach no meaning to that, and neither do you." And she glanced down at the front of her dress.

Benyon listened, but he went on as if he had not heard her. "What I came to say to you is this: that I should like your consent to my bringing a suit for divorce[147] against you."

"A suit for divorce? I never thought of that."

"So that I may marry another woman. I can easily obtain a divorce on the ground of your desertion. It will simplify our situation."

She stared a moment, then her smile solidified, as it were, and she looked grave; but he could see that her gravity, with her lifted eyebrows, was partly assumed. "Ah, you want to marry another woman!" she exclaimed, slowly, thoughtfully. He said nothing, and she went on, "Why don't you do as I have done?"

"Because I don't want my children to be——"

Before he could say the words she sprang up, checking him with a cry. "Don't say it; it isn't necessary! Of course I know what you mean; but they won't be if no one knows it."

"I should object to knowing it myself; it's enough for me to know it of yours."

"Of course I have been prepared for your saying that."

"I should hope so!" Benyon exclaimed. "You may be a bigamist, if it suits you, but to me the idea is not attractive. I wish to marry——" and, hesitating a moment, with his slight stammer, he repeated, "I wish to marry——"

"Marry, then, and have done with it!" cried Mrs. Roy.

He could already see that he should be able to extract no consent from her; he felt rather sick. "It's extraordinary to me that you shouldn't be more afraid of being found out," he said, after a moment's reflection. "There are two or three possible accidents."

"How do you know how much afraid I am? I have thought of every accident, in dreadful nights. How do you know what my life is, or what it has been all these horrid years? But every one is dead."

"You look wasted and worn, certainly."

"Ah, don't compliment me!" Georgina exclaimed. "If I had never known you—if I had not been through all this—I believe I should have been handsome. When did you hear of my marriage? Where were you at the time?"

"At Naples, more than six months ago, by a mere chance."

"How strange that it should have taken you so long! Is the lady a Neapolitan? They don't mind what they do over there."

"I have no information to give you beyond what I have just said," Benyon rejoined. "My life doesn't in the least regard you."

"Ah, but it does from the moment I refuse to let you divorce me."

"You refuse?" Benyon said, softly.

"Don't look at me that way! You haven't advanced so rapidly as I used to think you would; you haven't distinguished yourself so much," she went on, irrelevantly.

"I shall be promoted commodore one of these days," Benyon answered. "You don't know much about it, for my advancement has already been extraordinary rapid." He blushed as soon as the words were out of his mouth. She gave a light laugh on seeing it; but he took up his hat and added, "Think over a day or two what I have proposed to you. It's a perfectly possible proceeding. Think of the temper in which I ask it."

"The temper?" she stared. "Pray, what have you to do with temper?" And as he made no reply, smoothing his hat with his glove, she went on, "Years ago, as much as you please! you had a good right, I don't deny, and you raved, in your letters, to your heart's content. That's why I wouldn't see you;

I didn't wish to take it full in the face. But that's all over now; time is a healer; you have cooled off, and by your own admission you have consoled yourself. Why do you talk to me about temper? What in the world have I done to you but let you alone?"

"What do you call this business?" Benyon asked, with his eye flashing all over the room.

"Ah, excuse me, that doesn't touch you; it's my affair. I leave you your liberty, and I can live as I like. If I choose to live in this way, it may be queer (I admit it is, tremendously), but you have nothing to say to it. If I am willing to take the risk, you may be. If I am willing to play such an infernal trick upon a confiding gentleman (I will put it as strongly as you possibly could), I don't see what you have to say to it except that you are exceedingly glad such a woman as that isn't known to be your wife!" She had been cool and deliberate up to this time, but with these words her latent agitation broke out. "Do you think I have been happy? Do you think I have enjoyed existence? Do you see me freezing up into a stark old maid?"

"I wonder you stood out so long," said Benyon.

"I wonder I did! They were bad years."

"I have no doubt they were!"

"You could do as you pleased," Georgina went on. "You roamed about the world, you formed charming relations. I am delighted to hear it from your own lips. Think of my going back to my father's house—that family vault—and living there, year after year, as Miss Gressie! If you remember my father and mother—they are round in Twelfth Street, just the same—you must admit that I paid for my folly!"

"I have never understood you; I don't understand you now," said Benyon.

She looked at him a moment. "I adored you."

"I could damn you with a word!" he exclaimed.

XV

The moment he had spoken she grasped his arm and held up her other hand, as if she were listening to a sound outside the room. She had evidently had an inspiration, and she carried it into instant effect. She swept away to the door, flung it open, and passed into the hall, whence her voice came back to Benyon as she addressed a person who apparently was her husband. She had heard him enter the house at his habitual hour, after his long morning at business; the closing of the door of the vestibule had struck her ear. The parlour was on a level with the hall, and she greeted him without impediment. She asked him to come in and be introduced to Captain Benyon, and he responded with due solemnity. She returned in advance of him, her eyes fixed upon Benyon and lighted with defiance, her whole face saying to him vividly, "Here is your opportunity; I give it to you with my own hands. Break your promise and betray me if you dare! You say you can damn me with a word; speak the word and let us see!"

Benyon's heart beat faster, as he felt that it was indeed a chance; but half his emotion came from the spectacle, magnificent in its way, of her unparalleled impudence. A sense of all that he had escaped in not having had to live with her rolled over him like a wave, while he looked strangely at Mr. Roy, to whom this privilege had been vouchsafed. He saw in a moment his successor had a constitution that would carry it. Mr. Roy suggested squareness and solidity; he was a broad-based, comfortable, polished man, with a surface in which the rank tendrils of irritation would not easily obtain a foothold. He had a broad, blank face, a capacious mouth, and a small, light eye, to which, as he entered, he was engaged in adjusting a double gold-rimmed glass. He approached Benyon with a prudent, civil, punctual air, as if he habitually met a good many gentlemen in the course of business, and though, naturally, this was not that sort of occasion, he was not a man to waste time in preliminaries. Benyon had immediately the impression of having seen him, or his equivalent, a thousand times before. He was middle-aged, fresh-coloured, whiskered, prosperous, indefinite. Georgina introduced them to each other—she spoke of Benyon as an old friend, whom she had known long before she had known Mr. Roy, who had been very kind to her years ago, when she was a girl.

"He is in the navy. He has just come back from a long cruise."

Mr. Roy shook hands—Benyon gave him his before he knew it—said he was very happy, smiled, looked at Benyon from head to foot, then at Georgina, then round the room, then back at Benyon again—at Benyon, who stood there, without sound or movement, with a dilated eye and a pulse quickened to a degree of which Mr. Roy could have little idea. Georgina made some remark about their sitting down, but William Roy replied that he hadn't time for that, if Captain Benyon would excuse him. He should have to go straight into the library and write a note to send back to his office, where, as he just remembered, he had neglected to give, in leaving the place, an important direction.

"You can wait a moment, surely," Georgina said. "Captain Benyon wants so much to see you."

"Oh yes, my dear; I can wait a minute, and I can come back."

Benyon saw, accordingly, that he was waiting, and that Georgina was waiting too. Each was waiting for him to say something, though they were waiting for different things. Mr. Roy put his hands behind him, balanced himself on his toes, hoped that Captain Benyon had enjoyed his cruise—though he shouldn't care much for the navy himself—and evidently wondered at the vacuity of his wife's visitor. Benyon knew he was speaking, for he indulged in two or three more observations, after which he stopped. But his meaning was not present to our hero. This personage was conscious of only one thing, of his own momentary power, of everything that hung on his lips; all the rest swam before him; there was vagueness in his ears and eyes. Mr. Roy stopped, as I say, and there was a pause, which seemed to Benyon of tremendous length. He knew, while it lasted, that Georgina was as conscious as himself that he felt his opportunity, that he held it there in his hand, weighing it noiselessly in the palm, and that she braved and scorned, or rather that she enjoyed, the danger. He asked himself whether he should be able to speak if he were to try, and then he knew that he should not, that the words would stick in his throat,[148] that he should make sounds which would dishonour his cause. There was no real choice nor decision, then, on Benyon's part; his silence was after all the same old silence, the fruit of other hours and places, the stillness to which Georgina listened while he felt her eager eyes fairly eat into his face, so that his cheeks burned with the touch of them. The moments stood before him in their turn; each one was distinct. "Ah, well," said Mr. Roy, "perhaps I interrupt; I will just dash off my note." Benyon knew that he was rather bewildered, that he was making a protest, that he was leaving the room; knew presently that Georgina again stood before him alone.

"You are exactly the man I thought you!" she announced, as joyously as if she had won a bet.

"You are the most horrible woman I can imagine. Good God, if I had to live with you!" That is what he said to her in answer.

Even at this she never flinched; she continued to smile in triumph. "He adores me—but what's that to you? Of course you have all the future," she went on; "but I know you as if I had made you!"

Benyon considered a moment. "If he adores you, you are all right. If our divorce is pronounced you will be free, and then he can marry you properly, which he would like ever so much better."

"It's too touching to hear you reason about it. Fancy me telling such a hideous story—about myself—me—me!" And she touched her breasts with her white fingers.

Benyon gave her a look that was charged with all the sickness of his helpless rage. "You—you!" he repeated, as he turned away from her and passed through the door which Mr. Roy had left open.

She followed him into the hall, she was close behind him; he moved before her as she pressed. "There was one more reason," she said. "I wouldn't be forbidden. It was my hideous pride. That's what prevents me now."

"I don't care what it is," Benyon answered, wearily, with his hand on the knob of the door.

She laid hers on his shoulder; he stood there an instant, feeling it, wishing that her loathsome touch gave him the right to strike her to the earth, to strike her so that she should never rise again.

"How clever you are, and intelligent always, as you used to be; to feel so perfectly and know so well—without more scenes—that it's hopeless—my ever consenting! If I have, with you, the shame of having made you promise, let me at least have the profit!"[149]

His back had been turned to her, but at this he glanced round. "To hear you talk of shame——!"

"You don't know what I have gone through; but, of course, I don't ask any pity from you. Only I should like to say something kind to you before we part. I admire you so much. Who will ever tell her, if you don't? How will she ever know, then? She will be as safe as I am. You know what that is," said Georgina, smiling.

He had opened the door wide while she spoke, apparently not heeding her, thinking only of getting away from her for ever. In reality he heard every word she said, and felt to his marrow the lowered, suggestive tone in which she made him that last recommendation. Outside, on the steps—she stood there in the doorway— he gave her his last look. "I only hope you will die. I shall pray for that!" And he descended into the street and took his way.

It was after this that his real temptation came. Not the temptation to return betrayal for betrayal; that passed away even in a few days, for he simply knew that he couldn't break his promise, that it imposed itself on him as stubbornly as the colour of his eyes or the stammer of his lips; it had gone forth into the world to live for itself, and was far beyond his reach or his authority. But the temptation to go through the form of a marriage with Kate Theory, to let her suppose that he was as free as herself and that their children, if they should have any, would, before the law, have a right to exist—this attractive idea held him fast for many weeks, and caused him to pass some haggard nights and days. It was perfectly possible she might never learn his secret, and that, as no one could either suspect it or have an interest in bringing it to light, they both might live and die in security and honour. This vision fascinated him; it was, I say, a real temptation. He thought of other solutions—of telling her that he was married (without telling her to whom), and inducing her to overlook such an accident and content herself with a ceremony in which the world would see no flaw. But after all the contortions of his spirit it remained as clear to him as before that dishonour was in everything but renunciation. So, at last, he renounced. He took two steps which attested this act to himself. He addressed an urgent request to the Secretary of the Navy that he might, with as little delay as possible,

be despatched on another long voyage; and he returned to Boston to tell
Kate Theory that they must wait. He could explain so little that, say what he
would, he was aware that he could not make his conduct seem natural, and
he saw that the girl only trusted him, that she never understood. She trusted
without understanding, and she agreed to wait. When the writer of these
pages last heard of the pair they were waiting still.[150]

A New England Winter

I

MRS. DAINTRY[151] stood on her steps a moment, to address a parting injunction to her little domestic, whom she had induced a few days before, by earnest and friendly argument—the only coercion or persuasion this enlightened mistress was ever known to use—to crown her ruffled tresses with a cap; and then, slowly and with deliberation, she descended to the street. As soon as her back was turned, her maid-servant closed the door, not with violence, but inaudibly, quickly, and firmly; so that when she reached the bottom of the steps and looked up again at the front—as she always did before leaving it, to assure herself that everything was well— the folded wings of her portal were presented to her, smooth and shining, as wings should be, and ornamented with the large silver plate on which the name of her late husband was inscribed—which she had brought with her when, taking the inevitable course of good Bostonians, she had transferred her household goods from the "hill" to the "new land,"[152] and the exhibition of which, as an act of conjugal fidelity, she preferred—how much, those who knew her could easily understand—to the more distinguished modern fashion of suppressing the domiciliary label. She stood still for a minute on the pavement, looking at the closed aperture of her dwelling and asking herself a question; not that there was anything extraordinary in that, for she never spared herself in this respect. She would greatly have preferred that her servant should not shut the door till she had reached the sidewalk and dismissed her, as it were, with that benevolent, that almost maternal, smile with which it was a part of Mrs. Daintry's religion to encourage and reward her domestics. She liked to know that her door was being held open behind her until she should pass out of sight of the young woman standing in the hall. There was a want of respect in shutting her out so precipitately; it was almost like giving her a push down the steps. What Mrs. Daintry asked herself was, whether she should not do right to ascend the steps again, ring the bell, and request Beatrice, the parlour-maid, to be so good as to wait a little longer. She felt that this would have been a proceeding of some importance, and she presently decided against it. There were a good many reasons, and she thought them over as she took her way slowly up Newbury Street, turning as soon as possible into Commonwealth Avenue;[153] for she was very fond of the south side of this beautiful prospect, and the autumn sunshine to-day was delightful. During the moment that she paused, looking up at her house, she had had time to see that everything was as fresh and bright as she could desire. It looked a little too new, perhaps, and Florimond would not like that; for of course his great fondness was for the antique, which was the reason for his remaining year after year in Europe, where, as a young painter of considerable, if not of the highest, promise, he had opportunities to study the most dilapidated buildings.

It was a comfort to Mrs. Daintry, however, to be able to say to herself that he would be struck with her living really very nicely—more nicely, in many ways, than he could possibly be accommodated—that she was sure of—in a small dark *appartement de garçon* in Paris, on the uncomfortable side of the Seine.[154] Her state of mind at present was such that she set the highest value on anything that could possibly help to give Florimond a pleasant impression. Nothing could be too small to count, she said to herself; for she knew that Florimond was both fastidious and observant. Everything that would strike him agreeably would contribute to detain him, so that if there were only enough agreeable things he would perhaps stay four or five months, instead of three, as he had promised—the three that were to date from the day of his arrival in Boston, not from that (an important difference) of his departure from Liverpool,[155] which was about to take place. It was Florimond that Mrs. Daintry had had in mind when, on emerging from the little vestibule, she gave the direction to Beatrice about the position of the door-mat—in which the young woman, so carefully selected, as a Protestant, from the British Provinces,[156] had never yet taken the interest that her mistress expected from such antecedents. It was Florimond also that she had thought of in putting before her parlour-maid the question of donning a badge of servitude in the shape of a neat little muslin coif,[157] adorned with pink ribbon and stitched together by Mrs. Daintry's own beneficent fingers. Naturally there was no obvious connection between the parlour-maid's coiffure and the length of Florimond's stay; that detail was to be only a part of the general effect of American life. It was still Florimond that was uppermost as his mother, on her way up the hill, turned over in her mind that question of the ceremony of the front-door. He had been living in a country in which servants observed more forms, and he would doubtless be shocked at Beatrice's want of patience. An accumulation of such anomalies would at last undermine his loyalty. He would not care for them for himself, of course, but he would care about them for her; coming from France, where, as she knew by his letters, and indeed by her own reading—for she made a remarkably free use of the Athenæum[158]—that the position of a mother was one of the most exalted, he could not fail to be *froissé* at any want of consideration for his surviving parent. As an artist, he could not make up his mind to live in Boston; but he was a good son for all that. He had told her frequently that they might easily live together if she would only come to Paris; but of course she could not do that, with Joanna and her six children round in Clarendon Street,[159] and her responsibilities to her daughter multiplied in the highest degree. Besides, during that winter she spent in Paris, when Florimond was definitely making up his mind, and they had in the evening the most charming conversations, interrupted only by the repeated care of winding-up the lamp,[160] or applying the bellows to the obstinate little fire—during that winter she had felt that Paris was not her element. She had gone to the lectures at the Sorbonne, and she had visited the Louvre[161] as few people did it, catalogue in hand, taking the catalogue volume by volume; but all the while she was thinking of Joanna and her new baby, and how the other three (that was the number then) were getting on while their mother was so much absorbed with the last. Mrs. Daintry, familiar as she was with these anxieties, had not the step of a grandmother; for a mind that was always intent had the effect of refreshing and brightening her years. Responsibility with her was not a weariness, but a joy—at least it was the nearest approach to a joy that she knew, and she did not regard her life as especially cheerless; there were many others that were more denuded. She moved with circumspection, but without reluctance, holding up her head and looking at every one she met with a clear, unaccusing gaze. This expression showed that she took an interest, as she ought, in everything that concerned her fellow-creatures; but there was that also in her whole person which indicated that she went no farther than Christian charity required. It was only with regard to Joanna and that vociferous houseful—so fertile in problems, in opportunities for devotion—that she went really very far. And now to-day, of course, in this matter of Florimond's visit, after an absence of six years; which was perhaps more on her mind than anything had ever been. People who met Mrs. Daintry after she had traversed the Public Garden[162]—she always took that way—and begun to ascend the charming slope of Beacon Street,[163] would never, in spite of the relaxation of her pace as she measured this eminence, have mistaken her for a little old lady who should have crept out, vaguely and timidly, to inhale one of the last mild days. It was easy to see that she was not without a duty, or at least a reason— and indeed Mrs. Daintry had never in her life been left in this predicament. People who knew her ever so little would have felt that she was going to call on a relation; and if they had been to the manner born[164] they would have added a mental hope that her relation was prepared for her visit. No one would have doubted this, however, who had been aware that her steps were directed to the habitation of Miss Lucretia Daintry. Her sister-in-law, her husband's only sister, lived in that commodious nook which is known as Mount Vernon Place; and Mrs. Daintry therefore turned off at Joy Street.[165] By the time she did so, she had quite settled in her mind the question of Beatrice's behaviour in connection with the front-door. She had decided that it would never do to make a formal remonstrance, for it was plain that, in spite of the Old-World training which she hoped the girl might have imbibed in Nova Scotia (where, until lately, she learned, there had been an English garrison),[166] she would in such a case expose herself to the danger of desertion; Beatrice would not consent to stand there holding the door open for nothing. And after all, in the depths of her conscience Mrs. Daintry was not sure that she ought to; she was not sure that this was an act of homage that one human being had a right to exact of another, simply because this other happened to wear a little muslin cap with pink ribbons. It was a service that ministered to her importance, to her dignity, not to her hunger or thirst; and Mrs. Daintry, who had had other foreign advantages besides her winter in Paris, was quite aware that in the United States the machinery for that former kind of tribute was very undeveloped. It was a luxury that one ought not to pretend to enjoy—it was a luxury, indeed, that she probably ought not to presume to desire. At the bottom of her heart Mrs. Daintry suspected that such hankerings were criminal. And yet, turning the thing over, as she turned everything, she could not help coming back to the idea that it would be very pleasant, it would be really delightful, if Beatrice

herself, as a result of the growing refinement of her taste, her transplanta-
tion to a society after all more elaborate than that of Nova Scotia, should
perceive the fitness, the felicity, of such an attitude. This perhaps was too
much to hope; but it did not much matter, for before she had turned into
Mount Vernon Place Mrs. Daintry had invented a compromise. She would
continue to talk to her parlour-maid until she should reach the bottom of
her steps, making earnestly one remark after the other over her shoulder, so
that Beatrice would be obliged to remain on the threshold. It is true that it
occurred to her that the girl might not attach much importance to these
Parthian observations,[167] and would perhaps not trouble herself to wait for
their natural term; but this idea was too fraught with embarrassment to be
long entertained. It must be added that this was scarcely a moment for Mrs.
Daintry to go much into the ethics of the matter, for she felt that her call
upon her sister-in-law was the consequence of a tolerably unscrupulous
determination.

LUCRETIA DAINTRY was at home, for a wonder; but she kept her visitor waiting a quarter of an hour, during which this lady had plenty of time to consider her errand afresh. She was a little ashamed of it; but she did not so much mind being put to shame by Lucretia, for Lucretia did things that were much more ambiguous than any she should have thought of doing. It was even for this that Mrs. Daintry had picked her out, among so many relations, as the object of an appeal in its nature somewhat ambiguous. Nevertheless, her heart beat a little faster than usual as she sat in the quiet parlour, looking about her for the thousandth time at Lucretia's "things," and observing that she was faithful to her old habit of not having her furnace lighted until long after every one else. Miss Daintry had her own habits, and she was the only person her sister-in-law knew who had more reasons than herself. Her taste was of the old fashion, and her drawing-room embraced neither festoons nor Persian rugs, nor plates and *plaques* upon the wall, nor faded stuffs suspended[168] from unexpected projections. Most of the articles it contained dated from the year 1830; and a sensible, reasonable, rectangular arrangement of them abundantly answered to their owner's conception of the decorative. A rosewood sofa against the wall, surmounted by an engraving from Kaulbach;[169] a neatly drawn carpet, faded, but little worn, and sprigged with a floral figure; a chimney-piece of black marble, veined with yellow, garnished with an empire clock[170] and antiquated lamps; half a dozen large mirrors, with very narrow frames; and an immense glazed screen representing, in the livid tints of early worsted-work, a ruined temple overhanging a river—these were some of the more obvious of Miss Daintry's treasures. Her sister-in-law was a votary of the newer school, and had made sacrifices to have everything in black and gilt;[171] but she could not fail to see that Lucretia had some very good pieces. It was a wonder how she made them last, for Lucretia had never been supposed to know much about the keeping of a house, and no one would have thought of asking her how she treated the marble floor of her vestibule, or what measures she took in the spring with regard to her curtains. Her work in life lay outside. She took an interest in questions and institutions, sat on committees, and had views on Female Suffrage[172]—a movement which she strongly opposed. She even wrote letters sometimes to the *Transcript*,[173] not "chatty" and jocular, and signed with a fancy name, but "over" her initials, as the phrase was— every one recognised them—and bearing on some important topic. She was not, however, in the faintest degree slipshod or dishevelled, like some of the ladies of the newspaper and the forum; she had no ink on her fingers, and she wore her bonnet as scientifically poised as the dome of the State House.[174] When you rang at her door-bell you were never kept waiting, and when you entered her dwelling you were not greeted with those culinary odours which, pervading halls and parlours, had in certain other cases been described as the right smell in the wrong place. If Mrs. Daintry was made to wait some time before her hostess appeared, there was nothing extraordinary in this, for none of her friends came down directly, and she never did herself. To come down directly would have seemed to her to betray a frivolous eagerness for the social act.[175] The delay, moreover, not only gave her, as I have said, opportunity to turn over her errand afresh, but enabled her to say to herself, as she had often said before, that though Lucretia had no taste, she had some very good things, and to wonder both how she had kept them so well, and how she had originally got them. Mrs. Daintry knew that they proceeded from her mother and her aunts, who had been supposed to distribute among the children of the second generation the accumulations of the old house in Federal Street,[176] where many Daintrys had been born in the early part of the century. Of course she knew nothing of the principles on which the distribution had been made, but all she could say was that Lucretia had evidently been first in the field. There was apparently no limit to what had come to her. Mrs. Daintry was not obliged to look, to assure herself that there was another clock in the back parlour—which would seem to indicate that all the clocks had fallen to Lucretia. She knew of four other timepieces in other parts of the house, for of course in former years she had often been upstairs; it was only in comparatively recent times that she had renounced that practice. There had been a period when she ascended to the second story as a matter of course, without asking leave. On seeing that her sister-in-law was in neither of the parlours, she mounted and talked with Lucretia at the door of her bedroom, if it happened to be closed. And there had been another season when she stood at the foot of the staircase, and, lifting her voice, inquired of Miss Daintry—who called down with some shrillness in return—whether she might climb, while the maid-servant, wandering away with a vague cachinnation,[177] left her to her own devices. But both of these phases belonged to the past. Lucretia never came into *her* bedroom to-day, nor did she presume to penetrate into Lucretia's; so that she did not know for a long time whether she had renewed her chintz[178] nor whether she had hung in that bower the large photograph of Florimond, presented by Mrs. Daintry herself to his aunt, which had been placed in neither of the parlours. Mrs. Daintry would have given a good deal to know whether this memento had been honoured with a place in her sister-in-law's "chamber"—it was by this name, on each side, that these ladies designated their sleeping-apartment; but she could not bring herself to ask directly, for it would be embarrassing to learn—what was possible—that Lucretia had not paid the highest respect to Florimond's portrait. The point was cleared up by its being revealed to her accidentally that the photograph—an expensive and very artistic one, taken in Paris—had been relegated to the spare-room, or guest-chamber. Miss Daintry was very hospitable, and constantly had friends of her own sex staying with her. They were very apt to be young women in their twenties; and one of them had remarked to Mrs. Daintry that her son's portrait—he must be won-derfully handsome—was the first thing she saw when she woke up in the morning. Certainly Florimond was handsome; but his mother had a lurk-ing suspicion that, in spite of his beauty, his aunt was not fond of him. She doubtless thought he ought to come back and settle down in Boston; he was the first of the Daintrys who had had so much in common with Paris. Mrs. Daintry knew as a fact that, twenty-eight years before, Lucretia, whose opinions even at that period were already wonderfully formed, had not approved of the romantic name which, in a moment of pardonable weak-ness, she had conferred upon her rosy babe. The spinster (she had been as much of a spinster at twenty as she was to-day) had accused her of making a fool of the child. Every one was reading old ballads[179] in Boston then, and Mrs. Daintry had found the name in a ballad. It doubled any anxiety she might feel with regard to her present business to think that, as certain foreign newspapers which her son sent her used to say about ambassadors, Florimond was perhaps not a *persona grata* to his aunt. She reflected, how-ever, that if his fault were in his absenting himself, there was nothing that would remedy it so effectively as his coming home. She reflected, too, that if she and Lucretia no longer took liberties with each other, there was still something a little indiscreet in her purpose this morning. But it fortified and consoled her for everything to remember, as she sat looking at the empire clock, which was a very handsome one, that her husband at least had been disinterested.

Miss Daintry found her visitor in this attitude, and thought it was an expression of impatience; which led her to explain that she had been on the roof of her house with a man who had come to see about repairing it. She had walked all over it, and peeped over the cornice, and not been in the least dizzy; and had come to the conclusion that one ought to know a great deal more about one's roof than was usual.

"I am sure you have never been over yours," she said to her sister-in-law.

Mrs. Daintry confessed with some embarrassment that she had not, and felt, as she did so, that she was superficial and slothful. It annoyed her to reflect that while she supposed, in her new house, she had thought of every-thing, she had not thought of this important feature. There was no one like Lucretia for giving one such reminders.

"I will send Florimond up when he comes," she said; "he will tell me all about it."

"Do you suppose he knows about roofs, except tumbledown ones, in his little pictures? I am afraid it will make him giddy." This had been Miss Daintry's rejoinder, and the tone of it was not altogether reassuring. She was nearly fifty years old; she had a plain, fresh, delightful face, and in whatever part of the world she might have been met, an attentive observer of American life would not have had the least difficulty in guessing what phase of it she represented. She represented the various and enlightened activities which cast their rapid shuttle—in the comings and goings of eager workers—from one side to the other of Boston Common.[180] She had in an eminent degree the physiognomy, the accent, the costume, the con-science, and the little eye-glass, of her native place. She had never sacrificed to the graces, but she inspired unlimited confidence. Moreover, if she was thoroughly in sympathy with the New England capital,[181] she reserved her liberty; she had a great charity, but she was independent and witty; and if she was as earnest as other people, she was not quite so serious. Her voice was a little masculine; and it had been said of her that she didn't care in the least how she looked. This was far from true, for she would not for the world have looked better than she thought was right for so plain a woman.

Mrs. Daintry was fond of calculating consequences; but she was not a coward, and she arrived at her business as soon as possible.

"You know that Florimond sails on the 20th of this month. He will get home by the 1st of December."[182]

"Oh yes, my dear, I know it; everybody is talking about it. I have heard it thirty times. That's where Boston is so small," Lucretia Daintry remarked.

"Well, it's big enough for me," said her sister-in-law. "And of course people notice his coming back; it shows that everything that has been said is false, and that he really does like us."

"He likes his mother, I hope; about the rest I don't know that it matters."

"Well, it certainly will be pleasant to have him," said Mrs. Daintry, who was not content with her companion's tone, and wished to extract from her some recognition of the importance of Florimond's advent. "It will prove how unjust so much of the talk has been."

"My dear woman, I don't know anything about the talk. We make too much fuss about everything. Florimond was an infant when I last saw him."

This was open to the interpretation that too much fuss had been made about Florimond—an idea that accorded ill with the project that had kept Mrs. Daintry waiting a quarter of an hour while her hostess walked about on the roof. But Miss Daintry continued, and in a moment gave her sister-in-law the best opportunity she could have hoped for. "I don't suppose he will bring with him either salvation or the other thing; and if he has decided to winter among the bears,[183] it will matter much more to him than to any one else. But I shall be very glad to see him if he behaves himself; and I needn't tell you that if there is anything I can do for him—" and Miss Daintry, tightening her lips together a little, paused, suiting her action to the idea that professions were usually humbug.

"There is indeed something you can do for him," her sister-in-law hastened to respond; "or something you can do for me, at least," she added, more discreetly.

"Call it for both of you. What is it?" and Miss Daintry put on her eyeglass.

"I know you like to do kindnesses, when they are *real* ones; and you almost always have some one staying with you for the winter."

Miss Daintry stared. "Do you want to put him to live with me?"

"No, indeed! Do you think I could part with him? It's another person—a lady!"

"A lady! Is he going to bring a woman with him?"

"My dear Lucretia, you won't wait. I want to make it as pleasant for him as possible. In that case he may stay longer. He has promised three months; but I should so like to keep him till the summer. It would make me very happy."

"Well, my dear, keep him, then, if you can."

"But I can't, unless I am helped."

"And you want me to help you? Tell me what I must do. Should you wish me to make love to him?"

Mrs. Daintry's hesitation at this point was almost as great as if she had found herself obliged to say yes. She was well aware that what she had come to suggest was very delicate; but it seemed to her at the present moment more delicate than ever. Still, her cause was good, because it was the cause of maternal devotion. "What I should like you to do would be to ask Rachel Torrance to spend the winter with you."

Miss Daintry had not sat so much on committees without getting used to queer proposals, and she had long since ceased to waste time in expressing a vain surprise. Her method was Socratic;[184] she usually entangled her interlocutor in a net of questions.

"Ah, do you want *her* to make love to him?"

"No, I don't want any love at all. In such a matter as that I want Florimond to be perfectly free. But Rachel is such an attractive girl; she is so artistic and so bright."

"I don't doubt it; but I can't invite all the attractive girls in the country. Why don't you ask her yourself?!"

"It would be too marked. And then Florimond might not like her in the same house; he would have too much of her. Besides, she is no relation of mine, you know; the cousinship—such as it is, it is not very close—is on your side. I have reason to believe she would like to come; she knows so little of Boston, and admires it so much. It is astonishing how little idea the New York people have. She would be different from any one here, and that would make a pleasant change for Florimond. She was in Europe so much when she was young. She speaks French perfectly, and Italian, I think, too; and she was brought up in a kind of artistic way. Her father never did anything; but even when he hadn't bread to give his children, he always arranged to have a studio, and they gave musical parties. That's the way Rachel was brought up. But they tell me that it hasn't in the least spoiled her; it has only made her very familiar with life."

"Familiar with rubbish!" Miss Daintry ejaculated.

"My dear Lucretia, I assure you she is a very good girl, or I never would have proposed such a plan as this. She paints very well herself, and tries to sell her pictures. They are dreadfully poor—I don't mean the pictures, but Mrs. Torrance and the rest—and they live in Brooklyn,[185] in some second-rate boarding-house. With that, Rachel has everything about her that would enable her to appreciate Boston. Of course it would be a real kindness, because there would be one less to pay for at the boarding-house. You haven't a son, so you can't understand how a mother feels. I want to prepare everything, to have everything pleasantly arranged. I want to deprive him of every pretext for going away before the summer; because in August—I don't know whether I have told you—I have a kind of idea of going back with him myself. I am so afraid he will miss the artistic side. I don't mind saying that to you, Lucretia, for I have heard you say yourself that you thought it had been left out here. Florimond might go and see Rachel Torrance every day if he liked; of course, being his cousin, and calling her Rachel, it couldn't attract any particular attention. I shouldn't much care if it did," Mrs. Daintry went on, borrowing a certain bravado that in calmer moments was eminently foreign to her nature from the impunity with which she had hitherto proceeded. Her project, as she heard herself unfold it, seemed to hang together so well that she felt something of the intoxication of success. "I shouldn't care if it did," she repeated, "so long as Florimond had a little of the conversation that he is accustomed to, and I was not in perpetual fear of his starting off."

Miss Daintry had listened attentively while her sister-in-law spoke, with eager softness, passing from point to point with a *crescendo*[186] of lucidity, like a woman who had thought it all out and had the consciousness of many reasons on her side. There had been momentary pauses, of which Lucretia had not taken advantage, so that Mrs. Daintry rested at last in the enjoyment of a security that was almost complete and that her companion's first question was not of a nature to dispel.

"It's so long since I have seen her. Is she pretty?" Miss Daintry inquired.

"She is decidedly striking; she has magnificent hair!" her visitor answered, almost with enthusiasm.

"Do you want Florimond to marry her?"

This, somehow, was less pertinent. "Ah, no, my dear," Mrs. Daintry rejoined, very judicially. "That is not the kind of education—the kind of *milieu*—one would wish for the wife of one's son." She knew, moreover, that her sister-in-law knew her opinion about the marriage of young people. It was a sacrament more high and holy than any words could express, the propriety and timeliness of which lay deep in the hearts of the contracting parties, below all interference from parents and friends; it was an inspiration from above, and she would no more have thought of laying a train[187] to marry her son than she would have thought of breaking open his letters. More relevant even than this, however, was the fact that she did not believe he would wish to make a wife of a girl from a slipshod family in Brooklyn, however little he might care to lose sight of the artistic side. It will be observed that she gave Florimond the credit of being a very discriminating young man; and she indeed discriminated for him in cases in which she would not have presumed to discriminate for herself.

"My dear Susan, you are simply the most immoral woman in Boston!" These were the words of which, after a moment, her sister-in-law delivered herself.

Mrs. Daintry turned a little pale. "Don't you think it would be right?" she asked quickly.

"To sacrifice the poor girl to Florimond's amusement? What has she done that you should wish to play her such a trick?" Miss Daintry did not look shocked: she never looked shocked, for even when she was annoyed she was never frightened; but after a moment she broke into a loud, uncompromising laugh—a laugh which her sister-in-law knew of old and regarded as a peculiarly dangerous form of criticism.

"I don't see why she should be sacrificed. She would have a lovely time if she were to come on. She would consider it the greatest kindness to be asked."

"To be asked to come and amuse Florimond."

Mrs. Daintry hesitated a moment. "I don't see why she should object to that. Florimond is certainly not beneath a person's notice. Why, Lucretia, you speak as if there were something disagreeable about Florimond."

"My dear Susan," said Miss Daintry, "I am willing to believe that he is the first young man of his time; but, all the same, it isn't a thing to do."

"Well, I have thought of it in every possible way, and I haven't seen any harm in it. It isn't as if she were giving up anything to come."

"You have thought of it too much, perhaps. Stop thinking for a while. I should have imagined you were more scrupulous."

Mrs. Daintry was silent a moment; she took her sister-in-law's asperity very meekly, for she felt that if she had been wrong in what she proposed she deserved a severe judgment. But why was she wrong? She clasped her hands in her lap and rested her eyes with extreme seriousness upon Lucretia's little *pince-nez*, inviting her to judge her, and too much interested in having the question of her culpability settled to care whether or no she were hurt. "It is very hard to know what is right," she said presently. "Of course it is only a plan; I wondered how it would strike you."

"You had better leave Florimond alone," Miss Daintry answered. "I don't see why you should spread so many carpets for him. Let him shift for himself. If he doesn't like Boston, Boston can spare him."

"You are not nice about him; no, you are not, Lucretia!" Mrs. Daintry cried, with a slight tremor in her voice.

"Of course I am not as nice as you—he is not my son; but I am trying to be nice about Rachel Torrance."

"I am sure she would like him—she would delight in him!" Mrs. Daintry broke out.

"That's just what I'm afraid of; I couldn't stand that."

"Well, Lucretia, I am not convinced," Mrs. Daintry said, rising, with perceptible coldness. "It is very hard to be sure one is not unjust. Of course I shall not expect you to send for her; but I shall think of her with a good deal of compassion, all winter, in that dingy place in Brooklyn. And if you have some one else with you—and I am sure you will, because you always do, unless you remain alone on purpose this year, to put me in the wrong—if you have some one else I shall keep saying to myself: 'Well, after all, it might have been Rachel!'"

Miss Daintry gave another of her loud laughs at the idea that she might remain alone "on purpose." "I shall have a visitor, but it will be some one who will not amuse Florimond in the least. If he wants to go away, it won't be for anything in this house that he will stay."

"I really don't see why you should hate him," said poor Mrs. Daintry.

"Where do you find that? On the contrary, I appreciate him very highly. That's just why I think it very possible that a girl like Rachel Torrance—an odd, uninstructed girl, who hasn't had great advantages—may fall in love with him and break her heart."

Mrs. Daintry's clear eyes expanded, "Is *that* what you are afraid of?"

"Do you suppose my solicitude is for Florimond? An accident of that sort—if she were to show him her heels at the end—might perhaps do him good. But I am thinking of the girl, since you say you don't want him to marry her."

"It was not for that that I suggested what I did. I don't want him to marry any one—I have no plans for that," Mrs. Daintry said, as if she were resenting an imputation.

"Rachel Torrance least of all!" And Miss Daintry indulged still again in that hilarity, so personal to herself, which sometimes made the subject look so little jocular to others. "My dear Susan, I don't blame you," she said; "for I suppose mothers are necessarily unscrupulous. But that is why the rest of us should hold them in check."

"It's merely an assumption, that she would fall in love with him," Mrs. Daintry continued, with a certain majesty; "there is nothing to prove it, and I am not bound to take it for granted."

"In other words, you don't care if she should! Precisely; that, I suppose, is your *rôle*. I am glad I haven't any children; it is very sophisticating.[188] For so good a woman, you are very bad. Yes, you *are* good, Susan; and you *are* bad."

"I don't know that I pretend to be particularly good," Susan remarked, with the warmth of one who had known something of the burden of such a reputation, as she moved toward the door.

"You have a conscience, and it will wake up," her companion returned. "It will come over you in the watches of the night[189] that your idea was—as I have said—immoral."

Mrs. Daintry paused in the hall, and stood there looking at Lucretia. It was just possible that she was being laughed at, for Lucretia's deepest mirth was sometimes silent—that is, one heard the laughter several days later. Suddenly she coloured to the roots of her hair, as if the conviction of her error had come over her. Was it possible she had been corrupted by an affection in itself so pure? "I only want to do right," she said softly. "I would rather he should never come home than that I should go too far."

She was turning away, but her sister-in-law held her a moment and kissed her. "You are a delightful woman, but I won't ask Rachel Torrance!" This was the understanding on which they separated.

III

MISS DAINTRY, after her visitor had left her, recognised that she had been a little brutal; for Susan's proposition did not really strike her as so heinous. Her eagerness to protect the poor girl in Brooklyn was not a very positive quantity, inasmuch as she had an impression that this young lady was on the whole very well able to take care of herself. What her talk with Mrs. Daintry had really expressed was the lukewarmness of her sentiment with regard to Florimond. She had no wish to help his mother lay carpets for him, as she said. Rightly or wrongly, she had a conviction that he was selfish, that he was spoiled, that he was conceited; and she thought Lucretia Daintry meant for better things than the service of sugaring for the young man's lips the pill of a long-deferred visit to Boston. It was quite indifferent to her that he should be conscious, in that city, of unsatisfied needs. At bottom, she had never forgiven him for having sought another way of salvation. Moreover, she had a strong sense of humour, and it amused her more than a little that her sister-in-law—of all women in Boston—should have come to her on that particular errand. It completed the irony of the situation that one should frighten Mrs. Daintry—just a little—about what she had undertaken; and more than once that day Lucretia had, with a smile, the vision of Susan's countenance as she remarked to her that she was immoral. In reality, and speaking seriously, she did not consider Mrs. Daintry's inspiration unpardonable; what was very positive was simply that she had no wish to invite Rachel Torrance for the benefit of her nephew. She was by no means sure that she should like the girl for her own sake, and it was still less apparent that she should like her for that of Florimond. With all this, however, Miss Daintry had a high love of justice; she revised her social accounts from time to time to see that she had not cheated any one. She thought over her interview with Mrs. Daintry the next day, and it occurred to her that she had been a little unfair. But she scarcely knew what to do to repair her mistake, by which Rachel Torrance also had suffered, perhaps; for after all, if it had not been wicked of her sister-in-law to ask such a favour, it had at least been cool; and the penance that presented itself to

Lucretia Daintry did not take the form of despatching a letter to Brooklyn. An accident came to her help, and four days after the conversation I have narrated she wrote her a note which explains itself and which I will presently transcribe. Meanwhile Mrs. Daintry, on her side, had held an examination of her heart; and though she did not think she had been very civilly treated, the result of her reflections was to give her a fit of remorse. Lucretia was right: she had been anything but scrupulous; she had skirted the edge of an abyss. Questions of conduct had long been familiar to her; and the cardinal rule of life in her eyes was, that before one did anything which involved in any degree the happiness or the interest of another, one should take one's motives out of the closet in which they are usually laid away and give them a thorough airing. This operation, undertaken before her visit to Lucretia, had been cursory and superficial; for now that she repeated it, she discovered among the recesses of her spirit a number of nut-like scruples which she was astonished to think she should have overlooked. She had really been very wicked, and there was no doubt about *her* proper penance. It consisted of a letter to her sister-in-law, in which she completely disavowed her little project, attributing it to a momentary intermission of her reason. She saw it would never do, and she was quite ashamed of herself. She did not exactly thank Miss Daintry for the manner in which she had admonished her, but she spoke as one saved from a great danger, and assured her relative of Mount Vernon Place that she should not soon again expose herself. This letter crossed with Miss Daintry's missive, which ran as follows: —

"MY DEAR SUSAN—I have been thinking over our conversation of last Tuesday, and I am afraid I went rather too far in my condemnation of your idea with regard to Rachel Torrance. If I expressed myself in a manner to wound your feelings, I can assure you of my great regret. Nothing could have been further from my thoughts than the belief that you are wanting in delicacy. I know very well that you were prompted by the highest sense of duty. It is possible, however, I think, that your sense of duty to poor Florimond is a little too high. You think of him too much as that famous dragon of antiquity—wasn't it in Crete, or somewhere?—to whom young virgins had to be sacrificed.[190] It may relieve your mind, however, to hear that this particular virgin will probably, during the coming winter, be provided for. Yesterday, at Doll's, where I had gone in to look at the new pictures (there is a striking Appleton Brown[191]), I met Pauline Mesh, whom I had not seen for ages, and had half an hour's talk with her. She seems to me to have come out very much this winter, and to have altogether a higher tone. In short, she is much enlarged, and seems to want to take an interest in something. Of course you will say: Has she not her children? But, somehow, they don't seem to fill her life. You must remember that they are very small as yet to fill anything. Anyway, she mentioned to me her great disappointment in having had to give up her sister, who was to have come on from Baltimore to spend the greater part of the winter. Rosalie is very pretty, and Pauline expected to give a lot of Germans,[192] and make things generally pleasant. I shouldn't wonder if she thought something might happen that would make Rosalie a fixture in our city. She would have liked this immensely; for, whatever Pauline's faults may be, she has plenty of family feeling. But her sister has suddenly got engaged in Baltimore[193] (I believe it's much easier than here), so that the visit has fallen through. Pauline seemed to be quite in despair, for she had made all sorts of beautifications in one of her rooms, on purpose for Rosalie; and not only had she wasted her labour (you know how she goes into those things, whatever we may think, sometimes, of her taste), but she spoke as if it would make a great difference in her winter; said she should suffer a great deal from loneliness. She says Boston is no place for a married woman, standing on her own merits; she can't have any sort of time unless she hitches herself to some attractive girl who will help her to pull the social car. You know that isn't what every one says, and how much talk there has been the last two or three winters about the frisky young matrons. Well, however that may be, I don't pretend to know much about it, not being in the married set. Pauline spoke as if she were really quite high and dry, and I felt so sorry for her that it suddenly occurred to me to say something about Rachel Torrance. I remembered that she is related to Donald Mesh in about the same degree as she is to me—a degree nearer, therefore, than to Florimond. Pauline didn't seem to think much of the relationship—it's so remote; but when I told her that Rachel (strange as it might appear) would probably be thankful for a season in Boston, and might be a good substitute for Rosalie, why she quite jumped at the idea. She has never seen her, but she knows who she is—fortunately, for I could never begin to explain. She seems to think such a girl will be quite a novelty in this place. I don't suppose Pauline can do her any particular harm, from what you tell me of Miss Torrance; and, on the other hand, I don't know that she could injure Pauline. She is certainly very kind (Pauline, of course), and I have no doubt she will immediately write to Brooklyn, and that Rachel will come on. Florimond won't, of course, see as much of her as if she were staying with me, and I don't know that he will particularly care about Pauline Mesh, who, you know, is intensely American; but they will go out a great deal, and he will meet them (if he takes the trouble), and I have no doubt that

Rachel will take the edge off the east wind for him.[194] At any rate I have perhaps done her a good turn. I must confess to you—and it won't surprise you—that I was thinking of her, and not of him, when I spoke to Pauline. Therefore I don't feel that I have taken a risk, but I don't much care if I have. I have my views, but I never worry. I recommend you not to do so either—for you go, I know, from one extreme to the other. I have told you my little story; it was on my mind. Aren't you glad to see the lovely snow? —Ever affectionately yours, L. D.

"*P.S.* —The more I think of it, the more convinced I am that you *will* worry now about the danger for Rachel. Why did I drop the poison into your mind? Of course I didn't say a word about you or Florimond."

This epistle reached Mrs. Daintry, as I have intimated, about an hour after her letter to her sister-in-law had been posted; but it is characteristic of her that she did not for a moment regret having made a retractation rather humble in form, and which proved after all, scarcely to have been needed. The delight of having done that duty carried her over the sense of having given herself away. Her sister-in-law spoke from knowledge when she wrote that phrase about Susan's now beginning to worry from the opposite point of view. Her conscience, like the good Homer,[195] might sometimes nod; but when it woke, it woke with a start; and for many a day afterward its vigilance was feverish. For the moment her emotions were mingled. She thought Lucretia very strange, and that she was scarcely in a position to talk about one's going from one extreme to the other. It was good news to her that Rachel Torrance would probably be on the ground after all, and she was delighted that on Lucretia the responsibility of such a fact should rest. This responsibility, even after her revulsion, as we know, she regarded as grave; she exhaled an almost voluptuous sigh when she thought of having herself escaped from it. What she did not quite understand was Lucretia's apology, and her having, even if Florimond's happiness were not her motive, taken almost the very step which three days before she had so severely criticised. This was puzzling, for Lucretia was usually so consistent. But all the same Mrs. Daintry did not repent of her own penance; on the contrary, she took more and more comfort in it. If, with that, Rachel Torrance should be really useful, it would be delightful.

FLORIMOND DAINTRY had stayed at home for three days after his arrival; he had sat close to the fire, in his slippers, every now and then casting a glance over his shoulders at the hard white world which seemed to glare at him from the other side of the window-panes. He was very much afraid of the cold, and he was not in a hurry to go out and meet it. He had met it, on disembarking in New York, in the shape of a wave of frozen air, which had travelled from some remote point in the West (he was told), on purpose, apparently, to smite him in the face. That portion of his organism tingled yet with it, though the gasping, bewildered look which sat upon his features during the first few hours had quite left it. I am afraid it will be thought he was a young man of small courage; and on a point so delicate I do not hold myself obliged to pronounce. It is only fair to add that it was delightful to him to be with his mother and that they easily spent three days in talking. Moreover he had the company of Joanna and her children, who, after a lit-tle delay, occasioned apparently by their waiting to see whether he would not first come to them, had arrived in a body and had spent several hours. As regards the majority of them, they had repeated this visit several times in the three days, Joanna being obliged to remain at home with the two younger ones. There were four older ones, and their grandmother's house was open to them as a second nursery. The first day, their Uncle Florimond thought them charming; and, as he had brought a French toy for each, it is probable that this impression was mutual. The second day, their little ruddy bodies and woollen clothes seemed to him to have a positive odour of the cold—it was disagreeable to him, and he spoke to his mother about their "wintry smell." The third day they had become very familiar; they called him "Florry;" and he had made up his mind that, to let them loose in that way on his mother, Joanna must be rather wanting in delicacy—not men-tioning this deficiency, however, as yet, for he saw that his mother was not prepared for it. She evidently thought it proper, or at least it seemed inev-itable, that either she should be round at Joanna's or the children should be round in Newbury Street; for "Joanna's" evidently represented primarily the sound of small, loud voices, and the hard breathing that signalised the intervals of romps. Florimond was rather disappointed in his sister, seeing her after a long separation; he remarked to his mother that she seemed completely submerged. As Mrs. Daintry spent most of her time under the waves with her daughter, she had grown to regard this element as sufficiently favourable to life, and was rather surprised when Florimond said to her that he was sorry to see she and his sister appeared to have been converted into a pair of *bonnes d'enfants*. Afterward, however, she perceived what he meant; she was not aware, until he called her attention to it, that the little Merrimans[196] took up an enormous place in the intellectual economy of two households. "You ought to remember that they exist for you, and not you for them," Florimond said to her in a tone of friendly admonition; and he remarked on another occasion that the perpetual presence of children was a great injury to conversation—it kept it down so much; and that in Boston they seemed to be present even when they were absent, inasmuch as most of the talk was about them. Mrs. Daintry did not stop to ask herself what her son knew of Boston, leaving it years before, as a boy, and not having so much as looked out of the window since his return; she was taken up mainly with noting certain little habits of speech which he evidently had formed, and in wondering how they would strike his fellow-citizens. He was very definite and trenchant; he evidently knew perfectly what he thought; and though his manner was not defiant—he had, perhaps, even too many of the forms of politeness, as if sometimes, for mysterious reasons, he were playing upon you—the tone in which he uttered his opinions did not appear exactly to give you the choice. And then apparently he had a great many; there was a moment when Mrs. Daintry vaguely foresaw that the little house in Newbury Street would be more crowded with Florimond's views than it had ever been with Joanna's children. She hoped very much people would like him, and she hardly could see why they should fail to find him agreeable. To herself he was sweeter than any grandchild; he was as kind as if he had been a devoted parent. Florimond had but a small acquaintance with his brother-in-law; but after he had been at home forty-eight hours he found that he bore Arthur Merriman a grudge, and was ready to think rather ill of him—having a theory that he ought to have held up Joanna and interposed to save her mother. Arthur Merriman was a young and brilliant commission-merchant,[197] who had not married Joanna Daintry for the sake of Florimond, and, doing an active business all day in East Boston,[198] had a perfectly good conscience in leaving his children's mother and grandmother to establish their terms of intercourse.

Florimond, however, did not particularly wonder why his brother-in-law had not been round to bid him welcome. It was for Mrs. Daintry that this anxiety was reserved; and what made it worse was her uncertainty as to whether she should be justified in mentioning the subject to Joanna. It might wound Joanna to suggest to her that her husband was derelict— especially if she did not think so, and she certainly gave her mother no opening; and on the other hand Florimond might have ground for complaint if Arthur should continue not to notice him. Mrs. Daintry earnestly desired that nothing of this sort should happen, and took refuge in the hope that Florimond would have adopted the foreign theory of visiting, in accordance with which the newcomer was to present himself first. Meanwhile the young man, who had looked upon a meeting with his brother-in-law as a necessity rather than a privilege, was simply conscious of a reprieve; and up in Clarendon Street, as Mrs. Daintry said, it never occurred to Arthur Merriman to take this social step, nor to his wife to propose it to him. Mrs. Merriman simply took for granted that her brother would be round early some morning to see the children. A day or two later the couple dined at her mother's, and that virtually settled the question. It is true that Mrs. Daintry, in later days, occasionally recalled the fact that, after all, Joanna's husband never had called upon Florimond; and she even wondered why Florimond, who sometimes said bitter things, had not made more of it. The matter came back at moments when, under the pressure of circumstances which, it must be confessed, were rare, she found herself giving assent to an axiom that sometimes reached her ears. This axiom, it must be added, did not justify her in the particular case I have mentioned, for the full purport of it was that the queerness of Bostonians was collective, not individual.

There was no doubt, however, that it was Florimond's place to call first upon his aunt, and this was a duty of which she could not hesitate to remind him. By the time he took his way across the long expanse of the new land and up the charming hill which constitutes, as it were, the speaking face of Boston, the temperature either had relaxed, or he had got used, even in his

mother's hot little house, to his native air. He breathed the bright cold sunshine with pleasure; he raised his eyes to the arching blueness, and thought
he had never seen a dome so magnificently painted.[199] He turned his head
this way and that, as he walked (now that he had recovered his legs, he foresaw that he should walk a good deal), and freely indulged his most valued
organ, the organ that had won him such reputation as he already enjoyed. In
the little artistic circle in which he moved in Paris, Florimond Daintry was
thought to have a great deal of eye. His power of rendering was questioned,
his execution had been called pretentious and feeble; but a conviction had
somehow been diffused that he saw things with extraordinary intensity.
No one could tell better than he what to paint, and what not to paint, even
though his interpretation were sometimes rather too sketchy. It will have
been guessed that he was an impressionist;[200] and it must be admitted that
this was the character in which he proceeded on his visit to Miss Daintry. He
was constantly shutting one eye, to see the better with the other, making a little telescope by curving one of his hands together, waving these members in
the air with vague pictorial gestures, pointing at things which, when people
turned to follow his direction, seemed to mock the vulgar vision by eluding
it. I do not mean that he practised these devices as he walked along Beacon
Street, into which he had crossed shortly after leaving his mother's house;
but now that he had broken the ice he acted quite in the spirit of the reply he
had made to a friend in Paris, shortly before his departure, who asked him
why he was going back to America—"I am going to see how it looks." He
was of course very conscious of his eye; and his effort to cultivate it was both
intuitive and deliberate. He spoke of it freely, as he might have done of a
valuable watch or a horse. He was always trying to get the visual impression;
asking himself, with regard to such and such an object or a place, of what its
"character" would consist. There is no doubt he really saw with great intensity; and the reader will probably feel that he was welcome to this ambiguous privilege. It was not important for him that things should be beautiful;
what he sought to discover was their identity—the signs by which he should
know them. He began this inquiry as soon as he stepped into Newbury
Street from his mother's door, and he was destined to continue it for the first
few weeks of his stay in Boston. As time went on, his attention relaxed; for
one couldn't do more than see, as he said to his mother and another person;
and he had seen. Then the novelty wore off—the novelty which is often so

absurdly great in the eyes of the American who returns to his native land after a few years[201] spent in the foreign element—an effect to be accounted for only on the supposition that in the secret parts of his mind he recognises the aspect of life in Europe as, through long heredity, the more familiar; so that superficially, having no interest to oppose it, it quickly supplants the domestic type, which, upon his return, becomes supreme, but with its credit in many cases appreciably and permanently diminished. Florimond painted a few things while he was in America, though he had told his mother he had come home to rest; but when, several months later, in Paris, he showed his "notes," as he called them, to a friend, the young Frenchman asked him if Massachusetts were really so much like Andalusia.[202]

There was certainly nothing Andalusian in the prospect as Florimond traversed the artificial bosom of the Back Bay.[203] He had made his way promptly into Beacon Street, and he greatly admired that vista. The long straight avenue lay airing its newness in the frosty day, and all its individual facades, with their neat, sharp ornaments, seemed to have been scoured, with a kind of friction, by the hard, salutary light. Their brilliant browns and drabs, their rosy surfaces of brick, made a variety of fresh, violent tones, such as Florimond liked to memorise, and the large clear windows of their curved fronts faced each other, across the street, like candid, inevitable eyes. There was something almost terrible in the windows; Florimond had forgotten how vast and clean they were, and how, in their sculptured frames, the New England air seemed, like a zealous housewife, to polish and preserve them. A great many ladies were looking out, and groups of children, in the drawing-rooms, were flattening their noses against the transparent plate. Here and there, behind it, the back of a statuette or the symmetry of a painted vase, erect on a pedestal, presented itself to the street, and enabled the passer to construct, more or less, the room within—its frescoed ceilings, its new silk sofas, its untarnished fixtures. This continuity of glass constituted a kind of exposure, within and without, and gave the street the appearance of an enormous corridor, in which the public and the private were familiar and intermingled. But it was all very cheerful and commodious, and seemed to speak of diffused wealth, of intimate family life, of comfort constantly renewed. All sorts of things in the region of the temperature had happened during the few days that Florimond had been in the country. The cold wave had spent itself, a snowstorm had come and gone, and the air, after this temporary relaxation, had renewed its keenness. The snow, which had fallen in but moderate abundance, was heaped along the side of the pavement; it formed a radiant cornice on the housetops and crowned the windows with a plain white cap. It deepened the colour of everything else, made all surfaces look ruddy, and at a distance sent into the air a thin, delicate mist—a vaporous blur—which occasionally softened an edge. The upper part of Beacon Street seemed to Florimond charming—the long, wide, sunny slope, the uneven line of the older houses, the contrasted, differing, bulging fronts, the painted bricks, the tidy facings, the immaculate doors, the burnished silver plates, the denuded twigs of the far extent of the Common, on the other side; and to crown the eminence and complete the picture, high in the air, poised in the right place, over everything that clustered below, the most felicitous object in Boston—the gilded dome of the State House. It was in the shadow of this monument, as we know, that Miss Daintry lived; and Florimond, who was always lucky, had the good fortune to find her at home.

V

IT may seem that I have assumed on the part of the reader too great a curiosity about the impressions of this young man, who was not very remarkable, and who has not even the recommendation of being the hero of our perhaps too descriptive tale. The reader will already have discovered that a hero fails us here; but if I go on at all risks to say a few words about Florimond, he will perhaps understand the better why this part has not been filled. Miss Daintry's nephew was not very original; it was his own illusion that he had in a considerable degree the value of rareness. Even this youthful conceit was not rare, for it was not of heroic proportions, and was liable to lapses and discouragements. He was a fair, slim, civil young man, and you would never have guessed from his appearance that he was an impressionist. He was neat and sleek and quite anti-Bohemian,[204] and in spite of his looking about him as he walked, his figure was much more in harmony with the Boston landscape than he supposed. He was a little vain, a little affected, a little pretentious, a little good-looking, a little amusing, a little spoiled, and at times a little tiresome. If he was disagreeable, however, it was also only a little; he did not carry anything to a very high pitch; he was accomplished, industrious, successful—all in the minor degree. He was fond of his mother and fond of himself; he also liked the people who liked him. Such people could belong only to the class of good listeners, for Florimond, with the least encouragement (he was very susceptible to that), would chatter by the hour. As he was very observant, and knew a great many stories, his talk was often entertaining, especially to women, many of whom thought him wonderfully sympathetic. It may be added that he was still very young and fluid, and neither his defects nor his virtues had a great consistency. He was fond of the society of women, and had an idea that he knew a great deal about that element of humanity. He believed himself to know everything about art, and almost everything about life, and he expressed himself as much as possible in the phrases that are current in studios. He spoke French very well, and it had rubbed off on his English.

His aunt listened to him attentively, with her nippers on her nose. She
had been a little restless at first, and, to relieve herself, had vaguely punched
the sofa-cushion which lay beside her—a gesture that her friends always
recognised; they knew it to express a particular emotion. Florimond, whose
egotism was candid and confiding, talked for an hour about himself—about
what he had done, and what he intended to do, what he had said and what
had been said to him; about his habits, tastes, achievements, peculiarities,
which were apparently so numerous; about the decorations of his studio
in Paris; about the character of the French, the works of Zola,[205] the theory of art for art,[206] the American type, the "stupidity" of his mother's new
house—though of course it had some things that were knowing—the
pronunciation of Joanna's children,[207] the effect of the commission-busi-
ness on Arthur Merriman's conversation, the effect of everything on his
mother, Mrs. Daintry, and the effect of Mrs. Daintry on her son Florimond.
The young man had an epithet which he constantly introduced to express
disapproval; when he spoke of the architecture of his mother's house,
over which she had taken great pains (she remembered the gabled fronts
of Nuremberg[208]), he said that a certain effect had been dreadfully missed,
that the character of the doorway was simply "crass." He expressed, however, a lively sense of the bright cleanness of American interiors. "Oh, as
for that," he said, "the place is kept—it's kept;"[209] and, to give an image of
this idea, he put his gathered fingers to his lips[210] an instant, seemed to kiss
them or blow upon them, and then opened them into the air. Miss Daintry
had never encountered this gesture before; she had heard it described by
travelled persons; but to see her own nephew in the very act of it led her to
administer another thump to the sofa-cushion. She finally got this article
under control, and sat more quiet, with her hands clasped upon it, while her
visitor continued to discourse. In pursuance of his character as an impressionist, he gave her a great many impressions; but it seemed to her that as
he talked, he simply exposed himself—exposed his egotism, his little pretensions. Lucretia Daintry, as we know, had a love of justice, and though her
opinions were apt to be very positive, her charity was great and her judgments were not harsh; moreover, there was in her composition not a drop of
acrimony. Nevertheless, she was, as the phrase is, rather hard on poor little
Florimond; and to explain her severity we are bound to assume that in the
past he had in some way offended her. To-day, at any rate, it seemed to her

that he patronised his maiden-aunt. He scarcely asked about her health, but took for granted on her part an unlimited interest in his own sensations. It came over her afresh that his mother had been absurd in thinking that the usual resources of Boston would not have sufficed to maintain him; and she smiled a little grimly at the idea that a special provision should have been made. This idea presently melted into another, over which she was free to regale herself only after her nephew had departed. For the moment she contented herself with saying to him, when a pause in his young eloquence gave her a chance—"You will have a great many people to go and see. You pay the penalty of being a Bostonian; you have several hundred cousins. One pays for everything."

Florimond lifted his eyebrows. "I pay for that every day of my life. Have I got to go and see them all?"

"All—every one," said his aunt, who in reality did not hold this obligation in the least sacred.

"And to say something agreeable to them all?" the young man went on.

"Oh no, that is not necessary," Miss Daintry rejoined, with more exactness. "There are one or two, however, who always appreciate a pretty speech." She added in an instant, "Do you remember Mrs. Mesh?"

"Mrs. Mesh?" Florimond apparently did not remember.

"The wife of Donald Mesh; your grandfathers were first cousins. I don't mean her grandfather, but her husband's. If you don't remember her, I suppose he married her after you went away."

"I remember Donald; but I never knew he was a relation. He was single then, I think."

"Well, he's double now," said Miss Daintry; "he's triple, I may say, for there are two ladies in the house."

"If you mean he's a polygamist—are there Mormons even here?"[211] Florimond, leaning back in his chair, with his elbow on the arm, and twisting with his gloved fingers the point of a small fair moustache, did not appear to have been arrested by this account of Mr. Mesh's household; for he almost immediately asked, in a large, detached way—"Are there any nice women here?"

"It depends on what you mean by nice women: there are some very sharp ones."

"Oh, I don't like sharp ones," Florimond remarked, in a tone which made his aunt long to throw her sofa-cushion at his head. "Are there any pretty ones?"

She looked at him a moment, hesitating. "Rachel Torrance is pretty, in a strange, unusual way—black hair and blue eyes, a serpentine figure, old coins in her tresses; that sort of thing."[212]

"I have seen a good deal of that sort of thing," said Florimond, abstractedly.

"That I know nothing about. I mention Pauline Mesh's as one of the houses that you ought to go to, and where I know you are expected."

"I remember now that my mother has said something about that. But who is the woman with coins in her hair?—what has she to do with Pauline Mesh?"

"Rachel is staying with her; she came from New York a week ago, and I believe she means to spend the winter. She isn't a woman, she's a girl."

"My mother didn't speak of her," said Florimond; "but I don't think she would recommend me a girl with a serpentine figure."

"Very likely not," Miss Daintry answered, dryly. "Rachel Torrance is a far-away cousin of Donald Mesh, and consequently of mine and of yours. She's an artist, like yourself; she paints flowers on little panels and *plaques*."[213]

"Like myself?—I never painted a *plaque* in my life! "exclaimed Florimond, staring.

"Well, she's a model also; you can paint her if you like; she has often been painted, I believe."

Florimond had begun to caress the other tip of his moustache. "I don't care for women who have been painted before. I like to find them out. Besides, I want to rest this winter."

His aunt was disappointed; she wished to put him into relation with Rachel Torrance, and his indifference was an obstacle. The meeting was sure to take place sooner or later, but she would have been glad to precipitate it, and, above all, to quicken her nephew's susceptibilities. "Take care you are not found out yourself!" she exclaimed, tossing away her sofa-cushion and getting up.

Florimond did not see what she meant, and he accordingly bore her no rancour; but when, before he took his leave, he said to her, rather irrelevantly, that if he should find himself in the mood during his stay in Boston, he should like to do her portrait—she had such a delightful face—she almost thought the speech a deliberate impertinence. "Do you mean that you have discovered me—that no one has suspected it before?" she inquired with a laugh, and a little flush in the countenance that he was so good as to appreciate.

Florimond replied, with perfect coolness and good-nature, that he didn't know about this, but that he was sure no one had seen her in just the way he saw her; and he waved his hand in the air with strange circular motions, as if to evoke before him the image of a canvas, with a figure just rubbed in. He repeated this gesture, or something very like it, by way of farewell, when he quitted his aunt, and she thought him insufferably patronising.

This is why she wished him, without loss of time, to make the acquaintance of Rachel Torrance, whose treatment of his pretensions she thought would be salutary. It may now be communicated to the reader—after a delay proportionate to the momentousness of the fact—that this had been the idea which suddenly flowered in her brain, as she sat face to face with her irritating young visitor. It had vaguely shaped itself after her meeting with that strange girl from Brooklyn, whom Mrs. Mesh, all gratitude—for she liked strangeness—promptly brought to see her; and her present impression of her nephew rapidly completed it. She had not expected to take an interest in Rachel Torrance, and could not see why, through a freak of Susan's, she should have been called upon to think so much about her; but, to her surprise, she perceived that Mrs. Daintry's proposed victim was not the usual forward girl. She perceived at the same time that it had been ridiculous to think of Rachel as a victim—to suppose that she was in danger of vainly fixing her affections upon Florimond. She was much more likely to triumph than to suffer; and if her visit to Boston were to produce bitter fruits, it would not be she who should taste them. She had a striking, oriental head, a beautiful smile, a manner of dressing which carried out her exotic type, and a great deal of experience and wit. She evidently knew the world, as one knows it when one has to live by its help. If she had an aim in life, she would draw her bow well above the tender breast of Florimond Daintry. With all this, she certainly was an honest, obliging girl, and had a sense of humour which was a fortunate obstacle to her falling into a pose. Her coins and amulets and seamless garments were, for her, a part of the general joke of one's looking like a Circassian or a Smyrniote[214]—an accident for which nature was responsible; and it may be said of her that she took herself much less seriously than other people took her. This was a defect for which Lucretia Daintry had a great kindness; especially as she quickly saw that Rachel was not of an insipid paste, as even triumphant coquettes sometimes are. In spite of her poverty and the opportunities her beauty must have brought her, she had not yet seen fit to marry—which was a proof that she was clever as well as disinterested. It looks dreadfully cold-blooded as I write it here, but the notion that this capable creature might administer poetic justice to Florimond gave a measurable satisfaction to Miss Daintry. He was in distinct need of a snub, for down in Newbury Street his mother was perpetually swinging the censer;[215] and no young nature could stand that sort of thing—least of all such a nature as Florimond's. She said to herself that such a "putting in his place" as he might receive from Rachel Torrance would probably be a permanent correction. She wished his good, as she wished the good of every one; and that desire was at the bottom of her vision. She knew perfectly what she should like: she should like him to fall in love with Rachel, as he probably would, and to have no doubt of her feeling immensely honoured. She should like Rachel to encourage him just enough—just so far as she might, without being false. A little would do, for Florimond would always take his success for granted. To this point did the study of her nephew's moral regeneration bring the excellent woman who a few days before had accused his mother of a lack of morality. His mother was thinking only of his pleasure; *she* was thinking of his immortal spirit. She should like Rachel to tell him at the end that he was a presumptuous little boy, and that since it was his business to render "impressions" he might see what he could do with that of having been jilted. This extraordinary flight of fancy on Miss Daintry's part was caused in some degree by the high spirits which sprang from her conviction, after she met the young lady, that Mrs. Mesh's companion was not in danger; for even when she wrote to her sister-in-law in the manner the reader knows, her conscience was not wholly at rest. There was still a risk, and she knew not why she should take risks for Florimond. Now, however, she was prepared to be perfectly happy when she should hear that the young man was constantly in Arlington Street;[216] and at the end of a little month she enjoyed this felicity.

VI

MRS. MESH sat on one side of the fire, and Florimond on the other; he had by this time acquired the privilege of a customary seat. He had taken a general view of Boston. It was like a first introduction, for before his going to live in Paris he had been too young to judge; and the result of this survey was the conviction that there was nothing better than Mrs. Mesh's drawing-room. She was one of the few persons whom one was certain to find at home after five o'clock; and the place itself was agreeable to Florimond, who was very fastidious about furniture and decorations. He was willing to concede that Mrs. Mesh (the relationship had not yet seemed close enough to justify him in calling her Pauline) knew a great deal about such matters; though it was clear that she was indebted for some of her illumination to Rachel Torrance, who had induced her to make several changes. These two ladies, between them, represented a great fund of taste; with a difference that was a result of Rachel's knowing clearly beforehand what she liked (Florimond called her, at least, by her baptismal name), and Mrs. Mesh's only knowing it after a succession of experiments, of transposings and drapings, all more or less ingenious and expensive. If Florimond liked Mrs. Mesh's drawing-room better than any other corner of Boston, he also had his preference in regard to its phases and hours. It was most charming in the winter twilight, by the glow of the fire, before the lamps had been brought in. The ruddy flicker played over many objects, making them look more mysterious than Florimond had supposed anything could look in Boston, and, among others, upon Rachel Torrance, who, when she moved about the room in a desultory way (never so much *enfoncée*, as Florimond said, in a chair as Mrs. Mesh was) certainly attracted and detained the eye. The young man from his corner (he was almost as much *enfoncé* as Mrs. Mesh) used to watch her; and he could easily see what his aunt had meant by saying she had a serpentine figure. She was slim and flexible, she took attitudes which would have been awkward in other women, but which her charming pliancy made natural. She reminded him of a celebrated actress in Paris who was the ideal of tortuous thinness.[217] Miss Torrance used often

146

to seat herself for a short time at the piano; and though she never had been taught this art (she played only by ear), her musical feeling was such that she charmed the twilight hour. Mrs. Mesh sat on one side of the fire, as I have said, and Florimond on the other; the two might have been found in this relation—listening, face to face—almost any day in the week. Mrs. Mesh raved about her new friend, as they said in Boston—I mean about Rachel Torrance, not about Florimond Daintry. She had at last got hold of a mind that understood her own (Mrs. Mesh's mind contained depths of mystery), and she sacrificed herself, generally, to throw her companion into relief.[218] Her sacrifice was rewarded, for the girl was universally liked and admired; she was a new type altogether; she was the lioness of the winter.[219] Florimond had an opportunity to see his native town in one of its fits of enthusiasm. He had heard of the infatuations of Boston, literary and social; of its capacity for giving itself with intensity to a temporary topic; and he was now conscious, on all sides, of the breath of New England discussion. Some one had said to him—or had said to some one, who repeated it— that there was no place like Boston for taking up with such seriousness a second-rate spinster from Brooklyn. But Florimond himself made no criticism; for, as we know, he speedily fell under the charm of Rachel Torrance's personality. He was perpetually talking with Mrs. Mesh about it; and when Mrs. Mesh herself descanted on the subject, he listened with the utmost attention. At first, on his return, he rather feared the want of topics; he foresaw that he should miss the talk of the studios, of the theatres, of the boulevard, of a little circle of "naturalists" (in literature and art)[220] to which he belonged, without sharing all its views. But he presently perceived that Boston, too, had its actualities,[221] and that it even had this in common with Paris—that it gave its attention most willingly to a female celebrity. If he had had any hope of being himself the lion of the winter, it had been dissipated by the spectacle of his cousin's success. He saw that while she was there he could only be a subject of secondary reference. He bore her no grudge for this. I must hasten to declare that from the pettiness of this particular jealousy poor Florimond was quite exempt. Moreover, he was swept along by the general chorus; and he perceived that when one changes one's sky,[222] one inevitably changes, more or less, one's standard. Rachel Torrance was neither an actress, nor a singer, nor a beauty, nor one of the ladies who were chronicled in the *Figaro*,[223] nor the author of a successful book, nor a person of the great world; she had neither a future, nor a past, nor a position, nor even a husband, to make her identity more solid; she was a simple American girl, of the class that lived in *pensions* (a class of which Florimond had ever entertained a theoretic horror); and yet she had profited to the degree of which our young man was witness, by those treasures of sympathy constantly in reserve in the American public (as has already been intimated) for the youthful-feminine. If Florimond was struck with all this, it may be imagined whether or not his mother thought she had been clever when it occurred to her (before any one else) that Rachel would be a resource for the term of hibernation. She had forgotten all her scruples and hesitations; she only knew she had seen very far. She was proud of her prescience, she was even amused with it; and for the moment she held her head rather high. No one knew of it but Lucretia—for she had never confided it to Joanna, of whom she would have been more afraid in such a connection even than of her sister-in-law; but Mr. and Mrs. Merriman perceived an unusual lightness in her step, a fitful sparkle in her eye. It was of course easy for them to make up their mind that she was exhilarated to this degree by the presence of her son; especially as he seemed to be getting on beautifully in Boston.

"She stays out longer every day; she is scarcely ever home to tea," Mrs. Mesh remarked, looking up at the clock on the chimney-piece.

Florimond could not fail to know to whom she alluded, for it has been intimated that between these two there was much conversation about Rachel Torrance. "It's funny, the way the girls run about alone here," he said, in the amused, contemplative tone in which he frequently expressed himself on the subject of American life. "Rachel stays out after dark, and no one thinks any the worse of her."

"Oh, well, she's old enough," Mrs. Mesh rejoined, with a little sigh, which seemed to suggest that Rachel's age was really affecting. Her eyes had been opened by Florimond to many of the peculiarities of the society that surrounded her; and though she had spent only as many months in Europe as her visitor had spent years, she now sometimes spoke as if she thought the manners of Boston more odd even than he could pretend to do. She was very quick at picking up an idea, and there was nothing she desired more than to have the last on every subject. This winter, from her two new friends, Florimond and Rachel, she had extracted a great many that were new to her;

the only trouble was that, coming from different sources, they sometimes contradicted each other. Many of them, however, were very vivifying; they added a new zest to that prospect of life which had always, in winter, the denuded bushes, the solid pond, the plank-covered walks, the exaggerated bridge, the patriotic statues,[224] the dry, hard texture, of the Public Garden for its foreground, and for its middle distance the pale, frozen twigs, stiff in the windy sky that whistled over the Common, the domestic dome of the State House, familiar in the untinted air, and the competitive spires of a liberal faith.[225] Mrs. Mesh had an active imagination, and plenty of time on her hands. Her two children were young, and they slept a good deal; she had explained to Florimond, who observed that she was a great deal less in the nursery than his sister, that she pretended only to give her attention to their waking hours. "I have people for the rest of the time," she said; and the rest of the time was considerable; so that there were very few obstacles to her cultivation of ideas. There was one in her mind now, and I may as well impart it to the reader without delay. She was not quite so delighted with Rachel Torrance as she had been a month ago; it seemed to her that the young lady took up—socially speaking—too much room in the house; and she wondered how long she intended to remain, and whether it would be possible, without a direct request, to induce her to take her way back to Brooklyn. This last was the conception with which she was at present engaged; she was at moments much pressed by it, and she had thoughts of taking Florimond Daintry into her confidence. This, however, she determined not to do, lest he should regard it as a sign that she was jealous of her companion. I know not whether she was, but this I know—that Mrs. Mesh was a woman of a high ideal and would not for the world have appeared so. If she was jealous, this would imply that she thought Florimond was in love with Rachel; and she could only object to that on the ground of being in love with him herself. She was not in love with him, and had no intention of being; of this the reader, possibly alarmed, may definitely rest assured. Moreover, she did not think him in love with Rachel; as to her reason for this reserve, I need not, perhaps, be absolutely outspoken. She was not jealous, she would have said; she was only oppressed—she was a little over-ridden. Rachel pervaded her house, pervaded her life, pervaded Boston; every one thought it necessary to talk to her about Rachel, to rave about her in the Boston manner, which seemed to Mrs. Mesh, in spite of the Puritan tradition,[226] very much more unbridled than that of Baltimore. They thought it would give her pleasure; but by this time she knew everything about Rachel. The girl had proved rather more of a figure than she expected; and though she could not be called pretentious, she had the air, in staying with Pauline Mesh, of conferring rather more of a favour than she received. This was absurd for a person who was, after all, though not in her first youth, only a girl, and who, as Mrs. Mesh was sure from her biography—for Rachel had related every item—had never before had such unrestricted access to the fleshpots.[227] The fleshpots were full, under Donald Mesh's roof, and his wife could easily believe that the poor girl would not be in a hurry to return to her boarding-house in Brooklyn. For that matter there were lots of people in Boston who would be delighted that she should come to them. It was doubtless an inconsistency on Mrs. Mesh's part that if she was overdone with the praises of Rachel Torrance which fell from every lip, she should not herself have forborne to broach the topic. But I have sufficiently intimated that it had a perverse fascination for her; it is true she did not speak of Rachel only to praise her. Florimond, in truth, was a little weary of the young lady's name; he had plenty of topics of his own, and he had his own opinion about Rachel Torrance. He did not take up Mrs. Mesh's remark as to her being old enough.

"You must wait till she comes in. Please ring for tea," said Mrs. Mesh, after a pause. She had noticed that Florimond was comparing his watch with her clock; it occurred to her that he might be going.

"Oh, I always wait, you know; I like to see her when she has been any-where. She tells one all about it, and describes everything so well."

Mrs. Mesh looked at him a moment. "She sees a great deal more in things than I am usually able to discover. She sees the most extraordinary things in Boston."

"Well, so do I," said Florimond, placidly.

"Well, I don't, I must say!" She asked him to ring again; and then, with a slight irritation, accused him of not ringing hard enough; but before he could repeat the operation she left her chair and went herself to the bell. After this she stood before the fire a moment, gazing into it; then suggested to Florimond that he should put on a log.

"Is it necessary—when your servant is coming in a moment?" the young man asked, unexpectedly, without moving. In an instant, however, he rose; and then he explained that this was only his little joke.

"Servants are too stupid," said Mrs. Mesh. "But I spoil you. What would your mother say?" She watched him while he placed the log. She was plump, and she was not tall; but she was a very pretty woman. She had round brown eyes, which looked as if she had been crying a little—she had nothing in life to cry about; and dark, wavy hair, which here and there, in short, crisp tendrils, escaped artfully from the form in which it was dressed. When she smiled, she showed very pretty teeth; and the combination of her touching eyes and her parted lips was at such moments almost bewitching. She was accustomed to express herself in humorous superlatives, in pictorial circumlocutions; and had acquired in Boston the rudiments of a social dialect which, to be heard in perfection, should be heard on the lips of a native.[228] Mrs. Mesh had picked it up; but it must be confessed that she used it without originality. It was an accident that on this occasion she had not expressed her wish for her tea by saying that she should like a pint or two of that Chinese fluid.

"My mother believes I can't be spoiled," said Florimond, giving a little push with his toe to the stick that he had placed in the embers; after which he sank back into his chair, while Mrs. Mesh resumed possession of her own. "I am ever fresh—ever pure."

"You are ever conceited. I don't see what you find so extraordinary in Boston," Mrs. Mesh added, reverting to his remark of a moment before.

"Oh, everything! the ways of the people, their ideas, their peculiar *cachet*. The very expression of their faces amuses me."

"Most of them have no expression at all."

"Oh, you are used to it," Florimond said. "You have become one of themselves; you have ceased to notice."

"I am more of a stranger than you; I was born beneath other skies. Is it possible that you don't know yet that I am a native of Baltimore? 'Maryland, my Maryland!'"[229]

"Have they got so much expression in Maryland? No, I thank you; no tea. Is it possible," Florimond went on, with the familiarity of pretended irritation, "is it possible that you haven't noticed yet that I never take it? *Boisson fade, écœurante*,[230] as Balzac calls it."

"Ah, well, if you don't take it on account of Balzac!" said Mrs. Mesh. "I never saw a man who had such fantastic reasons. Where, by the way, is the volume of that depraved old author you promised to bring me?"

"When do you think he flourished? You call everything old, in this country, that isn't in the morning paper. I haven't brought you the volume,
because I don't want to bring you presents," Florimond said; "I want you to
love me for myself, as they say in Paris."

"Don't quote what they say in Paris! Don't profane this innocent bower
with those fearful words!" Mrs. Mesh rejoined, with a jocose intention.
"Dear lady, your son is not everything we could wish!" she added in the same
mock-dramatic tone, as the curtain of the door was lifted, and Mrs. Daintry
rather timidly advanced. Mrs. Daintry had come to satisfy a curiosity,
after all quite legitimate; she could no longer resist the impulse to ascertain for herself, so far as she might, how Rachel Torrance and Florimond
were getting on. She had had no definite expectation of finding Florimond
at Mrs. Mesh's; but she supposed that at this hour of the afternoon—it was
already dark, and the ice, in many parts of Beacon Street, had a polish which
gleamed through the dusk—she should find Rachel. "Your son has lived
too long in far-off lands; he has dwelt among outworn things,"²³¹ Mrs. Mesh
went on, as she conducted her visitor to a chair. "Dear lady, you are not as
Balzac was; do you start at the mention of his name? —therefore you will
have some tea in a little painted cup."

Mrs. Daintry was not bewildered, though it may occur to the reader that
she might have been; she was only a little disappointed. She had hoped she
might have occasion to talk about Florimond; but the young man's presence was a denial of this privilege. "I am afraid Rachel is not at home," she
remarked. "I am afraid she will think I have not been very attentive."

"She will be in in a moment; we are waiting for her," Florimond said.
"It's impossible she should think any harm of you. I have told her too much
good."

"Ah, Mrs. Daintry, don't build too much on what he has told her! He's a
false and faithless man!" Pauline Mesh interposed; while the good lady from
Newbury Street, smiling at this adjuration, but looking a little grave, turned
from one of her companions to the other. Florimond had relapsed into his
chair by the fireplace; he sat contemplating the embers, and fingering the tip
of his moustache. Mrs. Daintry imbibed her tea, and told how often she had
slipped coming down the hill. These expedients helped her to wear a quiet
face; but in reality she was nervous, and she felt rather foolish. It came over
her that she was rather dishonest; she had presented herself at Mrs. Mesh's

in the capacity of a spy. The reader already knows she was subject to sudden revulsions of feeling. There is an adage about repenting at leisure;[232] but Mrs. Daintry always repented in a hurry.

There was something in the air—something impalpable, magnetic— that told her she had better not have come; and even while she conversed with Mrs. Mesh she wondered what this mystic element could be. Of course she had been greatly preoccupied, these last weeks; for it had seemed to her that her plan with regard to Rachel Torrance was succeeding only too well. Florimond had frankly accepted her in the spirit in which she had been offered, and it was very plain that she was helping him to pass his winter. He was constantly at the house—Mrs. Daintry could not tell exactly how often; but she knew very well that in Boston, if one saw anything of a person, one saw a good deal. At first he used to speak of it; for two or three weeks he had talked a good deal about Rachel Torrance. More lately, his allusions had become few; yet to the best of Mrs. Daintry's belief his step was often in Arlington Street. This aroused her suspicions, and at times it troubled her conscience; there were moments when she wondered whether, in arranging a genial winter for Florimond, she had also prepared a season of torment for herself. Was he in love with the girl, or had he already discovered that the girl was in love with him? The delicacy of either situation would account for his silence. Mrs. Daintry said to herself that it would be a grim joke if she should prove to have plotted only too well. It was her sister-in-law's warning in especial that haunted her imagination, and she scarcely knew, at times, whether more to hope that Florimond might have been smitten, or to pray that Rachel might remain indifferent. It was impossible for Mrs. Daintry to shake off the sense of responsibility; she could not shut her eyes to the fact that she had been the prime mover.[233] It was all very well to say that the situation, as it stood, was of Lucretia's making; the thing never would have come into Lucretia's head if she had not laid it before her. Unfortunately, with the quiet life she led, she had very little chance to observe; she went out so little, that she was reduced to guessing what the manner of the two young persons might be to each other when they met in society, and she should have thought herself wanting in delicacy if she had sought to be intimate with Rachel Torrance. Now that her plan was in operation, she could make no attempt to foster it, to acknowledge it in the face of Heaven. Fortunately, Rachel had so many attentions, that there was no fear of her missing those of Newbury Street. She had dined there once, in the first days of her sojourn, without Pauline and Donald, who had declined, and with Joanna and Joanna's husband for all "company." Mrs. Daintry had noticed nothing particular then, save that Arthur Merriman talked rather more than usual—though he was always a free talker—and had bantered Rachel rather more familiarly than was perhaps necessary (considering that *he*, after all, was not her cousin) on her ignorance of Boston, and her thinking that Pauline Mesh could tell her anything about it. On this occasion Florimond talked very little; of course he could not say much when Arthur was in such extraordinary spirits. She knew by this time all that Florimond thought of his brother-in-law, and she herself had to confess that she liked Arthur better in his jaded hours, even though then he was a little cynical. Mrs. Daintry had been perhaps a little disappointed in Rachel, whom she saw for the first time in several years. The girl was less peculiar than she remembered her being, savoured less of the old studio, the musical parties, the creditors waiting at the door. However, people in Boston found her unusual, and Mrs. Daintry reflected, with a twinge at her depravity, that perhaps she had expected something too dishevelled.[234] At any rate, several weeks had elapsed since then, and there had been plenty of time for Miss Torrance to attach herself to Florimond. It was less than ever Mrs. Daintry's wish that he should (even in this case) ask her to be his wife. It seemed to her less than ever the way her son should marry—because he had got entangled with a girl in consequence of his mother's rashness. It occurred to her, of course, that she might warn the young man; but when it came to the point she could not bring herself to speak. She had never discussed the question of love with him, and she didn't know what ideas he might have brought with him from Paris. It was too delicate; it might put notions into his head. He might say something strange and French, which she shouldn't like; and then perhaps she should feel bound to warn Rachel herself—a complication from which she absolutely shrank. It was part of her embarrassment now, as she sat in Mrs. Mesh's drawing-room, that she should probably spoil Florimond's entertainment for this afternoon, and that such a crossing of his inclination would make him the more dangerous. He had told her that he was waiting for Rachel to come in; and at the same time, in view of the lateness of the hour and her being on foot, when she herself should take her leave he would be bound in decency to accompany her. As for remaining after Rachel should come in, that was an indiscretion which scarcely seemed to her possible. Mrs. Daintry was an American mother, and she knew what the elder generation owes to the younger. If Florimond had come there to call on a young lady, he didn't, as they used to say, want any mothers round. She glanced covertly at her son, to try and find some comfort in his countenance; for her perplexity was heavy. But she was struck only with his looking very handsome, as he lounged there in the firelight, and with his being very much at home. This did not lighten her burden, and she expressed all the weight of it—in the midst of Mrs. Mesh's flights of comparison—in an irrelevant little sigh. At such a time her only comfort could be the thought that at all events she had not betrayed herself to Lucretia. She had scarcely exchanged a word with Lucretia about Rachel since that young lady's arrival; and she had observed in silence that Miss Daintry now had a guest in the person of a young woman who had lately opened a kindergarten. This reticence might surely pass for natural.

Rachel came in before long, but even then Mrs. Daintry ventured to stay a little. The visitor from Brooklyn embraced Mrs. Mesh, who told her that, prodigal as she was, there was no fatted calf[235] for her return; she must content herself with cold tea. Nothing could be more charming than her manner, which was full of native archness; and it seemed to Mrs. Daintry that she directed her pleasantries at Florimond with a grace that was intended to be irresistible. The relation between them was a relation of "chaff,"[236] and consisted, on one side and the other, in alternations of attack and defence. Mrs. Daintry reflected that she should not wish her son to have a wife who should be perpetually turning him into a joke; for it seemed to her, perhaps, that Rachel Torrance put in her thrusts rather faster than Florimond could parry them. She was evidently rather wanting in the faculty of reverence, and Florimond panted a little. They presently went into an adjoining room, where the lamplight was brighter; Rachel wished to show the young man an old painted fan, which she had brought back from the repairer's. They remained there ten minutes. Mrs. Daintry, as she sat with Mrs. Mesh, heard their voices much intermingled. She wished very much to confide herself a little to Pauline—to ask her whether she thought Rachel was in love with Florimond. But she had a foreboding that this would not be safe; Pauline was capable of repeating her question to the others, of calling out to Rachel

155

to come back and answer it. She contented herself, therefore, with asking her hostess about the little Meshes, and regaling her with anecdotes of Joanna's progeny.

"Don't you ever have your little ones with you at this hour?" she inquired. "You know this is what Longfellow calls the children's hour."[237]

Mrs. Mesh hesitated a moment. "Well, you know, one can't have everything at once. I have my social duties now; I have my guests. I have Miss Torrance—you see she is not a person one can overlook."

"I suppose not," said poor Mrs. Daintry, remembering how little she herself had overlooked her.

"Have you done brandishing that superannuated relic?" Mrs. Mesh asked of Rachel and Florimond, as they returned to the fireside. "I should as soon think of fanning myself with the fire-shovel!"

"He has broken my heart," Rachel said. "He tells me it is not a Watteau."[238]

"Do you believe everything he tells you, my dear? His word is the word of the betrayer."

"Well, I know Watteau didn't paint fans," Florimond remarked, "any more than Michael Angelo."[239]

"I suppose you think he painted ceilings?" said Rachel Torrance. "I have painted a great many myself."

"A great many ceilings? I should like to see that!" Florimond exclaimed.

Rachel Torrance, with her usual promptness, adopted this fantasy. "Yes, I have decorated half the churches in Brooklyn; you know how many there are."

"If you mean fans, I wish men carried them," the young man went on; "I should like to have one *de votre façon*."

"You're cool enough as you are; I should be sorry to give you anything that would make you cooler!"

This retort, which may not strike the reader by its originality, was pregnant enough for Mrs. Daintry; it seemed to her to denote that the situation was critical; and she proposed to retire. Florimond walked home with her; but it was only as they reached their door that she ventured to say to him what had been on her tongue's end since they left Arlington Street.

"Florimond, I want to ask you something. I think it is important, and you mustn't be surprised. Are you in love with Rachel Torrance?"

Florimond stared, in the light of the street-lamp. The collar of his overcoat was turned up; he stamped a little as he stood still; the breath of the

February evening pervaded the empty vistas of the "new land."[240] "In love with Rachel Torrance? *Jamais de la vie*! What put that into your head?"

"Seeing you with her, that way, this evening. You know you are very attentive."

"How do you mean, attentive?"

"You go there very often. Isn't it almost every day?"

Florimond hesitated, and, in spite of the frigid dusk, his mother could see that there was irritation in his eye. "Where else can I go, in this precious place? It's the pleasantest house here."

"Yes, I suppose it's very pleasant," Mrs. Daintry murmured. "But I would rather have you return to Paris than go there too often," she added, with sudden energy.

"How do you mean, too often? *Qu'est-ce qui vous prend, ma mère?*" said Florimond.

"Is Rachel—Rachel in love with *you*?" she inquired solemnly. She felt that this question, though her heart beat as she uttered it, should not be mitigated by a circumlocution.

"Good heavens! mother, fancy talking about love in this temperature!" Florimond exclaimed. "Let one at least get into the house."

Mrs. Daintry followed him reluctantly; for she always had a feeling that if anything disagreeable were to be done one should not make it less drastic by selecting agreeable conditions. In the drawing-room, before the fire, she returned to her inquiry. "My son, you have not answered me about Rachel."

"Is she in love with me? Why, very possibly!"

"Are you serious, Florimond?"

"Why shouldn't I be? I have seen the way women go off."

Mrs. Daintry was silent a moment. "Florimond, is it true?" she said presently.

"Is what true? I don't see where you want to come out."

"Is it true that that girl has fixed her affections—" and Mrs. Daintry's voice dropped.

"Upon me, *ma mère*? I don't say it's true, but I say it's possible. You ask me, and I can only answer you. I am not swaggering, I am simply giving you decent satisfaction. You wouldn't have me think it impossible that a woman should fall in love with me? You know what women are, and how there is nothing, in that way, too queer for them to do."

Mrs. Daintry, in spite of the knowledge of her sex that she might be supposed to possess, was not prepared to rank herself on the side of this axiom. "I wished to warn you," she simply said; "do be very careful."

"Yes, I'll be careful; but I can't give up the house."

"There are other houses, Florimond."

"Yes, but there is a special charm there."

"I would rather you should return to Paris than do any harm."

"Oh, I shan't do any harm; don't worry, *ma mère*," said Florimond.

It was a relief to Mrs. Daintry to have spoken, and she endeavoured not to worry. It was doubtless this effort that, for the rest of the winter, gave her a somewhat rigid, anxious look. People who met her in Beacon Street missed something from her face. It was her usual confidence in the clearness of human duty; and some of her friends explained the change by saying that she was disappointed about Florimond—she was afraid he was not particularly liked.

VII

BY the first of March this young man had received a good many optical impressions, and had noted in water-colours several characteristic winter effects. He had perambulated Boston in every direction, he had even extended his researches to the suburbs; and if his eye had been curious, his eye was now almost satisfied. He perceived that even amid the simple civilisation of New England there was material for the naturalist; and in Washington Street[241] of a winter's afternoon, it came home to him that it was a fortunate thing the impressionist was not exclusively preoccupied with the beautiful. He became familiar with the slushy streets, crowded with thronging pedestrians and obstructed horse-cars, bordered with strange, promiscuous shops, which seemed at once violent and indifferent, overhung with snowbanks from the house-tops; the avalanche that detached itself at intervals, fell with an enormous thud amid the dense processions of women, made for a moment a clear space, splashed with whiter snow, on the pavement, and contributed to the gaiety of the Puritan capital. Supreme in the thoroughfare was the rigid groove of the railway,[242] where oblong receptacles, of fabulous capacity, governed by familiar citizens, jolted and jingled eternally, close on each other's rear, absorbing and emitting innumerable specimens of a single type. The road on either side, buried in mounds of pulverised, mud-coloured ice, was ploughed across by labouring vehicles, and traversed periodically by the sisterhood of "shoppers," laden with satchels and parcels, and protected by a round-backed policeman. Florimond looked at the shops, saw the women disgorged, surging, ebbing, dodged the avalanches, squeezed in and out of the horse-cars, made himself, on their little platforms, where flatness was enforced, as perpendicular as possible. The horses steamed in the sunny air, the conductor punched the tickets and poked the passengers, some of whom were under and some above, and all alike stabled in trampled straw. They were precipitated, collectively, by stoppages and starts; the tight, silent interior stuffed itself more and more, and the whole machine heaved and reeled in its interrupted course. Florimond had forgotten the look of many things, the details of American publicity;²⁴³ in some cases, indeed, he only pretended to himself that he had forgotten them, because it helped to entertain him. The houses—a bristling, jagged line of talls and shorts, a parti-coloured surface, expressively commercial—were spotted with staring signs, with labels and pictures, with advertisements familiar, colloquial, vulgar; the air was traversed with the tangle of the telegraph,²⁴⁴ with festoons of bunting, with banners not of war, with inexplicable loops and ropes; the shops, many of them enormous, had heterogeneous fronts, with queer juxtapositions in the articles that peopled them, an incompleteness of array, the stamp of the latest modern ugliness. They had pendant stuffs in the doorways, and flapping tickets outside. Every fifty yards there was a "candy store;" in the intervals was the painted panel of a chiropodist, representing him in his professional attitude. Behind the plates of glass, in the hot interiors, behind the counters, were pale, familiar, delicate, tired faces of women, with polished hair and glazed complexions. Florimond knew their voices; he knew how women would speak when their hair was "treated," as they said in the studios, like that. But the women that passed through the streets were the main spectacle. Florimond had forgotten their extraordinary numerosity, and the impression that they produced of a deluge of petticoats. He could see that they were perfectly at home on the road; they had an air of possession, of perpetual equipment, a look, in the eyes, of always meeting the gaze of crowds, always seeing people pass, noting things in shop-windows, and being on the watch at crossings; many of them evidently passed most of their time in these conditions, and Florimond wondered what sort of *intérieurs* they could have. He felt at moments that he was in a city of women, in a country of women. The same impression came to him *dans le monde*, as he used to say, for he made the most incongruous application of his little French phrases to Boston. The talk, the social life, were so completely in the hands of the ladies, the masculine note was so subordinate, that on certain occasions he could have believed himself (putting the brightness aside) in a country stricken by a war, where the men had all gone to the army, or in a seaport half depopulated by the absence of its vessels. This idea had intermissions; for instance, when he walked out to Cambridge. In this little excursion he often indulged; he used to go and see one of his college-mates, who was now a tutor at Harvard. It stretched away across the long, mean bridge that spans the mouth of the Charles²⁴⁵—a mile of wooden piles, supporting a brick pavement, a roadway deep in mire, and a rough timber fence, over which the pedestrian enjoys a view of the frozen bay, the backs of many new houses, and a big brown marsh. The horse-cars bore him company, relieved here of the press of the streets, though not of their internal congestion, and constituting the principal feature of the wide, blank avenue, where the puddles lay large across the bounding rails. He followed their direction through a middle region, in which the small wooden houses had an air of tent-like impermanence, and the February mornings, splendid and indiscreet, stared into bare windows and seemed to make civilisation transparent. Further, the suburb remained wooden, but grew neat, and the painted houses looked out on the car-track with an expression almost of superiority. At Harvard, the buildings were square and fresh; they stood in a yard planted with slender elms, which the winter had reduced to spindles; the town stretched away from the horizontal palings of the collegiate precinct, low, flat and immense, with vague, featureless spaces and the air of a clean encampment. Florimond remembered that when the summer came in, the whole place was transformed. It was pervaded by verdure and dust, the slender elms became profuse, arching over the unpaved streets, the green shutters bowed themselves before the windows, the flowers and creeping-plants bloomed in the small gardens, and on the piazzas, in the gaps of dropped awnings, light dresses arrested the eye. At night, in the warm darkness—for Cambridge is not festooned with lamps[246]—the bosom of nature would seem to palpitate, there would be a smell of earth and vegetation—a smell more primitive than the odour of Europe—and the air would vibrate with the sound of insects. All this was in reserve, if one would have patience, especially from March to June; but for the present the seat of the University struck our poor little critical Florimond as rather hard and bare. As the winter went on, and the days grew longer, he knew that Mrs. Daintry often believed him to be in Arlington Street when he was walking out to see his friend the tutor, who had once spent a winter in Paris, and never tired of talking about it. It is to be feared that he did not undeceive her so punctually as he might; for, in the first place, he was at Mrs. Mesh's very often; in the second, he failed to understand how worried his mother was; and in the third, the idea that he should be thought to have the peace of mind of a brilliant girl in his keeping was not disagreeable to him.

One day his Aunt Lucretia found him in Arlington Street; it occurred to her about the middle of the winter that, considering she liked Rachel Torrance so much, she had not been to see her very often. She had little time for such indulgences; but she caught a moment in its flight, and was told at Mrs. Mesh's door that this lady had not yet come in, but that her companion was accessible. Florimond was in his customary chair by the chimney-corner (his aunt perhaps did not know quite how customary it was), and Rachel, at the piano, was regaling him with a composition of Schubert.[247] Florimond, up to this time, had not become very intimate with his aunt, who had not, as it were, given him the key of her house, and in whom he detected a certain want of interest in his affairs. He had a limited sympathy with people who were interested only in their own, and perceived that Miss Daintry belonged to this preoccupied and ungraceful class. It seemed to him that it would have been more becoming in her to feign at least a certain attention to the professional and social prospects of the most promising of her nephews. If there was one thing that Florimond disliked more than another, it was an eager self-absorption; and he could not see that it was any better for people to impose their personality upon committees and charities than upon general society. He would have modified this judgment of his kinswoman, with whom he had dined but once, if he could have guessed with what anxiety she watched for the symptoms of that salutary change which she expected to see wrought in him by the fascinating independence of Rachel Torrance. If she had dared, she would have prompted the girl a little; she would have confided to her this secret desire. But the matter was delicate; and Miss Daintry was shrewd enough to see that everything must be spontaneous. When she paused at the threshold of Mrs. Mesh's drawing-room, looking from one of her young companions to the other, she felt a slight pang, for she feared they were getting on too well. Rachel was pouring sweet music into the young man's ears, and turning to look at him over her shoulder while she played; and he, with his head tipped back and his eyes on the ceiling, hummed an accompaniment which occasionally became an articulate remark. Harmonious intimacy was stamped upon the scene, and poor Miss Daintry was not struck with its being in any degree salutary. She was not reassured when, after ten minutes, Florimond took his departure; she could see that he was irritated by the presence of a third person; and this was a proof that Rachel had not yet begun to do her duty by him. It is possible that when the two ladies were left together, her disappointment would have led her to betray her views, had not Rachel almost immediately said to her: "My dear cousin, I am so glad you have come; I might not have seen you again. I go away in three days."

"Go away? Where do you go to?"

"Back to Brooklyn," said Rachel, smiling sweetly.

"Why on earth—I thought you had come here to stay for six months?"

"Oh, you know, six months would be a terrible visit for these good people; and of course no time was fixed. That would have been very absurd. I have been here an immense time already. It was to be as things should go."

"And haven't they gone well?"

"Oh yes, they have gone beautifully."

"Then why in the world do you leave?"

" Well, you know, I have duties at home. My mother coughs a good deal, and they write me dismal letters."

"They are ridiculous, selfish people. You are going home because your mother coughs? I don't believe a word of it!" Miss Daintry cried. "You have some other reason. Something has happened here; it has become disagreeable. Be so good as to tell me the whole story."

Rachel answered that there was not any story to tell, and that her reason consisted entirely of conscientious scruples as to absenting herself so long from her domestic circle. Miss Daintry esteemed conscientious scruples when they were well placed, but she thought poorly on the present occasion of those of Mrs. Mesh's visitor; they interfered so much with her own sense of fitness. "Has Florimond been making love to you?" she suddenly inquired. "You mustn't mind that—beyond boxing his ears."

Her question appeared to amuse Miss Torrance exceedingly; and the girl, a little inarticulate with her mirth, answered very positively that the young man had done her no such honour.

"I am very sorry to hear it," said Lucretia; "I was in hopes he would give you a chance to take him down. He needs it very much. He's dreadfully puffed up."

"He's an amusing little man!"

Miss Daintry put on her nippers. "Don't tell me it's you that are in love!"

"Oh, dear no! I like big, serious men; not small Frenchified gentlemen, like Florimond. Excuse me if he's your nephew, but you began it. Though I am fond of art," the girl added, "I don't think I am fond of artists."

163

"Do you call Florimond an artist?"

Rachel Torrance hesitated a little, smiling. "Yes, when he poses for Pauline Mesh."

This rejoinder for a moment left Miss Daintry in visible perplexity; then a sudden light seemed to come to her. She flushed a little; what she found was more than she was looking for. She thought of many things quickly, and among others she thought that she had accomplished rather more than she intended. "Have you quarrelled with Pauline?" she said presently.

"No, but she is tired of me."

"Everything has not gone well, then, and you *have* another reason for going home than your mother's cough?"

"Yes, if you must know, Pauline wants me to go. I didn't feel free to tell you that; but since you guess it—" said Rachel, with her rancourless smile.

"Has she asked you to decamp?"

"Oh, dear no! for what do you take us? But she absents herself from the house; she stays away all day. I have to play to Florimond to console him."

"So you *have* been fighting about him?" Miss Daintry remarked, perversely.

"Ah, my dear cousin, what have you got in your head? Fighting about sixpence! if you knew how Florimond bores me! I play to him to keep him silent. I have heard everything he has to say, fifty times over!"

Miss Daintry sank back in her chair; she was completely out of her reckoning. "I think he might have made love to you a little!" she exclaimed, incoherently.

"So do I! but he didn't—not a crumb. He is afraid of me—thank heaven!"

"It isn't for you he comes, then?" Miss Daintry appeared to cling to her theory.

"No, my dear cousin, it isn't!"

"Just now, as he sat there, one could easily have supposed it. He didn't at all like my interruption."

"That was because he was waiting for Pauline to come in. He will wait that way an hour. You may imagine whether he likes me for boring her so that, as I tell you, she can't stay in the house. I am out myself as much as possible. But there are days when I drop with fatigue; then I must rest. I can assure you that it's fortunate that I go so soon."

"Is Pauline in love with him?" Miss Daintry asked, gravely.

"Not a grain. She is the best little woman in the world."

"Except for being a goose. Why, then, does she object to your company—after being so enchanted with you?"

"Because even the best little woman in the world must object to something. She has everything in life, and nothing to complain of. Her children sleep all day, and her cook is a jewel. Her husband adores her, and she is perfectly satisfied with Mr. Mesh. I act on her nerves, and I think she believes I regard her as rather silly to care so much for Florimond. Excuse me again!"

"You contradict yourself. She *does* care for him, then?"

"Oh, as she would care for a new *coupé!*[248] She likes to have a young man of her own—fresh from Paris—quite to herself. She has everything else—why shouldn't she have that? She thinks your nephew very original, and he thinks her what she is—the prettiest woman in Boston. They have an idea that they are making a 'celebrated friendship'—like Horace Walpole and Madame du Deffand.[249] They sit there face to face—they are as innocent as the shovel and tongs. But, all the same, I am in the way, and Pauline is provoked that I am not jealous."

Miss Daintry got up with energy. "She's a vain, hollow, silly little creature, and you are quite right to go away; you are worthy of better company. Only you will not go back to Brooklyn, in spite of your mother's cough; you will come straight to Mount Vernon Place."

Rachel hesitated to agree to this. She appeared to think it was her duty to quit Boston altogether; and she gave as a reason that she had already refused other invitations. But Miss Daintry had a better reason than this—a reason that glowed in her indignant breast. It was she who had been the cause of the girl's being drawn into this sorry adventure; it was she who should charge herself with the reparation. The conversation I have related took place on a Tuesday; and it was settled that on the Friday Miss Torrance should take up her abode for the rest of the winter under her Cousin Lucretia's roof. This lady left the house without having seen Mrs. Mesh.

On Thursday she had a visit from her sister-in-law, the motive of which was not long in appearing. All winter Mrs. Daintry had managed to keep silent on the subject of her doubts and fears. Discretion and dignity recommended this course; and the topic was a painful one to discuss with Lucretia, for the bruises of their primary interview still occasionally throbbed. But at the first sign of alleviation the excellent woman overflowed, and she lost no time in announcing to Lucretia, as a heaven-sent piece of news, that Rachel had been called away by the illness of poor Mrs. Torrance and was to leave Boston from one day to the other. Florimond had given her this information the evening before, and it had made her so happy that she couldn't help coming to let Lucretia know that they were safe. Lucretia listened to her announcement in silence, fixing her eyes on her sister-in-law with an expression that the latter thought singular; but when Mrs. Daintry, expanding still further, went on to say that she had spent a winter of misery, that the harm the two together (she and Lucretia) might have done was never out of her mind, for Florimond's assiduity in Arlington Street had become notorious, and she had been told that the most cruel things were said—when Mrs. Daintry, expressing herself to this effect, added that from the present moment she breathed, the danger was over, the sky was clear, and her conscience might take a holiday—her hostess broke into the most prolonged, the most characteristic and most bewildering fit of laughter in which she had ever known her to indulge. They were safe, Mrs. Daintry had said? For Lucretia this was true, now, of herself, at least; she was secure from the dangers of her irritation; her sense of the whole affair had turned to hilarious music. The contrast that rose before her between her visitor's anxieties and the real position of the parties, her quick vision of poor Susan's dismay in case *that* reality should meet her eyes, among the fragments of her squandered scruples—these things smote the chords of mirth in Miss Daintry's spirit, and seemed to her in their high comicality to offer a sufficient reason for everything that had happened. The picture of her sister-in-law sitting all winter with her hands clasped and her eyes fixed on the wrong object was an image that would abide with her always; and it would render her an inestimable service—it would cure her of the tendency to worry. As may be imagined, it was eminently open to Mrs. Daintry to ask her what on earth she was laughing at; and there was a colour in the cheek of Florimond's mother that brought her back to propriety. She suddenly kissed this lady very tenderly—to the latter's great surprise, there having been no kissing since her visit in November—and told her that she would reveal to her some day, later, the cause of so much merriment. She added that Miss Torrance was leaving Arlington Street, yes; but only to go as far as Mount Vernon Place. She was engaged to spend three months in that very house. Mrs. Daintry's countenance at this fell several inches, and her joy appeared completely to desert her. She gave her sister-in-law a glance of ineffable reproach, and in a moment she exclaimed: "Then nothing is gained! it will all go on here!"

"Nothing will go on here. If you mean that Florimond will pursue the young lady into this mountain fastness,²⁵⁰ you may simply be quiet. He is not fond enough of me to wear out my threshold."

"Are you very sure?" Mrs. Daintry murmured, dubiously.

"I know what I say. Hasn't he told you he hates me?"

Mrs. Daintry coloured again, and hesitated. "I don't know how you think we talk," she said.

"Well, he does, and he will leave us alone."

Mrs. Daintry sprang up with an elasticity that was comical. "That's all I ask!" she exclaimed.

"I believe you hate me too!" Lucretia said, laughing; but at any risk she kissed her sister-in-law again before they separated.

Three weeks later Mrs. Daintry paid her another visit; and this time she looked very serious. "It's very strange. I don't know what to think. But perhaps you know it already?" This was her *entrée en matière*, as the French say. "Rachel's leaving Arlington Street has made no difference. He goes there as much as ever. I see no change at all. Lucretia, I have not the peace that I thought had come," said poor Mrs. Daintry, whose voice had failed, below her breath.

"Do you mean that he goes to see Pauline Mesh?"

"I am afraid so, every day."

"Well, my dear, what's the harm?" Miss Daintry asked. "He can't hurt *her* by not marrying her."

Mrs. Daintry stared; she was amazed at her sister-in-law's tone. "But it makes one suppose that all winter, for so many weeks, it has been for *her* that he has gone!" And the image of the *tête-à-tête* in which she had found them immersed that day, rose again before her; she could interpret it now.

"You wanted some one; why may not Pauline have served?"

Mrs. Daintry was silent, with the same expanded eyes. "Lucretia, it is not right!"

"My dear Susan, you are touching," Lucretia said.

Mrs. Daintry went on, without heeding her. "It appears that people are talking about it; they have noticed it for ever so long. Joanna never hears anything, or she would have told me. The children are too much. I have been the last to know."

"I knew it a month ago," said Miss Daintry, smiling.

"And you never told me?"

"I knew that you wanted to detain him. Pauline will detain him a year."

Mrs. Daintry gathered herself together. "Not a day, not an hour, that I can help! He shall go, if I have to take him."

"My dear Susan," murmured her sister-in-law on the threshold. Miss Daintry scarcely knew what to say; she was almost frightened at the rigidity of her face.

"My dear Lucretia, it is not right!" This ejaculation she solemnly repeated, and she took her departure as if she were decided upon action.

She had found so little sympathy in her sister-in-law that she made no answer to a note Miss Daintry wrote her that evening, to remark that she was really unjust to Pauline, who was silly, vain, and flattered by the development of her ability to monopolise an impressionist, but a perfectly innocent little woman and incapable of a serious flirtation. Miss Daintry had been careful to add to these last words no comment that could possibly shock Florimond's mother. Mrs. Daintry announced, about the 10th of April, that she had made up her mind she needed a change, and had determined to go abroad for the summer; and she looked so tired that people could see there was reason in it. Her summer began early; she embarked on the 20th of the month, accompanied by Florimond. Miss Daintry, who had not been obliged to dismiss the young lady of the kindergarten to make room for Rachel Torrance, never knew what had passed between the mother and the son, and she was disappointed at Mrs. Mesh's coolness in the face of this catastrophe. She disapproved of her flirtation with Florimond, and yet she was vexed at Pauline's pert resignation; it proved her to be so superficial. She disposed of everything with her absurd little phrases, which were half slang and half quotation. Mrs. Daintry was a native of Salem, and this gave Pauline, as a Baltimorean and a descendant of the Cavaliers,[251] an obvious opportunity. Rachel repeated her words to Miss Daintry, for she had spoken to Rachel of Florimond's departure, the day after he embarked. "Oh yes, he's in the midst of the foam, the cruel, crawling foam![252] I 'kind of' miss him, afternoons; he was so useful round the fire. It's his mother that charmed him away; she's a most uncanny old party. I don't care for Salem witches, anyway; she has worked on him with philters and spells!" Lucretia was obliged to recognise a grain of truth in this last assertion; she felt that her sister-in-law must indeed have worked upon Florimond, and she smiled to think that the conscientious Susan should have descended, in the last resort, to an artifice, to a pretext. She had probably persuaded him she was out of patience with Joanna's children.

The Path of Duty[253]

I AM glad I said to you the other night at Doubleton,[254] inquiring—too inquiring—compatriot, that I wouldn't undertake to tell you the story (about Ambrose Tester[255]), but would write it out for you; inasmuch as, thinking it over since I came back to town, I see that it may really be made interesting. It *is* a story, with a regular development, and for telling it I have the advantage that I happened to know about it from the first and was more or less in the confidence of every one concerned. Then it will amuse me to write it, and I shall do so as carefully and as cleverly as possible. The first winter days in London are not madly gay, so that I have plenty of time, and if the fog is brown outside, the fire is red within.[256] I like the quiet of this season; the glowing chimney-corner, in the midst of the December mirk, makes me think, as I sit by it, of all sorts of things. The idea that is almost always uppermost is the bigness and strangeness of this London world. Long as I have lived here—the sixteenth anniversary of my marriage is only ten days off—there is still a kind of novelty and excitement in it. It is a great pull, as they say here, to have remained sensitive—to have kept one's own point of view.[257] I mean it's more entertaining—it makes you see a thousand things (not that they are all very charming). But the pleasure of observation does not in the least depend on the beauty of what one observes. You see innumerable little dramas; in fact almost everything has acts and scenes, like a comedy. Very often it is a comedy with tears. There have been a good many of them, I am afraid, in the case I am speaking of. It is because this history of Sir Ambrose Tester and Lady Vandeleur[258] struck me, when you asked me about the relations of the parties, as having that kind of progression, that when I was on the point of responding I checked myself, thinking it a pity to tell you a little when I might tell you all. I scarcely know what made you ask, inasmuch as I had said nothing to excite your curiosity. Whatever you suspected you suspected on your own hook,[259] as they say. You had simply noticed the pair together that evening at Doubleton. If you suspected anything in particular, it is a proof that you are rather sharp, because they are very careful about the way they behave in public. At least they think they are; the result, perhaps, doesn't necessarily follow. If I have been in their confidence you may say that I make a strange use of my privilege in serving them up to feed the prejudices of an opinionated American. You think English society very wicked, and my little story will probably not correct the impression. Though, after all, I don't see why it should minister to it; for what I said to you (it was all I did say) remains the truth. They are treading together the path of duty. You would be quite right about its being base in me to betray them. It is very true that they have ceased to confide in me; even Joscelind[260] has said nothing to me for more than a year. That is doubtless a sign that the situation is more serious than before, all round—too serious to be talked about. It is also true that you are remarkably discreet, and that even if you were not it would not make much difference, inasmuch as if you were to repeat my revelations in America no one would know whom you were talking about. But, all the same, I should be base; and, therefore after I have written out my reminiscences for your delectation, I shall simply keep them for my own. You must content yourself with the explanation I have already given you of Sir Ambrose Tester and Lady Vandeleur: they are following—hand in hand, as it were—the path of duty. This will not prevent me from telling everything; on the contrary, don't you see?

I

His brilliant prospects dated from the death of his brother, who had no children, had indeed steadily refused to marry. When I say brilliant prospects, I mean the vision of the baronetcy,[261] one of the oldest in England, of a charming seventeenth-century house, with its park, in Dorsetshire,[262] and a property worth some twenty thousand a year.[263] Such a collection of items is still dazzling to me, even after what you would call, I suppose, a familiarity with British grandeur. My husband isn't a baronet (or we probably shouldn't be in London in December[264]), and he is far, alas, from having twenty thousand a year. The full enjoyment of these luxuries, on Ambrose Tester's part, was dependent naturally on the death of his father, who was still very much to the fore at the time I first knew the young man. The proof of it is the way he kept nagging at his sons, as the younger used to say, on the question of taking a wife. The nagging had been of no avail, as I have mentioned, with regard to Francis, the elder, whose affections were centred (his brother himself told me) on the wine-cup and the faro-table.[265] He was not a person to admire or imitate, and as the heir to an honourable name and a fine estate was very unsatisfactory indeed. It had been possible in those days to put him into the army, but it was not possible to keep him there, and he was still a very young man when it became plain that any parental dream of a "career" for Frank Tester was exceedingly vain. Old Sir Edmund had thought matrimony would perhaps correct him, but a sterner process than this was needed, and it came to him one day at Monaco[266]—he was most of the time abroad—after an illness so short that none of the family arrived in time. He was reformed altogether, he was utterly abolished. The second son, stepping into his shoes, was such an improvement that it was impossible there should be much simulation of mourning. You have seen him, you know what he is, there is very little mystery about him. As I am not going to show this composition to you, there is no harm in my writing here that he is—or, at any rate, he was—a remarkably attractive man. I don't say this because he made love to me, but precisely because he didn't. He was always in love with some one else—generally with Lady Vandeleur. You may say that in England that usually doesn't prevent; but Mr. Tester, though he had almost no intermissions, didn't, as a general thing, have duplicates. He was not provided with a second loved object, "under-studying," as they say, the part.[267] It was his practice to keep me accurately informed of the state of his affections—a matter about which he was never in the least vague. When he was in love he knew it and rejoiced in it, and when by a miracle he was not he greatly regretted it. He expatiated to me on the charms of other persons, and this interested me much more than if he had attempted to direct the conversation to my own, as regards which I had no illusions. He has told me some singular things, and I think I may say that for a considerable period my most valued knowledge of English society was extracted from this genial youth. I suppose he usually found me a woman of good counsel, for certain it is that he has appealed to me for the light of wisdom in very extraordinary predicaments. In his earlier years he was perpetually in hot water; he tumbled into scrapes as children tumble into puddles. He invited them, he invented them; and when he came to tell you how his trouble had come about (and he always told the whole truth) it was difficult to believe that a man should have been so idiotic.

And yet he was not an idiot; he was supposed to be very clever, and certainly is very quick and amusing. He was only reckless, and extraordinarily natural, as natural as if he had been an Irishman.[268] In fact, of all the Englishmen that I have known he is the most Irish in temperament (though he has got over it comparatively of late). I used to tell him that it was a great inconvenience that he didn't speak with a brogue, because then we should be forewarned and know with whom we were dealing. He replied that, by analogy, if he were Irish enough to have a brogue[269] he would probably be English; which seemed to me an answer wonderfully in character. Like most young Britons of his class he went to America, to see the great country, before he was twenty, and he took a letter to my father, who had occasion, à propos of some pickle, of course, to render him a considerable service. This led to his coming to see me—I had already been living here three or four years—on his return; and that, in the course of time, led to our becoming fast friends, without, as I tell you, the smallest philandering on either side. But I mustn't protest too much;[270] I shall excite your suspicion. "If he has made love to so many women, why shouldn't he have made love to you?"—some inquiry of that sort you will be likely to make. I have answered it already, "Simply on account of those very engagements." He couldn't make love to every one, and with me it wouldn't have done him the least good. It was a more amiable weakness than his brother's, and he has always behaved very well. How well he behaved on a very important occasion is precisely the subject of my story.

He was supposed to have embraced the diplomatic career, had been secretary of legation at some German capital;[271] but after his brother's death he came home and looked out for a seat in Parliament. He found it with no great trouble, and has kept it ever since. No one would have the heart to turn him out, he is so good-looking. It's a great thing to be represented by one of the handsomest men in England, it creates such a favourable association of ideas. Any one would be amazed to discover that the borough he sits for,[272] and the name of which I am always forgetting, is not a very pretty place. I have never seen it, and have no idea that it isn't, and I am sure he will survive every revolution. The people must feel that if they shouldn't keep him some monster would be returned. You remember his appearance, how tall, and fair, and strong he is, and always laughing, yet without looking silly. He is exactly the young man girls in America figure to themselves—in the place of the hero—when they read English novels and wish to imagine something very aristocratic and Saxon. A "bright Bostonian"[273] who met him once at my house, exclaimed as soon as he had gone out of the room, "At last, at last, I behold it, the moustache of Roland Tremayne!"

"Of Roland Tremayne?"

"Don't you remember in *A Lawless Love*,[274] how often it's mentioned, and how glorious and golden it was? Well, I have never seen it till now, but now I *have* seen it!"

If you hadn't seen Ambrose Tester, the best description I could give of him would be to say that he looked like Roland Tremayne. I don't know whether that hero was a "strong Liberal,"[275] but this is what Sir Ambrose is supposed to be. (He succeeded his father two years ago, but I shall come to that.) He is not exactly what I should call thoughtful, but he is interested, or thinks he is, in a lot of things that I don't understand, and that one sees and skips in the newspapers—volunteering, and redistribution, and sanitation, and the representation of minors[276]—minorities—what is it? When I said just now that he is always laughing, I ought to have explained that I didn't mean when he is talking to Lady Vandeleur. She makes him serious, makes him almost solemn; by which I don't mean that she bores him. Far from it; but when he is in her company he is thoughtful; he pulls his golden moustache, and Roland Tremayne looks as if his vision were turned in, and he were meditating on her words. He doesn't say much himself; it is she—she used to be so silent—who does the talking. She has plenty to say to him; she describes to him the charms that she discovers in the path of duty. He seldom speaks in the House, I believe, but when he does it's off-hand, and amusing, and sensible, and every one likes it. He will never be a great statesman, but he will add to the softness of Dorsetshire, and remain, in short, a very gallant, pleasant, prosperous, typical English gentleman, with a name, a fortune, a perfect appearance, a devoted, bewildered little wife, a great many reminiscences, a great many friends (including Lady Vandeleur and myself), and, strange to say, with all these advantages, something that faintly resembles a conscience.

II

Five years ago he told me his father insisted on his marrying—would not hear of his putting it off any longer. Sir Edmund had been harping on this string ever since he came back from Germany, had made it both a general and a particular request, not only urging him to matrimony in the abstract, but pushing him into the arms of every young woman in the country. Ambrose had promised, procrastinated, temporised; but at last he was at the end of his evasions, and his poor father had taken the tone of supplication. "He thinks immensely of the name, of the place, and all that, and he has got it into his head that if I don't marry before he dies I won't marry after." So much I remember Ambrose Tester said to me. "It's a fixed idea; he has got it on the brain. He wants to see me married with his eyes, and he wants to take his grandson in his arms. Not without that will he be satisfied that the whole thing will go straight. He thinks he is nearing his end, but he isn't—he will live to see a hundred, don't you think so?—and he has made me a solemn appeal to put an end to what he calls his suspense. He has an idea some one will get hold of me—some woman I can't marry. As if I were not old enough to take care of myself!"

"Perhaps he is afraid of me," I suggested, facetiously.

"No, it isn't you," said my visitor, betraying by his tone that it was some one, though he didn't say whom. "That's all rot, of course; one marries sooner or later, and I shall do like every one else. If I marry before I die it's as good as if I marry before he dies, isn't it? I should be delighted to have the governor at my wedding, but it isn't necessary for the legality, is it?"

I asked him what he wished me to do, and how I could help him. He knew already my peculiar views, that I was trying to get husbands for all the girls of my acquaintance and to prevent the men from taking wives. The sight of an unmarried woman afflicted me, and yet when my male friends changed their state I took it as a personal offence. He let me know that, so far as he was concerned, I must prepare myself for this injury, for he had given his father his word that another twelvemonth should not see him a bachelor.

The old man had given him *carte blanche,* he made no condition beyond exacting that the lady should have youth and health. Ambrose Tester, at any rate, had taken a vow, and now he was going seriously to look about him. I said to him that what must be must be, and that there were plenty of charming girls about the land, among whom he could suit himself easily enough. There was no better match in England, I said, and he would only have to make his choice. That, however, is not what I thought, for my real reflections were summed up in the silent exclamation, "What a pity Lady Vandeleur isn't a widow!" I hadn't the smallest doubt that if she were he would marry her on the spot; and after he had gone I wondered considerably what *she* thought of this turn in his affairs. If it was disappointing to me, how little it must be to *her* taste! Sir Edmund had not been so much out of the way in fearing there might be obstacles to his son's taking the step he desired. Margaret Vandeleur was an obstacle—I knew it as well as if Mr. Tester had told me.

I don't mean there was anything in their relation he might not freely have alluded to, for Lady Vandeleur, in spite of her beauty and her tiresome husband, was not a woman who could be accused of an indiscretion. Her husband was a pedant about trifles—the shape of his hat-brim, the *pose* of his coachman, and cared for nothing else; but she was as nearly a saint as one may be when one has rubbed shoulders for ten years with the best society in Europe. It is a characteristic of that society that even its saints are suspected, and I go too far in saying that little pin-pricks were not administered, in considerable numbers, to her reputation. But she didn't feel them, for, still more than Ambrose Tester, she was a person to whose happiness a good conscience was necessary. I should almost say that for her happiness it was sufficient, and, at any rate, it was only those who didn't know her that pretended to speak of her lightly. If one had the honour of her acquaintance one might have thought her rather shut up to her beauty and her grandeur, but one couldn't but feel there was something in her composition that would keep her from vulgar aberrations. Her husband was such a feeble type that she must have felt doubly she had been put upon her honour. To deceive such a man as that was to make him more ridiculous than he was already, and from such a result a woman bearing his name may very well have shrunk. Perhaps it would have been worse for Lord Vandeleur, who had every pretension of his order and none of its amiability, if he had been a better or, at least, a cleverer man.

When a woman behaves so well she is not obliged to be careful, and there is no need of consulting appearances when one is one's self an appearance. Lady Vandeleur accepted Ambrose Tester's attentions, and heaven knows they were frequent; but she had such an air of perfect equilibrium that one couldn't see her, in imagination, bend responsive. Incense was incense, but one saw her sitting quite serene among the fumes. That honour of her acquaintance of which I just now spoke it had been given me to enjoy; that is to say, I met her a dozen times in the season[277] in a hot crowd, and we smiled sweetly and murmured a vague question or two, without hearing, or even trying to hear, each other's answer. If I knew that Ambrose Tester was perpetually in and out of her house and always arranging with her that they should go to the same places, I doubt whether she, on her side, knew how often he came to see me. I don't think he would have let her know, and am conscious, in saying this, that it indicated an advanced state of intimacy (with her, I mean).

I also doubt very much whether he asked her to look about, on his behalf, for a future Lady Tester. This request he was so good as to make of me; but I told him I would have nothing to do with the matter. If Joscelind is unhappy, I am thankful to say the responsibility is not mine. I have found English husbands for two or three American girls, but providing English wives is a different affair. I know the sort of men that will suit women, but one would have to be very clever to know the sort of women that will suit men. I told Ambrose Tester that he must look out for himself, but, in spite of his promise, I had very little belief that he would do anything of the sort. I thought it probable that the old baronet would pass away without seeing a new generation come in; though when I intimated as much to Mr. Tester, he made answer in substance (it was not quite so crudely said) that his father, old as he was, would hold on till his bidding was done, and if it should not be done he would hold on out of spite. "Oh, he will tire me out": that I remember Ambrose Tester did say. I had done him injustice, for six months later he told me he was engaged. It had all come about very suddenly. From one day to the other the right young woman had been found. I forget who had found her; some aunt or cousin, I think; it had not been the young man himself. But when she was found, he rose to the occasion; he took her up seriously, he approved of her thoroughly, and I am not sure that he didn't fall a little in love with her, ridiculous (excuse my London tone) as this accident may appear. He told me that his father was delighted, and I knew afterwards that he had good reason to be. It was not till some weeks later that I saw the girl; but meanwhile I had received the pleasantest impression of her, and this impression came—must have come—mainly from what her intended told me. That proves that he spoke with some positiveness, spoke as if he really believed he was doing a good thing. I had it on my tongue's end to ask him how Lady Vandeleur liked her, but I fortunately checked this vulgar inquiry. He liked her, evidently, as I say; every one liked her, and when I knew her I liked her better even than the others. I like her to-day more than ever; it is fair you should know that, in reading this account of her situation. It doubt-less colours my picture, gives a point to my sense of the strangeness of my little story.

Joscelind Bernardstone[278] came of a military race, and had been brought up in camps—by which I don't mean she was one of those objectionable young women who are known as garrison-hacks.[279] She was in the flower of her freshness, and had been kept in the tent, receiving, as an only daugh-ter, the most "particular" education from the excellent Lady Emily (General Bernardstone married a daughter of Lord Clanduffy), who looks like a pink-faced rabbit, and is (after Joscelind) one of the nicest women I know. When I met them in a country-house, a few weeks after the marriage was "arranged," as they say here, Joscelind won my affections by saying to me, with her timid directness (the speech made me feel sixty years old), that she must thank me for having been so kind to Mr. Tester. You saw her at Doubleton, and you will remember that, though she has no regular beauty, many a prettier woman would be very glad to look like her. She is as fresh as a new-laid egg, as light as a feather, as strong as a mail-phaeton.[280] She is perfectly mild, yet she is clever enough to be sharp if she would. I don't know that clever women are necessarily thought ill-natured, but it is usu-ally taken for granted that amiable women are very limited. Lady Tester is a refutation of the theory, which must have been invented by a vixenish woman who was *not* clever. She has an adoration for her husband, which absorbs her without in the least making her silly, unless indeed it is silly to be modest, as in this brutal world I sometimes believe. Her modesty is so great that being unhappy has hitherto presented itself to her as a form of egotism—that egotism which she has too much delicacy to cultivate. She is by no means sure that, if being married to her beautiful baronet is not the ideal state she dreamed it, the weak point of the affair is not simply in her own presumption. It doesn't express her condition, at present, to say that she is unhappy or disappointed, or that she has a sense of injury. All this is latent; meanwhile, what is obvious is that she is bewildered—she simply doesn't understand, and her perplexity, to me, is unspeakably touching. She looks about her for some explanation, some light. She fixes her eyes on mine sometimes, and on those of other people, with a kind of searching dumbness, as if there were some chance that I—that they—may explain, may tell her what it is that has happened to her. I can explain very well—but not to her—only to you!

III

It was a brilliant match for Miss Bernardstone, who had no fortune at all, and all her friends were of the opinion that she had done very well. After Easter she was in London with her people, and I saw a good deal of them—in fact, I rather cultivated them. They might perhaps even have thought me a little patronising, if they had been given to thinking that sort of thing. But they were not; that is not in their line. English people are very apt to attribute motives—some of them attribute much worse ones than we poor simpletons in America recognise, than we have even heard of. But that is only some of them; others don't, but take everything literally and genially. That was the case with the Benardstones; you could be sure that on their way home, after dining with you, they wouldn't ask each other how in the world any one could call you pretty, or say that many people *did* believe, all the same, that you had poisoned your grandfather.

Lady Emily was exceedingly gratified at her daughter's engagement; of course she was very quiet about it, she didn't clap her hands or drag in Mr. Tester's name; but it was easy to see that she felt a kind of maternal peace, an abiding satisfaction. The young man behaved as well as possible, was constantly seen with Joscelind, and smiled down at her in the kindest, most protecting way. They looked beautiful together—you would have said it was a duty for people whose colour matched so well to marry. Of course he was immensely taken up, and didn't come very often to see me; but he came sometimes, and when he sat there he had a look which I didn't under-stand at first. Presently I saw what it expressed; in my drawing-room he was off duty, he had no longer to sit up and play a part; he would lean back and rest and draw a long breath, and forget that the day of his execution was fixed. There was to be no indecent haste about the marriage; it was not to take place till after the session,[281] at the end of August. It puzzled me and rather distressed me that his heart shouldn't be a little more in the matter; it seemed strange to be engaged to so charming a girl and yet go through with it as if it were simply a social duty. If one hadn't been in love with her at first, one ought to have been at the end of a week or two. If Ambrose Tester was not (and to me he didn't pretend to be), he carried it off, as I have said, better than I should have expected. He was a gentleman, and he behaved like a gentleman—with the added punctilio, I think, of being sorry for his betrothed. But it was difficult to see what, in the long run, he could expect to make of such a position. If a man marries an ugly, unattractive woman for reasons of state, the thing is comparatively simple; it is understood between them, and he need have no remorse at not offering her a sentiment of which there has been no question. But when he picks out a charming creature to gratify his father and *les convenances*, it is not so easy to be happy in not being able to care for her. It seemed to me that it would have been much better for Ambrose Tester to bestow himself upon a girl who might have given him an excuse for tepidity. His wife should have been healthy but stupid, prolific but morose. Did he expect to continue not to be in love with Joscelind, or to conceal from her the mechanical nature of his attentions? It was difficult to see how he could wish to do the one or succeed in doing the other. Did he expect such a girl as that would be happy if he didn't love her? and did he think himself capable of being happy if it should turn out that she was miserable? If she shouldn't be miserable—that is, if she should be indifferent, and, as they say, console herself, would he like that any better?

I asked myself all these questions and I should have liked to ask them of Mr. Tester; but I didn't, for after all he couldn't have answered them. Poor young man! he didn't pry into things as I do; he was not analytic, like us Americans, as they say in reviews. He thought he was behaving remarkably well, and so he was—for a man; that was the strange part of it. It had been proper that in spite of his reluctance he should take a wife, and he had dutifully set about it. As a good thing is better for being well done, he had taken the best one he could possibly find. He was enchanted with—with his young lady, you might ask? Not in the least; with himself; that is the sort of person a man is! Their virtues are more dangerous than their vices, and heaven preserve you when they want to keep a promise! It is never a promise to *you*, you will notice. A man will sacrifice a woman to live as a gentleman should, and then ask for your sympathy—for *him*! And I don't speak of the bad ones, but of the good. They, after all, are the worst. Ambrose Tester, as I say, didn't go into these details, but, synthetic as he might be,[282] was conscious that his position was false. He felt that sooner or later, and rather sooner than later, he would have to make it true—a process that couldn't possibly be agreeable. He would really have to make up his mind to care for his wife or not to care for her. What would Lady Vandeleur say to one alternative, and what would little Joscelind say to the other? That is what it was to have a pertinacious father and to be an accommodating son. With me it was easy for Ambrose Tester to be superficial, for, as I tell you, if I didn't wish to engage him, I didn't wish to disengage him, and I didn't insist. Lady Vandeleur insisted, I was afraid; to be with her was, of course, very complicated; even more than Miss Bernardstone she must have made him feel that his position was false. I must add that he once mentioned to me that she had told him he ought to marry. At any rate it is an immense thing to be a pleasant fellow. Our young fellow was so universally pleasant that, of course, his *fiancée* came in for her share. So did Lady Emily, suffused with hope, which made her pinker than ever; she told me he sent flowers even to her. One day in the Park, I was riding early; the Row²⁸³ was almost empty. I came up behind a lady and gentleman who were walking their horses, close to each other, side by side. In a moment I recognised her, but not before seeing that nothing could have been more benevolent than the way Ambrose Tester was bending over his future wife. If he struck me as a lover at that moment, of course he struck her so. But that isn't the way they ride to-day.

I V

One day, about the end of June, he came in to see me when I had two or three other visitors; you know that even at that season I am almost always at home from six to seven. He had not been three minutes in the room before I saw that he was different—different from what he had been the last time, and I guessed that something had happened in relation to his marriage. My visitors didn't, unfortunately, and they stayed and stayed until I was afraid he would have to go away without telling me what, I was sure, he had come for. But he sat them out; I think that, by exception, they didn't find him pleasant. After we were alone he abused them a little, and then he said, "Have you heard about Vandeleur? He's very ill. She's awfully anxious." I hadn't heard, and I told him so, asking a question or two; then my inquiries ceased, my breath almost failed me, for I had become aware of something very strange. The way he looked at me when he told me his news was a full confession—a confession so full that I had needed a moment to take it in. He was not too strong a man to be taken by surprise—not so strong but that in the presence of an unexpected occasion his first movement was to look about for a little help. I venture to call it help, the sort of thing he came to me for on that summer afternoon. It is always help when a woman who is not an idiot lets an embarrassed man take up her time. If he too is not an idiot, that doesn't diminish the service; on the contrary his superiority to the average helps him to profit. Ambrose Tester had said to me more than once, in the past, that he was capable of telling me things, because I was an American, that he wouldn't confide to his own people. He had proved it before this, as I have hinted, and I must say that being an American, with him, was sometimes a questionable honour. I don't know whether he thinks us more discreet and more sympathetic (if he keeps up the system : he has abandoned it with me), or only more insensible, more proof against shocks; but it is certain that, like some other Englishmen I have known, he has appeared, in delicate cases, to think I would take a comprehensive view. When I have inquired into the grounds of this discrimination in our favour, he has contented himself with saying, in the British-cursory manner, "Oh, I don't know; you are different!" I remember he remarked once that our impressions were fresher. And I am sure that now it was because of my nationality, in addition to other merits, that he treated me to the confession I have just alluded to. At least I don't suppose he would have gone about saying to people in general, "Her husband will probably die, you know; then why shouldn't I marry Lady Vandeleur?"

That was the question which his whole expression and manner asked of me, and of which, after a moment, I decided to take no notice. Why shouldn't he? There was an excellent reason why he shouldn't. It would just kill Joscelind Bernardstone; that was why he shouldn't! The idea that he should be ready to do it frightened me, and, independent as he might think my point of view, I had no desire to discuss such abominations. It struck me as an abomination at this very first moment, and I have never wavered in my judgment of it. I am always glad when I can take the measure of a thing as soon as I see it; it's a blessing to *feel* what we think, without balancing and comparing. It's a great rest, too, and a great luxury. That, as I say, was the case with the feeling excited in me by this happy idea of Ambrose Tester's. Cruel and wanton I thought it then, cruel and wanton I thought it later, when it was pressed upon me. I knew there were many other people that didn't agree with me, and I can only hope for them that their conviction was as quick and positive as mine; it all depends upon the way a thing strikes one. But I will add to this another remark. I thought I was right then, and I still think I was right; but it strikes me as a pity that I should have wished so much to be right. Why couldn't I be content to be wrong? to renounce my influence (since I appeared to possess the mystic article), and let my young friend do as he liked? As you observed the situation at Doubleton, shouldn't you say it was of a nature to make one wonder whether, after all, one did render a service to the younger lady?

At all events, as I say, I gave no sign to Ambrose Tester that I understood him, that I guessed what he wished to come to. He got no satisfaction out of me that day; it is very true that he made up for it later. I expressed regret at Lord Vandeleur's illness, inquired into its nature and origin, hoped it wouldn't prove as grave as might be feared, said I would call at the house and ask about him, commiserated discreetly her ladyship, and, in short, gave my young man no chance whatever. He knew that I had guessed his *arrière-pensée*, but he let me off for the moment, for which I was thankful; either because he was still ashamed of it, or because he supposed I was reserving myself for the catastrophe—should it occur. Well, my dear, it did occur, at the end of ten days. Mr. Tester came to see me twice in that interval, each time to tell me that poor Vandeleur was worse; he had some internal inflammation which, in nine cases out of ten, is fatal. His wife was all devotion; she was with him night and day. I had the news from other sources as well; I leave you to imagine whether in London, at the height of the season, such a situation could fail to be considerably discussed. To the discussion as yet, however, I contributed little, and with Ambrose Tester nothing at all. I was still on my guard. I never admitted for a moment that it was possible there should be any change in his plans. By this time, I think, he had quite ceased to be ashamed of his idea, he was in a state almost of exultation about it; but he was very angry with me for not giving him an opening.

As I look back upon the matter now, there is something almost amusing in the way we watched each other—he thinking that I evaded his question only to torment him (he believed me, or pretended to believe me, capable of this sort of perversity), and I determined not to lose ground by betraying an insight into his state of mind which he might twist into an expression of sympathy. I wished to leave my sympathy where I had placed it, with Lady Emily and her daughter, of whom I continued, bumping against them at parties, to have some observation. They gave no signal of alarm; of course it would have been premature. The girl, I am sure, had no idea of the existence of a rival. How they had kept her in the dark I don't know; but it was easy to see she was too much in love to suspect or to criticise. With Lady Emily it was different; she was a woman of charity, but she touched the world at too many points not to feel its vibrations. However, the dear little lady planted herself firmly; to the eye she was still enough. It was not from Ambrose Tester that I first heard of Lord Vandeleur's death; it was announced, with a quarter of a column of "padding," in the *Times*.[284] I have always known the *Times* was a wonderful journal, but this never came home to me so much as when it produced a quarter of a column about Lord Vandeleur. It was a triumph of word-spinning. If he had carried out his vocation, if he had been a tailor or a hatter (that's how I see him), there might have been something to say about him. But he missed his vocation, he missed everything but posthumous honours. I was so sure Ambrose Tester would come in that afternoon, and so sure he knew I should expect him, that I threw over an engagement on purpose. But he didn't come in, nor the next day, nor the next. There were two possible explanations of his absence. One was that he was giving all his time to consoling Lady Vandeleur; the other was that he was giving it all, as a blind, to Joscelind Bernardstone. Both proved incorrect, for when he at last turned up he told me he had been for a week in the country, at his father's. Sir Edmund also had been unwell; but he had pulled through better than poor Lord Vandeleur. I wondered at first whether his son had been talking over with him the question of a change of base; but guessed in a moment that he had not suffered this alarm. I don't think that Ambrose would have spared him if he had thought it necessary to give him warning; but he probably held that his father would have no ground for complaint so long as he should marry some one; would have no right to remonstrate if he simply transferred his contract. Lady Vandeleur had had two children (whom she had lost), and might, therefore, have others whom she shouldn't lose; that would have been a reply to nice discriminations on Sir Edmund's part.

V

In reality what the young man had been doing was thinking it over beneath his ancestral oaks and beeches. His countenance showed this—showed it more than Miss Bernardstone could have liked. He looked like a man who was crossed, not like a man who was happy, in love. I was no more disposed than before to help him out with his plot, but at the end of ten minutes we were articulately discussing it. When I say *we* were, I mean he was; for I sat before him quite mute, at first, and amazed at the clearness with which, before his conscience, he had argued his case. He had persuaded himself that it was quite a simple matter to throw over poor Joscelind and keep himself free for the expiration of Lady Vandeleur's term of mourning. The deliberations of an impulsive man sometimes land him in strange countries. Ambrose Tester confided his plan to me as a tremendous secret. He professed to wish immensely to know how it appeared to me, and whether my woman's wit couldn't discover for him some loophole big enough round, some honourable way of not keeping faith. Yet at the same time he seemed not to foresee that I should, of necessity, be simply horrified. Disconcerted and perplexed (a little), that he was prepared to find me; but if I had refused, as yet, to come to his assistance, he appeared to suppose it was only because of the real difficulty of suggesting to him that perfect pretext of which he was in want. He evidently counted upon me, however, for some illuminating proposal, and I think he would have liked to say to me, "You have always pretended to be a great friend of mine"—I hadn't; the pretension was all on his side—"and now is your chance to show it. Go to Joscelind and make her feel (women have a hundred ways of doing that sort of thing) that through Vandeleur's death the change in my situation is complete. If she is the girl I take her for, she will know what to do in the premises."

I was not prepared to oblige him to this degree, and I lost no time in telling him so, after my first surprise at seeing how definite his purpose had become. His contention, after all, was very simple. He had been in love with Lady

Vandeleur for years, and was now more in love with her than ever. There had been no appearance of her being, within a calculable period, liberated by the death of her husband. This nobleman was—he didn't say what just then (it was too soon)—but he was only forty years old, and in such health and preservation as to make such a contingency infinitely remote. Under these circumstances, Ambrose had been driven, for the most worldly reasons—he was ashamed of them, pah!—into an engagement with a girl he didn't love, and didn't pretend to love. Suddenly the unexpected occurred; the woman he did love had become accessible to him, and all the relations of things were altered. Why shouldn't he alter too?—why shouldn't Miss Bernardstone alter, Lady Emily alter, and every one alter? It would be *wrong* in him to marry Joscelind in so changed a world—a moment's consideration would certainly assure me of that. He could no longer carry out his part of the bargain, and the transaction must stop before it went any further. If Joscelind knew, she would be the first to recognise this, and the thing for her now was to know.

"Go and tell her, then, if you are so sure of it," I said. "I wonder you have put it off so many days."

He looked at me with a melancholy eye. "Of course I know it's beastly awkward."

It was beastly awkward certainly; there I could quite agree with him, and this was the only sympathy he extracted from me. It was impossible to be less helpful, less merciful, to an embarrassed young man than I was on that occasion. But other occasions followed very quickly, on which Mr. Tester renewed his appeal with greater eloquence. He assured me that it was torture to be with his intended, and every hour that he didn't break off committed him more deeply and more fatally. I repeated only once my previous question—asked him only once why then he didn't tell her he had changed his mind. The inquiry was idle, was even unkind, for my young man was in a very tight place. He didn't tell her, simply because he couldn't, in spite of the anguish of feeling that his chance to right himself was rapidly passing away. When I asked him if Joscelind appeared to have guessed nothing he broke out, "How in the world can she guess when I am so kind to her? I am so sorry for her, poor little wretch, that I can't help being nice to her. And from the moment I am nice to her she thinks it's all right."

I could see perfectly what he meant by that, and I liked him more for this little generosity than I disliked him for his nefarious scheme. In fact, I didn't dislike him at all when I saw what an influence my judgment would have on him. I very soon gave him the full benefit of it. I had thought over his case with all the advantages of his own presentation of it, and it was impossible for me to see how he could decently get rid of the girl. That, as I have said, had been my original opinion, and quickened reflection only confirmed it. As I have also said, I hadn't in the least recommended him to become engaged; but once he had done so I recommended him to abide by it. It was all very well being in love with Lady Vandeleur; he might be in love with her, but he hadn't promised to marry her. It was all very well not being in love with Miss Bernardstone; but, as it happened, he had promised to marry her, and in my country a gentleman was supposed to keep such promises. If it was a question of keeping them only so long as was convenient where would any of us be? I assure you I became very eloquent and moral—yes, moral, I maintain the word, in spite of your perhaps thinking (as you are very capable of doing) that I ought to have advised him in just the opposite sense. It was not a question of love, but of marriage, for he had never promised to love poor Joscelind. It was useless his saying it was dreadful to marry without love; he knew that he thought it, and the people he lived with thought it, nothing of the kind. Half his friends had married on those terms. "Yes, and a pretty sight their private life presented!" That might be, but it was the first time I had ever heard him say it. A fortnight before he had been quite ready to do like the others. I knew what I thought, and I suppose I expressed it with some clearness, for my arguments made him still more uncomfortable, unable as he was either to accept them or to act in contempt of them. Why he should have cared so much for my opinion is a mystery I can't elucidate; to understand my little story you must simply swallow it. That he did care is proved by the exasperation with which he suddenly broke out, "Well, then, as I understand you, what you recommend me is to marry Miss Bernardstone, and carry on an intrigue with Lady Vandeleur!"

He knew perfectly that I recommended nothing of the sort, and he must have been very angry to indulge in this *boutade.* He told me that other people didn't think as I did—that every one was of the opinion that between a woman he didn't love and a woman he had adored for years it was a plain moral duty not to hesitate. "Don't hesitate then!" I exclaimed; but I didn't get rid of him with this, for he returned to the charge more than once (he came to me so often that I thought he must neglect both his other alternatives), and let me know again that the voice of society was quite against my view. You will doubtless be surprised at such an intimation that he had taken "society" into his confidence, and wonder whether he went about asking people whether they thought he might back out. I can't tell you exactly, but I know that for some weeks his dilemma was a great deal talked about. His friends perceived he was at the parting of the roads, and many of them had no difficulty in saying which one *they* would take. Some observers thought he ought to do nothing, to leave things as they were. Others took very high ground and discoursed upon the sanctity of love and the wickedness of really deceiving the girl, as that would be what it would amount to (if he should lead her to the altar). Some held that it was too late to escape, others maintained that it is never too late. Some thought Miss Bernardstone very much to be pitied; some reserved their compassion for Ambrose Tester; others, still, lavished it upon Lady Vandeleur. The prevailing opinion, I think, was that he ought to obey the promptings of his heart—London cares so much for the heart! Or is it that London is simply ferocious, and always prefers the spectacle that is more entertaining? As it would prolong the drama for the young man to throw over Miss Bernardstone, there was a considerable readiness to see the poor girl sacrificed. She was like a Christian maiden in the Roman arena.[285] That is what Ambrose Tester meant by telling me that public opinion was on his side. I don't think he chattered about his quandary, but people, knowing his situation, guessed what was going on in his mind, and he, on his side, guessed what they said. London discussions might as well go on in the whispering-gallery of St. Paul's.[286]

I could, of course, do only one thing—I could but re-affirm my conviction that the Roman attitude, as I may call it, was cruel, was falsely sentimental. This naturally didn't help him as he wished to be helped—didn't remove the obstacle to his marrying in a year or two Lady Vandeleur. Yet he continued to look to me for inspiration—I must say it at the cost of making him appear a very feeble-minded gentleman. There was a moment when I thought him capable of an oblique movement, of temporising with a view to escape. If he succeeded in postponing his marriage long enough, the Bernardstones would throw *him* over, and I suspect that for a day he entertained the idea of fixing this responsibility on them. But he was too honest and too generous to do so for longer, and his destiny was staring him in the face when an accident gave him a momentary relief. General Bernardstone died, after an illness as sudden and short as that which had carried off Lord Vandeleur; his wife and daughter were plunged into mourning and immediately retired into the country. A week later we heard that the girl's marriage would be put off for several months—partly on account of her mourning and partly because her mother, whose only companion she had now become, could not bear to part with her at the time originally fixed and actually so near. People of course looked at each other—said it was the beginning of the end, a "dodge" of Ambrose Tester's. I wonder they didn't accuse him of poisoning the poor old general. I know to a certainty that he had nothing to do with the delay, that the proposal came from Lady Emily, who, in her bereavement, wished, very naturally, to keep a few months longer the child she was going to lose for ever. It must be said, in justice to her prospective son-in-law, that he was capable either of resigning himself or of frankly (with however many blushes) telling Joscelind he couldn't keep his agreement, but was not capable of trying to wriggle out of his difficulty. The plan of simply telling Joscelind he couldn't— this was the one he had fixed upon as the best, and this was the one of which I remarked to him that it had a defect which should be counted against its advantages. The defect was that it would kill Joscelind on the spot.

I think he believed me, and his believing me made this unexpected respite very welcome to him. There was no knowing what might happen in the interval, and he passed a large part of it in looking for an issue. And yet, at the same time, he kept up the usual forms with the girl whom in his heart he had renounced. I was told more than once (for I had lost sight of the pair during the summer and autumn) that these forms were at times very casual, that he neglected Miss Bernardstone most flagrantly, and had quite resumed his old intimacy with Lady Vandeleur. I don't exactly know what was meant by this, for she spent the first three months of her widowhood in complete seclusion, in her own old house in Norfolk,[287] where he certainly was not staying with her. I believe he stayed some time, for the partridge-shooting, at a place a few miles off. It came to my ears that if Miss Bernardstone didn't take the hint it was because she was determined to stick to him through thick and thin. She never offered to let him off, and I was sure she never would; but I was equally sure that, strange as it may appear, he had not ceased to be nice to her. I have never exactly understood why he didn't hate her, and I am convinced that he was not a comedian[288] in his conduct to her—he was only a good fellow. I have spoken of the satisfaction that Sir Edmund took in his daughter-in-law that was to be; he delighted in looking at her, longed for her when she was out of his sight, and had her, with her mother, staying with him in the country for weeks together. If Ambrose was not so constantly at her side as he might have been, this deficiency was covered by his father's devotion to her, by her appearance of being already one of the family. Mr. Tester was away as he might be away if they were already married.

V I

In October I met him at Doubleton; we spent three days there together. He was enjoying his respite, as he didn't scruple to tell me, and he talked to me a great deal—as usual—about Lady Vandeleur. He didn't mention Joscelind, except by implication, in this assurance of how much he valued his weeks of grace.

"Do you mean to say that, under the circumstances, Lady Vandeleur is willing to marry you?"

I made this inquiry more expressively, doubtless, than before; for when we had talked of the matter then he had naturally spoken of her consent as a simple contingency. It was contingent upon the lapse of the first months of her bereavement; it was not a question he could begin to press a few days after her husband's death.

"Not immediately, of course, but if I wait I think so." That, I remember, was his answer.

"If you wait till you get rid of that poor girl, of course."

"She knows nothing about that— it's none of her business."

"Do you mean to say she doesn't know you are engaged?"

"How should she know it, how should she believe it, when she sees how I love her?" the young man exclaimed; but he admitted afterwards that he had not deceived her, and that she rendered full justice to the motives that had determined him. He thought he could answer for it that she would marry him some day or other.

"Then she is a very cruel woman," I said, "and I should like, if you please, to hear no more about her." He protested against this, and, a month later, brought her up again, for a purpose. The purpose, you will see, was a very strange one. I had then come back to town; it was the early part of December. I supposed he was hunting, with his own hounds; but he appeared one afternoon in my drawing-room and told me I should do him a great favour if I would go and see Lady Vandeleur.

"Go and see her? where do you mean, in Norfolk?"

"She has come up to London—didn't you know it? She has a lot of business. She will be kept here till Christmas; I wish you would go."

194

"Why should I go?" I asked. "Won't you be kept here till Christmas too, and isn't that company enough for her?"

"Upon my word, you are cruel," he said, "and it's a great shame of you, when a man is trying to do his duty and is behaving like a saint."

"Is that what you call saintly, spending all your time with Lady Vandeleur? I will tell you whom I think a saint, if you would like to know."

"You needn't tell me, I know it better than you. I haven't a word to say against her; only she is stupid and hasn't any perceptions. If I am stopping a bit in London you don't understand why; it's as if you hadn't any perceptions either! If I am here for a few days I know what I am about."

"Why should I understand?" I asked—not very candidly, because I should have been glad to. "It's your own affair, you know what you are about, as you say, and of course you have counted the cost."

"What cost do you mean? It's a pretty cost, I can tell you." And then he tried to explain—if I would only enter into it, and not be so suspicious. He was in London for the express purpose of breaking off.

"Breaking off what—your engagement?"

"No, no, damn my engagement—the other thing. My acquaintance, my relations——"

"Your intimacy with Lady Van——?" It was not very gentle, but I believe I burst out laughing. "If this is the way you break off, pray, what would you do to keep up?"

He flushed, and looked both foolish and angry, for of course it was not very difficult to see my point. But he was—in a very clumsy manner of his own—trying to cultivate a good conscience, and he was getting no credit for it. "I suppose I may be allowed to look at her! It's a matter we have to talk over. One doesn't drop such a friend in half an hour."

"One doesn't drop her at all, unless one has the strength to make a sacrifice."

"It's easy for you to talk of sacrifice. You don't know what she is!" my visitor cried.

"I think I know what she is not. She is not a friend, as you call her, if she encourages you in the wrong, if she doesn't help you. No, I have no patience with her," I declared; "I don't like her, and I won't go to see her!"

Mr. Tester looked at me a moment, as if he were too vexed to trust himself to speak. He had to make an effort not to say something rude. That effort, however, he was capable of making, and though he held his hat as if he were going to walk out of the house, he ended by staying, by putting it down again, by leaning his head, with his elbows on his knees, in his hands, and groaning out that he had never heard of anything so impossible, and that he was the most wretched man in England. I was very sorry for him, and of course I told him so; but privately I didn't think he stood up to his duty as he ought. I said to him, however, that if he would give me his word of honour that he would not abandon Miss Bernardstone, there was no trouble I wouldn't take to be of use to him. I didn't think Lady Vandeleur was behaving well. He must allow me to repeat that; but if going to see her would give him any pleasure (of course there was no question of pleasure for *her*) I would go fifty times. I couldn't imagine how it would help him, but I would do it, as I would do anything else he asked me. He didn't give me his word of honour, but he said quietly, "*I* shall go straight; you needn't be afraid;" and as he spoke there was honour enough in his face. This left an opening, of course, for another catastrophe. There might be further postponements, and poor Lady Emily, indignant for the first time in her life, might declare that her daughter's situation had become intolerable, and that they withdrew from the engagement. But this was too odious a chance, and I accepted Mr. Tester's assurance. He told me that the good I could do by going to see Lady Vandeleur was that it would cheer her up, in that dreary, big house in Upper Brook Street,[289] where she was absolutely alone, with horrible overalls on the furniture, and newspapers—actually newspapers—on the mirrors. She was seeing no one, there was no one to see; but he knew she would see me. I asked him if she knew, then, he was to speak to me of coming, and whether I might allude to him, whether it was not too delicate. I shall never forget his answer to this, nor the tone in which he made it, blushing a little and looking away. "Allude to me? Rather!" It was not the most fatuous speech I had ever heard; it had the effect of being the most modest; and it gave me an odd idea, and especially a new one, of the condition in which, at any time, one might be destined to find Lady Vandeleur. If she, too, were engaged in a struggle with her conscience (in this light they were an edifying pair!) it had perhaps changed her considerably, made her more approachable; and I reflected, ingeniously, that it probably had a humanising effect upon her. Ambrose Tester didn't go away after I had told him that I would comply with his request. He lingered, fidgeting with his stick and gloves, and I perceived that he had more to tell me, and that the real reason why he wished me to go and see Lady Vandeleur was not that she had newspapers on her mirrors. He came out with it at last, for that "Rather!" of his (with the way I took it) had broken the ice.

"You say you don't think she behaves well" (he naturally wished to defend her). "But I daresay you don't understand her position. Perhaps you wouldn't behave any better in her place."

"It's very good of you to imagine me there!" I remarked, laughing.

"It's awkward for me to say. One doesn't want to dot one's i's to that extent."

"She would be delighted to marry you. That's not such a mystery."

"Well, she likes me awfully," Mr. Tester said, looking like a handsome child. "It's not all on one side, it's on both. That's the difficulty."

"You mean she won't let you go?—she holds you fast?"

But the poor fellow had, in delicacy, said enough, and at this he jumped up. He stood there a moment, smoothing his hat; then he broke out again. "Please do this. Let her know—make her feel. You can bring it in, you know." And here he paused, embarrassed.

"What can I bring in, Mr. Tester? That's the difficulty, as you say."

"What you told me the other day. You know. What you have told me before."

"What I have told you...?"

"That it would put an end to Joscelind! If you can't work round to it, what's the good of being—you?" And with this tribute to my powers he took his departure.

VII

It was all very well of him to be so flattering, but I really didn't see myself talking in that manner to Lady Vandeleur. I wondered why he didn't give her this information himself, and what particular value it could have as coming from me. Then I said to myself that of course he *had* mentioned to her the truth I had impressed upon him (and which by this time he had evidently taken home), but that to enable it to produce its full effect upon Lady Vandeleur the further testimony of a witness more independent was required. There was nothing for me but to go and see her, and I went the next day, fully conscious that to execute Mr. Tester's commission I should have either to find myself very brave or to find her strangely confidential; and fully prepared, also, not to be admitted. But she received me, and the house in Upper Brook Street was as dismal as Ambrose Tester had represented it. The December fog[290] (the afternoon was very dusky) seemed to pervade the muffled rooms, and her ladyship's pink lamp-light to waste itself in the brown atmosphere. He had mentioned to me that the heir to the title (a cousin of her husband), who had left her unmolested for several months, was now taking possession of everything, so that what kept her in town was the business of her "turning out," and certain formalities connected with her dower. This was very ample, and the large provision made for her included the London house. She was very gracious on this occasion, but she certainly had remarkably little to say. Still, she was different, or, at any rate (having taken that hint), I saw her differently. I saw, indeed, that I had never quite done her justice, that I had exaggerated her stiffness, attributed to her a kind of conscious grandeur which was in reality much more an accident of her appearance, of her figure, than a quality of her character. Her appearance is as grand as you know, and on the day I speak of, in her simplified mourning, under those vaguely-gleaming *lambris,* she looked as beautiful as a great white lily. She is very simple and good-natured; she will never make an advance, but she will always respond to one, and I saw, that evening, that the way to get on with her was to treat her as if she were not too imposing. I saw also that, with her nun-like robes and languid eyes,

198

she was a woman who might be immensely in love. All the same, we hadn't much to say to each other. She remarked that it was very kind of me to come, that she wondered how I could endure London at that season, that she had taken a drive and found the Park[291] too dreadful, that she would ring for some more tea if I didn't like what she had given me. Our conversation wandered, stumbling a little, among these platitudes, but no allusion was made on either side to Ambrose Tester. Nevertheless, as I have said, she was different, though it was not till I got home that I phrased to myself what I had detected.

Then, recalling her white face, and the deeper, stranger expression of her beautiful eyes, I entertained myself with the idea that she was under the influence of "suppressed exaltation."[292] The more I thought of her the more she appeared to me not natural; wound up, as it were, to a calmness beneath which there was a deal of agitation. This would have been nonsense if I had not, two days afterwards, received a note from her which struck me as an absolutely "exalted "production. Not superficially, of course; to the casual eye it would have been perfectly commonplace. But this was precisely its peculiarity, that Lady Vandeleur should have written me a note which had no apparent point save that she should like to see me again, a desire for which she did succeed in assigning a reason. She reminded me that she was paying no calls, and she hoped I wouldn't stand on ceremony, but come in very soon again, she had enjoyed my visit so much. We had not been on note-writing terms, and there was nothing in that visit to alter our relations; moreover, six months before, she would not have dreamed of addressing me in that way. I was doubly convinced, therefore, that she was passing through a crisis—that she was not in her normal equilibrium. Mr. Tester had not reappeared since the occasion I have described at length, and I thought it possible he had been capable of the bravery of leaving town. I had, however, no fear of meeting him in Upper Brook Street; for, according to my theory of his relations with Lady Vandeleur he regularly spent his evenings with her, it being clear to me that they must dine together. I could answer her note only by going to see her the next day, when I found abundant confirmation of that idea about the crisis. I must confess to you in advance that I have never really understood her behaviour—never understood why she should have taken to me so suddenly—with whatever reserves, and however much by implication merely—into her confidence.

All I can say is that this is an accident to which one is exposed with English people, who, in my opinion, and contrary to common report, are the most demonstrative, the most expansive, the most gushing in the world. I think she felt rather isolated at this moment, and she had never had many intimates of her own sex. That sex, as a general thing, disapproved of her proceedings during the last few months, held that she was making Joscelind Bernardstone suffer too cruelly. She possibly felt the weight of this censure, and at all events was not above wishing some one to know that, whatever injury had fallen upon the girl to whom Mr. Tester had so stupidly engaged himself, had not, so far as she was concerned, been wantonly inflicted. I was there, I was more or less aware of her situation, and I would do as well as any one else.

She seemed really glad to see me, but she was very nervous. Nevertheless, nearly half an hour elapsed, and I was still wondering whether she had sent for me only to discuss the question of how a London house whose appointments had the stamp of a debased period (it had been thought very handsome in 1850) could be "done up" without being made aesthetic.[293] I forget what satisfaction I gave her on this point; I was asking myself how I could work round in the manner prescribed by Joscelind's intended. At the last, however, to my extreme surprise, Lady Vandeleur herself relieved me of this effort.

"I think you know Mr. Tester rather well," she remarked abruptly, irrelevantly, and with a face more conscious of the bearings of things than any I had ever seen her wear. On my confessing to such an acquaintance, she mentioned that Mr. Tester (who had been in London a few days—perhaps I had seen him) had left town and wouldn't come back for several weeks. This, for the moment, seemed to be all she had to communicate; but she sat looking at me from the corner of her sofa as if she wished me to profit in some way by the opportunity she had given me. Did she want help from outside, this proud, inscrutable woman, and was she reduced to throwing out signals of distress? Did she wish to be protected against herself—applauded for such efforts as she had already made? I didn't rush forward, I was not precipitate, for I felt that now, surely, I should be able at my convenience to execute my commission. What concerned me was not to prevent Lady Vandeleur's marrying Mr. Tester, but to prevent Mr. Tester's marrying her. In a few moments—with the same irrelevance—she announced to me that he wished to, and asked whether I didn't know it. I saw that this was my chance, and instantly with extreme energy, I exclaimed—

"Ah, for heaven's sake, don't listen to him! It would kill Miss Bernardstone!"

The tone of my voice made her colour a little, and she repeated, "Miss Bernardstone?"

"The girl he is engaged to—or has been—don't you know? Excuse me, I thought every one knew."

"Of course I know he is dreadfully entangled. He was fairly hunted down." Lady Vandeleur was silent a moment, and then she added, with a strange smile, "Fancy, in such a situation, his wanting to marry me!"

"Fancy!" I replied. I was so struck with the oddity of her telling me her secrets that for the moment my indignation did not come to a head—my indignation, I mean, at her accusing poor Lady Emily (and even the girl herself) of having "trapped" our friend. Later I said to myself that I supposed she was within her literal right in abusing her rival, if she was trying sincerely to give him up. "I don't know anything about his having been hunted down," I said; "but this I do know, Lady Vandeleur, I assure you, that if he should throw Joscelind over she would simply go out like that!" And I snapped my fingers.

Lady Vandeleur listened to this serenely enough; she tried at least to take the air of a woman who has no need of new arguments. "Do you know her very well?" she asked, as if she had been struck by my calling Miss Bemardstone by her Christian name.

"Well enough to like her very much." I was going to say "to pity her;" but I thought better of it.

"She must be a person of very little spirit. If a man were to jilt me, I don't think I should go out!" cried her ladyship, with a laugh.

"Nothing is more probable than that she has not your courage or your wisdom. She may be weak, but she is passionately in love with him."

I looked straight into Lady Vandeleur's eyes as I said this, and I was conscious that it was a tolerably good description of my hostess.

"Do you think she would really die?" she asked in a moment.

"Die as if one should stab her with a knife. Some people don't believe in broken hearts," I continued. "I didn't till I knew Joscelind Bernardstone; then I felt that she had one that wouldn't be proof."

"One ought to live—one ought always to live," said Lady Vandeleur; "and always to hold up one's head."

"Ah, I suppose that one oughtn't to feel at all, if one wishes to be a great success."

"What do you call a great success?" she asked.

"Never having occasion to be pitied."

"Being pitied? That must be odious!" she said; and I saw that though she might wish for admiration, she would never wish for sympathy. Then, in a moment, she added that men, in her opinion, were very base—a remark that was deep, but not, I think, very honest; that is, in so far as the purpose of it had been to give me the idea that Ambrose Tester had done nothing but press her, and she had done nothing but resist. They were very odd, the discrepancies in the statements of each of this pair; but it must be said for Lady Vandeleur that now that she had made up her mind (as I believed she had) to sacrifice herself, she really persuaded herself that she had not had a moment of weakness. She quite unbosomed herself, and I fairly assisted at her crisis. It appears that she had a conscience—very much so, and even a high ideal of duty. She represented herself as moving heaven and earth to keep Ambrose Tester up to the mark, and you would never have guessed from what she told me that she had entertained, ever so faintly, the idea of marrying him. I am sure this was a dreadful perversion, but I forgave it on the score of that exaltation of which I have spoken. The things she said, and the way she said them, come back to me, and I thought that if she looked as handsome as that when she preached virtue to Mr. Tester, it was no wonder he liked the sermon to be going on perpetually.

"I daresay you know what old friends we are; but that doesn't make any difference, does it? Nothing would induce me to marry him—I haven't the smallest intention of marrying again. It is not a time for me to think of marrying, before his lordship has been dead six months. The girl is nothing to me; I know nothing about her, and I don't wish to know; but I should be very, very sorry if she were unhappy. He is the best friend I ever had, but I don't see that that's any reason I should marry him, do you?" Lady Vandeleur appealed to me, but without waiting for my answers, asking advice in spite of herself, and then remembering it was beneath her dignity to appear to be in need of it. "I have told him that if he doesn't act properly I shall never speak to him again. She's a charming girl, every one says, and

I have no doubt she will make him perfectly happy. Men don't feel things like women, I think, and if they are coddled and flattered they forget the rest. I have no doubt she is very sufficient for all that. For me, at any rate, once I see a thing in a certain way, I must abide by that. I think people are so dreadful—they do such horrible things. They don't seem to think what one's duty may be. I don't know whether you think much about that, but really one must at times, don't you think so? Every one is so selfish, and then, when they have never made an effort or a sacrifice themselves, they come to you and talk such a lot of hypocrisy. I know so much better than any one else whether I should marry or not. But I don't mind telling you that I don't see why I should. I am not in such a bad position—with my liberty and a decent maintenance."

In this manner she rambled on, gravely and communicatively, contradicting herself at times; not talking fast (she never did), but dropping one simple sentence, with an interval, after the other, with a certain richness of voice which always was part of the charm of her presence. She wished to be convinced against herself, and it was a comfort to her to hear herself argue. I was quite willing to be part of the audience, though I had to confine myself to very superficial remarks; for when I had said the event I feared would kill Miss Bernardstone I had said everything that was open to me. I had nothing to do with Lady Vandeleur's marrying, apart from that. I probably disappointed her. She had caught a glimpse of the moral beauty of self-sacrifice, of a certain ideal of conduct (I imagine it was rather new to her), and would have been glad to elicit from me, as a person of some experience of life, an assurance that such joys are not unsubstantial. I had no wish to wind her up to a spiritual ecstasy from which she would inevitably descend again, and I let her deliver herself according to her humour, without attempting to answer for it that she would find renunciation the road to bliss. I believed that if she should give up Mr. Tester she would suffer accordingly; but I didn't think that a reason for not giving him up. Before I left her she said to me that nothing would induce her to do anything that she didn't think right. "It would be no pleasure to me, don't you see? I should be always thinking that another way would have been better. Nothing would induce me—nothing, nothing!"

VIII

She protested too much, perhaps,[294] but the event seemed to show that she was in earnest. I have described these two first visits of mine in some detail, but they were not the only ones I paid her. I saw her several times again, before she left town, and we became intimate, as London intimacies are measured. She ceased to protest (to my relief, for it made me nervous), she was very gentle, and gracious, and reasonable, and there was something in the way she looked and spoke that told me that for the present she found renunciation its own reward. So far, my scepticism was put to shame; her spiritual ecstasy maintained itself. If I could have foreseen then that it would maintain itself till the present hour I should have felt that Lady Vandeleur's moral nature is finer indeed than mine. I heard from her that Mr. Tester remained at his father's, and that Lady Emily and her daughter were also there. The day for the wedding had been fixed, and the preparations were going rapidly forward. Meanwhile—she didn't tell me, but I gathered it from things she dropped—she was in almost daily correspondence with the young man. I thought this a strange concomitant of his bridal arrangements; but apparently, henceforth, they were bent on convincing each other that the torch of virtue lighted their steps, and they couldn't convince each other too much. She intimated to me that she had now effectually persuaded him (always by letter) that he would fail terribly if he should try to found his happiness on an injury done to another, and that of course she could never be happy (in a union with him) with the sight of his wretchedness before her. That a good deal of correspondence should be required to elucidate this is perhaps after all not remarkable. One day, when I was sitting with her (it was just before she left town), she suddenly burst into tears. Before we parted I said to her that there were several women in London I liked very much—that was common enough—but for her I had a positive respect, and that was rare. My respect continues still, and it sometimes makes me furious.

About the middle of January Ambrose Tester reappeared in town. He told me he came to bid me good-bye. He was going to be beheaded.[295] It was no use saying that old relations would be the same after a man was married; they would be different, everything would be different. I had wanted him to marry, and now I should see how I liked it. He didn't mention that I had also wanted him not to marry, and I was sure that if Lady Vandeleur had become his wife she would have been a much greater impediment to our harmless friendship than Joscelind Bernardstone would ever be. It took me but a short time to observe that he was in very much the same condition as Lady Vandeleur. He was finding how sweet it is to renounce, hand in hand with one we love. Upon him, too, the peace of the Lord had descended. He spoke of his father's delight at the nuptials being so near at hand; at the festivities that would take place in Dorsetshire when he should bring home his bride. The only allusion he made to what we had talked of the last time we were together was to exclaim suddenly, "How can I tell you how easy she has made it? She is so sweet, so noble! She really is a perfect creature!" I took for granted that he was talking of his future wife, but in a moment, as we were at cross-purposes, perceived that he meant Lady Vandeleur. This seemed to me really ominous—it stuck in my mind after he had left me. I was half tempted to write him a note, to say, "There is, after all, perhaps, something worse than your jilting Miss Bernardstone; and that is the danger that your rupture with Lady Vandeleur may become more of a bond than your marrying her would have been. For heaven's sake, let your sacrifice *be* a sacrifice; keep it in its proper place!"

Of course I didn't write; even the slight responsibility I had already incurred began to frighten me, and I never saw Mr. Tester again till he was the husband of Joscelind Bernardstone. They have now been married some four years; they have two children, the elder of whom is, as he should be, a boy. Sir Edmund waited till his grandson had made good his place in the world, and then, feeling it was safe, he quietly, genially, surrendered his trust. He died, holding the hand of his daughter-in-law, and giving it doubtless a pressure which was an injunction to be brave. I don't know what he thought of the success of his plan for his son; but perhaps, after all, he saw nothing amiss, for Joscelind is the last woman in the world to have troubled him with her sorrows. From him, no doubt, she successfully concealed that bewilderment on which I have touched. You see I speak of her sorrows as if they were a matter of common recognition; certain it is that any one who meets her must see that she doesn't pass her life in joy. Lady Vandeleur, as you know, has never married again; she is still the most beautiful widow in England. She enjoys the esteem of every one, as well as the approbation of her conscience, for every one knows the sacrifice she made, knows that she was even more in love with Sir Ambrose than he was with her. She goes out again, of course, as of old, and she constantly meets the baronet and his wife. She is supposed to be even "very nice" to Lady Tester, and she certainly treats her with exceeding civility. But you know (or perhaps you don't know) all the deadly things that, in London, may lie beneath that method. I don't in the least mean that Lady Vandeleur has any deadly intentions; she is a very good woman, and I am sure that in her heart she thinks she lets poor Joscelind off very easily. But the result of the whole situation is that Joscelind is in dreadful fear of her, for how can she help seeing that she has a very peculiar power over her husband? There couldn't have been a better occasion for observing the three together (if together it may be called, when Lady Tester is so completely outside) than those two days of ours at Doubleton. That's a house where they have met more than once before; I think she and Sir Ambrose like it. By "she" I mean, as he used to mean, Lady Vandeleur. You saw how Lady Tester was absolutely white with uneasiness. What can she do when she meets everywhere the implication that if two people in our time have distinguished themselves for their virtue, it is her husband and Lady Vandeleur? It is my impression that this pair are exceedingly happy. His marriage *has* made a difference, and I see him much less frequently and less intimately. But when I meet him I notice in him a kind of emanation of quiet bliss. Yes, they are certainly in felicity, they have trod the clouds together, they have soared into the blue, and they wear in their faces the glory of those altitudes. They encourage, they cheer, inspire, sustain each other; remind each other that they have chosen the better part. Of course they have to meet for this purpose, and their interviews are filled, I am sure, with its sanctity. He holds up his head, as a man may who on a very critical occasion behaved like a perfect gentleman. It is only poor Joscelind that droops. Haven't I explained to you now why she doesn't understand?

Mrs. Temperly

I

"Why, Cousin Raymond, how can you suppose? Why, she's only sixteen!"

"She told me she was seventeen," said the young man, as if it made a great difference.

"Well, only *just*!" Mrs. Temperly replied, in the tone of graceful, reasonable concession.

"Well, that's a very good age for me. I'm very young."

"You are old enough to know better," the lady remarked, in her soft, pleasant voice, which always drew the sting from a reproach, and enabled you to swallow it as you would a cooked plum, without the stone. "Why, she hasn't finished her education!"

"That's just what I mean," said her interlocutor. "It would finish it beautifully for her to marry me."

"Have you finished yours, my dear? "Mrs. Temperly inquired. "The way you young people talk about marrying!" she exclaimed, looking at the itinerant functionary with the long wand who touched into a flame the tall gas-lamp on the other side of the Fifth Avenue.[296] The pair were standing, in the recess of a window, in one of the big public rooms of an immense hotel,[297] and the October day was turning to dusk.

"Well, would you have us leave it to the old?" Raymond asked. "That's just what I think—she would be such a help to me," he continued. "I want to go back to Paris to study more. I have come home too soon. I don't know half enough; they know more here than I thought. So it would be perfectly easy, and we should all be together."

"Well, my dear, when you do come back to Paris we will talk about it," said Mrs. Temperly, turning away from the window.

"I should like it better, Cousin Maria, if you trusted me a little more," Raymond sighed, observing that she was not really giving her thoughts to what he said. She irritated him somehow; she was so full of her impending departure, of her arrangements, her last duties and memoranda. She was not exactly important, any more than she was humble; she was too conciliatory for the one and too positive for the other. But she bustled quietly and gave one the sense of being 'up to' everything; the successive steps of her enterprise were in advance perfectly clear to her, and he could see that her imagination (conventional as she was she had plenty of that faculty) had already taken up its abode on one of those fine *premiers* which she had never seen, but which by instinct she seemed to know all about, in the very best part of the quarter of the Champs Elysées.[298] If she ruffled him envy had perhaps something to do with it: she was to set sail on the morrow for the city of his affection and he was to stop in New York, where the fact that he was but half pleased did not alter the fact that he had his studio on his hands and that it was a bad one (though perhaps as good as any use he should put it to), which no one would be in a hurry to relieve him of.

It was easy for him to talk to Mrs. Temperly in that airy way about going back, but he couldn't go back unless the old gentleman gave him the means. He had already given him a great many things in the past, and with the others coming on (Marian's marriage-outfit, within three months, had cost literally thousands), Raymond had not at present the face to ask for more. He must sell some pictures first, and to sell them he must first paint them. It was his misfortune that he saw what he wanted to do so much better than he could do it. But he must really try and please himself—an effort that appeared more possible now that the idea of following Dora across the ocean had become an incentive. In spite of secret aspirations and even intentions, however, it was not encouraging to feel that he made really no impression at all on Cousin Maria. This certitude was so far from agreeable to him that he almost found it in him to drop the endearing title by which he had hitherto addressed her. It was only that, after all, her husband had been distantly related to his mother. It was not as a cousin that he was interested in Dora, but as something very much more intimate. I know not whether it occurred to him that Mrs. Temperly herself would never give his displeasure the benefit of dropping the affectionate form. She might shut her door to him altogether, but he would always be her kinsman and her dear. She was much addicted to these little embellishments of human intercourse—the friendly apostrophe and even the caressing hand—and there was something homely and cosy, a rustic, motherly *bonhomie*, in her use of them. She was as lavish of them as she was really careful in the selection of her friends.

She stood there with her hand in her pocket, as if she were feeling for something; her little plain, pleasant face was presented to him with a musing smile, and he vaguely wondered whether she were fumbling for a piece of money to buy him off from wishing to marry her daughter. Such an idea would be quite in keeping with the disguised levity with which she treated his state of mind. If her levity was wrapped up in the air of tender solicitude for everything that related to the feelings of her child, that only made her failure to appreciate his suit more deliberate. She struck him almost as impertinent (at the same time that he knew this was never her intention) as she looked up at him—her tiny proportions always made her throw back her head and set something dancing in her cap—and inquired whether he had noticed if she gave two keys, tied together by a blue ribbon, to Susan Winkle,[299] when that faithful but flurried domestic met them in the lobby. She was thinking only of questions of luggage, and the fact that he wished to marry Dora was the smallest incident in their getting off.

"I think you ask me that only to change the subject," he said. "I don't believe that ever in your life you have been unconscious of what you have done with your keys."

"Not often, but you make me nervous," she answered, with her patient, honest smile.

"Oh, Cousin Maria!" the young man exclaimed, ambiguously, while Mrs. Temperly looked humanely at some totally uninteresting people who came straggling into the great hot, frescoed, velvety drawing-room, where it was as easy to see you were in an hotel as it was to see that, if you were, you were in one of the very best. Mrs. Temperly, since her husband's death, had passed much of her life at hotels, where she flattered herself that she preserved the tone of domestic life free from every taint and promoted the refined development of her children; but she selected them as well as she selected her friends. Somehow they became better from the very fact of her being there, and her children were smuggled in and out in the most extraordinary way; one never met them racing and whooping, as one did hundreds of others, in the lobbies. Her frequentation of hotels, where she paid enormous bills, was part of her expensive but practical way of living, and also of her theory that, from one week to another, she was going to Europe for a series of years as soon as she had wound up certain complicated affairs which had devolved upon her at her husband's death. If these affairs had dragged on it was owing to their inherent troublesomeness and implied no doubt of her capacity to bring them to a solution and to administer the very considerable fortune that Mr. Temperly had left. She used, in a superior, unprejudiced way, every convenience that the civilisation of her time offered her, and would have lived without hesitation in a lighthouse if this had contributed to her general scheme. She was now, in the interest of this scheme, preparing to use Europe, which she had not yet visited and with none of whose foreign tongues she was acquainted. This time she was certainly embarking.

She took no notice of the discredit which her young friend appeared to throw on the idea that she had nerves, and betrayed no suspicion that he believed her to have them in about the same degree as a sound, productive Alderney cow.[300] She only moved toward one of the numerous doors of the room, as if to remind him of all she had still to do before night. They passed together into the long, wide corridor of the hotel—a vista of soft carpet, numbered doors, wandering women and perpetual gaslight[301]—and approached the staircase by which she must ascend again to her domestic duties. She counted over, serenely, for his enlightenment, those that were still to be performed; but he could see that everything would be finished by nine o'clock—the time she had fixed in advance. The heavy luggage was then to go to the steamer;[302] she herself was to be on board, with the children and the smaller things, at eleven o'clock the next morning. They had thirty pieces, but this was less than they had when they came from California[303] five years before. She wouldn't have done that again. It was true that at that time she had had Mr. Temperly to help: he had died, Raymond remembered, six months after the settlement in New York. But, on the other hand, she knew more now. It was one of Mrs. Temperly's amiable qualities that she admitted herself so candidly to be still susceptible of development. She never professed to be in possession of all the knowledge requisite for her career; not only did she let her friends know that she was always learning, but she appealed to them to instruct her, in a manner which was in itself an example.

When Raymond said to her that he took for granted she would let him come down to the steamer for a last good-bye, she not only consented graciously but added that he was free to call again at the hotel in the evening, if he had nothing better to do. He must come between nine and ten; she expected several other friends—those who wished to see the last of them, yet didn't care to come to the ship. Then he would see all of them—she meant all of themselves, Dora and Effie and Tishy,[304] and even Mademoiselle Bourde. She spoke exactly as if he had never approached her on the subject of Dora and as if Tishy, who was ten years of age, and Mademoiselle Bourde, who was the French governess and forty, were objects of no less an interest to him. He felt what a long pull[305] he should have ever to get round her, and the sting of this knowledge was in his consciousness that Dora was really in her mother's hands. In Mrs. Temperly's composition there was not a hint of the bully; but none the less she held her children—she would hold them for ever. It was not simply by tenderness; but what it was by she knew best herself. Raymond appreciated the privilege of seeing Dora again that evening as well as on the morrow; yet he was so vexed with her mother that his vexation betrayed him into something that almost savoured of violence—a fact which I am ashamed to have to chronicle, as Mrs. Temperly's own urbanity deprived such breaches of every excuse. It may perhaps serve partly as an excuse for Raymond Bestwick that he was in love, or at least that he thought he was. Before she parted from him at the foot of the staircase he said to her, "And of course, if things go as you like over there, Dora will marry some foreign prince."

She gave no sign of resenting this speech, but she looked at him for the first time as if she were hesitating, as if it were not instantly clear to her what to say. It appeared to him, on his side, for a moment, that there was something strange in her hesitation, that abruptly, by an inspiration, she was almost making up her mind to reply that Dora's marriage to a prince was, considering Dora's peculiarities (he knew that her mother deemed her peculiar, and so did he, but that was precisely why he wished to many her), so little probable that, after all, once such a union was out of the question, *he* might be no worse than another plain man. These, however, were not the words that fell from Mrs. Temperly's lips. Her embarrassment vanished in her clear smile. Do you know what Mr. Temperly used to say? He used to say that Dora was the pattern of an old maid—she would never make a choice."

"I hope—because that would have been too foolish—that he didn't say she wouldn't have a chance."

"Oh, a chance! what do you call by that fine name?" Cousin Maria exclaimed, laughing, as she ascended the stair.

II

When he came back, after dinner, she was again in one of the public rooms; she explained that a lot of the things for the ship were spread out in her own parlours: there was no space to sit down. Raymond was highly gratified by this fact; it offered an opportunity for strolling away a little with Dora, especially as, after he had been there ten minutes, other people began to come in. They were entertained by the rest, by Effie and Tishy, who was allowed to sit up a little, and by Mademoiselle Bourde, who besought every visitor to indicate her a remedy that was *really* effective against the sea—some charm, some philter, some potion or spell. "Never mind, ma'm'selle, I've got a remedy," said Cousin Maria, with her cheerful decision, each time; but the French instructress always began afresh.

As the young man was about to be parted for an indefinite period from the girl whom he was ready to swear that he adored, it is clear that he ought to have been equally ready to swear that she was the fairest of her species. In point of fact, however, it was no less vivid to him than it had been before that he loved Dora Temperly for qualities which had nothing to do with straightness of nose or pinkness of complexion. Her figure was straight, and so was her character, but her nose was not, and Philistines[306] and other vulgar people would have committed themselves, without a blush on their own flat faces, to the assertion that she was decidedly plain. In his artistic imagination he had analogies for her, drawn from legend and literature; he was perfectly aware that she struck many persons as silent, shy and angular,[307] while his own version of her peculiarities was that she was like a figure on the *predella* of an early Italian painting or a mediaeval maiden wandering about a lonely castle, with her lover gone to the Crusades.[308] To his sense, Dora had but one defect—her admiration for her mother was too undiscriminating. An ardent young man may well be slightly vexed when he finds that a young lady will probably never care for him so much as she cares for her parent; and Raymond Bestwick had this added ground for chagrin, that Dora had—if she chose to take it—so good a pretext for discriminating. For she had nothing whatever in common with the others; she was not of the same stuff as Mrs. Temperly and Effie and Tishy.

She was original and generous and uncalculating, besides being full of perception and taste in regard to the things *he* cared about. She knew nothing of conventional signs or estimates, but understood everything that might be said to her from an artistic point of view. She was formed to live in a studio, and not in a stiff drawing-room, amid upholstery horribly new; and moreover her eyes and her voice were both charming. It was only a pity she was so gentle; that is, he liked it for himself, but he deplored it for her mother. He considered that he had virtually given that lady his word that he would not make love to her; but his spirits had risen since his visit of three or four hours before. It seemed to him, after thinking things over more intently, that a way would be opened for him to return to Paris. It was not probable that in the interval Dora would be married off to a prince; for in the first place the foolish race of princes would be sure not to appreciate her, and in the second she would not, in this matter, simply do her mother's bidding—her gentleness would not go so far as that. She might remain single by the maternal decree, but she would not take a husband who was disagreeable to her. In this reasoning Raymond was obliged to shut his eyes very tight to the danger that some particular prince might not be disagreeable to her, as well as to the attraction proceeding from what her mother might announce that she would 'do.' He was perfectly aware that it was in Cousin Maria's power, and would probably be in her pleasure, to settle a handsome marriage-fee[309] upon each of her daughters. He was equally certain that this had nothing to do with the nature of his own interest in the eldest, both because it was clear that Mrs. Temperly would do very little for *him* and because he didn't care how little she did.

Effie and Tishy sat in the circle, on the edge of rather high chairs, while Mademoiselle Bourde surveyed in them with complacency the results of her own superiority. Tishy was a child, but Effie was fifteen, and they were both very nice little girls, arrayed in fresh travelling dresses and deriving a quaintness from the fact that Tishy was already armed, for foreign adventures, with a smart new reticule,[310] from which she could not be induced to part, and that Effie had her finger in her 'place' in a fat red volume of *Murray*.[311] Raymond knew that in a general way their mother would not have allowed them to appear in the drawing-room with these adjuncts, but something was to be allowed to the fever of anticipation. They were both pretty, with delicate features and blue eyes, and would grow up into worldly, conventional young ladies, just as Dora had not done. They looked at Mademoiselle Bourde for approval whenever they spoke, and, in addressing their mother alternately with that accomplished woman, kept their two languages neatly distinct.

Raymond had but a vague idea of who the people were who had come to bid Cousin Maria farewell, and he had no wish for a sharper one, though she introduced him, very definitely, to the whole group.[312] She might make light of him in her secret soul, but she would never put herself in the wrong by omitting the smallest form. Fortunately, however, he was not obliged to like all her forms, and he foresaw the day when she would abandon this particular one. She was not so well made up in advance about Paris but that it would be in reserve for her to detest the period when she had thought it proper to 'introduce all round.' Raymond detested it already, and tried to make Dora understand that he wished her to take a walk with him in the corridors. There was a gentleman with a curl on his forehead who especially displeased him; he made childish jokes, at which the others laughed all at once, as if they had rehearsed for it—jokes *à la portée* of Effie and Tishy and mainly about them. These two joined in the merriment, as if they followed perfectly, as indeed they might, and gave a small sigh afterward, with a little factitious air. Dora remained grave, almost sad; it was when she was different, in this way, that he felt how much he liked her. He hated, in general, a large ring of people who had drawn up chairs in the public room of an hotel: some one was sure to undertake to be funny.

He succeeded at last in drawing Dora away; he endeavoured to give the movement a casual air. There was nothing peculiar, after all, in their walking a little in the passage; a dozen other persons were doing the same. The girl had the air of not suspecting in the least that he could have anything particular to say to her—of responding to his appeal simply out of her general gentleness. It was not in her companion's interest that her mind should be such a blank; nevertheless his conviction that in spite of the ministrations of Mademoiselle Bourde she was not falsely ingenuous made him repeat to himself that he would still make her his own. They took several turns in the hall, during which it might still have appeared to Dora Temperly that her cousin Raymond had nothing particular to say to her. He remarked several times that he should certainly turn up in Paris in the spring; but when once she had replied that she was very glad that subject seemed exhausted. The young man cared little, however; it was not a question now of making any declaration: he only wanted to be with her. Suddenly, when they were at the end of the corridor furthest removed from the room they had left, he said to her: "Your mother is very strange. Why has she got such an idea about Paris?"

"How do you mean, such an idea?" He had stopped, making the girl stand there before him.

"Well, she thinks so much of it without having ever seen it, or really knowing anything. She appears to have planned out such a great life there."

"She thinks it's the best place," Dora rejoined, with the dim smile that always charmed our young man.

"The best place for what?"

"Well, to learn French." The girl continued to smile.

"Do you mean for her? She'll never learn it; she can't."

"No; for us. And other things."

"You know it already. And *you* know other things," said Raymond.

"She wants us to know them better—better than any girls know them."

"I don't know what things you mean," exclaimed the young man, rather impatiently.

"Well, we shall see," Dora returned, laughing.

He said nothing for a minute, at the end of which he resumed: "I hope you won't be offended if I say that it seems curious your mother should have such aspirations—such Napoleonic plans.[313] I mean being just a quiet little lady from California, who has never seen any of the kind of thing that she has in her head."

"That's just why she wants to see it, I suppose; and I don't know why her being from California should prevent. At any rate she wants us to have the best. Isn't the best taste in Paris?"

"Yes; and the worst." It made him gloomy when she defended the old lady, and to change the subject he asked: "Aren't you sorry, this last night, to leave your own country for such an indefinite time?"

It didn't cheer him up that the girl should answer: "Oh, I would go any-where with mother!"

"And with *her*?" Raymond demanded, sarcastically, as Mademoiselle Bourde came in sight, emerging from the drawing-room.

She approached them; they met her in a moment, and she informed Dora that Mrs. Temperly wished her to come back and play a part of that composition of Saint-Saens[314]—the last one she had been learning—for Mr. and Mrs. Parminter:[315] they wanted to judge whether their daughter could manage it.

"I don't believe she can," said Dora, smiling; but she was moving away to comply when her companion detained her a moment.

"Are you going to bid me good-bye?"

"Won't you come back to the drawing-room?"

"I think not; I don't like it."

"And to mamma—you'll say nothing?" the girl went on.

"Oh, we have made our farewell; we had a special interview this afternoon."

"And you won't come to the ship in the morning?"

Raymond hesitated a moment. "Will Mr. and Mrs. Parminter be there?"

"Oh, surely they will!" Mademoiselle Bourde declared, surveying the young couple with a certain tactful serenity, but standing very close to them, as if it might be her duty to interpose.

"Well then, I won't come."

"Well, good-bye then," said the girl gently, holding out her hand.

"Good-bye, Dora." He took it, while she smiled at him, but he said nothing more—he was so annoyed at the way Mademoiselle Bourde watched them. He only looked at Dora; she seemed to him beautiful.

"My dear child—that poor Madame Parminter," the governess murmured.

"I shall come over very soon," said Raymond, as his companion turned away.

"That will be charming." And she left him quickly, without looking back.

Mademoiselle Bourde lingered—he didn't know why, unless it was to make him feel, with her smooth, finished French assurance, which had the manner of extreme benignity, that she was following him up. He sometimes wondered whether she copied Mrs. Temperly or whether Mrs. Temperly tried to copy her. Presently she said, slowly rubbing her hands and smiling at him:

"You will have plenty of time. We shall be long in Paris."

"Perhaps you will be disappointed," Raymond suggested.

"How can we be—unless *you* disappoint us?" asked the governess, sweetly.

He left her without ceremony: the imitation was probably on the part of Cousin Maria.

"Only just ourselves," her note had said; and he arrived, in his natural impatience, a few moments before the hour. He remembered his Cousin Maria's habitual punctuality, but when he entered the splendid *salon* in the quarter of the Parc Monceau[316]—it was there that he had found her established— he saw that he should have it, for a little, to himself. This was pleasing, for he should be able to look round—there were admirable things to look at. Even to-day Raymond Bestwick was not sure that he had learned to paint, but he had no doubt of his judgment of the work of others, and a single glance showed him that Mrs. Temperly had 'known enough' to select, for the adornment of her walls, half a dozen immensely valuable specimens of contemporary French art.[317] Her choice of other objects had been equally enlightened, and he remembered what Dora had said to him five years before—that her mother wished them to have the best. Evidently now they had got it; if five years was a long time for him to have delayed (with his original plan of getting off so soon) to come to Paris, it was a very short one for Cousin Maria to have taken to arrive at the highest good.

Rather to his surprise the first person to come in was Effie, now so complete a young lady, and such a very pretty girl, that he scarcely would have known her. She was fair, she was graceful, she was lovely, and as she entered the room, blushing and smiling, with a little floating motion which suggested that she was in a liquid element, she brushed down the ribbons of a delicate Parisian *toilette de jeune fille*. She appeared to expect that he would be surprised, and as if to justify herself for being the first she said, "Mamma told me to come; she knows you are here; she said I was not to wait." More than once, while they conversed, during the next few moments, before any one else arrived, she repeated that she was acting by her mamma's directions. Raymond perceived that she had not only the costume but several other of the attributes of a *jeune fille*. They talked, I say, but with a certain difficulty, for Effie asked him no questions, and this made him feel a little stiff about thrusting information upon her. Then she was so pretty, so exquisite, that this by itself disconcerted him. It seemed to him almost that she had falsified a prophecy, instead of bringing one to pass. He had foretold that she would be like this; the only difference was that she was so much more like it. She made no inquiries about his arrival, his people in America, his plans; and they exchanged vague remarks about the pictures, quite as if they had met for the first time.

When Cousin Maria came in Effie was standing in front of the fire fastening a bracelet, and he was at a distance gazing in silence at a portrait of his hostess by Bastien-Lepage.[318] One of his apprehensions had been that Cousin Maria would allude ironically to the difference there had been between his threat (because it had been really almost a threat) of following them speedily to Paris and what had in fact occurred; but he saw in a moment how superficial this calculation had been. Besides, when had Cousin Maria ever been ironical? She treated him as if she had seen him last week (which did not preclude kindness), and only expressed her regret at having missed his visit the day before, in consequence of which she had immediately written to him to come and dine. He might have come from round the corner, instead of from New York and across the wintry ocean. This was a part of her 'cosiness,' her friendly, motherly optimism, of which, even of old, the habit had been never to recognise nor allude to disagreeable things; so that to-day, in the midst of so much that was not disagreeable, the custom would of course be immensely confirmed.

Raymond was perfectly aware that it was not a pleasure, even for her, that, for several years past, things should have gone so ill in New York with his family and himself. His father's embarrassments, of which Marian's silly husband had been the cause and which had terminated in general ruin and humiliation, to say nothing of the old man's 'stroke' and the necessity, arising from it, for a renunciation on his own part of all present thoughts of leaving home again and even for a partial relinquishment of present work, the old man requiring so much of his personal attention—all this constituted an episode which could not fail to look sordid and dreary in the light of Mrs. Temperly's high success. The odour of success was in the warm, slightly heavy air, which seemed distilled from rare old fabrics, from brocades and tapestries, from the deep, mingled tones of the pictures, the subdued radiance of cabinets and old porcelain and the jars of winter roses standing in soft circles of lamp-light. Raymond felt himself in the presence of an effect in regard to which he remained in ignorance of the cause—a mystery that required a key. Cousin Maria's success was unexplained so long as she simply stood there with her little familiar, comforting, upward gaze, talking in coaxing cadences, with exactly the same manner she had brought ten years ago from California, to a tall, bald, bending, smiling young man, evidently a foreigner, who had just come in and whose name Raymond had not caught from the lips of the *maître d'hôtel*. Was he just one of themselves—was he there for Effie, or perhaps even for Dora? The unexplained must preponderate till Dora came in; he found he counted upon her, even though in her letters (it was true that for the last couple of years they had come but at long intervals) she had told him so little about their life. She never spoke of people; she talked of the books she read, of the music she had heard or was studying (a whole page sometimes about the last concert at the Conservatoire[319]), the new pictures and the manner of the different artists.

When she entered the room three or four minutes after the arrival of the young foreigner, with whom her mother conversed in just the accents Raymond had last heard at the hotel in the Fifth Avenue (he was obliged to admit that she gave herself no airs; it was clear that her success had not gone in the least to her head); when Dora at last appeared she was accompanied by Mademoiselle Bourde. The presence of this lady—he didn't know she was still in the house—Raymond took as a sign that they were really dining *en famille*, so that the young man was either an actual or a prospective intimate. Dora shook hands first with her cousin, but he watched the manner of her greeting with the other visitor and saw that it indicated extreme friendliness—on the part of the latter. If there was a charming flush in her cheek as he took her hand, that was the remainder of the colour that had risen there as she came toward Raymond. It will be seen that our young man still had an eye for the element of fascination, as he used to regard it, in this quiet, dimly-shining maiden.[320]

He saw that Effie was the only one who had changed (Tishy remained yet to be judged), except that Dora really looked older, quite as much older as the number of years had given her a right to: there was as little difference in her as there was in her mother. Not that she was like her mother, but she was perfectly like herself. Her meeting with Raymond was bright, but very still; their phrases were awkward and commonplace, and the thing was mainly a contact of looks—conscious, embarrassed, indirect, but brightening every moment with old familiarities. Her mother appeared to pay no attention, and neither, to do her justice, did Mademoiselle Bourde, who, after an exchange of expressive salutations with Raymond, began to scrutinise Effie with little admiring gestures and smiles. She surveyed her from head to foot; she pulled a ribbon straight; she was evidently a flattering governess. Cousin Maria explained to Cousin Raymond that they were waiting for one more friend—a very dear lady. "But she lives near, and when people live near they are always late—haven't you noticed that?"

"Your hotel is far away, I know, and yet you were the first," Dora said, smiling to Raymond.

"Oh, even if it were round the corner I should be the first—to come to *you!*" the young man answered, speaking loud and clear, so that his words might serve as a notification to Cousin Maria that his sentiments were unchanged.

"You are more French than the French," Dora returned.

"You say that as if you didn't like them: I hope you don't," said Raymond, still with intentions in regard to his hostess.

"We like them more and more, the more we see of them," this lady interposed; but gently, impersonally, and with an air of not wishing to put Raymond in the wrong.

"*Mais j'espère bien!*" cried Mademoiselle Bourde, holding up her head and opening her eyes very wide. "Such friendships as we form, and, I may say, as we inspire! *Je m'en rapporte à Effie,*" the governess continued.

"We have received immense kindness; we have established relations that are so pleasant for us, Cousin Raymond. We have the *entrée* of so many charming homes," Mrs. Temperly remarked.

"But ours is the most charming of all; that I will say," exclaimed Mademoiselle Bourde. "Isn't it so, Effie?"

"Oh yes, I think it is; especially when we are expecting the Marquise," Effie responded. Then she added, "But here she comes now; I hear her carriage in the court."

The Marquise too was just one of themselves; she was a part of their charming home.

"She *is* such a love!" said Mrs. Temperly to the foreign gentleman, with an irrepressible movement of benevolence.

To which Raymond heard the gentleman reply that, Ah, she was the most distinguished woman in France.

"Do you know Madame de Brives?"[321] Effie asked of Raymond, while they were waiting for her to come in.

She came in at that moment, and the girl turned away quickly without an answer.

"How in the world should I know her?" That was the answer he would have been tempted to give. He felt very much out of Cousin Maria's circle. The foreign gentleman fingered his moustache and looked at him sidewise. The Marquise was a very pretty woman, fair and slender, of middle age, with a smile, a complexion, a diamond necklace, of great splendour, and a charming manner. Her greeting to her friends was sweet and familiar, and was accompanied with much kissing of a sisterly, motherly, daughterly kind; and yet with this expression of simple, almost homely sentiment there was something in her that astonished and dazzled. She might very well have been, as the foreign young man said, the most distinguished woman in France. Dora had not rushed forward to meet her with nearly so much *empressement* as Effie, and this gave him a chance to ask the former who she was. The girl replied that she was her mother's most intimate friend: to which he rejoined that that was not a description; what he wanted to know was her title to this exalted position.

"Why, can't you see it? She is beautiful and she is good."

"I see that she is beautiful; but how can I see that she is good?"

"Good to mamma, I mean, and to Effie and Tishy."

"And isn't she good to you?"

"Oh, I don't know her so well. But I delight to look at her."

"Certainly, that must be a great pleasure," said Raymond. He enjoyed it during dinner, which was now served, though his enjoyment was diminished by his not finding himself next to Dora. They sat at a small round table and he had at his right his Cousin Maria, whom he had taken in. On his left was Madame de Brives, who had the foreign gentleman for a neighbour. Then came Effie and Mademoiselle Bourde, and Dora was on the other side of her mother. Raymond regarded this as marked—a symbol of the fact that Cousin Maria would continue to separate them. He remained in ignorance of the other gentleman's identity, and remembered how he had prophesied at the hotel in New York that his hostess would give up introducing people.[322]

It was a friendly, easy little family repast, as she had said it would be, with just a marquise and a secretary of embassy—Raymond ended by guessing that the stranger was a secretary of embassy—thrown in. So far from interfering with the family tone Madame de Brives directly contributed to it. She eminently justified the affection in which she was held in the house; she was in the highest degree sociable and sympathetic, and at the same time witty (there was no insipidity in Madame de Brives), and was the cause of Raymond's making the reflection—as he had made it often in his earlier years—that an agreeable Frenchwoman is a triumph of civilisation. This did not prevent him from giving the Marquise no more than half of his attention; the rest was dedicated to Dora, who, on her side, though in common with Effie and Mademoiselle Bourde she bent a frequent, interested gaze on the splendid French lady, very often met our young man's eyes with mute, vague but, to his sense, none the less valuable intimations. It was as if she knew what was going on in his mind (it is true that he scarcely knew it himself), and might be trusted to clear things up at some convenient hour.

Madame de Brives talked across Raymond, in excellent English, to Cousin Maria, but this did not prevent her from being gracious, even encouraging, to the young man, who was a little afraid of her and thought her a delightful creature. She asked him more questions about himself than any of them had done. Her conversation with Mrs. Temperly was of an intimate, domestic order, and full of social, personal allusions, which Raymond was unable to follow. It appeared to be concerned considerably with the private affairs of the old French *noblesse*, into whose councils—to judge by the tone of the Marquise—Cousin Maria had been admitted by acclamation. Every now and then Madame de Brives broke into French, and it was in this tongue that she uttered an apostrophe to her hostess: "Oh, you, *ma toute-bonne*, you who have the genius of good sense!" And she appealed to Raymond to know if his Cousin Maria had not the genius of good sense—the wisdom of the ages. The old lady did not defend herself from the compliment; she let it pass, with her motherly, tolerant smile; nor did Raymond attempt to defend her, for he felt the justice of his neighbour's description: Cousin Maria's good sense was incontestable, magnificent. She took an affectionate, indulgent view of most of the persons mentioned, and yet her tone was far from being vapid or vague. Madame de Brives usually remarked that they were coming very soon again to see her, she did them so much good.

"The freshness of your judgment—the freshness of your judgment!" she repeated, with a kind of glee, and she narrated that Eldonore (a personage unknown to Raymond) had said that she was a woman of Plutarch.[323] Mrs. Temperly talked a great deal about the health of their friends; she seemed to keep the record of the influenzas and neuralgias of a numerous and susceptible circle. He did not find it in him quite to agree—the Marquise dropping the statement into his ear at a moment when their hostess was making some inquiry of Mademoiselle Bourde—that she was a nature absolutely marvellous; but he could easily see that to world-worn Parisians her quiet charities of speech and manner, with something quaint and rustic in their form, might be restorative and salutary. She allowed for everything, yet she was so good, and indeed Madame de Brives summed this up before they left the table in saying to her, "Oh, you, my dear, your success, more than any other that has ever taken place, has been a *succès de bonté*." Raymond was greatly amused at this idea of Cousin Maria's *succès de bonté*: it seemed to him delightfully Parisian.

Before dinner was over she inquired of him how he had got on 'in his profession' since they last met, and he was too proud, or so he thought, to tell her anything but the simple truth, that he had not got on very well. If he was to ask her again for Dora it would be just as he was, an honourable but not particularly successful man, making no show of lures and bribes. "I am not a remarkably good painter," he said. "I judge myself perfectly. And then I have been handicapped at home. I have had a great many serious bothers and worries."

"Ah, we were so sorry to hear about your dear father."

The tone of these words was kind and sincere; still Raymond thought that in this case her *bonté* might have gone a little further. At any rate this was the only allusion that she made to his bothers and worries. Indeed, she always passed over such things lightly; she was an optimist for others as well as for herself, which doubtless had a great deal to do (Raymond indulged in the reflection) with the headway she made in a society tired of its own pessimism.[324]

After dinner, when they went into the drawing-room, the young man noted with complacency that this apartment, vast in itself, communicated with two or three others into which it would be easy to pass without attracting attention, the doors being replaced by old tapestries, looped up and offering no barrier. With pictures and curiosities all over the place, there were plenty of pretexts for wandering away. He lost no time in asking Dora whether her mother would send Mademoiselle Bourde after them if she were to go with him into one of the other rooms, the same way she had done—didn't she remember?—that last night in New York, at the hotel. Dora didn't admit that she remembered (she was too loyal to her mother for that, and Raymond foresaw that this loyalty would be a source of irritation to him again, as it had been in the past), but he perceived, all the same, that she had not forgotten. She raised no difficulty, and a few moments later, while they stood in an adjacent *salon* (he had stopped to admire a bust of Effie, wonderfully living, slim and juvenile, the work of one of the sculptors who are the pride of contemporary French art[325]), he said to her, looking about him, "How has she done it so fast?"

"Done what, Raymond?"

"Why, done everything. Collected all these wonderful things; become intimate with Madame de Brives and every one else; organised her life—the life of all of you—so brilliantly."

"I have never seen mamma in a hurry," Dora replied.

"Perhaps she will be, now that I have come," Raymond suggested, laughing.

The girl hesitated a moment. "Yes, she was, to invite you—the moment she knew you were here."

"She has been most kind, and I talk like a brute. But I am liable to do worse—I give you notice. She won't like it any more than she did before, if she thinks I want to make up to you."

"Don't, Raymond—don't!" the girl exclaimed, gently, but with a look of sudden pain.

"Don't what, Dora?—don't make up to you?"

"Don't begin to talk of those things. There is no need. We can go on being friends."

"I will do exactly as you prescribe, and heaven forbid I should annoy you. But would you mind answering me a question? It is very particular, very intimate." He stopped, and she only looked at him, saying nothing. So he went on: "Is it an idea of your mother's that you should marry—some person here?" He gave her a chance to reply, but still she was silent, and he continued: "Do you mind telling me this? Could it ever be an idea of your own?"

"Do you mean some Frenchman?"

Raymond smiled. "Some protégé of Madame de Brives."

Then the girl simply gave a slow, sad headshake which struck him as the sweetest, proudest, most suggestive thing in the world. "Well, well, that's all right," he remarked, cheerfully, and looked again a while at the bust, which he thought extraordinarily clever. "And haven't *you* been done by one of these great fellows?"

"Oh dear no; only mamma and Effie. But Tishy is going to be, in a month or two. The next time you come you must see her. She remembers you vividly."

"And I remember her that last night, with her reticule. Is she always pretty?"

Dora hesitated a moment. "She is a very sweet little creature, but she is not so pretty as Effie."

"And have none of them wished to do you—none of the painters?"

"Oh, it's not a question of me. I only wish them to let me alone."

"For me it would be a question of you, if you would sit for me. But I daresay your mother wouldn't allow that."

"No, I think not," said Dora, smiling.

She smiled, but her companion looked grave. However, not to pursue the subject, he asked, abruptly, "Who is this Madame de Brives?"

"If you lived in Paris you would know. She is very celebrated."

"Celebrated for what?"

"For everything."

"And is she good—is she genuine?" Raymond asked. Then, seeing something in the girl's face, he added: "I told you I should be brutal again. Has she undertaken to make a great marriage for Effie?"

"I don't know what she has undertaken," said Dora, impatiently.

"And then for Tishy, when Effie has been disposed of?"

"Poor little Tishy!" the girl continued, rather inscrutably.

"And can she do nothing for you?" the young man inquired.

Her answer surprised him—after a moment. "She has kindly offered to exert herself, but it's no use."

"Well, that's good. And who is it the young man comes for—the secretary of embassy?"

"Oh, he comes for all of us," said Dora, laughing.

"I suppose your mother would prefer a preference," Raymond suggested.

To this she replied, irrelevantly, that she thought they had better go back; but as Raymond took no notice of the recommendation she mentioned that the secretary was no one in particular. At this moment Effie, looking very rosy and happy, pushed through the *portière* with the news that her sister must come and bid good-bye to the Marquise. She was taking her to the Duchess's— didn't Dora remember? To the *bal blanc*[326]—the *sauterie de jeunes filles*.

"I thought we should be called," said Raymond, as he followed Effie; and he remarked that perhaps Madame de Brives would find something suitable at the Duchess's.

"I don't know. Mamma would be very particular," the girl rejoined; and this was said simply, sympathetically, without the least appearance of deflection from that loyalty which Raymond deplored.

"You must come to us on the 17th; we expect to have a few people and some good music," Cousin Maria said to him before he quitted the house; and he wondered whether, the 17th being still ten days off, this might not be an intimation that they could abstain from his society until then. He chose, at any rate, not to take it as such, and called several times in the interval, late in the afternoon, when the ladies would be sure to have come in.

They were always there, and Cousin Maria's welcome was, for each occasion, maternal, though when he took leave she made no allusion to future meetings—to his coming again; but there were always other visitors as well, collected at tea round the great fire of logs, in the friendly, brilliant drawing-room where the luxurious was no enemy to the casual and Mrs. Temperly's manner of dispensing hospitality recalled to our young man somehow certain memories of his youthful time: visits in New England, at old homesteads[327] flanked with elms, where a talkative, democratic, delightful farmer's wife pressed upon her company rustic viands in which she herself had had a hand. Cousin Maria enjoyed the services of a distinguished *chef* and delicious *petits fours* were served with her tea; but Raymond had a sense that to complete the impression hot home-made gingerbread should have been produced.

The atmosphere was suffused with the presence of Madame de Brives. She was either there or she was just coming or she was just gone; her name, her voice, her example and encouragement were in the air. Other ladies came and went—sometimes accompanied by gentlemen who looked worn out, had waxed moustaches and knew how to talk—and they were sometimes designated in the same manner as Madame de Brives; but she remained the Marquise *par excellence*, the incarnation of brilliancy and renown. The conversation moved among simple but civilised topics, was not dull and, considering that it consisted largely of personalities, was not ill-natured. Least of all was it scandalous, for the girls were always there. Cousin Maria not having thought it in the least necessary, in order to put herself in accord with French traditions, to relegate her daughters to the middle distance. They occupied a considerable part of the foreground, in the prettiest, most modest, most becoming attitudes.

It was Cousin Maria's theory of her own behaviour that she did in Paris simply as she had always done; and though this would not have been a complete account of the matter Raymond could not fail to notice the good sense and good taste with which she laid down her lines and the quiet *bonhomie* of the authority with which she caused the tone of the American home to be respected. Scandal stayed outside, not simply because Effie and Tishy were there, but because, even if Cousin Maria had received alone, she never would have received evil-speakers. Indeed, for Raymond, who had been accustomed to think that in a general way he knew pretty well what the French capital was, this was a strange, fresh Paris altogether, destitute of the salt that seasoned it for most palates, and yet not insipid nor innutritive. He marvelled at Cousin Maria's air, in such a city, of knowing, of recognising nothing bad: all the more that it represented an actual state of mind. He used to wonder sometimes what she would do and how she would feel if some day, in consequence of researches made by the Marquise in the *grand monde*, she should find herself in possession of a son-in-law formed according to one of the types of which *he* had impressions. However, it was not credible that Madame de Brives would play her a trick. There were moments when Raymond almost wished she might—to see how Cousin Maria would handle the gentleman.

Dora was almost always taken up by visitors, and he had scarcely any direct conversation with her. She was there, and he was glad she was there, and she knew he was glad (he knew that), but this was almost all the communion he had with her. She was mild, exquisitely mild—this was the term he mentally applied to her now—and it amply sufficed him, with the conviction he had that she was not stupid. She attended to the tea (for Mademoiselle Bourde was not always free), she handed the *petits fours*, she rang the bell when people went out; and it was in connection with these offices that the idea came to him once—he was rather ashamed of it afterward—that she was the Cinderella of the house,[328] the domestic drudge, the one for whom there was no career, as it was useless for the Marquise to take up her case. He was ashamed of this fancy, I say, and yet it came back to him; he was even surprised that it had not occurred to him before. Her sisters were neither ugly nor proud[329] (Tishy, indeed, was almost touchingly delicate and timid, with exceedingly pretty points, yet with a little appealing, oldwomanish look, as if, small—very small—as she was, she was afraid she shouldn't grow any more); but her mother, like the mother in the fairy-tale, was a *femme forte*.[330] Madame de Brives could do nothing for Dora, not absolutely because she was too plain, but because she would never lend herself, and that came to the same thing. Her mother accepted her as recalcitrant, but Cousin Maria's attitude, at the best, could only be resignation. She would respect her child's preferences, she would never put on the screw;[331] but this would not make her love the child any more. So Raymond interpreted certain signs, which at the same time he felt to be very slight, while the conversation in Mrs. Temperly's *salon* (this was its preponderant tendency) rambled among questions of *bric-à-brac*, of where Tishy's portrait should be placed when it was finished, and the current prices of old Gobelins.[332] *Ces dames* were not in the least above the discussion of prices.

On the 17th it was easy to see that more lamps than usual had been lighted. They streamed through all the windows of the charming hotel and mingled with the radiance of the carriage-lanterns, which followed each other slowly, in couples, in a close, long rank, into the fine sonorous court, where the high stepping of valuable horses was sharp on the stones, and up to the ruddy portico. The night was wet, not with a downpour, but with showers interspaced by starry patches, which only added to the glitter of the handsome, clean Parisian surfaces. The *sergents de ville*[333] were about the place, and seemed to make the occasion important and official. These night aspects of Paris in the *beaux quartiers* had always for Raymond a particularly festive association, and as he passed from his cab under the wide permanent tin canopy, painted in stripes like an awning, which protected the low steps, it seemed to him odder than ever that all this established prosperity should be Cousin Maria's.

If the thought of how well she did it bore him company from the thresh-old, it deepened to admiration by the time he had been half an hour in the place. She stood near the entrance with her two elder daughters, distribut-ing the most familiar, most encouraging smiles, together with hand-shakes which were in themselves a whole system of hospitality. If her party was grand Cousin Maria was not; she indulged in no assumption of stateliness and no attempt at graduated welcomes. It seemed to Raymond that it was only because it would have taken too much time that she didn't kiss every one. Effie looked lovely and just a little frightened, which was exactly what she ought to have done; and he noticed that among the arriving guests those who were not intimate (which he could not tell from Mrs. Temperly's manner, but could from their own) recognised her as a daughter much more quickly than they recognised Dora, who hung back disinterestedly, as if not to challenge their discernment, while the current passed her, keeping her little sister in position on its brink meanwhile by the tenderest small gesture.

"May I talk with you a little, later?" he asked of Dora, with only a few seconds for the question, as people were pressing behind him. She answered evasively that there would be very little talk—they would all have to listen— it was very serious; and the next moment he had received a programme from the hand of a monumental yet gracious personage who stood beyond and who had a silver chain round his neck.

The place was arranged for music, and how well arranged he saw later, when every one was seated, spaciously, luxuriously, without pushing or overpeeping, and the finest talents in Paris performed selections at which the best taste had presided. The singers and players were all stars of the first magnitude.[334] Raymond was fond of music and he wondered whose taste it had been. He made up his mind it was Dora's—it was only she who could have conceived a combination so exquisite; and he said to himself: "How they all pull together! She is not in it, she is not of it, and yet she too works for the common end." And by 'all' he meant also Mademoiselle Bourde and the Marquise. This impression made him feel rather hopeless, as if, *en fin de compte*, Cousin Maria were too large an adversary. Great as was the pleasure of being present on an occasion so admirably organised, of sitting there in a beautiful room, in a still, attentive, brilliant company, with all the questions of temperature, space, light and decoration solved to the gratification of every sense, and listening to the best artists doing their best—happily constituted as our young man was to enjoy such a privilege as this, the total effect was depressing: it made him feel as if the gods were not on his side.

"And does she do it so well without a man? There must be so many details a woman can't tackle," he said to himself; for even counting in the Marquise and Mademoiselle Bourde this only made a multiplication of petticoats. Then it came over him that she *was* a man as well as a woman—the masculine element was included in her nature. He was sure that she bought her horses without being cheated, and very few men could do that. She had the American national quality—she had 'faculty'[335] in a supreme degree. "Faculty—faculty," the voices of the quartette of singers seemed to repeat, in the quick movement of a composition they rendered beautifully, while they swelled and went faster, till the thing became a joyous chant of praise, a glorification of Cousin Maria's practical genius.

During the intermission, in the middle of the concert, people changed places more or less and circulated, so that, walking about at this time, he came upon the Marquise, who, in her sympathetic, demonstrative way, appeared to be on the point of clasping her hostess in her arms. "Décidément, ma bonne, il n'y a que vous! C'est une perfection—" he heard her say. To which, gratified but unelated, Cousin Maria replied, according to her simple, sociable wont: "Well, it *does* seem quite a successful occasion. If it will only keep on to the end!"

Raymond, wandering far, found himself in a world that was mainly quite new to him, and explained his ignorance of it by reflecting that the people were probably celebrated: so many of them had decorations and stars[336] and a quiet of manner that could only be accounted for by renown. There were plenty of Americans with no badge[337] but a certain fine negativeness, and they were quiet for a reason which by this time had become very familiar to Raymond: he had heard it so often mentioned that his country-people were supremely 'adaptable.' He tried to get hold of Dora, but he saw that her mother had arranged things beautifully to keep her occupied with other people; so at least he interpreted the fact—after all very natural—that she had half a dozen fluttered young girls on her mind, whom she was providing with programmes, seats, ices, occasional murmured remarks and general support and protection.[338] When the concert was over she supplied them with further entertainment in the form of several young men who had pliable backs and flashing breastpins and whom she inarticulately introduced to them, which gave her still more to do, as after this serious step she had to stay and watch all parties. It was strange to Raymond to see her transformed by her mother into a precocious duenna. Him she introduced to no young girl, and he knew not whether to regard this as cold neglect or as high consideration. If he had liked he might have taken it as a sweet intimation that she knew he couldn't care for any girl but her.

232

On the whole he was glad, because it left him free—free to get hold of her mother, which by this time he had boldly determined to do. The conception was high, inasmuch as Cousin Maria's attention was obviously required by the ambassadors and other grandees who had flocked to do her homage. Nevertheless, while supper was going on (he wanted none, and neither apparently did she), he collared her, as he phrased it to himself, in just the right place—on the threshold of the conservatory. She was flanked on either side with a foreigner of distinction, but he didn't care for her foreigners now. Besides, a conservatory was meant only for couples; it was a sign of her comprehensive sociability that she should have been rambling among the palms and orchids with a double escort. Her friends would wish to quit her but would not wish to appear to give way to each other; and Raymond felt that he was relieving them both (though he didn't care) when he asked her to be so good as to give him a few minutes' conversation. He made her go back with him into the conservatory: it was the only thing he had ever made her do, or probably ever would. She began to talk about the great Gregorini[339]— how it had been too sweet of her to repeat one of her songs, when it had really been understood in advance that repetitions were not expected. Raymond had no interest at present in the great Gregorini. He asked Cousin Maria vehemently if she remembered telling him in New York—that night at the hotel, five years before—that when he should have followed them to Paris he would be free to address her on the subject of Dora. She had given him a promise that she would listen to him in this case, and now he must keep her up to the mark. It was impossible to see her alone, but, at whatever inconvenience to herself, he must insist on her giving him his opportunity.

"About Dora, Cousin Raymond?" she asked, blandly and kindly—almost as if she didn't exactly know who Dora was.

"Surely you haven't forgotten what passed between us the evening before you left America. I was in love with her then and I have been in love with her ever since. I told you so then, and you stopped me off, but you gave me leave to make another appeal to you in the future. I make it now—this is the only way I have—and I think you ought to listen to it. Five years have passed, and I love her more than ever. I have behaved like a saint in the interval: I haven't attempted to practise upon her without your knowledge."

"I am so glad; but she would have let me know," said Cousin Maria, looking round the conservatory as if to see if the plants were all there.

"No doubt. I don't know what you do to her. But I trust that to-day your opposition falls—in face of the proof that we have given you of mutual fidelity."

"Fidelity?" Cousin Maria repeated, smiling.

"Surely—unless you mean to imply that Dora has given me up. I have reason to believe that she hasn't."

"I think she will like better to remain just as she is."

"Just as she is?"

"I mean, not to make a choice," Cousin Maria went on, smiling.

Raymond hesitated a moment. "Do you mean that you have tried to make her make one?"

At this the good lady broke into a laugh. "My dear Raymond, how little you must think I know my child!"

"Perhaps, if you haven't tried to make her you have tried to prevent her. Haven't you told her I am unsuccessful, I am poor?"

She stopped him, laying her hand with unaffected solicitude on his arm. "*Are* you poor, my dear? I should be so sorry!"

"Never mind; I can support a wife," said the young man.

"It wouldn't matter, because I am happy to say that Dora has something of her own," Cousin Maria went on, with her imperturbable candour. "Her father thought that was the best way to arrange it. I had quite forgotten my opposition, as you call it; that was so long ago. Why, she was only a little girl. Wasn't that the ground I took? Well, dear, she's older now, and you can say anything to her you like. But I do think she wants to stay—" And she looked up at him, cheerily.

"Wants to stay?"

"With Effie and Tishy."

"Ah, Cousin Maria," the young man exclaimed, "you are modest about yourself!"

"Well, we are all together. Now is that all? I *must* see if there is enough champagne. Certainly—you can say to her what you like. But twenty years hence she will be just as she is to-day; that's how I see her."

"Lord, what is it you do to her?" Raymond groaned, as he accompanied his hostess back to the crowded rooms.

He knew exactly what she would have replied if she had been a French-woman; she would have said to him, triumphantly, overwhelmingly: "Que voulez-vous? Elle adore sa mère!" She was, however, only a Californian, unacquainted with the language of epigram, and her answer consisted simply of the words: "I am sorry you have ideas that make you unhappy. I guess you are the only person here who hasn't enjoyed himself to-night."

Raymond repeated to himself, gloomily, for the rest of the evening, "Elle adore sa mère—elle adore sa mère!" He remained very late, and when but twenty people were left and he had observed that the Marquise, passing her hand into Mrs. Temperly's arm, led her aside as if for some important confabulation (some new light doubtless on what might be hoped for Effie), he persuaded Dora to let the rest of the guests depart in peace³⁴⁰ (apparently her mother had told her to look out for them to the very last), and come with him into some quiet corner. They found an empty sofa in the outlasting lamp-light, and there the girl sat down with him. Evidently she knew what he was going to say, or rather she thought she did; for in fact, after a little, after he had told her that he had spoken to her mother and she had told him he might speak to *her*, he said things that she could not very well have expected.

"Is it true that you wish to remain with Effie and Tishy? That's what your mother calls it when she means that you will give me up."

"How can I give you up?" the girl demanded. "Why can't we go on being friends, as I asked you the evening you dined here?"

"What do you mean by friends?"

"Well, not making everything impossible."

"You didn't think anything impossible of old," Raymond rejoined, bitterly. "I thought you liked me then, and I have even thought so since."

"I like you more than I like any one. I like you so much that it's my principal happiness."

"Then why are there impossibilities?"

"Oh, some day I'll tell you!" said Dora, with a quick sigh. "Perhaps after Tishy is married. And meanwhile, are you not going to remain in Paris, at any rate? Isn't your work here? You are not here for me only. You can come to the house often. That's what I mean by our being friends."

Her companion sat looking at her with a gloomy stare, as if he were trying to make up the deficiencies in her logic.

"After Tishy is married? I don't see what that has to do with it. Tishy is little more than a baby; she may not be married for ten years."

"That is very true."

"And you dispose of the interval by a simple 'meanwhile'? My dear Dora, your talk is strange," Raymond continued, with his voice passionately lowered. "And I may come to the house—often? How often do you mean—in ten years? Five times—or even twenty?" He saw that her eyes were filling with tears, but he went on: "It has been coming over me little by little (I notice things very much if I have a reason), and now I think I understand your mother's system."

"Don't say anything against my mother," the girl broke in, beseechingly.

"I shall not say anything unjust. That is if I am unjust you must tell me. This is my idea, and your speaking of Tishy's marriage confirms it. To begin with she has had immense plans for you all; she wanted each of you to be a princess or a duchess—I mean a good one. But she has had to give *you* up."

"No one has asked for me," said Dora, with unexpected honesty.

"I don't believe it. Dozens of fellows have asked for you, and you have shaken your head in that divine way (divine for me, I mean) in which you shook it the other night."

"My mother has never said an unkind word to me in her life," the girl declared, in answer to this.

"I never said she had, and I don't know why you take the precaution of telling me so. But whatever you tell me or don't tell me," Raymond pursued, "there is one thing I see very well—that so long as you won't marry a duke Cousin Maria has found means to prevent you from marrying till your sisters have made rare alliances."

"Has found means?" Dora repeated, as if she really wondered what was in his thought.

"Of course I mean only through your affection for her. How she works that, you know best yourself."

"It's delightful to have a mother of whom every one is so fond," said Dora, smiling.

"She is a most remarkable woman. Don't think for a moment that I don't appreciate her. You don't want to quarrel with her, and I daresay you are right."

"Why, Raymond, of course I'm right!"

"It proves you are not madly in love with me. It seems to me that for you *I* would have quarreled——"

"Raymond, Raymond!" she interrupted, with the tears again rising.

He sat looking at her, and then he said, "Well, when they *are* married?"

"I don't know the future—I don't know what may happen."

"You mean that Tishy is so small—she doesn't grow—and will therefore be difficult? Yes, she *is* small." There was bitterness in his heart, but he laughed at his own words. "However, Effie ought to go off easily," he went on, as Dora said nothing. "I really wonder that, with the Marquise and all, she hasn't gone off yet. This thing, to-night, ought to do a great deal for her."

Dora listened to him with a fascinated gaze; it was as if he expressed things for her and relieved her spirit by making them clear and coherent. Her eyes managed, each time, to be dry again, and now a somewhat wan, ironical smile moved her lips. "Mamma knows what she wants—she knows what she will take. And she will take only that."

"Precisely—something tremendous. And she is willing to wait, eh? Well, Effie is very young, and she's charming. But she won't be charming if she has an ugly appendage in the shape of a poor unsuccessful American artist (not even a good one), whose father went bankrupt, for a brother-in-law. That won't smooth the way, of course; and if a prince is to come into the family, the family must be kept tidy to receive him." Dora got up quickly, as if she could bear his lucidity no longer, but he kept close to her as she walked away. "And she can sacrifice you like that, without a scruple, without a pang?"

"I might have escaped—if I would marry," the girl replied.

"Do you call that escaping? She has succeeded with you, but is it a part of what the Marquise calls her *succès de bonté*?"

"Nothing that you can say (and it's far worse than the reality) can prevent her being delightful."

"Yes, that's your loyalty, and I could shoot you for it!" he exclaimed, making her pause on the threshold of the adjoining room. "So you think it will take about ten years, considering Tishy's size—or want of size?" He himself again was the only one to laugh at this. "Your mother is closeted, as much as she can be closeted now, with Madame de Brives, and perhaps this time they are really settling something."

"I have thought that before and nothing has come. Mamma wants something so good; not only every advantage and every grandeur, but every virtue under heaven, and every guarantee. Oh, she wouldn't expose them!"

"I see; that's where her goodness comes in and where the Marquise is impressed." He took Dora's hand; he felt that he must go, for she exasperated him with her irony that stopped short and her patience that wouldn't stop. "You simply propose that I should wait?" he said, as he held her hand.

"It seems to me that you might, if *I* can." Then the girl remarked, "Now that you are here, it's far better."

There was a sweetness in this which made him, after glancing about a moment, raise her hand to his lips. He went away without taking leave of Cousin Maria, who was still out of sight, her conference with the Marquise apparently not having terminated. This looked (he reflected as he passed out) as if something might come of it. However, before he went home he fell again into a gloomy forecast. The weather had changed, the stars were all out, and he walked the empty streets for an hour. Tishy's perverse refusal to grow and Cousin Maria's conscientious exactions promised him a terrible probation. And in those intolerable years what further interference, what meddlesome, effective pressure, might not make itself felt? It may be added that Tishy is decidedly a dwarf and his probation is not yet over.

Louisa Pallant

I

NEVER say you know the last word about any human heart! I was once treated to a revelation which startled and touched me, in the nature of a person with whom I had been acquainted (well, as I supposed) for years, whose character I had had good reasons, heaven knows, to appreciate and in regard to whom I flattered myself that I had nothing more to learn.

It was on the terrace of the Kursaal at Homburg,[341] nearly ten years ago, one lovely night toward the end of July. I had come to the place that day from Frankfort,[342] with vague intentions, and was mainly occupied in waiting for my young nephew, the only son of my sister, who had been intrusted to my care by a very fond mother for the summer (I was expected to show him Europe—only the very best of it), and was on his way from Paris to join me. The excellent band[343] discoursed music not too abstruse, and the air was filled besides with the murmur of different languages, the smoke of many cigars, the creak on the gravel of the gardens of strolling shoes and the thick tinkle of beer-glasses. There were a hundred people walking about, there were some in clusters at little tables and many on benches and rows of chairs, watching the others as if they had paid for the privilege and were rather disappointed. I was among these last; I sat by myself, smoking my cigar and thinking of nothing very particular while families and couples passed and repassed me.

I scarcely know how long I had sat there when I became aware of a recognition which made my meditations definite. It was on my own part, and the object of it was a lady who moved to and fro, unconscious of my observation, with a young girl at her side. I had not seen her for ten years, and what first struck me was the fact not that she was Mrs. Henry Pallant but that the girl who was with her was remarkably pretty—or rather first of all that every one who passed her turned round to look at her. This led me to look at the young lady myself, and her charming face diverted my attention for some time from that of her companion. The latter, moreover, though it was night, wore a thin, light veil which made her features vague. The couple walked and walked, slowly, but though they were very quiet and decorous, and also very well dressed, they seemed to have no friends. Every one looked at them but no one spoke; they appeared even to talk very little to each other. Moreover they bore with extreme composure and as if they were thoroughly used to it the attention they excited. I am afraid it occurred to me to take for granted that they were not altogether honourable and that if they had been the elder lady would have covered the younger up a little more from the public stare and not have been so ashamed to exhibit her own face. Perhaps this question came into my mind too easily just then—in view of my prospective mentorship to my nephew. If I was to show him only the best of Europe I should have to be very careful about the people he should meet—especially the ladies—and the relations he should form. I suspected him of knowing very little of life and I was rather uneasy about my responsibilities. Was I completely relieved and reassured when I perceived that I simply had Louisa[344] Pallant before me and that the girl was her daughter—Linda, whom I had known as a child—Linda grown up into a regular beauty?

The question is delicate and the proof that I was not very sure is perhaps that I forbore to speak to the ladies immediately. I watched them awhile—I wondered what they would do. No great harm, assuredly; but I was anxious to see if they were really isolated. Homburg is a great resort of the English—the London season[345] takes up its tale there toward the first of August—and I had an idea that in such a company as that Louisa would naturally know people. It was my impression that she 'cultivated' the English, that she had been much in London and would be likely to have views in regard to a permanent settlement there. This supposition was quickened by the sight of Linda's beauty, for I knew there is no country in which a handsome person is more appreciated. You will see that I took time, and I confess that as I finished my cigar I thought it all over. There was no good reason in fact why I should have rushed into Mrs. Pallant's arms. She had not treated me well and we had never really made it up. Somehow even the circumstance that (after the first soreness) I was glad to have lost her had never put us quite right with each other; nor, for herself, had it made her less ashamed of her heartless behaviour that poor Pallant after all turned out no great catch. I had forgiven her; I had not felt that it was any thing but an escape not to have married a girl who had it in her to take back her given word and break a fellow's heart, for mere flesh-pots[346]—or the shallow promise, as it pitifully proved, of flesh-pots; moreover we had met since then, on the occasion of my former visit to Europe; we had looked each other in the eyes, we had pretended to be free friends and had talked of the wickedness of the world as composedly as if we were the only just, the only pure. I knew then what she had given out—that I had driven her off by my insane jealousy before she ever thought of Henry Pallant, before she had ever seen him. This had not been then and it could not be to-day a ground of real reunion, especially if you add to it that she knew perfectly what I thought of her. It is my belief that it does not often minister to friendship that your friend shall know your real opinion, for he knows it mainly when it is unfavourable, and this is especially the case when (if the solecism may pass) he is a woman. I had not followed Mrs. Pallant's fortunes; the years elapsed, for me, in my own country, whereas she led her life, which I vaguely believed to be difficult after her husband's death—virtually that of a bankrupt—in foreign lands. I heard of her from time to time; always as established somewhere, but on each occasion in a different place. She drifted from country to country, and if she had been of a hard composition at the beginning it could never occur to me that her struggle with society, as it might be called, would have softened the paste. Whenever I heard a woman spoken of as 'horribly worldly' I thought immediately of the object of my early passion. I imagined she had debts, and when I now at last made up my mind to recall myself to her it was present to me that she might ask me to lend her money. More than anything else, at this time of day, I was sorry for her, so that such an idea did not operate as a deterrent.

She pretended afterwards that she had not noticed me—expressing great surprise and wishing to know where I had dropped from; but I think the corner of her eye had taken me in and she was waiting to see what I would do. She had ended by sitting down with her girl on the same row of chairs with myself, and after a little, on the seat next to her becoming vacant, I went and stood before her. She looked up at me a moment, staring, as if she could not imagine who I was or what I wanted; then, smiling and extending her hands, she broke out, "Ah, my dear old friend—what a delight!" If she had waited to see what I would do, in order to choose her own line, she at least carried out this line with the utmost grace. She was cordial, friendly, artless, interested, and indeed I am sure she was very glad to see me. I may as well say immediately, however, that she gave neither then nor later any sign of a disposition to borrow money. She had none too much—that I learned—but for the moment she seemed able to pay her way. I took the empty chair and we remained talking for an hour. After a while she made me sit on the other side of her, next to her daughter, whom she wished to know me—to love me—as one of their oldest friends. "It goes back, back, back, doesn't it?" said Mrs. Pallant; "and of course she remembers you as a child." Linda smiled very sweetly and indefinitely, and I saw she remembered me not at all. When her mother intimated that they had often talked about me she failed to take it up, though she looked extremely nice. Looking nice was her strong point; she was prettier even than her mother had been. She was such a little lady that she made me ashamed of having doubted, however vaguely and for a moment, of her position in the scale of propriety. Her appearance seemed to say that if she had no acquaintances, it was because she did not want to—because there was nobody there who struck her as attractive: there was not the slightest difficulty about her choosing her friends. Linda Pallant, young as she was, and fresh and fair and charming and gentle and sufficiently shy, looked somehow exclusive—as if the dust of the common world had never been meant to settle upon her. She was simpler than her mother and was evidently not a young woman of professions—except in so far as she was committed to an interest in you by her bright, pure, intelligent smile. A girl who had such a lovely way of showing her teeth could never pass for heartless.

As I sat between the pair I felt that I had been taken possession of and that for better or worse my stay at Homburg would be intimately associated with theirs. We gave each other a great deal of news and expressed unlimited interest in each other's history since our last meeting. I know not what Mrs. Pallant kept back, but for myself I was frank enough. She let me see at any rate that her life had been a good deal what I supposed, though the terms she used to describe it were less crude than those of my thought. She confessed that they had drifted and that they were drifting still. Her narrative rambled and got what is vulgarly called somewhat mixed, as I thought Linda perceived while she sat watching the passers in a manner which betrayed no consciousness of their attention, without coming to her mother's aid. Once or twice Mrs. Pallant made me feel like a cross-questioner, which I had no intention of being. I took it that if the girl never put in a word it was because she had perfect confidence in her mother's ability to come out straight. It was suggested to me, I scarcely knew how, that this confidence between the two ladies went to a great length; that their union of thought, their system of reciprocal divination, was remarkable, and that they probably seldom needed to resort to the clumsy and in some cases dangerous expedient of putting their ideas into words. I suppose I made this reflection not all at once—it was not wholly the result of that first meeting. I was with them constantly for the next several days and my impressions had time to clarify.

I do remember however that it was on this first evening that Archie's name came up. She attributed her own stay at Homburg to no refined nor exalted motive—did not say that she was there because she always came or because a high medical authority had ordered her to drink the waters; she frankly admitted that the reason of her visit had been simply that she did not know where else to turn. But she appeared to assume that my behaviour rested on higher grounds and even that it required explanation, the place being frivolous and modern—devoid of that interest of antiquity which I used to value. "Don't you remember—ever so long ago—that you wouldn't look at anything in Europe that was not a thousand years old? Well, as we advance in life I suppose we don't think that's quite such a charm." And when I told her that I had come to Homburg because it was as good a place as another to wait for my nephew, she exclaimed: "Your nephew—what nephew? He must have come up of late." I answered that he was a youth named Archer Pringle[347] and very modern indeed; he was coming of age in a few months and was in Europe for the first time. My last news of him had been from Paris and I was expecting to hear from him from one day to the other. His father was dead, and though a selfish bachelor, little versed in the care of children, I was considerably counted on by his mother to see that he did not smoke too much nor fall off an Alp.[348]

Mrs. Pallant immediately guessed that his mother was my sister Charlotte, whom she spoke of familiarly, though I knew she had seen her but once or twice. Then in a moment it came to her which of the Pringles Charlotte had married; she remembered the family perfectly, in the old New York days—'that disgustingly rich lot.' She said it was very nice having the boy come out that way to my care; to which I replied that it was very nice for him. She declared that she meant for me—I ought to have had children; there was something so parental about me and I would have brought them up so well. She could make an allusion like that—to all that might have been and had not been—without a gleam of guilt in her eye; and I foresaw that before I left the place I should have confided to her that though I detested her and was very glad we had fallen out, yet our old relations had left me no heart for marrying another woman. If I was a maundering old bachelor to-day it was no one's fault but hers. She asked me what I meant to do with my nephew and I said it was much more a question of what he would do with me. She inquired whether he were a nice young man and had brothers and sisters and any particular profession. I told her that I had really seen but little of him; I believed him to be six feet high and of tolerable parts. He was an only son, but there was a little sister at home, a delicate, unsuccessful child, demanding all the mother's care.

"So that makes your responsibility greater, as it were, about the boy, doesn't it?" said Mrs. Pallant.

"Greater? I'm sure I don't know."

"Why, if the girl's life is uncertain he may be, some moment, all the mother has. So that being in your hands ——"

"Oh, I shall keep him alive, I suppose, if you mean that," I rejoined.

"Well, *we* won't kill him, shall we, Linda?" Mrs. Pallant went on, with a laugh.

"I don't know—perhaps we shall!" said the girl, smiling.

II

I CALLED on them the next day at their lodgings, the modesty of which was enhanced by a hundred pretty feminine devices—flowers and photographs and portable knick-knacks and a hired piano and morsels of old brocade flung over angular sofas. I asked them to drive; I met them again at the Kursaal; I arranged that we should dine together, after the Homburg fashion, at the same *table d'hôte*; and during several days this revived familiar intercourse continued, imitating intimacy if it did not quite achieve it. I liked it, for my companions passed my time for me and the conditions of our life were soothing—the feeling of summer and shade and music and leisure, in the German gardens and woods, where we strolled and sat and gossiped; to which may be added a kind of sociable sense that among people whose challenge to the curiosity was mainly not irresistible we kept quite to ourselves. We were on the footing of old friends who, with regard to each other, still had discoveries to make. We knew each other's nature but we did not know each other's experience; so that when Mrs. Pallant related to me what she had been 'up to' (as I called it) for so many years, the former knowledge attached a hundred interpretative footnotes (as if I had been editing an author who presented difficulties) to the interesting page. There was nothing new to me in the fact that I did not esteem her, but there was a sort of refreshment in finding that this was not necessary at Homburg and that I could like her in spite of it. She seemed to me, in the oddest way, both improved and degenerate, as if in her nature the two processes had gone on together. She was battered and world-worn and, spiritually speaking, vulgarised; something fresh had rubbed off her (it even included the vivacity of her early desire to do the best thing for herself), and something very stale had rubbed on. On the other hand she betrayed a scepticism, and that was rather becoming, as it quenched the eagerness of her prime, which had taken a form so unfortunate for me. She had grown weary and indifferent, and as she struck me as having seen more of the evil of the world than of the good, that was a gain; in other words the cynicism that had formed itself in her nature had a softer surface than some of her old ambitions. And

245

then I had to recognise that her devotion to her daughter had been a kind of religion; she had done the very best possible for Linda,

Linda was curious—Linda was interesting; I have seen girls I liked better (charming as she was), but I have never seen one who for the time I was with her (the impression passed, somehow, when she was out of sight) occupied me more. I can best describe the sort of attention that she excited by saying that she struck one above all things as a final product—just as some plant or fruit does, some waxen orchid or some perfect peach. More than any girl I ever saw she was the result of a process of calculation; a process patiently educative; a pressure exerted in order that she should reach a high point. This high point had been the star of her mother's heaven (it hung before her so definitely), and had been the source of the only light —in default of a better—that shone upon the poor lady's path. It stood her in stead of every other religion. The very most and the very best—that was what the girl had been led on to achieve; I mean, of course (for no real miracle had been wrought), the most and the best that she was capable of. She was as pretty, as graceful, as intelligent, as well-bred, as well-informed, as well-dressed, as it would have been possible for her to be; her music, her singing, her German, her French, her English, her step, her tone, her glance, her manner, and everything in her person and movement, from the shade and twist of her hair to the way you saw her finger-nails were pink when she raised her hand, had been carried so far that one found one's self accepting them as a kind of standard. I regarded her as a model, and yet it was a part of her perfection that she had none of the stiffness of a pattern. If she held the observation it was because one wondered where and when she would break down; but she never did, either in her French accent or in her *rôle* of educated angel.

After Archie had come the ladies were manifestly a great resource to him, and all the world knows that a party of four is more convenient than a party of three. My nephew kept me waiting a week, with a placidity all his own; but this same placidity was an element of success in our personal relations—so long, that is, as I did not lose my temper with it. I did not, for the most part, because my young man's unsurprised acceptance of the most various forms of good fortune had more than anything else the effect of amusing me. I had seen little of him for the last three or four years. I knew not what his impending majority would have made of him (he did not look himself in the least as if the wind were rising), and I watched him with a solicitude which usually ended in a joke. He was a tall, fresh-coloured youth, with a candid circular countenance and a love of cigarettes, horses and boats which had not been sacrificed to more transcendent studies. He was refreshingly natural, in a supercivilised age, and I soon made up my mind that the formula of his character was a certain simplifying serenity. After that I had time to meditate on the line which divides the serene from the inane and simplification from death. Archie was not clever—that theory it was not possible to maintain, though Mrs. Pallant tried it once or twice; but on the other hand it seemed to me that his want of wit was a good defensive weapon. It was not the sort of density that would let him in, but the sort that would keep him out. By which I don't mean that he had shortsighted suspicions, but on the contrary that imagination would never be needed to save him, because she would never put him in danger. In short he was a well-grown, well-washed, muscular young American, whose extreme good-nature might have made him pass for conceited. If he looked pleased with himself it was only because he was pleased with life (as well he might be, with the money he was on the point of stepping into), and his big healthy, independent person was an inevitable part of that. I am bound to add that he was accommodating—for which I was grateful. His own habits were active, but he did not insist on my adopting them and he made noteworthy sacrifices for the sake of my society. When I say for the sake of mine I must of course remember that mine and that of Mrs. Pallant and Linda were now very much the same thing. He was willing to sit and smoke for hours under the trees or, regulating his long legs to the pace of his three companions, stroll through the nearer woods of the charming little hill-range of the Taunus[349] to those rustic *Wirthschaften*[350] where coffee might be drunk under a trellis.

Mrs. Pallant took a great interest in him; she talked a great deal about him and thought him a delightful specimen, as a young gentleman of his period and country. She even asked me the sort of 'figure' that his fortune might really amount to and expressed the most hungry envy when I told her what I supposed it to be. While we talked together Archie, on his side, could not do less than converse with Linda, nor to tell the truth did he manifest the least inclination for any different exercise. They strolled away together while their elders rested; two or three times, in the evening, when the ballroom of the Kursaal was lighted and dance-music played, they whirled over the smooth floor in a waltz that made me remember. Whether it had the same effect on Mrs. Pallant I know not, for she held her peace. We had on certain occasions our moments, almost our half-hours, of unembarrassed silence while our young companions disported themselves. But if at other times her inquiries and comments were numerous on the subject of my ingenuous kinsman this might very well have passed for a courteous recognition of the frequent admiration that I expressed for Linda—an admiration to which I noticed that she was apt to give but a small direct response. I was struck with something anomalous in her way of taking my remarks about her daughter—they produced so little of a maternal flutter. Her detachment, her air of having no fatuous illusions and not being blinded by prejudice seemed to me at times to amount to an affectation. Either she answered me with a vague, slightly impatient sigh and changed the subject, or else she said before doing so: "Oh yes, yes, she's a very brilliant creature. She ought to be; God knows what I have done for her!"

The reader will have perceived that I am fond of looking at the explanations of things, and in regard to this I had my theory that she was disappointed in the girl. What had been her particular disappointment? As she could not possibly have wished her prettier or more pleasing it could only be that Linda had not made a successful use of her gifts. Had she expected her to capture a prince the day after she left the schoolroom? After all there was plenty of time for this, as Linda was only two and twenty. It did not occur to me to wonder whether the source of her mother's tepidity was that the young lady had not turned out so nice a nature as she had hoped, because in the first place Linda struck me as perfectly innocent and in the second I was not paid, as the French say,³⁵¹ for thinking that Louisa Pallant would much mind whether she were or not. The last hypothesis I should have resorted to was that of private despair at bad moral symptoms. And in relation to Linda's nature I had before me the daily spectacle of her manner with my nephew. It was as charming as it could be, without the smallest indication of a desire to lead him on. She was as familiar as a cousin, but as a distant one—a cousin who had been brought up to observe degrees. She was so much cleverer than Archie that she could not help laughing at him, but she did not laugh enough to exclude variety, being well aware, no doubt, that a woman's cleverness most shines in contrast with a man's stupidity when she pretends to take that stupidity for wisdom. Linda Pallant moreover was not a chatter-box; as she knew the value of many things she knew the value of intervals. There were a good many in the conversation of these young persons; my nephew's own speech, to say nothing of his thought, being not exempt from periods of repose; so that I sometimes wondered how their association was kept at that pitch of friendliness of which it certainly bore the stamp.

It was friendly enough, evidently, when Archie sat near her—near enough for low murmurs, if they had risen to his lips—and watched her with interested eyes and with liberty not to try too hard to make himself agreeable. She was always doing something—finishing a flower in a piece of tapestry, cutting the leaves of a magazine, sewing a button on her glove (she carried a little work-bag in her pocket and was a person of the daintiest habits), or plying her pencil in a sketchbook which she rested on her knee. When we were indoors, at her mother's house, she had always the resource of her piano, of which she was of course a perfect mistress. These avocations enabled her to bear such close inspection with composure (I ended by rebuking Archie for it—I told him he stared at the poor girl too much), and she sought further relief in smiling all over the place. When my young man's eyes shone at her those of Miss Pallant addressed themselves brightly to the trees and clouds and other surrounding objects, including her mother and me. Sometimes she broke out into a sudden embarrassed, happy, pointless laugh. When she wandered away from us she looked back at us in a manner which said that it was not for long—that she was with us still in spirit. If I was pleased with her it was for a good reason: it was many a day since any pretty girl had had the air of taking me so much into account. Sometimes, when they were so far away as not to disturb us, she read aloud a little to Mr. Archie. I don't know where she got her books—I never provided them, and certainly he did not. He was no reader and I daresay he went to sleep.

III

I REMEMBER well the first time—it was at the end of about ten days of this—that Mrs. Pallant remarked to me: "My dear friend, you are quite amazing! You behave for all the world as if you were perfectly ready to accept certain consequences." She nodded in the direction of our young companions, but I nevertheless put her at the pains of saying what consequences she meant. "What consequences?" she repeated. "Why, the consequences that ensued when you and I first became acquainted."

I hesitated a moment and then, looking her in the eyes, I said, "Do you mean that she would throw him over?"

"You are not kind, you are not generous," she replied, colouring quickly. "I am giving you a warning."

"You mean that my boy may fall in love with her?"

"Certainly. It looks even as if the harm might be already done."

"Then your warning is too late," I said, smiling. "But why do you call it a harm?"

"Haven't you any sense of responsibility?" she asked. "Is that what his mother sent him out to you for—that you should find him a wife—let him put his head into a noose the day after his arrival?"

"Heaven forbid I should do anything of the kind! I know moreover that his mother doesn't want him to marry young. She thinks it's a mistake and that at that age a man never really chooses. He doesn't choose till he has lived awhile—till he has looked about and compared."

"And what do you think yourself?"

"I should like to say I consider that love itself, however young, is a sufficient choice. But my being a bachelor at this time of day would contradict me too much."

"Well then, you're too primitive. You ought to leave this place to-morrow."

"So as not to see Archie tumble in?"

"You ought to fish him out now and take him with you."

"Do you think he is in very far?" I inquired.

"If I were his mother I know what I should think. I can put myself in her place—I am not narrow—I know perfectly well how she must regard such a question."

"And don't you know that in America that's not thought important—the way the mother regards it?"

Mrs. Pallant was silent a moment, as if I partly mystified and partly vexed her. "Well, we are not in America; we happen to be here."

"No; my poor sister is up to her neck in New York."

"I am almost capable of writing to her to come out," said Mrs. Pallant.

"You are warning me," I exclaimed, "but I hardly know of what. It seems to me that my responsibility would begin only at the moment when it should appear that your daughter herself was in danger."

"Oh, you needn't mind that; I'll take care of her."

"If you think she is in danger already I'll take him away to-morrow," I went on.

"It would be the best thing you could do."

"I don't know. I should be very sorry to act on a false alarm. I am very well here; I like the place and the life and your society. Besides, it doesn't strike me that—on her side—there is anything."

She looked at me with an expression that I had never seen in her face, and if I had puzzled her she repaid me in kind. "You are very annoying; you don't deserve what I would do for you."

What she would do for me she did not tell me that day, but we took up the subject again. I said to her that I did not really see why we should assume that a girl like Linda—brilliant enough to make one of the greatest matches—would fall into my nephew's arms. Might I inquire whether her mother had won a confession from her—whether she had stammered out her secret? Mrs. Pallant answered that they did not need to tell each other such things—they had not lived together twenty years in such intimacy for nothing. To this I rejoined that I had guessed as much but that there might be an exception for a great occasion like the present. If Linda had shown nothing it was a sign that for her the occasion was not great; and I mentioned that Archie had not once spoken to me of the young lady, save to remark casually and rather patronisingly, after his first encounter with her, that she was a regular little flower. (The little flower was nearly three years older than himself.) Apart from this he had not alluded to her and had taken up no allusion of mine. Mrs. Pallant informed me again (for which I was prepared) that I was quite too primitive; and then she said: "We needn't discuss the matter if you don't wish to, but I happen to know—how I obtained my knowledge is not important—that the moment Mr. Pringle should propose to my daughter she would gobble him down. Surely it's a detail worth mentioning to you."

"Very good. I will sound him. I will look into the matter to-night."

"Don't, don't; you will spoil everything!" she murmured, in a peculiar tone of discouragement. "Take him off—that's the only thing."

I did not at all like the idea of taking him off; it seemed too summary, unnecessarily violent, even if presented to him on specious grounds; and, moreover, as I had told Mrs. Pallant, I really had no wish to move. I did not consider it a part of my bargain with my sister that, with my middle-aged habits, I should duck and dodge about Europe. So I said: "Should you really object to the boy so much as a son-in-law? After all he's a good fellow and a gentleman."

"My poor friend, you are too superficial—too frivolous," Mrs. Pallant rejoined, with considerable bitterness.

There was a vibration of contempt in this which nettled me, so that I exclaimed, "Possibly; but it seems odd that a lesson in consistency should come from you."

I had no retort from her; but at last she said, quietly: "I think Linda and I had better go away. We have been here a month—that's enough."

"Dear me, that will be a bore!" I ejaculated; and for the rest of the evening, until we separated (our conversation had taken place after dinner, at the Kursaal), she remained almost silent, with a subdued, injured air. This, somehow, did not soothe me, as it ought to have done, for it was too absurd that Louisa Pallant, of all women, should propose to put me in the wrong. If ever a woman had been in the wrong herself——! Archie and I usually attended the ladies back to their own door—they lived in a street of minor accommodation, at a certain distance from the Rooms—and we parted for the night late, on the big cobble-stones, in the little sleeping German town, under the closed windows of which, suggesting stuffy interiors, our English farewells sounded gay. On this occasion however they were not gay, for the difficulty that had come up, for me, with Mrs. Pallant appeared to have extended by a mysterious sympathy to the young couple. They too were rather conscious and dumb.

As I walked back to our hotel with my nephew I passed my hand into his arm and asked him, by no roundabout approach to the question, whether he were in serious peril of love.

"I don't know, I don't know—really, uncle, I don't know!"—this was all the satisfaction I could extract from the youth, who had not the smallest vein of introspection. He might not know, but before we reached the inn (we had a few more words on the subject), it seemed to me that I did. His mind was not made to contain many objects at once, but Linda Pallant for the moment certainly constituted its principal furniture. She pervaded his consciousness she solicited his curiosity, she associated herself, in a manner as yet undefined and unformulated, with his future. I could see that she was the first intensely agreeable impression of his life. I did not betray to him, however, how much I saw, and I slept not particularly well, for thinking that, after all, it had been none of my business to provide him with intensely agreeable impressions. To find him a wife was the last thing that his mother had expected of me or that I had expected of myself. Moreover it was quite my opinion that he himself was too young to be a judge of wives. Mrs. Pallant was right and I had been strangely superficial in regarding her, with her beautiful daughter, as a 'resource.' There were other resources and one of them would be most decidedly to go away. What did I know after all about the girl except that I was very glad to have escaped from marrying her mother? That mother, it was true, was a singular person, and it was strange that her conscience should have begun to fidget before my own did and that she was more anxious on my nephew's behalf than I was. The ways of women were mysterious and it was not a novelty to me that one never knew where one would find them. As I have not hesitated in this narrative to reveal the irritable side of my own nature I will confess that I even wondered whether Mrs. Pallant's solicitude had not been a deeper artifice. Was it not possibly a plan of her own for making sure of my young man—though I did not quite see the logic of it? If she regarded him, as she might in view of his large fortune, as a great catch, might she not have arranged this little comedy, in their personal interest, with the girl?

That possibility at any rate only made it a happier thought that I should carry the boy away to visit other cities. There were many assuredly much more worthy of his attention than Homburg. In the course of the morning (it was after our early luncheon) I walked round to Mrs. Pallant's, to let her know that this truth had come over me with force; and while I did so I again felt the unlikelihood of the part attributed by my fears and by the mother's own, if they were real, to Linda. Certainly if she was such a girl as these fears represented her she would fly at higher game. It was with an eye to high game, Mrs. Pallant had frankly admitted to me, that she had been trained, and such an education, to say nothing of such a subject, justified a hope of greater returns. A young American who could give her nothing but pocket-money was a very moderate prize, and if she were prepared to marry for ambition (there was no such hardness in her face or tone, but then there never is), her mark would be at the least an English duke. I was received at Mrs. Pallant's lodgings with the announcement that she had left Homburg with her daughter half an hour before. The good woman who had entertained the pair professed to know nothing of their movements beyond the fact that they had gone to Frankfort, where however it was her belief that they did not intend to remain. They were evidently travelling beyond. Sudden? Oh yes, tremendously sudden. They must have spent the night in packing, they had so many things and such pretty ones; and their poor maid all the morning had scarcely had time to swallow her coffee. But they evidently were ladies accustomed to come and go. It did not matter: with such rooms as hers she never wanted; there was a new family coming in at three o'clock.

IV

THIS piece of strategy left me staring and I confess it made me rather angry. My only consolation was that Archie, when I told him, looked as blank as myself and that the trick touched him more nearly, for I was not in love with Louisa. We agreed that we required an explanation and we pretended to expect one the next day in the shape of a letter satisfactory even to the point of being apologetic. When I say 'we' pretended I mean that I did, for my suspicion that he knew (through an arrangement with Linda) what had become of our friends lasted only a moment. If his resentment was less than my own his surprise was equally great. I had been willing to bolt, but I felt rather slighted by the facility with which Mrs. Pallant had shown that she could part with us. Archie was not angry, because in the first place he was good-natured and in the second it was evidently not definite to him that he had been encouraged, having, I think, no very particular idea of what constituted encouragement. He was fresh from the wonderful country in which between the ingenuous young there may be so little question of 'intentions.' He was but dimly conscious of his own and would have had no opinion as to whether he had been provoked or jilted. I had no wish to exasperate him, but when at the end of three days more we were still without news of our late companions I remarked that it was very simple; it was plain they were just hiding from us; they thought us dangerous; they wished to avoid entanglements. They had found us too attentive and wished not to raise false hopes. He appeared to accept this explanation and even had the air (so at least I judged from his asking me no questions) of thinking that the matter might be delicate for myself. The poor youth was altogether much mystified, and I smiled at the image in his mind of Mrs. Pallant fleeing from his uncle's importunities.

We decided to leave Homburg, but if we did not pursue her it was not simply that we were ignorant of where she was. I could have found that out with a little trouble, but I was deterred by the reflection that this would be her own reasoning. She was dishonest and her departure was a provocation—I am afraid that it was in that stupid conviction that I made out a little independent itinerary with Archie. I even said to myself that we should learn where they were quite soon enough and that our patience—even my young man's—would be longer than theirs. Therefore I uttered a small private cry of triumph when three weeks later (we happened to be at Interlaken)[352] he told me that he had received a note from Miss Pallant. His manner of telling me was to inquire whether there were any particular reasons why we should longer delay our projected visit to the Italian lakes;[353] was not the fear of the hot weather, which was moreover in summer our native temperature, at an end, as it was already the middle of September? I answered that we would start on the morrow if he liked, and then, pleased apparently that I was so easy to deal with, he revealed his little secret. He showed me the letter, which was a graceful, natural document—it covered with a few flowing strokes but a single page of notepaper—not at all compromising to the young lady. If however it was almost the apology I had looked for (save that that should have come from the mother), it was not ostensibly in the least an invitation. It mentioned casually (the mention was mainly in the date) that they were on the Lago Maggiore, at Baveno;[354] but it consisted mainly of the expression of a regret that they had to leave us at Homburg without giving notice. Linda did not say under what necessity they had found themselves; she only hoped we had not judged them too harshly and would accept 'these few hasty words' as a substitute for the omitted goodbye. She also hoped we were passing our time in an interesting manner and having the same lovely weather that prevailed south of the Alps; and she remained very sincerely, with the kindest remembrances to me.

The note contained no message from her mother and it was open to me to suppose, as I should judge, either that Mrs. Pallant had not known she was writing or that they wished to make us think she had not known. The letter might pass as a common civility of the girl's to a person with whom she had been on very familiar terms. It was however as something more than this that my nephew took it; at least so I was warranted in inferring from the very distinct nature of his determination to go to Baveno. I saw it was useless to drag him another way; he had money in his own pocket and was quite capable of giving me the slip. Yet—such are the sweet incongruities of youth—when I asked him if he had been thinking of Linda Pallant ever since they left us in the lurch he replied, "Oh dear no; why should I?" This fib was accompanied by an exorbitant blush. Since he must obey the young lady's call I must also go and see where it would take him, and one splendid morning we started over the Simplon in a post-chaise.[355]

I represented to him successfully that it would be in much better taste for us to alight at Stresa,[356] which as every one knows is a resort of tourists, also on the shore of the major lake, at about a mile's distance from Baveno. If we stayed at the latter place we should have to inhabit the same hotel as our friends, and this would be indiscreet, considering our peculiar relations with them. Nothing would be easier than to go and come between the two points, especially by the water, which would give Archie a chance for unlimited paddling. His face lighted up at the vision of a pair of oars; he pretended to take my plea for discretion very seriously and I could see that he immediately began to calculate opportunities for being afloat with Linda. Our post-chaise (I had insisted on easy stages and we were three days on the way) deposited us at Stresa toward the middle of the afternoon, and it was within an amazingly short time that I found myself in a small boat with my nephew, who pulled us over to Baveno with vigorous strokes. I remember the sweetness of the whole impression (I had had it before, but to my companion it was new and he thought it as pretty as the opera); the enchanting beauty of the place and hour, the stillness of the air and water, with the romantic, fantastic Borromean Islands[357] in the midst of them. We disembarked at the steps at the garden-foot of the hotel, and somehow it seemed a perfectly natural part of the lovely situation that I should immediately become conscious Mrs. Pallant and her daughter were sitting there—on the terrace—quietly watching us. They had all the air of expecting us and I think we looked for it in them. I had not even asked Archie if he had answered Linda's note; that was between themselves and in the way of supervision I had done enough in coming with him.

There is no doubt there was something very odd in our meeting with our friends—at least as between Louisa and me. I was too much taken up with that part of it to notice very much what was the manner of the encounter of the young people. I have sufficiently indicated that I could not get it out of my head that Mrs. Pallant was 'up to' something, and I am afraid she saw in my face that this suspicion had been the motive of my journey. I had come there to find her out. The knowledge of my purpose could not help her to make me very welcome, and that is why I say we met in strange conditions.

However, on this occasion we observed all forms and the admirable scene gave us plenty to talk about. I made no reference before Linda to the retreat from Homburg. She looked even prettier than she had done on the eve of that manœuvre and gave no sign of an awkward consciousness. She struck me so, afresh, as a charming, clever girl that I was puzzled afresh to know why we should get—or should have got—into a tangle about her. People had to want to complicate a situation to do it on so simple a pretext as that Linda was admirable. So she was, and why should not the consequences be equally so? One of them, on the spot, was that at the end of a very short time Archie proposed to her to take a turn with him in his boat,[358] which awaited us at the foot of the steps. She looked at her mother with a smiling "May I, mamma?" and Mrs. Pallant answered, "Certainly, darling, if you are not afraid." At this—I scarcely knew why—I burst out laughing; it seemed so droll to me somehow that timidity should be imputed to this competent young lady. She gave me a quick, slightly sharp look as she turned away with my nephew; it appeared to challenge me a little—to say, "Pray what is the matter with *you?*" It was the first expression of the kind I had ever seen in her face. Mrs. Pallant's eyes, on the other hand, were not turned to mine; after we had been left there together she sat silent, not heeding me, looking at the lake and mountains—at the snowy crests which wore the flush of evening. She seemed not even to watch our young companions as they got into their boat and pushed off. For some minutes I respected her reverie; I walked slowly up and down the terrace and lighted a cigar, as she had always permitted me to do at Homburg. I noticed that she had an expression of weariness which I had never seen before; her delicate, agreeable face was pale; I made out that there were new lines of fatigue, almost of age, in it. At last I stopped in front of her and asked her, since she looked so sad, if she had any bad news.

"The only bad news was when I learned—through your nephew's note to Linda that you were coming to us."

"Ah, then he wrote?" I exclaimed.

"Certainly he wrote."

"You take it all harder than I do," I remarked, sitting down beside her. And then I added, smiling, "Have you written to his mother?"

She slowly turned her face to me and rested her eyes on mine. "Take care, take care, or you'll insult me," she said, with an air of patience before the inevitable.

"Never, never! Unless you think I do so if I ask you if you knew when Linda wrote."

She hesitated a moment. "Yes; she showed me her letter. She wouldn't have done anything else. I let it go because I didn't know what it was best to do. I am afraid to oppose her, to her face."

"Afraid, my dear friend, with that girl?"

"That girl? Much you know about her! It didn't follow that you would come—I didn't think it need follow."

"I am like you," I said—"I am afraid of my nephew. I don't venture to oppose him to his face. The only thing I could do under the circumstances was to come with him."

"I see; I'm glad you have done it," said Mrs. Pallant, thoughtfully.

"Oh, I was conscientious about that! But I have no authority; I can't order him nor forbid him—I can use no force. Look at the way he is pulling that boat and see if you can fancy me."

"You could tell him she's a bad, hard girl, who would poison any good man's life!" my companion suddenly broke out, with a kind of passion.

"Dear Mrs. Pallant, what do you mean?" I murmured, staring.

She bent her face into her hands, covering it over with them, and remained so for a minute; then she went on, in a different manner, as if she had not heard my question: "I hoped you were too disgusted with us, after the way we left you planted."

"It was disconcerting, assuredly, and it might have served if Linda hadn't written. That patched it up," I said, laughing. But my laughter was hollow, for I had been exceedingly impressed with her little explosion of a moment before. "Do you really mean she is bad?" I added.

Mrs. Pallant made no immediate answer to this; she only said that it did not matter after all whether the crisis should come a few weeks sooner or a few weeks later, since it was destined to come at the first opening. Linda had marked my young man—and when Linda had marked a thing!

"Bless my soul—how very grim! Do you mean she's in love with him?" I demanded, incredulous.

"It's enough if she makes him think she is—though even that isn't essential."

"If she makes him think so? Dearest lady, what do you mean? I have observed her, I have watched her, and after all what has she done? She has been nice to him, but it would have been much more marked if she hadn't. She has really shown him nothing but the common friendliness of a bright, good-natured girl. Her note was nothing; he showed it to me."

"I don't think you have heard every word that she has said to him," Mrs. Pallant rejoined, with a persistence that struck me as unnatural.

"No more have you, I take it!" I exclaimed. She evidently meant more than she said, and this impression chilled me, made me really uncomfortable.

"No, but I know my own daughter. She's a very rare young woman."

"You have a singular tone about her," I responded—"such a tone as I think I have never heard on a mother's lips. I have observed it before, but never so accentuated."

At this Mrs. Pallant got up; she stood there an instant, looking down at me. "You make my reparation—my expiation—difficult!" And leaving me rather startled, she began to move along the terrace.

I overtook her presently and repeated her words. "Your reparation—your expiation? What on earth do you mean by that?"

"You know perfectly what I mean—it is too magnanimous of you to pretend you don't."

"Well, at any rate I don't see what good it does me or what it makes up to me for that you should abuse your daughter."

"Oh, I don't care; I shall save him!" she exclaimed, as we went, with a kind of perverse cheerfulness. At the same moment two ladies, apparently English, came toward us (scattered groups had been sitting there and the inmates of the hotel were moving to and fro), and I observed the immediate charming transition (it seemed to me to show such years of social practice), by which, as they greeted us, she exchanged her excited, almost fevered expression for an air of recognition and pleasure. They stopped to speak to her and she asked with eagerness whether their mother were better. I strolled on and she presently rejoined me; after which she said impatiently, "Come away from this—come down into the garden." We descended into the garden, strolled through it and paused on the border of the lake.

V

THE charm of the evening had deepened, the stillness was like a solemn expression on a beautiful face and the whole air of the place divine. In the fading light my nephew's boat was too far out to be perceived. I looked for it a little and then, as I gave it up, I remarked that from such an excursion as that, on such a lake, at such an hour, a young man and a young woman of ordinary sensibility could only come back doubly pledged to each other. To this observation Mrs. Pallant's answer was, superficially at least, irrelevant; she said after a pause:

"With you, my dear sir, one has certainly to dot one's 'i's'. Haven't you discovered, and didn't I tell you at Homburg, that we are miserably poor?"

"Isn't 'miserably' rather too much, when you are living at an expensive hotel?"

"They take us *en pension*, for ever so little a day. I have been knocking about Europe long enough to learn there are certain ways of doing things. Besides, don't speak of hotels; we have spent half our life in them and Linda told me only last night that she hoped never to put her foot into one again. She thinks that when she comes to such a place as this it's the least that she should find a villa of her own."

"Well, her companion there is perfectly competent to give her one. Don't think I have the least desire to push them into each other's arms; I only ask to wash my hands of them. But I should like to know why you want, as you said just now, to save him. When you speak as if your daughter were a monster I take it that you are not serious."

She was facing me there in the twilight, and to let me know that she was more serious perhaps than she had ever been in her life she had only to look at me awhile without protestation. "It's Linda's standard. God knows I myself could get on! She is ambitious, luxurious, determined to have what she wants, more than any one I have ever seen. Of course it's open to you to tell me that it's my fault, that I was so before her and have made her so. But does that make me like it any better?"

"Dear Mrs. Pallant, you are most extraordinary," I stammered, infinitely surprised and not a little pained.

"Oh yes, you have made up your mind about me; you see me in a certain way and you don't like the trouble of changing. *Votre siège est fait.*[359] But you will have to change—if you have any generosity!" Her eyes shone in the summer dusk and she looked remarkably handsome.

"Is this a part of the reparation, of the expiation?" I inquired. "I don't see what you ever did to Archie."

"It's enough that he belongs to you. But it isn't for you that I do it; it's for myself," she went on.

"Doubtless you have your own reasons, which I can't penetrate. But can't you sacrifice something else?— must you sacrifice your child?"

"She's my punishment and she's my stigma!" cried Louisa Pallant, with veritable exaltation.

"It seems to me rather that you are hers."

"Hers? What does *she* know of such things?—what can she ever feel? She's cased in steel;[360] she has a heart of marble. It's true—it's true. She appals me!"

I laid my hand upon the poor lady's; I uttered, with the intention of checking and soothing her, the first incoherent words that came into my head and I drew her toward a bench which I perceived a few yards away. She dropped upon it; I placed myself near her and besought her to consider well what she was saying. She owed me nothing and I wished no one injured, no one denounced or exposed for my sake.

"For your sake? Oh, I am not thinking of you!" she answered; and indeed the next moment I thought my words rather fatuous. "It's a satisfaction to my own conscience—for I have one, little as you think I have a right to speak of it. I have been punished by my sin itself. I have been hideously worldly, I have thought only of that, and I have taught her to be so—to do the same. That's the only instruction I have ever given her, and she has learned the lesson so well that now that I see it printed there in all her nature I am horrified at my work. For years we have lived that way; we have thought of nothing else. She has learned it so well that she has gone far beyond me. I say I am horrified, because she is horrible."

"My poor extravagant friend," I pleaded, "isn't it still more so to hear a mother say such things?"

"Why so, if they are abominably true? Besides, I don't care what I say, if I save him."

"Do you expect me to repeat to him——?"

"Not in the least," she broke in; "I will do it myself." At this I uttered some strong inarticulate protest, and she went on with a sort of simplicity: "I was very glad at first, but it would have been better if we hadn't met."

"I don't agree to that, for you interest me immensely."

"I don't care for that—if I can interest him."

"You must remember then that your charges are strangely vague, considering how violent they are. Never had a girl a more innocent appearance. You know how I have admired it."

"You know nothing about her. *I* do, for she is the work of my hand!"[361] Mrs. Pallant declared, with a bitter laugh. "I have watched her for years and little by little, for the last two or three, it has come over me. There is not a tender spot in her whole composition. To arrive at a brilliant social position, if it were necessary, she would see me drown in this lake without lifting a finger, she would stand there and see it—she would push me in— and never feel a pang. That's my young lady! To climb up to the top and be splendid and envied there—to do it at any cost or by any meanness and cruelty, is the only thing she has a heart for. She would lie for it, she would steal for it, she would kill for it!" My companion brought out these words with a tremendous low distinctness and an air of sincerity that was really solemn. I watched her pale face and glowing eyes; she held me in a kind of stupor, but her strange, almost vindictive earnestness imposed itself. I found myself believing her, pitying her more than I pitied the girl. It was as if she had been bottled up for longer than she could bear, suffering more and more from the ferment of her knowledge. It relieved her to warn and denounce and expose. "God has let me see it in time, in his mercy," she continued; "but his ways are strange, that he has let me see it in my daughter. It is myself that he has let me see, myself as I was for years. But she's worse— she is, I assure you; she's worse than I ever intended or dreamed." Her hands were clasped tightly together in her lap; her low voice quavered and her breath came short; she looked up at the faint stars with religious perversity.

"Have you ever spoken to her as you speak to me?" I asked. "Have you ever admonished her, reproached her?"

"Reproached her? How can I? when all she would have to say would be, 'You—*you*—you base one—who made me!'"

"Then why do you want to play her a trick?"

"I'm not bound to tell you and you wouldn't understand if I did. I should play that boy a far worse trick if I were to hold my tongue."

"If he loves her he won't believe a word you say."

"Very possibly, but I shall have done my duty."

"And shall you say to him simply what you have said to me?"

"Never mind what I shall say to him. It will be something that will perhaps affect him, if I lose no time."

"If you are so bent on gaining time," I said, "why did you let her go out in the boat with him?"

"Let her? how could I prevent it?"

"But she asked your permission."

"That's a part of all the comedy!"

We were silent a moment, after which I resumed: "Then she doesn't know you hate her?"

"I don't know what she knows. She has depths and depths, and all of them bad. Besides, I don't hate her in the least; I pity her simply, for what I have made of her. But I pity still more the man who may find himself married to her."

"There's not much danger of there being any such person, at the rate you go on."

"Oh, perfectly; she'll marry some one. She'll marry a title as well as a fortune."

"It's a pity my nephew hasn't a title," I murmured, smiling.

She hesitated a moment. "I see you think I want that and that I am acting a part. God forgive you! Your suspicion is perfectly natural: how can any one tell, with people like us?"

The way she uttered these last words brought tears to my eyes. I laid my hand on her arm, holding her awhile, and we looked at each other through the dusk. "You couldn't do more if he were my son," I said at last.

"Oh, if he had been your son he would have kept out of it! I like him for himself; he's simple and honest—he needs affection."

"He would have an admirable, a devoted, mother-in-law," I went on.

Mrs. Pallant gave a little impatient sigh and replied that she was not joking. We sat there some time longer, while I thought over what she had said to me and she apparently did the same. I confess that even close at her side, with the echo of her passionate, broken voice still in the air, some queer ideas came into my head. Was the comedy on *her* side and not on the girl's, and was she posturing as a magnanimous woman at poor Linda's expense? Was she determined, in spite of the young lady's preference, to keep her daughter for a grander personage than a young American whose dollars were not numerous enough (numerous as they were) to make up for his want of high relationships, and had she brought forth these cruel imputations to help her to her end? If she was prepared really to denounce the girl to Archie she would have to go very far to overcome the suspicion he would be sure to feel at so unnatural a proceeding. Was she prepared to go far enough? The answer to these doubts was simply the way I had been touched—it came back to me the next moment—when she used the words, 'people like us.' The effect of them was poignant. She made herself humble indeed and I felt in a manner ashamed, on my own side, that I saw her in the dust. She said to me at last that I must wait no longer; I must go away before the young people came back. They were staying very long, too long; all the more reason that she should deal with Archie that evening. I must drive back to Stresa or, if I liked, I could go on foot: it was not far—for a man. She disposed of me freely, she was so full of her purpose; and after we had quitted the garden and returned to the terrace of the hotel she seemed almost to push me to leave her—I felt her fine hands, quivering a little, on my shoulders. I was ready to do what she liked: she affected me painfully and I wanted to get away from her. Before I went I asked her why Linda should regard my young man as such a *parti*; it did not square after all with her account of the girl's fierce ambitions. By that picture it would seem that a reigning prince was the least she would look at.

"Oh, she has reflected well; she has regarded the question in every light," said Mrs. Pallant. "If she has made up her mind it is because she sees what she can do."

"Do you mean that she has talked it over with you?"

"Lord! for what do you take us? We don't talk over things to-day. We know each other's point of view and we only have to act. We can take reasons, which are awkward things, for granted."

"But in this case she certainly doesn't know your point of view, poor thing."

THE ASPERN PAPERS AND OTHER TALES

"No—that's because I haven't played fair. Of course she couldn't expect I would cheat. There ought to be honour among thieves.[362] But it was open to her to do the same."

"How do you mean, to do the same?"

"She might have fallen in love with a poor man; then I should have been done."

"A rich one is better; he can do more," I replied, with conviction.

"So you would have reason to know if you had led the life that we have! Never to have had really enough—I mean to do just the few simple things we have wanted; never to have had the sinews of war,[363] I suppose you would call them—the funds for a campaign; to have felt every day and every hour the hard, monotonous pinch and found the question of dollars and cents (and so horridly few of them) mixed up with every experience, with every impulse that *does* make one mercenary, it does make money seem a good beyond all others, and it's quite natural it should. That is why Linda is of the opinion that a fortune is always a fortune. She knows all about that of your nephew, how it's invested, how it may be expected to increase, exactly on what sort of footing it would enable her to live. She has decided that it's enough, and enough is as good as a feast. She thinks she could lead him by the nose, and I daresay she could. She will make him live here: she has not the least intention of settling in America. I think she has views upon London,[364] because in England he can hunt and shoot, and that will make him let her alone."

"It strikes me that he would like that very much," I interposed; "that's not at all a bad programme, even from Archie's point of view."

"It's no use of talking about princes," Mrs. Pallant pursued, as if she had not heard me. "Yes, they are most of them more in want of money even than we are. Therefore a title is out of the question, and we recognised that at an early stage. Your nephew is exactly the sort of young man we had constructed in advance—he was made on purpose. Dear Linda was her mother's own daughter when she recognised him on the spot! It's enough of a title to-day to be an American—with the way they have come up. It does as well as anything and it's a great simplification. If you don't believe me go to London and see."

She had come with me out to the road. I had said I would walk back to Stresa and we stood there in the complete evening. As I took her hand, bidding her good-night, I exclaimed, "Poor Linda—poor Linda!"

"Oh, she'll live to do better," said Mrs. Pallant.

"How can she do better, since you have described this as perfection?"

She hesitated a moment. "I mean better for Mr. Pringle."

I still had her hand—I remained looking at her. "How came it that you could throw me over—such a woman as you?"

"Ah, my friend, if I hadn't thrown you over I couldn't do this for you?" And disengaging herself she turned away quickly and went back to the hotel.

VI

I DON'T know whether she blushed as she made this avowal, which was
a retraction of a former denial and the real truth, as I permitted myself
to believe; but I did, while I took my way to Stresa—it is a walk of half an
hour—in the darkness. The new and singular character in which she had
appeared to me produced an effect of excitement which would have made
it impossible for me to sit still in a carriage. This same agitation kept me
up late after I had reached my hotel; as I knew that I should not sleep it was
useless to go to bed. Long, however, as I deferred this ceremony Archie had
not turned up when the lights in the hotel began to be put out. I felt even
slightly nervous about him and wondered whether he had had an accident
on the lake. I reflected that in this case—if he had not brought his companion back to Baveno—Mrs. Pallant would already have sent after me.
It was foolish moreover to suppose that anything could have happened to
him after putting off from Baveno by water to rejoin me, for the evening
was absolutely windless and more than sufficiently clear and the lake as
calm as glass. Besides I had unlimited confidence in his power to take care
of himself in circumstances much more difficult. I went to my room at
last; his own was at some distance, the people of the hotel not having been
able—it was the height of the autumn season—to place us together. Before
I went to bed I had occasion to ring for a servant, and then I learned by a
chance inquiry that my nephew had returned an hour before and had gone
straight to his own apartment. I had not supposed he could come in without my seeing him—I was wandering about the saloons and terraces—and
it had not occurred to me to knock at his door. I had half a mind to do so
then—I had such a curiosity as to how I should find him; but I checked
myself, for evidently he had not wished to see me. This did not diminish
my curiosity, and I slept even less than I had expected. His dodging me that
way (for if he had not perceived me downstairs he might have looked for
me in my room) was a sign that Mrs. Pallant's interview with him had really
come off. What had she said to him? What strong measures had she taken?

The impression of almost morbid eagerness of purpose that she had given me suggested possibilities that I was afraid to think of. She had spoken of these things as we parted there as something she would do for me; but I had made the mental comment, as I walked away from her, that she had not done it yet. It would not really be done till Archie had backed out. Perhaps it was done by this time; his avoiding me seemed almost a proof. That was what I thought of most of the night. I spent a considerable part of it at my window, looking out at the sleeping mountains. *Had* he backed out?—was he making up his mind to back out?

There was a strange contradiction in it; there were in fact more contradictions than ever. I believed what Mrs. Pallant had told me about Linda, and yet that other idea made me ashamed of my nephew. I was sorry for the girl; I regretted her loss of a great chance, if loss it was to be; and yet I hoped that the manner in which her mother had betrayed her (there was no other word) to her lover had been thoroughgoing. It would need very radical measures on Mrs. Pallant's part to excuse Archie. For him too I was sorry, if she had made an impression on him—the impression she desired. Once or twice I was on the point of going in to condole with him, in my dressing-gown; I was sure he too had jumped up from his bed and was looking out of his window at the everlasting hills.

I am bound to say that he showed few symptoms when we met in the morning and breakfasted together. Youth is strange; it has resources that experience seems only to take away from us. One of these is simply (in the given case) to do nothing—to say nothing. As we grow older and cleverer we think that is too simple, too crude; we dissimulate more elaborately, but with an effect much less baffling. My young man looked not in the least as if he had lain awake or had something on his mind; and when I asked him what he had done after my premature departure (I explained this by saying I had been tired of waiting for him—I was weary with my journey and wanted to go to bed), he replied: "Oh, nothing in particular. I hung about the place; I like it better than this. We had an awfully jolly time on the water. *I* wasn't in the least tired." I did not worry him with questions; it seemed to me indelicate to try to probe his secret. The only indication he gave was on my saying after breakfast that I should go over again to see our friends and my appearing to take for granted that he would be glad to accompany me. Then he remarked that he would stop at Stresa—he had paid them such a tremendous visit; also he had some letters to write. There was a freshness in his scruples about the length of his visits, and I knew something about his correspondence, which consisted entirely of twenty pages every week from his mother. But he satisfied my curiosity so little that it was really this senti-ment that carried me back to Baveno. This time I ordered a conveyance, and as I got into it he stood watching me in the porch of the hotel with his hands in his pockets. Then it was for the first time that I saw in this young man's face the expression of a person slightly dazed, slightly foolish even, to whom something disagreeable has happened. Our eyes met as I observed him, and I was on the point of saying, "You had really better come with me," when he turned away. He went into the house as if he wished to escape from my call. I said to myself that Mrs. Pallant had warned him off but that it would not take much to bring him back.

The servant to whom I spoke at Baveno told me that my friends were in a certain summer-house in the garden, to which he led the way. The place had an empty air; most of the inmates of the hotel were dispersed on the lake, on the hills, in picnics, excursions, visits to the Borromean Islands. My guide was so far right as that Linda was in the summer-house, but she was there alone. On finding this to be the case I stopped short, rather awkwardly, for I had a sudden sense of being an unmasked hypocrite—a conspirator against her security and honour. But there was no awkwardness about Linda Pallant; she looked up with a little cry of pleasure from the book she was reading and held out her hand with the most engaging frankness. I felt as if I had no right to touch her hand and I pretended not to see it. But this gave no chill to her pretty manner; she moved a roll of tapestry off the bench, so that I might sit down, and praised the place as a delightful shady corner. She had never been fresher, fairer, kinder; she made her mother's damning talk about her seem a hideous dream. She told me Mrs. Pallant was coming to join her; she had remained indoors to write a letter. One could not write out there, though it was so nice in other respects: the table was too rick-ety. They too then had pretexts between them in the way of letters: I judged this to be a token that the situation was tense. It was the only one however that Linda gave: like Archie she was young enough to carry it off. She had been used to seeing us always together and she made no comment on my having come over without him. I waited in vain for her to say something about it; this would only be natural—it was almost unfriendly to omit it. At last I observed that my nephew was very unsociable that morning; I had expected him to join me but he had left me to come alone.

"I am very glad," she answered. "You can tell him that if you like."

"If I tell him that he will come immediately."

"Then don't tell him; I don't want him to come. He stayed too long last night," Linda went on, "and kept me out on the water till the most dreadful hours. That isn't done here, you know, and every one was shocked when we came back—or rather when we didn't come back. I begged him to bring me in, but he wouldn't. When we did return—I almost had to take the oars myself—I felt as if every one had been sitting up to time us, to stare at us. It was very embarrassing."

These words made an impression upon me; and as I have treated the reader to most of the reflections—some of them perhaps rather morbid—in which I indulged on the subject of this young lady and her mother I may as well complete the record and let him know that I now wondered whether Linda—candid and accomplished maiden—had conceived the fine idea of strengthening her hold of Archie by attempting to prove that he had compromised her. "Ah, no doubt that was the reason he had a bad conscience last evening!" I exclaimed. "When he came back to Stresa he sneaked off to his room; he wouldn't look me in the face."

"Mamma was so vexed that she took him apart and gave him a scolding," the girl went on. "And to punish *me* she sent me straight to bed. She has very old-fashioned ideas—haven't you, mamma?" she added, looking over my head at Mrs. Pallant, who had just come in behind me.

I forget what answer Mrs. Pallant made to Linda's appeal; she stood there with two letters, sealed and addressed, in her hand. She greeted me gaily and then asked her daughter if she had any postage-stamps. Linda consulted a somewhat shabby pocket-book and confessed that she was destitute; whereupon her mother gave her the letters, with the request that she would go into the hotel, buy the proper stamps at the office, carefully affix them and put the letters into the box. She was to pay for the stamps, not have them put on the bill—a preference for which Mrs. Pallant gave her reasons. I had bought some at Stresa that morning and I was on the point of offering them, when, apparently having guessed my intention, the elder lady silenced me with a look. Linda told her she had no money and she fumbled in her pocket for a franc. When she had found it and the girl had taken it Linda kissed her before going off with the letters.

"Darling mother, you haven't any too many of them, have you?" she murmured; and she gave me, sidelong, as she left us, the prettiest half comical, half pitiful smile.

"She's amazing—she's amazing," said Mrs. Pallant, as we looked at each other.

"Does she know what you have done?"

"She knows I have done something and she is making up her mind what it is—or she will in the course of the next twenty-four hours, if your nephew doesn't come back. I think I can promise you he won't."

"And won't she ask you?"

"Never!"

"Shall you not tell her? Can you sit down together in this summer-house, this divine day, with such a dreadful thing as that between you?"

"Don't you remember what I told you about our relations—that everything was implied between us and nothing expressed? The ideas we have had in common—our perpetual worldliness, our always looking out for chances—are not the sort of thing that can be uttered gracefully between persons who like to keep up forms, as we both do: so that if we understood each other it was enough. We shall understand each other now, as we have always done, and nothing will be changed, because there has always been something between us that couldn't be talked about."

"Certainly, she is amazing—she is amazing," I repeated; "but so are you." And then I asked her what she had said to my boy.

She seemed surprised. "Hasn't he told you?"

"No, and he never will."

"I am glad of that," she said, simply.

"But I am not sure he won't come back. He didn't this morning, but he had already half a mind to."

"That's your imagination," said Mrs. Pallant, decisively. "If you knew what I told him you would be sure."

"And you won't let me know?"

"Never, my near friend."

"And did he believe you?"

272

"Time will show; but I think so."

"And how did you make it plausible to him that you should take so unnatural a course?"

For a moment she said nothing, only looking at me. Then at last—"I told him the truth."

"The truth?" I repeated.

"Take him away—take him away!" she broke out. "That's why I got rid of Linda, to tell you that you mustn't stay—you must leave Stresa to-morrow. This time it's you that must do it; I can't fly from you again—it costs too much!" And she smiled strangely.

"Don't be afraid; don't be afraid. We will leave to-morrow; I want to go myself." I took her hand in farewell, and while I held it I said, "The way you put it, about Linda, was very bad?"

"It was horrible."

I turned away—I felt indeed that I wanted to leave the neighbourhood. She kept me from going to the hotel, as I might meet Linda coming back, which I was far from wishing to do, and showed me another way into the road. Then she turned round to meet her daughter and spend the rest of the morning in the summer-house with her, looking at the bright blue lake and the snowy crests of the Alps. When I reached Stresa again I found that Archie had gone off to Milan (to see the cathedral,[365] the servant said), leaving a message for me to the effect that, as he should not be back for a day or two (though there were numerous trains), he had taken a small portmanteau[366] with him. The next day I got a telegram from him notifying me that he had determined to go on to Venice and requesting me to forward the rest of his luggage. "Please don't come after me," this missive added; "I want to be alone; I shall do no harm." That sounded pathetic to me, in the light of what I knew, and I was glad to leave the poor boy to his own devices. He proceeded to Venice and I recrossed the Alps. For several weeks after this I expected to discover that he had rejoined Mrs. Pallant; but when we met in Paris, in November, I saw that he had nothing to hide from me, except indeed the secret of what that lady had told him. This he concealed from me then and has concealed ever since. He returned to America before Christmas and then I felt that the crisis had passed. I have never seen my old friend since. About a year after the time to which my story refers, Linda married, in London, a young Englishman, the possessor of a large fortune, a fortune acquired by his father in some useful industry. Mrs. Gimingham's photographs (such is her present name) may be obtained from the principal stationers.[367] I am convinced her mother was sincere. My nephew has not changed his state yet, and now even my sister is beginning, for the first time, to desire it. I related to her as soon as I saw her the substance of the story I have written here, and (such is the inconsequence of women) nothing can exceed her reprobation of Louisa Pallant.

The Aspern Papers

I

I HAD taken Mrs. Prest[368] into my confidence; in truth without her I should have made but little advance, for the fruitful idea in the whole business dropped from her friendly lips. It was she who invented the short cut, who severed the Gordian knot.[369] It is not supposed to be the nature of women to rise as a general thing to the largest and most liberal view—I mean of a practical scheme; but it has struck me that they sometimes throw off a bold conception—such as a man would not have risen to—with singular serenity. "Simply ask them to take you in on the footing of a lodger"—I don't think that unaided I should have risen to that. I was beating about the bush, trying to be ingenious, wondering by what combination of arts I might become an acquaintance, when she offered this happy suggestion that the way to become an acquaintance was first to become an inmate. Her actual knowledge of the Misses Bordereau was scarcely larger than mine, and indeed I had brought with me from England some definite facts which were new to her. Their name had been mixed up ages before with one of the greatest names of the century, and they lived now in Venice in obscurity, on very small means, unvisited, unapproachable, in a dilapidated old palace[370] on an out-of-the-way canal: this was the substance of my friend's impression of them. She herself had been established in Venice for fifteen years and had done a great deal of good there; but the circle of her benevolence did not include the two shy, mysterious and, as it was somehow supposed, scarcely respectable Americans (they were believed to have lost in their long exile all national quality, besides having had, as their name implied,[371] some French strain in their origin), who asked no favours and desired no attention. In the early years of her residence she had made an attempt to see them, but this had been successful only as regards the little one, as Mrs. Prest called the niece; though in reality as I afterwards learned she was considerably the bigger of the two. She had heard Miss Bordereau was ill and had a suspicion that she was in want; and she had gone to the house to offer assistance, so that if there were suffering (and American suffering), she should at least not have it on her conscience. The 'little one' received her in the great cold, tarnished Venetian *sala*,[372] the central hall of the house, paved with marble and roofed with dim crossbeams, and did not even ask her to sit down. This was not encouraging for me, who wished to sit so fast, and I remarked as much to Mrs. Prest. She however replied with profundity, "Ah, but there's all the difference: I went to confer a favour and you will go to ask one. If they are proud you will be on the right side." And she offered to show me their house to begin with—to row me thither in her gondola. I let her know that I had already been to look at it half a dozen times; but I accepted her invitation, for it charmed me to hover about the place. I had made my way to it the day after my arrival in Venice (it had been described to me in advance by the friend in England to whom I owed definite information as to their possession of the papers), and I had besieged it with my eyes while I considered my plan of campaign. Jeffrey Aspern[373] had never been in it that I knew of; but some note of his voice seemed to abide there by a roundabout implication, a faint reverberation.

Mrs. Prest knew nothing about the papers, but she was interested in my curiosity, as she was always interested in the joys and sorrows of her friends. As we went, however, in her gondola, gliding there under the sociable hood[374] with the bright Venetian picture framed on either side by the movable window, I could see that she was amused by my infatuation, the way my interest in the papers had become a fixed idea. "One would think you expected to find in them the answer to the riddle of the universe," she said; and I denied the impeachment only by replying that if I had to choose between that precious solution and a bundle of Jeffrey Aspern's letters I knew indeed which would appear to me the greater boon. She pretended to make light of his genius and I took no pains to defend him. One doesn't defend one's god: one's god is in himself a defence. Besides, to-day, after his long comparative obscuration, he hangs high in the heaven of our literature, for all the world to see; he is a part of the light by which we walk.[375] The most I said was that he was no doubt not a woman's poet: to which she rejoined aptly enough that he had been at least Miss Bordereau's. The strange thing had been for me to discover in England that she was still alive: it was as if I had been told Mrs. Siddons was, or Queen Caroline, or the famous Lady Hamilton,[376] for it seemed to me that she belonged to a generation as extinct. "Why, she must be tremendously old—at least a hundred," I had said; but on coming to consider dates I saw that it was not strictly necessary that she should have exceeded by very much the common span. None the less she was very far advanced in life and her relations with Jeffrey Aspern had occurred in her early womanhood. "That is her excuse," said Mrs. Prest, half sententiously and yet also somewhat as if she were ashamed of making a speech so little in the real tone of Venice. As if a woman needed an excuse for having loved the divine poet! He had been not only one of the most brilliant minds of his day (and in those years, when the century was young, there were, as every one knows, many), but one of the most genial men and one of the handsomest.

The niece, according to Mrs. Prest, was not so old, and she risked the conjecture that she was only a grand-niece. This was possible; I had nothing but my share in the very limited knowledge of my English fellow-worshipper John Cumnor,[377] who had never seen the couple. The world, as I say, had recognised Jeffrey Aspern, but Cumnor and I had recognised him most. The multitude, to-day, flocked to his temple, but of that temple he and I regarded ourselves as the ministers. We held, justly, as I think, that we had done more for his memory than any one else, and we had done it by opening lights into his life. He had nothing to fear from us because he had nothing to fear from the truth, which alone at such a distance of time we could be interested in establishing. His early death had been the only dark spot in his life, unless the papers in Miss Bordereau's hands should perversely bring out others. There had been an impression about 1825 that he had "treated her badly," just as there had been an impression that he had "served," as the London populace says,[378] several other ladies in the same way. Each of these cases Cumnor and I had been able to investigate, and we had never failed to acquit him conscientiously of shabby behaviour. I judged him perhaps more indulgently than my friend; certainly, at any rate, it appeared to me that no man could have walked straighter in the given circumstances. These were almost always awkward. Half the women of his time, to speak liberally, had flung themselves at his head, and out of this pernicious fashion many complications, some of them grave, had not failed to arise. He was not a woman's poet, as I had said to Mrs. Prest, in the modern phase of his reputation; but the situation had been different when the man's own voice was mingled with his song. That voice, by every testimony, was one of the sweetest ever heard. "Orpheus and the

Maenads!"[379] was the exclamation that rose to my lips when I first turned over his correspondence. Almost all the Maenads were unreasonable and many of them insupportable; it struck me in short that he was kinder, more considerate than, in his place (if I could imagine myself in such a place!) I should have been.

It was certainly strange beyond all strangeness, and I shall not take up space with attempting to explain it, that whereas in all these other lines of research we had to deal with phantoms and dust, the mere echoes of echoes, the one living source of information that had lingered on into our time had been unheeded by us. Every one of Aspern's contemporaries had, according to our belief, passed away; we had not been able to look into a single pair of eyes into which his had looked or to feel a transmitted contact in any aged hand that his had touched. Most dead of all did poor Miss Bordereau appear, and yet she alone had survived. We exhausted in the course of months our wonder that we had not found her out sooner, and the substance of our explanation was that she had kept so quiet. The poor lady on the whole had had reason for doing so. But it was a revelation to us that it was possible to keep so quiet as that in the latter half of the nineteenth century—the age of newspapers and telegrams and photographs and interviewers.[380] And she had taken no great trouble about it either: she had not hidden herself away in an undiscoverable hole; she had boldly settled down in a city of exhibition.[381] The only secret of her safety that we could perceive was that Venice contained so many curiosities that were greater than she. And then accident had somehow favoured her, as was shown for example in the fact that Mrs. Prest had never happened to mention her to me, though I had spent three weeks in Venice—under her nose, as it were—five years before. Mrs. Prest had not mentioned this much to any one; she appeared almost to have forgotten she was there. Of course she had not the responsibilities of an editor. It was no explanation of the old woman's having eluded us to say that she lived abroad, for our researches had again and again taken us (not only by correspondence but by personal inquiry) to France, to Germany, to Italy,[382] in which countries, not counting his important stay in England, so many of the too few years of Aspern's career were spent. We were glad to think at least that in all our publishings (some people consider I believe that we have overdone them), we had only touched in passing and in the most discreet manner on Miss Bordereau's connection. Oddly enough, even if we had had the material (and we often wondered what had become of it), it would have been the most difficult episode to handle.

The gondola stopped, the old palace was there; it was a house of the class which in Venice carries even in extreme dilapidation the dignified name. "How charming! It's gray and pink!" my companion exclaimed; and that is the most comprehensive description of it. It was not particularly old, only two or three centuries; and it had an air not so much of decay as of quiet discouragement, as if it had rather missed its career. But its wide front, with a stone balcony from end to end of the *piano nobile* or most important floor, was architectural enough, with the aid of various pilasters and arches; and the stucco with which in the intervals it had long ago been endued was rosy in the April afternoon. It overlooked a clean, melancholy, unfrequented canal, which had a narrow *riva* or convenient footway on either side. "I don't know why there are no brick gables," said Mrs. Prest, "but this corner has seemed to me before more Dutch than Italian, more like Amsterdam than like Venice.[383] It's perversely clean, for reasons of its own; and though you can pass on foot scarcely any one ever thinks of doing so. It has the air of a Protestant Sunday.[384] Perhaps the people are afraid of the Misses Bordereau. I daresay they have the reputation of witches."

I forget what answer I made to this—I was given up to two other reflections. The first of these was that if the old lady lived in such a big, imposing house she could not be in any sort of misery and therefore would not be tempted by a chance to let a couple of rooms. I expressed this idea to Mrs. Prest, who gave me a very logical reply. "If she didn't live in a big house how could it be a question of her having rooms to spare? If she were not amply lodged herself you would lack ground to approach her. Besides, a big house here, and especially in this *quartier perdu*,[385] proves nothing at all: it is perfectly compatible with a state of penury. Dilapidated old palazzi, if you will go out of the way for them, are to be had for five shillings a year.[386] And as for the people who live in them—no, until you have explored Venice socially as much as I have you can form no idea of their domestic desolation. They live on nothing, for they have nothing to live on." The other idea that had come into my head was connected with a high blank wall which appeared to confine an expanse of ground on one side of the house. Blank I call it, but it was figured over with the patches that please a painter, repaired breaches, crumblings of plaster, extrusions of brick that had turned pink with time; and a few thin trees, with the poles of certain rickety trellises, were visible over the top. The place was a garden and apparently it belonged to the house. It suddenly occurred to me that if it did belong to the house I had my pretext.

I sat looking out on all this with Mrs. Prest (it was covered with the golden glow of Venice) from the shade of our *felze*, and she asked me if I would go in then, while she waited for me, or come back another time. At first I could not decide—it was doubtless very weak of me. I wanted still to think I *might* get a footing, and I was afraid to meet failure, for it would leave me, as I remarked to my companion, without another arrow for my bow. "Why not another?" she inquired, as I sat there hesitating and thinking it over; and she wished to know why even now and before taking the trouble of becoming an inmate (which might be wretchedly uncomfortable after all, even if it succeeded), I had not the resource of simply offering them a sum of money down. In that way I might obtain the documents without bad nights.

"Dearest lady," I exclaimed, "excuse the impatience of my tone when I suggest that you must have forgotten the very fact (surely I communicated it to you) which pushed me to throw myself upon your ingenuity. The old woman won't have the documents spoken of; they are personal, delicate, intimate, and she hasn't modern notions, God bless her! If I should sound that note first I should certainly spoil the game. I can arrive at the papers only by putting her off her guard, and I can put her off her guard only by ingratiating diplomatic practices. Hypocrisy, duplicity are my only chance. I am sorry for it, but for Jeffrey Aspern's sake I would do worse still. First I must take tea with her; then tackle the main job." And I told over what had happened to John Cumnor when he wrote to her. No notice whatever had been taken of his first letter, and the second had been answered very sharply, in six lines, by the niece. "Miss Bordereau requested her to say that she could not imagine what he meant by troubling them. They had none of Mr. Aspern's papers, and if they had should never think of showing them to any one on any account whatever. She didn't know what he was talking about and begged he would let her alone." I certainly did not want to be met that way.

"Well," said Mrs. Prest, after a moment, provokingly, "perhaps after all they haven't any of his things. If they deny it flat how are you sure?"

"John Cumnor is sure, and it would take me long to tell you how his conviction, or his very strong presumption—strong enough to stand against the old lady's not unnatural fib—has built itself up. Besides, he makes much of the internal evidence of the niece's letter."

"The internal evidence?"

"Her calling him 'Mr. Aspern'."[387]

"I don't see what that proves."

"It proves familiarity, and familiarity implies the possession of mementoes, of relics. I can't tell you how that 'Mr.' touches me—how it bridges over the gulf of time[388] and brings our hero near to me—nor what an edge it gives to my desire to see Juliana. You don't say 'Mr.' Shakespeare."

"Would I, any more, if I had a box full of his letters?"

"Yes, if he had been your lover and some one wanted them!" And I added that John Cumnor was so convinced, and so all the more convinced by Miss Bordereau's tone, that he would have come himself to Venice on the business were it not that for him there was the obstacle that it would be difficult to disprove his identity with the person who had written to them, which the old ladies would be sure to suspect in spite of dissimulation and a change of name. If they were to ask him point-blank if he were not their correspondent it would be too awkward for him to lie; whereas I was fortunately not tied in that way. I was a fresh hand and could say no without lying.

"But you will have to change your name," said Mrs. Prest. "Juliana lives out of the world as much as it is possible to live, but none the less she has probably heard of Mr. Aspern's editors; she perhaps possesses what you have published."

"I have thought of that," I returned; and I drew out of my pocket-book a visiting-card, neatly engraved with a name that was not my own.

"You are very extravagant; you might have written it," said my companion.

"This looks more genuine."

"Certainly, you are prepared to go far! But it will be awkward about your letters; they won't come to you in that mask."

"My banker will take them in and I will go every day to fetch them. It will give me a little walk."

"Shall you only depend upon that?" asked Mrs. Prest. "Aren't you coming to see me?"

"Oh, you will have left Venice, for the hot months, long before there are any results. I am prepared to roast all summer—as well as hereafter, perhaps you'll say! Meanwhile, John Cumnor will bombard me with letters addressed, in my feigned name, to the care of the *padrona*."

"She will recognise his hand," my companion suggested.

"On the envelope he can disguise it."

"Well, you're a precious pair! Doesn't it occur to you that even if you are able to say you are not Mr. Cumnor in person they may still suspect you of being his emissary?"

"Certainly, and I see only one way to parry that."

"And what may that be?"

I hesitated a moment. "To make love to the niece."

"Ah," cried Mrs. Prest, "wait till you see her!"

"I MUST work the garden—I must work the garden," I said to myself, five minutes later, as I waited, upstairs, in the long, dusky sala, where the bare scagliola floor[389] gleamed vaguely in a chink of the closed shutters. The place was impressive but it looked cold and cautious. Mrs. Prest had floated away, giving me a rendezvous at the end of half an hour by some neighbouring water-steps; and I had been let into the house, after pulling the rusty bell-wire, by a little red-headed, white-faced maid-servant, who was very young and not ugly and wore clicking pattens[390] and a shawl in the fashion of a hood. She had not contented herself with opening the door from above by the usual arrangement of a creaking pulley, though she had looked down at me first from an upper window, dropping the inevitable challenge[391] which in Italy precedes the hospitable act. As a general thing I was irritated by this survival of mediaeval manners, though as I liked the old I suppose I ought to have liked it; but I was so determined to be genial that I took my false card out of my pocket and held it up to her, smiling as if it were a magic token. It had the effect of one indeed, for it brought her, as I say, all the way down. I begged her to hand it to her mistress, having first written on it in Italian the words, "Could you very kindly see a gentleman, an American, for a moment?" The little maid was not hostile, and I reflected that even that was perhaps something gained. She coloured, she smiled and looked both frightened and pleased. I could see that my arrival was a great affair, that visits were rare in that house, and that she was a person who would have liked a sociable place. When she pushed forward the heavy door behind me I felt that I had a foot in the citadel. She pattered across the damp, stony lower hall and I followed her up the high staircase—stonier still, as it seemed—without an invitation. I think she had meant I should wait for her below, but such was not my idea, and I took up my station in the sala. She flitted, at the far end of it, into impenetrable regions, and I looked at the place with my heart beating as I had known it to do in the dentist's parlour. It was gloomy and stately, but it owed its character almost entirely to its noble shape and to the fine architectural doors—as high as the doors of houses—which, leading into the various rooms, repeated themselves on either side at intervals. They were surmounted with old faded painted escutcheons,[392] and here and there, in the spaces between them, brown pictures, which I perceived to be bad, in battered frames, were suspended. With the exception of several straw-bottomed chairs with their backs to the wall, the grand obscure vista contained nothing else to minister to effect. It was evidently never used save as a passage, and little even as that. I may add that by the time the door opened again through which the maid-servant had escaped, my eyes had grown used to the want of light.

I had not meant by my private ejaculation that I must myself cultivate the soil of the tangled enclosure which lay beneath the windows, but the lady who came toward me from the distance over the hard, shining floor might have supposed as much from the way in which, as I went rapidly to meet her, I exclaimed, taking care to speak Italian: "The garden, the garden—do me the pleasure to tell me if it's yours!"

She stopped short, looking at me with wonder; and then, "Nothing here is mine," she answered in English, coldly and sadly.

"Oh, you are English; how delightful!" I remarked, ingenuously. "But surely the garden belongs to the house?"

"Yes, but the house doesn't belong to me." She was a long, lean, pale person, habited apparently in a dull-coloured dressing-gown, and she spoke with a kind of mild literalness. She did not ask me to sit down, any more than years before (if she were the niece) she had asked Mrs. Prest, and we stood face to face in the empty pompous hall.

"Well then, would you kindly tell me to whom I must address myself? I'm afraid you'll think me odiously intrusive, but you know I *must* have a garden—upon my honour I must!"

Her face was not young, but it was simple; it was not fresh, but it was mild. She had large eyes which were not bright, and a great deal of hair which was not "dressed,"[393] and long fine hands which were—possibly—not clean. She clasped these members almost convulsively as, with a confused, alarmed look, she broke out, "Oh, don't take it away from us; we like it ourselves!"

"You have the use of it then?"

"Oh yes. If it wasn't for that!" And she gave a shy, melancholy smile.

"Isn't it a luxury, precisely? That's why, in tending to be in Venice some weeks, possibly all summer, and having some literary work, some reading and writing to do, so that I must be quiet, and yet if possible a great deal in the open air—that's why I have felt that a garden is really indispensable. I appeal to your own experience," I went on, smiling. "Now can't I look at yours?"

"I don't know, I don't understand," the poor woman murmured, planted there and letting her embarrassed eyes wander all over my strangeness.

"I mean only from one of those windows—such grand ones as you have here—if you will let me open the shutters." And I walked toward the back of the house. When I had advanced half-way I stopped and waited, as if I took it for granted she would accompany me. I had been of necessity very abrupt, but I strove at the same time to give her the impression of extreme courtesy. "I have been looking at furnished rooms all over the place, and it seems impossible to find any with a garden attached. Naturally in a place like Venice gardens are rare. It's absurd if you like, for a man, but I can't live without flowers."

"There are none to speak of down there." She came nearer to me, as if, though she mistrusted me, I had drawn her by an invisible thread. I went on again, and she continued as she followed me: "We have a few, but they are very common. It costs too much to cultivate them; one has to have a man."

"Why shouldn't I be the man?" I asked. "I'll work without wages; or rather I'll put in a gardener. You shall have the sweetest flowers in Venice."

She protested at this, with a queer little sigh which might also have been a gush of rapture at the picture I presented. Then she observed, "We don't know you—we don't know you."

"You know me as much as I know you; that is much more, because you know my name. And if you are English I am almost a countryman."

"We are not English," said my companion, watching me helplessly while I threw open the shutters of one of the divisions of the wide high window.

"You speak the language so beautifully: might I ask what you are?" Seen from above the garden was certainly shabby; but I perceived at a glance that it had great capabilities.[394] She made no rejoinder, she was so lost in staring at me, and I exclaimed, "You don't mean to say you are also by chance American?"

"I don't know; we used to be."

"Used to be? Surely you haven't changed?"

"It's so many years ago—we are nothing."

"So many years that you have been living here? Well, I don't wonder at that; it's a grand old house. I suppose you all use the garden," I went on, "but I assure you I shouldn't be in your way. I would be very quiet and stay in one corner."

"We all use it?" she repeated after me, vaguely, not coming close to the window but looking at my shoes. She appeared to think me capable of throwing her out.

"I mean all your family, as many as you are."

"There is only one other; she is very old—she never goes down."

"Only one other, in all this great house!" I feigned to be not only amazed but almost scandalised. "Dear lady, you must have space then to spare!"

"To spare?" she repeated, in the same dazed way.

"Why, you surely don't live (two quiet women—I see *you* are quiet, at any rate) in fifty rooms!" Then with a burst of hope and cheer I demanded: "Couldn't you let me two or three? That would set me up!"

I had now struck the note that translated my purpose and I need not reproduce the whole of the tune I played. I ended by making my interlocutress believe that I was an honourable person, though of course I did not even attempt to persuade her that I was not an eccentric one. I repeated that I had studies to pursue; that I wanted quiet; that I delighted in a garden and had vainly sought one up and down the city; that I would undertake that before another month was over the dear old house should be smothered in flowers. I think it was the flowers that won my suit, for I afterwards found that Miss Tita (for such the name of this high tremulous spinster[395] proved somewhat incongruously to be) had an insatiable appetite for them. When I speak of my suit as won I mean that before I left her she had promised that she would refer the question to her aunt. I inquired who her aunt might be and she answered, "Why, Miss Bordereau!" with an air of surprise, as if I might have been expected to know. There were contradictions like this in Tita Bordereau which, as I observed later, contributed to make her an odd and affecting person. It was the study of the two ladies to live so that the world should not touch them, and yet they had never altogether accepted the idea that it never heard of them. In Tita at any rate a grateful susceptibility to human contact had not died out, and contact of a limited order there would be if I should come to live in the house.

"We have never done anything of the sort; we have never had a lodger or any kind of inmate." So much as this she made a point of saying to me. "We are very poor, we live very badly. The rooms are very bare—that you might take; they have nothing in them. I don't know how you would sleep, how you would eat."

"With your permission, I could easily put in a bed and a few tables and chairs. *C'est la moindre des choses* and the affair of an hour or two. I know a little man from whom I can hire what I should want for a few months, for a trifle, and my gondolier[396] can bring the things round in his boat. Of course in this great house you must have a second kitchen, and my servant, who is a wonderfully handy fellow" (this personage was an evocation of the moment), "can easily cook me a chop there. My tastes and habits are of the simplest; I live on flowers!" And then I ventured to add that if they were very poor it was all the more reason they should let their rooms. They were bad economists—I had never heard of such a waste of material.

I saw in a moment that the good lady had never before been spoken to in that way, with a kind of humorous firmness which did not exclude sympathy but was on the contrary founded on it. She might easily have told me that my sympathy was impertinent, but this by good fortune did not occur to her. I left her with the understanding that she would consider the matter with her aunt and that I might come back the next day for their decision.

"The aunt will refuse; she will think the whole proceeding very *louche!*" Mrs. Prest declared shortly after this, when I had resumed my place in her gondola. She had put the idea into my head and now (so little are women to be counted on) she appeared to take a despondent view of it. Her pessimism provoked me and I pretended to have the best hopes; I went so far as to say that I had a distinct presentiment that I should succeed. Upon this Mrs. Prest broke out, "Oh, I see what's in your head! You fancy you have made such an impression in a quarter of an hour that she is dying for you to come and can be depended upon to bring the old one round. If you do get in you'll count it as a triumph."

I did count it as a triumph, but only for the editor (in the last analysis), not for the man, who had not the tradition of personal conquest. When I went back on the morrow the little maid-servant conducted me straight through the long sala (it opened there as before in perfect perspective and was lighter now, which I thought a good omen) into the apartment from which the recipient of my former visit had emerged on that occasion. It was a large shabby parlour, with a fine old painted ceiling and a strange figure sitting alone at one of the windows. They come back to me now almost with the palpitation they caused, the successive feelings that accompanied my consciousness that as the door of the room closed behind me I was really face to face with the Juliana of some of Aspern's most exquisite and most renowned lyrics. I grew used to her afterwards, though never completely; but as she sat there before me my heart beat as fast as if the miracle of resurrection had taken place for my benefit. Her presence seemed somehow to contain his, and I felt nearer to him at that first moment of seeing her than I ever had been before or ever have been since. Yes, I remember my emotions in their order, even including a curious little tremor that took me when I saw that the niece was not there. With her, the day before, I had become sufficiently familiar, but it almost exceeded my courage (much as I had longed for the event) to be left alone with such a terrible relic as the aunt. She was too strange, too literally resurgent. Then came a check, with the perception that we were not really face to face, inasmuch as she had over her eyes a horrible green shade[397] which, for her, served almost as a mask. I believed for the instant that she had put it on expressly, so that from underneath it she might scrutinise me without being scrutinised herself. At the same time it increased the presumption that there was a ghastly death's-head lurking behind it. The divine Juliana as a grinning skull—the vision hung there until it passed. Then it came to me that she *was* tremendously old—so old that death might take her at any moment, before I had time to get what I wanted from her. The next thought was a correction to that; it lighted up the situation. She would die next week, she would die to-morrow—then I could seize her papers. Meanwhile she sat there neither moving nor speaking. She was very small and shrunken, bent forward, with her hands in her lap. She was dressed in black and her head was wrapped in a piece of old black lace which showed no hair.

My emotion keeping me silent she spoke first, and the remark she made was exactly the most unexpected.

III

"OUR house is very far from the centre, but the little canal is very *comme il faut.*"

"It's the sweetest corner of Venice and I can imagine nothing more charming," I hastened to reply. The old lady's voice was very thin and weak, but it had an agreeable, cultivated murmur and there was wonder in the thought that that individual note had been in Jeffrey Aspern's ear.

"Please to sit down there. I hear very well," she said quietly, as if perhaps I had been shouting at her; and the chair she pointed to was at a certain distance. I took possession of it, telling her that I was perfectly aware that I had intruded, that I had not been properly introduced and could only throw myself upon her indulgence. Perhaps the other lady, the one I had had the honour of seeing the day before, would have explained to her about the garden. That was literally what had given me courage to take a step so unconventional. I had fallen in love at sight with the whole place (she herself probably was so used to it that she did not know the impression it was capable of making on a stranger), and I had felt it was really a case to risk something. Was her own kindness in receiving me a sign that I was not wholly out in my calculation? It would render me extremely happy to think so. I could give her my word of honour that I was a most respectable, inoffensive person and that as an inmate they would be barely conscious of my existence. I would conform to any regulations, any restrictions if they would only let me enjoy the garden. Moreover I should be delighted to give her references, guarantees; they would be of the very best, both in Venice and in England as well as in America.

She listened to me in perfect stillness and I felt that she was looking at me with great attention, though I could see only the lower part of her bleached and shrivelled face. Independently of the refining process of old age it had a delicacy which once must have been great. She had been very fair, she had had a wonderful complexion. She was silent a little after I had ceased speaking; then she inquired, "If you are so fond of a garden why don't you go to *terra firma*,[398] where there are so many far better than this?"

"Oh, it's the combination!" I answered, smiling; and then, with rather a flight of fancy, "It's the idea of a garden in the middle of the sea."

"It's not in the middle of the sea; you can't see the water."

I stared a moment, wondering whether she wished to convict me of fraud. "Can't see the water? Why, dear madam, I can come up to the very gate in my boat."

She appeared inconsequent, for she said vaguely in reply to this, "Yes, if you have got a boat. I haven't any; it's many years since I have been in one of the gondolas." She uttered these words as if the gondolas were a curious faraway craft which she knew only by hearsay.

"Let me assure you of the pleasure with which I would put mine at your service!" I exclaimed. I had scarcely said this however before I became aware that the speech was in questionable taste and might also do me the injury of making me appear too eager, too possessed of a hidden motive. But the old woman remained impenetrable and her attitude bothered me by suggesting that she had a fuller vision of me than I had of her. She gave me no thanks for my somewhat extravagant offer but remarked that the lady I had seen the day before was her niece; she would presently come in. She had asked her to stay away a little on purpose, because she herself wished to see me at first alone. She relapsed into silence and I asked myself why she had judged this necessary and what was coming yet; also whether I might venture on some judicious remark in praise of her companion. I went so far as to say that I should be delighted to see her again: she had been so very courteous to me, considering how odd she must have thought me—a declaration which drew from Miss Bordereau another of her whimsical speeches.

"She has very good manners; I bred her up myself!" I was on the point of saying that that accounted for the easy grace of the niece, but I arrested myself in time, and the next moment the old woman went on: "I don't care who you may be—I don't want to know; it signifies very little today." This had all the air of being a formula of dismissal, as if her next words would be that I might take myself off now that she had had the amusement of looking on the face of such a monster of indiscretion. Therefore I was all the more surprised when she added, with her soft, venerable quaver, "You may have as many rooms as you like—if you will pay a good deal of money."

I hesitated but for a single instant, long enough to ask myself what she meant in particular by this condition. First it struck me that she must have really a large sum in her mind; then I reasoned quickly that her idea of a large sum would probably not correspond to my own. My deliberation, I think, was not so visible as to diminish the promptitude with which I replied, "I will pay with pleasure and of course in advance whatever you may think it proper to ask me."

"Well then, a thousand francs a month,"[399] she rejoined instantly, while her baffling green shade continued to cover her attitude.

The figure, as they say, was startling and my logic had been at fault. The sum she had mentioned was, by the Venetian measure of such matters, exceedingly large; there was many an old palace in an out-of-the-way corner that I might on such terms have enjoyed by the year. But so far as my small means allowed I was prepared to spend money, and my decision was quickly taken. I would pay her with a smiling face what she asked, but in that case I would give myself the compensation of extracting the papers from her for nothing. Moreover if she had asked five times as much I should have risen to the occasion; so odious would it have appeared to me to stand chaffering[400] with Aspern's Juliana. It was queer enough to have a question of money with her at all. I assured her that her views perfectly met my own and that on the morrow I should have the pleasure of putting three months rent into her hand. She received this announcement with serenity and with no apparent sense that after all it would be becoming of her to say that I ought to see the rooms first. This did not occur to her and indeed her serenity was mainly what I wanted. Our little bargain was just concluded when the door opened and the younger lady appeared on the threshold. As soon as Miss Bordereau saw her niece she cried out almost gaily, "He will give three thousand—three thousand to-morrow!"

Miss Tita stood still, with her patient eyes turning from one of us to the other; then she inquired, scarcely above her breath, "Do you mean francs?"

"Did you mean francs or dollars?" the old woman asked of me at this.

"I think francs were what you said," I answered, smiling.

"That is very good," said Miss Tita, as if she had become conscious that her own question might have looked over-reaching.

"What do *you* know? You are ignorant," Miss Bordereau remarked; not with acerbity but with a strange, soft coldness.

"Yes, of money—certainly of money!" Miss Tita hastened to exclaim.

"I am sure you have your own branches of knowledge," I took the liberty of saying, genially. There was something painful to me, somehow, in the turn the conversation had taken, in the discussion of the rent.

"She had a very good education when she was young. I looked into that myself," said Miss Bordereau. Then she added, "But she has learned nothing since."

"I have always been with you," Miss Tita rejoined very mildly, and evidently with no intention of making an epigram.

"Yes, but for that!" her aunt declared, with more satirical force. She evidently meant that but for this her niece would never have got on at all; the point of the observation however being lost on Miss Tita, though she blushed at hearing her history revealed to a stranger. Miss Bordereau went on, addressing herself to me: "And what time will you come to-morrow with the money?"

"The sooner the better. If it suits you I will come at noon."

"I am always here but I have my hours," said the old woman, as if her convenience were not to be taken for granted.

"You mean the times when you receive?"[401]

"I never receive. But I will see you at noon, when you come with the money."

"Very good, I shall be punctual"; and I added, "May I shake hands with you, on our contract?" I thought there ought to be some little form, it would make me really feel easier, for I foresaw that there would be no other. Besides, though Miss Bordereau could not to-day be called personally attractive and there was something even in her wasted antiquity[402] that bade one stand at one's distance, I felt an irresistible desire to hold in my own for a moment the hand that Jeffrey Aspern had pressed.

For a minute she made no answer and I saw that my proposal failed to meet with her approbation. She indulged in no movement of withdrawal, which I half expected; she only said coldly, "I belong to a time when that was not the custom."

I felt rather snubbed but I exclaimed good-humouredly to Miss Tita, "Oh, you will do as well!" I shook hands with her while she replied, with a small flutter, "Yes, yes, to show it's all arranged!"

"Shall you bring the money in gold?"[403] Miss Bordereau demanded, as I was turning to the door.

I looked at her a moment. "Aren't you a little afraid, after all, of keeping such a sum as that in the house?" It was not that I was annoyed at her avidity but I was really struck with the disparity between such a treasure and such scanty means of guarding it.

"Whom should I be afraid of if I am not afraid of you?" she asked with her shrunken grimness.

"Ah well," said I, laughing, "I shall be in point of fact a protector and I will bring gold if you prefer."

"Thank you," the old woman returned with dignity and with an inclination of her head which evidently signified that I might depart. I passed out of the room, reflecting that it would not be easy to circumvent her. As I stood in the sala again I saw that Miss Tita had followed me and I supposed that as her aunt had neglected to suggest that I should take a look at my quarters it was her purpose to repair the omission. But she made no such suggestion; she only stood there with a dim, though not a languid smile, and with an effect of irresponsible, incompetent youth which was almost comically at variance with the faded facts of her person. She was not infirm, like her aunt, but she struck me as still more helpless, because her inefficiency was spiritual, which was not the case with Miss Bordereau's. I waited to see if she would offer to show me the rest of the house, but I did not precipitate the question, inasmuch as my plan was from this moment to spend as much of my time as possible in her society. I only observed at the end of a minute:

"I'll have had better fortune than I hoped. It was very kind of her to see me. Perhaps you said a good word for me."

"It was the idea of the money," said Miss Tita.

"And did you suggest that?"

"I told her that you would perhaps give a good deal."

"What made you think that?"

"I told her I thought you were rich."

"And what put that idea into your head?"

"I don't know; the way you talked."

"Dear me, I must talk differently now," I declared. "I'm sorry to say it's not the case."

"Well," said Miss Tita, "I think that in Venice the *forestieri*, in general, often give a great deal for something that after all isn't much." She appeared to make this remark with a comforting intention, to wish to remind me that if I had been extravagant I was not really foolishly singular. We walked together along the sala, and as I took its magnificent measure I said to her that I was afraid it would not form a part of my *quartiere*. Were my rooms by chance to be among those that opened into it? "Not if you go above, on the second floor," she answered with a little startled air, as if she had rather taken for granted I would know my proper place.

"And I infer that that's where your aunt would like me to be."

"She said your apartments ought to be very distinct."

"That certainly would be best." And I listened with respect while she told me that up above I was free to take whatever I liked; that there was another staircase, but only from the floor on which we stood, and that to pass from it to the garden-story or to come up to my lodging I should have in effect to cross the great hall. This was an immense point gained; I foresaw that it would constitute my whole leverage in my relations with the two ladies. When I asked Miss Tita how I was to manage at present to find my way up she replied with an access of that sociable shyness which constantly marked her manner.

"Perhaps you can't. I don't see—unless I should go with you." She evidently had not thought of this before.

We ascended to the upper floor and visited a long succession of empty rooms. The best of them looked over the garden; some of the others had a view of the blue lagoon, above the opposite rough-tiled housetops. They were all dusty and even a little disfigured with long neglect, but I saw that by spending a few hundred francs I should be able to convert three or four of them into a convenient habitation. My experiment was turning out costly, yet now that I had all but taken possession I ceased to allow this to trouble me. I mentioned to my companion a few of the things that I should put in, but she replied rather more precipitately than usual that I might do exactly what I liked; she seemed to wish to notify me that the Misses Bordereau would take no overt interest in my proceedings. I guessed that her aunt had instructed her to adopt this tone, and I may as well say now that I came afterwards to distinguish perfectly (as I believed) between the speeches she made on her own responsibility and those the old lady imposed upon her. She took no notice of the unswept condition of the rooms and indulged in no explanations nor apologies. I said to myself that this was a sign that Juliana and her niece (disenchanting idea!) were untidy persons, with a low Italian standard; but I afterwards recognised that a lodger who had forced an entrance had no *locus standi* as a critic. We looked out of a good many windows, for there was nothing within the rooms to look at, and still I wanted to linger. I asked her what several different objects in the prospect might be, but in no case did she appear to know. She was evidently not familiar with the view—it was as if she had not looked at it for years—and I presently saw that she was too preoccupied with something else to pretend to care for it. Suddenly she said—the remark was not suggested:

"I don't know whether it will make any difference to you, but the money is for me."

"The money?"

"The money you are going to bring."

"Why, you'll make me wish to stay here two or three years." I spoke as benevolently as possible, though it had begun to act on my nerves that with these women so associated with Aspern the pecuniary question should constantly come back.

"That would be very good for me," she replied, smiling.

"You put me on my honour!"

She looked as if she failed to understand this, but went on: "She wants me to have more. She thinks she is going to die."

"Ah, not soon, I hope!" I exclaimed, with genuine feeling. I had perfectly considered the possibility that she would destroy her papers on the day she should feel her end really approach. I believed that she would cling to them till then and I think I had an idea that she read Aspern's letters over every night or at least pressed them to her withered lips. I would have given a good deal to have a glimpse of the latter spectacle. I asked Miss Tita if the old lady were seriously ill and she replied that she was only very tired—she had lived so very, very long. That was what she said herself—she wanted to die for a change. Besides, all her friends were dead long ago; either they ought to have remained or she ought to have gone. That was another thing her aunt often said—she was not at all content.

"But people don't die when they like, do they?" Miss Tita inquired. I took the liberty of asking why, if there was actually enough money to maintain both of them, there would not be more than enough in case of her being left alone. She considered this difficult problem a moment and then she said, "Oh, well, you know, she takes care of me. She thinks that when I'm alone I shall be a great fool, I shall not know how to manage."

"I should have supposed rather that you took care of her. I'm afraid she is very proud."

"Why, have you discovered that already?" Miss Tita cried, with the glimmer of an illumination in her face.

"I was shut up with her there for a considerable time, and she struck me, she interested me extremely. It didn't take me long to make my discovery. She won't have much to say to me while I'm here."

"No, I don't think she will," my companion averred.

"Do you suppose she has some suspicion of me?"

Miss Tita's honest eyes gave me no sign that I had touched a mark. "I shouldn't think so—letting you in after all so easily."

"Oh, so easily! she has covered her risk. But where is it that one could take an advantage of her?"

"I oughtn't to tell you if I knew, ought I?" And Miss Tita added, before I had time to reply to this, smiling dolefully, "Do you think we have any weak points?"

"That's exactly what I'm asking. You would only have to mention them for me to respect them religiously."

She looked at me, at this, with that air of timid but candid and even gratified curiosity with which she had confronted me from the first; and then she said, "There is nothing to tell. We are terribly quiet. I don't know how the days pass. We have no life."

"I wish I might think that I should bring you a little."

"Oh, we know what we want," she went on. "It's all right."

There were various things I desired to ask her: how in the world they did live; whether they had any friends or visitors, any relations in America or in other countries. But I judged such an inquiry would be premature; I must leave it to a later chance. "Well, don't *you* be proud," I contented myself with saying. "Don't hide from me altogether."

"Oh, I must stay with my aunt," she returned, without looking at me. And at the same moment, abruptly, without any ceremony of parting, she quitted me and disappeared, leaving me to make my own way downstairs. I remained a while longer, wandering about the bright desert (the sun was pouring in) of the old house, thinking the situation over on the spot. Not even the pattering little *serva* came to look after me and I reflected that after all this treatment showed confidence.

IV

PERHAPS it did, but all the same, six weeks later, towards the middle of June, the moment when Mrs. Prest undertook her annual migration,[404] I had made no measureable advance. I was obliged to confess to her that I had no results to speak of. My first step had been unexpectedly rapid, but there was no appearance that it would be followed by a second. I was a thousand miles from taking tea with my hostesses—that privilege of which, as I reminded Mrs. Prest, we both had had a vision. She reproached me with wanting boldness and I answered that even to be bold you must have an opportunity: you may push on through a breach but you can't batter down a dead wall.[405] She answered that the breach I had already made was big enough to admit an army and accused me of wasting precious hours in whimpering in her salon when I ought to have been carrying on the struggle in the field. It is true that I went to see her very often, on the theory that it would console me (I freely expressed my discouragement) for my want of success on my own premises. But I began to perceive that it did not console me to be perpetually chaffed for my scruples, especially when I was really so vigilant; and I was rather glad when my derisive friend closed her house for the summer. She had expected to gather amusement from the drama of my intercourse with the Misses Bordereau and she was disappointed that the intercourse, and consequently the drama, had not come off. "They'll lead you on to your ruin," she said before she left Venice. "They'll get all your money without showing you a scrap." I think I settled down to my business with more concentration after she had gone away.

It was a fact that up to that time I had not, save on a single brief occasion, had even a moment's contact with my queer hostesses. The exception had occurred when I carried them according to my promise the terrible three thousand francs. Then I found Miss Tita waiting for me in the hall, and she took the money from my hand so that I did not see her aunt. The old lady had promised to receive me, but she apparently thought nothing of breaking that vow. The money was contained in a bag of chamois leather, of respectable dimensions, which my banker had given me, and Miss Tita had to make a big fist to receive it. This she did with extreme solemnity, though I tried to treat the affair a little as a joke. It was in no jocular strain, yet it was with simplicity, that she inquired, weighing the money in her two palms: "Don't you think it's too much?" To which I replied that that would depend upon the amount of pleasure I should get for it. Hereupon she turned away from me quickly, as she had done the day before, murmuring in a tone different from any she had used hitherto: "Oh, pleasure, pleasure—there's no pleasure in this house!"

After this, for a long time, I never saw her, and I wondered that the common chances of the day should not have helped us to meet. It could only be evident that she was immensely on her guard against them; and in addition to this the house was so big that for each other we were lost in it. I used to look out for her hopefully as I crossed the sala in my comings and goings, but I was not rewarded with a glimpse of the tail of her dress. It was as if she never peeped out of her aunt's apartment. I used to wonder what she did there week after week and year after year. I had never encountered such a violent *parti pris* of seclusion;[406] it was more than keeping quiet— it was like hunted creatures feigning death.[407] The two ladies appeared to have no visitors whatever and no sort of contact with the world. I judged at least that people could not have come to the house and that Miss Tita could not have gone out without my having some observation of it. I did what I disliked myself for doing (reflecting that it was only once in a way): I questioned my servant about their habits and let him divine that I should be interested in any information he could pick up. But he picked up amazingly little for a knowing Venetian: it must be added that where there is a perpetual fast there are very few crumbs on the floor. His cleverness in other ways was sufficient, if it was not quite all that I had attributed to him on the occasion of my first interview with Miss Tita. He had helped my gondolier to bring me round a boat-load of furniture; and when these articles had been carried to the top of the palace and distributed according to our associated wisdom he organised my household with such promptitude as was consistent with the fact that it was composed exclusively of himself. He made me in short as comfortable as I could be with my indifferent prospects. I should have been glad if he had fallen in love with Miss Bordereau's maid or, failing this, had taken her in aversion; either event might have brought about some kind of catastrophe and a catastrophe might have led to some parley. It was my idea that she would have been sociable, and I myself on various occasions saw her flit to and fro on domestic errands, so that I was sure she was accessible. But I tasted of no gossip from that fountain, and I afterwards learned that Pasquale's[408] affections were fixed upon an object that made him heedless of other women. This was a young lady with a powdered face, a yellow cotton gown and much leisure, who used often to come to see him. She practised, at her convenience, the art of a stringer of beads[409] (these ornaments are made in Venice, in profusion; she had her pocket full of them and I used to find them on the floor of my apartment), and kept an eye on the maiden in the house. It was not for me of course to make the domestics tattle, and I never said a word to Miss Bordereau's cook.

It seemed to me a proof of the old lady's determination to have nothing to do with me that she should never have sent me a receipt for my three months' rent. For some days I looked out for it and then, when I had given it up, I wasted a good deal of time in wondering what her reason had been for neglecting so indispensable and familiar a form. At first I was tempted to send her a reminder, after which I relinquished the idea (against my judgment as to what was right in the particular case), on the general ground of wishing to keep quiet. If Miss Bordereau suspected me of ulterior aims she would suspect me less if I should be businesslike, and yet I consented not to be so. It was possible she intended her omission as an impertinence, a visible irony, to show how she could overreach people who attempted to overreach her. On that hypothesis it was well to let her see that one did not notice her little tricks. The real reading of the matter, I afterwards perceived, was simply the poor old woman's desire to emphasise the fact that I was in the enjoyment of a favour as rigidly limited as it had been liberally bestowed. She had given me part of her house and now she would not give me even a morsel of paper with her name on it. Let me say that even at first this did not make me too miserable, for the whole episode was essentially delightful to me. I foresaw that I should have a summer after my own literary heart, and the sense of holding my opportunity was much greater than the sense of losing it. There could be no Venetian business without patience, and since I adored the place I was much more in the spirit of it for having laid in a large provision. That spirit kept me perpetual company and seemed to look out at me from the revived immortal face—in which all his genius shone—of the great poet who was my prompter. I had invoked him and he had come; he hovered before me half the time; it was as if his bright ghost[410] had returned to earth to tell me that he regarded the affair as his own no less than mine and that we should see it fraternally, cheerfully to a conclusion. It was as if he had said, "Poor dear, be easy with her; she has some natural prejudices; only give her time. Strange as it may appear to you she was very attractive in 1820. Meanwhile are we not in Venice together, and what better place is there for the meeting of dear friends? See how it glows with the advancing summer; how the sky and the sea and the rosy air[411] and the marble of the palaces all shimmer and melt together." My eccentric private errand became a part of the general romance and the general glory—I felt even a mystic companionship, a moral fraternity with all those who in the past had been in the service of art. They had worked for beauty, for a devotion; and what else was I doing? That element was in everything that Jeffrey Aspern had written and I was only bringing it to the light.

I lingered in the sala when I went to and fro; I used to watch—as long as I thought decent—the door that led to Miss Bordereau's part of the house. A person observing me might have supposed I was trying to cast a spell upon it or attempting some odd experiment in hypnotism. But I was only praying it would open or thinking what treasure probably lurked behind it. I hold it singular, as I look back, that I should never have doubted for a moment that the sacred relics were there; never have failed to feel a certain joy at being under the same roof with them. After all they were under my hand—they had not escaped me yet; and they made my life continuous, in a fashion, with the illustrious life they had touched at the other end. I lost myself in this satisfaction to the point of assuming—in my quiet extravagance— that poor Miss Tita also went back, went back, as I used to phrase it.[412] She did indeed, the gentle spinster, but not quite so far as Jeffrey Aspern, who was simple hearsay to her, quite as he was to me. Only she had lived for years with Juliana, she had seen and handled the papers and (even though she was stupid) some esoteric knowledge had rubbed off on her. That was what the old woman represented—esoteric knowledge; and this was the idea with which my editorial heart used to thrill. It literally beat faster often, of an evening, when I had been out, as I stopped with my candle in the re-echoing hall on my way up to bed. It was as if at such a moment as that, in the stillness, after the long contradiction of the day, Miss Bordereau's secrets were in the air, the wonder of her survival more palpable. These were the acute impressions. I had them in another form, with more of a certain sort of reciprocity, during the hours that I sat in the garden looking up over the top of my book at the closed windows of my hostess. In these windows no sign of life ever appeared; it was as if, for fear of my catching a glimpse of them, the two ladies passed their days in the dark. But this only proved to me that they had something to conceal; which was what I had wished to demonstrate. Their motionless shutters became as expressive as eyes consciously closed, and I took comfort in thinking that at all events though invisible themselves they saw me between the lashes.

I made a point of spending as much time as possible in the garden, to justify the picture I had originally given of my horticultural passion. And I not only spent time, but (hang it! as I said) I spent money. As soon as I had got my rooms arranged and could give the proper thought to the matter I surveyed the place with a clever expert and made terms for having it put in order. I was sorry to do this, for personally I liked it better as it was, with its weeds and its wild, rough tangle, its sweet, characteristic Venetian shabbiness. I had to be consistent, to keep my promise that I would smother the house in flowers. Moreover I formed this graceful project that by flowers I would make my way—I would succeed by big nosegays. I would batter the old women with lilies—I would bombard their citadel with roses. Their door would have to yield to the pressure when a mountain of carnations should be piled up against it. The place in truth had been brutally neglected. The Venetian capacity for dawdling is of the largest, and for a good many days unlimited litter was all my gardener had to show for his ministrations. There was a great digging of holes and carting about of earth, and after a while I grew so impatient that I had thoughts of sending for my bouquets to the nearest stand. But I reflected that the ladies would see through the chinks of their shutters that they must have been bought and might make up their minds from this that I was a humbug. So I composed myself and finally, though the delay was long, perceived some appearances of bloom. This encouraged me and I waited serenely enough till they multiplied. Meanwhile the real summer days arrived and began to pass, and as I look back upon them they seem to me almost the happiest of my life. I took more and more care to be in the garden whenever it was not too hot. I had an arbour arranged and a low table and an armchair put into it; and I carried out books and portfolios (I had always some business of writing in hand), and worked and waited and mused and hoped, while the golden hours elapsed and the plants drank in the light and the inscrutable old palace turned pale and then, as the day waned, began to flush in it and my papers rustled in the wandering breeze of the Adriatic.[413]

Considering how little satisfaction I got from it at first it is remarkable that I should not have grown more tired of wondering what mystic rites of ennui the Misses Bordereau celebrated in their darkened rooms; whether this had always been the tenor of their life and how in previous years they had escaped elbowing their neighbours. It was clear that they must have had other habits and other circumstances; that they must once have been young or at least middle-aged. There was no end to the questions it was possible to ask about them and no end to the answers it was not possible to frame. I had known many of my country-people in Europe and was familiar with the strange ways they were liable to take up there; but the Misses Bordereau formed altogether a new type of the American absentee. Indeed it was plain that the American name had ceased to have any application to them—I had seen this in the ten minutes I spent in the old woman's room. You could never have said whence they came, from the appearance of either of them; wherever it was they had long ago dropped the local accent and fashion. There was nothing in them that one recognised, and putting the question of speech aside they might have been Norwegians or Spaniards. Miss Bordereau, after all, had been in Europe nearly threequarters of a century; it appeared by some verses addressed to her by Aspern on the occasion of his own second absence from America—verses of which Cumnor and I had after infinite conjecture established solidly enough the date—that she was even then, as a girl of twenty, on the foreign side of the sea. There was an implication in the poem (I hope not just for the phrase) that he had come back for her sake. We had no real light upon her circumstances at that moment, any more than we had upon her origin, which we believed to be of the sort usually spoken of as modest. Cumnor had a theory that she had been a governess in some family in which the poet visited and that, in consequence of her position, there was from the first something unavowed, or rather something positively clandestine, in their relations. I on the other hand had hatched a little romance according to which she was the daughter of an artist, a painter or a sculptor, who had left the western world when the century was fresh, to study in the ancient schools.[414] It was essential to my hypothesis that this amiable man should have lost his wife, should have been poor and unsuccessful and should have had a second daughter, of a disposition quite different from Juliana's. It was also indispensable that he should have been accompanied to Europe by these young ladies and should have established himself there for the remainder of a struggling, saddened life. There was a further implication that Miss Bordereau had had in her youth a perverse and adventurous, albeit a generous and fascinating character, and that she had passed through some singular vicissitudes. By what passions had she been ravaged, by what sufferings had she been blanched, what store of memories had she laid away for the monotonous future?

I asked myself these things as I sat spinning theories about her in my arbour and the bees droned in the flowers. It was incontestable that, whether for right or for wrong, most readers of certain of Aspern's poems (poems not as ambiguous as the sonnets—scarcely more divine, I think— of Shakespeare)[415] had taken for granted that Juliana had not always adhered to the steep footway of renunciation.[416] There hovered about her name a perfume of reckless passion, an intimation that she had not been exactly as the respectable young person in general. Was this a sign that her singer had betrayed her, had given her away, as we say nowadays, to posterity? Certain it is that it would have been difficult to put one's finger on the passage in which her fair fame suffered an imputation. Moreover was not any fame fair enough that was so sure of duration and was associated with works immortal through their beauty? It was a part of my idea that the young lady had had a foreign lover (and an unedifying tragical rupture) before her meeting with Jeffrey Aspern. She had lived with her father and sister in a queer old-fashioned, expatriated, artistic Bohemia, in the days when the aesthetic was only the academic[417] and the painters who knew the best models for a *contadina* and *pifferaro*[418] wore peaked hats and long hair.[419] It was a society less furnished than the coteries of today (in its ignorance of the wonderful chances, the opportunities of the early bird, with which its path was strewn), with tatters of old stuff and fragments of old crockery; so that Miss Bordereau appeared not to have picked up or have inherited many objects of importance. There was no enviable *bric-à-brac*,[420] with its provoking legend of cheapness, in the room in which I had seen her. Such a fact as that suggested bareness, but none the less it worked happily into the sentimental interest I had always taken in the early movements of my countrymen

as visitors to Europe. When Americans went abroad in 1820[421] there was
something romantic, almost heroic in it, as compared with the perpetual
ferryings of the present hour, when photography and other conveniences
have annihilated surprise. Miss Bordereau sailed with her family on a tossing brig,[422] in the days of long voyages and sharp differences; she had her
emotions on the top of yellow diligences,[423] passed the night at inns where
she dreamed of travellers' tales,[424] and was struck, on reaching the eternal
city, with the elegance of Roman pearls and scarfs. There was something
touching to me in all that and my imagination frequently went back to the
period. If Miss Bordereau carried it there of course Jeffrey Aspern at other
times had done so a great deal more. It was a much more important fact, if
one were looking at his genius critically, that he had lived in the days before
the general transfusion. It had happened to me to regret that he had known
Europe at all; I should have liked to see what he would have written without
that experience, by which he had incontestably been enriched. But as his
fate had ordered otherwise I went with him—I tried to judge how the old
world would have struck him. It was not only there, however, that I watched
him; the relations he had entertained with the new had even a livelier interest. His own country after all had had most of his life, and his muse, as they
said at that time, was essentially American. That was originally what I had
loved him for: that at a period when our native land was nude and crude
and provincial, when the famous "atmosphere" it is supposed to lack was
not even missed, when literature was lonely there and art and form almost
impossible,[425] he had found means to live and write like one of the first; to
be free and general and not at all afraid; to feel, understand and express
everything.

V

I WAS seldom at home in the evening, for when I attempted to occupy myself in my apartments the lamplight brought in a swarm of noxious insects, and it was too hot for closed windows. Accordingly I spent the late hours either on the water (the moonlight of Venice is famous), or in the splendid square which serves as a vast forecourt to the strange old basilica of Saint Mark.[426] I sat in front of Florian's *cafè*,[427] eating ices, listening to music, talking with acquaintances: the traveller will remember how the immense cluster of tables and little chairs stretches like a promontory into the smooth lake of the Piazza. The whole place, of a summer's evening, under the stars and with all the lamps, all the voices and light footsteps on marble (the only sounds of the arcades that enclose it), is like an open-air saloon dedicated to cooling drinks and to a still finer degustation—that of the exquisite impressions received during the day. When I did not prefer to keep mine to myself there was always a stray tourist, disencumbered of his Bädeker,[428] to discuss them with, or some domesticated painter rejoicing in the return of the season of strong effects. The wonderful church, with its low domes and bristling embroideries, the mystery of its mosaic and sculpture, looked ghostly in the tempered gloom, and the sea-breeze passed between the twin columns of the Piazzetta,[429] the lintels of a door no longer guarded, as gently as if a rich curtain were swaying there. I used sometimes on these occasions to think of the Misses Bordereau and of the pity of their being shut up in apartments which in the Venetian July even Venetian vastness did not prevent from being stuffy. Their life seemed miles away from the life of the Piazza, and no doubt it was really too late to make the austere Juliana change her habits. But poor Miss Tita would have enjoyed one of Florian's ices, I was sure; sometimes I even had thoughts of carrying one home to her. Fortunately my patience bore fruit and I was not obliged to do anything so ridiculous.

One evening about the middle of July I came in earlier than usual—I forget what chance had led to this—and instead of going up to my quarters made my way into the garden. The temperature was very high; it was such a night as one would gladly have spent in the open air and I was in no hurry to go to bed. I had floated home in my gondola, listening to the slow splash of the oar in the narrow dark canals, and now the only thought that solicited me was the vague reflection that it would be pleasant to recline at one's length in the fragrant darkness on a garden bench. The odour of the canal[430] was doubtless at the bottom of that aspiration and the breath of the garden, as I entered it, gave consistency to my purpose. It was delicious— just such an air as must have trembled with Romeo's vows[431] when he stood among the flowers and raised his arms to his mistress's balcony. I looked at the windows of the palace to see if by chance the example of Verona (Verona being not far off) had been followed; but everything was dim, as usual, and everything was still. Juliana, on summer nights in her youth, might have murmured down from open windows at Jeffrey Aspern, but Miss Tita was not a poet's mistress any more than I was a poet. This however did not prevent my gratification from being great as I became aware on reaching the end of the garden that Miss Tita was seated in my little bower. At first I only made out an indistinct figure, not in the least counting on such an overture from one of my hostesses; it even occurred to me that some sentimental maidservant had stolen in to keep a tryst with her sweetheart. I was going to turn away, not to frighten her, when the figure rose to its height and I recognised Miss Bordereau's niece. I must do myself the justice to say that I did not wish to frighten her either, and much as I had longed for some such accident I should have been capable of retreating. It was as if I had laid a trap for her by coming home earlier than usual and adding to that eccentricity by creeping into the garden. As she rose she spoke to me, and then I reflected that perhaps, secure in my almost inveterate absence, it was her nightly practice to take a lonely airing. There was no trap, in truth, because I had had no suspicion. At first I took for granted that the words she uttered expressed discomfiture at my arrival; but as she repeated them—I had not caught them clearly—I had the surprise of hearing her say, "Oh, dear, I'm so very glad you've come!" She and her aunt had in common the property of unexpected speeches. She came out of the arbour almost as if she were going to throw herself into my arms.

I hasten to add that she did nothing of the kind; she did not even shake hands with me. It was a gratification to her to see me and presently she told me why—because she was nervous when she was out-of-doors at night

307

alone. The plants and bushes looked so strange in the dark, and there were all sorts of queer sounds—she could not tell what they were—like the noises of animals. She stood close to me, looking about her with an air of greater security but without any demonstration of interest in me as an individual. Then I guessed that nocturnal prowlings were not in the least her habit, and I was also reminded (I had been struck with the circumstance in talking with her before I took possession) that it was impossible to overestimate her simplicity.

"You speak as if you were lost in the backwoods," I said, laughing. "How you manage to keep out of this charming place when you have only three steps to take to get into it, is more than I have yet been able to discover. You hide away mighty well so long as I am on the premises, I know; but I had a hope that you peeped out a little at other times. You and your poor aunt are worse off than Carmelite nuns[432] in their cells. Should you mind telling me how you exist without air, without exercise, without any sort of human contact? I don't see how you carry on the common business of life."

She looked at me as if I were talking some strange tongue and her answer was so little of an answer that I was considerably irritated. "We go to bed very early—earlier than you would believe." I was on the point of saying that this only deepened the mystery when she gave me some relief by adding, "Before you came we were not so private. But I never have been out at night."

"Never in these fragrant alleys, blooming here under your nose?"

"Ah," said Miss Tita, "they were never nice till now!" There was an unmistakable reference in this and a flattering comparison, so that it seemed to me I had gained a small advantage. As it would help me to follow it up to establish a sort of grievance I asked her why, since she thought my garden nice, she had never thanked me in any way for the flowers I had been sending up in such quantities for the previous three weeks. I had not been discouraged—there had been, as she would have observed, a daily armful; but I had been brought up in the common forms and a word of recognition now and then would have touched me in the right place.

"Why I didn't know they were for me!"

"They were for both of you. Why should I make a difference?"

Miss Tita reflected as if she might be thinking of a reason for that, but she failed to produce one. Instead of this she asked abruptly, "Why in the world do you want to know us?"

"I ought after all to make a difference," I replied. "That question is your aunt's; it isn't yours. You wouldn't ask it if you hadn't been put up to it."

"She didn't tell me to ask you," Miss Tita replied, without confusion; she was the oddest mixture of the shrinking and the direct.

"Well, she has often wondered about it herself and expressed her wonder to you. She has insisted on it, so that she has put the idea into your head that I am unsufferably pushing. Upon my word I think I have been very discreet. And how completely your aunt must have lost every tradition of sociability, to see anything out of the way in the idea that respectable intelligent people, living as we do under the same roof, should occasionally exchange a remark! What could be more natural? We are of the same country and we have at least some of the same tastes, since, like you, I am intensely fond of Venice."

My interlocutress appeared incapable of grasping more than one clause in any proposition, and she declared quickly, eagerly, as if she were answering my whole speech: "I am not in the least fond of Venice. I should like to go far away!"

"Has she always kept you back so?" I went on, to show her that I could be as irrelevant as herself.

"She told me to come out to-night; she has told me very often," said Miss Tita. "It is I who wouldn't come. I don't like to leave her."

"Is she too weak, is she failing?" I demanded, with more emotion, I think, than I intended to show. I judged this by the way her eyes rested upon me in the darkness. It embarrassed me a little, and to turn the matter off I continued genially: "Do let us sit down together comfortably somewhere and you will tell me all about her."

Miss Tita made no resistance to this. We found a bench less secluded, less confidential, as it were, than the one in the arbour; and we were still sitting there when I heard midnight ring out from those clear bells of Venice[433] which vibrate with a solemnity of their own over the lagoon and hold the air so much more than the chimes of other places. We were together more than an hour and our interview gave, as it struck me, a great lift to my undertaking. Miss Tita accepted the situation without a protest; she had avoided me for three months, yet now she treated me almost as if these three months had made me an old friend. If I had chosen I might have inferred from this that though she had avoided me she had given a good deal of consideration to doing so. She paid no attention to the flight of time—never worried at my keeping her so long away from her aunt. She talked freely, answering questions and asking them and not even taking advantage of certain long-ish pauses with which they inevitably alternated to say she thought she had better go in. It was almost as if she were waiting for something—something I might say to her—and intended to give me my opportunity. I was the more struck by this as she told me that her aunt had been less well for a good many days and in a way that was rather new. She was weaker; at moments it seemed as if she had no strength at all; yet more than ever before she wished to be left alone. That was why she had told her to come out—not even to remain in her own room, which was alongside; she said her niece irritated her, made her nervous. She sat still for hours together, as if she were asleep; she had always done that, musing and dozing; but at such times formerly she gave at intervals some small sign of life, of interest, liking her companion to be near her with her work. Miss Tita confided to me that at present her aunt was so motionless that she sometimes feared she was dead; moreover she took hardly any food—one couldn't see what she lived on. The great thing was that she still on most days got up; the serious job was to dress her, to wheel her out of her bedroom. She clung to as many of her old habits as pos-sible and she had always, little company as they had received for years, made a point of sitting in the parlour.

I scarcely knew what to think of all this—of Miss Tita's sudden conver-sion to sociability and of the strange circumstance that the more the old lady appeared to decline toward her end the less she should desire to be looked after. The story did not hang together, and I even asked myself whether it were not a trap laid for me, the result of a design to make me show my hand. I could not have told why my companions (as they could only by courtesy be called) should have this purpose—why they should try to trip up so lucra-tive a lodger. At any rate I kept on my guard, so that Miss Tita should not have occasion again to ask me if I had an *arrière-pensée*. Poor woman, before we parted for the night my mind was at rest as to *her* capacity for entertain-ing one.

She told me more about their affairs than I had hoped; there was no need to be prying, for it evidently drew her out simply to feel that I listened, that I cared. She ceased wondering why I cared, and at last, as she spoke of the brilliant life they had led years before, she almost chattered. It was Miss Tita who judged it brilliant; she said that when they first came to live in Venice, years and years before (I saw that her mind was essentially vague about dates and the order in which events had occurred), there was scarcely a week that they had not some visitor or did not make some delightful *passeggio* in the city. They had seen all the curiosities; they had even been to the Lido[434] in a boat (she spoke as if I might think there was a way on foot); they had had a collation there, brought in three baskets and spread out on the grass. I asked her what people they had known and she said, Oh! very nice ones— the Cavaliere Bombicci and the Contessa Altemura, with whom they had had a great friendship. Also English people—the Churtons and the Goldies and Mrs. Stock-Stock,[435] whom they had loved dearly; she was dead and gone, poor dear. That was the case with most of their pleasant circle (this expression was Miss Tita's own), though a few were left, which was a wonder considering how they had neglected them. She mentioned the names of two or three Venetian old women; of a certain doctor, very clever, who was so kind—he came as a friend, he had really given up practice; of the *avvocato* Pochintesta,[436] who wrote beautiful poems and had addressed one to her aunt. These people came to see them without fail every year, usually at the *capo d'anno*, and of old her aunt used to make them some little present— her aunt and she together: small things that she, Miss Tita, made herself, like paper lamp-shades or mats for the decanters of wine at dinner or those woollen things that in cold weather were worn on the wrists. The last few years there had not been many presents; she could not think what to make and her aunt had lost her interest and never suggested. But the people came all the same; if the Venetians liked you once they liked you for ever.

There was something affecting in the good faith of this sketch of former social glories; the picnic at the Lido had remained vivid through the ages and poor Miss Tita evidently was of the impression that she had had a brilliant youth. She had in fact had a glimpse of the Venetian world in its gossiping, home-keeping, parsimonious, professional walks; for I observed for the first time that she had acquired by contact something of the trick of the familiar, soft-sounding, almost infantile speech of the place. I judged that she had imbibed this invertebrate dialect,[437] from the natural way the names of things and people—mostly purely local—rose to her lips. If she knew little of what they represented she knew still less of anything else. Her aunt had drawn in—her failing interest in the table-mats and lamp-shades was a sign of that—and she had not been able to mingle in society or to entertain it alone; so that the matter of her reminiscences struck one as an old world altogether. If she had not been so decent her references would have seemed to carry one back to the queer rococo Venice of Casanova.[438] I found myself falling into the error of thinking of her too as one of Jeffrey Aspern's contemporaries; this came from her having so little in common with my own. It was possible, I said to myself, that she had not even heard of him; it might very well be that Juliana had not cared to lift even for her the veil that covered the temple[439] of her youth. In this case she perhaps would not know of the existence of the papers, and I welcomed that presumption—it made me feel more safe with her—until I remembered that we had believed the letter of disavowal received by Cumnor to be in the handwriting of the niece. If it had been dictated to her she had of course to know what it was about; yet after all the effect of it was to repudiate the idea of any connection with the poet. I held it probable at all events that Miss Tita had not read a word of his poetry. Moreover if, with her companion, she had always escaped the interviewer there was little occasion for her having got it into her head that people were "after" the letters. People had not been after them, inasmuch as they had not heard of them; and Cumnor's fruitless feeler would have been a solitary accident.

When midnight sounded Miss Tita got up; but she stopped at the door of the house only after she had wandered two or three times with me round the garden. "When shall I see you again?" I asked, before she went in; to which she replied with promptness that she should like to come out the next night. She added however that she should not come—she was so far from doing everything she liked.

"You might do a few things that *I* like," I said with a sigh.

"Oh, you—I don't believe you!" she murmured, at this, looking at me with her simple solemnity.

"Why don't you believe me?"

"Because I don't understand you."

"That is just the sort of occasion to have faith." I could not say more, though I should have liked to, as I saw that I only mystified her; for I had no wish to have it on my conscience that I might pass for having made love to her. Nothing less should I have seemed to do had I continued to beg a lady to "believe in me" in an Italian garden on a midsummer night. There was some merit in my scruples, for Miss Tita lingered and lingered: I perceived that she felt that she should not really soon come down again and wished therefore to protract the present. She insisted too on making the talk between us personal to ourselves; and altogether her behaviour was such as would have been possible only to a completely innocent woman.

"I shall like the flowers better now that I know they are also meant for me."

"How could you have doubted it? If you will tell me the kind you like best I will send a double lot of them."

"Oh, I like them all best!" Then she went on, familiarly: "Shall you study—shall you read and write—when you go up to your rooms?"

"I don't do that at night, at this season. The lamplight brings in the animals."

"You might have known that when you came."

"I did know it!"

"And in winter do you work at night?"

"I read a good deal, but I don't often write." She listened as if these details had a rare interest, and suddenly a temptation quite at variance with the prudence I had been teaching myself associated itself with her plain, mild face. Ah yes, she was safe and I could make her safer! It seemed to me from one moment to another that I could not wait longer—that I really must take a sounding. So I went on: "In general before I go to sleep—very often in bed (it's a bad habit, but I confess to it), I read some great poet. In nine cases out of ten it's a volume of Jeffrey Aspern."

I watched her well as I pronounced that name but I saw nothing wonderful. Why should I indeed—was not Jeffrey Aspern the property of the human race?

"Oh, we read him—we *have* read him," she quietly replied.

"He is my poet of poets—I know him almost by heart."

For an instant Miss Tita hesitated; then her sociability was too much for her.

"Oh, by heart—that's nothing!" she murmured, smiling. "My aunt used to know him—to know him"—she paused an instant and I wondered what she was going to say— "to know him as a visitor."

"As a visitor?" I repeated, staring.

"He used to call on her and take her out."

I continued to stare. "My dear lady, he died a hundred years ago!"

"Well," she said, mirthfully, "my aunt is a hundred and fifty."

"Mercy on us!" I exclaimed; "why didn't you tell me before? I should like so to ask her about him."

"She wouldn't care for that—she wouldn't tell you," Miss Tita replied.

"I don't care what she cares for! She *must* tell me—it's not a chance to be lost."

"Oh, you should have come twenty years ago: then she still talked about him."

"And what did she say?" I asked, eagerly.

"I don't know—that he liked her immensely."

"And she—didn't she like him?"

"She said he was a god." Miss Tita gave me this information flatly, without expression; her tone might have made it a piece of trivial gossip. But it stirred me deeply as she dropped the words into the summer night; it seemed such a direct testimony.

"Fancy, fancy!" I murmured. And then, "Tell me this, please—has she got a portrait of him? They are distressingly rare."

"A portrait? I don't know," said Miss Tita; and now there was discomfiture in her face. "Well, good-night!" she added; and she turned into the house.

I accompanied her into the wide, dusky, stone-paved passage which on the ground floor corresponded with our grand sala. It opened at one end into the garden, at the other upon the canal, and was lighted now only by the small lamp that was always left for me to take up as I went to bed. An extinguished candle which Miss Tita apparently had brought down with her stood on the same table with it. "Good night, good-night!" I replied, keeping beside her as she went to get her light. "Surely you would know, shouldn't you, if she had one?"

"If she had what?" the poor lady asked, looking at me queerly over the flame of her candle.

"A portrait of the god. I don't know what I wouldn't give to see it."

"I don't know what she has got. She keeps her things locked up." And Miss Tita went away, toward the staircase, with the sense evidently that she had said too much.

I let her go—I wished not to frighten her—and I contented myself with remarking that Miss Bordereau would not have locked up such a glorious possession as that—a thing a person would be proud of and hang up in a prominent place on the parlour-wall. Therefore of course she had not any portrait. Miss Tita made no direct answer to this and candle in hand, with her back to me, ascended two or three stairs. Then she stopped short and turned round, looking at me across the dusky space.

"Do you write—do you write?" There was a shake in her voice—she could scarcely bring out what she wanted to ask.

"Do I write? Oh, don't speak of my writing on the same day with Aspern's!"

"Do you write about *him*—do you pry into his life?"

"Ah, that's your aunt's question; it can't be yours!" I said, in a tone of slightly wounded sensibility.

"All the more reason then that you should answer it. Do you, please?"

I thought I had allowed for the falsehoods I should have to tell; but I found that in fact when it came to the point I had not. Besides, now that I had an opening there was a kind of relief in being frank. Lastly (it was perhaps fanciful, even fatuous), I guessed that Miss Tita personally would not in the last resort be less my friend. So after a moment's hesitation I answered, "Yes, I have written about him and I am looking for more material. In heaven's name have you got any?"

"*Santo Dio!*" she exclaimed, without heeding my question; and she hurried upstairs and out of sight. I might count upon her in the last resort, but for the present she was visibly alarmed. The proof of it was that she began to hide again, so that for a fortnight I never beheld her. I found my patience ebbing and after four or five days of this I told the gardener to stop the flowers.

VI

ONE afternoon, as I came down from my quarters to go out, I found Miss Tita in the sala: it was our first encounter on that ground since I had come to the house. She put on no air of being there by accident; there was an ignorance of such arts in her angular, diffident directness. That I might be quite sure she was waiting for me she informed me of the fact and told me that Miss Bordereau wished to see me: she would take me into the room at that moment if I had time. If I had been late for a love-tryst I would have stayed for this, and I quickly signified that I should be delighted to wait upon the old lady. "She wants to talk with you—to know you," Miss Tita said, smiling as if she herself appreciated that idea; and she led me to the door of her aunt's apartment. I stopped her a moment before she had opened it, looking at her with some curiosity. I told her that this was a great satisfaction to me and a great honour; but all the same I should like to ask what had made Miss Bordereau change so suddenly. It was only the other day that she wouldn't suffer me near her. Miss Tita was not embarrassed by my question; she had as many little unexpected serenities as if she told fibs, but the odd part of them was that they had on the contrary their source in her truthfulness. "Oh, my aunt changes," she answered; "it's so terribly dull—I suppose she's tired."

"But you told me that she wanted more and more to be alone."

Poor Miss Tita coloured, as if she found me over-insistent. "Well, if you don't believe she wants to see you—I haven't invented it! I think people often are capricious when they are very old."

"That's perfectly true. I only wanted to be clear as to whether you have repeated to her what I told you the other night."

"What you told me?"

"About Jeffrey Aspern—that I am looking for materials."

"If I had told her do you think she would have sent for you?"

"That's exactly what I want to know. If she wants to keep him to herself she might have sent for me to tell me so."

"She won't speak of him," said Miss Tita. Then as she opened the door she added in a lower tone, "I have told her nothing."

The old woman was sitting in the same place in which I had seen her last, in the same position, with the same mystifying bandage over her eyes. Her welcome was to turn her almost invisible face to me and show me that while she sat silent she saw me clearly. I made no motion to shake hands with her; I felt too well on this occasion that that was out of place for ever. It had been sufficiently enjoined upon me that she was too sacred for that sort of reciprocity—too venerable to touch. There was something so grim in her aspect (it was partly the accident of her green shade), as I stood there to be measured, that I ceased on the spot to feel any doubt as to her knowing my secret, though I did not in the least suspect that Miss Tita had not just spoken the truth. She had not betrayed me, but the old woman's brooding instinct had served her; she had turned me over and over in the long, still hours and she had guessed. The worst of it was that she looked terribly like an old woman who at a pinch would burn her papers. Miss Tita pushed a chair forward, saying to me, "This will be a good place for you to sit." As I took possession of it I asked after Miss Bordereau's health; expressed the hope that in spite of the very hot weather it was satisfactory. She replied that it was good enough—good enough; that it was a great thing to be alive.

"Oh, as to that, it depends upon what you compare it with!" I exclaimed, laughing.

"I don't compare—I don't compare. If I did that I should have given everything up long ago."

I liked to think that this was a subtle allusion to the rapture she had known in the society of Jeffrey Aspern—though it was true that such an allusion would have accorded ill with the wish I imputed to her to keep him buried in her soul. What it accorded with was my constant conviction that no human being had ever had a more delightful social gift than his, and what it seemed to convey was that nothing in the world was worth speaking of if one pretended to speak of that. But one did not! Miss Tita sat down beside her aunt, looking as if she had reason to believe some very remarkable conversation would come off between us.

"It's about the beautiful flowers," said the old lady; "you sent us so many—I ought to have thanked you for them before. But I don't write letters and I receive only at long intervals."

She had not thanked me while the flowers continued to come, but she departed from her custom so far as to send for me as soon as she began to fear that they would not come any more. I noted this; I remembered what an acquisitive propensity she had shown when it was a question of extracting gold from me, and I privately rejoiced at the happy thought I had had in suspending my tribute. She had missed it and she was willing to make a concession to bring it back. At the first sign of this concession I could only go to meet her. "I am afraid you have not had many, of late, but they shall begin again immediately—to-morrow, to-night."

"Oh, do send us some to-night!" Miss Tita cried, as if it were an immense circumstance.

"What else should you do with them? It isn't a manly taste to make a bower of your room," the old woman remarked.

"I don't make a bower of my room, but I am exceedingly fond of growing flowers, of watching their ways. There is nothing unmanly in that: it has been the amusement of philosophers, of statesmen in retirement; even I think of great captains."[440]

"I suppose you know you can sell them—those you don't use," Miss Bordereau went on. "I dare say they wouldn't give you much for them; still, you could make a bargain."

"Oh, I have never made a bargain, as you ought to know. My gardener disposes of them and I ask no questions."

"I would ask a few, I can promise you!" said Miss Bordereau; and it was the first time I had heard her laugh. I could not get used to the idea that this vision of pecuniary profit was what drew out the divine Juliana most.

"Come into the garden yourself and pick them; come as often as you like; come every day. They are all for you," I pursued, addressing Miss Tita and carrying off this veracious statement by treating it as an innocent joke. "I can't imagine why she doesn't come down," I added, for Miss Bordereau's benefit.

"You must make her come; you must come up and fetch her," said the old woman, to my stupefaction. "That odd thing you have made in the corner would be a capital place for her to sit."

The allusion to my arbour was irreverent; it confirmed the impression I had already received that there was a flicker of impertinence in Miss Bordereau's talk, a strange mocking lambency which must have been a part of her adventurous youth and which had outlived passions and faculties. None the less I asked, "Wouldn't it be possible for you to come down there yourself? Wouldn't it do you good to sit there in the shade, in the sweet air?"

"Oh, sir, when I move out of this it won't be to sit in the air, and I'm afraid that any that may be stirring around me won't be particularly sweet! It will be a very dark shade indeed. But that won't be just yet," Miss Bordereau continued, cannily, as if to correct any hopes that this courageous allusion to the last receptacle of her mortality might lead me to entertain. "I have sat here many a day and I have had enough of arbours in my time. But I'm not afraid to wait till I'm called."

Miss Tita had expected some interesting talk, but perhaps she found it less genial on her aunt's side (considering that I had been sent for with a civil intention) than she had hoped. As if to give the conversation a turn that would put our companion in a light more favourable she said to me, "Didn't I tell you the other night that she had sent me out? You see that I can do what I like!"

"Do you pity her—do you teach her to pity herself?" Miss Bordereau demanded, before I had time to answer this appeal. "She has a much easier life than I had when I was her age."

"You must remember that it has been quite open to me to think you rather inhuman."

"Inhuman? That's what the poets used to call the women a hundred years ago. Don't try that; you won't do as well as they!" Juliana declared. "There is no more poetry in the world—that I know of at least. But I won't bandy words with you," she pursued, and I well remember the old-fashioned, artificial sound she gave to the speech. "You have made me talk, talk! It isn't good for me at all." I got up at this and told her I would take no more of her time; but she detained me to ask, "Do you remember, the day I saw you about the rooms, that you offered us the use of your gondola?" And when I assented, promptly, struck again with her disposition to make a "good thing" of being there and wondering what she now had in her eye, she broke out, "Why don't you take that girl out in it and show her the place?"

"Oh dear aunt, what do you want to do with me?" cried the "girl," with a piteous quaver. "I know all about the place!"

"Well then, go with him as a cicerone!" said Miss Bordereau, with an effect of something like cruelty in her implacable power of retort—an incongruous suggestion that she was a sarcastic, profane, cynical old woman. "Haven't we heard that there have been all sorts of changes in all these years? You ought to see them and at your age (I don't mean because you're so young), you ought to take the chances that come. You're old enough, my dear, and this gentleman won't hurt you. He will show you the famous sunsets, if they still go on—*do* they go on? The sun set for me so long ago. But that's not a reason. Besides, I shall never miss you; you think you are too important. Take her to the Piazza; it used to be very pretty," Miss Bordereau continued, addressing herself to me. "What have they done with the funny old church?[441] I hope it hasn't tumbled down. Let her look at the shops; she may take some money, she may buy what she likes."

Poor Miss Tita had got up, discountenanced and helpless, and as we stood there before her aunt it would certainly have seemed to a spectator of the scene that the old woman was amusing herself at our expense. Miss Tita protested, in a confusion of exclamations and murmurs; but I lost no time in saying that if she would do me the honour to accept the hospitality of my boat I would engage that she should not be bored. Or if she did not want so much of my company the boat itself, with the gondolier, was at her service; he was a capital oar and she might have every confidence. Miss Tita, without definitely answering this speech, looked away from me, out of the window, as if she were going to cry; and I remarked that once we had Miss Bordereau's approval we could easily come to an understanding. We would take an hour, whichever she liked, one of the very next days. As I made my obeisance to the old lady I asked her if she would kindly permit me to see her again.

For a moment she said nothing; then she inquired, "Is it very necessary to your happiness?"

"It diverts me more than I can say."

"You are wonderfully civil. Don't you know it almost kills *me*?"

"How can I believe that when I see you more animated, more brilliant than when I came in?"

"That is very true, aunt," said Miss Tita. "I think it does you good."

"Isn't it touching, the solicitude we each have that the other shall enjoy herself?" sneered Miss Bordereau. "If you think me brilliant to-day you don't know what you are talking about; you have never seen an agreeable woman. Don't try to pay me a compliment; I have been spoiled," she went on. "My door is shut, but you may sometimes knock."

With this she dismissed me and I left the room. The latch closed behind me, but Miss Tita, contrary to my hope, had remained within. I passed slowly across the hall and before taking my way downstairs I waited a little. My hope was answered; after a minute Miss Tita followed me. "That's a delightful idea about the Piazza," I said. "When will you go—to-night, to-morrow?"

She had been disconcerted, as I have mentioned, but I had already perceived and I was to observe again that when Miss Tita was embarrassed she did not (as most women would have done) turn away from you and try to escape, but came closer, as it were, with a deprecating, clinging appeal to be spared, to be protected. Her attitude was perpetually a sort of prayer for assistance, for explanation; and yet no woman in the world could have been less of a comedian.[442] From the moment you were kind to her she depended on you absolutely; her self-consciousness dropped from her and she took the greatest intimacy, the innocent intimacy which was the only thing she could conceive, for granted. She told me she did not know what had got into her aunt; she had changed so quickly, she had got some idea. I replied that she must find out what the idea was and then let me know; we would go and have an ice together at Florian's and she should tell me while we listened to the band.

"Oh, it will take me a long time to find out!" she said, rather ruefully; and she could promise me this satisfaction neither for that night nor for the next. I was patient now, however, for I felt that I had only to wait; and in fact at the end of the week, one lovely evening after dinner, she stepped into my gondola, to which in honour of the occasion I had attached a second oar.

We swept in the course of five minutes into the Grand Canal;[443] whereupon she uttered a murmur of ecstasy as fresh as if she had been a tourist just arrived. She had forgotten how splendid the great water-way looked on a clear, hot summer evening, and how the sense of floating between marble palaces and reflected lights disposed the mind to sympathetic talk. We floated long and far, and though Miss Tita gave no high-pitched voice to her satisfaction I felt that she surrendered herself. She was more than pleased, she was transported; the whole thing was an immense liberation. The gondola moved with slow strokes, to give her time to enjoy it, and she listened to the plash of the oars, which grew louder and more musically liquid as we passed into narrow canals, as if it were a revelation of Venice. When I asked her how long it was since she had been in a boat she answered, "Oh, I don't know; a long time—not since my aunt began to be ill." This was not the only example she gave me of her extreme vagueness about the previous years and the line which marked off the period when Miss Bordereau flourished. I was not at liberty to keep her out too long, but we took a considerable *giro* before going to the Piazza.[444] I asked her no questions, keeping the conversation on purpose away from her domestic situation and the things I wanted to know; I poured treasures of information about Venice into her ears, described Florence and Rome, discoursed to her on the charms and advantages of travel. She reclined, receptive, on the deep leather cushions, turned her eyes conscientiously to everything I pointed out to her, and never mentioned to me till some time afterwards that she might be supposed to know Florence better than I, as she had lived there for years with Miss Bordereau. At last she asked, with the shy impatience of a child, "Are we not really going to the Piazza? That's what I want to see!" I immediately gave the order that we should go straight; and then we sat silent with the expectation of arrival. As some time still passed, however, she said suddenly, of her own movement, "I have found out what is the matter with my aunt: she is afraid you will go!"

"What has put that into her head?"

"She has had an idea you have not been happy. That is why she is different now."

"You mean she wants to make me happier?"

"Well, she wants you not to go; she wants you to stay."

"I suppose you mean on account of the rent," I remarked candidly.

Miss Tita's candour showed itself a match for my own. "Yes, you know; so that I shall have more."

"How much does she want you to have?" I asked, laughing. "She ought to fix the sum, so that I may stay till it's made up."

"Oh, that wouldn't please me," said Miss Tita. "It would be unheard of, your taking that trouble."

"But suppose I should have my own reasons for staying in Venice?"

"Then it would be better for you to stay in some other house."

"And what would your aunt say to that?"

"She wouldn't like it at all. But I should think you would do well to give up your reasons and go away altogether."

"Dear Miss Tita," I said, "it's not so easy to give them up!"

She made no immediate answer to this, but after a moment she broke out: "I think I know what your reasons are!"

"I daresay, because the other night I almost told you how I wish you would help me to make them good."

"I can't do that without being false to my aunt."

"What do you mean, being false to her?"

"Why, she would never consent to what you want. She has been asked, she has been written to. It made her fearfully angry."

"Then she *has* got papers of value?" I demanded, quickly.

"Oh, she has got everything!" sighed Miss Tita, with a curious weariness, a sudden lapse into gloom.

These words caused all my pulses to throb, for I regarded them as precious evidence. For some minutes I was too agitated to speak, and in the interval the gondola approached the Piazzetta.[445] After we had disembarked I asked my companion whether she would rather walk round the square or go and sit at the door of the café; to which she replied that she would do whichever I liked best—I must only remember again how little time she had. I assured her there was plenty to do both, and we made the circuit of the long arcades.[446] Her spirits revived at the sight of the bright shop-windows, and she lingered and stopped, admiring or disapproving of their contents, asking me what I thought of things, theorising about prices. My attention wandered from her; her words of a while before, "Oh, she has got everything!" echoed so in my consciousness. We sat down at last in the crowded circle at Florian's, finding an unoccupied table among those that were ranged in the square. It was a splendid night and all the world was out-of-doors; Miss Tita could not have wished the elements more auspicious for her return to society. I saw that she enjoyed it even more than she told; she was agitated with the multitude of her impressions. She had forgotten what an attractive thing the world is, and it was coming over her that somehow she had for the best years of her life been cheated of it. This did not make her angry; but as she looked all over the charming scene her face had, in spite of its smile of appreciation, the flush of a sort of wounded surprise. She became silent, as if she were thinking with a secret sadness of opportunities, for ever lost, which ought to have been easy; and this gave me a chance to say to her, "Did you mean a while ago that your aunt has a plan of keeping me on by admitting me occasionally to her presence?"

THE ASPERN PAPERS AND OTHER TALES

"She thinks it will make a difference with you if you sometimes see her. She wants you so much to stay that she is willing to make that concession."

"And what good does she consider that I think it will do me to see her?"

"I don't know; she thinks it's interesting," said Miss Tita, simply. "You told her you found it so."

"So I did; but every one doesn't think so."

"No, of course not, or more people would try."

"Well, if she is capable of making that reflection she is capable also of making this further one," I went on: "that I must have a particular reason for not doing as others do, in spite of the interest she offers—for not leaving her alone." Miss Tita looked as if she failed to grasp this rather complicated proposition; so I continued, "If you have not told her what I said to you the other night may she not at least have guessed it?"

"I don't know; she is very suspicious."

"But she has not been made so by indiscreet curiosity, by persecution?"

"No, no; it isn't that," said Miss Tita, turning on me a somewhat troubled face. "I don't know how to say it: it's on account of something—ages ago, before I was born—in her life."

"Something? What sort of thing?" I asked, as if I myself could have no idea.

"Oh, she has never told me," Miss Tita answered; and I was sure she was speaking the truth.

Her extreme limpidity was almost provoking, and I felt for the moment that she would have been more satisfactory if she had been less ingenuous. "Do you suppose it's something to which Jeffrey Aspern's letters and papers—I mean the things in her possession—have reference?"

"I daresay it is!" my companion exclaimed, as if this were a very happy suggestion. "I have never looked at any of those things."

"None of them? Then how do you know what they are?"

"I don't," said Miss Tita, placidly. "I have never had them in my hands. But I have seen them when she has had them out."

"Does she have them out often?"

"Not now, but she used to. She is very fond of them."

"In spite of their being compromising?"

"Compromising?" Miss Tita repeated, as if she was ignorant of the meaning of the word. I felt almost as one who corrupts the innocence of youth.

324

"I mean their containing painful memories."

"Oh, I don't think they are painful."

"You mean you don't think they affect her reputation?"

At this a singular look came into the face of Miss Bordereau's niece—a kind of confession of helplessness, an appeal to me to deal fairly, generously with her. I had brought her to the Piazza, placed her among charming influences, paid her an attention she appreciated, and now I seemed to let her perceive that all this had been a bribe—a bribe to make her turn in some way against her aunt. She was of a yielding nature and capable of doing almost anything to please a person who was kind to her; but the greatest kindness of all would be not to presume too much on this. It was strange enough, as I afterwards thought, that she had not the least air of resenting my want of consideration for her aunt's character, which would have been in the worst possible taste if anything less vital (from my point of view) had been at stake. I don't think she really measured it. "Do you mean that she did something bad?" she asked in a moment.

"Heaven forbid I should say so, and it's none of my business. Besides, if she did," I added, laughing, "it was in other ages, in another world. But why should she not destroy her papers?"

"Oh, she loves them too much."

"Even now, when she may be near her end?"

"Perhaps when she's sure of that she will."

"Well, Miss Tita," I said, "it's just what I should like you to prevent."

"How can I prevent it?"

"Couldn't you get them away from her?"

"And give them to you?"

This put the case very crudely, though I am sure there was no irony in her intention. "Oh, I mean that you might let me see them and look them over. It isn't for myself; there is no personal avidity in my desire. It is simply that they would be of such immense interest to the public, such immeasurable importance as a contribution to Jeffrey Aspern's history."

She listened to me in her usual manner, as if my speech were full of reference to things she had never heard of, and I felt particularly like the reporter of a newspaper who forces his way into a house of mourning. This was especially the case when after a moment she said, "There was a gentleman who some time ago wrote to her in very much those words. He also wanted her papers."

"And did she answer him?" I asked, rather ashamed of myself for not having her rectitude.

"Only when he had written two or three times. He made her very angry."

"And what did she say?"

"She said he was a devil," Miss Tita replied, simply.

"She used that expression in her letter?"

"Oh no; she said it to me. She made me write to him."

"And what did you say?"

"I told him there were no papers at all."

"Ah, poor gentleman!" I exclaimed.

"I knew there were, but I wrote what she bade me."

"Of course you had to do that. But I hope I shall not pass for a devil."

"It will depend upon what you ask me to do for you," said Miss Tita, smiling.

"Oh, if there is a chance of *your* thinking so my affair is in a bad way! I sha'n't ask you to steal for me, nor even to fib—for you can't fib, unless on paper. But the principal thing is this—to prevent her from destroying the papers."

"Why, I have no control of her," said Miss Tita. "It's she who controls me."

"But she doesn't control her own arms and legs, does she? The way she would naturally destroy her letters would be to burn them. Now she can't burn them without fire, and she can't get fire unless you give it to her."

"I have always done everything she has asked," my companion rejoined. "Besides, there's Olimpia."

I was on the point of saying that Olimpia was probably corruptible, but I thought it best not to sound that note. So I simply inquired if that faithful domestic could not be managed.

"Every one can be managed by my aunt," said Miss Tita. And then she observed that her holiday was over; she must go home.

I laid my hand on her arm, across the table, to stay her a moment. "What I want of you is a general promise to help me."

"Oh, how can I—how can I?" she asked, wondering and troubled. She was half surprised, half frightened at my wishing to make her play an active part.

"This is the main thing: to watch her carefully and warn me in time, before she commits that horrible sacrilege."

"I can't watch her when she makes me go out."

"That's very true."

"And when you do too."

"Mercy on us; do you think she will have done anything to-night?"

"I don't know; she is very cunning."

"Are you trying to frighten me?" I asked.

I felt this inquiry sufficiently answered when my companion murmured in a musing, almost envious way, "Oh, but she loves them—she loves them!"

This reflection, repeated with such emphasis, gave me great comfort; but to obtain more of that balm I said, "If she shouldn't intend to destroy the objects we speak of before her death she will probably have made some disposition by will."

"By will?"

"Hasn't she made a will for your benefit?"

"Why, she has so little to leave. That's why she likes money," said Miss Tita.

"Might I ask, since we are really talking things over, what you and she live on?"

"On some money that comes from America, from a lawyer. He sends it every quarter. It isn't much!"

"And won't she have disposed of that?"

My companion hesitated—I saw she was blushing. "I believe it's mine," she said; and the look and tone which accompanied these words betrayed so the absence of the habit of thinking of herself that I almost thought her charming. The next instant she added, "But she had a lawyer once, ever so long ago. And some people came and signed something."

"They were probably witnesses. And you were not asked to sign? Well then," I argued, rapidly and hopefully, "it is because you are the legatee; she has left all her documents to you!"

"If she has it's with very strict conditions," Miss Tita responded, rising quickly, while the movement gave the words a little character of decision. They seemed to imply that the bequest would be accompanied with a command that the articles bequeathed should remain concealed from every inquisitive eye and that I was very much mistaken if I thought she was the person to depart from an injunction so solemn.

"Oh, of course you will have to abide by the terms," I said; and she uttered nothing to mitigate the severity of this conclusion. None the less, later, just before we disembarked at her own door, on our return, which had taken place almost in silence, she said to me abruptly, "I will do what I can to help you." I was grateful for this—it was very well so far as it went; but it did not keep me from remembering that night in a worried waking hour that I now had her word for it to reinforce my own impression that the old woman was very cunning.

VII

THE fear of what this side of her character might have led her to do made me nervous for days afterwards. I waited for an intimation from Miss Tita; I almost figured to myself that it was her duty to keep me informed, to let me know definitely whether or no Miss Bordereau had sacrificed her treasures. But as she gave no sign I lost patience and determined to judge so far as was possible with my own senses. I sent late one afternoon to ask if I might pay the ladies a visit, and my servant came back with surprising news. Miss Bordereau could be approached without the least difficulty; she had been moved out into the sala and was sitting by the window that overlooked the garden. I descended and found this picture correct; the old lady had been wheeled forth into the world and had a certain air, which came mainly perhaps from some brighter element in her dress, of being prepared again to have converse with it. It had not yet, however, begun to flock about her; she was perfectly alone and, though the door leading to her own quarters stood open, I had at first no glimpse of Miss Tita. The window at which she sat had the afternoon shade and, one of the shutters having been pushed back, she could see the pleasant garden, where the summer sun had by this time dried up too many of the plants—she could see the yellow light and the long shadows.

"Have you come to tell me that you will take the rooms for six months more?" she asked, as I approached her, startling me by something coarse in her cupidity almost as much as if she had not already given me a specimen of it. Juliana's desire to make our acquaintance lucrative had been, as I have sufficiently indicated, a false note in my image of the woman who had inspired a great poet with immortal lines; but I may say here definitely that I recognised after all that it behoved me to make a large allowance for her. It was I who had kindled the unholy flame;[447] it was I who had put into her head that she had the means of making money. She appeared never to have thought of that; she had been living wastefully for years, in a house five times too big for her, on a footing that I could explain only by the presumption that, excessive as it was, the space she enjoyed cost her next to nothing and that small as were her revenues they left her, for Venice, an appreciable margin. I had descended on her one day and taught her to calculate, and my almost extravagant comedy on the subject of the garden had presented me irresistibly in the light of a victim. Like all persons who achieve the miracle of changing their point of view when they are old she had been intensely converted; she had seized my hint with a desperate, tremulous clutch.

I invited myself to go and get one of the chairs that stood, at a distance, against the wall (she had given herself no concern as to whether I should sit or stand); and while I placed it near her I began, gaily, "Oh, dear madam, what an imagination you have, what an intellectual sweep! I am a poor devil of a man of letters who lives from day to day. How can I take palaces by the year? My existence is precarious. I don't know whether six months hence I shall have bread to put in my mouth. I have treated myself for once; it has been an immense luxury. But when it comes to going on——!"

"Are your rooms too dear? if they are you can have more for the same money," Juliana responded. "We can arrange, we can *combinare*, as they say here."

"Well yes, since you ask me, they are too dear," I said. "Evidently you suppose me richer than I am."

She looked at me in her barricaded way. "If you write books don't you sell them?"

"Do you mean don't people buy them? A little—not so much as I could wish. Writing books, unless one be a great genius—and even then!—is the last road to fortune. I think there is no more money to be made by literature."

"Perhaps you don't choose good subjects. What do you write about?" Miss Bordereau inquired.

"About the books of other people. I'm a critic, an historian, in a small way." I wondered what she was coming to.

"And what other people, now?"

"Oh, better ones than myself: the great writers mainly—the great philosophers and poets of the past; those who are dead and gone and can't speak for themselves."

"And what do you say about them?"

"I say they sometimes attached themselves to very clever women!" I answered, laughing. I spoke with great deliberation, but as my words fell upon the air they struck me as imprudent. However, I risked them and I was not sorry, for perhaps after all the old woman would be willing to treat. It seemed to be tolerably obvious that she knew my secret: why therefore drag the matter out? But she did not take what I had said as a confession; she only asked:

"Do you think it's right to rake up the past?"

"I don't know that I know what you mean by raking it up; but how can we get at it unless we dig a little? The present has such a rough way of treading it down."[448]

"Oh, I like the past, but I don't like critics," the old woman declared, with her fine tranquillity.

"Neither do I, but I like their discoveries."

"Aren't they mostly lies?"

"The lies are what they sometimes discover," I said, smiling at the quiet impertinence of this. "They often lay bare the truth."

"The truth is God's, it isn't man's; we had better leave it alone. Who can judge of it—who can say?"

"We are terribly in the dark, I know," I admitted; "but if we give up trying what becomes of all the fine things? What becomes of the work I just mentioned, that of the great philosophers and poets? It is all vain words if there is nothing to measure by it."

"You talk as if you were a tailor," said Miss Bordereau, whimsically; and then she added quickly, in a different manner, "This house is very fine; the proportions are magnificent. To-day I wanted to look at this place again. I made them bring me out here. When your man came, just now, to learn if I would see you, I was on the point of sending for you, to ask if you didn't mean to go on. I wanted to judge what I'm letting you have. This sala is very grand," she pursued, like an auctioneer, moving a little, as I guessed, her invisible eyes. "I don't believe you often have lived in such a house, eh?"

"I can't often afford to!" I said.

"Well then, how much will you give for six months?"

I was on the point of exclaiming—and the air of excruciation in my face would have denoted a moral fact—"Don't, Juliana; for *his* sake, don't!" But I controlled myself and asked less passionately: "Why should I remain so long as that?"

"I thought you liked it," said Miss Bordereau, with her shrivelled dignity.

"So I thought I should."

For a moment she said nothing more, and I left my own words to suggest to her what they might. I half expected her to say, coldly enough, that if I had been disappointed we need not continue the discussion, and this in spite of the fact that I believed her now to have in her mind (however it had come there), what would have told her that my disappointment was natural. But to my extreme surprise she ended by observing: "If you don't think we have treated you well enough perhaps we can discover some way of treating you better." This speech was somehow so incongruous that it made me laugh again, and I excused myself by saying that she talked as if I were a sulky boy, pouting in the corner, to be "brought round." I had not a grain of complaint to make; and could anything have exceeded Miss Tita's graciousness in accompanying me a few nights before to the Piazza? At this the old woman went on: "Well, you brought it on yourself!" And then in a different tone, "She is a very nice girl." I assented cordially to this proposition, and she expressed the hope that I did so not merely to be obliging, but that I really liked her. Meanwhile I wondered still more what Miss Bordereau was coming to. "Except for me, to-day," she said, "she has not a relation in the world." Did she by describing her niece as amiable and unencumbered wish to represent her as a *parti*?

It was perfectly true that I could not afford to go on with my rooms at a fancy price and that I had already devoted to my undertaking almost all the hard cash I had set apart for it. My patience and my time were by no means exhausted, but I should be able to draw upon them only on a more usual Venetian basis. I was willing to pay the venerable woman with whom my pecuniary dealings were such a discord twice as much as any other *padrona di casa* would have asked, but I was not willing to pay her twenty times as much. I told her so plainly, and my plainness appeared to have some success, for she exclaimed, "Very good; you have done what I asked—you have made an offer!"

"Yes, but not for half a year. Only by the month."

"Oh, I must think of that then." She seemed disappointed that I would not tie myself to a period, and I guessed that she wished both to secure me and to discourage me; to say, severely, "Do you dream that you can get off with less than six months? Do you dream that even by the end of that time you will be appreciably nearer your victory?" What was more in my mind was that she had a fancy to play me the trick of making me engage myself when in fact she had annihilated the papers. There was a moment when my suspense on this point was so acute that I all but broke out with the question, and what kept it back was but a kind of instinctive recoil (lest it should be a mistake), from the last violence of self-exposure. She was such a subtle old witch that one could never tell where one stood with her. You may imagine whether it cleared up the puzzle when, just after she had said she would think of my proposal and without any formal transition, she drew out of her pocket with an embarrassed hand a small object wrapped in crumpled white paper. She held it there a moment and then she asked, "Do you know much about curiosities?"

"About curiosities?"

"About antiquities, the old gimcracks that people pay so much for to-day. Do you know the kind of price they bring?"

I thought I saw what was coming, but I said ingenuously, "Do you want to buy something?"

"No, I want to sell. What would an amateur give me for that?" She unfolded the white paper and made a motion for me to take from her a small oval portrait.[449] I possessed myself of it with a hand of which I could only hope that she did not perceive the tremor, and she added, "I would part with it only for a good price."

At the first glance I recognised Jeffrey Aspern, and I was well aware that I flushed with the act. As she was watching me however I had the consistency to exclaim, "What a striking face! Do tell me who it is."

"It's an old friend of mine, a very distinguished man in his day. He gave it to me himself, but I'm afraid to mention his name, lest you never should have heard of him, critic and historian as you are. I know the world goes fast and one generation forgets another. He was all the fashion when I was young."

She was perhaps amazed at my assurance, but I was surprised at hers; at her having the energy, in her state of health and at her time of life, to wish to sport with me that way simply for her private entertainment—the humour to test me and practise on me. This, at least, was the interpretation that I put upon her production of the portrait, for I could not believe that she really desired to sell it or cared for any information I might give her. What she wished was to dangle it before my eyes and put a prohibitive price on it. "The face comes back to me, it torments me," I said, turning the object this way and that and looking at it very critically. It was a careful but not a supreme work of art, larger than the ordinary miniature and representing a young man with a remarkably handsome face, in a high-collared green coat and a buff waistcoat.[450] I judged the picture to have a valuable quality of resemblance and to have been painted when the model was about twenty-five years old. There are, as all the world knows, three other portraits of the poet in existence, but none of them is of so early a date as this elegant production. "I have never seen the original but I have seen other likenesses," I went on. "You expressed doubt of this generation having heard of the gentleman, but he strikes me for all the world as a celebrity. Now who is he? I can't put my finger on him—I can't give him a label. Wasn't he a writer? Surely he's a poet." I was determined that it should be she, not I, who should first pronounce Jeffrey Aspern's name.

My resolution was taken in ignorance of Miss Bordereau's extremely resolute character, and her lips never formed in my hearing the syllables that meant so much for her. She neglected to answer my question but raised her hand to take back the picture, with a gesture which though ineffectual was in a high degree peremptory. "It's only a person who should know for himself that would give me my price," she said with a certain dryness.

"Oh, then, you have a price?" I did not restore the precious thing; not from any vindictive purpose but because I instinctively clung to it. We looked at each other hard while I retained it.

"I know the least I would take. What it occurred to me to ask you about is the most I shall be able to get."

She made a movement, drawing herself together as if, in a spasm of dread at having lost her treasure, she were going to attempt the immense effort of rising to snatch it from me. I instantly placed it in her hand again, saying as I did so, "I should like to have it myself, but with your ideas I could never afford it."

She turned the small oval plate over in her lap, with its face down, and I thought I saw her catch her breath a little, as if she had had a strain or an escape. This however did not prevent her saying in a moment, "You would buy a likeness of a person you don't know, by an artist who has no reputation?"

"The artist may have no reputation, but that thing is wonderfully well painted," I replied, to give myself a reason.

"It's lucky you thought of saying that, because the painter was my father."

"That makes the picture indeed precious!" I exclaimed, laughing; and I may add that a part of my laughter came from my satisfaction in finding that I had been right in my theory of Miss Bordereau's origin. Aspern had of course met the young lady when he went to her father's studio as a sitter. I observed to Miss Bordereau that if she would entrust me with her property for twenty-four hours I should be happy to take advice upon it; but she made no answer to this save to slip it in silence into her pocket. This convinced me still more that she had no sincere intention of selling it during her life-time, though she may have desired to satisfy herself as to the sum her niece, should she leave it to her, might expect eventually to obtain for it. "Well, at any rate I hope you will not offer it without giving me notice," I said, as she remained irresponsive. "Remember that I am a possible purchaser."

"I should want your money first!" she returned, with unexpected rude-ness; and then, as if she bethought herself that I had just cause to complain of such an insinuation and wished to turn the matter off, asked abruptly what I talked about with her niece when I went out with her that way in the evening.

"You speak as if we had set up the habit," I replied. "Certainly I should be very glad if it were to become a habit. But in that case I should feel a still greater scruple at betraying a lady's confidence."

"Her confidence? Has she got confidence?"

"Here she is—she can tell you herself," I said; for Miss Tita now appeared on the threshold of the old woman's parlour. "Have you got confidence, Miss Tita? Your aunt wants very much to know."

"Not in her, not in her!" the younger lady declared, shaking her head with a dolefulness that was neither jocular nor affected. "I don't know what to do with her; she has fits of horrid imprudence. She is so easily tired—and yet she has begun to roam—to drag herself about the house." And she stood looking down at her immemorial companion with a sort of helpless won-der, as if all their years of familiarity had not made her perversities, on occa-sion, any more easy to follow.

"I know what I'm about. I'm not losing my mind. I daresay you would like to think so," said Miss Bordereau, with a cynical little sigh.

"I don't suppose you came out here yourself. Miss Tita must have had to lend you a hand," I interposed, with a pacifying intention.

"Oh, she insisted that we should push her; and when she insists!" said Miss Tita, in the same tone of apprehension; as if there were no knowing what service that she disapproved of her aunt might force her next to render.

"I have always got most things done I wanted, thank God! The people I have lived with have humoured me," the old woman continued, speaking out of the gray ashes of her vanity.

"I suppose you mean that they have obeyed you."

"Well, whatever it is, when they like you."

"It's just because I like you that I want to resist," said Miss Tita, with a nervous laugh.

"Oh, I suspect you'll bring Miss Bordereau upstairs next, to pay me a visit," I went on; to which the old lady replied:

"Oh no; I can keep an eye on you from here!"

"You are very tired; you will certainly be ill tonight!" cried Miss Tita.

"Nonsense, my dear; I feel better at this moment than I have done for a month. To-morrow I shall come out again. I want to be where I can see this clever gentleman."

"Shouldn't you perhaps see me better in your sitting-room?" I inquired.

"Don't you mean shouldn't you have a better chance at me?" she returned, fixing me a moment with her green shade.

"Ah, I haven't that anywhere! I look at you but I don't see you."

"You excite her dreadfully—and that is not good," said Miss Tita, giving me a reproachful, appealing look.

"I want to watch you— I want to watch you!" the old lady went on.

"Well then, let us spend as much of our time together as possible—I don't care where—and that will give you every facility."

"Oh, I've seen you enough for to-day. I'm satisfied. Now I'll go home." Miss Tita laid her hands on the back of her aunt's chair and began to push, but I begged her to let me take her place. "Oh yes, you may move me this way—you sha'n't in any other!" Miss Bordereau exclaimed, as she felt herself propelled firmly and easily over the smooth, hard floor. Before we reached the door of her own apartment she commanded me to stop, and she took a long, last look up and down the noble sala. "Oh, it's a magnificent house!" she murmured; after which I pushed her forward. When we had entered the parlour Miss Tita told me that she should now be able to manage, and at the same moment the little red-haired *donna* came to meet her mistress. Miss Tita's idea was evidently to get her aunt immediately back to bed. I confess that in spite of this urgency I was guilty of the indiscretion of lingering; it held me there to think that I was nearer the documents I coveted—that they were probably put away somewhere in the faded, unsociable room. The place had indeed a bareness which did not suggest hidden treasures; there were no dusky nooks nor curtained corners, no massive cabinets nor chests with iron bands. Moreover it was possible, it was perhaps even probable that the old lady had consigned her relics to her bedroom, to some battered box that was shoved under the bed, to the drawer of some lame dressing-table, where they would be in the range of vision by the dim night-lamp. None the less I scrutinised every article of furniture, every conceivable cover for a hoard, and noticed that there were half a dozen things with drawers, and in particular a tall old secretary, with brass ornaments of the style of the Empire[451]—a receptacle somewhat rickety but still capable of keeping a great many secrets. I don't know why this article fascinated me so, inasmuch as I certainly had no definite purpose of breaking into it; but I stared at it so hard that Miss Tita noticed me and changed colour. Her doing this made me think I was right and that wherever they might have been before the Aspern papers at that moment languished behind the peevish little lock of the secretary. It was hard to remove my eyes from the dull mahogany front when I reflected that a simple panel divided me from the goal of my hopes; but I remembered my prudence and with an effort took leave of Miss Bordereau. To make the effort graceful I said to her that I should certainly bring her an opinion about the little picture.

"The little picture?" Miss Tita asked, surprised.

"What do *you* know about it, my dear?" the old woman demanded. "You needn't mind. I have fixed my price."

"And what may that be?"

"A thousand pounds."

"Oh Lord!" cried poor Miss Tita, irrepressibly.

"Is that what she talks to you about?" said Miss Bordereau.

"Imagine your aunt's wanting to know!" I had to separate from Miss Tita with only those words, though I should have liked immensely to add, "For heaven's sake meet me to-night in the garden!"

VIII

As it turned out the precaution had not been needed, for three hours later, just as I had finished my dinner, Miss Bordereau's niece appeared, unannounced, in the open doorway of the room in which my simple repasts were served. I remember well that I felt no surprise at seeing her; which is not a proof that I did not believe in her timidity. It was immense, but in a case in which there was a particular reason for boldness it never would have prevented her from running up to my rooms. I saw that she was now quite full of a particular reason; it threw her forward—made her seize me, as I rose to meet her, by the arm.

"My aunt is very ill; I think she is dying!"

"Never in the world," I answered, bitterly. "Don't you be afraid!"

"Do go for a doctor—do, do! Olimpia is gone for the one we always have, but she doesn't come back; I don't know what has happened to her. I told her that if he was not at home she was to follow him where he had gone; but apparently she is following him all over Venice. I don't know what to do—she looks so as if she were sinking."

"May I see her, may I judge?" I asked. "Of course I shall be delighted to bring some one; but hadn't we better send my man instead, so that I may stay with you?"

Miss Tita assented to this and I despatched my servant for the best doctor in the neighbourhood. I hurried downstairs with her, and on the way she told me that an hour after I quitted them in the afternoon Miss Bordereau had had an attack of "oppression", a terrible difficulty in breathing. This had subsided but had left her so exhausted that she did not come up: she seemed all gone. I repeated that she was not gone, that she would not go yet; whereupon Miss Tita gave me a sharper sidelong glance than she had ever directed at me and said, "Really what do you mean? I suppose you don't accuse her of making-believe!" I forget what reply I made to this, but I grant that in my heart I thought the old woman capable of any weird manœuvre. Miss Tita wanted to know what I had done to her; her aunt had told her that I had made her so angry. I declared I had done nothing—I had been exceedingly careful; to which my companion rejoined that Miss Bordereau had assured her she had had a scene with me—a scene that had upset her. I answered with some resentment that it was a scene of her own making—that I couldn't think what she was angry with me for unless for not seeing my way to give a thousand pounds for the portrait of Jeffrey Aspern. "And did she show you that? Oh gracious—oh deary me!" groaned Miss Tita, who appeared to feel that the situation was passing out of her control and that the elements of her fate were thickening around her. I said that I would give anything to possess it, yet that I had not a thousand pounds; but I stopped when we came to the door of Miss Bordereau's room. I had an immense curiosity to pass it, but I thought it my duty to represent to Miss Tita that if I made the invalid angry she ought perhaps to be spared the sight of me. "The sight of you? Do you think she can *see*?" my companion demanded, almost with indignation. I did think so but forbore to say it, and I softly followed my conductress.

I remember that what I said to her as I stood for a moment beside the old woman's bed was, "Does she never show you her eyes then? Have you never seen them?" Miss Bordereau had been divested of her green shade, but (it was not my fortune to behold Juliana in her nightcap) the upper half of her face was covered by the fall of a piece of dingy lacelike muslin, a sort of extemporised hood which, wound round her head, descended to the end of her nose, leaving nothing visible but her white withered cheeks and puckered mouth, closed tightly and, as it were, consciously. Miss Tita gave me a glance of surprise, evidently not seeing a reason for my impatience. "You mean that she always wears something? She does it to preserve them."

"Because they are so fine?"

"Oh, to-day, to-day!" And Miss Tita shook her head, speaking very low. "But they used to be magnificent!"

"Yes indeed, we have Aspern's word for that." And as I looked again at the old woman's wrappings I could imagine that she had not wished to allow people a reason to say that the great poet had overdone it. But I did not waste my time in considering Miss Bordereau, in whom the appearance of respiration was so slight as to suggest that no human attention could ever help her more. I turned my eyes all over the room, rummaging with them the closets, the chests of drawers, the tables. Miss Tita met them quickly and read, I think, what was in them; but she did not answer it, turning away restlessly, anxiously, so that I felt rebuked, with reason, for a preoccupation that was almost profane in the presence of our dying companion. All the same I took another look, endeavouring to pick out mentally the place to try first, for a person who should wish to put his hand on Miss Bordereau's papers directly after her death. The room was a dire confusion; it looked like the room of an old actress. There were clothes hanging over chairs, odd-looking, shabby bundles here and there, and various pasteboard boxes piled together, battered, bulging and discoloured, which might have been fifty years old. Miss Tita after a moment noticed the direction of my eyes again and, as if she guessed how I judged the air of the place (forgetting I had no business to judge it at all), said, perhaps to defend herself from the imputation of complicity in such untidiness:

"She likes it this way; we can't move things. There are old bandboxes[452] she has had most of her life." Then she added, half taking pity on my real thought, "Those things were *there*." And she pointed to a small, low trunk which stood under a sofa where there was just room for it. It appeared to be a queer, superannuated coffer, of painted wood, with elaborate handles and shrivelled straps and with the colour (it had last been endued with a coat of light green) much rubbed off. It evidently had travelled with Juliana in the olden time—in the days of her adventures, which it had shared. It would have made a strange figure arriving at a modern hotel.

"*Were* there—they aren't now?" I asked, startled by Miss Tita's implication.

She was going to answer, but at that moment the doctor came in—the doctor whom the little maid had been sent to fetch and whom she had at last overtaken. My servant, going on his own errand, had met her with her companion in tow, and in the sociable Venetian spirit, retracing his steps with them, had also come up to the threshold of Miss Bordereau's room, where I saw him peeping over the doctor's shoulder. I motioned him away the more instantly that the sight of his prying face reminded me that I myself had almost as little to do there—an admonition confirmed by the sharp way the little doctor looked at me, appearing to take me for a rival who had the field before him. He was a short, fat, brisk gentleman who wore the tall hat of his profession[453] and seemed to look at everything but his patient. He looked particularly at me, as if it struck him that I should be better for a dose, so that I bowed to him and left him with the women, going down to smoke a cigar in the garden. I was nervous; I could not go further; I could not leave the place. I don't know exactly what I thought might happen, but it seemed to me important to be there. I wandered about in the alleys—the warm night had come on—smoking cigar after cigar and looking at the light in Miss Bordereau's windows. They were open now, I could see; the situation was different. Sometimes the light moved, but not quickly; it did not suggest the hurry of a crisis. Was the old woman dying or was she already dead? Had the doctor said that there was nothing to be done at her tremendous age but to let her quietly pass away; or had he simply announced with a look a little more conventional that the end of the end had come? Were the other two women moving about to perform the offices that follow in such a case? It made me uneasy not to be nearer, as if I thought the doctor himself might carry away the papers with him. I bit my cigar hard as it came over me again that perhaps there were now no papers to carry!

I wandered about for an hour—for an hour and a half. I looked out for Miss Tita at one of the windows, having a vague idea that she might come there to give me some sign. Would she not see the red tip of my cigar moving about in the dark and feel that I wanted eminently to know what the doctor had said? I am afraid it is a proof my anxieties had made me gross that I should have taken in some degree for granted that at such an hour, in the midst of the greatest change that could take place in her life, they were uppermost also in poor Miss Tita's mind. My servant came down and spoke to me; he knew nothing save that the doctor had gone after a visit of half an hour. If he had stayed half an hour then Miss Bordereau was still alive: it could not have taken so much time as that to enunciate the contrary. I sent the man out of the house; there were moments when the sense of his curiosity annoyed me and this was one of them. *He* had been watching my cigar-tip from an upper window, if Miss Tita had not; he could not know what I was after and I could not tell him, though I was conscious he had fantastic private theories about me which he thought fine and which I, had I known them, should have thought offensive.

I went upstairs at last but I ascended no higher than the sala. The door of Miss Bordereau's apartment was open, showing from the parlour the dimness of a poor candle. I went toward it with a light tread and at the same moment Miss Tita appeared and stood looking at me as I approached. "She's better—she's better," she said, even before I had asked. "The doctor has given her something; she woke up, came back to life while he was there. He says there is no immediate danger."

"No immediate danger? Surely he thinks her condition strange!"

"Yes, because she had been excited. That affects her dreadfully."

"It will do so again then, because she excites herself. She did so this afternoon."

"Yes; she mustn't come out any more," said Miss Tita, with one of her lapses into a deeper placidity.

"What is the use of making such a remark as that if you begin to rattle her about again the first time she bids you?"

"I won't—I won't do it any more."

"You must learn to resist her," I went on.

"Oh yes, I shall; I shall do so better if you tell me it's right."

"You mustn't do it for me; you must do it for yourself. It all comes back to you, if you are frightened."

"Well, I am not frightened now," said Miss Tita, cheerfully. "She is very quiet."

"Is she conscious again—does she speak?"

"No, she doesn't speak, but she takes my hand. She holds it fast."

"Yes," I rejoined, "I can see what force she still has by the way she grabbed that picture this afternoon. But if she holds you fast how comes it that you are here?"

Miss Tita hesitated a moment; though her face was in deep shadow (she had her back to the light in the parlour and I had put down my own candle far off, near the door of the sala), I thought I saw her smile ingenuously. "I came on purpose—I heard your step."

"Why, I came on tiptoe, as inaudibly as possible."

"Well, I heard you," said Miss Tita.

"And is your aunt alone now?"

"Oh no; Olimpia is sitting there."

On my side I hesitated. "Shall we then step in there?" And I nodded at the parlour; I wanted more and more to be on the spot.

"We can't talk there—she will hear us."

I was on the point of replying that in that case we would sit silent, but I was too conscious that this would not do, as there was something I desired immensely to ask her. So I proposed that we should walk a little in the sala, keeping more at the other end, where we should not disturb the old lady. Miss Tita assented unconditionally; the doctor was coming again, she said, and she would be there to meet him at the door. We strolled through the fine super-fluous hall, where on the marble floor—particularly as at first we said noth-ing—our footsteps were more audible than I had expected. When we reached the other end—the wide window, inveterately closed, connecting with the balcony that overhung the canal—I suggested that we should remain there, as she would see the doctor arrive still better. I opened the window and we passed out on the balcony. The air of the canal seemed even heavier, hotter than that of the sala. The place was hushed and void; the quiet neighbourhood had gone to sleep. A lamp, here and there, over the narrow black water, glim-mered in double; the voice of a man going homeward singing, with his jacket on his shoulder and his hat on his ear, came to us from a distance. This did not prevent the scene from being very *comme il faut*, as Miss Bordereau had called it the first time I saw her. Presently a gondola passed along the canal with its slow rhythmical plash, and as we listened we watched it in silence. It did not stop, it did not carry the doctor; and after it had gone on I said to Miss Tita:

"And where are they now—the things that were in the trunk?"

"In the trunk?"

"That green box you pointed out to me in her room. You said her papers had been there; you seemed to imply that she had transferred them."

"Oh yes; they are not in the trunk," said Miss Tita.

"May I ask if you have looked?"

"Yes, I have looked—for you."

"How for me, dear Miss Tita? Do you mean you would have given them to me if you had found them?" I asked, almost trembling.

She delayed to reply and I waited. Suddenly she broke out, "I don't know what I would do—what I wouldn't!"

"Would you look again—somewhere else?"

She had spoken with a strange, unexpected emotion, and she went on in the same tone: "I can't—I can't—while she lies there. It isn't decent."

"No, it isn't decent," I replied, gravely. "Let the poor lady rest in peace." And the words, on my lips, were not hypocritical, for I felt reprimanded and shamed.

Miss Tita added in a moment, as if she had guessed this and were sorry for me, but at the same time wished to explain that I did drive her on or at least did insist too much: "I can't deceive her that way. I can't deceive her—perhaps on her deathbed."

"Heaven forbid I should ask you, though I have been guilty myself!"

"You have been guilty?"

"I have sailed under false colours." I felt now as if I must tell her that I had given her an invented name, on account of my fear that her aunt would have heard of me and would refuse to take me in. I explained this and also that I had really been a party to the letter written to them by John Cumnor months before.

She listened with great attention, looking at me with parted lips, and when I had made my confession she said, "Then your real name[454]—what is it?" She repeated it over twice when I had told her, accompanying it with the exclamation "Gracious, gracious!" Then she added, "I like your own best."

"So do I," I said, laughing. "Ouf! it's a relief to get rid of the other."

"So it was a regular plot—a kind of conspiracy?"

"Oh, a conspiracy—we were only two," I replied, leaving out Mrs. Prest of course.

She hesitated; I thought she was perhaps going to say that we had been very base. But she remarked after a moment, in a candid, wondering way, "How much you must want them!"

"Oh, I do, passionately!" I conceded, smiling. And this chance made me go on, forgetting my compunction of a moment before. "How can she possibly have changed their place herself? How can she walk? How can she arrive at that sort of muscular exertion? How can she lift and carry things?"

"Oh, when one wants and when one has so much will!" said Miss Tita, as if she had thought over my question already herself and had simply had no choice but that answer—the idea that in the dead of night, or at some moment when the coast was clear, the old woman had been capable of a miraculous effort.

"Have you questioned Olimpia? Hasn't she helped her—hasn't she done it for her?" I asked; to which Miss Tita replied promptly and positively that their servant had had nothing to do with the matter, though without admitting definitely that she had spoken to her. It was as if she were a little shy, a little ashamed now of letting me see how much she had entered into my

344

uneasiness and had me on her mind. Suddenly she said to me, without any immediate relevance:

"I feel as if you were a new person, now that you have got a new name."

"It isn't a new one; it is a very good old one, thank heaven!"

She looked at me a moment. "I do like it better."

"Oh, if you didn't I would almost go on with the other!"

"Would you really?"

I laughed again, but for all answer to this inquiry I said, "Of course if she can rummage about that way she can perfectly have burnt them."

"You must wait—you must wait," Miss Tita moralised mournfully; and her tone ministered little to my patience, for it seemed after all to accept that wretched possibility. I would teach myself to wait, I declared nevertheless; because in the first place I could not do otherwise and in the second I had her promise, given me the other night, that she would help me.

"Of course if the papers are gone that's no use," she said; not as if she wished to recede, but only to be conscientious.

"Naturally. But if you could only find out!" I groaned, quivering again.

"I thought you said you would wait."

"Oh, you mean wait even for that?"

"For what then?"

"Oh, nothing," I replied, rather foolishly, being ashamed to tell her what had been implied in my submission to delay—the idea that she would do more than merely find out. I know not whether she guessed this; at all events she appeared to become aware of the necessity for being a little more rigid.

"I didn't promise to deceive, did I? I don't think I did."

"It doesn't much matter whether you did or not, for you couldn't!"

I don't think Miss Tita would have contested this even had she not been diverted by our seeing the doctor's gondola shoot into the little canal and approach the house. I noted that he came as fast as if he believed that Miss Bordereau was still in danger. We looked down at him while he disembarked and then went back into the sala to meet him. When he came up however I naturally left Miss Tita to go off with him alone, only asking her leave to come back later for news.

I went out of the house and took a long walk, as far as the Piazza, where my restlessness declined to quit me. I was unable to sit down (it was very late now but there were people still at the little tables in front of the cafés);

I could only walk round and round, and I did so half a dozen times. I was uncomfortable, but it gave me a certain pleasure to have told Miss Tita who I really was. At last I took my way home again, slowly getting all but inextricably lost, as I did whenever I went out in Venice: so that it was considerably past midnight when I reached my door. The sala, upstairs, was as dark as usual and my lamp as I crossed it found nothing satisfactory to show me. I was disappointed, for I had notified Miss Tita that I would come back for a report, and I thought she might have left a light there as a sign. The door of the ladies' apartment was closed; which seemed an intimation that my faltering friend had gone to bed, tired of waiting for me. I stood in the middle of the place, considering, hoping she would hear me and perhaps peep out, saying to myself too that she would never go to bed with her aunt in a state so critical; she would sit up and watch—she would be in a chair, in her dressing-gown. I went nearer the door; I stopped there and listened. I heard nothing at all and at last I tapped gently. No answer came and after another minute I turned the handle. There was no light in the room; this ought to have prevented me from going in, but it had no such effect. If I have candidly narrated the importunities, the indelicacies, of which my desire to possess myself of Jeffrey Aspern's papers had rendered me capable I need not shrink from confessing this last indiscretion. I think it was the worst thing I did; yet there were extenuating circumstances. I was deeply though doubtless not disinterestedly anxious for more news of the old lady, and Miss Tita had accepted from me, as it were, a rendezvous which it might have been a point of honour with me to keep. It may be said that her leaving the place dark was a positive sign that she released me, and to this I can only reply that I desired not to be released.

The door of Miss Bordereau's room was open and I could see beyond it the faintness of a taper. There was no sound—my footstep caused no one to stir. I came further into the room; I lingered there with my lamp in my hand. I wanted to give Miss Tita a chance to come to me if she were with her aunt, as she must be. I made no noise to call her; I only waited to see if she would not notice my light. She did not, and I explained this (I found afterwards I was right) by the idea that she had fallen asleep. If she had fallen asleep her aunt was not on her mind, and my explanation ought to have led me to go out as I had come. I must repeat again that it did not, for I found myself at the same moment thinking of something else. I had no definite purpose, no bad intention, but I felt myself held to the spot by an acute, though absurd, sense of opportunity. For what I could not have said, inasmuch as it was not in my mind that I might commit a theft. Even if it had been I was confronted with the evident fact that Miss Bordereau did not leave her secretary, her cupboard and the drawers of her tables gaping. I had no keys, no tools and no ambition to smash her furniture. None the less it came to me that I was now, perhaps alone, unmolested, at the hour of temptation and secrecy, nearer to the tormenting treasure than I had ever been. I held up my lamp, let the light play on the different objects as if it could tell me something. Still there came no movement from the other room. If Miss Tita was sleeping she was sleeping sound. Was she doing so—generous creature—on purpose to leave me the field? Did she know I was there and was she just keeping quiet to see what I would do—what I *could* do? But what could I do, when it came to that? She herself knew even better than I how little.

I stopped in front of the secretary, looking at it very idiotically; for what had it to say to me after all? In the first place it was locked, and in the second it almost surely contained nothing in which I was interested. Ten to one the papers had been destroyed; and even if they had not been destroyed the old woman would not have put them in such a place as that after removing them from the green trunk—would not have transferred them, if she had the idea of their safety on her brain, from the better hiding-place to the worse. The secretary was more conspicuous, more accessible in a room in which she could no longer mount guard. It opened with a key, but there was a little brass handle, like a button, as well; I saw this as I played my lamp over it. I did something more than this at that moment: I caught a glimpse of the possibility that Miss Tita wished me really to understand. If she did not wish me to understand, if she wished me to keep away, why had she not locked the door of communication between the sitting-room and the sala? That would have been a definite sign that I was to leave them alone. If I did not leave them alone she meant me to come for a purpose—a purpose now indicated by the quick, fantastic idea that to oblige me she had unlocked the secretary. She had not left the key, but the lid would probably move if I touched the button. This theory fascinated me, and I bent over very close to judge. I did not propose to do anything, not even—not in the least—to let down the lid; I only wanted to test my theory, to see if the cover *would* move. I

347

touched the button with my hand—a mere touch would tell me; and as I did so (it is embarrassing for me to relate it), I looked over my shoulder. It was a chance, an instinct, for I had not heard anything. I almost let my luminary drop and certainly I stepped back, straightening myself up at what I saw. Miss Bordereau stood there in her night-dress, in the doorway of her room, watching me; her hands were raised, she had lifted the everlasting curtain that covered half her face, and for the first, the last, the only time I beheld her extraordinary eyes. They glared at me, they made me horribly ashamed. I never shall forget her strange little bent white tottering figure, with its lifted head, her attitude, her expression; neither shall I forget the tone in which as I turned, looking at her, she hissed out passionately, furiously:

"Ah, you publishing scoundrel!"

I know not what I stammered, to excuse myself, to explain; but I went towards her, to tell her I meant no harm. She waved me off with her old hands, retreating before me in horror; and the next thing I knew she had fallen back with a quick spasm, as if death had descended on her,[455] into Miss Tita's arms.

IX

I LEFT Venice the next morning, as soon as I learnt that the old lady had not succumbed, as I feared at the moment, to the shock I had given her— the shock I may also say she had given me. How in the world could I have supposed her capable of getting out of bed by herself? I failed to see Miss Tita before going; I only saw the *donna*, whom I entrusted with a note for her younger mistress. In this note I mentioned that I should be absent but for a few days. I went to Treviso, to Bassano, to Castelfranco;[456] I took walks and drives and looked at musty old churches with ill-lighted pictures and spent hours seated smoking at the doors of cafés, where there were flies and yellow curtains, on the shady side of sleepy little squares. In spite of these pastimes, which were mechanical and perfunctory, I scantily enjoyed my journey: there was too strong a taste of the disagreeable in my life. It had been devilish awkward, as the young men say, to be found by Miss Bordereau in the dead of night examining the attachment of her bureau; and it had not been less so to have to believe for a good many hours afterward that it was highly probable I had killed her. In writing to Miss Tita I attempted to minimise these irregularities; but as she gave me no word of answer I could not know what impression I made upon her. It rankled in my mind that I had been called a publishing scoundrel, for certainly I did publish and certainly I had not been very delicate. There was a moment when I stood convinced that the only way to make up for this latter fault was to take myself away altogether on the instant; to sacrifice my hopes and relieve the two poor women for ever of the oppression of my inter- course. Then I reflected that I had better try a short absence first, for I must already have had a sense (unexpressed and dim) that in disappearing completely it would not be merely my own hopes that I should condemn to extinction. It would perhaps be sufficient if I stayed away long enough to give the elder lady time to think she was rid of me. That she would wish to be rid of me after this (if I was not rid of her) was now not to be doubted: that nocturnal scene would have cured her of the disposition to put up with my company for the sake of my dollars. I said to myself that after all I could not abandon Miss Tita, and I continued to say this even while I observed that she quite failed to comply with my earnest request (I had given her two or three addresses, at little towns, *poste restante*) that she would let me know how she was getting on. I would have made my servant write to me but that he was unable to manage a pen. It struck me there was a kind of scorn in Miss Tita's silence (little disdainful as she had ever been), so that I was uncomfortable and sore. I had scruples about going back and yet I had others about not doing so, for I wanted to put myself on a better footing. The end of it was that I did return to Venice on the twelfth day; and as my gondola gently bumped against Miss Bordereau's steps a certain palpitation of suspense told me that I had done myself a violence in holding off so long.

I had faced about so abruptly that I had not telegraphed to my servant. He was therefore not at the station to meet me, but he poked out his head from an upper window when I reached the house. "They have put her into the earth, *la vecchia*,"[457] he said to me in the lower hall, while he shouldered my valise; and he grinned and almost winked, as if he knew I should be pleased at the news.

"She's dead!" I exclaimed, giving him a very different look.

"So it appears, since they have buried her."

"It's all over? When was the funeral?"

"The other yesterday. But a funeral you could scarcely call it, signore; it was a dull little passeggio[458] of two gondolas. Poveretta!" the man continued, referring apparently to Miss Tita. His conception of funerals was apparently that they were mainly to amuse the living.

I wanted to know about Miss Tita—how she was and where she was—but I asked him no more questions till we had got upstairs. Now that the fact had met me I took a bad view of it, especially of the idea that poor Miss Tita had had to manage by herself after the end. What did she know about arrangements, about the steps to take in such a case? Poveretta indeed! I could only hope that the doctor had given her assistance and that she had not been neglected by the old friends of whom she had told me, the little band of the faithful whose fidelity consisted in coming to the house once a year. I elicited from my servant that two old ladies and an old gentleman had in fact rallied round Miss Tita and had supported her (they had come for her in a gondola of their own) during the journey to the cemetery,[459] the little red-walled island of tombs which lies to the north of the town, on the way to Murano. It appeared from these circumstances that the Misses Bordereau were Catholics, a discovery I had never made, as the old woman could not go to church and her niece, so far as I perceived, either did not or went only to early mass in the parish, before I was stirring. Certainly even the priests respected their seclusion; I had never caught the whisk of the curato's skirt. That evening, an hour later, I sent my servant down with five words written on a card, to ask Miss Tita if she would see me for a few moments. She was not in the house, where he had sought her, he told me when he came back, but in the garden walking about to refresh herself and gathering flowers. He had found her there and she would be very happy to see me.

I went down and passed half an hour with poor Miss Tita. She had always had a look of musty mourning (as if she were wearing out old robes of sorrow that would not come to an end), and in this respect there was no appreciable change in her appearance. But she evidently had been crying, crying a great deal—simply, satisfyingly, refreshingly, with a sort of primitive, retarded sense of loneliness and violence. But she had none of the formalism or the self-consciousness of grief, and I was almost surprised to see her standing there in the first dusk with her hands full of flowers, smiling at me with her reddened eyes. Her white face, in the frame of her mantilla, looked longer, leaner than usual. I had had an idea that she would be a good deal disgusted with me—would consider that I ought to have been on the spot to advise her, to help her; and, though I was sure there was no rancour in her composition and no great conviction of the importance of her affairs, I had prepared myself for a difference in her manner, for some little injured look, half familiar, half estranged, which should say to my conscience, "Well, you are a nice person to have professed things!" But historic truth compels me to declare that Tita Bordereau's countenance expressed unqualified pleasure in seeing her late aunt's lodger. That touched him extremely and he thought it simplified his situation until he found it did not. I was as kind to her that evening as I knew how to be, and I walked about the garden with her for half an hour. There was no explanation of any sort between us; I did not ask her why she had not answered my letter. Still less did I repeat what I had said to her in that communication; if she chose to let me suppose that she had forgotten the position in which Miss Bordereau surprised me that night and the effect of the discovery on the old woman I was quite willing to take it that way: I was grateful to her for not treating me as if I had killed her aunt.

We strolled and strolled and really not much passed between us save the recognition of her bereavement, conveyed in my manner and in a visible air that she had of depending on me now, since I let her see that I took an interest in her. Miss Tita had none of the pride that makes a person wish to preserve the look of independence; she did not in the least pretend that she knew at present what would become of her. I forbore to touch particularly on that however, for I certainly was not prepared to say that I would take charge of her. I was cautious; not ignobly, I think, for I felt that her knowledge of life was so small that in her unsophisticated vision there would be no reason why—since I seemed to pity her—I should not look after her. She told me how her aunt had died, very peacefully at the last, and how everything had been done afterwards by the care of her good friends (fortunately, thanks to me, she said, smiling, there was money in the house; and she repeated that when once the Italians like you they are your friends for life); and when we had gone into this she asked me about my *giro*, my impressions, the places I had seen. I told her what I could, making it up partly, I am afraid, as in my depression I had not seen much; and after she had heard me she exclaimed, quite as if she had forgotten her aunt and her sorrow, "Dear, dear, how much I should like to do such things—to take a little journey!" It came over me for the moment that I ought to propose some tour, say I would take her anywhere she liked; and I remarked at any rate that some excursion—to give her a change—might be managed: we would think of it, talk it over. I said never a word to her about the Aspern documents; asked no questions as to what she had ascertained or what had otherwise happened with regard to them before Miss Bordereau's death. It was not that I was not on pins and needles to know, but that I thought it more decent not to betray my anxiety so soon after the catastrophe. I hoped she herself would say something, but she never glanced that way, and I thought this natural at the time. Later however, that night, it occurred to me that her silence was somewhat strange; for if she had talked of my movements, of anything so detached as the Giorgione at Castelfranco,[460] she might have alluded to what she could easily remember was in my mind. It was not to be supposed that

352

the emotion produced by her aunt's death had blotted out the recollection that I was interested in that lady's relics, and I fidgeted afterwards as it came to me that her reticence might very possibly mean simply that nothing had been found. We separated in the garden (it was she who said she must go in); now that she was alone in the rooms I felt that (judged, at any rate, by Venetian ideas) I was on rather a different footing in regard to visiting her there. As I shook hands with her for good-night I asked her if she had any general plan—had thought over what she had better do. "Oh yes, oh yes, but I haven't settled anything yet," she replied, quite cheerfully. Was her cheerfulness explained by the impression that I would settle for her?

I was glad the next morning that we had neglected practical questions, for this gave me a pretext for seeing her again immediately. There was a very practical question to be touched upon. I owed it to her to let her know formally that of course I did not expect her to keep me on as a lodger, and also to show some interest in her own tenure, what she might have on her hands in the way of a lease. But I was not destined, as it happened, to converse with her for more than an instant on either of these points. I sent her no message; I simply went down to the sala and walked to and fro there. I knew she would come out; she would very soon discover I was there. Somehow I preferred not to be shut up with her; gardens and big halls seemed better places to talk. It was a splendid morning, with something in the air that told of the waning of the long Venetian summer; a freshness from the sea which stirred the flowers in the garden and made a pleasant draught in the house, less shuttered and darkened now than when the old woman was alive. It was the beginning of autumn, of the end of the golden months. With this it was the end of my experiment—or would be in the course of half an hour, when I should really have learned that the papers had been reduced to ashes. After that there would be nothing left for me but to go to the station;[461] for seriously (and as it struck me in the morning light) I could not linger there to act as guardian to a piece of middle-aged female helplessness. If she had not saved the papers wherein should I be indebted to her? I think I winced a little as I asked myself how much, if she *had* saved them, I should have to recognise and, as it were, to reward such a courtesy. Might not that circumstance after all saddle me with a guardianship? If this idea did not make me more uncomfortable as I walked up and down it was because I was convinced I had nothing to look to. If the old woman had not destroyed everything before she pounced upon me in the parlour she had done so afterwards.

It took Miss Tita rather longer than I had expected to guess that I was there; but when at last she came out she looked at me without surprise. I said to her that I had been waiting for her and she asked why I had not let her know. I was glad the next day that I had checked myself before remarking that I had wished to see if a friendly intuition would not tell her: it became a satisfaction to me that I had not indulged in that rather tender joke. What I did say was virtually the truth—that I was too nervous, since I expected her now to settle my fate.

"Your fate?" said Miss Tita, giving me a queer look; and as she spoke I noticed a rare change in her. She was different from what she had been the evening before—less natural, less quiet. She had been crying the day before and she was not crying now, and yet she struck me as less confident. It was as if something had happened to her during the night, or at least as if she had thought of something that troubled her—something in particular that affected her relations with me, made them more embarrassing and complicated. Had she simply perceived that her aunt's not being there now altered my position?

"I mean about our papers. *Are* there any? You must know now."

"Yes, there are a great many; more than I supposed." I was struck with the way her voice trembled as she told me this.

"Do you mean that you have got them in there—and that I may see them?"

"I don't think you can see them," said Miss Tita, with an extraordinary expression of entreaty in her eyes, as if the dearest hope she had in the world now was that I would not take them from her. But how could she expect me to make such a sacrifice as that after all that had passed between us? What had I come back to Venice for but to see them, to take them? My delight at learning they were still in existence was such that if the poor woman had gone down on her knees to beseech me never to mention them again I would have treated the proceeding as a bad joke. "I have got them but I can't show them," she added.

"Not even to me? Ah, Miss Tita!" I groaned, with a voice of infinite remonstrance and reproach.

She coloured and the tears came back to her eyes; I saw that it cost her a kind of anguish to take such a stand but that a dreadful sense of duty had descended upon her. It made me quite sick to find myself confronted with that particular obstacle; all the more that it appeared to me I had been extremely encouraged to leave it out of account. I almost considered that Miss Tita had assured me that if she had no greater hindrance than that——! "You don't mean to say you made her a deathbed promise? It was precisely against your doing anything of that sort that I thought I was safe. Oh, I would rather she had burned the papers outright than that!"

"No, it isn't a promise," said Miss Tita.

"Pray what is it then?"

She hesitated and then she said, "She tried to burn them, but I prevented it. She had hid them in her bed."

"In her bed?"

"Between the mattresses. That's where she put them when she took them out of the trunk. I can't understand how she did it, because Olimpia didn't help her. She tells me so and I believe her. My aunt only told her afterwards, so that she shouldn't touch the bed—anything but the sheets. So it was badly made," added Miss Tita, simply.

"I should think so! And how did she try to burn them?"

"She didn't try much; she was too weak, those last days. But she told me—she charged me. Oh, it was terrible! She couldn't speak after that night; she could only make signs."

"And what did you do?"

"I took them away. I locked them up."

"In the secretary?"

"Yes, in the secretary," said Miss Tita, reddening again.

"Did you tell her you would burn them?"

"No, I didn't—on purpose."

"On purpose to gratify me?"

"Yes, only for that."

"And what good will you have done me if after all you won't show them?"

"Oh, none; I know that—I know that."

"And did she believe you had destroyed them?"

"I don't know what she believed at the last. I couldn't tell—she was too far gone."

"Then if there was no promise and no assurance I can't see what ties you."

"Oh, she hated it so—she hated it so! She was so jealous. But here's the portrait—you may have that," Miss Tita announced, taking the little picture, wrapped up in the same manner in which her aunt had wrapped it, out of her pocket.

"I may have it—do you mean you give it to me?" I questioned, staring, as it passed into my hand.

"Oh yes."

"But it's worth money—a large sum."

"Well!" said Miss Tita, still with her strange look.

I did not know what to make of it, for it could scarcely mean that she wanted to bargain like her aunt. She spoke as if she wished to make me a present. "I can't take it from you as a gift," I said, "and yet I can't afford to pay you for it according to the ideas Miss Bordereau had of its value. She rated it at a thousand pounds."

"Couldn't we sell it?" asked Miss Tita.

"God forbid! I prefer the picture to the money."

"Well then keep it."

"You are very generous."

"So are you."

"I don't know why you should think so," I replied; and this was a truthful speech, for the singular creature appeared to have some very fine reference in her mind, which I did not in the least seize.

"Well, you have made a great difference for me," said Miss Tita.

I looked at Jeffrey Aspern's face in the little picture, partly in order not to look at that of my interlocutress, which had begun to trouble me, even to frighten me a little—it was so self-conscious, so unnatural. I made no answer to this last declaration; I only privately consulted Jeffrey Aspern's delightful eyes with my own (they were so young and brilliant, and yet so wise, so full of vision); I asked him what on earth was the matter with Miss Tita. He seemed to smile at me with friendly mockery, as if he were amused at my case. I had got into a pickle for him—as if he needed it! He was unsatisfactory, for the only moment since I had known him. Nevertheless, now that I held the little picture in my hand I felt that it would be a precious possession.

"Is this a bribe to make me give up the papers?" I demanded in a moment, perversely. "Much as I value it, if I were to be obliged to choose, the papers are what I should prefer. Ah, but ever so much!"

"How can you choose—how can you choose?" Miss Tita asked, slowly, lamentably.

"I see! Of course there is nothing to be said, if you regard the interdiction that rests upon you as quite insurmountable. In this case it must seem to you that to part with them would be an impiety of the worst kind, a simple sacrilege!"

Miss Tita shook her head, full of her dolefulness. "You would understand if you had known her. I'm afraid," she quavered suddenly—"I'm afraid! She was terrible when she was angry."

"Yes, I saw something of that, that night. She was terrible. Then I saw her eyes. Lord, they were fine!"

"I see them—they stare at me in the dark!" said Miss Tita.

"You are nervous, with all you have been through."

"Oh yes, very—very!"

"You mustn't mind; that will pass away," I said, kindly. Then I added, resignedly, for it really seemed to me that I must accept the situation, "Well, so it is, and it can't be helped. I must renounce." Miss Tita, at this, looking at me, gave a low, soft moan, and I went on: "I only wish to heaven she had destroyed them; then there would be nothing more to say. And I can't understand why, with her ideas, she didn't."

"Oh, she lived on them!" said Miss Tita.

"You can imagine whether that makes me want less to see them," I answered, smiling. "But don't let me stand here as if I had it in my soul to tempt you to do anything base. Naturally you will understand I give up my rooms. I leave Venice immediately." And I took up my hat, which I had placed on a chair. We were still there rather awkwardly, on our feet, in the middle of the sala. She had left the door of the apartments open behind her but she had not led me that way.

A kind of spasm came into her face as she saw me take my hat. "Immediately—do you mean today?" The tone of the words was tragical—they were a cry of desolation.

"Oh no; not so long as I can be of the least service to you."

"Well, just a day or two more—just two or three days," she panted. Then controlling herself she added in another manner, "She wanted to say something to me—the last day—something very particular, but she couldn't."

"Something very particular?"

"Something more about the papers."

"And did you guess—have you any idea?"

"No, I have thought—but I don't know. I have thought all kinds of things."

"And for instance?"

"Well, that if you were a relation it would be different."

"If I were a relation?"

"If you were not a stranger. Then it would be the same for you as for me. Anything that is mine—would be yours, and you could do what you like. I couldn't prevent you—and you would have no responsibility."

She brought out this droll explanation with a little nervous rush, as if she were speaking words she had got by heart. They gave me an impression of subtlety and at first I failed to follow. But after a moment her face helped me to see further, and then a light came into my mind. It was embarrassing, and I bent my head over Jeffrey Aspern's portrait. What an odd expression was in his face! "Get out of it as you can, my dear fellow!" I put the picture into the pocket of my coat and said to Miss Tita, "Yes, I'll sell it for you. I sha'n't get a thousand pounds by any means, but I shall get something good."

She looked at me with tears in her eyes, but she seemed to try to smile as she remarked, "We can divide the money."

"No, no, it shall be all yours." Then I went on, "I think I know what your poor aunt wanted to say. She wanted to give directions that her papers should be buried with her."

Miss Tita appeared to consider this suggestion for a moment; after which she declared, with striking decision, "Oh no, she wouldn't have thought that safe!"

"It seems to me nothing could be safer."

"She had an idea that when people want to publish they are capable——" And she paused, blushing.

"Of violating a tomb? Mercy on us, what must she have thought of me!"

"She was not just, she was not generous!" Miss Tita cried with sudden passion.

The light that had come into my mind a moment before increased. "Ah, don't say that, for we *are* a dreadful race." Then I pursued, "If she left a will, that may give you some idea."

"I have found nothing of the sort—she destroyed it. She was very fond of me," Miss Tita added, incongruously. "She wanted me to be happy. And if any person should be kind to me—she wanted to speak of that."

I was almost awestricken at the astuteness with which the good lady found herself inspired, transparent astuteness as it was and sewn, as the phrase is, with white thread.[462] "Depend upon it she didn't want to make any provision that would be agreeable to me."

"No, not to you but to me. She knew I should like it if you could carry out your idea. Not because she cared for you but because she did think of me," Miss Tita went on, with her unexpected, persuasive volubility. "You could see them—you could use them." She stopped, seeing that I perceived the sense of that conditional—stopped long enough for me to give some sign which I did not give. She must have been conscious however that though my face showed the greatest embarrassment that was ever painted on a human countenance it was not set as a stone, it was also full of compassion. It was a comfort to me a long time afterwards to consider that she could not have seen in me the smallest symptom of disrespect. "I don't know what to do; I'm too tormented, I'm too ashamed!" she continued, with vehemence. Then turning away from me and burying her face in her hands she burst into a flood of tears. If she did not know what to do it may be imagined whether I did any better. I stood there dumb, watching her while her sobs resounded in the great empty hall. In a moment she was facing me again, with her streaming eyes. "I would give you everything—and she would understand, where she is—she would forgive me!"

"Ah, Miss Tita—ah, Miss Tita," I stammered, for all reply. I did not know what to do, as I say, but at a venture I made a wild, vague movement, in consequence of which I found myself at the door. I remember standing there and saying, "It wouldn't do—it wouldn't do!" pensively, awkwardly, grotesquely, while I looked away to the opposite end of the sala as if there were a beautiful view there. The next thing I remember is that I was downstairs and out of the house. My gondola was there and my gondolier, reclining on the cushions, sprang up as soon as he saw me. I jumped in and to his usual "*Dove commanda?*"[463] I replied, in a tone that made him stare, "Anywhere, anywhere; out into the lagoon!"

359

He rowed me away and I sat there prostrate, groaning softly to myself, with my hat pulled over my face.[464] What in the name of the preposterous did she mean if she did not mean to offer me her hand? That was the price—that was the price! And did she think I wanted it, poor deluded, infatuated, extravagant lady? My gondolier, behind me, must have seen my ears red as I wondered, sitting there under the fluttering *tenda,* with my hidden face, noticing nothing as we passed—wondered whether her delusion, her infatuation had been my own reckless work. Did she think I had made love to her, even to get the papers? I had not, I had not; I repeated that over to myself for an hour, for two hours, till I was wearied if not convinced. I don't know where my gondolier took me; we floated aimlessly about on the lagoon, with slow, rare strokes. At last I became conscious that we were near the Lido, far up, on the right hand, as you turn your back to Venice, and I made him put me ashore. I wanted to walk, to move, to shed some of my bewilderment. I crossed the narrow strip and got to the seabeach—I took my way toward Malamocco.[465] But presently I flung myself down again on the warm sand, in the breeze, on the coarse dry grass. It took it out of me to think I had been so much at fault, that I had unwittingly but none the less deplorably trifled. But I had not given her cause—distinctly I had not. I had said to Mrs. Prest that I would make love to her; but it had been a joke without consequences and I had never said it to Tita Bordereau. I had been as kind as possible, because I really liked her; but since when had that become a crime where a woman of such an age and such an appearance was concerned? I am far from remembering clearly the succession of events and feelings during this long day of confusion, which I spent entirely in wandering about, without going home, until late at night; it only comes back to me that there were moments when I pacified my conscience and others when I lashed it into pain. I did not laugh all day—that I do recollect; the case, however it might have struck others, seemed to me so little amusing. It would have been better perhaps for me to feel the comic side of it. At any rate, whether I had given cause or not it went without saying that I could not pay the price. I could not accept. I could not, for a bundle of tattered papers, marry a ridiculous, pathetic, provincial old woman. It was a proof that she did not think the idea would come to me, her having determined to suggest it herself in that practical, argumentative, heroic way, in which the timidity however had been so much more striking than the boldness that her reasons appeared to come first and her feelings afterward.

As the day went on I grew to wish that I had never heard of Aspern's relics, and I cursed the extravagant curiosity that had put John Cumnor on the scent of them. We had more than enough material without them and my predicament was the just punishment of that most fatal of human follies, our not having known when to stop. It was very well to say it was no predicament, that the way out was simple, that I had only to leave Venice by the first train in the morning, after writing a note to Miss Tita, to be placed in her hand as soon as I got clear of the house; for it was a strong sign that I was embarrassed that when I tried to make up the note in my mind in advance (I would put it on paper as soon as I got home, before going to bed), I could not think of anything but "How can I thank you for the rare confidence you have placed in me?" That would never do; it sounded exactly as if an acceptance were to follow. Of course I might go away without writing a word, but that would be brutal and my idea was still to exclude brutal solutions. As my confusion cooled I was lost in wonder at the importance I had attached to Miss Bordereau's crumpled scraps; the thought of them became odious to me and I was as vexed with the old witch for the superstition that had prevented her from destroying them as I was with myself for having already spent more money than I could afford in attempting to control their fate. I forget what I did, where I went after leaving the Lido and at what hour or with what recovery of composure I made my way back to my boat. I only know that in the afternoon, when the air was aglow with the sunset, I was standing before the church of Saints John and Paul[466] and looking up at the small square-jawed face of Bartolommeo Colleoni, the terrible *condottiere*[467] who sits so sturdily astride of his huge bronze horse, on the high pedestal on which Venetian gratitude maintains him. The statue is incomparable, the finest of all mounted figures, unless that of Marcus Aurelius, who rides benignant before the Roman Capitol,[468] be finer: but I was not thinking of that; I only found myself staring at the triumphant captain as if he had an oracle on his lips. The western light shines into all his grimness at that hour and makes it wonderfully personal. But he continued to look far over my head, at the red immersion of another day—he had seen so many go down into the lagoon through the centuries—and if he were thinking of battles and stratagems they were of a different quality from any I had to tell him of. He could not direct me what to do, gaze up at him as I might. Was it before this or after that I wandered about for an hour in the small canals, to the continued stupefaction of my gondolier, who had never seen me so restless and yet so void of a purpose and could extract from me no order but "Go any-where—everywhere—all over the place"? He reminded me that I had not lunched and expressed therefore respectfully the hope that I would dine earlier. He had had long periods of leisure during the day, when I had left the boat and rambled, so that I was not obliged to consider him, and I told him that that day, for a change, I would touch no meat. It was an effect of poor Miss Tita's proposal, not altogether auspicious, that I had quite lost my appetite. I don't know why it happened that on this occasion I was more than ever struck with that queer air of sociability, of cousinship and family life, which makes up half the expression of Venice. Without streets and vehicles, the uproar of wheels, the brutality of horses, and with its little winding ways where people crowd together, where voices sound as in the corridors of a house, where the human step circulates as if it skirted the angles of furniture and shoes never wear out, the place has the character of an immense collective apartment, in which Piazza San Marco is the most ornamented corner and palaces and churches, for the rest, play the part of great divans of repose, tables of entertainment, expanses of decoration. And somehow the splendid common domicile, familiar, domestic and res-onant, also resembles a theatre, with actors clicking over bridges and, in straggling processions, tripping along fondamentas.[469] As you sit in your gondola the footways that in certain parts edge the canals assume to the eye the importance of a stage, meeting it at the same angle, and the Venetian figures, moving to and fro against the battered scenery of their little houses of comedy, strike you as members of an endless dramatic troupe.[470]

I went to bed that night very tired, without being able to compose a let-ter to Miss Tita. Was this failure the reason why I became conscious the next morning as soon as I awoke of a determination to see the poor lady again the first moment she would receive me? That had something to do with it, but what had still more was the fact that during my sleep a very odd revulsion had taken place in my spirit. I found myself aware of this almost as soon as I opened my eyes; it made me jump out of my bed with the movement of a man who remembers that he has left the house-door ajar or a candle burning under a shelf. Was I still in time to save my goods? That question was in my heart; for what had now come to pass was that in the unconscious cerebration of sleep[471] I had swung back to a passionate appreciation of Miss Bordereau's papers. They were now more precious than ever and a kind of ferocity had come into my desire to possess them. The condition Miss Tita had attached to the possession of them no longer appeared an obstacle worth thinking of, and for an hour, that morning, my repentant imagination brushed it aside. It was absurd that I should be able to invent nothing; absurd to renounce so easily and turn away helpless from the idea that the only way to get hold of the papers was to unite myself to her for life. I would not unite myself and yet I would have them. I must add that by the time I sent down to ask if she would see me I had invented no alternative, though to do so I had had all the time that I was dressing. This failure was humiliating, yet what could the alternative be? Miss Tita sent back word that I might come; and as I descended the stairs and crossed the sala to her door—this time she received me in her aunt's forlorn parlour—I hoped she would not think my errand was to tell her I accepted her hand. She certainly would have made the day before the reflection that I declined it.

As soon as I came into the room I saw that she had drawn this inference, but I also saw something which had not been in my forecast. Poor Miss Tita's sense of her failure had produced an extraordinary alteration in her, but I had been too full of my literary concupiscence to think of that. Now I perceived it; I can scarcely tell how it startled me. She stood in the middle of the room with a face of mildness bent upon me, and her look of forgiveness, of absolution made her angelic. It beautified her; she was younger; she was not a ridiculous old woman. This optical trick gave her a sort of phantasmagoric brightness, and while I was still the victim of it I heard a whisper somewhere in the depths of my conscience: "Why not, after all—why not?" It seemed to me I was ready to pay the price. Still more distinctly however than the whisper I heard Miss Tita's own voice. I was so struck with the different effect she made upon me that at first I was not clearly aware of what she was saying; then I perceived she had bade me good-bye—she said something about hoping I should be very happy.

"Good-bye—good-bye?" I repeated, with an inflection interrogative and probably foolish.

I saw she did not feel the interrogation, she only heard the words; she had strung herself up to accepting our separation and they fell upon her ear as a proof. "Are you going to-day?" she asked. "But it doesn't matter, for whenever you go I shall not see you again. I don't want to." And she smiled strangely, with an infinite gentleness. She had never doubted that I had left her the day before in horror. How could she, since I had not come back before night to contradict, even as a simple form, such an idea? And now she had the force of soul[472]—Miss Tita with force of soul was a new conception—to smile at me in her humiliation.

"What shall you do—where shall you go?" I asked.

"Oh, I don't know. I have done the great thing. I have destroyed the papers."

"Destroyed them?" I faltered.

"Yes; what was I to keep them for? I burnt them last night, one by one, in the kitchen."

"One by one?" I repeated, mechanically.

"It took a long time—there were so many." The room seemed to go round me as she said this and a real darkness for a moment descended upon my eyes. When it passed Miss Tita was there still, but the transfiguration was over and she had changed back to a plain, dingy, elderly person. It was in this character she spoke as she said, "I can't stay with you longer, I can't;" and it was in this character that she turned her back upon me, as I had turned mine upon her twenty-four hours before, and moved to the door of her room. Here she did what I had not done when I quitted her—she paused long enough to give me one look. I have never forgotten it and I sometimes still suffer from it, though it was not resentful. No, there was no resentment, nothing hard or vindictive in poor Miss Tita; for when, later, I sent her in exchange for the portrait of Jeffrey Aspern a larger sum of money than I had hoped to be able to gather for her, writing to her that I had sold the picture, she kept it with thanks; she never sent it back. I wrote to her that I had sold the picture, but I admitted to Mrs. Prest, at the time (I met her in London, in the autumn), that it hangs above my writing-table. When I look at it my chagrin at the loss of the letters becomes almost intolerable.

The Liar

I

The train was half an hour late and the drive from the station longer than he had supposed, so that when he reached the house its inmates had dispersed to dress for dinner and he was conducted straight to his room. The curtains were drawn in this asylum, the candles were lighted, the fire was bright, and when the servant had quickly put out his clothes the comfortable little place became suggestive—seemed to promise a pleasant house, a various party, talks, acquaintances, affinities, to say nothing of very good cheer. He was too occupied with his profession to pay many country visits, but he had heard people who had more time for them speak of establishments where "they do you very well." He foresaw that the proprietors of Stayes[473] would do him very well. In his bedroom at a country house he always looked first at the books on the shelf and the prints on the walls; he considered that these things gave a sort of measure of the culture and even of the character of his hosts. Though he had but little time to devote to them on this occasion a cursory inspection assured him that if the literature, as usual, was mainly American and humorous[474] the art consisted neither of the water-colour studies of the children nor of "goody" engravings.[475] The walls were adorned with old-fashioned lithographs, principally portraits of country gentlemen with high collars and riding gloves: this suggested—and it was encouraging—that the tradition of portraiture was held in esteem. There was the customary novel of Mr. Le Fanu,[476] for the bedside; the ideal reading in a country house for the hours after midnight. Oliver Lyon could scarcely forbear beginning it while he buttoned his shirt.

Perhaps that is why he not only found every one assembled in the hall when he went down, but perceived from the way the move to dinner was instantly made that they had been waiting for him. There was no delay, to introduce him to a lady, for he went out in a group of unmatched men, without this appendage. The men, straggling behind, sidled and edged as usual at the door of the dining-room, and the *dénouement* of this little comedy was that he came to his place last of all. This made him think that he was in a sufficiently distinguished company, for if he had been humiliated (which he was not), he could not have consoled himself with the reflection that such a fate was natural to an obscure, struggling young artist. He could no longer think of himself as very young, alas, and if his position was not so brilliant as it ought to be he could no longer justify it by calling it a struggle. He was something of a celebrity and he was apparently in a society of celebrities. This idea added to the curiosity with which he looked up and down the long table as he settled himself in his place.

It was a numerous party—five and twenty people; rather an odd occasion to have proposed to him, as he thought. He would not be surrounded by the quiet that ministers to good work; however, it had never interfered with his work to see the spectacle of human life before him in the intervals. And though he did not know it, it was never quiet at Stayes. When he was working well he found himself in that happy state—the happiest of all for an artist—in which things in general contribute to the particular idea and fall in with it, help it on and justify it, so that he feels for the hour as if nothing in the world can happen to him, even if it come in the guise of disaster or suffering, that will not be an enhancement of his subject. Moreover there was an exhilaration (he had felt it before) in the rapid change of scene—the jump, in the dusk of the afternoon, from foggy London[477] and his familiar studio to a centre of festivity in the middle of Hertfordshire[478] and a drama half acted, a drama of pretty women and noted men and wonderful orchids in silver jars. He observed as a not unimportant fact that one of the pretty women was beside him: a gentleman sat on his other hand. But he went into his neighbours little as yet: he was busy looking out for Sir David, whom he had never seen and about whom he naturally was curious.

Evidently, however, Sir David was not at dinner, a circumstance sufficiently explained by the other circumstance which constituted our friend's principal knowledge of him—his being ninety years of age. Oliver Lyon had looked forward with great pleasure to the chance of painting a nonagenarian, and though the old man's absence from table was something of a disappointment (it was an opportunity the less to observe him before going to work), it seemed a sign that he was rather a sacred and perhaps therefore an impressive relic. Lyon looked at his son with the greater interest—wondered whether the glazed bloom of his cheek had been transmitted from Sir David.

That would be jolly to paint, in the old man—the withered ruddiness[479] of a winter apple, especially if the eye were still alive and the white hair carried out the frosty look. Arthur Ashmore's hair had a midsummer glow, but Lyon was glad his commission had been to delineate the father rather than the son, in spite of his never having seen the one and of the other being seated there before him now in the happy expansion of liberal hospitality.

Arthur Ashmore was a fresh-coloured, thick-necked English gentleman, but he was just not a subject; he might have been a farmer and he might have been a banker: you could scarcely paint him in characters. His wife did not make up the amount; she was a large, bright, negative woman, who had the same air as her husband of being somehow tremendously new; a sort of appearance of fresh varnish (Lyon could scarcely tell whether it came from her complexion or from her clothes), so that one felt she ought to sit in a gilt frame, suggesting reference to a catalogue or a price-list. It was as if she were already rather a bad though expensive portrait, knocked off by an eminent hand, and Lyon had no wish to copy that work. The pretty woman on his right was engaged with her neighbour and the gentleman on his other side looked shrinking and scared, so that he had time to lose himself in his favourite diversion of watching face after face. This amusement gave him the greatest pleasure he knew, and he often thought it a mercy that the human mask[480] did interest him and that it was not less vivid than it was (sometimes it ran its success in this line very close) since he was to make his living by reproducing it. Even if Arthur Ashmore would not be inspiring to paint (a certain anxiety rose in him lest if he should make a hit with her father-in-law Mrs. Arthur should take it into her head that he had now proved himself worthy to *aborder* her husband); even if he had looked a little less like a page (fine as to print and margin) without punctuation, he would still be a refreshing, iridescent surface. But the gentleman four persons off—what was he? Would he be a subject, or was his face only the legible door-plate of his identity, burnished with punctual washing and shaving—the least thing that was decent that you would know him by?

This face arrested Oliver Lyon: it struck him at first as very handsome. The gentleman might still be called young, and his features were regular: he had a plentiful, fair moustache that curled up at the ends, a brilliant, gallant, almost adventurous air, and a big shining breastpin in the middle of his shirt. He appeared a fine satisfied soul, and Lyon perceived that wherever he rested his friendly eye there fell an influence as pleasant as the September sun—as if he could make grapes and pears or even human affection ripen by looking at them. What was odd in him was a certain mixture of the correct and the extravagant: as if he were an adventurer imitating a gentleman with rare perfection or a gentleman who had taken a fancy to go about with hidden arms. He might have been a dethroned prince or the war-correspondent of a newspaper: he represented both enterprise and tradition, good manners and bad taste. Lyon at length fell into conversation with the lady beside him—they dispensed, as he had had to dispense at dinner-parties before, with an introduction—by asking who this personage might be.

"Oh, he's Colonel Capadose,[481] don't you know?" Lyon didn't know and he asked for further information. His neighbour had a sociable manner and evidently was accustomed to quick transitions; she turned from her other interlocutor with a methodical air, as a good cook lifts the cover of the next saucepan. "He has been a great deal in India[482]—isn't he rather celebrated?" she inquired. Lyon confessed he had never heard of him, and she went on, "Well, perhaps he isn't; but he says he is, and if you think it, that's just the same, isn't it?"

"If you *think* it?"

"I mean if he thinks it—that's just as good, I suppose."

"Do you mean that he says that which is not?"[483]

"Oh dear, no—because I never know. He is exceedingly clever and amusing—quite the cleverest person in the house, unless indeed you are more so. But that I can't tell yet, can I? I only know about the people I know; I think that's celebrity enough!"

"Enough for them?"

"Oh, I see you're clever. Enough for me! But I have heard of you," the lady went on. I know your pictures; I admire them. But I don't think you look like them."

"They are mostly portraits," Lyon said; "and what I usually try for is not my own resemblance."

"I see what you mean. But they have much more colour. And now you are going to do some one here?"

"I have been invited to do Sir David. I'm rather disappointed at not seeing him this evening."

"Oh, he goes to bed at some unnatural hour—eight o'clock or something of that sort. You know he's rather an old mummy."[484]

"An old mummy?" Oliver Lyon repeated.

"I mean he wears half a dozen waistcoats, and that sort of thing. He's always cold."

"I have never seen him and never seen any portrait or photograph of him," Lyon said. "I'm surprised at his never having had anything done—at their waiting all these years."

"Ah, that's because he was afraid, you know; it was a kind of superstition. He was sure that if anything were done he would die directly afterwards. He has only consented to-day."

"He's ready to die then?"

"Oh, now he's so old he doesn't care."

"Well, I hope I shan't kill him," said Lyon. "It was rather unnatural in his son to send for me."

"Oh, they have nothing to gain—everything is theirs already!" his companion rejoined, as if she took this speech quite literally. Her talkativeness was systematic—she fraternised as seriously as she might have played whist.[485] "They do as they like—they fill the house with people—they have *carte blanche*!"

"I see—but there's still the title."

"Yes, but what is it?"

Our artist broke into laughter at this, whereat his companion stared. Before he had recovered himself she was scouring the plain with her other neighbour. The gentleman on his left at last risked an observation, and they had some fragmentary talk. This personage played his part with difficulty: he uttered a remark as a lady fires a pistol, looking the other way. To catch the ball Lyon had to bend his ear, and this movement led to his observing a handsome creature who was seated on the same side, beyond his interlocutor. Her profile was presented to him and at first he was only struck with its beauty; then it produced an impression still more agreeable—a sense of undimmed remembrance and intimate association. He had not recognised her on the instant only because he had so little expected to see her there; he had not seen her anywhere for so long, and no news of her ever came to him. She was often in his thoughts, but she had passed out of his life. He thought of her twice a week; that may be called often in relation to a person one has not seen for twelve years. The moment after he recognised her he felt how true it was that it was only she who could look like that; of the most charming head in the world (and this lady had it) there could never be a replica. She was leaning forward a little; she remained in profile, apparently listening to some one on the other side of her. She was listening, but she was also looking, and after a moment Lyon followed the direction of her eyes. They rested upon the gentleman who had been described to him as Colonel Capadose—rested, as it appeared to him, with a kind of habitual, visible complacency. This was not strange, for the Colonel was unmistakably formed to attract the sympathetic gaze of woman; but Lyon was slightly disappointed that she could let *him* look at her so long without giving him a glance. There was nothing between them to-day and he had no rights, but she must have known he was coming (it was of course not such a tremendous event, but she could not have been staying in the house without hearing of it), and it was not natural that that should absolutely fail to affect her.

She was looking at Colonel Capadose as if she were in love with him—a queer accident for the proudest, most reserved of women. But doubtless it was all right, if her husband liked it or didn't notice it: he had heard indefinitely, years before, that she was married, and he took for granted (as he had not heard that she had become a widow) the presence of the happy man on whom she had conferred what she had refused to *him*, the poor art-student at Munich.[486] Colonel Capadose appeared to be aware of nothing, and this circumstance, incongruously enough, rather irritated Lyon than gratified him. Suddenly the lady turned her head, showing her full face to our hero. He was so prepared with a greeting that he instantly smiled, as a shaken jug overflows; but she gave him no response, turned away again and sank back in her chair. All that her face said in that instant was, "You see I'm as handsome as ever." To which he mentally subjoined, "Yes, and as much good it does me!" He asked the young man beside him if he knew who that beautiful being was—the fifth person beyond him. The young man leaned forward, considered and then said, "I think she's Mrs. Capadose."

"Do you mean his wife—that fellow's?" And Lyon indicated the subject of the information given him by his other neighbour.

"Oh, is *he* Mr. Capadose?" said the young man, who appeared very vague. He admitted his vagueness and explained it by saying that there were so many people and he had come only the day before. What was definite to Lyon was that Mrs. Capadose was in love with her husband; so that he wished more than ever that he had married her.

"She's very faithful," he found himself saying three minutes later to the lady on his right. He added that he meant Mrs. Capadose.

"Ah, you know her then?"

"I knew her once upon a time—when I was living abroad."

"Why then were you asking me about her husband?"

"Precisely for that reason. She married after that—I didn't even know her present name."

"How then do you know it now?"

"This gentleman has just told me—he appears to know."

"I didn't know he knew anything," said the lady, glancing forward.

"I don't think he knows anything but that."

"Then you have found out for yourself that she is faithful. What do you mean by that?"

"Ah, you mustn't question me—I want to question you," Lyon said. "How do you all like her here?"

"You ask too much! I can only speak for myself. I think she's hard."

"That's only because she's honest and straightforward."

"Do you mean I like people in proportion as they deceive?"

"I think we all do, so long as we don't find them out," Lyon said. "And then there's something in her face—a sort of Roman type, in spite of her having such an English eye. In fact she's English down to the ground; but her complexion, her low forehead and that beautiful close little wave in her dark hair make her look like a glorified *contadina*!"

"Yes, and she always sticks pins and daggers into her head,[487] to increase that effect. I must say I like her husband better: he is so clever."

"Well, when I knew her there was no comparison that could injure her. She was altogether the most delightful thing in Munich."

"In Munich?"

"Her people lived there; they were not rich—in pursuit of economy in fact, and Munich was very cheap. Her father was the younger son of some noble house; he had married a second time and had a lot of little mouths to feed. She was the child of the first wife and she didn't like her stepmother, but she was charming to her little brothers and sisters. I once made a sketch of her as Werther's Charlotte,[488] cutting bread and butter while they clustered all round her. All the artists in the place were in love with her but she wouldn't look at "the likes" of us. She was too proud—I grant you that; but she wasn't stuck up nor young ladyish; she was simple and frank and kind about it. She used to remind me of Thackeray's Ethel Newcome.[489] She told me she must marry well: it was the one thing she could do for her family. I suppose you would say that she has married well."

"She told *you*?" smiled Lyon's neighbour.

"Oh, of course I proposed to her too. But she evidently thinks so herself!" he added.

When the ladies left the table the host as usual bade the gentlemen draw together, so that Lyon found himself opposite to Colonel Capadose. The conversation was mainly about the "run," for it had apparently been a great day in the hunting-field. Most of the gentlemen communicated their adventures and opinions, but Colonel Capadose's pleasant voice was the most audible in the chorus. It was a bright and fresh but masculine organ, just such a voice as, to Lyon's sense, such a "fine man" ought to have had. It appeared from his remarks that he was a very straight rider, which was also very much what Lyon would have expected. Not that he swaggered, for his allusions were very quietly and casually made; but they were all to dangerous experiments and close shaves. Lyon perceived after a little that the attention paid by the company to the Colonel's remarks was not in direct relation to the interest they seemed to offer; the result of which was that the speaker, who noticed that he at least was listening, began to treat him as his particular auditor and to fix his eyes on him as he talked. Lyon had nothing to do but to look sympathetic and assent—Colonel Capadose appeared to take so much sympathy and assent for granted. A neighbouring squire had had an accident; he had come a cropper[490] in an awkward place—just at the finish—with consequences that looked grave. He had struck his head; he remained insensible, up to the last accounts: there had evidently been concussion of the brain. There was some exchange of views as to his recovery—how soon it would take place or whether it would take place at all; which led the Colonel to confide to our artist across the table that *he* shouldn't despair of a fellow even if he didn't come round for weeks—for weeks and weeks and weeks—for months, almost for years. He leaned forward; Lyon leaned forward to listen, and

Colonel Capadose mentioned that he knew from personal experience that there was really no limit to the time one might lie unconscious without being any the worse for it. It had happened to him in Ireland, years before; he had been pitched out of a dogcart, had turned a sheer somersault and landed on his head. They thought he was dead, but he wasn't; they carried him first to the nearest cabin, where he lay for some days with the pigs, and then to an inn in a neighbouring town—it was a near thing they didn't put him under ground. He had been completely insensible—without a ray of recognition of any human thing—for three whole months; had not a glimmer of consciousness of any blessed thing. It was touch and go[491] to that degree that they couldn't come near him, they couldn't feed him, they could scarcely look at him. Then one day he had opened his eyes—as fit as a flea!

"I give you my honour it had done me good—it rested my brain." He appeared to intimate that with an intelligence so active as his these periods of repose were providential. Lyon thought his story very striking, but he wanted to ask him whether he had not shammed a little—not in relating it, but in keeping so quiet. He hesitated however, in time, to imply a doubt—he was so impressed with the tone in which Colonel Capadose said that it was the turn of a hair that they hadn't buried him alive. That had happened to a friend of his in India—a fellow who was supposed to have died of jungle fever[492]—they clapped him into a coffin. He was going on to recite the further fate of this unfortunate gentleman when Mr. Ashmore made a move and every one got up to adjourn to the drawing-room. Lyon noticed that by this time no one was heeding what his new friend said to him. They came round on either side of the table and met while the gentlemen dawdled before going out.

"And do you mean that your friend was literally buried alive?" asked Lyon, in some suspense.

Colonel Capadose looked at him a moment, as if he had already lost the thread of the conversation. Then his face brightened—and when it brightened it was doubly handsome. "Upon my soul he was chucked into the ground!"

"And was he left there?"

"He was left there till I came and hauled him out."

"*You* came?"

"I dreamed about him—it's the most extraordinary story: I heard him calling to me in the night. I took upon myself to dig him up. You know there are people in India—a kind of beastly race, the ghouls[493]—who violate graves. I had a sort of presentiment that they would get at him first. I rode straight, I can tell you; and, by Jove, a couple of them had just broken ground! Crack—crack, from a couple of barrels, and they showed me their heels, as you may believe. Would you credit that I took him out myself? The air brought him to and he was none the worse. He has got his pension—he came home the other day; he would do anything for me."

"He called to you in the night?" said Lyon, much startled.

"That's the interesting point. Now *what was it*? It wasn't his ghost, because he wasn't dead. It wasn't himself, because he couldn't. It was something or other! You see India's a strange country—there's an element of the mysterious: the air is full of things you can't explain."

They passed out of the dining-room, and Colonel Capadose, who went among the first, was separated from Lyon; but a minute later, before they reached the drawing-room, he joined him again. "Ashmore tells me who you are. Of course I have often heard of you—I'm very glad to make your acquaintance; my wife used to know you."

"I'm glad she remembers me. I recognised her at dinner and I was afraid she didn't."

"Ah, I daresay she was ashamed," said the Colonel, with indulgent humour.

"Ashamed of me?" Lyon replied, in the same key.

"Wasn't there something about a picture? Yes; you painted her portrait."

"Many times," said the artist; "and she may very well have been ashamed of what I made of her."

"Well, I wasn't, my dear sir; it was the sight of that picture, which you were so good as to present to her, that made me first fall in love with her."

"Do you mean that one with the children—cutting bread and butter?"

"Bread and butter? Bless me, no—vine leaves and a leopard skin—a kind of Bacchante."[494]

"Ah, yes," said Lyon; "I remember. It was the first decent portrait I painted. I should be curious to see it to-day."

"Don't ask her to show it to you—she'll be mortified!" the Colonel exclaimed.

"Mortified?"

"We parted with it—in the most disinterested manner," he laughed. "An old friend of my wife's—her family had known him intimately when they lived in Germany—took the most extraordinary fancy to it: the Grand Duke of Silberstadt-Schreckenstein,[495] don't you know? He came out to Bombay while we were there and he spotted your picture (you know he's one of the greatest collectors in Europe), and made such eyes at it that, upon my word—it happened to be his birthday—she told him he might have it, to get rid of him. He was perfectly enchanted—but we miss the picture."

"It is very good of you," Lyon said. "If it's in a great collection—a work of my incompetent youth—I am infinitely honoured."

"Oh, he has got it in one of his castles; I don't know which—you know he has so many. He sent us, before he left India—to return the compliment— a magnificent old vase."

"That was more than the thing was worth," Lyon remarked.

Colonel Capadose gave no heed to this observation; he seemed to be thinking of something. After a moment he said, "If you'll come and see us in town she'll show you the vase." And as they passed into the drawing-room he gave the artist a friendly propulsion. "Go and speak to her; there she is— she'll be delighted."

Oliver Lyon took but a few steps into the wide saloon; he stood there a moment looking at the bright composition of the lamplit group of fair women, the single figures, the great setting of white and gold, the panels of old damask, in the centre of each of which was a single celebrated picture. There was a subdued lustre in the scene and an air as of the shining trains of dresses tumbled over the carpet. At the furthest end of the room sat Mrs. Capadose, rather isolated; she was on a small sofa, with an empty place beside her. Lyon could not flatter himself she had been keeping it for him; her failure to respond to his recognition at table contradicted that, but he felt an extreme desire to go and occupy it. Moreover he had her husband's sanction; so he crossed the room, stepping over the tails of gowns, and stood before his old friend.

"I hope you don't mean to repudiate me," he said.

She looked up at him with an expression of unalloyed pleasure. "I am so glad to see you. I was delighted when I heard you were coming."

"I tried to get a smile from you at dinner—but I couldn't."

"I didn't see—I didn't understand. Besides, I hate smirking and telegraphing. Also I'm very shy—you won't have forgotten that. Now we can communicate comfortably." And she made a better place for him on the little sofa. He sat down and they had a talk that he enjoyed, while the reason for which he used to like her so came back to him, as well as a good deal of the very same old liking. She was still the least spoiled beauty he had ever seen, with an absence of coquetry or any insinuating art that seemed almost like an omitted faculty; there were moments when she struck her interlocutor as some fine creature from an asylum—a surprising deaf-mute or one of the operative blind. Her noble pagan head[496] gave her privileges that she neglected, and when people were admiring her brow she was wondering whether there were a good fire in her bedroom. She was simple, kind and good; inexpressive but not inhuman or stupid. Now and again she dropped something that had a sifted, selected air—the sound of an impression at first hand. She had no imagination, but she had added up her feelings, some of her reflections, about life. Lyon talked of the old days in Munich, reminded her of incidents, pleasures and pains, asked her about her father and the others; and she told him in return that she was so impressed with his own fame, his brilliant position in the world, that she had not felt very sure he would speak to her or that his little sign at table was meant for her. This was plainly a perfectly truthful speech—she was incapable of any other—and he was affected by such humility on the part of a woman whose grand line was unique. Her father was dead; one of her brothers was in the navy and the other on a ranch in America; two of her sisters were married and the youngest was just coming out and very pretty. She didn't mention her stepmother. She asked him about his own personal history and he said that the principal thing that had happened to him was that he had never married.[497]

"Oh, you ought to," she answered. "It's the best thing."

"I like that—from you!" he returned.

"Why not from me? I am very happy."

"That's just why I can't be. It's cruel of you to praise your state. But I have had the pleasure of making the acquaintance of your husband. We had a good bit of talk in the other room."

"You must know him better—you must know him really well," said Mrs. Capadose.

"I am sure that the further you go the more you find. But he makes a fine show, too."

She rested her good gray eyes on Lyon. "Don't you think he's handsome?"

"Handsome and clever and entertaining. You see I'm generous."

"Yes; you must know him well," Mrs. Capadose repeated.

"He has seen a great deal of life," said her companion.

"Yes, we have been in so many places. You must see my little girl. She is nine years old—she's too beautiful."

"You must bring her to my studio some day—I should like to paint her."

"Ah, don't speak of that," said Mrs. Capadose. "It reminds me of something so distressing."

"I hope you don't mean when *you* used to sit to me—though that may well have bored you."

"It's not what you did—it's what we have done. It's a confession I must make—it's a weight on my mind! I mean about that beautiful picture you gave me—it used to be so much admired. When you come to see me in London (I count on your doing that very soon) I shall see you looking all round. I can't tell you I keep it in my own room because I love it so, for the simple reason——" And she paused a moment.

"Because you can't tell wicked lies," said Lyon.

"No, I can't. So before you ask for it——"

"Oh, I know you parted with it—the blow has already fallen," Lyon interrupted.

"Ah then, you have heard? I was sure you would! But do you know what we got for it? Two hundred pounds."[498]

"You might have got much more," said Lyon, smiling.

"That seemed a great deal at the time. We were in want of the money—it was a good while ago, when we first married. Our means were very small then, but fortunately that has changed rather for the better. We had the chance; it really seemed a big sum, and I am afraid we jumped at it. My husband had expectations which have partly come into effect, so that now we do well enough. But meanwhile the picture went."

"Fortunately the original remained. But do you mean that two hundred was the value of the vase?" Lyon asked.

"Of the vase?'

"The beautiful old Indian vase—the Grand Duke's offering."

"The Grand Duke?"

"What's his name?—Silberstadt-Schreckenstein. Your husband mentioned the transaction."

"Oh, my husband," said Mrs. Capadose; and Lyon saw that she coloured a little.

Not to add to her embarrassment, but to clear up the ambiguity, which he perceived the next moment he had better have left alone, he went on: "He tells me it's now in his collection."

"In the Grand Duke's? Ah, you know its reputation? I believe it contains treasures." She was bewildered, but she recovered herself, and Lyon made the mental reflection that for some reason which would seem good when he knew it the husband and the wife had prepared different versions of the same incident. It was true that he did not exactly see Everina Brant[499] preparing a version; that was not her line of old, and indeed it was not in her eyes to-day. At any rate they both had the matter too much on their conscience. He changed the subject, said Mrs. Capadose must really bring the little girl. He sat with her some time longer and thought—perhaps it was only a fancy—that she was rather absent, as if she were annoyed at their having been even for a moment at cross-purposes. This did not prevent him from saying to her at the last, just as the ladies began to gather themselves together to go to bed: "You seem much impressed, from what you say, with my renown and my prosperity, and you are so good as greatly to exaggerate them. Would you have married me if you had known that I was destined to success?"

"I did know it."

"Well, I didn't."

"You were too modest."

"You didn't think so when I proposed to you."

"Well, if I had married you I couldn't have married *him*—and he's so nice," Mrs. Capadose said. Lyon knew she thought it—he had learned that at dinner—but it vexed him a little to hear her say it. The gentleman designated by the pronoun came up, amid the prolonged hand-shaking for goodnight, and Mrs. Capadose remarked to her husband as she turned away, "He wants to paint Amy."

"Ah, she's a charming child, a most interesting little creature," the Colonel said to Lyon.

"She does the most remarkable things."

Mrs. Capadose stopped, in the rustling procession that followed the hostess out of the room.

"Don't tell him, please don't," she said.

"Don't tell him what?"

"Why, what she does. Let him find out for himself." And she passed on.

"She thinks I swagger about the child—that I bore people," said the Colonel. "I hope you smoke." He appeared ten minutes later in the smoking-room, in a brilliant equipment, a suit of crimson foulard[500] covered with little white spots. He gratified Lyon's eye, made him feel that the modern age has its splendour too and its opportunities for costume. If his wife was an antique he was a fine specimen of the period of colour: he might have passed for a Venetian of the sixteenth century.[501] They were a remarkable couple, Lyon thought, and as he looked at the Colonel standing in bright erectness before the chimney-piece while he emitted great smoke-puffs he did not wonder that Everina could not regret she had not married *him*. All the gentlemen collected at Stayes were not smokers and some of them had gone to bed. Colonel Capadose remarked that there probably would be a smallish muster, they had had such a hard day's work. That was the worst of a hunting house—the men were so sleepy after dinner; it was devilish stupid for the ladies, even for those who hunted themselves—for women were so extraordinary, they never showed it. But most fellows revived under the stimulating influences of the smoking-room, and some of them, in this confidence, would turn up yet. Some of the grounds of their confidence— not all of them—might have been seen in a cluster of glasses and bottles on a table near the fire, which made the great salver and its contents twinkle sociably. The others lurked as yet in various improper corners of the minds of the most loquacious. Lyon was alone with Colonel Capadose for some moments before their companions, in varied eccentricities of uniform, straggled in, and he perceived that this wonderful man had but little loss of vital tissue to repair.

They talked about the house, Lyon having noticed an oddity of construction in the smoking-room; and the Colonel explained that it consisted of two distinct parts, one of which was of very great antiquity. They were two complete houses in short, the old one and the new, each of great extent and each very fine in its way. The two formed together an enormous structure—Lyon must make a point of going all over it. The modern portion had been erected by the old man when he bought the property; oh yes, he had bought it, forty years before—it hadn't been in the family: there hadn't been any particular family for it to be in. He had had the good taste not to spoil the original house—he had not touched it beyond what was just necessary for joining it on. It was very curious indeed—a most irregular, rambling, mysterious pile, where they every now and then discovered a walled-up room or a secret staircase. To his mind it was essentially gloomy, however; even the modern additions, splendid as they were, failed to make it cheerful. There was some story about a skeleton having been found years before, during some repairs under a stone slab of the floor of one of the passages; but the family were rather shy of its being talked about. The place they were in was of course in the old part, which contained after all some of the best rooms: he had an idea it had been the primitive kitchen, half modernised at some intermediate period.

"My room is in the old part too then—I'm very glad," Lyon said. "It's very comfortable and contains all the latest conveniences, but I observed the depth of the recess of the door and the evident antiquity of the corridor and staircase—the first short one—after I came out. That panelled corridor is admirable; it looks as if it stretched away, in its brown dimness (the lamps didn't seem to me to make much impression on it), for half a mile."

"Oh, don't go to the end of it!" exclaimed the Colonel, smiling.

"Does it lead to the haunted room?"[502] Lyon asked. His companion looked at him a moment.

"Ah, you know about that?"

"No, I don't speak from knowledge, only from hope. I have never had any luck—I have never stayed in a dangerous house. The places I go to are always as safe as Charing Cross.[503] I want to see—whatever there is, the regular thing. *Is* there a ghost here?"

"Of course there is—a rattling good one."

"And have you seen him?"

"Oh, don't ask me what *I've* seen—I should tax your credulity. I don't like to talk of these things. But there are two or three as bad—that is, as good!—rooms as you'll find anywhere."

"Do you mean in my corridor?" Lyon asked.

"I believe the worst is at the far end. But you would be ill-advised to sleep there."

"Ill-advised?"

"Until you've finished your job. You'll get letters of importance the next morning, and you'll take the 10.20."

"Do you mean I will invent a pretext for running away?"

"Unless you are braver than almost any one has ever been. They don't often put people to sleep there, but sometimes the house is so crowded that they have to. The same thing always happens—ill-concealed agitation at the breakfast-table and letters of the greatest importance. Of course it's a bachelor's room, and my wife and I are at the other end of the house. But we saw the comedy three days ago—the day after we got here. A young fellow had been put there—I forget his name—the house was so full; and the usual consequence followed. Letters at breakfast—an awfully queer face—an urgent call to town—so very sorry his visit was cut short. Ashmore and his wife looked at each other, and off the poor devil went."

"Ah, that wouldn't suit me; I must paint my picture," said Lyon. "But do they mind your speaking of it? Some people who have a good ghost are very proud of it, you know."

What answer Colonel Capadose was on the point of making to this inquiry our hero was not to learn, for at that moment their host had walked into the room accompanied by three or four gentlemen. Lyon was conscious that he was partly answered by the Colonel's not going on with the subject. This however on the other hand was rendered natural by the fact that one of the gentlemen appealed to him for an opinion on a point under discussion, something to do with the everlasting history of the day's run. To Lyon himself Mr. Ashmore began to talk, expressing his regret at having had so little direct conversation with him as yet. The topic that suggested itself was naturally that most closely connected with the motive of the artist's visit. Lyon remarked that it was a great disadvantage to him not to have had some preliminary acquaintance with Sir David—in most cases he found that so important. But the present sitter was so far advanced in life that there was doubtless no time to lose. "Oh, I can tell you all about him," said Mr. Ashmore; and for half an hour he told him a good deal. It was very interesting as well as very eulogistic, and Lyon could see that he was a very nice old man, to have endeared himself so to a son who was evidently not a gusher. At last he got up—he said he must go to bed if he wished to be fresh for his work in the morning. To which his host replied, "Then you must take your candle; the lights are out; I don't keep my servants up."

In a moment Lyon had his glimmering taper in hand, and as he was leaving the room (he did not disturb the others with a good-night; they were absorbed in the lemon-squeezer and the soda-water cork) he remembered other occasions on which he had made his way to bed alone through a darkened country-house; such occasions had not been rare, for he was almost always the first to leave the smoking-room. If he had not stayed in houses conspicuously haunted he had, none the less (having the artistic temperament), sometimes found the great black halls and staircases rather "creepy":[504] there had been often a sinister effect, to his imagination, in the sound of his tread in the long passages or the way the winter moon peeped into tall windows on landings. It occurred to him that if houses without super-natural pretensions could look so wicked at night, the old corridors of Stayes would certainly give him a sensation. He didn't know whether the proprietors were sensitive; very often, as he had said to Colonel Capadose, people enjoyed the impeachment. What determined him to speak, with a certain sense of the risk, was the impression that the Colonel told queer stories. As he had his hand on the door he said to Arthur Ashmore, "I hope I shan't meet any ghosts."

"Any ghosts?"

"You ought to have some—in this fine old part."

"We do our best, but *que voulez-vous?*" said Mr. Ashmore. "I don't think they like the hot-water pipes."

"They remind them too much of their own climate? But haven't you a haunted room—at the end of my passage?"

"Oh, there are stories—we try to keep them up."

"I should like very much to sleep there," Lyon said.

"Well, you can move there to-morrow if you like."

"Perhaps I had better wait till I have done my work."

"Very good; but you won't work there, you know. My father will sit to you in his own apartments."

"Oh, it isn't that; it's the fear of running away, like that gentleman three days ago."

"Three days ago? What gentleman?" Mr. Ashmore asked.

"The one who got urgent letters at breakfast and fled by the 10.20. Did he stand more than one night?"

"I don't know what you are talking about. There was no such gentleman—three days ago."

"Ah, so much the better," said Lyon, nodding good-night and departing. He took his course, as he remembered it, with his wavering candle, and, though he encountered a great many gruesome objects, safely reached the passage out of which his room opened. In the complete darkness it seemed to stretch away still further, but he followed it, for the curiosity of the thing, to the end. He passed several doors with the name of the room painted upon them, but he found nothing else. He was tempted to try the last door—to look into the room of evil fame; but he reflected that this would be indiscreet, since Colonel Capadose handled the brush—as a *raconteur*—with such freedom. There might be a ghost and there might not; but the Colonel himself, he inclined to think, was the most mystifying figure in the house.

II

Lyon found Sir David Ashmore a capital subject and a very comfortable sitter into the bargain. Moreover he was a very agreeable old man, tremendously puckered but not in the least dim; and he wore exactly the furred dressing-gown that Lyon would have chosen. He was proud of his age but ashamed of his infirmities, which however he greatly exaggerated and which did not prevent him from sitting there as submissive as if portraiture in oils had been a branch of surgery. He demolished the legend of his having feared the operation would be fatal, giving an explanation which pleased our friend much better. He held that a gentleman should be painted but once in his life—that it was eager and fatuous to be hung up all over the place. That was good for women, who made a pretty wall-pattern; but the male face didn't lend itself to decorative repetition. The proper time for the likeness was at the last, when the whole man was there—you got the totality of his experience. Lyon could not reply that that period was not a real compendium—you had to allow so for leakage; for there had been no crack in Sir David's crystallisation. He spoke of his portrait as a plain map of the country, to be consulted by his children in a case of uncertainty. A proper map could be drawn up only when the country had been travelled. He gave Lyon his mornings, till luncheon, and they talked of many things, not neglecting, as a stimulus to gossip, the people in the house. Now that he did not "go out," as he said, he saw much less of the visitors at Stayes: people came and went whom he knew nothing about, and he liked to hear Lyon describe them. The artist sketched with a fine point and did not caricature, and it usually befell that when Sir David did not know the sons and daughters he had known the fathers and mothers. He was one of those terrible old gentlemen who are a repository of antecedents. But in the case of the Capadose family, at whom they arrived by an easy stage, his knowledge embraced two, or even three, generations. General Capadose was an old crony, and he remembered his father before him. The general was rather a smart soldier, but in private life of too speculative a turn—always sneaking into the City to put his money into some rotten thing. He married a girl who brought him something and they had half a dozen children. He scarcely knew what had become of the rest of them, except that one was in the Church and had found preferment—wasn't he Dean of Rockingham?[505] Clement, the fellow who was at Stayes, had some military talent; he had served in the East, he had married a pretty girl. He had been at Eton[506] with his son, and he used to come to Stayes in his holidays. Lately, coming back to England, he had turned up with his wife again; that was before he—the old man—had been put to grass.[507] He was a taking dog, but he had a monstrous foible.

"A monstrous foible?" said Lyon.

"He's a thumping liar."

Lyon's brush stopped short, while he repeated, for somehow the formula startled him, "A thumping liar?"

"You are very lucky not to have found it out."

'Well, I confess I have noticed a romantic tinge——"

"Oh, it isn't always romantic. He'll lie about the time of day, about the name of his hatter. It appears there are people like that."

"Well, they are precious scoundrels," Lyon declared, his voice trembling a little with the thought of what Everina Brant had done with herself.

"Oh, not always," said the old man. "This fellow isn't in the least a scoundrel. There is no harm in him and no bad intention; he doesn't steal nor cheat nor gamble nor drink; he's very kind—he sticks to his wife, is fond of his children. He simply can't give you a straight answer."

"Then everything he told me last night, I suppose, was mendacious: he delivered himself of a series of the stiffest statements. They stuck, when I tried to swallow them, but I never thought of so simple an explanation."

"No doubt he was in the vein," Sir David went on. "It's a natural peculiarity—as you might limp or stutter or be left-handed. I believe it comes and goes, like intermittent fever. My son tells me that his friends usually understand it and don't haul him up—for the sake of his wife."

"Oh, his wife—his wife!" Lyon murmured, painting fast.

"I daresay she's used to it."

"Never in the world, Sir David. How can she be used to it?"

"Why, my dear sir, when a woman's fond!—And don't they mostly handle the long bow[508] themselves? They are connoisseurs—they have a sympathy for a fellow performer."

Lyon was silent a moment; he had no ground for denying that Mrs. Capadose was attached to her husband. But after a little he rejoined: "Oh, not this one! I knew her years ago—before her marriage; knew her well and admired her. She was as clear as a bell."

"I like her very much," Sir David said, "but I have seen her back him up."

Lyon considered Sir David for a moment, not in the light of a model. "Are you very sure?"

The old man hesitated; then he answered, smiling, "You're in love with her."

"Very likely. God knows I used to be!"

"She must help him out—she can't expose him."

"She can hold her tongue," Lyon remarked.

"Well, before you probably she will."

"That's what I am curious to see." And Lyon added, privately, "Mercy on us, what he must have made of her!" He kept this reflection to himself, for he considered that he had sufficiently betrayed his state of mind with regard to Mrs. Capadose. None the less it occupied him now immensely, the question of how such a woman would arrange herself in such a predicament. He watched her with an interest deeply quickened when he mingled with the company; he had had his own troubles in life, but he had rarely been so anxious about anything as he was now to see what the loyalty of a wife and the infection of an example would have made of an absolutely truthful mind. Oh, he held it as immutably established that whatever other women might be prone to do she, of old, had been perfectly incapable of a deviation. Even if she had not been too simple to deceive she would have been too proud; and if she had not had too much conscience she would have had too little eagerness. It was the last thing she would have endured or condoned—the particular thing she would not have forgiven. Did she sit in torment while her husband turned his somersaults, or was she now too so perverse that she thought it a fine thing to be striking at the expense of one's honour? It would have taken a wondrous alchemy—working backwards, as it were—to produce this latter result. Besides these two alternatives (that she suffered tortures in silence and that she was so much in love that her husband's humiliating idiosyncrasy seemed to her only an added richness—a proof of life and talent), there was still the possibility that she had not found him out, that she took his false pieces at his own valuation. A little reflection rendered this hypothesis untenable; it was too evident that the account he gave of things must repeatedly have contradicted her own knowledge. Within an hour or two of his meeting them Lyon had seen her confronted with that perfectly gratuitous invention about the profit they had made off his early picture. Even then indeed she had not, so far as he could see, smarted, and—but for the present he could only contemplate the case.

Even if it had not been interfused, through his uneradicated tenderness for Mrs. Capadose, with an element of suspense, the question would still have presented itself to him as a very curious problem, for he had not painted portraits during so many years without becoming something of a psychologist. His inquiry was limited for the moment to the opportunity that the following three days might yield, as the Colonel and his wife were going on to another house. It fixed itself largely of course upon the Colonel too—this gentleman was such a rare anomaly. Moreover it had to go on very quickly. Lyon was too scrupulous to ask other people what they thought of the business—he was too afraid of exposing the woman he once had loved. It was probable also that light would come to him from the talk of the rest of the company: the Colonel's queer habit, both as it affected his own situation and as it affected his wife, would be a familiar theme in any house in which he was in the habit of staying. Lyon had not observed in the circles in which he visited any marked abstention from comment on the singularities of their members. It interfered with his progress that the Colonel hunted all day, while he plied his brushes and chatted with Sir David; but a Sunday intervened and that partly made it up. Mrs. Capadose fortunately did not hunt, and when his work was over she was not inaccessible. He took a couple of longish walks with her (she was fond of that), and beguiled her at tea into a friendly nook in the hall. Regard her as he might he could not make out to himself that she was consumed by a hidden shame; the sense of being married to a man whose word had no worth was not, in her spirit, so far as he could guess, the canker within the rose.[509] Her mind appeared to have nothing on it but its own placid frankness, and when he looked into her eyes (deeply, as he occasionally permitted himself to do), they had no uncomfortable consciousness. He talked to her again and still again of the dear old days—reminded her of things that he had not (before this reunion) the least idea that he remembered. Then he spoke to her of her husband, praised his appearance, his talent for conversation, professed to have felt a quick friendship for him and asked (with an inward audacity at which he trembled a little) what manner of man he was. "What manner?" said Mrs. Capadose. "Dear me, how can one describe one's husband? I like him very much."

"Ah, you have told me that already!" Lyon exclaimed, with exaggerated ruefulness.

"Then why do you ask me again?" She added in a moment, as if she were so happy that she could afford to take pity on him, "He is everything that's good and kind. He's a soldier—and a gentleman—and a dear! He hasn't a fault. And he has great ability."

"Yes; he strikes one as having great ability. But of course I can't think him a dear."

"I don't care what you think him!" said Mrs. Capadose, looking, it seemed to him, as she smiled, handsomer than he had ever seen her. She was either deeply cynical or still more deeply impenetrable, and he had little prospect of winning from her the intimation that he longed for—some hint that it had come over her that after all she had better have married a man who was not a by-word for the most contemptible, the least heroic, of vices. Had she not seen—had she not felt—the smile go round when her husband executed some especially characteristic conversational caper? How could a woman of her quality endure that day after day, year after year, except by her quality's altering? But he would believe in the alteration[510] only when he should have heard *her* lie. He was fascinated by his problem and yet half exasperated, and he asked himself all kinds of questions. Did she not lie, after all, when she let his falsehoods pass without a protest? Was not her life a perpetual complicity, and did she not aid and abet him by the simple fact that she was not disgusted with him? Then again perhaps she was disgusted and it was the mere desperation of her pride that had given her an inscrutable mask. Perhaps she protested in private, passionately; perhaps every night, in their own apartments, after the day's hideous performance, she made him the most scorching scene. But if such scenes were of no avail and he took no more trouble to cure himself, how could she regard him, and after so many years of marriage too, with the perfectly artless complacency that Lyon had surprised in her in the course of the first day's dinner? If our friend had not been in love with her he could have taken the diverting view of the Colonel's

388

delinquencies; but as it was they turned to the tragical in his mind, even while he had a sense that his solicitude might also have been laughed at.

The observation of these three days showed him that if Capadose was an abundant he was not a malignant liar and that his fine faculty exercised itself mainly on subjects of small direct importance. "He is the liar platonic,"[511] he said to himself; "he is disinterested, he doesn't operate with a hope of gain or with a desire to injure. It is art for art[512] and he is prompted by the love of beauty. He has an inner vision of what might have been, of what ought to be, and he helps on the good cause by the simple substitution of a *nuance*. He paints, as it were, and so do I!" His manifestations had a considerable variety, but a family likeness ran through them, which consisted mainly of their singular futility. It was this that made them offensive; they encumbered the field of conversation, took up valuable space, converted it into a sort of brilliant sun-shot fog. For a fib told under pressure a convenient place can usually be found, as for a person who presents himself with an author's order[513] at the first night of a play. But the supererogatory lie is the gentleman without a voucher or a ticket who accommodates himself with a stool in the passage.

In one particular Lyon acquitted his successful rival; it had puzzled him that irrepressible as he was he had not got into a mess in the service. But he perceived that he respected the service—that august institution was sacred from his depredations. Moreover though there was a great deal of swagger in his talk it was, oddly enough, rarely swagger about his military exploits. He had a passion for the chase, he had followed it in far countries and some of his finest flowers were reminiscences of lonely danger and escape. The more solitary the scene the bigger of course the flower. A new acquaintance, with the Colonel, always received the tribute of a bouquet: that generalisation Lyon very promptly made. And this extraordinary man had inconsistencies and unexpected lapses—lapses into flat veracity. Lyon recognised what Sir David had told him, that his aberrations came in fits or periods—that he would sometimes keep the truce of God for a month at a time. The muse breathed upon him at her pleasure; she often left him alone. He would neglect the finest openings and then set sail in the teeth of the breeze. As a general thing he affirmed the false rather than denied the true; yet this proportion was sometimes strikingly reversed. Very often he joined in the laugh against himself—he admitted that he was trying it on and that a good many of his anecdotes had an experimental character. Still he never completely retracted nor retreated—he dived and came up in another place. Lyon divined that he was capable at intervals of defending his position with violence, but only when it was a very bad one. Then he might easily be dangerous—then he would hit out and become calumnious. Such occasions would test his wife's equanimity—Lyon would have liked to see her there. In the smoking-room and elsewhere the company, so far as it was composed of his familiars, had an hilarious protest always at hand; but among the men who had known him long his rich tone was an old story, so old that they had ceased to talk about it, and Lyon did not care, as I have said, to elicit the judgment of those who might have shared his own surprise.

The oddest thing of all was that neither surprise nor familiarity prevented the Colonel's being liked; his largest drafts on a sceptical attention passed for an overflow of life and gaiety—almost of good looks. He was fond of portraying his bravery and used a very big brush, and yet he was unmistakably brave. He was a capital rider and shot, in spite of his fund of anecdote illustrating these accomplishments: in short he was very nearly as clever and his career had been very nearly as wonderful as he pretended. His best quality however remained that indiscriminate sociability which took interest and credulity for granted and about which he bragged least. It made him cheap, it made him even in a manner vulgar; but it was so contagious that his listener was more or less on his side as against the probabilities. It was a private reflection of Oliver Lyon's that he not only lied but made one feel one's self a bit of a liar, even (or especially) if one contradicted him. In the evening, at dinner and afterwards, our friend watched his wife's face to see if some faint shade or spasm never passed over it. But she showed nothing, and the wonder was that when he spoke she almost always listened. That was her pride: she wished not to be even suspected of not facing the music. Lyon had none the less an importunate vision of a veiled figure coming the next day in the dusk to certain places to repair the Colonel's ravages, as the relatives of kleptomaniacs punctually call at the shops that have suffered from their pilferings.

"I must apologise, of course it wasn't true, I hope no harm is done, it is only his incorrigible——" Oh, to hear that woman's voice in that deep abasement! Lyon had no nefarious plan, no conscious wish to practise upon her shame or her loyalty; but he did say to himself that he should like to bring her round to feel that there would have been more dignity in a union with a certain other person. He even dreamed of the hour when, with a burning face, she would ask *him* not to take it up. Then he should be almost consoled—he would be magnanimous.

Lyon finished his picture and took his departure, after having worked in a glow of interest which made him believe in his success, until he found he had pleased every one, especially Mr. and Mrs. Ashmore, when he began to be sceptical. The party at any rate changed: Colonel and Mrs. Capadose went their way. He was able to say to himself however that his separation from the lady was not so much an end as a beginning, and he called on her soon after his return to town. She had told him the hours she was at home—she seemed to like him. If she liked him why had she not married him or at any rate why was she not sorry she had not? If she was sorry she concealed it too well. Lyon's curiosity on this point may strike the reader as fatuous, but something must be allowed to a disappointed man. He did not ask much after all; not that she should love him to-day or that she should allow him to tell her that he loved her, but only that she should give him some sign she was sorry. Instead of this, for the present, she contented herself with exhibiting her little daughter to him. The child was beautiful and had the prettiest eyes of innocence he had ever seen: which did not prevent him from wondering whether she told horrid fibs. This idea gave him much entertainment—the picture of the anxiety with which her mother would watch as she grew older for the symptoms of heredity. That was a nice occupation for Everina Brant! Did she lie to the child herself, about her father—was that necessary, when she pressed her daughter to her bosom, to cover up his tracks? Did he control himself before the little girl—so that she might not hear him say things she knew to be other than he said? Lyon doubted this: his genius would be too strong for him, and the only safety for the child would be in her being too stupid to analyse. One couldn't judge yet—she was too young. If she should grow up clever she would be sure to tread in his steps—a delightful improvement in her mother's situation! Her little face was not shifty, but neither was her father's big one: so that proved nothing.

Lyon reminded his friends more than once of their promise that Amy should sit to him, and it was only a question of his leisure. The desire grew in him to paint the Colonel also—an operation from which he promised himself a rich private satisfaction. He would draw him out, he would set

him up in that totality about which he had talked with Sir David, and none
but the initiated would know. They, however, would rank the picture high,
and it would be indeed six rows deep[514]—a masterpiece of subtle characterization, of legitimate treachery. He had dreamed for years of producing
something which should bear the stamp of the psychologist as well as of the
painter, and here at last was his subject. It was a pity it was not better, but
that was not *his* fault. It was his impression that already no one drew the
Colonel out more than he, and he did it not only by instinct but on a plan.
There were moments when he was almost frightened at the success of his
plan—the poor gentleman went so terribly far. He would pull up some day,
look at Lyon between the eyes—guess he was being played upon—which
would lead to his wife's guessing it also. Not that Lyon cared much for that
however, so long as she failed to suppose (as she must) that *she* was a part of
his joke. He formed such a habit now of going to see her of a Sunday afternoon that he was angry when she went out of town. This occurred often,
as the couple were great visitors and the Colonel was always looking for
sport, which he liked best when it could be had at other people's expense.
Lyon would have supposed that this sort of life was particularly little to her
taste, for he had an idea that it was in country-houses that her husband
came out strongest. To let him go off without her, not to see him expose
himself—that ought properly to have been a relief and a luxury to her. She
told Lyon in fact that she preferred staying at home; but she neglected to
say it was because in other people's houses she was on the rack: the reason she gave was that she liked so to be with the child. It was not perhaps
criminal to draw such a bow,[515] but it was vulgar: poor Lyon was delighted
when he arrived at that formula. Certainly some day too he would cross
the line—he would become a noxious animal. Yes, in the meantime he was
vulgar, in spite of his talents, his fine person, his impunity. Twice, by exception, toward the end of the winter, when he left town for a few days' hunting,
his wife remained at home. Lyon had not yet reached the point of asking
himself whether the desire not to miss two of his visits had something to
do with her immobility. That inquiry would perhaps have been more in
place later, when he began to paint the child and she always came with her.
But it was not in her to give the wrong name, to pretend, and Lyon could
see that she had the maternal passion, in spite of the bad blood in the little
girl's veins.

She came inveterately, though Lyon multiplied the sittings: Amy was never entrusted to the governess or the maid. He had knocked off poor old Sir David in ten days, but the portrait of the simple-faced child bade fair to stretch over into the following year. He asked for sitting after sitting, and it would have struck any one who might have witnessed the affair that he was wearing the little girl out. He knew better however and Mrs. Capadose also knew: they were present together at the long intermissions he gave her, when she left her pose and roamed about the great studio, amusing herself with its curiosities, playing with the old draperies and costumes, having unlimited leave to handle. Then her mother and Mr. Lyon sat and talked; he laid aside his brushes and leaned back in his chair; he always gave her tea. What Mrs. Capadose did not know was the way that during these weeks he neglected other orders: women have no faculty of imagination with regard to a man's work beyond a vague idea that it doesn't matter. In fact Lyon put off everything and made several celebrities wait. There were half-hours of silence, when he plied his brushes, during which he was mainly conscious that Everina was sitting there. She easily fell into that if he did not insist on talking, and she was not embarrassed nor bored by it. Sometimes she took up a book—there were plenty of them about; sometimes, a little way off, in her chair, she watched his progress (though without in the least advising or correcting), as if she cared for every stroke that represented her daughter. These strokes were occasionally a little wild; he was thinking so much more of his heart than of his hand. He was not more embarrassed than she was, but he was agitated: it was as if in the sittings (for the child, too, was beautifully quiet) something was growing between them or had already grown—a tacit confidence, an inexpressible secret. He felt it that way; but after all he could not be sure that she did. What he wanted her to do for him was very little; it was not even to confess that she was unhappy. He would be superabundantly gratified if she should simply let him know, even by a silent sign, that she recognised that with him her life would have been finer. Sometimes he guessed—his presumption went so far—that he might see this sign in her contentedly sitting there.

III

At last he broached the question of painting the Colonel: it was now very late in the season—there would be little time before the general dispersal.[516] He said they must make the most of it; the great thing was to begin; then in the autumn, with the resumption of their London life, they could go forward. Mrs. Capadose objected to this that she really could not consent to accept another present of such value. Lyon had given her the portrait of herself of old, and he had seen what they had had the indelicacy to do with it. Now he had offered her this beautiful memorial of the child—beautiful it would evidently be when it was finished, if he could ever satisfy himself; a precious possession which they would cherish for ever. But his generosity must stop there—they couldn't be so tremendously 'beholden' to him. They couldn't order the picture—of course he would understand that, without her explaining: it was a luxury beyond their reach, for they knew the great prices he received. Besides, what had they ever done—what above all had *she* ever done, that he should overload them with benefits? No, he was too dreadfully good; it was really good that Clement should sit. Lyon listened to her without protest, without interruption, while he bent forward at his work, and at last he said: "Well, if you won't take it why not let him sit for me for my own pleasure and profit? Let it be a favour, a service I ask of him. It will do me a lot of good to paint him and the picture will remain in my hands."

"How will it do you a lot of good?" Mrs. Capadose asked.

"Why, he's such a rare model—such an interesting subject. He has such an expressive face. It will teach me no end of things."

"Expressive of what?" said Mrs. Capadose.

"Why, of his nature."

"And do you want to paint his nature?"

"Of course I do. That's what a great portrait gives you, and I shall make the Colonel's a great one. It will put me up high. So you see my request is eminently interested."

"How can you be higher than you are?"

"Oh, I'm insatiable! Do consent," said Lyon.

"Well, his nature is very noble," Mrs. Capadose remarked.

"Ah, trust me, I shall bring it out!" Lyon exclaimed, feeling a little ashamed of himself.

Mrs. Capadose said before she went away that her husband would probably comply with his invitation, but she added, "Nothing would induce me to let you pry into *me* that way!"

"Oh, you," Lyon laughed—"I could do you in the dark!"

The Colonel shortly afterwards placed his leisure at the painter's disposal and by the end of July had paid him several visits. Lyon was disappointed neither in the quality of his sitter nor in the degree to which he himself rose to the occasion; he felt really confident that he should produce a fine thing. He was in the humour; he was charmed with his *motif* and deeply interested in his problem. The only point that troubled him was the idea that when he should send his picture to the Academy[517] he should not be able to give the title, for the catalogue, simply as "The Liar." However, it little mattered, for he had now determined that this character should be perceptible even to the meanest intelligence—as overtopping as it had become to his own sense in the living man. As he saw nothing else in the Colonel to-day, so he gave himself up to the joy of painting nothing else. How he did it he could not have told you, but it seemed to him that the mystery of how to do it was revealed to him afresh every time he sat down to his work. It was in the eyes and it was in the mouth, it was in every line of the face and every fact of the attitude, in the indentation of the chin, in the way the hair was planted, the moustache was twisted, the smile came and went, the breath rose and fell. It was in the way he looked out at a bamboozled world in short—the way he would look out for ever. There were half a dozen portraits in Europe that Lyon rated as supreme; he regarded them as immortal, for they were as perfectly preserved as they were consummately painted. It was to this small exemplary group that he aspired to annex the canvas on which he was now engaged. One of the productions that helped to compose it was the magnificent Moroni of the National Gallery[518]—the young tailor, in the white jacket, at his board with his shears. The Colonel was not a tailor, nor was Moroni's model, unlike many tailors, a liar; but as regards the masterly clearness with which the individual should be rendered his work would be on the same line as that. He had to a degree in which he had rarely had it before the satisfaction of feeling life grow and grow under his brush. The Colonel, as it turned out, liked to sit and he liked to talk while he was sitting: which was very fortunate, as his talk largely constituted Lyon's inspiration. Lyon put into practice that idea of drawing him out which he had been nursing for so many weeks: he could not possibly have been in a better relation to him for the purpose. He encouraged, beguiled, excited him, manifested an unfathomable credulity, and his only interruptions were when the Colonel did not respond to it. He had his intermissions, his hours of sterility, and then Lyon felt that the picture also languished. The higher his companion soared, the more gyrations he executed, in the blue, the better he painted; he couldn't make his flights long enough. He lashed him on when he flagged; his apprehension became great at moments that the Colonel would discover his game. But he never did, apparently; he basked and expanded in the fine steady light of the painter's attention. In this way the picture grew very fast; it was astonishing what a short business it was, compared with the little girl's. By the fifth of August it was pretty well finished: that was the date of the last sitting the Colonel was for the present able to give, as he was leaving town the next day with his wife. Lyon was amply content—he saw his way so clear: he should be able to do at his convenience what remained, with or without his friend's attendance. At any rate, as there was no hurry, he would let the thing stand over till his own return to London, in November, when he would come back to it with a fresh eye. On the Colonel's asking him if his wife might come and see it the next day, if she should find a minute—this was so greatly her desire— Lyon begged as a special favour that she would wait: he was so far from satisfied as yet. This was the repetition of a proposal Mrs. Capadose had made on the occasion of his last visit to her, and he had then asked for a delay—declared that he was by no means content. He was really delighted, and he was again a little ashamed of himself.

By the fifth of August the weather was very warm, and on that day, while the Colonel sat straight and gossiped, Lyon opened for the sake of ventilation a little subsidiary door which led directly from his studio into the garden and sometimes served as an entrance and an exit for models and for visitors of the humbler sort, and as a passage for canvases, frames, packing-boxes, and other professional gear. The main entrance was through the house and his own apartments, and this approach had the charming effect of admitting you first to a high gallery, from which a crooked picturesque staircase enabled you to descend to the wide, decorated, encumbered room. The view of this room, beneath them, with all its artistic ingenuities and the objects of value that Lyon had collected, never failed to elicit exclamations of delight from persons stepping into the gallery. The way from the garden was plainer and at once more practicable and more private. Lyon's domain, in St. John's Wood,[519] was not vast, but when the door stood open of a summer's day it offered a glimpse of flowers and trees, you smelt something sweet and you heard the birds. On this particular morning the side-door had been found convenient by an unannounced visitor, a youngish woman who stood in the room before the Colonel perceived her and whom he perceived before she was noticed by his friend. She was very quiet, and she looked from one of the men to the other. "Oh, dear, here's another!" Lyon exclaimed, as soon as his eyes rested on her. She belonged, in fact, to a somewhat importunate class—the model in search of employment, and she explained that she had ventured to come straight in, that way, because very often when she went to call upon gentlemen the servants played her tricks, turned her off and wouldn't take in her name.

"But how did you get into the garden?" Lyon asked.

"The gate was open, sir—the servants' gate. The butcher's cart was there."

"The butcher ought to have closed it," said Lyon.

"Then you don't require me, sir?" the lady continued.

Lyon went on with his painting; he had given her a sharp look at first, but now his eyes lighted on her no more. The Colonel, however, examined her with interest. She was a person of whom you could scarcely say whether being young she looked old or old she looked young; she had at any rate evidently rounded several of the corners of life and had a face that was rosy but that somehow failed to suggest freshness. Nevertheless she was pretty and even looked as if at one time she might have sat for the complexion. She wore a hat with many feathers, a dress with many bugles,[520] long black gloves, encircled with silver bracelets, and very bad shoes. There was something about her that was not exactly of the governess out of place nor completely of the actress seeking an engagement, but that savoured of an interrupted profession or even of a blighted career. She was rather soiled and tarnished, and after she had been in the room a few moments the air, or at any rate the nostril, became acquainted with a certain alcoholic waft. She was unpractised in the *h*,[521] and when Lyon at last thanked her and said he didn't want her—he was doing nothing for which she could be useful—she replied with rather a wounded manner, "Well, you know you *'ave* 'ad me!"

"I don't remember you," Lyon answered.

"Well, I daresay the people that saw your pictures do! I haven't much time, but I thought I would look in."

"I am much obliged to you."

"If ever you should require me, if you just send me a postcard——"

"I never send postcards," said Lyon.

"Oh well, I should value a private letter! Anything to Miss Geraldine, Mortimer Terrace Mews, Notting 'ill[522]—"

"Very good; I'll remember," said Lyon. Miss Geraldine lingered. "I thought I'd just stop, on the chance."

"I'm afraid I can't hold out hopes, I'm so busy with portraits," Lyon continued.

"Yes; I see you are. I wish I was in the gentleman's place."

"I'm afraid in that case it wouldn't look like me," said the Colonel, laughing.

"Oh, of course it couldn't compare—it wouldn't be so 'andsome! But I do hate them portraits!" Miss Geraldine declared. "It's so much bread out of our mouths."

"Well, there are many who can't paint them," Lyon suggested, comfortingly.

"Oh, I've sat to the very first—and only to the first! There's many that couldn't do anything without me."

"I'm glad you're in such demand." Lyon was beginning to be bored and he added that he wouldn't detain her—he would send for her in case of need.

"Very well; remember it's the Mews[523]—more's the pity! You don't sit so well as *us*!" Miss Geraldine pursued, looking at the Colonel.

"If *you* should require me, sir——"

"You put him out; you embarrass him," said Lyon.

"Embarrass him, oh gracious!" the visitor cried, with a laugh which diffused a fragrance.

"Perhaps send postcards, eh?" she went on to the Colonel; and then she retreated with a wavering step. She passed out into the garden as she had come.

"How very dreadful—she's drunk!" said Lyon. He was painting hard, but he looked up, checking himself: Miss Geraldine, in the open doorway, had thrust back her head.

"Yes, I do hate it—that sort of thing!" she cried with an explosion of mirth which confirmed Lyon's declaration. And then she disappeared.

"What sort of thing—what does she mean?" the Colonel asked.

"Oh, my painting you, when I might be painting her."

"And have you ever painted her?"

"Never in the world; I have never seen her. She is quite mistaken."

The Colonel was silent a moment; then he remarked, "She was very pretty—ten years ago."

"I daresay, but she's quite ruined. For me the least drop too much spoils them; I shouldn't care for her at all."

"My dear fellow, she's not a model," said the Colonel, laughing.

"To-day, no doubt, she's not worthy of the name; but she has been one."

"*Jamais de la vie!* That's all a pretext."

"A pretext?" Lyon pricked up his ears—he began to wonder what was coming now.

"She didn't want you—she wanted me."

"I noticed she paid you some attention. What does she want of you?"

"Oh, to do me an ill turn. She hates me—lots of women do. She's watching me—she follows me."

Lyon leaned back in his chair—he didn't believe a word of this. He was all the more delighted with it and with the Colonel's bright, candid manner. The story had bloomed, fragrant, on the spot. "My dear Colonel!" he murmured, with friendly interest and commiseration.

"I was annoyed when she came in—but I wasn't startled," his sitter continued.

"You concealed it very well, if you were."

"Ah, when one has been through what I have! To-day however I confess I was half prepared. I have seen her hanging about—she knows my movements. She was near my house this morning—she must have followed me.'

"But who is she then—with such a *toupet?*"

"Yes, she has that," said the Colonel; "but as you observe she was primed. Still, there was a cheek, as they say, in her coming in. Oh, she's a bad one! She isn't a model and she never was; no doubt she has known some of those women and picked up their form.[524] She had hold of a friend of mine ten years ago—a stupid young gander who might have been left to be plucked but whom I was obliged to take an interest in for family reasons. It's a long story—I had really forgotten all about it. She's thirty-seven if she's a day. I cut in and made him get rid of her—I sent her about her business. She knew it was me she had to thank. She has never forgiven me—I think she's off her head. Her name isn't Geraldine at all and I doubt very much if that's her address."

"Ah, what is her name?" Lyon asked, most attentive. The details always began to multiply, to abound, when once his companion was well launched—they flowed forth in battalions.

"It's Pearson—Harriet Pearson; but she used to call herself Grenadine—wasn't that a rum appellation? Grenadine—Geraldine—the jump was easy." Lyon was charmed with the promptitude of this response, and his interlocutor went on: "I hadn't thought of her for years—I had quite lost sight of her. I don't know what her idea is, but practically she's harmless. As I came in I thought I saw her a little way up the road. She must have found out I come here and have arrived before me. I daresay—or rather I'm sure—she is waiting for me there now."

"Hadn't you better have protection?" Lyon asked, laughing.

"The best protection is five shillings—I'm willing to go that length. Unless indeed she has a bottle of vitriol.[525] But they only throw vitriol on the men who have deceived them, and I never deceived her—I told her the first time I saw her that it wouldn't do. Oh, if she's there we'll walk a little way together and talk it over and, as I say, I'll go as far as five shillings."

"Well," said Lyon, "I'll contribute another five." He felt that this was little to pay for his entertainment.

That entertainment was interrupted however for the time by the Colonel's departure. Lyon hoped for a letter recounting the fictive sequel; but apparently his brilliant sitter did not operate with the pen. At any rate he left town without writing; they had taken a rendezvous for three months later. Oliver Lyon always passed the holidays in the same way; during the first weeks he paid a visit to his elder brother, the happy possessor, in the south of England, of a rambling old house with formal gardens, in which he delighted, and then he went abroad—usually to Italy or Spain. This year he carried out his custom after taking a last look at his all but finished work and feeling as nearly pleased with it as he ever felt with the translation of the idea by the hand—always, as it seemed to him, a pitiful compromise. One yellow afternoon, in the country, as he was smoking his pipe on one of the old terraces he was seized with the desire to see it again and do two or three things more to it: he had thought of it so often while he lounged there. The impulse was too strong to be dismissed, and though he expected to return to town in the course of another week he was unable to face the delay. To look at the picture for five minutes would be enough—it would clear up certain questions which hummed in his brain; so that the next morning, to give himself this luxury, he took the train for London. He sent no word in advance; he would lunch at his club and probably return into Sussex by the 5.45.

In St. John's Wood the tide of human life flows at no time very fast, and in the first days of September Lyon found unmitigated emptiness in the straight sunny roads where the little plastered garden-walls, with their incommunicative doors, looked slightly Oriental. There was definite stillness in his own house, to which he admitted himself by his pass-key, having a theory that it was well sometimes to take servants unprepared. The good woman who was mainly in charge and who cumulated the functions of cook and housekeeper was, however, quickly summoned by his step, and (he cultivated frankness of intercourse with his domestics) received him without the confusion of surprise. He told her that she needn't mind the place being not quite straight, he had only come up for a few hours—he should be busy in the studio. To this she replied that he was just in time to see a lady and a gentleman who were there at the moment—they had arrived five minutes before. She had told them he was away from home but they said it was all right; they only wanted to look at a picture and would be very careful of everything. "I hope it is all right, sir," the housekeeper concluded. "The gentleman says he's a sitter and he gave me his name—rather an odd name; I think it's military. The lady's a very fine lady, sir; at any rate there they are."

"Oh, it's all right," Lyon said, the identity of his visitors being clear. The good woman couldn't know, for she usually had little to do with the comings and goings; his man, who showed people in and out, had accompanied him to the country. He was a good deal surprised at Mrs. Capadose's having come to see her husband's portrait when she knew that the artist himself wished her to forbear; but it was a familiar truth to him that she was a woman of a high spirit. Besides, perhaps the lady was not Mrs. Capadose; the Colonel might have brought some inquisitive friend, a person who wanted a portrait of *her* husband. What were they doing in town, at any rate, at that moment? Lyon made his way to the studio with a certain curiosity; he wondered vaguely what his friends were "up to." He pushed aside the curtain that hung in the door of communication—the door opening upon the gallery which it had been found convenient to construct at the time the studio was added to the house. When I say he pushed it aside I should amend my phrase; he laid his hand upon it, but at that moment he was arrested by a very singular sound. It came from the floor of the room beneath him and it startled him extremely, consisting apparently as it did of a passionate wail—a sort of smothered shriek—accompanied by a violent burst of tears. Oliver Lyon listened intently a moment, and then he passed out upon the balcony, which was covered with an old thick Moorish rug.[526] His step was noiseless, though he had not endeavoured to make it so, and after that first instant he found himself profiting irresistibly by the accident of his not having attracted the attention of the two persons in the studio, who were some twenty feet below him. In truth they were so deeply and so strangely engaged that their unconsciousness of observation was explained. The scene that took place before Lyon's eyes was one of the most extraordinary they had ever rested upon. Delicacy and the failure to comprehend kept him at first from interrupting it—for what he saw was a woman who had thrown herself in a flood of tears on her companion's bosom—and these influences were succeeded after a minute (the minutes were very few and very short) by a definite motive which presently had the force to make him step back behind the curtain. I may add that it also had the force to make him avail himself for further contemplation of a crevice formed by his gathering together the two halves of the *portière*. He was perfectly aware of what he was about—he was for the moment an eavesdropper, a spy; but he was also aware that a very odd business, in which his confidence had been trifled with, was going forward, and that if in a measure it didn't concern him, in a measure it very definitely did. His observation, his reflections, accomplished themselves in a flash.

His visitors were in the middle of the room; Mrs. Capadose clung to her husband, weeping, sobbing as if her heart would break. Her distress was horrible to Oliver Lyon but his astonishment was greater than his horror when he heard the Colonel respond to it by the words, vehemently uttered, "Damn him, damn him, damn him!" What in the world had happened? why was she sobbing and whom was he damning? What had happened, Lyon saw the next instant, was that the Colonel had finally rummaged out his unfinished portrait (he knew the corner where the artist usually placed it, out of the way, with its face to the wall) and had set it up before his wife on an empty easel. She had looked at it a few moments and then—apparently—what she saw in it had produced an explosion of dismay and resentment. She was too busy sobbing and the Colonel was too busy holding her and reiterating his objurgation, to look round or look up. The scene was so unexpected to Lyon that he could not take it, on the spot, as a proof of the triumph of his hand—of a tremendous hit: he could only wonder what on earth was the matter. The idea of the triumph came a little later. Yet he could see the portrait from where he stood; he was startled with its look of life—he had not thought it so masterly. Mrs. Capadose flung herself away from her husband—she dropped into the nearest chair, buried her face in her arms, leaning on a table. Her weeping suddenly ceased to be audible, but she shuddered there as if she were overwhelmed with anguish and shame. Her husband remained a moment staring at the picture; then he went to her, bent over her, took hold of her again, soothed her. "What is it, darling, what the devil is it?" he demanded.

Lyon heard her answer. "It's cruel—oh, it's too cruel!"

"Damn him—damn him—damn him!" the Colonel repeated.

"It's all there—it's all there!" Mrs. Capadose went on.

"Hang it, what's all there?"

"Everything there oughtn't to be—everything he has seen—it's too dreadful!"

"Everything he has seen? Why, ain't I a good-looking fellow? He has made me rather handsome."

Mrs. Capadose had sprung up again; she had darted another glance at the painted betrayal. "Handsome? Hideous, hideous! Not that—never, never!"

"Not *what*, in heaven's name?" the Colonel almost shouted. Lyon could see his flushed, bewildered face.

"What he has made of you—what you know! *He* knows—he has seen. Every one will know—every one will see. Fancy that thing in the Academy!"

"You're going wild, darling; but if you hate it so it needn't go."

403

"Oh, he'll send it —it's so good! Come away—come away!' Mrs. Capadose wailed, seizing her husband.

"It's so good?" the poor man cried.

"Come away—come away," she only repeated; and she turned toward the staircase that ascended to the gallery.

"Not that way—not through the house, in the state you're in," Lyon heard the Colonel object. "This way—we can pass," he added; and he drew his wife to the small door that opened into the garden. It was bolted, but he pushed the bolt and opened the door. She passed out quickly, but he stood there looking back into the room. "Wait for me a moment!" he cried out to her; and with an excited stride he re-entered the studio. He came up to the picture again, and again he stood looking at it. "Damn him—damn him —damn him!" he broke out once more. It was not clear to Lyon whether this malediction had for its object the original or the painter of the portrait. The Colonel turned away and moved rapidly about the room, as if he were looking for something; Lyon was unable for the instant to guess his intention. Then the artist said to himself, below his breath, "He's going to do it a harm!" His first impulse was to rush down and stop him; but he paused, with the sound of Everina Brant's sobs still in his ears. The Colonel found what he was looking for—found it among some odds and ends on a small table and rushed back with it to the easel. At one and the same moment Lyon perceived that the object he had seized was a small Eastern dagger and that he had plunged it into the canvas. He seemed animated by a sudden fury, for with extreme vigour of hand he dragged the instrument down[527] (Lyon knew it to have no very fine edge) making a long, abominable gash. Then he plucked it out and dashed it again several times into the face of the likeness, exactly as if he were stabbing a human victim: it had the oddest effect—that of a sort of figurative suicide. In a few seconds more the Colonel had tossed the dagger away—he looked at it as he did so, as if he expected it to reek with blood—and hurried out of the place, closing the door after him.

The strangest part of all was—as will doubtless appear—that Oliver Lyon made no movement to save his picture. But he did not feel as if he were losing it or cared not if he were, so much more did he feel that he was gaining a certitude. His old friend *was* ashamed of her husband, and he had made her so, and he had scored a great success, even though the picture had been reduced to rags. The revelation excited him so—as indeed the whole scene did—that when he came down the steps after the Colonel had gone he trembled with his happy agitation; he was dizzy and had to sit down a moment. The portrait had a dozen jagged wounds—the Colonel literally had hacked it to death. Lyon left it where it was, never touched it, scarcely looked at it; he only walked up and down his studio, still excited, for an hour. At the end of this time his good woman came to recommend that he should have some luncheon; there was a passage under the staircase from the offices.

"Ah, the lady and gentleman have gone, sir? I didn't hear them."

"Yes; they went by the garden."

But she had stopped, staring at the picture on the easel. "Gracious, how you 'ave served it, sir!"

Lyon imitated the Colonel. "Yes, I cut it up—in a fit of disgust."

"Mercy, after all your trouble! Because they weren't pleased, sir?"

"Yes; they weren't pleased."

"Well, they must be very grand! Blessed if I would!"

"Have it chopped up; it will do to light fires," Lyon said.

He returned to the country by the 3.30 and a few days later passed over to France. During the two months that he was absent from England he expected something—he could hardly have said what; a manifestation of some sort on the Colonel's part. Wouldn't he write, wouldn't he explain, wouldn't he take for granted Lyon had discovered the way he had, as the cook said, served him and deem it only decent to take pity in some fashion or other on his mystification? Would he plead guilty or would he repudiate suspicion? The latter course would be difficult and make a considerable draft upon his genius, in view of the certain testimony of Lyon's housekeeper, who had admitted the visitors and would establish the connection between their presence and the violence wrought. Would the Colonel proffer some apology or some amends, or would any word from him be only a further expression of that destructive petulance which our friend had seen his wife so suddenly and so potently communicate to him? He would have either to declare that he had not touched the picture or to admit that he had, and in either case he would have to tell a fine story. Lyon was impatient for the story and, as no letter came, disappointed that it was not produced. His impatience however was much greater in respect to Mrs. Capadose's version, if version there was to be; for certainly that would be the real test, would show

how far she would go for her husband, on the one side, or for him, Oliver Lyon, on the other. He could scarcely wait to see what line she would take; whether she would simply adopt the Colonel's, whatever it might be. He wanted to draw her out without waiting, to get an idea in advance. He wrote to her, to this end, from Venice, in the tone of their established friendship, asking for news, narrating his wanderings, hoping they should soon meet in town and not saying a word about the picture. Day followed day, after the time, and he received no answer; upon which he reflected that she couldn't trust herself to write—was still too much under the influence of the emotion produced by his "betrayal." Her husband had espoused that emotion and she had espoused the action he had taken in consequence of it, and it was a complete rupture and everything was at an end. Lyon considered this prospect rather ruefully, at the same time that he thought it deplorable that such charming people should have put themselves so grossly in the wrong. He was at last cheered, though little further enlightened, by the arrival of a letter, brief but breathing good-humour and hinting neither at a grievance nor at a bad conscience. The most interesting part of it to Lyon was the postscript, which consisted of these words: "I have a confession to make to you. We were in town for a couple of days, the 1st of September, and I took the occasion to defy your authority—it was very bad of me but I couldn't help it. I made Clement take me to your studio—I wanted so dreadfully to see what you had done with him, your wishes to the contrary notwithstanding. We made your servants let us in and I took a good look at the picture. It is really wonderful!" "Wonderful" was non-committal, but at least with this letter there was no rupture.

The third day after Lyon's return to London was a Sunday, so that he could go and ask Mrs. Capadose for luncheon. She had given him in the spring a general invitation to do so and he had availed himself of it several times. These had been the occasions (before he sat to him) when he saw the Colonel most familiarly. Directly after the meal his host disappeared (he went out, as he said, to call on *his* women) and the second half-hour was the best, even when there were other people. Now, in the first days of December, Lyon had the luck to find the pair alone, without even Amy, who appeared but little in public. They were in the drawing-room, waiting for the repast to be announced, and as soon as he came in the Colonel broke out, "My dear fellow, I'm delighted to see you! I'm so keen to begin again."

"Oh, do go on, it's so beautiful," Mrs. Capadose said, as she gave him her hand.

Lyon looked from one to the other; he didn't know what he had expected, but he had not expected this. "Ah, then, you think I've got something?"

"You've got everything," said Mrs. Capadose, smiling from ·her golden-brown eyes.

"She wrote you of our little crime?" her husband asked. "She dragged me there—I had to go." Lyon wondered for a moment whether he meant by their little crime the assault on the canvas; but the Colonel's next words didn't confirm this interpretation. "You know I like to sit—it gives such a chance to my *bavardise*. And just now I have time."

"You must remember I had almost finished," Lyon remarked.

"So you had. More's the pity. I should like you to begin again."

"My dear fellow, I shall have to begin again!" said Oliver Lyon with a laugh, looking at Mrs. Capadose. She did not meet his eyes—she had got up to ring for luncheon. "The picture has been smashed," Lyon continued.

"Smashed? Ah, what did you do that for?" Mrs. Capadose asked, standing there before him in all her clear, rich beauty. Now that she looked at him she was impenetrable.

"I didn't—I found it so—with a dozen holes punched in it!"

"I say!" cried the Colonel.

Lyon turned his eyes to him, smiling. "I hope *you* didn't do it?"

"Is it ruined?" the Colonel inquired. He was as brightly true as his wife and he looked simply as if Lyon's question could not be serious. "For the love of sitting to you? My dear fellow, if I had thought of it I would!"

"Nor you either?" the painter demanded of Mrs. Capadose.

Before she had time to reply her husband had seized her arm, as if a highly suggestive idea had come to him. "I say, my dear, that woman—that woman!"

"That woman?" Mrs. Capadose repeated; and Lyon too wondered what woman he meant.

"Don't you remember when we came out, she was at the door—or a little way from it? I spoke to you of her—I told you about her. Geraldine—Grenadine—the one who burst in that day," he explained to Lyon. "We saw her hanging about—I called Everina's attention to her."

"Do you mean she got at my picture?"

"Ah yes, I remember," said Mrs. Capadose, with a sigh.

"She burst in again—she had learned the way—she was waiting for her chance," the Colonel continued. "Ah, the little brute!"

Lyon looked down; he felt himself colouring. This was what he had been waiting for—the day the Colonel should wantonly sacrifice some innocent person. And could his wife be a party to that final atrocity? Lyon had reminded himself repeatedly during the previous weeks that when the Colonel perpetrated his misdeed she had already quitted the room; but he had argued none the less—it was a virtual certainty—that he had on rejoining her immediately made his achievement plain to her. He was in the flush of performance; and even if he had not mentioned what he had done she would have guessed it. He did not for an instant believe that poor Miss Geraldine had been hovering about his door, nor had the account given by the Colonel the summer before of his relations with this lady deceived him in the slightest degree. Lyon had never seen her before the day she planted herself in his studio; but he knew her and classified her as if he had made her. He was acquainted with the London female model in all her varieties—in every phase of her development and every step of her decay. When he entered his house that September morning just after the arrival of his two friends there had been no symptoms whatever, up and down the road, of Miss Geraldine's reappearance. That fact had been fixed in his mind by his recollecting the vacancy of the prospect when his cook told him that a lady and a gentleman were in his studio: he had wondered there was not a carriage nor a cab at his door. Then he had reflected that they would have come by the underground railway; he was close to the Marlborough Road station[528] and he knew the Colonel, coming to his sittings, more than once had availed himself of that convenience. "How in the world did she get in?" He addressed the question to his companions indifferently.

"Let us go down to luncheon," said Mrs. Capadose, passing out of the room.

"We went by the garden—without troubling your servant—I wanted to show my wife." Lyon followed his hostess with her husband and the Colonel stopped him at the top of the stairs. "My dear fellow, I *can't* have been guilty of the folly of not fastening the door?"

"I am sure I don't know, Colonel," Lyon said as they went down. "It was a very determined hand—a perfect wild-cat."

"Well, she *is* a wild-cat—confound her! That's why I wanted to get him away from her."

"But I don't understand her motive."

"She's off her head—and she hates me; that was her motive."

"But she doesn't hate me, my dear fellow!" Lyon said, laughing.

"She hated the picture—don't you remember she said so? The more portraits there are the less employment for such as her."

"Yes; but if she is not really the model she pretends to be, how can that hurt her?" Lyon asked.

The inquiry baffled the Colonel an instant—but only an instant. "Ah, she was in a vicious muddle! As I say, she's off her head."

They went into the dining-room, where Mrs. Capadose was taking her place. "It's too bad, it's too horrid!" she said. "You see the fates are against you. Providence won't let you be so disinterested—painting masterpieces for nothing."

"Did *you* see the woman?" Lyon demanded, with something like a sternness that he could not mitigate.

Mrs. Capadose appeared not to perceive it or not to heed it if she did. "There was a person, not far from your door, whom Clement called my attention to. He told me something about her but we were going the other way."

"And do you think she did it?"

"How can I tell? If she did she was mad, poor wretch."

"I should like very much to get hold of her," said Lyon. This was a false statement, for he had no desire for any further conversation with Miss Geraldine. He had exposed his friends to himself, but he had no desire to expose them to any one else, least of all to themselves.

"Oh, depend upon it she will never show again. You're safe!" the Colonel exclaimed.

"But I remember her address—Mortimer Terrace Mews, Notting Hill."

"Oh, that's pure humbug; there isn't any such place."

"Lord, what a deceiver!" said Lyon.

"Is there any one else you suspect?" the Colonel went on.

"Not a creature."

"And what do your servants say?"

"They say it wasn't *them* and I reply that I never said it was. That's about the substance of our conferences."

"And when did they discover the havoc?"

"They never discovered it at all. I noticed it first—when I came back."

"Well, she could easily have stepped in," said the Colonel. "Don't you remember how she turned up that day, like the clown in the ring?"

"Yes, yes; she could have done the job in three seconds, except that the picture wasn't out."

"My dear fellow, don't curse me!—but of course I dragged it out."

"You didn't put it back?" Lyon asked tragically.

"Ah, Clement, Clement, didn't I tell you to?" Mrs. Capadose exclaimed in a tone of exquisite reproach.

The Colonel groaned, dramatically; he covered his face with his hands. His wife's words were for Lyon the finishing touch; they made his whole vision crumble—his theory that she had secretly kept herself true. Even to her old lover she wouldn't be so! He was sick; he couldn't eat; he knew that he looked very strange. He murmured something about it being useless to cry over spilled milk—he tried to turn the conversation to other things. But it was a horrid effort and he wondered whether they felt it as much as he. He wondered all sorts of things: whether they guessed he disbelieved them (that he had seen them of course they would never guess); whether they had arranged their story in advance or it was only an inspiration of the moment; whether she had resisted, protested, when the Colonel proposed it to her, and then had been borne down by him; whether in short she didn't loathe herself as she sat there.

The cruelty, the cowardice of fastening their unholy act upon the wretched woman struck him as monstrous—no less monstrous indeed than the levity that could make them run the risk of her giving them, in her righteous indignation, the lie. Of course that risk could only exculpate her and not inculpate them—the probabilities protected them so perfectly; and what the Colonel counted on (what he would have counted upon the day he delivered himself, after first seeing her, at the studio, if he had thought about the matter then at all and not spoken from the pure spontaneity of his genius) was simply that Miss Geraldine had really vanished for ever into her native unknown. Lyon wanted so much to quit the subject that when after a little Mrs. Capadose said to him, "But can nothing be done, can't the picture be repaired? You know they do such wonders in that way now," he only replied, "I don't know, I don't care, it's all over, *n'en parlons plus!*" Her hypocrisy revolted him. And yet, by way of plucking off the last veil of her shame, he broke out to her again, shortly afterward, "And you did like it, really?" To which she returned, looking him straight in his face, without a blush, a pallor, an evasion, "Oh, I loved it!" Truly her husband had trained her well. After that Lyon said no more and his companions forbore temporarily to insist, like people of tact and sympathy aware that the odious accident had made him sore.

When they quitted the table the Colonel went away without coming upstairs; but Lyon returned to the drawing-room with his hostess, remarking to her however on the way that he could remain but a moment. He spent that moment—it prolonged itself a little—standing with her before the chimneypiece. She neither sat down nor asked him to; her manner denoted that she intended to go out. Yes, her husband had trained her well; yet Lyon dreamed for a moment that now he was alone with her she would perhaps break down, retract, apologise, confide, say to him, "My dear old friend, forgive this hideous comedy—you understand!" And then how he would have loved her and pitied her, guarded her, helped her always! If she were not ready to do something of that sort why had she treated him as if he were a dear old friend; why had she let him for months suppose certain things—or almost; why had she come to his studio day after day to sit near him on the pretext of her child's portrait, as if she liked to think what might have been? Why had she come so near a tacit confession, in a word, if she was not willing to go an inch further? And she was not willing—she was not; he could see that as he lingered there. She moved about the room a little, rearranging two or three objects on the tables, but she did nothing more. Suddenly he said to her: "Which way was she going, when you came out?"

"She—the woman we saw?"

"Yes, your husband's strange friend. It's a clew worth following." He had no desire to frighten her; he only wanted to communicate the impulse which would make her say, "Ah, spare me—and spare *him*! There was no such person."

Instead of this Mrs. Capadose replied, "She was going away from us—she crossed the road. We were coming towards the station."

"And did she appear to recognise the Colonel—did she look round?"

"Yes; she looked round, but I didn't notice much. A hansom came along and we got into it. It was not till then that Clement told me who she was: I remember he said that she was there for no good. I suppose we ought to have gone back."

"Yes; you would have saved the picture."

For a moment she said nothing; then she smiled. "For you, I am very sorry. But you must remember that I possess the original!"

At this Lyon turned away. "Well, I must go," he said; and he left her without any other farewell and made his way out of the house As he went slowly up the street the sense came back to him of that first glimpse of her he had had at Stayes—the way he had seen her gaze across the table at her husband. Lyon stopped at the corner, looking vaguely up and down. He would never go back—he couldn't. She was still in love with the Colonel—he had trained her too well.

The Modern Warning

I

WHEN he reached the hotel Macarthy Grice[529] was apprised, to his great disappointment, of the fact that his mother and sister were absent for the day, and he reproached himself with not having been more definite in announcing his arrival to them in advance. It was a little his nature to expect people to know things about himself that he had not told them and to be vexed when he found they were ignorant of them. I will not go so far as to say that he was inordinately conceited, but he had a general sense that he himself knew most things without having them pumped into him. He had been uncertain about his arrival and, since he disembarked at Liverpool,[530] had communicated his movements to the two ladies who after spending the winter in Rome were awaiting him at Cadenabbia[531] only by notes as brief as telegrams and on several occasions by telegrams simply. It struck his mother that he spent a great deal of money on these latter missives— which were mainly negative, mainly to say that he could not yet say when he *should* be able to start for the Continent. He had had business in London and had apparently been a good deal vexed by the discovery that, most of the people it was necessary for him to see being out of town, the middle of August was a bad time[532] for transacting it. Mrs. Grice gathered that he had had annoyances and disappointments, but she hoped that by the time he should join them his serenity would have been restored. She had not seen him for a year and her heart hungered for her boy. Family feeling was strong among these three though Macarthy's manner of showing it was sometimes peculiar, and her affection for her son was jealous and passionate; but she and Agatha made no secret between themselves of the fact that the privilege of being his mother and his sister was mainly sensible when things were going well with him. They were a little afraid they were not going well just now and they asked each other why he could not leave his affairs alone for a few weeks anyway and treat his journey to Europe as a complete holiday—a course which would do him infinitely more good. He

413

took life too hard and was overworked and overstrained. It was only to each other however that the anxious and affectionate women made these reflections, for they knew it was of no use to say such things to Macarthy. It was not that he answered them angrily; on the contrary he never noticed them at all. The answer was in the very essence of his nature: he was indomitably ambitious.

They had gone on the steamboat to the other end of the lake[533] and could not possibly be back for several hours. There was a *festa* going on at one of the villages—in the hills, a little way from the lake—and several ladies and gentlemen had gone from the hotel to be present at it. They would find carriages at the landing and they would drive to the village, after which the same vehicles would bring them back to the boat. This information was given to Macarthy Grice by the secretary of the hotel, a young man with a very low shirt collar, whose nationality puzzled and even defied him by its indefiniteness (he liked to know whom he was talking to even when he could not have the satisfaction of feeling that it was an American), and who suggested to him that he might follow and overtake his friends in the next steamer. As however there appeared to be some danger that in this case he should cross them on their way back he determined simply to lounge about the lake-side and the grounds of the hotel. The place was lovely, the view magnificent, and there was a coming and going of little boats, of travellers of every nationality, of itinerant vendors of small superfluities. Macarthy observed these things as patiently as his native restlessness allowed—and indeed that quality was reinforced to-day by an inexplicable tendency to fidget. He changed his place twenty times; he lighted a cigar and threw it away; he ordered some luncheon and when it came had no appetite for it. He felt nervous and he wondered what he was nervous about; whether he were afraid that during their excursion an accident had befallen his mother or Agatha. He was not usually a prey to small timidities, and indeed it cost him a certain effort to admit that a little Italian lake could be deep enough to drown a pair of independent Americans or that Italian horses could have the high spirit to run away with them. He talked with no one, for the Americans seemed to him all taken up with each other and the English all taken up with themselves. He had a few elementary principles for use in travelling (he had travelled little, but he had an abundant supply of theory on the subject), and one of them was that with Englishmen an American should never open the conversation. It was his belief that in doing so an American was exposed to be snubbed, or even insulted, and this belief was unshaken by the fact that Englishmen very often spoke to him, Macarthy, first.

The afternoon passed, little by little, and at last, as he stood there with his hands in his pockets and his hat pulled over his nose to keep the western sun out of his eyes, he saw the boat that he was waiting for round a distant point. At this stage the little annoyance he had felt at the trick his relations had unwittingly played him passed completely away and there was nothing in his mind but the eagerness of affection, the joy of reunion—of the prospective embrace. This feeling was in his face, in the fixed smile with which he watched the boat grow larger and larger. If we watch the young man himself as he does so we shall perceive him to be a tallish, lean personage, with an excessive slope of the shoulders, a very thin neck, a short light beard and a bright, sharp, expressive eye. He almost always wore his hat too much behind or too much in front; in the former case it showed a very fine high forehead. He looked like a man of intellect whose body was not much to him and its senses and appetites not importunate. His feet were small and he always wore a double-breasted frockcoat,[534] which he never buttoned. His mother and sister thought him very handsome. He had this appearance especially of course when, making them out on the deck of the steamer, he began to wave his hat and his hand to them. They responded in the most demonstrative manner and when they got near enough his mother called out to him over the water that she could not forgive herself for having lost so much of his visit. This was a bold proceeding for Mrs. Grice, who usually held back. Only she had been uncertain—she had not expected him that day in particular. "It's my fault!—it's my fault!" exclaimed a gentleman beside her, whom our young man had not yet noticed, raising his hat slightly as he spoke. Agatha, on the other side, said nothing—she only smiled at her brother. He had not seen her for so many months that he had almost forgotten how pretty she was. She looked lovely, under the shadow of her hat and of the awning of the steamer, as she stood there with happiness in her face and a big bunch of familiar flowers in her hand. Macarthy was proud of many things, but on this occasion he was proudest of having such a charming sister. Before they all disembarked he had time to observe the gentleman

415

who had spoken to him—an extraordinarily fair, clean-looking man, with a white waistcoat, a white hat, a glass in one eye and a flower in his button hole. Macarthy wondered who he was, but only vaguely, as it explained him sufficiently to suppose that he was a gentleman staying at the hotel who had made acquaintance with his mother and sister and taken part in the excursion. The only thing Grice had against him was that he had the air of an American who tried to look like an Englishman—a definite and conspicuous class to the young man's sense and one in regard to which he entertained a peculiar abhorrence. He was sorry his relatives should associate themselves with persons of that stamp; he would almost have preferred that they should become acquainted with the genuine English. He happened to perceive that the individual in question looked a good deal at him; but he disappeared instantly and discreetly when the boat drew up at the landing and the three Grices—I had almost written the three Graces[535]—pressed each other in their arms.

Half an hour later Macarthy sat between the two ladies at the table d'hôte, where he had a hundred questions to answer and to ask. He was still more struck with Agatha's improvement; she was older, handsomer, brighter: she had turned completely into a young lady and into a very accomplished one. It seemed to him that there had been a change for the better in his mother as well, the only change of that sort of which the good lady was susceptible, an amelioration of health, a fresher colour and a less frequent cough. Mrs. Grice was a gentle, sallow, serious little woman, the main principle of whose being was the habit of insisting that nothing that concerned herself was of the least consequence. She thought it indelicate to be ill and obtrusive even to be better, and discouraged all conversation of which she was in any degree the subject. Fortunately she had not been able to prevent her children from discussing her condition sufficiently to agree—it took but few words, for they agreed easily, that is Agatha always agreed with her brother—that she must have a change of climate and spend a winter or two in the south of Europe. Mrs. Grice kept her son's birthday all the year and knew an extraordinary number of stitches in knitting. Her friends constantly received from her, by post, offerings of little mats for the table, done up in an envelope, usually without any writing. She could make little mats in forty or fifty different ways. Toward the end of the dinner Macarthy, who up to this moment had been wholly occupied with his companions, began to look around him and to ask questions about the people opposite. Then he leaned forward a little and turned his eye up and down the row of their fellow-tourists on the same side. It was in this way that he perceived the gentleman who had said from the steamer that it was *his* fault that Mrs. Grice and her daughter had gone away for so many hours and who now was seated at some distance below the younger lady. At the moment Macarthy leaned forward this personage happened to be looking toward him, so that he caught his eye. The stranger smiled at him and nodded, as if an acquaintance might be considered to have been established between them, rather to Macarthy's surprise. He drew back and asked his sister who he was—the fellow who had been with them on the boat.

"He's an Englishman—Sir Rufus Chasemore," said the girl. Then she added, "Such a nice man."

"Oh, I thought he was an American making a fool of himself!" Macarthy rejoined.

"There's nothing of the fool about him," Agatha declared, laughing; and in a moment she added that Sir Rufus's usual place was beside hers, on her left hand. On this occasion he had moved away.

"What do you mean by this occasion?" her brother inquired.

"Oh, because you are here."

"And is he afraid of me?"

"Yes, I think he is."

"He doesn't behave so, anyway."

"Oh, he has very good manners," said the girl.

"Well, I suppose he's bound to do that. Isn't he a kind of nobleman?" Macarthy asked.

"Well no, not exactly a nobleman."

"Well, some kind of a panjandarum.[536] Hasn't he got one of their titles?"

"Yes, but not a very high one," Agatha explained. "He's only a K.C.B. And also an M.P."[537]

"A K.C.B. and an M.P.? What the deuce is all that?" And when Agatha had elucidated these mystic signs, as to which the young man's ignorance was partly simulated, he remarked that the Post-office ought to charge her friend double for his letters—for requiring that amount of stuff in his address. He also said that he owed him one for leading them astray at a time when they were bound to be on hand to receive one who was so dear to them. To this Agatha replied:

"Ah, you see, Englishmen are like that. They expect women to be so much honoured by their wanting them to do anything. And it must always be what *they* like, of course."

"What the men like? Well, that's all right, only they mustn't be Englishmen," said Macarthy Grice.

"Oh, if one is going to be a slave I don't know that the nationality of one's master matters!" his sister exclaimed. After which his mother began to ask him if he had seen anything during the previous months of their Philadelphia[538] cousins—some cousins who wrote their name Gryce and for whom Macarthy had but a small affection.

After dinner the three sat out on the terrace of the hotel, in the delicious warmth of the September night. There were boats on the water, decked with coloured lanterns; music and song proceeded from several of them and every influence was harmonious. Nevertheless by the time Macarthy had finished a cigar it was judged best that the old lady should withdraw herself from the evening air. She went into the salon of the hotel, and her children accompanied her, against her protest, so that she might not be alone. Macarthy liked better to sit with his mother in a drawing-room which the lamps made hot than without her under the stars. At the end of a quarter of an hour he became aware that his sister had disappeared, and as some time elapsed without her returning he asked his mother what had become of her.

"I guess she has gone to walk with Sir Rufus," said the old lady, candidly.

"Why, you seem to do everything Sir Rufus wants, down here!" her son exclaimed. "How did he get such a grip on you?"

"Well, he has been most kind, Macarthy," Mrs. Grice returned, not appearing to deny that the Englishman's influence was considerable.

"I have heard it stated that it's not the custom, down here, for young girls to walk round—at night[539]—with foreign lords."

"Oh, he's not foreign and he's most reliable," said the old lady, very earnestly. It was not in her nature to treat such a question, or indeed any question, as unimportant.

"Well, that's all right," her son remarked, in a tone which implied that he was in good-humour and wished not to have his equanimity ruffled. Such accidents with Macarthy Grice were not light things. All the same at the end of five minutes more, as Agatha did not reappear, he expressed the hope that nothing of any kind had sprung up between her and the K.C.B.

"Oh, I guess they are just conversing by the lake. I'll go and find them if you like," said Mrs. Grice.

"Well, haven't they been conversing by the lake—and on the lake—all day?" asked the young man, without taking up her proposal.

"Yes, of course we had a great deal of bright talk while we were out. It was quite enough for me to listen to it. But he is most kind—and he knows everything, Macarthy."

"Well, that's all right!" exclaimed the young man again. But a few moments later he returned to the charge and asked his mother if the Englishman were paying any serious attention—she knew what he meant—to Agatha. "Italian lakes and summer evenings and glittering titles and all that sort of thing—of course you know what they may lead to."

Mrs. Grice looked anxious and veracious, as she always did, and appeared to consider a little. "Well, Macarthy, the truth is just this. Your sister is so attractive and so admired that it seems as if wherever she went there was a great interest taken in her. Sir Rufus certainly does like to converse with her, but so have many others—and so would any one in their place. And Agatha is full of conscience. For me that's her highest attraction."

"I'm very much pleased with her—she's a lovely creature," Macarthy remarked.

"Well, there's no one whose appreciation could gratify her more than yours. She has praised you up to Sir Rufus," added the old lady, simply.

"Dear mother, what has *he* got to do with it?" her son demanded, staring. "I don't care what Sir Rufus thinks of me."

Fortunately the good lady was left only for a moment confronted with this inquiry, for Agatha now re-entered the room, passing in from the terrace by one of the long windows and accompanied precisely by the gentleman whom her relatives had been discussing. She came toward them smiling and perhaps even blushing a little, but with an air of considerable resolution, and she said to Macarthy, "Brother, I want to make you acquainted with a good friend of ours, Sir Rufus Chasemore."

"Oh, I asked Miss Grice to be so good." The Englishman laughed, looking easy and genial.

Macarthy got up and extended his hand, with a "Very happy to know you, sir," and the two men stood a moment looking at each other while Agatha, beside them, bent her regard upon both. I shall not attempt to translate the reflections which rose in the young lady's mind as she did so, for they were complicated and subtle and it is quite difficult enough to reproduce our own more casual impression of the contrast between her companions. This contrast was extreme and complete, and it was not weakened by the fact that both the men had the signs of character and ability. The American was thin, dry, fine, with something in his face which seemed to say that there was more in him of the spirit than of the letter. He looked unfinished and yet somehow he looked mature, though he was not advanced in life. The Englishman had more detail about him, something stippled and retouched,[540] an air of having been more artfully fashioned, in conformity with traditions and models. He wore old clothes which looked new, while his transatlantic brother wore new clothes which looked old. He thought he had never heard the American tone so marked as on the lips of Mr. Macarthy Grice, who on his side found in the accent of his sister's friend a strange, exaggerated, even affected variation of the tongue in which he supposed himself to have been brought up. In general he was much irritated by the tricks which the English played with the English language, deprecating especially their use of familiar slang.

"Miss Grice tells me that you have just crossed the ditch,[541] but I'm afraid you are not going to stay with us long," Sir Rufus remarked, with much pleasantness.

"Well, no, I shall return as soon as I have transacted my business," Macarthy replied. "That's all I came for."

"You don't do us justice; you ought to follow the example of your mother and sister and take a look round," Sir Rufus went on, with another laugh. He was evidently of a mirthful nature.

"Oh, I have been here before; I've seen the principal curiosities."

"He has seen everything thoroughly," Mrs. Grice murmured over her crotchet.

"Ah, I daresay you have seen much more than we poor natives. And your own country is so interesting. I have an immense desire to see that."

"Well, it certainly repays observation," said Macarthy Grice.

"You wouldn't like it at all; you would find it awful," his sister remarked, sportively, to Sir Rufus.

"Gracious, daughter!" the old lady exclaimed, trying to catch Agatha's eye.

"That's what she's always telling me, as if she were trying to keep me from going. I don't know what she has been doing over there that she wants to prevent me from finding out." Sir Rufus's eyes, while he made this observation, rested on the young lady in the most respectful yet at the same time the most complacent manner.

She smiled back at him and said with a laugh still clearer than his own, "I know the kind of people who will like America and the kind of people who won't."

"Do you know the kind who will like *you* and the kind who won't?" Sir Rufus Chasemore inquired.

"I don't know that in some cases it particularly matters what people like," Macarthy interposed, with a certain severity.

"Well, I must say I like people to like my country," said Agatha.

"You certainly take the best way to make them, Miss Grice!" Sir Rufus exclaimed.

"Do you mean by dissuading them from visiting it, sir?" Macarthy asked.

"Oh dear no; by being so charming a representative of it. But I shall most positively go on the first opportunity."

"I hope it won't be while we are on this side," said Mrs. Grice, very civilly.

"You will need us over there to explain everything," her daughter added.

The Englishman looked at her a moment with his glass in his eye. "I shall certainly pretend to be very stupid." Then he went on, addressing himself to Macarthy: "I have an idea that you have some rocks ahead,[542] but that doesn't diminish—in fact it increases—my curiosity to see the country."

"Oh, I suspect we'll scratch along all right," Macarthy replied, with rather a grim smile, in a tone which conveyed that the success of American institutions might not altogether depend on Sir Rufus's judgment of them. He was on the point of expressing his belief, further, that there were European countries which would be glad enough to exchange their "rocks" for those of the United States; but he kept back this reflection, as it might appear too pointed and he wished not to be rude to a man who seemed on such sociable terms with his mother and sister. In the course of a quarter of an hour the ladies took their departure for the upper regions and Macarthy Grice went off with them. The Englishman looked for him again however, as something had been said about their smoking a cigar together before they went to bed; but he never turned up, so that Sir Rufus puffed his own weed in solitude, strolling up and down the terrace without mingling with the groups that remained and looking much at the starlit lake and mountains.

THE next morning after breakfast Mrs. Grice had a conversation with her son in her own room. Agatha had not yet appeared, and she explained that the girl was sleeping late, having been much fatigued by her excursion the day before as well as by the excitement of her brother's arrival. Macarthy thought it a little singular that she should bear her fatigue so much less well than her mother, but he understood everything in a moment, as soon as the old lady drew him toward her with her little conscious, cautious face, taking his hand in hers. She had had a long and important talk with Agatha the previous evening, after they went upstairs, and she had extracted from the girl some information which she had within a day or two begun very much to desire.

"It's about Sir Rufus Chasemore. I couldn't but think you would wonder—just as I was wondering myself," said Mrs. Grice. "I felt as if I couldn't be satisfied till I had asked. I don't know how you will feel about it. I am afraid it will upset you a little; but anything that you may think—well, yes, it *is* the case."

"Do you mean she is engaged to be married to your Englishman?" Macarthy demanded, with a face that suddenly flushed.

"No, she's not engaged. I presume she wouldn't take that step without finding out how you'd feel. In fact that's what she said last night."

"I feel like thunder, I feel like hell!" Macarthy exclaimed; "and I hope you'll tell her so."

Mrs. Grice looked frightened and pained. "Well, my son, I'm glad you've come, if there is going to be any trouble."

"Trouble—what trouble should there be? He can't marry her if she won't have him."

"Well, she didn't say she wouldn't have him; she said the question hadn't come up. But she thinks it would come up if she were to give him any sort of opening. That's what I thought and that's what I wanted to make sure of."

Macarthy looked at his mother for some moments in extreme seriousness; then he took out his watch and looked at that. "What time is the first
boat?" he asked.

"I don't know—there are a good many."

"Well, we'll take the first—we'll quit this." And the young man put back
his watch and got up with decision.

His mother sat looking at him rather ruefully. "Would you feel so badly if
she were to do it?"

"She may do it without my consent; she shall never do it with," said
Macarthy Grice.

"Well, I could see last evening, by the way you acted—" his mother murmured, as if she thought it her duty to try and enter into his opposition.

"How did I act, ma'am?"

"Well, you acted as if you didn't think much of the English."

"Well, I don't," said the young man.

"Agatha noticed it and she thought Sir Rufus noticed it too."

"They have such thick hides in general that they don't notice anything.
But if he is more sensitive than the others perhaps it will keep him away."

"Would you like to wound him, Macarthy?" his mother inquired, with an
accent of timid reproach.

"Wound him? I should like to kill him! Please to let Agatha know that
we'll move on," the young man added.

Mrs. Grice got up as if she were about to comply with this injunction, but
she stopped in the middle of the room and asked of her son, with a quaint
effort at conscientious impartiality which would have made him smile if he
had been capable of smiling in such a connection, "Don't you think that in
some respects the English are a fine nation?"

"Well, yes; I like them for pale ale and note-paper and umbrellas; and I
got a firstrate trunk there the other day. But I want my sister to marry one of
her own people."

"Yes, I presume it would be better," Mrs. Grice remarked. "But Sir Rufus
has occupied very high positions in his own country."

"I know the kind of positions he has occupied; I can tell what they were
by looking at him. The more he has done of that the more intensely he represents what I don't like."

"Of course he would stand up for England," Mrs. Grice felt herself compelled to admit.

"Then why the mischief doesn't he do so instead of running round after Americans?" Macarthy demanded.

"He doesn't run round after us; but we knew his sister, Lady Bolitho,[543] in Rome. She is a most sweet woman and we saw a great deal of her; she took a great fancy to Agatha. I surmise that she mentioned us to him pretty often when she went back to England, and when he came abroad for his autumn holiday, as he calls it—he met us first in the Engadine,[544] three or four weeks ago, and came down here with us—it seemed as if we already knew him and he knew us. He is very talented and he is quite well off."

"Mother," said Macarthy Grice, going close to the old lady and speaking very gravely, "why do you know so much about him? Why have you gone into it so?"

"I haven't gone into it; I only know what he has told us."

"But why have you given him the right to tell you? How does it concern you whether he is well off?"

The poor woman began to look flurried and scared. "My son, I have given him no right; I don't know what you mean. Besides, it wasn't he who told us he is well off; it was his sister."

"It would have been better if you hadn't known his sister," said the young man, gloomily.

"Gracious, Macarthy, we must know some one!" Mrs. Grice rejoined, with a flicker of spirit.

"I don't see the necessity of your knowing the English."

"Why Macarthy, can't we even *know* them?" pleaded his mother.

"You see the sort of thing it gets you into."

"It hasn't got us into anything. Nothing has been done."

"So much the better, mother darling," said the young man. "In that case we will go on to Venice.[545] Where is he going?"

"I don't know, but I suppose he won't come on to Venice if we don't ask him."

"I don't believe any delicacy would prevent him," Macarthy rejoined. "But he loathes me; that's an advantage."

"He *loathes* you—when he wanted so to know you?"

"Oh yes, I understand. Well, now he knows me! He knows he hates everything I like and I hate everything he likes."

"He doesn't imagine you hate your sister, I suppose!" said the old lady, with a little vague laugh.

"Mother," said Macarthy, still in front of her with his hands in his pockets, "I verily believe I should hate her if she were to marry him."

"Oh, gracious, my son, don't, don't!" cried Mrs. Grice, throwing herself into his arms with a shudder of horror and burying her face on his shoulder.

Her son held her close and as he bent over her he went on: "Dearest mother, don't you see that we must remain together, that at any rate we mustn't be separated by different ideas, different associations and institutions? I don't believe any family has ever had more of the feeling that holds people closely together than we have had: therefore for heaven's sake let us keep it, let us find our happiness in it as we always have done. Of course Agatha will marry some day; but why need she marry in such a way as to make a gulf? You and she are all I have, and—I may be selfish—I should like very much to keep you."

"Of course I will let her know the way you feel," said the old lady, a moment later, rearranging her cap and her shawl and putting away her pocket-handkerchief.

"It's a matter she certainly ought to understand. She would wish to, unless she is very much changed," Macarthy added, as if he saw all this with high lucidity.

"Oh, she isn't changed—she'll never change!" his mother exclaimed, with rebounding optimism. She thought it wicked not to take cheerful views.

"She wouldn't if she were to marry an Englishman," he declared, as Mrs. Grice left him to go to her daughter.

She told him an hour later that Agatha would be quite ready to start for Venice on the morrow and that she said he need have no fear that Sir Rufus Chasemore would follow them. He was naturally anxious to know from her what words she had had with Agatha, but the only very definite information he extracted was to the effect that the girl had declared with infinite feeling that she would never marry an enemy of her country. When he saw her later in the day he thought she had been crying; but there was nothing in her manner to show that she resented any pressure her mother might have represented to her that he had put upon her or that she was making a reluctant sacrifice. Agatha Grice was very fond of her brother, whom she knew to be upright, distinguished and exceedingly mindful of the protection and support that he owed her mother and herself. He was perverse and obstinate, but she was aware that in essentials he was supremely tender, and he had always been very much the most eminent figure in her horizon.

No allusion was made between them to Sir Rufus Chasemore, though the silence on either side was rather a conscious one, and they talked of the prospective pleasures of Venice and of the arrangements Macarthy would be able to make in regard to his mother's spending another winter in Rome.[546] He was to accompany them to Venice and spend a fortnight with them there, after which he was to return to London to terminate his business and then take his way back to New York. There was a plan of his coming to see them again later in the winter, in Rome, if he should succeed in getting six weeks off. As a man of energy and decision, though indeed of a somewhat irritable stomach, he made light of the Atlantic voyage: it was a rest and a relief, alternating with his close attention to business. That the disunion produced by the state of Mrs. Grice's health was a source of constant regret and even of much depression to him was well known to his mother and sister, who would not have broken up his home by coming to live in Europe if he had not insisted upon it. Macarthy was in the highest degree conscientious; he was capable of suffering the extremity of discomfort in a cause which he held to be right. But his mother and sister *were* his home, all the same, and in their absence he was perceptibly desolate. Fortunately it had been hoped that a couple of southern winters would quite set Mrs. Grice up again and that then everything in America would be as it had been before. Agatha's affection for her brother was very nearly as great as his affection for herself; but it took the form of wishing that his loneliness might be the cause of his marrying some thoroughly nice girl, inasmuch as after all her mother and she might not always be there. Fraternal tenderness in Macarthy's bosom followed a different logic. He was so fond of his sister that he had a secret hope that she would never marry at all. He had spoken otherwise to his mother, because that was the only way not to seem offensively selfish; but the essence of his thought was that on the day Agatha should marry she would throw him over. On the day she should marry an Englishman she would not throw him over—she would betray him. That is she would betray her country, and it came to the same thing. Macarthy's

427

patriotism was of so intense a hue that to his own sense the national life and his own life flowed in an indistinguishable current.

The particular Englishman he had his eye upon now was not, as a general thing, visible before luncheon. He had told Agatha, who mentioned it to her brother, that in the morning he was immersed in work in letter-writing. Macarthy wondered what his work might be, but did not condescend to inquire. He was enlightened however by happening by an odd chance to observe an allusion to Sir Rufus in a copy of the London *Times*[547] which he took up in the reading-room of the hotel. This occurred in a letter to the editor of the newspaper, the writer of which accused Agatha's friend of having withheld from the public some information to which the public was entitled. The information had respect to "the situation in South Africa,"[548] and Sir Rufus was plainly an agent of the British government, the head of some kind of department or sub-department. This did not make Macarthy like him any better. He was displeased with the idea of England's possessing colonies at all and considered that she had acquired them by force and fraud[549] and held them by a frail and unnatural tenure. It appeared to him that any man who occupied a place in this unrighteous system must have false, detestable views.

Sir Rufus Chasemore turned up on the terrace in the afternoon and bore himself with the serenity of a man unconscious of the damaging inferences that had been formed about him. Macarthy neither avoided him nor sought him out—he even relented a little toward him mentally when he thought of the loss he was about to inflict on him; but when the Englishman approached him and appeared to wish to renew their conversation of the evening before it struck him that he was wanting in delicacy. There was nothing strange in that however, for delicacy and tact were not the strong point of one's transatlantic cousins, with whom one had always to dot one's i's. It seemed to Macarthy that Sir Rufus Chasemore ought to have guessed that he cared little to keep up an acquaintance with him, though indeed the young American would have been at a loss to say how he was to guess it, inasmuch as he would have resented the imputation that he himself had been rude enough to make such a fact patent. The American ladies were in their apartments, occupied in some manner connected with their intended retreat, and there was nothing for Macarthy but to stroll up and down for nearly half an hour with the personage who was so provokingly the cause of it. It had come over him now that he should have liked extremely to spend several days on the lake of Como.[550] The place struck him as much more delicious than it had done while he chafed the day before at the absence of his relations. He was angry with the Englishman for forcing him to leave it and still more angry with him for showing so little responsibility or even perception in regard to the matter. It occurred to him while he was in this humour that it might be a good plan to make himself so disagreeable that Sir Rufus would take to his heels and never reappear, fleeing before the portent of such an insufferable brother-in-law. But this plan demanded powers of execution which Macarthy did not flatter himself that he possessed: he felt that it was impossible to him to divest himself of his character of a polished American gentleman.

If he found himself dissenting from most of the judgments and opinions which Sir Rufus Chasemore happened to express in the course of their conversation there was nothing perverse in that: it was a simple fact apparently that the Englishman had nothing in common with him and was predestined to enunciate propositions to which it was impossible for him to assent. Moreover how could he assent to propositions enunciated in that short, offhand, clipping tone, with the words running into each other and the voice rushing up and down the scale? Macarthy, who spoke very slowly, with great distinctness and in general with great correctness, was annoyed not only by his companion's intonation but by the odd and, as it seemed to him, licentious application that he made of certain words. He struck him as wanting in reverence for the language, which Macarthy had an idea, not altogether unjust, that he himself deeply cherished. He would have admitted that these things were small and not great, but in the usual relations of life the small things count more than the great, and they sufficed at any rate to remind him of the essential antipathy and incompatibility which he had always believed to exist between an Englishman and an American. They were, in the very nature of things, disagreeable to each other—both mentally and physically irreconcilable. In cases where this want of correspondence had been bridged over it was because the American had made weak concessions, had been shamefully accommodating. That was a kind of thing the Englishman, to do him justice, never did; he had at least the courage of his prejudices.[551] It was not unknown to Macarthy that the repugnance in question appeared to be confined to the American male, as was shown by a thousand international marriages,[552] which had transplanted as many of his countrywomen to unnatural British homes. That variation had to be allowed for, and the young man felt that he was allowing for it when he reflected that probably his own sister liked the way Sir Rufus Chasemore spoke. In fact he was intimately convinced she liked it, which was a reason the more for their quitting Cadenabbia the next morning.

Sir Rufus took the opposite point of view quite as much as himself, only he took it gaily and familiarly and laughed about it, as if he were amused at the preferences his companion betrayed and especially amused that he should hold them so gravely, so almost gloomily. This sociable jocosity, as if they had known each other three months was what appeared to Macarthy so indelicate. They talked no politics and Sir Rufus said nothing more about America; but it stuck out of the Englishman at every pore that he was a resolute and consistent conservative, a prosperous, accomplished, professional, official Tory.[553] It gave Macarthy a kind of palpitation to think that his sister had been in danger of associating herself with such arrogant doctrines. Not that a woman's political creed mattered; but that of her husband did. He had an impression that he himself was a passionate democrat, an unshrinking radical. It was a proof of how far Sir Rufus's manner was from being satisfactory to his companion that the latter was unable to guess whether he already knew of the sudden determination of his American friends to leave Cadenabbia or whether their intention was first revealed to him in Macarthy's casual mention of it, which apparently put him out not at all, eliciting nothing more than a frank, cheerful expression of regret. Macarthy somehow mistrusted a man who could conceal his emotions like that. How could he have known they were going unless Agatha had told him, and how could Agatha have told him, since she could not as yet have seen him? It did not even occur to the young man to suspect that she might have conveyed the unwelcome news to him by a letter. And if he had not known it why was he not more startled and discomfited when Macarthy dealt the blow? The young American made up his mind at last that the reason why Sir Rufus was not startled was that he had thought in advance it would be no more than natural that the newly-arrived brother should wish to spoil his game. But in that case why was he not angry with him for such a disposition? Why did he come after him and insist on talking with him? There seemed to Macarthy something impudent in this incongruity—as if to the mind of an English statesman the animosity of a Yankee lawyer were really of too little account.

IT may be intimated to the reader that Agatha Grice had written no note to her English friend, and she held no communication with him of any sort, till after she had left the table d'hôte with her mother and brother in the evening. Sir Rufus had seated himself at dinner in the same place as the night before; he was already occupying it and he simply bowed to her with a smile, from a distance, when she came into the room. As she passed out to the terrace later with her companions he overtook her and said to her in a lower tone of voice than usual that he had been exceedingly sorry to hear that she was leaving Cadenabbia so soon. Was it really true? could not they put it off a little? should not they find the weather too hot in Venice and the mosquitoes too numerous? Agatha saw that Sir Rufus asked these questions with the intention of drawing her away, engaging her in a walk, in some talk to which they should have no listeners; and she resisted him at first a little, keeping near the others because she had made up her mind that morning in deep and solitary meditation that she would force him to understand that further acquaintance could lead to nothing profitable for either party. It presently came over her, however, that it would take some little time to explain this truth and that the time might be obtained by their walking a certain distance along the charming shore of the lake together. The windows of the hotel and of the little water-side houses and villas projected over the place long shafts of lamplight which shimmered on the water, broken by the slow-moving barges laden with musicians, and gave the whole region the air of an illuminated garden surrounding a magnificent pond. Agatha made the further reflection that it would be only common kindness to give Sir Rufus an opportunity to say anything he wished to say; that is within the limits she was prepared to allow: they had been too good friends to separate without some of the forms of regret, without a backward look at least, since they might not enjoy a forward one. In short she had taken in the morning a resolution so virtuous, founded on so high and large a view of the whole situation, that she felt herself entitled to some reward, some present liberty of action. She turned away from her relatives with Sir Rufus—she observed that they paid no attention to her—and in a few moments she was strolling by his side at a certain distance from the hotel.

"I will tell you what I should like to do," he said, as they went; "I should like to turn up in Venice—about a week hence."

"I don't recommend you to do that," the girl replied, promptly enough; though as soon as she had spoken she bethought herself that she could give him no definite reason why he should not follow her; she could give him no reason at all that would not be singularly wanting in delicacy. She had a movement of vexation with her brother for having put her in a false position; it was the first, for in the morning when her mother repeated to her what Macarthy had said and she perceived all that it implied she had not been in the least angry with him—she sometimes indeed wondered why she was not—and she did not propose to become so for Sir Rufus Chasemore. What she had been was sad—touched too with a sense of horror—horror at the idea that she might be in danger of denying, under the influence of an insinuating alien, the pieties and sanctities in which she had been brought up. Sir Rufus *was* a tremendous conservative, though perhaps that did not matter so much, and he had let her know at an early stage of their acquaintance that he had never liked Americans in the least as a people. As it was apparent that he liked her—all American and very American as she was—she had regarded this shortcoming only in its minor bearings, and it had even gratified her to form a private project of converting him to a friendlier view. If she had not found him a charming man she would not have cared what he thought about her country-people; but, as it happened, she did find him a charming man, and it grieved her to see a mind that was really worthy of the finest initiations (as regarded the American question) wasting itself on poor prejudices. Somehow, by showing him how nice she was herself she could make him like the people better with whom she had so much in common, and as he admitted that his observation of them had after all been very restricted she would also make him know them better. This prospect drew her on till suddenly her brother sounded the note of warning. When it came she understood it perfectly; she could not pretend that she did not. If she were not careful she would give her country away: in the privacy of her own room she had coloured up to her hair at the thought. She had a lurid vision in which the chance seemed to be greater that Sir

Rufus Chasemore would bring her over to his side than that she should make him like anything he had begun by disliking; so that she resisted, with the conviction that the complications which might arise from allowing a prejudiced English man to possess himself, as he evidently desired to do, of her affections, would be much greater than a sensitive girl with other loyalties to observe might be able to manage. A moment after she had said to her companion that she did not recommend him to come to Venice she added that of course he was free to do as he liked: only why should he come if he was sure the place was so uncomfortable? To this Sir Rufus replied that it signified little how uncomfortable it was if she should be there and that there was nothing he would not put up with for the sake of a few days more of her society.

"Oh, if it's for that you are coming," the girl replied, laughing and feeling nervous—feeling that something was in the air which she had wished precisely to keep out of it—"Oh, if it's for that you are coming you had very much better not take the trouble. You would have very little of my society. While my brother is with us all my time will be given up to him."

"Confound your brother!" Sir Rufus exclaimed. Then he went on: "You told me yourself he wouldn't be with you long. After he's gone you will be free again and you will still be in Venice, shan't you? I do want to float in a gondola with you."

"It's very possible my brother may be with us for weeks."

Sir Rufus hesitated a moment. "I see what you mean—that he won't leave you so long as I am about the place. In that case if you are so fond of him you ought to take it as a kindness of me to hover about." Before the girl had time to make a rejoinder to this ingenious proposition he added, "Why in the world has he taken such a dislike to me?"

"I know nothing of any dislike," Agatha said, not very honestly. "He has expressed none to me."

"He has to me then. He quite loathes me."

She was silent a little; then she inquired, "And do you like him very much?"

"I think he's immense fun! He's very clever, like most of the Americans I have seen, including yourself. I should like to show him I like him, and I have salaamed and kowtowed[554] to him whenever I had a chance; but he won't let me get near him. Hang it, it's cruel!"

433

"It's not directed to you in particular, any dislike he may have. I have told you before that he doesn't like the English," Agatha remarked.

"Bless me—no more do I! But my best friends have been among them."

"I don't say I agree with my brother and I don't say I disagree with him," Sir Rufus's companion went on. "I have told you before that we are of Irish descent,[555] on my mother's side. Her mother was a Macarthy. We have kept up the name and we have kept up the feeling."

"I see—so that even if the Yankee were to let me off the Paddy would come down![556] That's a most unholy combination. But you remember, I hope, what I have also told you—that I am quite as Irish as you can ever be. I had an Irish grandmother—a beauty of beauties, a certain Lady Laura Fitzgibbon,[557] *qui vaut bien la vôtre*. A charming old woman she was."

"Oh, well, she wasn't of our kind!" the girl exclaimed, laughing.

"You mean that yours wasn't charming? In the presence of her granddaughter permit me to doubt it."

"Well, I suppose that those hostilities of race—transmitted and hereditary, as it were—are the greatest of all." Agatha Grice uttered this sage reflection by no means in the tone of successful controversy and with the faintest possible tremor in her voice.

"Good God! do you mean to say that an hostility of race, a legendary feud, is to prevent you and me from meeting again?" The Englishman stopped short as he made this inquiry, but Agatha continued to walk, as if that might help her to elude it. She had come out with a perfectly sincere determination to prevent Sir Rufus from saying what she believed he wanted to say, and if her voice had trembled just now it was because it began to come over her that her preventive measures would fail. The only tolerably efficacious one would be to turn straight round and go home. But there would be a rudeness in this course and even a want of dignity; and besides she did not wish to go home. She compromised by not answering her companion's question, and though she could not see him she was aware that he was looking after her with an expression in his face of high impatience momentarily baffled. She knew that expression and thought it handsome; she knew all his expressions and thought them all handsome. He overtook her in a few moments and then she was surprised that he should be laughing as he exclaimed: "It's too absurd!—it's too absurd!" It was not long however before she understood the nature of his laughter, as she understood everything else. If she was nervous he was scarcely less so; his whole manner now expressed the temper of a man wishing to ascertain rapidly whether he may enjoy or must miss great happiness. Before she knew it he had spoken the words which she had flattered herself he should not speak; he had said that since there appeared to be a doubt whether they should soon meet again it was important he should seize the present occasion. He was very glad after all, because for several days he had been wanting to speak. He loved her as he had never loved any woman and he besought her earnestly to believe it. What was this crude stuff about disliking the English and disliking the Americans? what had questions of nationality to do with it any more than questions of ornithology? It was a question simply of being his wife, and that was rather between themselves, was it not? He besought *her* to consider it, as he had been turning it over from almost the first hour he met her. It was not in Agatha's power to go her way now, because he had laid his hand upon her in a manner that kept her motionless, and while he talked to her in low, kind tones, touching her face with the breath of supplication, she stood there in the warm darkness, very pale, looking as if she were listening to a threat of injury rather than to a declaration of love. "Of course I ought to speak to your mother," he said; "I ought to have spoken to her first. But your leaving at an hour's notice and apparently wishing to shake me off has given me no time. For God's sake give me your permission and I will do it to-night."

"Don't—don't speak to my mother," said Agatha, mournfully.

"Don't tell me to-morrow then that she won't hear of it!"

"She likes you, Sir Rufus," the girl rejoined, in the same singular, hopeless tone.

"I hope you don't mean to imply by that that you don't!"

"No; I like you of course; otherwise I should never have allowed myself to be in this position, because I hate it!" The girl uttered these last words with a sudden burst of emotion and an equally sudden failure of sequence, and turning round quickly began to walk in the direction from which they had come. Her companion, however, was again beside her, close to her, and he found means to prevent her from going as fast as she wished. History has lost the record of what at that moment he said to her; it was something that made her exclaim in a voice which seemed on the point of breaking into tears: "Please don't say that or anything like it again, Sir Rufus, or I shall have to take leave of you for ever this instant, on the spot." He strove to be obedient and they walked on a little in silence; after which she resumed, with a slightly different manner: "I am very sorry you have said this to-night. You have troubled and distressed me; it isn't a good time."

"I wonder if you would favour me with your idea of what might be a good time?"

"I don't know. Perhaps never. I am greatly obliged to you for the honour you have done me. I beg you to believe me when I say this. But I don't think I shall ever marry. I have other duties. I can't do what I like with my life."

At this Sir Rufus made her stop again, to tell him what she meant by such an extraordinary speech. What overwhelming duties had she, pray, and what restrictions upon her life that made her so different from other women? He could not, for his part, imagine a woman more free. She explained that she had her mother, who was terribly delicate and who must be her first thought and her first care. Nothing would induce her to leave her mother. She was all her mother had except Macarthy, and he was absorbed in his profession.

"What possible question need there be of your leaving her?" the Englishman demanded. "What could be more delightful than that she should live with us and that we should take care of her together? You say she is so good as to like me, and I assure you I like *her*—most uncommonly."

"It would be impossible that we should take her away from my brother," said the girl, after an hesitation.

"Take her away?" And Sir Rufus Chasemore stood staring. "Well, if he won't look after her himself—you say he is so taken up with his work—he has no earthly right to prevent other people from doing so."

"It's not a man's business—it's mine—it's her daughter's."

"That's exactly what I think, and what in the world do I wish but to help you? If she requires a mild climate we will find some lovely place in the south of England[558] and be as happy there as the day is long."

"So that Macarthy would have to come *there* to see his mother? Fancy Macarthy in the south of England—especially as happy as the day is long! He would find the day very long," Agatha Grice continued, with the strange little laugh which expressed—or rather which disguised—the mixture of her feelings. "He would never consent."

"Never consent to what? Is what you mean to say that he would never consent to your marriage? I certainly never dreamed that you would have to ask him. Haven't you defended to me again and again the freedom, the independence with which American girls marry? Where is the independence when it comes to your own case?" Sir Rufus Chasemore paused a moment and then he went on with bitterness: "Why don't you say outright that you are afraid of your brother? Miss Grice, I never dreamed that that would be your answer to an offer of everything that a man—and a man of some distinction, I may say, for it would be affectation in me to pretend that I consider myself a nonentity—can lay at the feet of a woman."

The girl did not reply immediately; she appeared to think over intently what he had said to her, and while she did so she turned her white face and her charming serious eyes upon him. When at last she spoke it was in a very gentle, considerate tone. "You are wrong in supposing that I am afraid of my brother. How can I be afraid of a person of whom I am so exceedingly fond?"

"Oh, the two things are quite consistent," said Sir Rufus Chasemore, impatiently. "And is it impossible that I should ever inspire you with a sentiment which you would consent to place in the balance with this intense fraternal affection?" He had no sooner spoken those somewhat sarcastic words than he broke out in a different tone: "Oh Agatha, for pity's sake don't make difficulties where there are no difficulties!"

"I don't make them; I assure you they exist. It is difficult to explain them, but I can see them, I can feel them. Therefore we mustn't talk this way any more. Please, please don't," the girl pursued, imploringly. "Nothing is possible to-day. Some day or other very likely there will be changes. Then we shall meet; then we shall talk again."

"I like the way you ask me to wait ten years. What do you mean by 'changes'? Before heaven, I shall never change," Sir Rufus declared.

Agatha Grice hesitated. "Well, perhaps you will like us better."

"Us? Whom do you mean by 'us'? Are you coming back to that beastly question of one's feelings—real or supposed it doesn't matter—about your great and glorious country? Good God, it's too monstrous! One tells a girl one adores her and she replies that she doesn't care so long as one doesn't adore her compatriots. What do you want me to do to them? What do you want me to say? I will say anything in the English language, or in the American, that you like. I'll say that they're the greatest of the great and have every charm and virtue under heaven. I'll go down on my stomach before them and remain there for ever. I can't do more than that!"

Whether this extravagant profession had the effect of making Agatha Grice ashamed of having struck that note in regard to her companion's international attitude, or whether her nerves were simply upset by his vehemence, his insistence, is more than I can say: what is certain is that her rejoinder to this last speech was a sudden burst of tears. They fell for a moment rapidly, soundlessly, but she was quicker still in brushing them away. "You may laugh at me or you may despise me," she said when she could speak, "and I daresay my state of mind is deplorably narrow. But I couldn't be happy with you if you hated my country."

"You would hate mine back and we should pass the liveliest, jolliest days!" returned the Englishman, gratified, softened, enchanted by her tears. "My dear girl, what is a woman's country? It's her house and her garden, her children and her social world. You exaggerate immensely the difference which that part of the business makes. I assure you that if you were to marry me it would be the last thing you would find yourself thinking of. However, to prove how little I hate your country I am perfectly willing to go there and live with you."

"Oh, Sir Rufus Chasemore!" murmured Agatha Grice, protestingly.

"You don't believe me?"

She believed him not a bit and yet to hear him make such an offer was sweet to her, for it gave her a sense of the reality of his passion. "I shouldn't ask that—I shouldn't even like it," she said; and then he wished to know what she would like. "I should like you to let me go—not to press me, not to distress me any more now. I shall think of everything—of course you know that. But it will take me a long time. That's all I can tell you now, but I think you ought to be content." He was obliged to say that he was content, and they resumed their walk in the direction of the hotel. Shortly before they reached it Agatha exclaimed with a certain irrelevance, "You ought to go there first; then you would know."

"Then I should know what?"

"Whether you would like it."

"Like your great country? Good Lord, what difference does it make whether I like it or not?"

"No—that's just it—you don't care," said Agatha; "yet you said to my brother that you wanted immensely to go."

438

"So I do; I am ashamed not to have been; that's an immense drawback to-day, in England, to a man in public life. Something has always stopped me off, tiresomely, from year to year. Of course I shall go the very first moment I can take the time."

"It's a pity you didn't go this year instead of coming down here," the girl observed, rather sententiously.

"I thank my stars I didn't!" he responded, in a very different tone.

"Well, I should try to make you like it," she went on. "I think it very probable I should succeed."

"I think it very probable you could do with me exactly whatever you might attempt."

"Oh, you hypocrite!" the girl exclaimed; and it was on this that she separated from him and went into the house. It soothed him to see her do so instead of rejoining her mother and brother, whom he distinguished at a distance sitting on the terrace. She had perceived them there as well, but she would go straight to her room; she preferred the company of her thoughts. It suited Sir Rufus Chasemore to believe that those thoughts would plead for him and eventually win his suit. He gave a melancholy, loverlike sigh, however, as he walked toward Mrs. Grice and her son. He could not keep away from them, though he was so interested in being and appearing discreet. The girl had told him that her mother liked him, and he desired both to stimulate and to reward that inclination. Whatever he desired he desired with extreme definiteness and energy. He would go and sit down beside the little old lady (with whom hitherto he had no very direct conversation), and talk to her and be kind to her and amuse her. It must be added that he rather despaired of the success of these arts as he saw Macarthy Grice, on becoming aware of his approach, get up and walk away.

IV

"IT sometimes seems to me as if he didn't marry on purpose to make me feel badly." That was the only fashion, as yet, in which Lady Chasemore had given away her brother to her husband. The words fell from her lips some five years after Macarthy's visit to the lake of Como—two years after her mother's death—a twelvemonth after her marriage. The same idea came into her mind—a trifle whimsically perhaps, only this time she forbore to express it—as she stood by her husband's side, on the deck of the steamer, half an hour before they reached the wharf at New York. Six years had elapsed between the scenes at Cadenabbia and their disembarkation in that city. Agatha knew that Macarthy would be on the wharf to meet them, and that he should be there alone was natural enough. But she had a prevision of their return with him—she also knew he expected that—to the house, so narrow but fortunately rather deep, in Thirty-seventh street,[559] in which such a happy trio had lived in the old days before this unexpressed but none the less perceptible estrangement. As her marriage had taken place in Europe (Sir Rufus coming to her at Bologna,[560] in the very midst of the Parliamentary session,[561] the moment he heard, by his sister, of her mother's death: this was really the sign of devotion that had won her); as the ceremony of her nuptials, I say—a very simple one—had been performed in Paris, so that her absence from her native land had had no intermission, she had not seen the house since she left it with her mother for that remedial pilgrimage in the course of which poor Mrs. Grice, travelling up from Rome in the spring, after her third winter there (two had been so far from sufficing), was to succumb, from one day to the other, to inflammation of the lungs. She saw it over again now, even before she left the ship, and felt in advance all that it would imply to find Macarthy living there as a bachelor, struggling with New York servants, unaided and unrelieved by the sister whose natural place might by many people have been thought to be the care of his establishment, as her natural reward would have been the honours of such a position. Lady Chasemore was prepared to feel pang upon pang when she should perceive how much less comfortably he lived than he would have lived if she had not quitted him. She knew that their second cousins in Boston, whose sense of duty was so terrible (even her poor mother, who never had a thought for herself, used to try as much as possible to conceal her life from them), considered that she had in a manner almost immoral deserted him for the sake of an English title.[562] When they went ashore and drove home with Macarthy Agatha received exactly the impression she had expected: her brother's life struck her as bare, ungarnished, helpless, socially and domestically speaking. He had not the art of keeping house, naturally, and in New York, unless one were a good deal richer than he, it was very difficult to do that sort of thing by deputy. But Lady Chasemore made no further allusion to the idea that he remained single out of perversity. The situation was too serious for that or for any other flippant speech.

It was a delicate matter for the brothers-in-law to spend two or three weeks together; not however because when the moment for her own real decision came Macarthy had protested in vivid words against her marriage. By the time he arrived from America after his mother's death the Englishman was in possession of the field and it was too late to save her. He had had the opportunity to show her kindness for which her situation made her extremely grateful—he had indeed rendered her services which Macarthy himself, though he knew they were the result of an interested purpose, could not but appreciate. When her brother met her in Paris he saw that she was already lost to him: she had ceased to struggle, she had accepted the fate of a Briton's bride. It appeared that she was much in love with her Briton—that was necessarily the end of it. Macarthy offered no opposition, and she would have liked it better if he had, as it would have given her a chance to put him in the wrong a little more than, formally at least, she had been able to do. He knew that she knew what he thought and how he felt, and there was no need of saying any more about it. No doubt he would not have accepted a sacrifice from her even if she had been capable of making it (there were moments when it seemed to her that even at the last, if he had appealed to her directly and with tenderness, she would have renounced); but it was none the less clear to her that he was deeply disappointed at her having found it in her heart to separate herself so utterly. And there was something in his whole attitude which seemed to say that it was not only from him that she separated herself, but from all her fellow-countrymen besides and from everything that was best and finest in American life. He regarded her marriage as an abjuration, an apostasy, a kind of moral treachery. It was of no use to say to him that she was doing nothing original or extraordinary, to ask him if he did not know that in England, at the point things had come to, American wives were as thick as blackberries, so that if she were doing wrong she was doing wrong with—well, almost the majority: for he had an answer to such cheap arguments, an answer according to which it appeared that the American girls who had done what she was about to do were notoriously poor specimens, the most frivolous and feather-headed young persons in the country. They had no conception of the great meaning of American institutions, no appreciation of their birthright, and they were doubtless very worthy recruits to a debauched and stultified aristocracy. The pity of Agatha's desertion was that *she* had been meant for better things, she had appreciated her birthright, or if she had not it had not been the fault of a brother who had taken so much pains to form her mind and character. The sentiment of her nationality had been cultivated in her; it was not a mere brute instinct or customary prejudice—it was a responsibility, a faith, a religion. She was not a poor specimen but a remarkably fine one; she was intelligent, she was clever, she was sensitive, she could understand difficult things and feel great ones.

Of course in those days of trouble in Paris, when it was arranged that she should be married immediately (as if there had really been an engagement to Sir Rufus from the night before their flight from Cadenabbia), of course she had had a certain amount of talk with Macarthy about the matter, and at such moments she had almost wished to drive him to protest articulately, so that she might as explicitly reassure him, endeavour to bring him round. But he had never said to her personally what he had said to her mother at Cadenabbia—what her mother, frightened and distressed, had immediately repeated to her. The most he said was that he hoped she was conscious of all the perfectly different and opposed things she and her husband would represent when they should find themselves face to face. He hoped she had measured in advance the strain that might arise from the fact that in so many ways her good would be his evil, her white his black and *vice versa*—the fact in a word that by birth, tradition, convictions, she was the product of a democratic society, while the very breath of Sir Rufus's nostrils was the denial of human equality. She had replied, "Oh yes, I have thought of everything;" but in reality she had not thought that she was in any very aggressive manner a democrat or even that she had a representative function. She had not thought that Macarthy in his innermost soul was a democrat either; and she had even wondered what would happen if in regard to some of those levelling theories he had suddenly been taken at his word. She knew however that nothing would have made him more angry than to hint that anything could happen which would find him unprepared, and she was ashamed to repudiate the opinions, the general character her brother attributed to her, to fall below the high standard he had set up for her. She had moreover no wish to do so. She was well aware that there were many things in English life that she should not like, and she was never a more passionate American than the day she married Sir Rufus Chasemore.

To what extent she remained one an observer of the deportment of this young lady would at first have had considerable difficulty in judging. The question of the respective merits of the institutions of the two countries came up very little in her life. Her husband had other things to think of than the great republic beyond the sea, and her horizon, social and political, had practically the same large but fixed line as his. Sir Rufus was immersed in politics and in administrative questions; but these things belonged wholly to the domestic field; they were embodied in big blue-books[563] with terrible dry titles (Agatha had tried conscientiously to acquaint herself with the contents of some of them), which piled themselves up on the table of his library. The conservatives had come into power[564] just after his marriage, and he had held honourable though not supereminent office. His duties had nothing to do with foreign relations; they were altogether of an economical and statistical kind. He performed them in a manner which showed perhaps that he was conscious of some justice in the reproach usually addressed to the Tories—the taunt that they always came to grief in the department of industry and finance. His wife was sufficiently in his confidence to know how much he had it at heart to prove that a conservative administration could be strong in ciphering. He never spoke to her of her own country— they had so many other things to talk about—but if there was nothing in his behaviour to betray the assumption that she had given it up, so on the other hand there was nothing to show that he doubted of her having done so. What he had said about a woman's country being her husband and children, her house and garden and visiting list, was very considerably verified; for it was certain that her ladyship's new career gave her, though she had no children, plenty of occupation. Even if it had not however she would have found a good deal of work to her hand in loving her husband, which she continued to do with the most commendable zeal. He seemed to her a very magnificent person, bullying her not half so much as she expected. There were times when it even occurred to her that he really did not bully her enough, for she had always had an idea that it would be agreeable to be subjected to this probation by some one she should be very fond of.

After they had been married a year he became a permanent official,[565] in succession to a gentleman who was made a peer on his retirement[566] from the post to which Sir Rufus was appointed. This gave Lady Chasemore an opportunity to reflect that she might some day be a peeress, it being reasonable to suppose that the same reward would be meted out to her husband on the day on which, in the fulness of time and of credit, he also should retire. She was obliged to admit to herself that the reflection was unattended with any sense of horror; it exhilarated her indeed to the point of making her smile at the contingency of Macarthy's finding himself the brother of a member of the aristocracy. As a permanent official her husband was supposed to have no active political opinions; but she could not flatter herself that she perceived any diminution of his conservative zeal. Even if she had done so it would have made little difference, for it had not taken her long to discover that she had married into a tremendous Tory "set"[567]—a set in which people took for granted she had feelings that she was not prepared to publish on the housetops.[568] It was scarcely worth while however to explain at length that she had not been brought up in that way, partly because the people would not have understood and partly because really after all they did not care. How little it was possible in general to care her career in England helped her in due time to discover. The people who cared least appeared to be those who were most convinced that everything in the national life was going to the dogs. Lady Chasemore was not struck with this tendency herself; but if she had been the belief would have worried her more than it seemed to worry her friends. She liked most of them extremely and thought them very kind, very easy to live with; but she liked London

444

much better than the country, rejoiced much when her husband's new post added to the number of months he would have annually to spend there (they ended by being there as much as any one), and had grave doubts as to whether she would have been able to "stand" it if her lot had been cast among those members of her new circle who lived mainly on their acres.

All the same, though what she had to bear she bore very easily, she indulged in a good deal of private meditation on some of the things that failed to catch her sympathy. She did not always mention them to her husband, but she always intended to mention them. She desired he should not think that she swallowed his country whole, that she was stupidly undiscriminating. Of course he knew that she was not stupid and of course also he knew that she could not fail to be painfully impressed by the misery and brutality of the British populace. She had never anywhere else seen anything like that. Of course, furthermore, she knew that Sir Rufus had given and would give in the future a great deal of thought to legislative measures directed to elevating gradually the condition of the lower orders. It came over Lady Chasemore at times that it would be well if some of these measures might arrive at maturity with as little delay as possible.

The night before she quitted England with her husband they slept at an hotel at Liverpool, in order to embark early on the morrow. Sir Rufus went out to attend to some business and, the evening being very close, she sat at the window of their sitting-room and looked out on a kind of square which stretched in front of the hotel. The night was muggy, the window was open and she was held there by a horrible fascination. Dusky forms of vice and wretchedness moved about in the stuffy darkness, visions of grimy, half-naked, whining beggary hovered before her, curses and the sound of blows came to her ears; there were young girls, frousy and violent, who evidently were drunk, as every one seemed to be, more or less, which was little wonder, as four public-houses flared into the impure night, visible from where Lady Chasemore sat, and they appeared to be gorged with customers, half of whom were women. The impression came back to her that the horrible place had made upon her and upon her mother when they landed in England years before, and as she turned from the window she liked to think that she was going to a country where, at any rate, there would be less of that sort of thing. When her husband came in he said it was of course a beastly place but much better than it used to be—which she was glad to hear. She made some allusion to the confidence they might have that they should be treated to no such scenes as that in *her* country: whereupon he remonstrated, jocosely expressing a hope that they should not be deprived of a glimpse of the celebrated American drinks and bar-room fights.

It must be added that in New York he made of his brother-in-law no inquiry about these phenomena—a reserve, a magnanimity keenly appreciated by his wife. She appreciated altogether the manner in which he conducted himself during their visit to the United States and felt that if she had not already known that she had married a perfect gentleman the fact would now have been revealed to her. For she had to make up her mind to this, that after all (it was vain to shut one's eyes to it) Sir Rufus personally did not like the United States: he did not like them yet he made an immense effort to behave as if he did. She was grateful to him for that; it assuaged her nervousness (she was afraid there might be 'scenes' if he should break out with some of his displeasures); so grateful that she almost forgot to be disappointed at the failure of her own original intent, to be distressed at seeing or rather at guessing (for he was reserved about it even to her), that a nearer view of American institutions had not had the effect which she once promised herself a nearer view should have. She had married him partly to bring him over to an admiration of her country (she had never told any one this, for she was too proud to make the confidence to an English person and if she had made it to an American the answer would have been so prompt, "What on earth does it signify what he thinks of it?" no one, of course, being obliged to understand that it might signify to *her*); she had united herself to Sir Rufus in this missionary spirit and now not only did her proselyte prove unamenable but the vanity of her enterprise became a fact of secondary importance. She wondered a little that she did not suffer more from it, and this is partly why she rejoiced that her husband kept most of his observations to himself: it gave her a pretext for not being ashamed. She had flattered herself before that in general he had the manners of a diplomatist (she did not suspect that this was not the opinion of all his contemporaries), and his behaviour during the first few weeks at least of their stay in the western world struck her as a triumph of diplomacy. She had really passed from caring whether he disliked American manners to caring primarily whether he showed he disliked them—a transition which on her own side she was very sensible it was important to conceal from Macarthy. To love a man who could feel no tenderness for the order of things which had encompassed her early years and had been intimately mixed with her growth, which was a part of the conscience, the piety of many who had been most dear to her and whose memory would be dear to her always—that was an irregularity which was after all shut up in her own breast, where she could trust her dignity to get some way or other the upper hand of it. But to be pointed at as having such a problem as that on one's back was quite another affair; it was a kind of exposure of one's sanctities, a surrender of private judgment. Lady Chasemore had by this time known her husband long enough to enter into the logic of his preferences; if he disliked or disapproved what he saw in America his reasons for doing so had ceased to be a mystery. They were the very elements of his character, the joints and vertebration of his general creed. All the while she was absent from England with him (it was not very long, their whole tour, including the two voyages, being included in ten weeks), she knew more or less the impression that things would have made upon him; she knew that both in the generals and in the particulars American life would have gone against his grain, contradicted his traditions, violated his taste.

V

ALL the same he was determined to see it thoroughly, and this is doubtless one of the reasons why after the first few days she cherished the hope that they should be able to get off at the end without any collision with Macarthy. Of course it was to be taken into account that Macarthy's own demeanour was much more that of a man of the world than she had ventured to hope. He appeared for the time almost to have smothered his national consciousness, which had always been so acute, and to have accepted his sister's perfidious alliance. She could see that he was delighted that she should be near him again—so delighted that he neglected to look for the signs of corruption in her or to manifest any suspicion that in fact, now that she was immersed in them again, she regarded her old associations with changed eyes. So, also, if she had not already been aware of how much Macarthy was a gentleman she would have seen it from the way he rose to the occasion. Accordingly they were all superior people and all was for the best in Lady Chasemore's simple creed. Her brother asked her no questions whatever about her life in England, but his letters had already enlightened her as to his determination to avoid that topic. They had hitherto not contained a single inquiry on the subject of her occupations and pursuits, and if she had been domiciled in the moon he could not have indulged in less reference to public or private events in the British islands. It was a tacit form of disapprobation of her being connected with that impertinent corner of the globe; but it had never prevented her from giving him the fullest information on everything he never asked about. He never took up her allusions, and when she poured forth information to him now in regard to matters concerning her life in her new home (on these points she was wilfully copious and appealing), he listened with a sort of exaggerated dumb deference, as if she were reciting a lesson and he must sit quiet till she should come to the end. Usually when she stopped he simply sighed, then directed the conversation to something as different as possible. It evidently pleased him however to see that she enjoyed her native air and her temporary reunion with some of her old familiars. This was a graceful inconsistency on his part: it showed that he had not completely given her up. Perhaps he thought Sir Rufus would die and that in this case she would come back and live in New York. She was careful not to tell him that such a calculation was baseless, that with or without Sir Rufus she should never be able to settle in her native city as Lady Chasemore. He was scrupulously polite to Sir Rufus, and this personage asked Agatha why he never by any chance addressed him save by his title. She could see what her husband meant, but even in the privacy of the conjugal chamber she was loyal enough to Macarthy not to reply, "Oh, it's a mercy he doesn't say simply 'Sir!'"

The English visitor was prodigiously active; he desired to leave nothing unexplored, unattempted; his purpose was to inspect institutions, to collect statistics, to talk with the principal people, to see the workings of the political machine, and Macarthy acquitted himself scrupulously, even zealously, in the way of giving him introductions and facilities. Lady Chasemore reflected with pleasure that it was in her brother's power to do the honours of his native land very completely. She suspected indeed that as he did not like her husband (he *couldn't* like him, in spite of Sir Rufus's now comporting himself so sweetly), it was a relief to him to pass him on to others—to work him off, as it were, into penitentiaries and chambers of commerce.[569] Sir Rufus's frequent expeditions to these establishments and long interviews with local worthies of every kind kept him constantly out of the house and removed him from contact with his host, so that as Macarthy was extremely busy with his own profession (Sir Rufus was greatly struck with the way he worked; he had never seen a gentleman work so hard, without any shooting or hunting or fishing), it may be said, though it sounds odd, that the two men met very little directly—met scarcely more than in the evening or in other words always in company. During the twenty days the Chasemores spent together in New York they either dined out or were members of a party given at home by Macarthy, and on these occasions Sir Rufus found plenty to talk about with his new acquaintance. His wife flattered herself he was liked, he was so hilarious and so easy. He had a very appreciative manner, but she really wished sometimes that he might have subdued his hilarity a little; there were moments when perhaps it looked as if he took everything in the United States as if it were more than all else amusing. She knew exactly how it must privately affect Macarthy, this implication that it was merely a comical country; but after all it was not very easy to say how Macarthy would have preferred that a stranger, or that Sir Rufus in particular, should take the great republic. A cheerful view, yet untinged by the sense of drollery—that would have been the right thing if it could have been arrived at. At all events (and this was something gained), if Sir Rufus was in his heart a pessimist in regard to things he did not like he was not superficially sardonic. And then he asked questions by the million; and what was curiosity but an homage?

It will be inferred, and most correctly, that Macarthy Grice was not personally in any degree for his brother-in-law the showman of the exhibition. He caused him to be conducted, but he did not conduct him. He listened to his reports of what he had seen (it was at breakfast mainly that these fresh intimations dropped from Sir Rufus's lips), with very much the same cold patience (as if he were civilly forcing his attention) with which he listened to Agatha's persistent anecdotes of things that had happened to her in England. Of course with Sir Rufus there could be no question of persistence; he cared too little whether Macarthy cared or not and he did not stick to this everlasting subject of American institutions either to entertain him or to entertain himself—all he wanted was to lead on to further researches and discoveries. Macarthy always met him with the same response, "Oh, So-and-So is the man to tell you all about that. If you wish I will give you a letter to him." Sir Rufus always wished and certainly Macarthy wrote a prodigious number of letters. The inquiries and conclusions of his visitor (so far as Sir Rufus indulged in the latter) all bore on special points; he was careful to commit himself to no crude generalisations. He had to remember that he had still the rest of the country to see, and after a little discussion (which was confined to Lady Chasemore and her husband) it was decided that he should see it without his wife, who would await his return among her friends in New York. This arrangement was much to her taste, but it gives again the measure of the degree to which she had renounced her early dream of interpreting the western world to Sir Rufus. If she was not to be at his side at the moment, on the spot, of course she could not interpret—he would get a tremendous start of her. In short by staying quietly with Macarthy during his absence she almost gave up the great advantage she had hitherto had of knowing more about America than her husband could. She liked however to feel that she was making a sacrifice—making one indeed both to Sir Rufus and to her brother. The idea of giving up something for Macarthy (she only wished it had been something more) did her great good—sweetened the period of her husband's absence.

The whole season had been splendid, but at this moment the golden days of the Indian summer[570] descended upon the shining city and steeped it in a kind of fragrant haze. For two or three weeks New York seemed to Lady Chasemore poetical; the marble buildings looked yellow in the sleeping sunshine and her native land exhibited for the occasion an atmosphere. Vague memories came back to her of her younger years, of things that had to do somehow with the blurred brightness of the late autumn in the country. She walked about, she walked irresponsibly for hours; she did not care, as she had to care in London. She met friends in the streets and turned and walked with them; and pleasures as simple as this acquired an exaggerated charm for her. She liked walking and as an American girl had indulged the taste freely; but in London she had no time but to drive—besides which there were other tiresome considerations. Macarthy came home from his office earlier and she went to meet him in Washington Square and walked up the Fifth Avenue[571] with him in the rich afternoon. It was many years since she had been in New York and she found herself taking a kind of relapsing interest in changes and improvements. There were houses she used to know, where friends had lived in the old days and where they lived no more (no one in New York seemed to her to live where they used to live), which reminded her of incidents she had long ago forgotten, incidents that it pleased and touched her now to recall. Macarthy became very easy and sociable; he even asked her a few questions about her arrangements and habits in England and struck her (though she had never been particularly aware of it before) as having a great deal of the American humour.[572] On one occasion he stayed away from work altogether and took her up the Hudson, on the steamer, to West Point[573]—an excursion in which she found a peculiar charm. Every day she lunched intimately with a dozen ladies, at the house of one or other of them.

In due time Sir Rufus returned from Canada, the Mississippi, the Rocky Mountains and California; he had achieved marvels in the way of traversing distances and seeing manners and men with rapidity and facility. Everything had been settled in regard to their sailing for England almost directly after his return; there were only to be two more days in New York, then a rush to Boston, followed by another rush to Philadelphia and Washington.[574] Macarthy made no inquiry whatever of his brother-in-law touching his impression of the great West; he neglected even to ask him if he had been favourably impressed with Canada. There would not have been much opportunity however, for Sir Rufus on his side was extremely occupied with the last things he had to do. He had not even time as yet to impart his impressions to his wife, and she forbore to interrogate him, feeling that the voyage close at hand would afford abundant leisure for the history of his adventures. For the moment almost the only light that he threw upon them was by saying to Agatha (not before Macarthy) that it was a pleasure to him to see a handsome woman again, as he had not had that satisfaction in the course of his travels. Lady Chasemore wondered, exclaimed, protested, eliciting from him the declaration that to his sense, and in the interior at least, the beauty of the women was, like a great many other things, a gigantic American fraud. Sir Rufus had looked for it in vain—he went so far as to say that he had, in the course of extensive wanderings about the world, seen no female type on the whole less to his taste than that of the ladies in whose society, in hundreds (there was no paucity of specimens), in the long, hot, heaving trains, he had traversed a large part of the American continent. His wife inquired whether by chance he preferred the young persons they had (or at least she had) observed at Liverpool the night before their departure; to which he replied that they were no doubt sad creatures, but that the looks of a woman mattered only so long as one lived with her, and he did not live, and never should live, with the daughters of that grimy seaport. With the women in the American cars he had been living—oh, tremendously! and they were deucedly plain. Thereupon Lady Chasemore wished to know whether he did not think Mrs. Eugene had beauty, and Mrs. Ripley, and her sister Mrs. Redwood, and Mrs. Long,[575] and several other ornaments of the society in which they had mingled during their stay in New York. "Mrs. Eugene is Mrs. Eugene and Mrs. Redwood is Mrs. Redwood," Sir Rufus retorted; "but the women in the cars weren't either, and all the women I saw were like the women in the cars."—"Well, there may be something in the cars," said Lady Chasemore, pensively; and she mentioned that it was very odd that during her husband's absence, as she roamed about New York, she should have made precisely the opposite reflection and been struck with the number of pretty faces. "Oh, pretty faces, pretty faces, I daresay!" But Sir Rufus had no time to develop this vague rejoinder.

When they came back from Washington to sail Agatha told her brother that he was going to write a book about America:[576] it was for this he had made so many inquiries and taken so many notes. She had not known it before; it was only while they were in Washington that he told her he had made up his mind to it. Something he saw or heard in Washington appeared to have brought this resolution to a point. Lady Chasemore privately thought it rather a formidable fact; her husband had startled her a good deal in announcing his intention. She had said, "Of course it will be friendly—you'll say nice things?" And he had replied, "My poor child, they will abuse me like a pickpocket." This had scarcely been reassuring, so that she had had it at heart to probe the question further, in the train, after they left Washington. But as it happened, in the train, all the way, Sir Rufus was engaged in conversation with a Democratic Congressman whom he had picked up she did not know how—very certainly he had not met him at any respectable house in Washington. They sat in front of her in the car, with their heads almost touching, and although she was a better American than her husband she should not have liked hers to be so close to that of the Democratic Congressman. Now of course she knew that Sir Rufus was taking in material for his book. This idea made her uncomfortable and she would have liked immensely to separate him from his companion—she scarcely knew why, after all, except that she could not believe the Representative represented anything very nice. She promised herself to ascertain thoroughly, after they should be comfortably settled in the ship, the animus with which the book was to be written. She was a very good sailor and she liked to talk at sea; there her husband would not be able to escape from her, and she foresaw the manner in which she should catechise him. It exercised her greatly in advance and she was more agitated than she could easily have expressed by the whole question of the book. Meanwhile, however, she was careful not to show her agitation to Macarthy. She referred to her husband's project as casually as possible, and the reason she referred to it was that this seemed more loyal—more loyal to Macarthy. If the book, when written, should attract attention by the severity of its criticism (and that by many qualities it would attract attention of the widest character Lady Chasemore could not doubt), she should feel more easy not to have had the air of concealing from her brother that such a work was in preparation, which would also be the air of having a bad conscience about it. It was to prove, both to herself and Macarthy, that she had a good conscience that she told him of Sir Rufus's design. The habit of detachment from matters connected with his brother-in-law's activity was strong in him; nevertheless he was not able to repress some sign of emotion—he flushed very perceptibly. Quickly, however, he recovered his appearance of considering that the circumstance was one in which he could not hope to interest himself much; though the next moment he observed, with a certain inconsequence, "I am rather sorry to hear it."

"Why are you sorry?" asked Agatha. She was surprised and indeed gratified that he should commit himself even so far as to express regret. What she had supposed he would say, if he should say anything, was that he was obliged to her for the information, but that if it was given him with any expectation that he might be induced to read the book he must really let her know that such an expectation was extremely vain. He could have no more affinity with Sir Rufus's printed ideas than with his spoken ones.

"Well, it will be rather disagreeable for you," he said, in answer to her question. "Unless indeed you don't care what he says."

"But I do care. The book will be sure to be very able. Do you mean if it should be severe—that would be disagreeable for me? Very certainly it would; it would put me in a false, in a ridiculous position, and I don't see how I should bear it," Lady Chasemore went on, feeling that her candour was generous and wishing it to be. "But I shan't allow it to be severe. To prevent that, if it's necessary, I will write every word of it myself."

She laughed as she took this vow, but there was nothing in Macarthy's face to show that *he* could lend himself to a mirthful treatment of the question. "I think an Englishman had better look at home," he said, "and if he does so I don't easily see how the occupation should leave him any leisure or any assurance for reading lectures to other nations.[577] The self-complacency of your husband's countrymen is colossal, imperturbable. Therefore, with the tight place they find themselves in to-day and with the judgment of the rest of the world upon them being what it is, it's grotesque to see them still sitting in their old judgment-seat and pronouncing upon the shortcomings of people who are full of the life that has so long since left *them*." Macarthy Grice spoke slowly, mildly, with a certain dryness, as if he were delivering himself once for all and would not return to the subject. The quietness of his manner made the words solemn for his sister, and she stared at him a moment, wondering, as if they pointed to strange things which she had hitherto but imperfectly apprehended.

"The judgment of the rest of the world—what is that?"

"Why, that they are simply finished; that they don't count."

"Oh, a nation must count which produces such men as my husband," Agatha rejoined, with another laugh. Macarthy was on the point of retorting that it counted as the laughing-stock of the world (that of course was something), but he checked himself and she moreover checked him by going on: "Why Macarthy, you ought to come out with a book yourself about the English. You would steal my husband's thunder."

"Nothing would induce me to do anything of the sort; I pity them too much."

"You pity them?" Lady Chasemore exclaimed. "It would amuse my husband to hear that."

"Very likely, and it would be exactly a proof of what is so pitiable—the contrast between their gross pretensions and the real facts of their condition. They have pressing upon them at once every problem, every source of weakness, every danger that can threaten the life of a people, and they have nothing to meet the situation with but their classic stupidity."

"Well, that has been useful to them before," said Lady Chasemore, smiling. Her smile was a little forced and she coloured as her brother had done when she first spoke to him. She found it impossible not to be impressed by what he said and yet she was vexed that she was, because this was far from her desire.

He looked at her as if he saw some warning in her face and continued: "Excuse my going so far. In this last month that we have spent together so happily for me I had almost forgotten that you are one of them."

Lady Chasemore said nothing—she did not deny that she was one of them. If her husband's country was denounced—after all he had not written his book yet—she felt as if such a denial would be a repudiation of one of the responsibilities she had taken in marrying him.

THE postman was at the door in Grosvenor Crescent[578] when she came
back from her drive; the servant took the letters from his hand as she passed
into the house. In the hall she stopped to see which of the letters were for
her; the butler gave her two and retained those that were for Sir Rufus. She
asked him what orders Sir Rufus had given about his letters and he replied
that they were to be forwarded up to the following night. This applied only
to letters, not to parcels, pamphlets and books. "But would he wish this
to go, my lady?" the man asked, holding up a small packet; he added that
it appeared to be a kind of document. She took it from him: her eye had
caught a name printed on the wrapper and though she made no great profession of literature she recognised the name as that of a distinguished publisher and the packet as a roll of proof-sheets. She turned it up and down
while the servant waited; it had quite a different look from the bundles
of printed official papers which the postman was perpetually leaving and
which, when she scanned the array on the hall-table in her own interest,
she identified even at a distance. They were certainly the sheets, at least
the first, of her husband's book—those of which he had said to her on the
steamer, on the way back from New York a year before, "My dear child,
when I tell you that you shall see them—every page of them—that you shall
have complete control of them!" Since she was to have complete control of
them she began with telling the butler not to forward them—to lay them
on the hall-table. She went upstairs to dress—she was dining out in her
husband's absence—and when she came down to re-enter her carriage she
saw the packet lying where it had been placed. So many months had passed
that she had ended by forgetting that the book was on the stocks;[579] nothing had happened to remind her of it. She had believed indeed that it was
not on the stocks and even that the project would die a natural death. Sir
Rufus would have no time to carry it out—he had returned from America
to find himself more than ever immersed in official work—and if he did
not put his hand to it within two or three years at the very most he would

never do so at all, for he would have lost the freshness of his impressions, on which the success of the whole thing would depend. He had his notes of course, but none the less a delay would be fatal to the production of the volume (it was to be only a volume and not a big one), inasmuch as by the time it should be published it would have to encounter the objection that everything changed in America in two or three years and no one wanted to know anything about a dead past.

Such had been the reflections with which Lady Chasemore consoled herself for the results of those inquiries she had promised herself, in New York, to make when once she should be ensconced in a sea-chair by her husband's side and which she had in fact made to her no small discomposure. Meanwhile apparently he had stolen a march upon her, he had put his hand to *The Modern Warning* (that was to be the title, as she had learned on the ship), he had worked at it in his odd hours, he had sent it to the printers and here were the first-fruits of it. Had he had a bad conscience about it— was that the reason he had been so quiet? She did not believe much in his bad conscience, for he had been tremendously, formidably explicit when they talked the matter over; had let her know as fully as possible what he intended to do. Then it was that he relieved himself, that in the long, unoccupied hours of their fine voyage (he was in wonderful "form" at sea) he took her into the confidence of his real impressions—made her understand how things had struck him in the United States. They had not struck him well; oh no, they had not struck him well at all! But at least he had prepared her and therefore since then he had nothing to hide. It was doubtless an accident that he appeared to have kept his work away from her, for sometimes, in other cases, he had paid her intelligence the compliment (was it not for that in part he had married her?) of supposing that she could enter into it. It was probable that in this case he had wanted first to see for himself how his chapters would look in print. Very likely even he had not written the whole book, nor even half of it; he had only written the opening pages and had them "set up:" she remembered to have heard him speak of this as a very convenient system. It would be very convenient for her as well and she should also be much interested in seeing how they looked. On the table, in their neat little packet, they seemed half to solicit her, half to warn her off.

They were still there of course when she came back from her dinner, and this time she took possession of them. She carried them upstairs and in her dressing-room, when she had been left alone in her wrapper, she sat down with them under the lamp. The packet lay in her lap a long time, however, before she decided to detach the envelope. Her hesitation came not from her feeling in any degree that this roll of printed sheets had the sanctity of a letter, a seal that she might not discreetly break, but from an insurmountable nervousness as to what she might find within. She sat there for an hour, with her head resting on the back of her chair and her eyes closed; but she had not fallen asleep—Lady Chasemore was very wide-awake indeed. She was living for the moment in a kind of concentration of memory, thinking over everything that had fallen from her husband's lips after he began, as I have said, to relieve himself. It turned out that the opinion he had formed of the order of society in the United States was even less favourable than she had had reason to fear. There were not many things it would have occurred to him to commend, and the few exceptions related to the matters that were not most characteristic of the country—not idiosyncrasies of American life. The idiosyncrasies he had held to be one and all detestable. The whole spectacle was a vivid warning, a consummate illustration of the horrors of democracy. The only thing that had saved the misbegotten republic as yet was its margin, its geographical vastness; but that was now discounted and exhausted. For the rest every democratic vice was in the ascendant and could be studied there *sur le vif*; he could not be too thankful that he had not delayed longer to go over and master the subject. He had come back with a head full of lessons and a heart fired with the resolve to enforce them upon his own people, who, as Agatha knew, had begun to move in the same lamentable direction. As she listened to him she perceived the mistake she had made in not going to the West with him, for it was from that part of the country that he had drawn his most formidable anecdotes and examples. Of these he produced a terrific array; he spoke by book, he overflowed with facts and figures, and his wife felt herself submerged by the deep, bitter waters. She even felt what a pity it was that she had not dragged him away from that vulgar little legislator whom he had stuck to so in the train, coming from Washington; yet it did not matter—a little more or a little less—the whole affair had rubbed him so the wrong way, exasperated his taste, confounded his traditions. He proved to have disliked quite unspeakably things that she supposed he liked, to have suffered acutely on occasions when she thought he was really pleased. It would appear that there had been no occasion, except once sitting at dinner between Mrs. Redwood and Mrs. Eugene, when he was really pleased. Even his long chat with the Pennsylvania representative had made him almost ill at the time. His wife could be none the less struck with the ability which had enabled him to absorb so much knowledge in so short a time; he had not only gobbled up facts, he had arranged them in a magnificent order, and she was proud of his being so clever even when he made her bleed by the way he talked. He had had no intention whatever of this, and he was as much surprised as touched when she broke out into a passionate appeal to him not to publish such horrible misrepresentations. She defended her country with exaltation, and so far as was possible in the face of his own flood of statistics, of anecdotes of "lobbying,"[580] of the corruption of public life, for which she was unprepared, endeavouring to gainsay him in the particulars as well as in the generals, she maintained that he had seen everything wrong, seen it through the distortion of prejudice, of a hostile temperament, in the light—or rather in the darkness—of wishing to find weapons to worry the opposite party in England. Of course America had its faults, but on the whole it was a much finer country than any other, finer even than his clumsy, congested old England, where there was plenty to do to sweep the house clean, if he would give a little more of his time to that. Scandals for scandals she had heard more since she came to England than all the years she had lived at home. She forbore to quote Macarthy to him (she had reasons for not doing so), but something of the spirit of Macarthy flamed up in her as she spoke.

Sir Rufus smiled at her vehemence; he took it in perfectly good part, though it evidently left him not a little astonished. He had forgotten that America was hers—that she had any allegiance but the allegiance of her marriage. He had made her his own and, being the intense Englishman that he was, it had never occurred to him to doubt that she now partook of his quality in the same degree as himself. He had assimilated her, as it were, completely, and he had assumed that she had also assimilated him and his country with him—a process which would have for its consequence that the other country, the ugly, vulgar, importunate one, would be, as he mentally phrased it to himself, "shunted."[581] That it had not been was the proof of rather a morbid sensibility, which tenderness and time would still assuage. Sir Rufus was tender, he reassured his wife on the spot, in the first place by telling her that she knew nothing whatever about the United States (it was astonishing how little many of the people in the country itself knew about them), and in the second by promising her that he would not print a word to which her approval should not be expressly given. She should countersign every page before it went to press, and none should leave the house without her *visé*. She wished to know if he possibly could have forgotten—so strange would it be—that she had told him long ago, at Cadenabbia, how horrible it would be to her to find herself married to a man harbouring evil thoughts of her fatherland. He remembered this declaration perfectly and others that had followed it, but was prepared to ask if she on her side recollected giving him notice that she should convert him into an admirer of transatlantic peculiarities. She had had an excellent opportunity, but she had not carried out her plan. He had been passive in her hands, she could have done what she liked with him (had not he offered, that night by the lake of Como, to throw up his career and go and live with her in some beastly American town? and he had really meant it—upon his honour he had!), so that if the conversion had not come off whose fault was it but hers? She had not gone to work with any sort of earnestness. At all events now it was too late; he had seen for himself—the impression was made. Two points were vivid beyond the others in Lady Chasemore's evocation of the scene on the ship; one was her husband's insistence on the fact that he had not the smallest animosity to the American people, but had only his own English brothers in view, wished only to protect and save them, to point a certain moral as it never had been pointed before; the other was his pledge that nothing should be made public without her assent.

As at last she broke the envelope of the packet in her lap she wondered how much she should find to assent to. More perhaps than a third person judging the case would have expected; for after what had passed between them Sir Rufus must have taken great pains to tone down his opinions—or at least the expression of them.

HE came back to Grosvenor Place the next evening very late and on asking for his wife was told that she was in her apartments. He was furthermore informed that she was to have dined out but had given it up, countermanding the carriage at the last moment and despatching a note instead. On Sir Rufus's asking if she were ill it was added that she had seemed not quite right and had not left the house since the day before. A minute later he found her in her own sitting-room, where she appeared to have been walking up and down. She stopped when he entered and stood there looking at him; she was in her dressing-gown, very pale, and she received him without a smile. He went up to her, kissed her, saw something strange in her eyes and asked with eagerness if she had been suffering. "Yes, yes," she said, "but I have not been ill," and the next moment flung herself upon his neck and buried her face there, sobbing yet at the same time stifling her sobs. Inarticulate words were mingled with them and it was not till after a moment he understood that she was saying, "How could you? ah, how *could* you?" He failed to understand her allusion, and while he was still in the dark she recovered herself and broke away from him. She went quickly to a drawer and possessed herself of a parcel of papers which she held out to him, this time without meeting his eyes. "Please take them away—take them away for ever. It's your book—the things from the printers. I saw them on the table—I guessed what they were—I opened them to see. I read them—I read them. Please take them away."

He had by this time become aware that even though she had flung herself upon his breast his wife was animated by a spirit of the deepest reproach, an exquisite sense of injury. When he first saw the papers he failed to recognise his book: it had not been in his mind. He took them from her with an exclamation of wonder, accompanied by a laugh which was meant in kindness, and turned them over, glancing at page after page. Disconcerted as he was at the condition in which Agatha presented herself he was still accessible to that agreeable titillation which a man feels on seeing his prose "set up."

Sir Rufus had been quoted and reported by the newspapers and had put into circulation several little pamphlets, but this was his first contribution to the regular literature of his country, and his publishers had given him a very handsome page. Its striking beauty held him a moment; then his eyes passed back to his wife, who with her grand, cold, wounded air was also very handsome. "My dear girl, do you think me an awful brute? have I made you ill?" he asked. He declared that he had no idea he had gone so far as to shock her—he had left out such a lot; he had tried to keep the sting out of everything; he had made it all butter and honey. But he begged her not to get into a state; he would go over the whole thing with her if she liked—make any changes she should require. It would spoil the book, but he would rather do that than spoil her perfect temper. It was in a highly jocular manner that he made this allusion to her temper, and it was impressed upon her that he was not too much discomposed by her discomposure to be able to joke. She took notice of two things: the first of which was that he had a perfectly good conscience and that no accusing eye that might have been turned upon him would have made him change colour. He had no sense that he had broken faith with her, and he really thought his horrible book was very mild. He spoke the simple truth in saying that for her sake he had endeavoured to qualify his strictures, and strange as it might appear he honestly believed he had succeeded. Later, at other times, Agatha wondered what he would have written if he had felt himself free. What she observed in the second place was that though he saw she was much upset he did not in the least sound the depth of her distress or, as she herself would have said, of her shame. He never would—he never would; he could not enter into her feelings, because he could not believe in them: they could only strike him as exaggerated and factitious. He had given her a country, a magnificent one, and why in the name of common sense was she making him a scene about another? It was morbid—it was mad.

When he accused her of this extravagance it was very simple for her to meet his surprise with a greater astonishment—astonishment at his being able to allow so little for her just susceptibility. He could not take it seriously that she had American feelings; he could not believe that it would make a terrible difference in her happiness to go about the world as the wife, the cynical, consenting wife of the author of a blow dealt with that brutality at a breast to which she owed filial honour. She did not say to him that she should never hold her head up before Macarthy again (her strength had been that hitherto, as against Macarthy, she was perfectly straight), but it was in a great degree the prefigurement of her brother's cold, lifelong scorn that had kindled in her, while she awaited her husband's return, the passion with which she now protested. He would never read *The Modern Warning* but he would hear all about it; he would meet it in the newspapers, in every one's talk; the very voices of the air would distil the worst pages into his ear and make the scandal of her participation even greater than—as heaven knew—it would deserve to be. She thought of the month of renewed association, of happy, pure impressions that she had spent a year before in the midst of American kindness, in the midst of memories more innocent than her visions of to-day; and the effect of this retrospect was galling in the face of her possible shame. Shame—shame: she repeated that word to Sir Rufus in a tone which made him stare, as if it dawned upon him that her reason was perhaps deserting her. That shame should attach itself to his wife in consequence of any behaviour of *his* was an idea that he had to make a very considerable effort to embrace; and while his candour betrayed it his wife was touched even through her resentment by seeing that she had not made him angry. He thought she was strangely unreasonable, but he was determined not to fall into that vice on his own side.

She was silent about Macarthy because Sir Rufus had accused her before her marriage of being afraid of him, and she had then resolved never again to incur such a taunt; but before things had gone much further between them she reminded her husband that she had Irish blood, the blood of the people, in her veins and that he must take that into account in measuring the provocation he might think it safe to heap upon her. She was far from being a fanatic on this subject, as he knew; but when America was made out to be an object of holy horror to virtuous England she could not but remember that millions of her Celtic cousins had found refuge there from the blessed English dispensation[582] and be struck with his recklessness in challenging comparisons which were better left to sleep.

When his wife began to represent herself as Irish Sir Rufus evidently thought her "off her head" indeed: it was the first he had heard of it since she communicated the mystic fact to him on the lake of Como. Nevertheless he argued with her for half an hour as if she were sane, and before they separated he made her a liberal concession, such as only a perfectly lucid mind would be able to appreciate. This was a simple indulgence, at the end of their midnight discussion; it was not dictated by any recognition of his having been unjust; for though his wife reiterated this charge with a sacred fire in her eyes which made them more beautiful than he had ever known them he took his stand, in his own stubborn opinion, too firmly upon piles of evidence, revelations of political fraud and corruption, and the "whole tone of the newspapers"—to speak only of that. He remarked to her that clearly he must simply give way to her opposition. If she were going to suffer so inordinately it settled the question. The book should not be published and they would say no more about it. He would put it away, he would burn it up and *The Modern Warning* should be as if it had never been. Amen! amen! Lady Chasemore accepted this sacrifice with eagerness, although her husband (it must be added) did not fail to place before her the exceeding greatness of it. He did not lose his temper, he was not petulant nor spiteful, he did not throw up his project and his vision of literary distinction in a huff; but he called her attention very vividly and solemnly to the fact that in deferring to the feelings she so uncompromisingly expressed he renounced the dream of rendering a signal service to his country. There was a certain bitterness in his smile as he told her that *her* wish was the only thing in the world that could have made him throw away such a golden opportunity. The rest of his life would never offer him such another; but patriotism might go to the dogs if only it were settled that she should not have a grudge. He did not care what became of poor old England if once that precious result were obtained; poor old England might pursue impure delusions and rattle down hill as fast as she chose for want of the word his voice would have spoken—really inspired as he held it to be by the justice of his cause.

Lady Chasemore flattered herself that they did not drop the subject that night in acrimony; there was nothing of this in the long kiss which she took from her husband's lips, with wet eyes, with a grateful, comprehensive murmur. It seemed to her that nothing could be fairer or finer than their mutual confidence; her husband's concession was gallant in the extreme; but even more than this was it impressed upon her that her own affection was perfect, since it could accept such a renunciation without a fear of the aftertaste. She had been in love with Sir Rufus from the day he sought her hand at Cadenabbia, but she was never so much in love with him as during the weeks that immediately followed his withdrawal of his book. It was agreed between them that neither of them would speak of the circumstance again, but she at least, in private, devoted an immense deal of meditation to it. It gave her a tremendous reprieve, lifted a nightmare off her breast, and that in turn gave her freedom to reflect that probably few men would have made such a graceful surrender. She wanted him to understand, or at any rate she wanted to understand herself, that in all its particulars too she thoroughly appreciated it; if he really was unable to conceive how she could feel as she did, it was all the more generous of him to comply blindly, to take her at her word, little as he could make of it. It did not become less obvious to Lady Chasemore, but quite the contrary, as the weeks went on, that *The Modern Warning* would have been a masterpiece of its class. In her room, that evening, her husband had told her that the best of him intellectually had gone into it, that he believed he had uttered certain truths there as they never would be uttered again—contributed his grain of gold to the limited sum of human wisdom. He had done something to help his country, and then— to please her—he had undone it. Above all it was delightful to her that he had not been sullen or rancorous about it, that he never made her pay for his magnanimity. He neither sighed nor scowled nor took on the air of a domestic martyr; he came and went with his usual step and his usual smile, remaining to all appearance the same fresh-coloured, decided, accomplished high official.

Therefore it is that I find it difficult to explain how it was that Lady Chasemore began to feel at the end of a few months that their difficulties had after all not become the mere reminiscence of a flurry, making present security more deep. What if the flurry continued impalpably, insidiously, under the surface? She thought there had been no change, but now she suspected that there was at least a difference. She had read Tennyson and she knew the famous phrase about the little rift within the lute.[583] It came back to her with a larger meaning, it haunted her at last, and she asked herself whether when she accepted her husband's relinquishment it had been her happiness and his that she staked and threw away. In the light of this fear she struck herself as having lived in a fool's paradise—a misfortune from which she had ever prayed to be delivered. She wanted in every situation to know the worst, and in this case she had not known it; at least she knew it only now, in the shape of the formidable fact that Sir Rufus's outward good manners misrepresented his real reaction. At present she began anxiously, broodingly to take this reaction for granted and to see signs of it in the very things which she had regarded at first as signs of resignation. She secretly watched his face; she privately counted his words. When she began to do this it was no very long time before she made up her mind that the latter had become much fewer—that Sir Rufus talked to her very much less than he had done of old. He took no revenge, but he was cold, and in his coldness there was something horribly inevitable. He looked at her less and less, whereas formerly his eyes had had no more agreeable occupation. She tried to teach herself that her suspicions were woven of air and were an offence to a just man's character; she remembered that Sir Rufus had told her she was morbid, and if the charge had not been true at the time it might very well be true now. But the effect of this reflection was only to suggest to her that Sir Rufus himself was morbid and that her behaviour had made him so. It was the last thing that would be in his nature, but she had subjected that nature to an injurious strain. He was feeling it now; he was feeling that he had failed in the duty of a good citizen: a good citizen being what he had ever most earnestly proposed to himself to be. Lady Chasemore pictured to herself that his cheek burned for this when it was turned away from her— that he ground his teeth with shame in the watches of the night.[584] Then it came over her with unspeakable bitterness that there had been no real solution of their difficulty; that it was too great to be settled by so simple an arrangement as that—an arrangement too primitive for a complicated world. Nothing was less simple than to bury one's gold and live without the interest.

It is a singular circumstance, and suggesting perhaps a perversion of the imagination under the influence of distress, but Lady Chasemore at this time found herself thinking with a kind of baffled pride of the merits of *The Modern Warning* as a literary composition, a political essay. It would have been dreadful for her, but at least it would have been superb, and that was what was naturally enough present to the defeated author as he tossed through the sleepless hours. She determined at last to question him, to confess her fears, to make him tell her whether his weakness—if he considered it a weakness—really did rankle; though when he made the sacrifice months before (nearly a year had come round) he had let her know that he wished the subject buried between them for evermore. She approached it with some trepidation, and the manner in which he looked at her as she stammered out her inquiry was not such as to make the effort easier. He waited in silence till she had expressed herself as she best could, without helping her, without showing that he guessed her trouble, her need to be assured that he did not feel her to have been cruel. Did he?—*did* he? that was what she wanted to be certain of. Sir Rufus's answer was in itself a question; he demanded what she meant by imputing to him such hypocrisy, such bad faith. What did she take him for and what right had he given her to make a new scene, when he flattered himself the last pretext had been removed? If he had been dissatisfied she might be very sure he would have told her so; and as he had not told her she might pay him the compliment to believe he was honest. He expressed the hope and for the first time in his life he was stern with her that this would be the last endeavour on her part to revive an odious topic. His sternness was of no avail; it neither wounded her nor comforted her; it only had the effect of making her perfectly sure that he suffered and that he regarded himself as a kind of traitor. He was one more in the long list of those whom a woman had ruined, who had sold themselves, sold their honour and the commonwealth, for a fair face, a quiet life, a show of tears, a bribe of caresses. The vision of this smothered pain, which he tried to carry off as a gentleman should, only ministered to the love she had ever borne him—the love that had had the power originally to throw her into his arms in the face of an opposing force. As month followed month all her nature centred itself in this feeling; she loved him more than ever and yet she had been the cause of the most tormenting thing that had ever happened to him. This was a tragic contradiction, impossible to bear, and she sat staring at it with tears of rage.

One day she had occasion to tell him that she had received a letter from Macarthy, who announced that he should soon sail for Europe, even intimated that he should spend two or three weeks in London. He had been overworked, it was years since he had had a proper holiday, and the doctor threatened him with nervous prostration unless he very soon broke off everything. His sister had a vision of his reason for offering to let her see him in England; it was a piece of appreciation on Macarthy's part, a reward for their having behaved—that is, for Sir Rufus's having behaved, apparently under her influence—better than might have been expected. He had the good taste not to bring out his insolent book, and Macarthy gave this little sign, the most mollified thing he had done as yet, that he noticed. If Lady Chasemore had not at this moment been thinking of something else it might have occurred to her that nervous prostration, in her brother's organism, had already set in. The prospect of his visit held Sir Rufus's attention very briefly, and in a few minutes Agatha herself ceased to dwell upon it. Suddenly, illogically, fantastically, she could not have told why, at that moment and in that place, for she had had no such intention when she came into the room, she broke out: "My own darling, do you know what has come over me? I have changed entirely—I see it differently; I want you to publish that grand thing." And she stood there smiling at him, expressing the transformation of her feeling so well that he might have been forgiven for not doubting it.

Nevertheless he did doubt it, especially at first. But she repeated, she pressed, she insisted; once she had spoken in this sense she abounded and overflowed. It went on for several days (he had begun by refusing to listen to her, for even in touching the question she had violated his express command), and by the end of a week she persuaded him that she had really come round. She was extremely ingenious and plausible in tracing the process by which she had done so, and she drew from him the confession (they kissed a great deal after it was made) that the manuscript of *The Modern Warning* had not been destroyed at all, but was safely locked up in a cabinet, together with the interrupted proofs. She doubtless placed her tergiversation in a more natural light than her biographer has been able to do: he however will spare the reader the exertion of following the impalpable clue which leads to the heart of the labyrinth. A month was still to elapse before Macarthy would show himself, and during this time she had the leisure and freedom of mind to consider the sort of face with which she should meet him, her husband having virtually promised that he would send the book back to the printers. Now, of course, she renounced all pretension of censorship; she had nothing to do with it; it might be whatever he liked; she gave him formal notice that she should not even look at it after it was printed. It was his affair altogether now—it had ceased to be hers. A hard crust had formed itself in the course of a year over a sensibility that was once so tender; this she admitted was very strange, but it would be stranger still if (with the value that he had originally set upon his opportunity) he should fail to feel that he might hammer away at it. In this case would not the morbidness be quite on *his* side? Several times, during the period that preceded Macarthy's arrival, Lady Chasemore saw on the table in the hall little packets which reminded her of the roll of proofs she had opened that evening in her room. Her courage never failed her, and an observer of her present relations with her husband might easily have been excused for believing that the solution which at one time appeared so illusory was now valid for earthly purposes. Sir Rufus was immensely taken up with the resumption of his task; the revision of his original pages went forward the more rapidly that in fact, though his wife was unaware of it, they had repeatedly been in his hands since he put them away. He had retouched and amended them, by the midnight lamp, disinterestedly, platonically, hypothetically; and the alterations and improvements which suggest themselves when valuable ideas are laid by to ripen, like a row of pears on a shelf, started into life and liberty. Sir Rufus was as happy as a man who after having been obliged for a long time to entertain a passion in secret finds it recognised and legitimated, finds that the obstacles are removed and he may conduct his beloved to the altar.

Nevertheless when Macarthy Grice alighted at the door of his sister's house—he had assented at the last to her urgent request that he would make it his habitation during his stay in London—he stepped into an atmosphere of sudden alarm and dismay. It was late in the afternoon, a couple of hours before dinner, and it so happened that Sir Rufus drove up at the moment the American traveller issued from the carriage that had been sent for him. The two men exchanged greetings on the steps of the house, but in the next breath Macarthy's host asked what had become of Agatha, whether she had not gone to the station to meet him, as she had announced at noon, when Sir Rufus saw her last, that she intended.

It appeared that she had not accompanied the carriage; Macarthy had been met only by one of the servants, who had been with the Chasemores to America and was therefore in a position to recognise him. This functionary said to Sir Rufus that her ladyship had sent him down word an hour before the carriage started that she had altered her intention and he was to go on without her. By this time the door of the house had been thrown open; the butler and the other footman had come to the front. They had not, however, their usual perpendicular demeanour, and the master's eye immediately saw that there was something wrong in the house. This apprehension was confirmed by the butler on the instant, before he had time to ask a question.

"We are afraid her ladyship is ill, sir; rather seriously, sir; we have but this moment discovered it, sir; her maid is with her, sir, and the other women."

Sir Rufus started; he paused but a single instant, looking from one of the men to the other. Their faces were very white; they had a strange, scared expression. "What do you mean by rather seriously?—what the devil has happened?" But he had sprung to the stairs—he was half-way up before they could answer.

"You had better go up, sir, really," said the butler to Macarthy, who was planted there and had turned as white as himself. "We are afraid she has taken something."

"Taken something?"

"By mistake, sir, you know, sir," quavered the footman, looking at his companion. There were tears in the footman's eyes. Macarthy felt sick.

"And there's no doctor? You don't send? You stand gaping?"

"We are going, sir—we have already gone!" cried both the men together. "He'll come from the hospital, round the corner;⁵⁸⁵ he'll be here by the time you're upstairs. It was but this very moment, sir, just before you rang the bell," one of them went on. The footman who had come with Macarthy from Euston⁵⁸⁶ dashed out of the house and he himself followed the direction his brother-in-law had taken. The butler was with him, saying he didn't know what—that it was only while they were waiting—that it would be a stroke for Sir Rufus. He got before him, on the upper landing; he led the way to Lady Chasemore's room, the door of which was open, revealing a horrible hush and, beyond the interior, a flurried, gasping flight of female domestics. Sir Rufus was there, he was at the bed still; he had cleared the room; two of the women had remained, they had hold of Lady Chasemore, who lay there passive, with a lifeless arm that caught Macarthy's eye—calling her, chafing her, pushing each other, saying that she would come to in a minute. Sir Rufus had apparently been staring at his wife in stupefaction and horror, but as Macarthy came to the bed he caught her up in his arms, pressing her to his bosom, and the American visitor met his face glaring at him over her shoulder, convulsed and transformed. "She has taken something, but only by mistake:" he was conscious that the butler was saying that again, behind him, in his ear.

"By God, you have killed her! It's *your* infernal work!" cried Sir Rufus, in a voice that matched his terrible face.

"*I* have killed her?" answered Macarthy, bewildered and appalled.

"Your damned fantastic opposition—the fear of meeting you," Sir Rufus went on. But his words lost themselves, as he bent over her, in violent kisses and imprecations, in demands whether nothing could be done, why the doctor was not there; in clumsy passionate attempts to arouse, to revive.

"Oh, I am sure she wanted you to come. She was very well this morning, sir," the waiting-maid broke out, to Macarthy, contradicting Sir Rufus in her fright and protesting again that it was nothing, that it was a faint, for the very pleasure, that her ladyship would come round. The other woman had picked up a little phial. She thrust it at Macarthy with the boldness of their common distress, and as he took it from her mechanically he perceived that it was empty and had a strange odour. He sniffed it—then with a shout of horror flung it away. He rushed at his sister and for a moment almost had a struggle with her husband for the possession of her body, in which, as soon as he touched it, he felt the absence of life. Then she was on the bed again, beautiful, irresponsive, inanimate, and they were both beside her for an instant, after which Sir Rufus broke away and staggered out of the room. It seemed an eternity to Macarthy while he waited, though it had already come over him that he was waiting only for something still worse. The women talked, tried to tell him things; one of them said something about the pity of his coming all the way from America on purpose. Agatha was beautiful; there was no disfigurement. The butler had gone out with Sir Rufus and he came back with him, reappearing first, and with the doctor. Macarthy did not even heed what the doctor said. By this time he knew it all for himself. He flung himself into a chair, overwhelmed, covering his face with the cape of his ulster. The odour of the little phial was in his nostrils. He let the doctor lead him out without resistance, scarcely with consciousness, after some minutes.

Lady Chasemore had taken something—the doctor gave it a name but it was not by mistake.[587] In the hall, downstairs, he stood looking at Macarthy, kindly, soothingly, tentatively, with his hand on his shoulder. "Had she—a—had she some domestic grief?" Macarthy heard him ask. He could not stay in the house—not with Chasemore. The servant who had brought him from the station took him to an hotel, with his luggage, in the carriage, which was still at the door—a horrible hotel where, in a dismal, dingy back room, with chimney-pots outside, he spent a night of unsurpassable anguish. He could not understand, and he howled to himself, "Why, *why,* just now?" Sir Rufus, in the other house, had exactly such another vigil: it was plain enough that this was the case when, the next morning, he came to the hotel. He held out his hand to Macarthy—he appeared to take back his monstrous words of the evening before. He made him return to Grosvenor Crescent; he made him spend three days there, three days during which the two men scarcely exchanged a word. But the rest of the holiday that Macarthy had undertaken for the benefit of his health was passed upon the Continent, with little present evidence that he should find what he had sought. *The Modern Warning* has not yet been published, but it may still appear. This doubtless will depend upon whether, this time, the sheets have really been destroyed—buried in Lady Chasemore's grave or only put back into the cabinet.

THE END.

GLOSSARY OF FOREIGN WORDS
AND PHRASES

All French unless stated otherwise. The foreign word or phrase is (or is not) capitalized and/or italicized based on how it is found in the text; if there is more than one usage, it is (or is not) italicized and/or capitalized based on the first usage in the texts. Words or phrases which may have a text-specific meaning are cross-referenced in the notes.

à la portée (de)	at the level of, acceptable to
à perte de vue	as far as the eye can see
à propos (de)	concerning
aborder	to approach
appartement de garçon	apartment, young man's lodgings
arrière-pensée	ulterior motive, lurking idea
avvocato	lawyer or barrister (Italian)
bal blanc	literally, a white dance, young girls' dance
bavardise	garrulity
beaux quartiers	elegant areas
boisson fade, écœurante	a plain, disgusting drink
bonhomie	geniality, good nature
bonnes d'enfants	children's nurses
bonté	goodness
boutade	wisecrack, joke
bric-à-brac	knick-knacks, objects without much value
cachet	particular qualities
campi	lit. fields (Venetian squares) (Italian)
capo d'anno	New Year's eve (Italian)
cara	dear (Italian) (f.)
carte blanche	full permission
cavaliere	knight (honorific title, term of address) (Italian)
ces dames	these ladies

C'est la moindre des choses	it is the least important thing
chef	cook
cher grand maître / cher maître	dear great master, dear master
cicerone	cultural guide (Italian)
combinare	to arrange, to find an agreement (Italian)
comme il faut	proper
condottiere	mercenary troops commander (Italian)
contadina	peasant woman (Italian)
contessa	countess (Italian)
(les) convenances	(the) rules of society, propriety
coupé	short, four-wheeled close carriage
curato	priest (Italian)
dans cette galère	in this galley, fig. in this business
dans le monde	in society, at social gatherings
de votre façon	in your style
Décidément, ma bonne, il n'y a que vous! C'est une perfection.	decidedly, my dear, you are the only one! It is perfect.
dénouement	conclusion
diligance	stage-coach (correctly *diligence*)
Donau	Danube (German)
donna	woman servant, maid (Italian)
D'où tombez vous	where on earth do you come from?
dove commanda?	where do you order? (correctly *comanda*; Italian)
duenna	chaperon (Spanish-Latin origin: *dueña-domina*)
Elle adore sa mère	she adores her mother
empressement	alacrity
en famille	simply, just with the members of the family
en fin de comte	all said and done
en herbe	budding
en pension	lodging and meals
enfoncée/enfoncé	sunk, ensconced (f./m.)
ennui	boredom

entourage	circle, surroundings, environment
entrée	literally entrance, invitation
entrée en matière	broaching the subject
felze	black wooden cover for a gondola (Italian)
femme forte	strong woman
festa	a public festival, a popular celebration (Italian)
fondamentas	streets alongside canals (correctly pl. *fondamente*; Italian)
froissé	irritated, annoyed
forestieri	foreigners, or people coming from other cities (Italian)
gemüthlich	comfortable, cosy (obs., now *gemütlich*; German)
giro	tour (Italian)
grand monde	high society
gondola, gondolas	gondola (correctly pl. *gondole*; Italian)
horresco referens	I shudder to relate (Latin)
intérieurs	interiors
Jamais de la vie!	Never ever!
Je m'en rapporte à Effie	Effie can tell
jeune fille	girl, young woman
Kursaal	the place of treatment in a spa town, the Hotel (German)
la vecchia / quella vecchia	the old woman / that old woman (Italian)
lambris	panelling
lazzarone	one of the lowest class at Naples, who lounge about the streets, living by odd jobs or by begging (*OED*; Italian)
locus standi	status, authority (Latin)
louche	shady, not correct
Mädchen	unmarried girl, young woman (German)

mantilla	shawl (Spanish)
ma mère	mother
ma toute-bonne	my very good woman
Mais j'espère bien	I do hope so
maître d'hôtel	a major-domo, butler
Marquise	marchioness
milieu	social surroundings
motif	motif, subject
n'en parlons plus!	enough of that! (lit. let's not talk about it any more)
noblesse	aristocracy
nuance	shade
padrona, padrona di casa	house mistress, landlady (Italian)
par excellence	quintessential
parti	rich husband or wife
parti pris	fixed decision
passeggio	walk or promenade; also, tour in a gondola (Italian)
pater patriæ	father of the country (Latin)
pension	boarding-house
persona grata	welcome person (Latin)
petits fours	small cakes, usually served with coffee
piano nobile	main and most important floor in Venetian buildings (Italian)
Piazza	St Mark's Square (lit. a square; Italian)
Piazzetta	the square near St Mark's overlooking the lagoon (lit. a small square; Italian)
(un) piccolo passeggio	(a) poor gondola procession (obs. Italian)
pifferaro	pipe-playing character (Italian)
pince-nez	spectacles without support, posed on the bridge of the nose
Pisana	woman from the Tuscan city of Pisa (Italian)

plaques	ornamental plates or tablets, made of metal or porcelain, and painted with figures or flowers
portière	door, curtain
pose	posture
post-chaise	hired vehicle
poste restante	P.O. Box
poveretta, *poverina*	poor thing (f.) (Italian)
predella	lowest part of a painting, diptych, or triptych (Italian)
premiers	first floors (UK), second floors (US)
promenade historique	walk through history
protégé	person who receives the protection or patronage of another
quartiere	part of the city (Italian)
quartier perdu	distant part of the city
quelconque	any, ordinary
Qu'est-ce qui vous prend, ma mère?	What's the matter with you, mother?
Que voulez-vous? Elle adore sa mère!	What can you do about it? She adores her mother.
Qui vaut bien la vôtre	Who is just as good as yours
raconteur	storyteller
rendezvous	arranged meeting
riva	quay, landing place (Italian)
roba da niente	not much (Italian)
rôle	role
sala	main hall (Italian)
salon	sitting room
Santissima Madonna!	Holy Mary! (Italian)
Santo Dio	Holy God (Italian)
sauterie de jeunes filles	young girls' dance
scagliola	terrazzo marble floor (Italian)
sergents de ville	police constables
serva	female servant, maid (Italian)
signore	sir (Italian)
succès de bonté	success of goodness

477

sur le vif	on the spot, in reality
table d'hôte	table where hotel guests sat together for dinner
tace	be silent (Latin)
tenda	gondola cover (lit. awning; Italian)
tenue	conduct (lit.); also outfit
terra firma	mainland (Latin)
tête-à-tête	the meeting of two persons in private
toga	cloak or mantle (Latin)
toilette de jeune fille	clothes fit for a girl
toupet	nerve
Trasteverina	woman from Trastevere (Italian)
vieux jeu	old-fashioned
villa	country mansion (Italian)
villeggiatura	holiday resort, holiday period (Italian)
visé	approved
votre siège est fait	you've done what you could (lit. your siege is done)
Wirthschaften	inns (obs., now *Wirtschaften*; German)

NOTES

We are indebted to previous editors of and commentators on these tales: to Adrian Poole, *The Aspern Papers and Other Tales* (Oxford University Press, 1983 and 2013), hereafter Poole; to Jean Gooder, *Daisy Miller and Other Stories* (Oxford University Press, 1985) hereafter *DMOS* ; to Edward W. Said, *Henry James: Complete Stories 1884–1891* (New York: Library of America, 1999) hereafter *S1884–1891*; to Évelyne Labbé, *Henry James. Nouvelles Complètes 1877–1888 II* (Paris: Éditions de la Pléiade, 2003), hereafter *NC2*, and to Adrian Dover's electronic edition at the Henry James website, 'The Ladder' (no longer available at the time of writing in 2021).

Biblical references are to the King James Bible (KJV). Quotations from Shakespeare are from *The Riverside Shakespeare*, general editor G. Blakemore Evans (Boston, MA: Houghton Mifflin, 1974).

The following notes have benefited from many suggestions from friends and colleagues thanked in the Acknowledgements.

'Pandora'

1   **North German Lloyd steamers [...] Southampton:** Founded in Bremen (Germany) in 1857, the North German Lloyd (Norddeutscher Lloyd) became one of the most important transatlantic shipping companies of the late nineteenth and early twentieth centuries. SS *Donau* (Danube) was the name given to several steamships that could cross the Atlantic in ten days. The port of Southampton on the south coast of England was a historical and renowned boarding location for people travelling to the United States and the Orient. It features in the short story 'A Tragedy of Error' (1864), and in *The Golden Bowl* (1904): Charlotte Stant disembarks at Southampton (Ch. 4) and from there departs to the United States with Adam Verver (Ch. 41). James also left from this port when he travelled to New York in August 1904.

2   **the German legation at Washington:** See Introduction, pp. xlviii–xlix.

3   **at present the German Empire:** The German Empire (Deutsches Kaiserreich) was created by Otto von Bismarck (1815–98) after the Franco-Prussian War through the unification of twenty-five German states under Wilhelm I (1797–1888), the king of Prussia; it lasted until the abdication of Kaiser Wilhelm II in 1918.

4   **a Junker of Junkers**: This phrase was used to denote a member of the landed nobility in Prussia and the eastern part of Germany. It also refers to 'a member of the reactionary party of the aristocracy whose aim it is to maintain the exclusive social and political privileges of their class' (*OED*).

5   **German emigrants**: The largest flow of German emigration to America occurred between 1820 and World War One, and involved nearly 6 million people. From 1840 to 1880 Germans were the largest group of immigrants in the United States.

6   **Some were yellow Germans and some were black**: Evelyn A. Hovanec comments upon this rather obscure passage, arguing that in this story 'social class, apparently, has some impact on physical appearance' (*Henry James and Germany* (Amsterdam: Rodopi, 1979), p. 77, note 66).

7   **a lady in Dresden**: Once the capital of the Kingdom of Saxony (part of the German Empire since 1871), Dresden was a major economic and manufacturing centre for most of the nineteenth century and is occasionally mentioned in James's works ('The Pension Beaurepas' and *Confidence* (both 1879), for example). During his 1867–8 European visit, James's brother William sojourned in Dresden, writing several letters to his family. In one of these, addressed to Henry (26 September 1867), he described the city as follows: 'Dresden was a place in which it always seemed afternoon; and as I used to sit in my cool and darksome room, and see through the ancient window the long dusty sunbeams slanting past the roof angles opposite down into the deep well of a street, and hear the distant droning of the market and think of no reason why it should not thus continue in secula seculorum, I used to have the same sort of feeling as that which now comes over me when I remember days passed in Grandma's old house in Albany' (*The Correspondence of William James*, vol. 1, *William and Henry 1861–1884*, ed. Ignas K. Skrupselis and Elizabeth M. Berkeley (Charlottesville, VA: University of Virginia Press, 1992), p. 19). James went to Dresden in December 1891 to attend the funeral of the young American writer Walcott Balestier (1861–91).

8   **Jews and commercial**: In the mid-nineteenth century Jewish immigrants to the United States were mostly Yiddish-speaking Ashkenazis coming from diasporic communities in Germany and eastern Europe. They found employment in trade and manufacturing in many American cities.

9   **Tauchnitz novel**: Tauchnitz was a German publishing house (established in 1798) which began to publish English-language editions in the 1840s with a series of books by British and American authors (1841–1939). Popular

with English-speaking travellers on the Continent throughout the late nineteenth and early twentieth centuries, these inexpensive, small paper-bound editions – direct precursors to mass-market paperbacks – eventually ran to over 5,000 volumes. James had sixteen volumes published by Tauchnitz, beginning with *The American* (1877) and ending with *The Outcry* (1912): see Leon Edel and Dan H. Laurence, *A Bibliography of Henry James*, 3rd edn, revised with the assistance of James Rambeau (Oxford: Clarendon Press, 1985), p. 384. In Book III of *The Wings of the Dove* (1902) Susan Stringham finds a Tauchnitz volume left behind by Milly Theale, before discovering her seated on an Alpine promontory.

10 **enormous German characters**: Written in Gothic German, i.e. *Fraktur*, a German style of black-letter type very common until the early twentieth century.

11 **the Needles [...] the Isle of Wight**: Spectacular row of three stacks of chalk that rise from the sea off the western tip of the Isle of Wight, not far from Southsea (Portsmouth). See note 145. In 'English Vignettes' (first published 1879) James had complained that the Isle of Wight had been spoilt by its 'detestable little railway [...] The place is pure picture or is nothing at all. It is ornamental only—it exists for exclamation and the water-colour brush' (*PPL* 292).

12 **the story [...] of a flighty, forward little American girl, who plants herself in front of a young man in the garden of an hotel**: An obvious echo of James's own 'Daisy Miller' (1878): 'a pretty American girl coming and standing in front of you in a garden' (Ch. 1). The novella was published by Tauchnitz in 1879 with 'An International Episode' and 'Four Meetings' as vol. 1819. See Introduction, p. liii.

13 **felt more than ever like the young man in his American tale**: The young man is Frederick Winterbourne.

14 **Teuton**: 'A German; in extended ethnic sense, any member of the races or peoples speaking a Germanic or Teutonic language' (*OED*). In *Roderick Hudson* (1875), Madame Grandoni is often referred to as Teutonic: she displays 'an interminable Teutonic pedigree' and 'a deep-welling fund of Teutonic sentiment'. In *The Princess Casamassima* (1886), Madame Grandoni laughs 'with her Teutonic homeliness' (*CFHJ* 9, p. 166).

15 **Miss Day was exceedingly provincial**: Pandora will turn out to hail from Utica (see note 30). She shares with Daisy Miller (from Schenectady) the fate of many young women in James's fiction to be declared 'provincial' by ladies from New York and Boston.

481

16 **"nuby"**: A variant for 'nubia', 'a soft fleecy scarf for the head and neck, usually worn by women' in nineteenth-century America (*OED*).

17 **Pandora**: See Introduction, pp. xlvii–xlix.

18 **fez**: 'A skull-cap formerly of wool, now of felt, of a dull crimson colour, in the form of a truncated cone, ornamented with a long black tassel; formerly the national head-dress of the Turks' (*OED*).

19 **yellow paper**: Until the early twentieth century, books of French fiction were usually covered with yellow or yellowish dust jackets.

20 **Sainte-Beuve […] Renan […] de Musset**: Charles Augustin Sainte-Beuve (1804–69) was a French literary critic whose work and correspondence were reviewed by James. In his review of Sainte-Beuve's *Premiers Lundis* (1874), James called him 'the acutest critic the world has seen' (*LC2* 669). Joseph Ernest Renan (1823–92) was a French historian and philosopher, renowned for his works on early Christianity and his theories of nationalism and national identity. James met him in Paris in 1875. He reviewed his *Dialogues et fragments philosophiques* (1876) and *Souvenirs d'enfance et de jeunesse* (1883), praising both the man and his style: 'At the present moment he is the first writer in France; […] Renan is the great apostle of the delicate; he upholds this waning fashion on every occasion. His mission is to say delicate things, to plead the cause of intellectual good manners, and he is wonderfully competent to discharge it' (*LC2* 634). Alfred Louis Charles de Musset (1810–57) was a French dramatist, poet, and novelist, and author of the autobiographical *La Confession d'un enfant du siècle* (*The Confession of a Child of the Century*, 1836). James reviewed an anthology of his works (1870) as well as a biography written by Musset's brother, Paul (1877, reprinted in *French Poets and Novelists*, 1878). In the latter review James describes Musset as 'beyond question one of the first poets of our day […] Half the beauty of Musset's writing is its simple suggestion of youthfulness—of something fresh and fair, slim and tremulous, with a tender epidermis […] What makes him valuable is just this gift for the expression of that sort of emotion which the conventions and proprieties of life, the dryness of ordinary utterance, the stiffness of most imaginations, leave quite in the vague, and yet which forms part of human nature important enough to have its exponent' (*LC2* 609–10).

21 **euchre**: A card game of American origin, played by two, three, or four persons, with a pack of thirty-two cards (the two, three, four, five, and six of each suit being rejected). A player may, if he pleases, 'pass' or decline

to play, but if he undertakes to play and fails to take three tricks, he or his side is said to be 'euchred' and the other side gains two points. Reputedly played on the old Mississippi steamboats (*DMOS* 277).

22 **a certain small brother,—a candy-loving Madison, Hamilton or Jefferson**: Vogelstein seems to imagine both young Mr Day and the fictional character of the book he is reading (Daisy Miller's brother, Randolph) as possible American statesmen, like those mentioned who belonged to the early period of American independence. James Madison was the fourth president of the United States (1809–17), succeeding Thomas Jefferson (1801–9), the principal author of the Declaration of Independence. Like Jefferson, Alexander Hamilton was one of the Founding Fathers of the United States, promoting the Constitution and serving as first secretary of the Treasury (1789–95). Monteiro reads Vogelstein's inexact memory of Daisy Miller's brother (Randolph) in connection with these statesmen as alluding to two works by Henry Adams, *John Randolph* and *History of the United States of America during the Administration of Jefferson and Madison* ('Washington Friends and National Reviewers: Henry James's "Pandora"', *Research Studies*, 43.1 (March 1975), 38–44; 41–3).

23 **The Germans […] a transcendental people**: The philosophers of German idealism (J. G. Fichte (1762–1814), G. W. F. Hegel (1770–1831), and F. W. J. Schelling (1775–1854)) had an important influence on the development of Transcendentalism, the loose philosophical movement which bloomed in New England in the first half of the nineteenth century thanks to figures such as Ralph Waldo Emerson (1803–82), Theodore Parker (1810–60), and proto-feminist Margaret Fuller (1810–50). The Transcendentalists strongly emphasized individualism and nonconformity.

24 **heavy little burghers**: A phrase expressing the condescension of 'a young man of the upper class' for his social inferiors, suggesting something like 'tradesmen' (*DMOS* 278).

25 **the rise in prices, the telephone, the discovery of dynamite, the Chassepôt rifle, the socialistic spirit**: The telephone was invented by P. Reis in 1861. The Swedish chemist and engineer Alfred Nobel patented dynamite in 1867. In the original magazine version and in the Osgood edition of this tale, James gives emphasis to other elements such as 'the railway, the telegraph' (see Textual Variants, p. 581). The Chassepôt, officially known as Fusil modèle 1866, was a type of rifle, famous as the weapon of the French armed forces in the Franco-Prussian War of 1870–1. Most likely, 'Socialistic spirit' refers

to those economic and social theories advanced by thinkers such as Robert Owen (1771–1858) and Charles Fourier (1772–1837), which were sources of inspiration for many utopian communities both in Europe and America in the mid nineteenth century. Karl Marx's *Das Kapital* was only translated into English in 1886, but his voice began to be heard through articles in Horace Greeley's *New York Tribune* between 1852 and 1862, and in the 1880s his writings were increasingly influential on leaders of various British social-ist groups, including those led by Henry Hyndman (1842–1921) and William Morris (1834–96). During the German Empire, socialists and Marxists rep-resented one of the main targets of Bismarck's repressive politics.

26 **mesmeric influence**: Mesmerism was a therapeutic doctrine or system, first popularized by German physician Franz Anton Mesmer (1734–1815), according to which a trained practitioner could induce a hypnotic state in a patient by the exercise of a force (called by Mesmer 'animal magnetism'). This doctrine was influential and generally accepted until the end of the nineteenth century. References to mesmerism were quite common in nineteenth-century literature. See, for instance, Edgar Allan Poe's short stories 'The Facts in the Case of Mr. Valdemar' (1845), 'A Tale of the Ragged Mountain' (1844), and 'Mesmeric Revelation' (1844), Hawthorne's *The Blithedale Romance* (1852), and Edward Bellamy's *Looking Backward* (1888). In *The Bostonians* (1886) Doctor Tarrant (Verena's father) is referred to as a 'mesmeric healer' or 'mesmerist'. Spiritualism and magnetism are also the subject of James's short story 'Professor Fargo' (1874).

27 **I'm chalked**: In the nineteenth century, to mark an item with chalk was a way to show that it had been officially admitted, e.g. by a customs officer, or directed.

28 **Acropolis [...] Pheidias and Pericles**: The Acropolis is the ancient citadel of Athens, comprising the Parthenon and other notable buildings mostly dating from the fifth century BCE. Pheidias, or Phidias (*c.* 480–430 BCE), was one of the most celebrated sculptors of antiquity and believed to be responsible for many sculptures on the Acropolis, including the statue of Athena featuring the birth of Pandora at its base (*DMOS* 277). Pheidias was a contemporary of Pericles (*c.* 495–429 BCE), the great statesman and general of Athens. In *The American Scene* (1907, Ch. 11) James draws an analogy between the newest wings of Washington's Capitol and the Greek Acropolis: 'These parts of the Capitol, on their Acropolis height, are ideally constructed for "raking," [in one or more of the senses of the verb 'to rake', under *OED* 10, esp. (d) 'to command or afford a view' and (e) 'to sweep

with the eyes'] and for this suggestion of their dominating the American scene in playhouse gallery fashion' (*CTW1* 652).

29 **something of that sort in Goethe, somewhere**: As Edel has shown (*Henry James*, vol. 1, *The Untried Years, 1843–1870* (Philadelphia: J. B. Lippincott, 1953), p. 260), James was competent in German and familiar with the works of Goethe, which he read during his stay in Bonn in 1860 and his tour of Europe in 1869. He also reviewed Thomas Carlyle's translation of *Wilhelm Meister* (*North American Review*, 1865) and a new translation of *Faust* (*Nation*, 1873). See note 32. Between 1807 and 1808 Goethe wrote a theatrical work titled *Pandora* that remained a fragment. Other references to Goethe in James's fiction can be found in *The American*, where he is favourite reading of Mr Babcock, *Watch and Ward* (1878), *The Bostonians*, in which he is distinguished as the 'only foreign author' Olive Chancellor cares about, in the short stories 'Travelling Companions' (1870), 'Owen Wingrave' (1893), 'The Birthplace' (1903), and in James's early play *Pyramus and Thisbe* (1869). See also note 488 to 'The Liar'.

30 **Utica**: The capital of Oneida County in upstate New York. In the late nineteenth century it became a commercial centre of considerable note.

31 **Parthenon [...] the Mount of Olives**: The Parthenon (448–438 BCE) is a temple on the Acropolis, dedicated to the Goddess Athena, patron of the city. It is held to be one of the most important monuments of Greek art, as well as a symbol of democracy and Western civilization. The Classical style of architecture was highly favoured in eighteenth- and nineteenth-century America, for both public buildings and substantial domestic homes, as is evident by James's remark in the travel essay 'Abbeys and Castles': 'For myself, I have never been in a country so unattractive that it did not seem a peculiar felicity to be able to purchase the most considerable house it contained. In New England and other portions of the United States I have coveted the large mansion with Doric columns and a pediment of white-painted timber' (*PPL* 271). The Mount of Olives is a mountain ridge east of Jerusalem's Old City, named after the olive groves that used to cover its slopes. It is a famous biblical site, in both the Old and New Testaments. See also note 28.

32 **Goethe's dictum**: Gooder (*DMOS* 278) interprets this as a reference to Goethe's *Wilhelm Meister* (1796) in Carlyle's translation: 'Let no one think that he can conquer the first impression of his youth' (Book 11, Ch. 9).

33 **the landing-place of the German steamers, at Jersey City**: Located on a peninsula facing Manhattan on the west side of the Hudson, Jersey City was a dock and manufacturing town for much of the nineteenth and

twentieth centuries. Like New York, Jersey City has always been a destination for newly arrived immigrants to the United States. As noted by Patrick B. Shaloub, 'Between 1830 and 1880 waves of Irish, German and British immigrants settled throughout Jersey City, which had become a thriving center of industry and transportation' (*Jersey City* (Charleston, SC: Arcadia Publishing, 1995), p. 36). James landed there in 1904.

34 **chalk-marks**: See note 27.

35 **thirty shillings to take you to the inn**: The rough equivalent of thirty shillings then (£1.50) would be well over £100 in 2021. It should be noted that shillings were not the official US currency at this time.

36 **Mrs. Bonnycastle**: This name appears in a list of names attached to an undated notebook entry, probably written in late December 1880 or early January 1881, in which James sketches the plot of *The Portrait of a Lady* (*CN* 13). See Introduction, p. l.

37 **soft, scented days of the Washington spring**: James is remembering his visit to Washington in the spring of 1883, when he wrote to his editor at the *Atlantic Monthly*, T. B. Aldrich: 'You should be in this place, editor & Bostonian. The sky is turquoise & pearl; & the robe of the earth is trimmed (most tastefully) with pink & white bloom' (letter of 22 April 1883, *CLHJ 1883–1884* 1:101).

38 **a plan so ingenious, yet so bewildering**: In the early 1870s, thanks to the powerful Republican politician Alexander Robey Shepherd (1835–1902), the city of Washington underwent a radical urban renewal which significantly improved it and turned it into a modern capital.

39 **Alfred Bonnycastle**: See Introduction, p. l.

40 **a new tenant**: Three presidents have been proposed as possible models: Rutherford B. Hayes (4 March 1877 – 4 March 1881), James A. Garfield (4 March – 19 September 1881), and Chester A. Arthur (19 September 1881 – 4 March 1885). Given that Garfield was assassinated, the bland description here of the change of 'tenancy' makes it unlikely that James had Garfield's successor, Chester A. Arthur, specifically in mind. Nevertheless, Edel suggests (*Henry James: The Conquest of London, 1870–1883* (London: Rupert Hart-Davis, 1962), p. 10), that this passage was inspired by a meeting James had with Arthur in January 1882. James wrote to Isabella Stewart Gardner from Washington (23 January 1882): 'I met the President [Chester A. Arthur] the other day, (at dinner at Mr. Blaine's) & thought him a good fellow—even attractive. He is a gentleman & evidently has that amiable quality, a desire

to please; he also had a well-made coat & well-cut whiskers. But he told me none of the secrets of state and I couldn't judge of him as a ruler of Men. He seemed so genial, however that I was much disposed to ask him for a foreign mission' (*CHJL 1880–1883* 2: 90). He wrote in similar terms on the same day to Sir John Clark, that Arthur 'has the art of pleasing rather more than some of his predecessors', while adding that the White House was 'shrouded in gloom', haunted by 'the ghosts of Lincoln & Garfield' (*CHJL 1880–1883* 2: 87–88). Robert Gale argues, however, that 'the new tenant' refers to President Garfield, whom James mentioned in several letters written between November 1880 and October 1881 ('"Pandora" and Her President', *Studies in Short Fiction*, 1 (Spring 1964), 222–5). In a letter to his sister Alice dated 30 January 1881, in which he thanked her for enclosing a portrait of Garfield, James wrote: 'I am grateful for the photograph of the president-elect—the more so that I like his face, which though, I think, peculiarly "self-made", is a good type of the self-made, & pleasant & manly in expression; much more potent than poor Hayes's' (*CLHJ 1880–1883* 1:153). But Gooder, and also Gale (see *HJE* 485), take into account the possibility that James is referring to Garfield's predecessor, Rutherford B. Hayes (see *DMOS* 279). James was in Washington, 23 December 1881 – 30 January 1882, after the shooting of President Garfield on 2 July 1881 (he died on 19 September).

41   **a distribution of spoils**: This expression refers to the systematic sacking of one's opponent's appointees and substitution by appointees of one's own, on winning an election, that was an accepted part of the American federal government in the nineteenth century. The 'spoils system' of distributing government jobs as a reward for political services began during the presidency of Andrew Jackson (1829–37). In the 1870s good-government reformers attempted to eradicate this system but were opposed by congressional party chieftains. President Garfield's assassination by a 'disappointed office-seeker' finally undermined resistance and led to the passage of the Pendleton Civil Service Act (1883), which partially modified it. Gooder (*DMOS* 279–80) suggests a comparison of this passage in James's story with Henry Adams's treatment of the distribution of the spoils of office in his novel *Democracy* (1880).

42   **the legislative session [...] the congressional season**: Congress, the national legislative body of the United States of America (composed of two bodies, the House of Representatives and the Senate), has two-year terms with one session each year. A term is divided into two sessions, one for each year (plus a special session, occasionally). Before the Twentieth

Amendment (ratified in 1933), Congress met from the first Monday in December to April or May in the first session of a term (the 'long session'); and from December to 4 March in the second 'short session'.

43 **something of the toga**: 'The outer garment of a Roman citizen in time of peace, but also a robe of office, a professional gown, a cloak, a "mantle"' (*OED*).

44 **lettered and numbered streets**: With few exceptions, the streets in Washington are set out in a grid pattern, where east–west streets are named with letters and north–south streets with numbers.

45 **a society in which familiarity reigned**: On Washington society, see James's letter to Sir John Clark dated 8 January 1882, quoted in note 40.

46 **Steuben**: A name with some resonance. The Prussian-born Baron Friedrich Wilhelm von Steuben (1730–94) served as a general in the American Revolution and was George Washington's chief of staff in the final years of the war. Von Steuben Day is celebrated every September in many US cities, most notably in New York. Gooder reads Mrs Steuben as a 'caricature of the Southern lady with literary pretensions' (*DMOS* 280). James briefly mentioned Steuben Street in Albany in *A Small Boy and Others*, p. 13.

47 **Spielhagen's novels**: Friedrich Spielhagen (1829–1911) was a popular German novelist, literary theorist, and translator, best known for his lengthy novel *Problematische Naturen* (1861; translated into English as *Problematic Characters* (1869)). Gooder suggests that the young lady who reads his work represents 'Bostonian earnestness' outdoing 'the Teutonic kind' (*DMOS* 280).

48 **Washington had become the fashion**: The post-Civil War reconstruction saw an amelioration of the city and its architecture, as well as an improvement of its social life. In the 1870s Washington became one of the main attractions of the nation. Despite some reservations, James had warm feelings towards the city, as can be seen in a series of letters he wrote while sojourning there in January 1882. To Sir John Clark, on 8 January, he observed: 'I believe that Washington is the place in the world where money—or the absence of it, matters least. It is very queer & yet extremely pleasant; informal, familiar, heterogeneous, good-natured, essentially social & conversational, enormously big & yet extremely provincial, indefinably ridiculous & yet eminently agreeable. It is the only place in America where there is no business, where an air of leisure hangs over the enormous streets, where every one walks slowly & doesn't look

488

keen & preoccupied. The sky is blue, the sun is warm, the women are charming, & at dinners the talk is always general' (*CLHJ 1880–1883* 2: 66–67). On 10 January he told Grace Norton that Washington seemed 'queer, but genial' (*CLHJ 1880–1883* 2: 74). The most unequivocally positive impression surfaces in this letter to Isabella Stewart Gardner on 23 January: 'Washington is really very good; too much of a village materially, but socially & conversationally bigger & more varied, I think, than anything we have. I shouldn't care to live here—it is too rustic & familiar; but I should certainly come here for a part of every winter if I lived in the United States' (*CLHJ 1880–1883* 2: 89–90). James wrote extensively about Washington in Chapter 11 of *The American Scene*.

49 **Hegelian element [...] a monstrous, mystical *Werden*:** *Das Werden* ('becoming') is the category of Hegelian philosophy which synthesizes opposed abstractions such as being and not being, encompassing this pair in a higher category which is reality itself. See Simon Blackburn, *The Oxford Dictionary of Philosophy* (Oxford: Oxford University Press, 2005), p. 71). In James's 'The Coxon Fund' (1894) one of the characters, George Gravener, uses 'Werden' as a synonym for 'process' (Ch. 8). Gooder suggests that the expression 'carries over to the description of Washington itself – a city planned to a vast scale on geometrical principles, monumental but unfinished' (*DMOS* 280).

50 **the ruler of fifty millions:** The 1880 census determined the resident population of the United States to be 50,189,209, an increase of 30.2 per cent over the 39,818,449 persons enumerated during the 1870 census.

51 **Mrs. Runkle, from Natchez:** Natchez, founded by the French in 1716, is the oldest colony established on the Mississippi River, located in the southwest area of the state of Mississippi. The city had a prominent role in Mississippi River commerce throughout the nineteenth century.

52 **the mission to England [...] a lady at the head over there:** The position of Envoy Extraordinary and Minister Plenipotentiary to the Court of St James, known since 1893 as 'Ambassador'. At the time of the tale's writing the post was held by James's friend James Russell Lowell (1819–91). The lady was of course Queen Victoria.

53 **watery waste:** Clichéd expression originally used by John Dryden in his 1697 translation of *The Aeneid* (*NC2* 1478, note 35).

54 **a commodore:** Naval officer, 'ranking above captain and below rear-admiral' (*OED*).

55 **like the queen in *Hamlet***: Gertrude, queen of Denmark, mother of young Hamlet in Shakespeare's eponymous tragedy (*c.* 1601).

56 **the accent of Savannah**: Savannah is the largest city and the county seat of Chatham County, in the southern state of Georgia. James was very sensitive to the sound of language; see in particular his reflections on English as spoken in New York's Lower East Side in Chapter 3 of *The American Scene* and the essay *The Question of Our Speech* (1905). On the distinctness of the Southern accent, see the passage that introduces the character Basil Ransom in *The Bostonians* (Ch. 1): 'He came, in fact, from Mississippi, and he spoke very perceptibly with the accent of that country. It is not in my power to reproduce by any combination of characters this charming dialect; but the initiated reader will have no difficulty in evoking the sound, which is to be associated in the present instance with nothing vulgar or vain. [...] the reader who likes a complete image, who desires to read with the senses as well as with the reason, is entreated not to forget that he prolonged his consonants and swallowed his vowels, that he was guilty of elisions and interpolations which were equally unexpected, and that his discourse was pervaded by something sultry and vast, something almost African in its rich, basking tone, something that suggested the teeming expanse of the cotton-field' (*CFHJ* 8, p. 6).

57 **another weakness as well**: Her grammar is faulty – 'we Southerners' should be 'us Southerners'.

58 **the Revolution**: The war between America and Britain which began in 1775, with the Battles of Lexington and Concord, resulted in the Declaration of Independence (4 July 1776); hostilities formally ended on 3 September 1783, with the signing of the Treaty of Paris.

59 **Pennsylvania Avenue**: A major street in Washington connecting the White House and the Capitol.

60 **Down the Potomac to Mount Vernon**: The Potomac river flows near Alexandria in Virginia. In *The American Scene* (Ch. 11) James lingers on the beauty of this natural landscape: 'The light of nature was there, splendid and serene; the Potomac opened out in its grandest manner, the bluff above the river, before the sweep of its horizon, raised its head for the historic crown' (*CTW1* 628). Mount Vernon, a large estate located on the banks of the Potomac, was the plantation home of George Washington, first president of the United States (1789–97); it is also his burial place. James again: 'The old high-placed house, unquestionably, is charming, and the felicity of the whole scene, on such a day as that of my impression, scarce to be

uttered. The little hard facts, facts of form, of substance, of scale, facts of essential humility and exiguity, none the less, look us straight in the face, present themselves literally to be counted over—and reduce us thereby to the recognition of our supreme example of the rich interference of association [...] The whole thing *is* Washington—not his invention and his property, but his presence and his person [...] The great soft fact, as opposed to the little hard ones, is the beauty of the site itself' (*CTW1* 630–1).

61 **self-made girl:** See Introduction, pp. xlvi–xlvii.

62 **silver spoon:** From the proverbial phrase 'to be born with a silver spoon in one's mouth', i.e. blessed with some kind of inherited advantage, usually wealth.

63 **blackamoor:** Archaic (and now offensive) word for a black American or any dark-skinned person.

64 **the Capitol:** Located on the top of Capitol Hill in Washington DC, it is the meeting place of Congress and the federal courts. The construction of the neoclassical-style building began in 1793. It was rebuilt with its central white dome after being almost completely burnt down by the British in 1814 (*DMOS* 281).

65 **Prince Bismarck:** Bismarck, the famous conservative *Ministerpräsident* of Prussia (1862–90). See note 3.

66 **the rotunda:** The highest ceilinged part of the Capitol. Located below the dome, it displays the large fresco *The Apotheosis of Washington* (1865) by Italian Costantino Brumidi (1805–80) (See Rosella Mamoli Zorzi, 'Il sogno americano nel Campidoglio di Washington', in *Il sogno delle Americhe, Promesse e tradimenti*, Francesca Bisutti De Riz, Patrizio Rigobon, Bernard Vincents (eds.) (Padua: Studio Editoriale Gordini, 2007), 180–2.). The rotunda features a frieze painted in grisaille (a monochrome of whites and browns that resembles sculpture) depicting nineteen scenes from American history. Brumidi was able to paint only seven and a half scenes, and his work was completed in 1889 by Filippo Costaggini (1839–1904) with a later addition by Allyn Cox (1896–1982). In the lower part of the rotunda eight niches hold large, framed historical paintings. Four of these paintings, installed between 1817 and 1824, feature scenes from the American Revolution, painted by John Trumbull (*Declaration of Independence, Surrender of General Burgoyne, Surrender of Lord Cornwallis*, and *General George Washington Resigning His Commission*). The other four, added between 1840 and 1855, centre on the exploration and colonization of America (*Landing of Columbus* by John Vanderlyn, *Discovery of the Mississippi* by

William Henry Powell, *Baptism of Pocahontas* by John Gadsby Chapman, and *Embarkation of the Pilgrims* by Robert Walter Weir.) James wrote unfavourably about the rotunda subsequent to his 1905 visit to Washington: 'the interference of the monumental spittoons, that of the immense amount of vulgar, of barbaric, decoration, that of the terrible artistic tributes from, and scarce less to, the different States—the unassorted marble mannikins in particular, each a portrayal by one of the commonwealths of her highest worthy, which make the great Rotunda, the intended Valhalla, resemble a stonecutter's collection of priced sorts and sizes' (*American Scene*, Ch. 11).

67 **the lower House […] the uncanny statues of local worthies, presented by the different States:** The passage refers to the former meeting place of the US House of Representatives (1807–57) which later became the National Statuary Hall, displaying statues donated by the states of the Federal Republic (two statues by each) to honour notable figures in their history (see note 66).

68 **the magnificent terrace that surrounds the Capitol:** The current grounds of the Capitol were designed by famous landscape architect Frederick Law Olmstead (1822–1903), who also planned the subsequent interventions (from 1874 to 1892). In 1875 Olmsted proposed the construction of the marble terraces on the north, west, and south sides of the building. In *The American Scene* (Ch. 11) James wrote: 'the question is positively of the impressiveness of the great terraced Capitol hill, with its stages and slopes, staircases and fountains, its general presentation of its charge. And if the whole mass and prospect "amuse," as I say, from the moment they are embraced, the visitor curious of the *democratic assimilation* of the greater dignities and majesties will least miss the general logic' (*CTW1* 650).

69 **the far-gleaming pediment of Arlington:** The pediment of Arlington House, a neoclassical mansion located on a high point of a 1,100-acre estate in Arlington, on the side of the Potomac opposite Washington. The house was built between 1802 and 1818 by George Custis (1781–1857), the step-grandson of President Washington and father-in-law of Confederate General Robert E. Lee, who was residing there at the start of the Civil War, although the house was occupied by Union troops soon after the war began. The mansion stands in the famous Arlington National Cemetery, established during the Civil War.

70 **Alexandria:** The city of Alexandria is located on the western bank of the Potomac River and is approximately six miles south of downtown Washington DC. It was founded in 1749, and its port and market flourished

during the slave trade period but declined rapidly after slavery was outlawed. In May 1861 Union troops breached the city, which remained under military occupation until the end of the Civil War.

71 "fly": Slang for 'a trick, dodge' (*OED*).

72 *gemüthlich*: The use of this old-fashioned spelling (now, *gemütlich*) is to be found also in James's letters, where for example he writes 'ungemüthlich' (4 March 1879 to William, *CLHJ 1878–1880* 1:125).

73 **Pomeranian**: Pomerania is on the south shore of the Baltic Sea, straddling the border between Germany and Poland. At the time of writing it was under Prussian control and part of the German Empire.

74 **the classic ice-house**: This anecdote either circulated in various versions or was incorrectly remembered by James. Labbé (*NC2*, note 46, p. 1479) notices that an anonymous 1859 article in *Harper's New Monthly Magazine* ascribed the mistake to a young lady rather than to an old one: 'On the right of the carriage entrance to the mansion is an ice-house, built by Washington, and still used. It is well preserved, and to the highly imaginative mind its form suggests the idea of a tomb. It is affirmed that a sentimental young lady was once seen, with an embroidered kerchief pressed to her eyes, weeping softly at the door of the ice-house, under the impression that she was standing at the tomb of Washington!' ('Mount Vernon as it is.' *Harper's New Monthly Magazine*, 18 March 1859, 433–51, 441). The ice-house built at Mount Vernon was based on a model Washington saw in the house of senator Robert Morris (1734–1806) in Philadelphia.

75 **K Street**: Major thoroughfare in Washington DC. See note 44.

'Georgina's Reasons'

76 **Georgina**: This name is also used in 'A Bundle of Letters' (1879), where Georgina is the sick sister of Miss Evelyn Vane.

77 **Raymond Benyon**: 'Benyon' was listed among other names in a notebook entry dated 2 January 1884 (*CN* 23). Raymond is an uncommon name in James's fiction, though Raymond Bestwick is the name of the hero of the 1887 tale 'Mrs. Temperly' elsewhere in this volume.

78 **Valparaiso [...] Halifax [...] Cape of Good Hope**: James couples here port cities in the northern and southern hemispheres: New York and Valparaiso (Chile), and Halifax (Nova Scotia) and the Cape of Good Hope, the rocky

headland on the Atlantic coast of South Africa. Valparaiso also appears in *Watch and Ward*. He never travelled to any of these places.

79 **Georgina Gressie:** Gressie is not a common name in Britain or America, but in 1807 the captain of the British ship *Psyché*, Rear Admiral Sir Edward Pellew, destroyed two Dutch ships at the port of Gressie or Griessie on Java.

80 **Brooklyn navy-yard:** Founded in 1801, the Brooklyn Navy Yard was one of America's premier ship-building facilities until 1966. On a site of 144 acres, 'including more than a mile of the most eligible wharfage in the harbor', according to *Appleton's 1879*, the yard also boasted an 'immense dry dock' which cost over 2 million dollars. Madame Merle declares in *The Portrait of a Lady* that 'I came into the world in the Brooklyn navy yard' (Ch. 18).

81 **God-fearing relations in New Hampshire:** Like the other states of New England, New Hampshire is marked by the heritage of Puritanism. A mainly inland state, it has a very short stretch of coast.

82 **a slight impediment in his speech:** According to Edith Wharton in her autobiography *A Backward Glance* (1934), James himself had suffered from a stammer 'which in his boyhood had been thought incurable' (*Novellas and Other Writings* (New York: Library of America, 1990), p. 917).

83 **the piazza of an hotel at Fort Hamilton [...] Brooklyn:** Built between 1825 and 1831, Fort Hamilton was one of the oldest army garrisons of the United States, but *Appleton's 1879* states that 'Fort Hamilton is the name not only of a fort, but of a pretty little village which has grown up around it'. It is located in the far south-western corner of Brooklyn, in the township formerly called New Utrecht, now Bensonhurst. In 1913 James recalls thinking, when a child, of 'New York and Albany, Fort Hamilton and New Brighton' as forming 'so fallacious a maximum' in opposition to the 'ancient order' of Europe, of '[t]he very names of places and things in the other world' (*SBOC* 72). The farthest western part of Long Island, Brooklyn became an independent city in the 1840s and a borough of New York City in 1898.

84 **Twelfth Street:** See note 86.

85 **Napoleon [...] Empress Josephine:** The French emperor (1769–1821) and his first wife, Joséphine de Beauharnais (1763–1814), whom he divorced in 1810. On the possible relation between the story's characters and these historical figures, see Charles Johanningsmeier ('Henry James's Dalliance with the Newspaper World', *Henry James Review*, 19.1 (1998), 47). Corsica is a French island in the Mediterranean Sea, north of the Italian island of Sardinia. Napoleon was born in its capital, Ajaccio, in 1769. A reference

to Empress Josephine also occurs in *The Europeans*, where Gertrude Wentworth's expectation that Baroness Munster will 'resemble a very pretty portrait of the Empress Josephine, of which there hung an engraving in one of the parlors', is disappointed (*CFHJ* 4, p. 31–2).

86 **when Twelfth Street had but lately ceased to be suburban:** The story is set in the mid-1840s (see p. 61). At that time the frontier of urbanization in New York was at the level of Fourteenth Street. James was born in 1843, at 21 Washington Place, north of Fourth Street. From 1847 to 1855 the James family resided at 58 West Fourteenth Street, near Sixth Avenue. The evocation of this part of New York in this story is similar to James's recollections in *Washington Square* (1880) and *A Small Boy and Others* (1913, Ch. 8).

87 **when the theatres [...] expensive vocal music [...] Castle Garden:** New York's theatre area, originally located near the City Hall, extended progressively northwards, following Broadway, and towards 1870 reached Twenty-third Street, south of Madison Square (see *NC2* 1485, note 8). Built between 1808 and 1811 in Battery Park, Castle Garden began to be used as a concert hall and theatre in 1823. It was the principal venue for opera before the opening of the Academy of Music, in 1854, on Fourteenth Street and Irving Place (*SBOC* 98, note 225). Castle Garden is mentioned in *A Small Boy and Others* (Ch. 9) and in *The American Scene* (Ch. 2, 'New York Revisited'), where James describes it as a 'shabby, shrunken, barely discernible [...] ancient rotunda buried in a city of skyscrapers' (*CTW1* 422). In both these works, James remembered it as the place where he had listened to the young singing prodigy Adelina Patti (1843–1919), 'poised in an armchair that had been pushed to the footlights and announcing her incomparable gift' (*SBOC* 98).

88 **when "the park" [...] the City Hall:** Located in downtown Manhattan, this was a communal pasture ground until the end of the eighteenth century; in 1812 it was turned into the park surrounding the third City Hall of New York. *Appleton's 1879* remarks that 'During the day-time the halls and steps of the City Hall are infested by small-fry politicians and officeholders, who make the place a rendez-vous.' In *A Small Boy and Others* James remembers the park as the site of Barnum's great American Museum (Ch. 5). In the third chapter of *Washington Square* he briefly traces the development of this area: '[Dr. Sloper] had been living ever since his marriage in an edifice of red brick, with granite copings and an enormous fanlight over the door, standing in a street within five minutes' walk of the City Hall, which saw its best days (from the social point of view) about 1820. After this, the

495

tide of fashion began to set steadily northward, as, indeed, in New York, thanks to the narrow channel in which it flows, it is obliged to do, and the great hum of traffic rolled farther to the right and left of Broadway.' In *The American Scene* (Ch. 2, 'New York Revisited') James offers a few remarks on City Hall, noticing how at the beginning of the twentieth century the building still 'lives on securely, by the mercy of fate—lives on in the delicacy of its beauty, speaking volumes again (more volumes, distinctly, than are anywhere else spoken) [...] the pale yellow marble (or whatever it may be) of the City Hall has lost, by some late excoriation, the remembered charm of its old surface, the pleasant promiscuous patina of time; but the perfect taste and finish, the reduced yet ample scale, the harmony of parts, the just proportions, the modest classic grace, the living look of the type aimed at, these things, with gaiety of detail undiminished and "quaintness" of effect augmented, are all there' (*CTW1* 436).

89 **Bloomingdale Road [...] Hoboken [...] Fifth Avenue:** The road, today known as Broadway, opened in 1703 and led from lower Manhattan to the Bloomingdale Insane Asylum (established in the 1820s and relocated in the 1890s) in the neighbourhood of Morningside Heights, now the site of a number of renowned educational institutions, among them Columbia University. Located west of Manhattan on the Hudson River, the city of Hoboken was originally founded by the Dutch. In the nineteenth century German and Irish immigration changed its character. The city was an integral part of the Port of New York and New Jersey and home to major industries for most of the twentieth century. Hoboken is mentioned at the very beginning of *The American Scene* (Ch. 1, 'New England: An Autumn Impression'; *CWT1* 357), as James describes the experience of arriving in New York. Fifth Avenue is a major thoroughfare in the centre of Manhattan which became prestigious as mid-nineteenth-century wealthy New Yorkers – such as Henry Benkard or, later, Caroline Astor and Cornelius Vanderbilt – started building their stylish residences there. In *The American Scene* (Ch. 4, 'New York: Social Notes') James remarked: 'Uppermost Fifth Avenue, for example, is lined with dwellings the very intention both of the spread and of the finish of which would seem to be to imply that they are "entailed" as majestically as red tape can entail them' (*CTW1* 488).

90 **Brooklyn ferry:** A ferry that connected Manhattan to Brooklyn on the East River before the construction of the Brooklyn Bridge (1870–83), celebrated in Walt Whitman's poem 'Crossing Brooklyn Ferry', included in *Leaves of Grass* (second edition of 1856).

91 **Portsmouth, N.H.:** A city in New Hampshire and one of the most important seaports in the United States until the nineteenth century. In *Hawthorne* (1879) James mentions it, along with Plymouth, New Bedford, Newburyport, and Newport, as belonging to 'that rather melancholy group of old coast-towns, scattered along the great sea-face of New England [...]—superannuated centres of the traffic with foreign lands, which have seen their trade carried away from them by the greater cities' (Ch. 1, 'Early Years'; *LC1* 329–30).

92 **"cellarettes":** 'Cases of cabinet-work made to hold wine bottles, etc. Later also: a sideboard with compartments for the same purpose' (*OED*).

93 **Stuyvesant Square:** Once the farmland of Peter Stuyvesant (1610–72), the last Dutch governor of the colonial province of the New Netherlands. The land was sold by the Stuyvesant family to the city of New York in 1836, and a public park was formally established there in 1850. Today it is bisected by 2nd Avenue and lies between 15th and 17th Streets on the East Side.

94 **Twelfth Street Juliet [...] Brooklyn Romeo:** Obvious reference to Shakespeare's famous tragedy (1597).

95 **the pretty Gothic church:** Probably the First Presbyterian Church at 12th Street and 5th Avenue, built in the Gothic style and first used in 1846.

96 **Wall Street:** Located in lower Manhattan at the heart of New York's world-famous financial district, this street is a symbol of a capitalist and future-oriented society. On his return to America in 1904, James bitterly remarked: 'If it had been the final function of the Bay to make one feel one's age, so, assuredly, the mouth of Wall Street proclaimed it, for one's private ear, distinctly enough; the breath of existence being taken, wherever one turned, as that of youth on the run and with the prize of the race in sight, and the new landmarks crushing the old quite as violent children stamp on snails and caterpillars' (*AS*, Ch. 2, 'New York Revisited'; *CTW1* 423).

97 **in New York, about 1845:** The chronological setting of the story is here made explicit if not exact.

98 **Schleswig-Holstein:** The two duchies, located in the southern part of the Jutland peninsula, were annexed as a province of Prussia in 1867; it is the northernmost state of modern Germany. At the time of the tale's setting, however, the territory was in dispute between Denmark and Germany, leading to the First Schleswig War (1848–51) and Danish victory; this was conclusively reversed in the Second Schleswig War of 1864.

99 **Episcopal church at Haarlem:** James is probably thinking of St Mary's Episcopal Church, a Protestant church belonging to the Anglican Communion, established in 1823 on what is now West 126th Street in Manhattanville, also known as West Harlem, a 'dusty suburb' in the 1840s, as James calls it.

100 **under the rose:** 'Privately, secretly, in strict confidence' (*OED*), from Latin, '*sub rosa*'.

101 **Genoa:** Italian port city in north-eastern Italy incorporated into the Kingdom of Sardinia after the Congress of Vienna (1815), now the capital of the Liguria region. James was initially disappointed with this city. In a letter to his father from Genoa dated 14 January 1870, he described it 'as an humble step-sister—a poor fifth Cousin, of my Florence' (*CLHJ 1855–1872* 2:256). A few years later he showed more appreciation of 'the queerest place in the world', in 'Italy revisited' (1878): 'In the wonderful crooked, twisting, climbing, soaring, burrowing Genoese alleys the traveller is really up to his neck in the old Italian sketchability' (*PPL* 48). James stopped in Genoa again briefly in 1881, on his way to Milan: see the letter to his mother dated 16 March 1881 (*CHJL 1880–1883* 1:189–193).

102 **Charlestown, near Boston:** Charlestown is the oldest neighbourhood in Boston, Massachusetts, located on a peninsula north of the Charles River. It became a city in 1848 and was annexed by Boston in 1874. Its navy-yard was established in 1800.

103 **false position:** A phrase much used by James, in e.g. *Hawthorne, The Bostonians, The Princess Casamassima,* 'The Patagonia' (1888), *What Maisie Knew* (1897), and *The Sense of the Past* (1917).

104 **the South Seas:** The United States Navy was increasingly active in the South Pacific in the nineteenth century, notably when Commodore Matthew Perry, great-uncle of James's boyhood friend Thomas Sergeant Perry, sailed into Tokyo Bay in 1853 (shortly before the action of this story) and when Admiral George Dewey defeated the Spanish Pacific fleet in 1898 at Manila.

105 **a palace painted in fresco by Vandyke and Titian:** Sir Anthony Van Dyck (1599–1641), Flemish Baroque artist and leading court painter in England; the Italian Titian (Tiziano Vecellio) (1488?–1576), the most important painter of the so-called Venetian School. Both artists appear recurrently among the many who populate James's fiction and essays. It is unclear what

frescoes James might be thinking of in this passage, as these two artists are known to have painted only portraits and canvasses in the Genoese palaces.

106 **Medusa-mask**: A reference to the mythological monster who petrified those who gazed into her eyes. Further references to the mask of Medusa in James's writings occur in *The Other House* (1896), where 'Rose [Armiger]'s mask was the mask of Medusa' (Ch. 27), and 'The Way It Came' (1896, Ch. 7; retitled 'The Friends of the Friends' for the *NYE*). In a notebook entry by the graves of his sister Alice and the rest of the family (29 March 1905) James reflected on 'the cold Medusa-face of life' (*CN* 40).

107 **devastated by brigands**: The phenomenon of brigandage, which particularly affected the southern regions of Italy from the late eighteenth century to the early years after unification, was largely overestimated in nineteenth-century American culture. Writers like Washington Irving dedicated part of their work to debunking the 'myth' of Italian brigandage (see the section 'The Italian Banditti' in Irving's 1824 collection *Tales of a Traveller*). Nonetheless, it was reported by the Naples correspondent for the London *Times* of 3 June 1875, for instance, that 'a band of brigands' had 'appeared near Casabuono and captured a shepherd boy of the age of 14 years and a well-to-do peasant. For the release of the former they demand a ransom of 4,250 lire, and that of the latter 6,375 lire.'

108 **a creature of clay and iron**: Compare Daniel 2:42: 'And as the toes of the feet were part of iron, and part of clay, so the kingdom shall be partly strong, and partly broken' (KJV).

109 **in Chinese waters**: There was some marginal US involvement in the Opium Wars of 1839–42 and 1856–60, which mainly pitted the British (and to some extent the French) against the Chinese Qing Dynasty; Western powers imported opium into China, making immense profits. Robert Acton in *The Europeans* has a houseful of 'chinoiseries—trophies of his sojourn in the Celestial Empire' (*CFHJ* 4, Ch. 6, p. 174, notes 73 and 74 (Susan Griffin)).

110 **Secretary of the Navy**: A presidential appointee, and by statute a civilian; the post was held in the 1840s by a succession of people: David Henshaw (1843–4); Thomas W. Gilmer (1844); John Y. Mason (1844–5); George Bancroft (1845–6); John Y. Mason (1846–9); William B. Preston (1849–50).

111 **Rome [...] the Seven Hills [...] malarial fever**: The Seven Hills (Aventine, Caelian, Capitoline, Esquiline, Palatine, Quirinal, Viminal) are a symbol

of Rome. They are located east of the Tiber River and constitute the heart of the ancient city. Rome was notorious for the malaria that proved fatal to the title character of James's 'Daisy Miller'.

112 **Theory:** This name was listed among others in a notebook entry dated 16 March 1879 (*CN* 13). See Introduction, p. lv.

113 **dates of the different eruptions:** According to Baedeker's *Italy: Handbook for Travellers: Third Part, Southern Italy, Sicily, etc.* (1867), the first recorded eruption of Mount Vesuvius was in 79 CE and the most recent were in 1804, 1805, and 1822 and (perhaps after the action of the tale) in 1850, 1855, 1858, and 1861.

114 **the museum:** The Royal Bourbon Museum, founded by Charles III of Spain in the 1750s. In the nineteenth century the museum was considerably expanded with materials from private collections and archaeological sites around Pompeii and Vesuvius. James visited it in December 1869 (*CLHJ 1855–1872* 2:230–1); so too did the title character of *Roderick Hudson* a few years later. A reference to this museum, as well as impressions of the Naples area, can also be found in James's travel essay 'The Saint's Afternoon and Others' (1901, *CTW2* 600–19).

115 **Magna Graecia:** A Latin name ('Great Greece') which designates the coastal areas of southern Italy, extensively colonized by Greek settlers.

116 **Mildred's beauty [...] mortal disease:** See Introduction, p. lviii.

117 **excavations at Pompeii:** Roman city near Naples, partially destroyed and buried during the eruption of Mount Vesuvius in 79 CE. The archaeological excavations began in the mid-eighteenth century. James wrote: 'Pompei is simply the great Roman world on a reduced scale & you get there in a deeply concentrated form, the emotion you feel, diffused & diluted, in Rome' (21 December 1869, *CLHJ 1855–1872* 2:231). An October 1841 report on 'Vesuvius, Herculaneum, and Pompeii' in *Bradshaw's Manchester Journal* noted that 'The excavations proceed [...] with dismal slowness', owing to a reduction in the budget and workforce employed.

118 **the Neapolitan winter had been remarkably soft:** James's stay in Naples in December 1869 had not been so fortunate: he told his mother that 'the pleasure of my visit has been seriously diminished by obstinate bad weather—& that I shall probably be condemned to leave with hardly more than a glimpse of that Southern Sunshine which fills the sky & sea with color & calls out the latent beauty of the place' (*CLHJ 1855–1872* 2:229).

119 **crest of the volcano [...] the great sea-vision of Capri:** The Theory sisters seem to be residing in a villa in Posillipo (see note 121), a residential quarter of Naples, located along the northern coast of its bay. There is a breathtaking view of the bay, looking southwards. According to Collister (*SBOC* 307–8, note 665) James visited Naples several times between 1869 and 1907. In an 1869 letter to his mother he wrote: 'My hotel directly faces the sea and my room is perched aloft in the 5th story on a terrace which commands all the immensity of the view. On each side of me the bay stretches out its mighty arms—holding in one hand the sullen mass of Vesuvius & in the other, veiled in a mist which shadows forth the dimness of their classicism, the antique sites of Baiae and Cumae— all haunted with Horatian & Virgilian memories. Into its vast embrace the grey Mediterranean comes roaring & tumbling, distressed by many winds. Directly opposite, in the middle of the immensely uplifted horizon, Capri uplifts into the watery sky the vague steepness of its beautiful shape. Cast aloft over all this an immeasurable sky in which a faint sunset is fighting with a compacted army of clouds & then evoke in your mind's ears the tremendous clamour of the troubled waves—& you'll have a notion of what my window treats me to' (21 December 1869, *CLHJ 1855–1872* 2:229–30). On James's impressions of Naples see his essay 'The Saint's Afternoon and Others' (1901, *CTW*2 600–19).

120 **Percival:** This name is also used in *The Tragic Muse* (Percival Dormer).

121 **Posilippo:** *Correctly:* Posillipo. See note 463 to 'The Aspern Papers'. The hill of Posillipo separates the bay of Naples from the gulf of Pozzuoli. In a letter to Grace Norton from Sorrento, 9 April 1880, James wrote: 'The bay of Naples lies before me like a vast pale-blue floor, streaked in all sorts of fantastic ways with currents both of lighter & darker colour. The opposite coast—Posilippo, Baiae etc.—is wonderfully distinct in the clear still light, & I can almost see the shapes of the villas, & the boats pulled up along the strand. Vesuvius sits there on my right, looking wonderfully serene as he smokes his morning pipe, and just beneath my window a boatful of fishermen in red caps sends up a murmur of lazy sounds which mingles with the clash of little waves at the base of the cliff on which the hotel is planted' (*CLHJ 1878–1880* 2: 153). In *The Portrait of a Lady* Madame Merle goes to visit a friend of hers who owns a villa at Posillipo (Ch. 47).

122 *Louisiana:* The most famous episode regarding a steamboat called *Louisiana* was an explosion on 12 August 1844 which killed seventeen persons, 15 miles above the settlement of Bayou Sara in the New Orleans area.

123   **the commodore, who had gone to Constantinople:** After the Greek War of Independence (1821–32), the Ottoman Empire signed a treaty of commerce with the United States government that included a secret clause for American assistance in rebuilding the Turkish navy with the help of naval architects such as Henry Eckford and Foster Rhodes. Such cooperation was further improved with a supplementary treaty of 1862. See Şuhnaz Yilmaz, *Turkish–American Relations, 1800–1952: Between the Stars, Stripes and the Crescent* (London: Routledge, 2015), pp. 18–19.

124   **a glass of cold "orangeade":** The inverted commas suggest that this orange drink was a new phenomenon. Along with 'lemonade', it had in fact existed since the late seventeenth century, but, like so much else at the time James was writing, it was being produced, advertised, and consumed on a wholly new scale.

125   **the American consul:** One of the United States' oldest Foreign Service posts, the Consulate General Naples was established in 1796. In 1853 the post had been filled for the previous forty-four years by Alexander Hammett.

126   **Miss Mildred […] the pleasant American habit of using the lady's personal name:** James underlines the difference between the British usage and the American usage. In Britain, 'Miss' is followed by the family name.

127   **advertisements of quack medicines:** Patent medicines (pseudo-medical remedies available without prescription) were particularly popular in nineteenth-century America. In New York, in particular, English-born Benjamin Brandreth (1809–80) pioneered modern mass merchandizing and advertising in the sale of purgative pills which allegedly cured a variety of illnesses related to the 'impurity' of the blood.

128   **Lago Maggiore:** Lake Maggiore is located on the south side of the Alps. It is the second largest lake in Italy and largest lake of the canton of Ticino, Switzerland. The lake and its renowned locations, such as Stresa, are also employed by James as a setting for the short story 'Louisa Pallant' and are briefly mentioned in *The Wings of the Dove*. See note 354.

129   **not from Boston, but from New York:** See Introduction, p. xlv.

130   **"diligance":** The misspelling of the word 'diligence' is used to emphasize the bad French displayed by Percival Theory's wife.

131   **in filigree, in tartan lacquer:** 'filigree' refers to small jewels made with very light silver thread; 'tartan lacquer' may refer to card or tobacco tins or boxes with that pattern.

132   **Coliseum:** The world-renowned ancient amphitheatre in the heart of Rome, whose construction was begun by the Emperor Vespasian in 70 CE on the marshy site of a lake in the grounds of Nero's palace. James commented on this ancient ruin in 'A Roman Holiday' (1873) and in the later essay 'Very Modern Rome' (1878, unpublished until 1954; *CTW2* 752–63), where he lamented the results of the excavations that had been concluded in 1874. The Colosseum also features in crucial passages of both *Roderick Hudson* and *Daisy Miller* (Part 2).

133   **the Drapers [...] to Twenty-fourth Street [...] the Vanderdeckens [...] to the Twenty-third Street:** These addresses show the fast pace of urbanization in Manhattan in the mid-nineteenth century. At the beginning of the story, Twelfth Street has just ceased to be suburban, while ten years later the city limit is at the level of Madison Square. The name 'Draper' appears in 'Madame de Mauves' (1874); the variant 'Vanderdecker' in 'Lady Barberina' (1884).

134   **Mr. Henry Platt:** Another character named Platt (William) appears in the short story 'A Bundle of Letters' (1878).

135   **purchase of coral:** Coral jewellery and cameo-making have a very old history in the town of Torre del Greco, south of Naples. Although coral fishing had been a traditional practice in the area since ancient times, a large manufacturing industry related to this material boomed at the beginning of the nineteenth century. Local artisans took inspiration from the ancient jewellery found in the excavations in Pompeii and Herculaneum. In 1879 a 'School of Coral Carving' also opened, giving an additional impulse to the development of this industry.

136   **Alps and Apennines:** The two mountain ranges north of the Italian peninsula and along the spine of the same. James 'descended' into Italy over the Alps more than once.

137   **the royal palace:** Located in the heart of Naples, it was one of the four residences used by the Bourbon kings during their rule of the Kingdom of Two Sicilies (1730–1860). Since the eighteenth century, they mostly resided in the newly erected and much safer palace of Caserta, away from the many revolts which took place in Naples. After the big fire which damaged many of its rooms (1837), the royal palace remained under restoration until 1858. The king until his death in 1859 was the repressive Ferdinand II, who was followed by his son Francesco II until the kingdom was dissolved upon Italian unification in 1861.

138 **a Bostonian converted to New York; a very special type:** The most notable other example in James's work is the Europeanized Mrs Luna, Olive Chancellor's sister in *The Bostonians*.

139 **the royal apartments:** They consist of thirty adjoining rooms.

140 **scagliola floor:** Type of floor made with small pieces of marble or other stone mixed with plaster and then polished. See note 389 to 'The Aspern Papers'.

141 **a modern portrait of a Bourbon princess:** *Murray's 1868* notes the existence of paintings by 'modern artists' in the private rooms of the royal apartments on the second floor (179). No portrait in the palace at present seems to correspond to this description, but the princess could be identified with Maria Amalia of Saxony (1724–60), the queen consort of Naples and Sicily (1738–59) and then queen consort of Spain (1759–60). Rococo painter Giuseppe Bonito (1707–89) made a very famous painting of her (*c.* 1745), now in the Prado Museum in Madrid. Another possibility might be a portrait by Anton Raphael Mengs of Archduchess Maria Carolina of Austria, who married Ferdinand IV of Naples in 1768.

142 **Do you see who she looks like?:** Compare with the scene in *The Wings of the Dove* where Milly Theale's resemblance to the young woman in a Bronzino painting becomes an important turning point in the story.

143 **a big bill at Tiffany's:** Founded by Charles Lewis Tiffany and John B. Young in lower Manhattan in 1837, the store originally sold a wide variety of luxury items.

144 **my sister Cora:** Other occurrences of the name occur in *The Reverberator* (1888), where 'Mr. and Mrs. D. S. Rosenheim and Miss Cora Rosenheim and Master Samuel Rosenheim had "left for Brussels"' (*CFHJ 10*, p. 17) and Cora Prodmore is a character in James's one-act play *Summersoft* (1895), converted into a story, 'Covering End' (1898) and subsequently reworked for his three-act play, *The High Bid* (1907).

145 **Isle of Wight:** Island in the English Channel off the coast of Hampshire that was popular with Victorians, including Queen Victoria and the poet laureate, Alfred Lord Tennyson, both of whom had residences there. See note 11 to 'Pandora'.

146 **anti-slavery conventions:** Anti-slavery conventions were organized by the Abolitionists, who were particularly active in Boston in the 1830s. William Lloyd Garrison founded the Boston-based New England Anti-Slavery Society in 1831.

147 **a suit for divorce:** In pre-bellum America divorce was heavily debated and divided legislators, journalists, and activists, who lamented the national disunion on such an important question. In most states the process of obtaining the act of legislature to end a marriage could be very protracted, expensive, and above all publicly humiliating. See Norma Basch, *Framing American Divorce: From the Revolutionary Generation to the Victorians* (Berkeley and Los Angeles: University of California Press, 1999). On James and divorce, see Lynn Wardley's 'Courtship, marriage, family' in *Henry James in Context*, ed. David McWhirter (Cambridge: Cambridge University Press, 2010), pp. 150–160.

148 **James's story 'The Siege of London' (1883) also uses this allusion to Macbeth:** 'And yet he couldn't give her away, as they said in New York; that stuck in his throat.' (*S1874–1884* 628) The connection seems to come in Mrs Headway's need of vouched-for respectability, of social blessing; Macbeth asks, 'But wherefore could not I pronounce 'Amen'? / I had most need of blessing, and 'Amen' Stuck in my throat. (2.2.30–32)

149 **If I have […] the shame […], let me at least have the profit!:** The distorted echo of a notorious declaration by the eponymous tragic heroine of Jean Racine's *Phèdre*: 'Hélas! du crime affreux dont la honte me suit / Jamais mon triste coeur n'a recueilli le fruit' (4.6.40–1): 'Alas! Of the terrible crime whose shame pursues me, never has my sad heart gathered the fruit.'

150 **When the writer of these pages last heard of the pair they were waiting still:** The last encounter between Benyon and Georgina, who had met in the 1840s, probably takes place in the 1850s. On p. 61 we read that 'Georgina came very early, earlier even than visits were paid in New York thirty years ago.'

'A New England Winter'

151 MRS. DAINTRY: James wrote down a list of names which included 'Daintry' and 'Florimond' on 2 January 1884, noting: 'Most of them are out of the *Times* of the above date, very rich.—' (*CN* 23). *The Times* lists a Mr. J. T. Daintree as a contributor to the Homeless Boys of London ('Universal Week Prayer'). For the 'romantic' associations of Florimond's name, see note 179. James may have heard the name Florimond in France, where there was at least one fairly well-known Florimond in the 1870s: Louis-Auguste Florimond Ronger, better known as Hervé (1825–92), one of the initiators of *opéra bouffe*. The name was common in France.

152 **from the "hill" to the "new land":** The hill is Beacon Hill, the old part of Boston, contrasted here with what was called the Back Bay, south of the Charles River, mudland filled in, and built upon, from 1857. In the story there are several references to Beacon Hill and the artificial ground of the 'Back Bay', as this well-to-do residential area came to be called (see also Daniel Karlin's Introduction to *The Bostonians, CFHJ* 8, p. lxxi). The use of the article in front of 'Back Bay' seems to be the norm in the nineteenth century (see Howells's *The Rise of Silas Lapham*, 1885), but it is uncertain nowadays. From 2 February 1882 James lived on Beacon Hill, at 102 Mount Vernon Street, for about three months, renting a place there after the death of his mother. Coming back from Europe on his father's death, he lived in his father's house at 131 Mount Vernon Street, from 21 December 1882 to August 1883, until he returned to Europe. The topography of Boston is quite detailed in this story.

153 **Newbury Street [...] Commonwealth Avenue:** In the Back Bay, Newbury is a street mostly parallel to the much longer and wider Commonwealth Avenue, which has now a grassy, tree-lined central reservation for pedestrians. The *Yale Review* (n.s. 13.1 (October 1923), 206–8) has a James letter of 8 August 1901 to a Mrs Frances Carruth Prindle about topographic details in this tale and *The Bostonians* (we are indebted to Philip Horne for pointing this out). On the latter work James wrote: 'I only remember in the N.E.W. Mrs. Daintry as in Marlborough St.' This would have made Mrs Daintry's itinerary quite complicated, as Marlborough Street is parallel to Commonwealth Avenue to the north, while Newbury Street is parallel to it on the south. Therefore if Mrs Daintry had lived on Marlborough, she would have turned into Newbury after crossing Commonwealth, and then back again into Commonwealth. But in 1901 James must have misremembered, because in the story Mrs Daintry lives on Newbury.

154 **on the uncomfortable side of the Seine:** Presumably the *rive gauche*, although Mrs Daintry appears to have in mind the Latin Quarter, the artistic section, rather than the conservative and elegant Faubourg Saint-Germain. In *The American* it is in this latter quarter (the Faubourg Saint-Germain), on the rue de l'Université, that the old Bellegarde family house is situated, while in *The Ambassadors* Madame de Vionnet lives on the rue de Bellechasse, not far from the same street. In *The Reverberator* this area is referred to as 'the conservative *faubourg*' (*CFHJ* 10, p. 67). The Paris Baedeker for 1884 defines the left bank as the area where there are 'numerous learned institutions' and the adjoining Quartier Saint-Germain-des-Prés as an 'aristocratic quarter' (p. 213). Horne quotes a Baedeker describing the quarter as 'more or less sacred to the aristocracy

of blood' (notes to *A London Life and The Reverberator* (Oxford: Oxford University Press, 1989), p. 365). Mrs Daintry's knowledge of the 'uncomfortable side of the Seine' is thus limited; she appears to be merely contrasting it to the other side of the river, the right bank, where the Louvre and other significant buildings and institutions are situated.

155 **Liverpool:** Liverpool was one of the usual departure and arrival British ports to and from the United States.

156 **the British Provinces:** Ontario, Nova Scotia, and New Brunswick, with French Québec, were the four original provinces of Canada.

157 **a badge of servitude in the shape of a neat little muslin coif:** In the Victorian era women servants usually wore a uniform with an apron and a coif.

158 **the Athenæum:** This famous and exclusive literary club, founded as the Anthology Club in 1805, became the Boston Athenæum in 1807, and was established in 1847 at 10½ Beacon Street. A pamphlet listed its functions: 'a Reading Room, a Library, a Museum, and a Laboratory' (*The First One Hundred Years of the Boston Athenæum from 1807 to 1907* (1907), p. 26). R. L. Midgley's 1865 *Boston Sights: Or, Handbook for Visitors* declares that 'The library is hardly surpassed, either in size or in value, by any other in the country; and its regulations are framed with the design that it shall answer the highest purposes of a public library' (Boston: A. Williams and Company, 1865 p. 43). It gradually became one of the most important cultural centres and libraries in Boston. The Jameses were members of the Athenæum and often borrowed books. In *The American Scene* (Ch. 7) James saw it as an element of a precious past ('this honoured haunt of all the most civilized— library, gallery, temple of culture') squeezed to nothingness by the 'mere masses of brute ugliness beside it' (*CTW1* 546).

159 **Clarendon Street:** A street to the west of Boston Common, perpendicular to Newbury Street and Commonwealth Avenue.

160 **winding-up the lamp:** A reference to the cotton wick that had to be adjusted in oil lamps.

161 **the Sorbonne [...] the Louvre:** The famous Paris university, founded in 1257 by Robert de Sorbon as a college, and called La Sorbonne in 1554 when theology courses were taught there; the Louvre is the equally famous museum, inaugurated in 1793 as the central Museum of the French Republic, in the former residence of the French kings. It is often used by James as a setting for his fiction, e.g. in *The American*, and referred to in *A Small Boy and Others* as the place where the young James had the

revelation of 'Style' and 'the most appalling yet admirable nightmare of [his] life' in the Galerie d'Apollon (Ch. 25).

162 **the Public Garden:** The Boston Public Garden was laid out in 1859–60 by landscape architect John F. Meacham, on reclaimed land that had been reserved for a public garden as early as 1839.

163 **Beacon Street:** The very long street slightly ascending the north side of Boston Common. It runs along the Common, the Public Garden and through the Back Bay, parallel to the Charles River.

164 **to the manner born:** The phrase comes from *Hamlet* 1.4.12–16: '*Horatio*: Is it a custom? / *Hamlet*: Ay, marry, is't, / But to my mind, though I am native here / And to the manner born, it is a custom / More honor'd in the breach than the observance.'

165 **Mount Vernon Place [...] Joy Street:** On Beacon Hill, Mount Vernon Place is a cul-de-sac near the corner of Mount Vernon Street and Joy Street, the street joining Beacon Street to Cambridge Street.

166 **Nova Scotia, where, until lately [...] there had been an English garrison:** The most populous of the four British provinces in Canada, with a mainly Catholic population; the 78th (Highlanders) Regiment of Foot were stationed at Halifax, 1869–71, and British troops guarded the city's Citadel fort. As most of James's readers knew, Nova Scotia was the place where the eponymous heroine of the epic poem by Henry Wadsworth Longfellow (1807–82), 'Evangeline, A Tale of Acadie' (1847), came from. In view of the reference to Bostonians reading ballads, the association with Longfellow may have influenced the choice of Nova Scotia. Longfellow is also explicitly quoted for his *Children's Hour* (see note 237). See Introduction, pp. lxi–lxii.

167 **Parthian observations:** Parthian is used figuratively with reference to the fighting tactics of the Parthians in ancient Iran: a 'Parthian shot' indicates 'a pointed glance, cutting remark, etc., delivered by a person at the moment of departure', as 'Parthian horsemen were accustomed to baffle their enemies with their rapid manœuvres, and to discharge missiles backwards while fleeing or pretending to flee' (*OED*).

168 **neither festoons nor Persian rugs, nor plates and *plaques* upon the wall nor faded stuffs suspended:** The description of Lucretia's house is that of a house in the style of the 1830s, rather than of a later period, characterized by decorations in the Aesthetic style (see note 293 to 'The Path of Duty').

169 **Kaulbach:** Wilhelm von Kaulbach (1805–74), German painter noted for his Munich murals but also for his engravings from Shakespeare and

the Gospels. James commented on his 'Era of the Reformation' and its 'incredible amount of science and skill' in his 1874 unsigned article 'Art' [The Duke of Montpensier's pictures exhibited at the Boston Athenaeum] (*CWAD1* 93). On 27 May 1867 William James wrote to his father from Dresden that he was in a beer-garden, met a person 'and found out afterwards that he was no less a person than the illustrious Kaulbach' (*Correspondence of William James*, vol. 4, *1856–1877*, p. 163).

170   **an empire clock**: A clock in the style that became popular after Napoleon's campaign in Egypt and Italy, from 1803 onwards. See note 451.

171   **in black and gilt**: This type of house decoration goes together with the festoons and Persian rugs quoted above. See note 168.

172   **Female Suffrage**: The campaign to secure women's right to vote, supported by Olive Chancellor and Verena Tarrant in *The Bostonians*, was publicly launched at the women's rights convention held at Seneca Falls, New York, in 1848. The Civil War slowed the movement's progress. A proposed eighteenth amendment (1869), giving the vote to black men, caused different reactions in women activists. Some of them thought that giving the right to vote to black men might further the women's cause, some that it would hinder it. Women's right to vote (through the Nineteenth Amendment) was obtained in 1920.

173   **the *Transcript***: The *Boston Transcript* (or *Boston Evening Transcript*), a Boston newspaper founded in 1830. In 1842 it had the first woman editor in the United States, Cornelia Wells Walter (1813?–98), sister of the founder, Lynde Walter. It lasted until 1941. There is a poem by T.S. Eliot called 'The Boston Evening Transcript' (1915) that underlines the conservative type of the readers of the *Boston Transcript*. It is also mentioned in *The Bostonians* and *The Wings of the Dove*.

174   **the dome of the State House**: The gilded cupola of the (new) Boston State House, built by Charles Bulfinch (1795–8) on the southern slope of Beacon Hill. The State House itself is mentioned in *The American Scene* (Ch. 7): 'the old uplifted front of the State House, surely, in its spare and austere, its ruled and pencilled kind, a thing of beauty, more delightful and harmonious even than I had remembered it; one of the inestimable values again, in the eye of the town, for taste and temperance' (*CTW1* 544).

175   **a frivolous eagerness for the social act**: Compare Mrs. Luna's account of why Olive Chancellor keeps Basil Ransom waiting at the very start of *The Bostonians*: 'Olive will come down in about ten minutes; she told me to tell you that. About ten; that is exactly like Olive. Neither five nor fifteen,

and yet not ten exactly, but either nine or eleven. She didn't tell me to say she was glad to see you, because she doesn't know whether she is or not, and she wouldn't for the world expose herself to telling a fib. She is very honest, is Olive Chancellor; she is full of rectitude. Nobody tells fibs in Boston; I don't know what to make of them all.' (*CFHJ 8*, p. 5).

176 **Federal Street:** Now in the financial district, it was in Mrs Daintry's mother's time, the pre-Civil War years, still residential, part of the old Boston. The street was called Long Lane up to 1788.

177 **cachinnation:** 'Loud or immoderate laughter' (*OED*). Used in Chapter 4 of Thomas Carlyle's *Sartor Resartus* (1833–4), where he denounces those who can only produce 'some whiffling husky cachinnation, as if they were laughing through wool: of none such comes good'. Thereafter it was mostly adopted by American writers in humorous contexts.

178 **her chintz:** Upholstery material made of cotton with a glossy finish, often with flower patterns.

179 **romantic name [...] old ballads:** The name of Florimond is found in a medieval Scottish ballad, 'The tale of Florimond of Albanye / that sléu the dragon be the see', in John Leyden's *The Complaint of Scotland written in 1548* (Edinburgh, A. Constable 1801). This might be the ballad referred to. The reading of ballads was influenced by the popularity of Longfellow (see Introduction, p. lxi). The fact that the young people's magazine *Wide Awake* could publish a story from December 1887 to May 1888 by Henry Harland (pseud. Sidney Luska), called *Uncle Florimond*, suggests that the name had become popular. It is the story of a boy who dreams of his French uncle, Florimond Charles Marie Auguste de la Bourbonnaye, a marquis, who lives in France but eventually arrives in the United States in total poverty.

180 **Boston Common:** The green area, or park, south of Beacon Hill, which used to be the 'common' ground for cows' pasture in Puritan times. Cows were allowed on it until 1830. Midgley's 1865 *Boston Sights* proclaims that 'Were we to be asked, What is *the* great feature of Boston city, we should assuredly reply, BOSTON COMMON' (68).

181 **the New England capital:** The city of Boston.

182 **sails on the 20th [...] home by the 1st of December:** Ten days was the average time a steamer took to cross the Atlantic at this period.

183 **winter among the bears:** A reference to the cold of Boston. Any more specific association of Boston with bears would have to wait until the

formation of their celebrated ice hockey team, the Boston Bruins, in 1924.

184 **Her method was Socratic:** Method of teaching based on questions and answers, used by the Greek philosopher Socrates, made famous by the dialogues of Plato. At one point in *The Awkward Age* (1899) 'Mrs Brook was almost Socratic' (Ch. 30).

185 **they live in Brooklyn:** One of the five boroughs of New York City since 1898. For the Brooklyn navy-yard, see note 80 to 'Georgina's Reasons'.

186 **with a *crescendo*:** Italian musical term indicating the intensification of sound, or voice, here used in a figurative sense.

187 **laying a train:** Laying a trap, deceiving, in order to marry her son.

188 **it is very sophisticating:** A term of denigration in this context: 'to corrupt or spoil [...] to render less genuine or honest' (*OED*), with reference to the speaker's 'Socratic method'. In 'The Solution' (1892), the guilty narrator says that there was 'something in the sophisticating Roman air which converted all life into a pleasant comedy'.

189 **in the watches of the night:** Adrian Poole notes that this phrase, with biblical associations (Psalm 63:6), was 'absorbed into the English literary tradition, as for example in Tennyson's *In Memoriam* (xci): "Come: not in watches of the night, / But where the sunbeam broodeth warm." The phrase occurs with some frequency in James's writings, as for instance in *The Bostonians* (Ch. 16), 'The Tree of Knowledge' (Ch. 3), *The Spoils of Poynton* (Ch. 7) *The Ambassadors* (*CFHJ* 18 Chs. 7 and 14) and *The Princess Casamassima* (*CFHJ* 9 p. 495, note 28). Tamara Follini adds its occurrence in *The Wings of the Dove* (1902: Vol. I, Book Fourth: Ch. 2), noting in *CFHJ* that New Englander Susan Stringham may be also remembering a sonnet by Henry Wadsworth Longfellow written in memory of his wife, 'The Cross of Snow', composed in 1879, in which 'In the long, sleepless watches of the night', the speaker ruminates upon 'the face of one long dead'. See note 584 to 'The Modern Warning'.

190 **that famous dragon of antiquity,—wasn't it in Crete [...] sacrificed:** Miss Daintry appears to be referring to the myth of the Minotaur, the creature who was not a dragon but half man, half bull, and who devoured young virgins in the labyrinth in Crete, built by Daedalus and his son Icarus, on the order of King Minos of Crete. The monster was defeated by the Athenian hero Theseus, who found his way through the labyrinth

thanks to the thread given to him by Ariadne, one of the daughters of Minos, who had fallen in love with him. On 17 May 1874 James wrote to his mother from Florence, about delaying his return to the US, 'I shall be wondering whether if I were to stay another year I shouldn't propitiate the Minotaur & return more resignedly' (*CLHJ 1872–1876* 2:169).

191 **at Doll's […] Appleton Brown**: Doll & Richards was an important Boston art gallery, dating, with different names, from the late 1830s or the mid-1840s. It had several locations on Beacon Hill, and was at 145 Tremont Street from 1871 until 1880 (*PE* 43), taking over the Warren Building at no. 2 Park Street in 1878. For a photo of the gallery in 1878, see *CLHJ 1877–1878* 1: illus. 6. James wrote on at least five Doll & Richards exhibitions, in 1872 ('French Pictures in Boston', 'Pictures by William Morris Hunt, Gerôme and Others', 'Art: Boston', 'Art') and in 1875 ('Duveneck and Copley'). John Appleton Brown (1844–1902) was an American painter, nicknamed 'Apple Blossom Brown' for his paintings of spring trees. In 1875 James had commented of Brown's French-influenced work at Doll's, though calling him 'a truly discreet painter', that 'Muddy streams, rusty trees, and homely verity sometimes strike us as rather savorless diet, and we almost pray for a turn of the tide in favor of old-fashioned composition and selection' (*CWAD1* 100). Some of his paintings, owned by Doll & Richards, were exhibited at the Cincinnati Industrial Expositions of 1874 and 1875. He joined Sargent, Abbey, Millet, and other impressionist painters in the village of Broadway, in England, in 1886. In the 1880s and 1890s Doll & Richards had exhibitions of Winslow Homer (1880), Elizabeth Boott (1884), John La Farge, and Childe Hassam (1893). A possible reference to Doll's is to be found in *The Ambassadors* (Book xi, Ch. 2), when Strether remembers, while in France, the Lambinet painting of the French countryside that he had seen and admired in a dealer's shop in Tremont Street (one address of Doll's, as mentioned above).

192 **to give a lot of Germans**: Allusion to the 'German cotillion', a type of dance, or to a party where the German cotillion was danced. In *A Small Boy and Others*, after talking about the passion for dancing in his youth, James remembers that on a yacht belonging to a member of the extended James family circle, 'the deck must have been more used for the "German" than for other diphthong – manœuvres' (*SBOC* 37). The dance must have been quite fashionable, as we see in a letter to Lizzie Boott from New York (8 March 1875), where James tells of a visit to the Italian Bottas: Vincenzo Botta, an Italian scholar and his wife Charlotte Lynch Botta, a

painter. Their home on West Thirty-ninth Street was a literary and artistic salon (*CLHJ 1872–1876* 2:214), and James, writing in Italian, puns on nationalities: 'trovai invece un *German*, ballato da giovani New Yorkesi' ('I found instead a *German*, danced by young New Yorkers'). (Letter to Lizzie Booth, *CLHJ 1872–1876* 2:212).

193 **Baltimore:** The capital city of Maryland, visited by James on his first encounter with the South in June 1905, and described in Chapter 10 of *The American Scene*.

194 **take the edge off the east wind:** The cold wind of Boston, symbolic of the Puritan tradition of the city.

195 **like the good Homer:** American proverb, deriving from Horace's *Ars Poetica*, 359: 'et idem indignor quandoque bonus dormitat Homerus' ('and yet I too get indignant whenever the good Homer nods off'), often misquoted as 'aliquando bonus dormitat Homerus' ('sometimes good Homer dozes'), meaning that even the best writer can have some blemishes in his work.

196 **the little Merrimans:** James gave the same name to Miss Merriman, the governess in *The Awkward Age* (1899).

197 **commission-merchant:** An American term: 'A person who conducts business or trade on behalf of another; an agent, a factor' (*OED*).

198 **East Boston:** Established in 1836, East Boston became a multi-ethnic neighbourhood populated by immigrants. It was the port for transoceanic vessels, and became rich in shipyards and maritime industries. Joined to downtown Boston by an underground tunnel (1900–4), it is now partly the site of Boston Logan International Airport.

199 **a dome so magnificently painted:** See note 174.

200 **an impressionist:** James's use of the term in this story is ironic. He was initially critical of impressionism, an artistic movement that originated in France in the 1870s. The term, first used in a satirical way with reference to Monet's *Impression, Soleil levant* (1872), which caused a scandal when exhibited in 1874, became the label for a number of painters who believed in painting *en plein air*, in the use of short, broken brushstrokes, and derived their ideas from optical theories of light. They also represented a reaction against academic, studio painting. James wrote on the impressionists in a negative way in 1876, and again against Whistler in 1877 and in 1878. In later years, joining the group of impressionists

which included Sargent at Broadway, in the Cotswolds, in 1885 (see note 191), James became more sympathetic to this type of painting. See Peter Brooks, *Henry James Goes to Paris* (Princeton, NJ: Princeton University Press, 2007).

201 **the American who returns to his native land after a few years**: James returned to the United States in October 1881, after being in Europe since November 1875, an absence of almost six years. His next absence, from the summer of 1883, lasted over twenty years.

202 **Massachusetts [...] Andalusia**: Massachusetts is a northern state while Andalusia, in Spain, is a southern region. Here it is apparently the way in which Florimond paints that makes the two very different countries look similar. James made a similar observation in a January 1875 article in the *Atlantic Monthly*, where he praised John Appleton Brown's painting *Newburyport*, but wrote that this 'painter is rather open to the imputation of believing that Newburyport is in the pleasant land of France' (*CWAD1* 99–100).

203 **the Back Bay**: The vast marshy land, south of the Charles River, reclaimed after the building of the Mill Dam, which closed off part of the river's estuary in 1821. It was not built up until the 1860s. See note 151.

204 **anti-Bohemian**: Not looking Bohemian, as painters and artists, including impressionists, were supposed to look in Paris, following the tradition set by Henri Mürger in the 1840s with his influential *Scènes de la vie de Bohème* (published in book form, 1851). In *The Tragic Muse* a theatrical party in St John's Wood, an artists' district of London, is described thus: 'It was all very Bohemian and journalistic and picturesque' (Vol. II, Ch. 17). For 'Bohemia' in James, especially in the novels of his 'middle period', see Julián Jiménez Heffernan, '"On the Outer Edge": The Temptation of Bohemia in Henry James', *Studies in American Fiction*, 44.1 (2017), 53–86. See note 417 to 'The Aspern Papers'.

205 **Zola**: Émile Zola (1840–1902), leader of the 'naturalists', author of many novels, among them *Nana* (1880), which focused on prostitution, a subject hardly acceptable to American realists, such as William Dean Howells, and their readers. James first met Zola at Flaubert's in 1875, and saw more of him again in 1884; he wrote several essays on Zola, whom he respected and even gradually came to admire in spite of the 'naturalist', or low-life, subjects of his novels. In 1884 the Anglo-American reaction against Zola was not yet as violent as it would become.

206 **the theory of art for art:** The phrase is attributed to the French philosopher, Victor Cousin (1792–1867) but was further disseminated by
Théophile Gautier, who famously used it in the preface to his 1835 novel,
Mademoiselle de Maupin. It refers to the Aesthetic movement which started
in France in the nineteenth century, detaching art from any didactic and
moral purpose. It flourished in England from the 1860s, promoted by such
writers as Walter Pater (1839–94) and later by Oscar Wilde (1854–1900). In
his 1876 essay, 'Charles Baudelaire', James was hostile about 'the crudity of
sentiment of the advocates of "art for art"' (*LC2* 157). He staged the conflict
between an aesthetic and a moralistic attitude in 'The Author of Beltraffio'
(1884), where the main character, an aesthete, states: 'Nothing had been
done in that line from the point of view of art for art. That served me as a
fond formula.' The phrase also occurs in 'The Liar' (1889): 'It is art for art
and he is prompted by the love of beauty.' See note 512.

207 **the pronunciation of Joanna's children:** James expressed himself more
than once as regards pronunciation. In *The Question of Our Speech* (1905),
and then in *The Speech of American Women* (1906–7), he commented at
length on the necessity to utter speech in a clear and conscious way. In
the second essay, remembering the period when he was living on Mount
Vernon Street, 'years ago—so many that I might […] hesitate now to produce it', he wrote that he had heard 'a whole group of Boston maidens
[who] slobbered unchecked'. The 'slovenly speech' of American women was
due, James went on, to the very success of American women, a product of
democracy. Unchecked by anyone, women were 'all articulating as from sore
mouths, all mumbling and whining and vocally limping and shuffling, as it
were, together' (*The Speech of American Women*, in *Henry James on Culture,
Collected Essays on Politics and the American Social Scene*, ed. Pierre A. Walker
(Lincoln, NE: University of Nebraska Press, 2004), pp. 69, 74, 74–5).

208 **Nuremberg:** A northern German city with gabled roofs and decorations
on the façades of the houses. In describing his journey 'From Venice to
Strasburg' in 1873, James had only grudgingly moderated his general judgment that Germany was 'ugly', when he observed that 'even Nuremberg
[was] not a joy forever' (*TS* 95).

209 **it's kept:** Or as we would now be more likely to say, 'well-kept'.

210 **he put his gathered fingers to his lips:** This piece of French body language is a gesture expressing appreciation.

211 **a polygamist—are there Mormons even here?:** Mormons were allowed
to have more than one wife until 1890 (despite the practice being

prohibited by US law in 1862), when polygamy was officially ended by the church president, although it survived longer in practice. The church of the Mormons, or the Church of Jesus Christ of Latter-Day Saints, was founded by Joseph Smith in 1830.

212 **old coins in her tresses; that sort of thing**: In his work James has a number of characters described with Oriental accessories, from Eugenia Munster in *The Europeans* to Fanny Assingham in *The Golden Bowl*: 'she put pearls in her hair and crimson and gold in her tea-gown for the same reason: it was her theory that nature itself had overdressed her and that her only course was to drown, as it was hopeless to try to chasten, the overdressing' (Book 1, Ch. 2). See note 214.

213 *plaques*: French word indicating ornamental plates or tablets, made of metal or porcelain, and painted with figures or flowers.

214 **a Circassian or a Smyrniote**: A woman from Circassia, in the Caucasus, or a woman from Smyrna, now in Turkey (Izmir), on the Mediterranean, in Asia Minor. However, the indications symbolically suggest the image of a vaguely Eastern woman as imagined by painters and writers in the nineteenth century, according to the fashion of Orientalism.

215 **swinging the censer**: The container where incense burns, used in religious ceremonies, meaning here an excess of worship.

216 **Arlington Street**: The street running northwards along the western side of Boston Common, up to Beacon Street.

217 **a celebrated actress in Paris who was the ideal of tortuous thinness**: James may have thought of the French actress Mademoiselle Rachel (Elizabeth Félix, 1821–58), who was known for her slim build, and is mentioned in *The Tragic Muse* and in his *Tribune* articles from Paris (1876); though he was too young ever to have seen Rachel, in 'The Théâtre Français' of 1877 'it was something of a consolation to think that those very footlights had illumined her finest moments' (*CWAD2* 190). Tintner instead identifies Rachel Torrance with Sarah Bernhardt, who was also described as thin (1844–1923) (*Pop World*, p. 90). James was a keen, quizzical observer of Bernhardt's performances. In his *Tribune* articles he names her several times, albeit without too much enthusiasm (*PS* 150). However, at the end of the essay 'The Théâtre Français' (1877) he mentions that she would deserve a whole chapter to herself (*CWAD2* 203), and in 'Occasional Paris' (1877) he praises her 'singular intelligence' and 'the fineness of her artistic nature' (*CTW2* 732). But James's judgment became increasingly severe

over the years. When the Comédie Française visited London in 1879, he judged her to be more of a celebrity than an artist (*CWAD2* 245). In 1880, writing to Grace Norton (28 December), he defined her as 'the great humbug of the age' (*CLHJ 1880–1883* 1:136) and by 1895 he had decided that 'Sarah, for a long time, has bored me to death' (Fred Kaplan, *Henry James: The Imagination of Genius* (New York: William Morrow, 1992), p. 399). Bernhardt performed one of her most celebrated roles as Theodora, Empress of Byzantium, in Victorien Sardou's play of the same name in the year 'A New England Winter' was published.

218 **to throw her companion into relief**: James developed the theme of a beautiful woman with an unattractive companion, whose plainness highlights the other's attractiveness, in the story 'The Beldonald Holbein' (1903); there, however, it is the old, lined face of the companion that attracts a painter's attention.

219 **the lioness of the winter**: To lionize is to entertain and make prominent a celebrity, or to treat someone as such (as in James's tale 'The Death of the Lion', 1894). James's Preface to *The Reverberator* (1888) calls its heroine Francie Dosson 'our roaring young lioness of the old-world salons' (*CFHJ* 10, p. 297).

220 **"naturalists" (in literature and art)**: The followers of a literary movement which developed from realism in the 1880s, notably Zola, Edmond de Goncourt (1822–96), and Alphonse Daudet (1840–97). Naturalists wanted to present reality as conditioned by heredity, social environment, evolution, according to theories popularized by Darwin and his followers. Their subjects were taken from lower-class life. See note 205 on Zola. In the visual arts, the naturalists were associated with Gustave Courbet (1819–77), Jules Breton (1827–1906), Auguste Rodin (1840–1917), and Jules Bastien-Lepage (1848–84).

221 **Boston, too, had its actualities**: James, or Florimond, is thinking in French, where *actualité* means something of topical interest, or in the plural, 'news'.

222 **when one changes one's sky**: A faint echo of Horace's 'Coelum non animum mutant qui trans mare currunt' (*Epistulae* 1.2.27), which may be translated 'Those who race across the sea change the sky over their heads but not who they are.'

223 **in the *Figaro***: The French politically conservative daily newspaper, founded in 1826, probably often read by James, as he mentions it in his

travel writing and essays (e.g. 'The Théâtre Français'). Several of his characters are described as reading the *Figaro* (e.g. Christopher Newman in *The American*). Works by Daudet and Edmond de Goncourt appeared in the newspaper.

224 **the exaggerated bridge, the patriotic statues:** The ornamental suspension bridge in the Public Gardens, designed in 1867 to cross the central pond. Among the statues are those of George Washington by Thomas Ball (1819–1911), dedicated in 1869, and Senator Charles Sumner (1811–74), a powerful opponent of slavery during the antebellum period, by the same sculptor, unveiled in 1878.

225 **the competitive spires of a liberal faith:** A reference to the spires of different churches in Boston, such as the spire of Old South Meeting House, a Congregationalist church which had been the organizing point for the Boston Tea Party (1773); the spire of Park Street Church, founded 1809 (primarily by members of the Old South Meeting House), where W. L. Garrison gave his first public speech against slavery – its spire made it the highest building in Boston until after the Civil War. Other churches, such as Arlington Street Church, North Church, and the Catholic St Francis de Sales Church, also have spires.

226 **the Puritan tradition:** Boston was founded by the Pilgrim Fathers and grew as a Puritan city. Its strict theocratic beginnings conditioned many writers, including Hawthorne. James's father was part of the reaction against Puritanism also inspired by German Romantic ideas and resulting in the Transcendentalist movement. Its main representative, R. W. Emerson, was a friend of Henry James Sr and like him was strongly influenced by the idealism of Emanuel Swedenborg (1688–1772).

227 **the fleshpots:** In this context, abundance of food and other material comforts, with reference to Exodus 16.3 (KJV): 'And the children of Israel said unto them, Would to God we had died by the hand of the Lord in the land of Egypt, when we sat by the flesh pots, and when we did eat bread to the full; for ye have brought us forth into this wilderness, to kill this whole assembly with hunger.' See note 346 to 'Louisa Pallant'.

228 **a social dialect which […] should be heard on the lips of a native:** Harry Thurston Peck cites this passage in an essay called 'The Little Touches': 'Allied somewhat with a prim preference for the superficially elegant is that jocular

use of "literary" language, which is common with certain people, especially with women, and most of all perhaps New England women, with whom literary allusion is something of a fad. It has been neatly caught by Henry James in his story, *A New England Winter*, where one of the characters, Pauline Mesh, speaks this sort of Bostonese'. (*What Is Good English? and Other Essays* (New York: Dodd, Mead, 1899), p. 43)

229 **'Maryland, my Maryland!'**: The title of a poem by James Ryder Randall (1839–1908), written in 1861, with the purpose of persuading Maryland to secede from the Union. In spite of its inflammatory words – 'The despot's heel is on thy shore' refers to Lincoln, and 'Huzza! she spurns the Northern scum!' – it became the state song in 1939. It was set to the music of 'O Tannenbaum', an anonymous German folk song, possibly of mediaeval origin.

230 *Boisson fade, écœurante*: French, an insipid, disgusting drink. Allegedly a quotation from the great French writer Honoré de Balzac (1799–1850), who drank much coffee to keep himself awake in order to finish his novels. Balzac's lovely porcelain coffee pot is quite famous. Balzac wrote a *Traité des excitants modernes* (1838), on alcohol, sugar, tea, coffee, tobacco, and chocolate, but the quotation does not appear there. It seems possible that Florimond (or James) is misremembering and misattributing to Balzac a phrase from George Sand's *L'Homme de neige* (1859), in which tea is described as 'cette boisson fade et mélancolique'. James mentioned this novel more than once in his 1877 essay on Sand (*LC2* 721, 730).

231 **far-off lands [...] dwelt among outworn things**: Mrs. Mesh's allusive speech echoes the idiom of William Wordsworth in poems that celebrate figures of elusive or fugitive innocence, such as 'The Solitary Reaper' who sings of 'old, unhappy, far-off things' and 'Lucy' who 'dwelt among the untrodden ways'.

232 **an adage about repenting at leisure**: The proverb, or adage, is: 'Marry in haste, repent at leisure.'

233 **the prime mover**: Ironic echo of the 'prime mover', God in mediaeval theology and in Dante.

234 **something too dishevelled**: James used this adjective, often in conjunction with the word 'nymph', to describe vaguely unconventional young women, as in the essay *In Warwickshire* (1877): 'When they came back to

the house, after the games, flushed a little and a little dishevelled, they might have passed for the attendant nymphs of Diana flocking in from the chase.' (*English Hours*, London: William Heinemann, 1905, p. 193). Italy in 1869 was for James a 'beautiful dishevelled nymph' (*CLHJ 1855–1872* 2:95)

235 **no fatted calf**: Reference to the parable of the prodigal son (Luke 15:11–32), who returns home after wasting his fortune. To celebrate his return a great feast is made ('And bring hither the fatted calf, and kill it; and let us eat, and be merry'). Felix in *The Europeans* says of his Wentworth cousins that 'They took me to their hearts; they killed the fatted calf' (*CFHJ* 4, p. 25)

236 **a relation of "chaff"**: Teasing, irrelevant subjects.

237 **what Longfellow calls the children's hour**: The popular poem 'The Children's Hour', source of the phrase 'The patter of little feet', written in 1859 by Longfellow. In the poem the three little girls of the poet rush downstairs to kiss him in his study, an obvious contrast to the absence of Mrs Mesh's children.

238 **not a Watteau**: Jean-Antoine Watteau (1684–1721), the French rococo painter. Apparently Watteau did paint fans, and Florimond's denial of this is further proof of his basic ignorance (Adeline R. Tintner, *The Museum World of Henry James* (Ann Arbor, MI: UMI Research Press, 1986), p. 48). See also *Le Cousin Pons* (1847) by Balzac, ed. André Lorant (Paris: Gallimard, 1973), and Susan Hiner, 'Fan Fashion in Balzac's *Le Cousin Pons*', *Romance Studies*, 25.3 (July 2007), 175–87.

239 **Michael Angelo**: The great Renaissance artist Michelangelo Buonarroti (1475–1564), best known for his frescoes in the Sistine Chapel in the Vatican. James was a great admirer of Michelangelo's sculpture and drawings, as his letters of 1869–70 show, in particular that of 7 November to his sister, where he wrote that the beauty of Michelangelo's Florence statues "far surpasses my prior conception" (*CLHJ 1855–1872* 2:172), his letters of 27 November to William about the *Moses* in St. Pietro in Vincoli (238–9), and of 1 January again on the Medici Chapels.

240 **the "new land"**: The filled-in ground of the Back Bay; see note 151.

241 **Washington Street**: The longest street in Boston, running south-west from Chinatown to Dudley Square.

242 **the rigid groove of the railway**: A reference to horse-drawn street-cars, which became a popular means of transportation in Boston in 1856.

Compare *The Europeans*: 'a huge, low omnibus, painted in brilliant colours, and decorated apparently with jangling bells, attached to a species of groove in the pavement, through which it was dragged, with a great deal of rumbling, bouncing and scratching, by a couple of remarkably small horses' (*CFHJ* 4, p. 2). James took a dim view of the horse-car, calling it, in a letter to Grace Norton, 'so much the ugliest thing in a country where so much is ugly', and agreed with Matthew Arnold regarding 'the horrors of the horsecars'. In the same letter, he also declared: 'Surely (for the impression they make on the arrived European especially) they [the horrors] can scarcely be exaggerated. To me, all the while I was in the US, they were unspeakable' (11 December 1883, *CHJL 1883–1884* 1:280–281). Horne notes that Henry James Sr wrote an unpublished piece, 'The Omnibus, and Its Morality' (*LL* 150 note), in which he saw it as an almost sublime emblem of democracy.

243 **American publicity**: By the 1870s modern publicity, i.e. large billboards, had replaced the old way of advertising by means of street criers and shop signs, as part of the huge development of industrial production and consumerism.

244 **the air was traversed with the tangle of the telegraph**: By 1846 the telegraph in the form patented in 1837 by painter Samuel F. B. Morse was spreading fast. Telegraph wires were suspended from high poles, and could cause complaints, as in New York in March 1881: 'In many places these huge, ugly excrescences, on being set up, occupied more than one-half of the sidewalk, and in one place (one of the narrowest in the narrow street) actually took up the whole of the sidewalk with the exception of six inches, thus forcing the unfortunate pedestrian into the mud-filled gutter' ('The Unsightly Telegraph Poles: Suit by the Attorney-General to Remove the Pine-Street Obstructions', *New York Times*, 1 March 1881, 3).

245 **Cambridge […] Harvard […] the long, mean bridge that spans the mouth of the Charles**: The town on the north side of the Charles River, the seat of Harvard University, founded in 1636. James briefly attended Harvard Law School (1862–3), following his brother William, who enrolled in 1861 to study chemistry and anatomy, and would teach there for the whole of his professional life. The Jameses moved to 20 Quincy Street, in Cambridge, in November 1866. James wrote at length on Harvard and Cambridge in *The American Scene*, especially in the latter part of Chapter 1, 'New England: An Autumn Impression', sections VII–IX. The Charles River Dam Bridge, or Craigie Bridge, is named after the

businessman behind its construction, Edward Craigie. It was opened in 1809, and replaced in 1910.

246 **for Cambridge is not festooned with lamps**: Not 'festooned' perhaps, yet the Cambridge Gas Light Company, founded in 1852, was supplying the Cambridge area quite extensively by the 1870s (www.cambridgehistory .org/discover/industry/cambridgegaslight.html).

247 **a composition of Schubert**: Franz Schubert (1797–1828), the Viennese composer, whose large *oeuvre* included compositions for voice, symphony and chamber orchestras and many piano sonatas. In *The Portrait of a Lady* (Ch. 18) we first meet Madame Merle playing Schubert on the piano at Gardencourt (in the revised *New York Edition*, 1908; in the earlier version, 1881, it had been Beethoven).

248 **a new *coupé***: A 'short, four-wheeled close carriage with an inside seat for two, and outside seat for the driver' (*OED*).

249 **Horace Walpole and Madame du Deffand**: At 70, blind, Madame du Deffand (1697–1780), famous for her witty salon and friendships with Voltaire and others, and for her *Correspondance*, began a celebrated friendship with the effeminate Horace Walpole (1717–97), the British writer and author of the Gothic novel *The Castle of Otranto* (1764), connoisseur and Member of Parliament.

250 **this mountain fastness**: Indicating ironically a stronghold, i.e. Lucretia Daintry's house on Beacon Hill.

251 **Salem [...] Cavaliers**: The contrast here is between the Puritans (Salem) and the Cavaliers, the followers of Lord Baltimore (1605–75), who received a charter from Charles I in order to found the initially Catholic colony of Maryland in 1635, named after Charles I's Catholic Queen Henrietta Maria. Lord Baltimore also had the right to establish a colonial nobility. The Cavaliers, or Royalists, left England after the execution of Charles I in 1649 and the institution of the Puritan Commonwealth. Although they mainly went to Virginia, Maryland was a colony where religious tolerance was decreed in 1649, with the Maryland Toleration Act. As evident in the mention of the Salem witches a few lines below, Mrs Daintry, as a native of Salem, is presented as a witch who persuades her son with 'philters and spells'. The Salem trials in 1692–3, which took place throughout Massachusetts, represented the most notorious persecution of innocent women, accused of witchcraft, in early American annals.

252 **he's in the midst of the foam, the cruel, crawling foam:** A quotation from the ballad 'The Sands of Dee' (1849) by Charles Kingsley (1819–75). In the ballad, Mary, who has gone out to call the cattle back home, is caught by the high tide, and her body is rowed back 'across the rolling foam / The cruel crawling foam' to 'her grave beside the sea'. James wrote three essays on Kingsley, one in 1866 on his novels, one on the occasion of his death in 1875, and the third, a review of the correspondence and memoirs published by his widow, in 1877. James appreciated only two of his early novels, *Hereward* (1866) and *Westward Ho!* (1855), but on the whole his opinion of the religious and political man was not of the highest order. At the very end of the 1875 essay there are three lines of appreciation for 'three or four' of his 'admirable songs, which indeed posterity, left to itself, is likely to continue to sing' (*LC1* 1105).

'The Path of Duty'

253 **The Path of Duty:** James almost certainly draws this title from Tennyson's 'Ode on the Death of the Duke of Wellington' (1852), ll. 218–24: 'his work is done. / But while the races of mankind endure, / Let his great example stand / Colossal, seen of every land, / And keep the soldier firm, the statesman pure: / Till in all lands and thro' all human story / The path of duty be the way to glory'.

254 **Doubleton:** Fictitious country house.

255 **Tester:** This name appears on a list in a notebook entry dated 26 March 1884 (*CN* 28).

256 **if the fog is brown outside, the fire is red within:** James was happy to perpetuate the Dickensian image of London fog, writing in 'An English New Year' (1879) that 'It is of course a very old story that London is foggy'. But in his essay on 'London', first published in 1888, reprinted in *Essays in London and Elsewhere* (1893) and *English Hours* (1905), he laid particular emphasis on the pleasure and inspiration to be drawn from retreating within from the fog without: 'The friendly fog seems to protect and enrich' the idea of 'experiments and excursions'; 'it is most in the winter months that the imagination weaves such delights', especially in 'the strictly social desolation of Christmas week'. Then it is, James writes, that he is 'most haunted by the London of Dickens', when 'the big fires blaze in the lone twilight of the clubs', and that 'to a man of letters, [...] this is the best time for writing' (*EL* 30–1). See note 477.

257 **one's own point of view**: Though this is one of James's characteristic phrases ('The Point of View' is the title of an 1882 tale), it carries a particular value in the face of London's 'bigness and strangeness'. Recalling his first night in 'the stupendous city' in 1869, James recorded his gratitude for 'a shelter and a point of view' ('London', *EL* 4).

258 **Vandeleur**: This name appears on a notebook list dated 2 January 1884 (*CN* 23).

259 **on your own hook**: A colloquialism, more common in the nineteenth century than now, meaning 'in dependence on oneself or one's own efforts; on one's own account; at one's own risk' (*OED*).

260 **Joscelind**: This name (the usual form is 'Josceline') appears on a notebook list dated 9 July 1884 (*CN* 30).

261 **the baronetcy**: A titled order, the lowest that is hereditary, ranking next below a barony, having precedence over all orders of knighthood, except that of the Garter. A baronet is a commoner – the principle of the order being 'to give rank, precedence, and title without privilege' – but able to use the prefix 'Sir'. This title, awarded by the British crown, was originally introduced in England in the fourteenth century. In James's story, Ambrose's older brother (Francis 'Frank' Tester) dies, leaving him as the only successor to the baronetcy.

262 **Dorsetshire**: A county in the middle of the south coast of England, now called Dorset. James had been to the seaside resort of Bournemouth to see his sister Alice in the spring of 1885 (see Introduction, p. xxxvi). There he also visited his friend Robert Louis Stevenson, residing in his newly acquired cottage 'Skerryvore'. Other stories by James associated with Bournemouth are 'Glasses' (1893), 'The Middle Years' (1896), and 'In the Cage' (1898).

263 **twenty thousand a year**: With all the caveats about the difficulty of translating such figures into modern terms, the Bank of England website calculates that in 2021 this would have the approximate equivalent purchasing power of £2,589,000: see www.bankofengland.co.uk/monetary-policy/inflation/inflation-calculator.

264 **London in December**: James noted that '[t]he London year is studded with holidays, [...] intervals of absence for good society', when 'the wonderful English faculty for "going out of town for a little change" comes into illimitable play'. December was one of the months 'when the country-houses are filled at the expense of the metropolis' ('London', *EL* 29–30).

265 **the faro-table**: Faro is 'a gambling game at cards, in which the players bet on the order in which certain cards will appear when taken singly from the top of the pack' (*OED*).

266 **Monaco**: The sovereign city state located on the French Riviera, renowned for its casino. In a letter to his sister Alice from Avignon dated 25–27 January 1870, James wrote: 'Of course I went to that wicked little Monaco—the famous principality of six-miles square, supported by its great gambling house. I tried to do my duty by Monaco as a conscientious observer but I'm afraid I rather failed. I took the midday train from Nice & was deposited with a cargo of dissolute persons of both sexes, at the Casino station after half an hour's journey. I made my way into the gambling-rooms & watched the play at the various tables with vague projects of learning the *modus operandi* & staking a napoleon for that 1ˢᵗ time which is always so highly profitable. After a while—however I turned from the greedy human throng & the vulgar chink of gold to the nobler face of the great blue ocean without & the deeper music of its waves. Monaco out of doors is as divinely beautiful as Monaco in-doors is godlessly ugly.' (*CLHJ 1855–1872* 2:270)

267 **"under-studying"** [...] **the part**: As the inverted commas indicate, the verb (and its related noun), meaning 'To study (a part or character) in order to be able to take the place of a principal actor or actress if necessary', was just gaining currency in the 1880s; the *OED*'s first citation is from 1874.

268 **as natural as if he had been an Irishman**: This was one among the many clichés attributed to Irish people in the nineteenth century. In his essay 'La Poésie des races celtiques' (1854) the French historian Ernest Renan – whom James particularly admired (see note 20 to 'Pandora') – argued that the Irish were particularly emotional, playful, and passionate. According to the Victorian mentality, they were therefore closer to children and nature and thus in need of guidance. James himself had Irish ancestry; his paternal grandfather, William James (1771–1832), founder of the family fortunes, had emigrated from Ireland to the United States towards the end of the eighteenth century. See L. P. Curtis, *Anglo-Saxons and Celts: A Study of Anti-Irish Prejudice in Victorian England* (New York: New York University Press, 1968).

269 **a brogue**: 'A strongly marked dialectal pronunciation or accent; now particularly used of the peculiarities that generally mark the English speech of Ireland' (*OED*).

270 **But I mustn't protest too much**: Compare *Hamlet* 3.2.229–30, during the performance of *The Mousetrap*, the play within a play: '*Hamlet*: Madam, how like you this play? / *Queen*: The lady doth protest too much, methinks.'

271 **secretary of legation at some German capital**: '*Secretary of Embassy or Legation*: an official of an embassy or diplomatic mission ranking next to the ambassador or envoy, and empowered to some extent to supply his place in his absence' (*OED*).

272 **the borough he sits for**: That he represents in Parliament.

273 **"bright Bostonian"**: The inverted commas highlight a recognizable 'type', such as James had portrayed in the Bostonian Bessie Alden, whose preconceptions of Englishness, in 'An International Episode' (1879), are strongly shaped by her reading.

274 **Roland Tremayne [...] *A Lawless Love***: According to Robert Gale, the hero and title of an imaginary novel (*HJE* 670).

275 **a "strong Liberal"**: Another 'type' indicated by inverted commas. James was on friendly terms with prominent Liberal politicians including the Earl of Rosebery (1847–1929), who served twice as foreign secretary under Gladstone, succeeding him as leader of the Liberal Party (1894), and (briefly) prime minister (1894–5). In 1878 James became a member of the Reform Club, vouched for as a good Liberal by Frank Hill, Charles Robarts, and Sir Charles Dilke: as Greg Zacharias says, 'Its by-laws required each nominee and each member to be "Reformers"' ('Liberal London, Home, and Henry James's Letters from the Later 1870s', *Henry James Review*, 35.2 (2014), 127–40; 135–6).

276 **volunteering, and redistribution, and sanitation, and the representation of minors**: A series of topical political issues. The Volunteer Force was a citizen army created as a popular movement in 1859, after the Crimean War and the increase of tension between the United Kingdom and France. The Redistribution of Seats Act introduced by Gladstone in 1885 was a piece of electoral reform legislation that introduced the concept of equally populated constituencies, in an attempt to create just representation across the UK. As for 'sanitation, and the representation of minors', James is referring to contemporary parliamentary debates on legislation regarding public health and child labour in Britain. In the 1870s the minimum age for (half-time) employment in various manufactures was raised from 8 to 10 and childhood was deemed to end at

13. See Pamela Horn, *Children's Work and Welfare 1780–1890* (Cambridge: Cambridge University Press, 1995).

277 **a dozen times in the season**: That is, the season from spring to midsummer at which high society congregated in London at a series of exclusive social and cultural events. See note 281 on its relation to the sitting of Parliament, and further references to its significance for English social life in 'Louisa Pallant' (note 345), 'The Liar' (notes 480, 516), and 'The Modern Warning' (note 532).

278 **Bernardstone**: The variant 'Bernardistone' appears on a list in a notebook entry dated 26 March 1884 (*CN* 28).

279 **one of those objectionable young women who are known as garrison-hacks**: A slang term for 'a woman who flirts indiscriminately with the officers of a garrison'; the *OED* cites James Grant's 1876 novel *One of Six Hundred*: 'The garrison hacks, or *passé belles*, whose names and flirtations are standing jokes.'

280 **a mail-phaeton**: A phaeton was '[a] type of light four-wheeled open carriage, usually drawn by a pair of horses' (*OED*), strong enough, in this more specialized usage, to carry loads of mail.

281 **after the session**: Of Parliament, that is, in the 'summer recess'. The London season (see note 277) notionally coincided with the sitting of Parliament, but by the 1880s the session frequently extended deep into August, and the timing of the recess varied a good deal: see note 571 to 'The Modern Warning', on the differing length of parliamentary sessions. See also the references to 'the general dispersal' in 'The Liar' (note 516), and to the middle of August as 'a bad time' in 'The Modern Warning' (note 562).

282 **synthetic as he might be**: This picks up the previous statement that 'he was not analytic, like us Americans, as they say in reviews'. 'Analytic' and 'synthetic' are terms commonly opposed to each other in philosophical discourse: synthesis being '[t]he action of proceeding in thought from causes to effects, or from laws or principles to their consequences', and analysis '[t]he action or method of proceeding from effects to causes, or of inferring general laws or principles from particular instances' (*OED*). James may also be hinting at Howells's comment on *The Portrait of a Lady* ('an analytic study rather than a story') in the *Century*, 25.1 (1882), 24–9. In *The American Scene* James often defines his narrating persona as 'the restless analyst'.

283 **the Park [...] the Row:** Rotten Row is a broad track used for riding, running along the south side of Hyde Park in London. During the eighteenth and nineteenth centuries Rotten Row was a fashionable place where one could see many upper-class Londoners. It provides the setting for significant scenes in 'An International Episode' (1879) and 'Lady Barberina' (1884).

284 **a quarter of a column of "padding" in the *Times*:** 'Padding' is another comparatively recent colloquialism at the time of the tale's writing, first attested by the *OED* in 1861, to mean 'superfluous or inferior material introduced into or included in a book, speech, etc., in order to make up a required or expected length'. The *Times*, which James read regularly, was founded by John Walter in 1785 as the *Daily Universal Register*.

285 **Christian maiden in the Roman arena:** This image seems to be particularly cherished by James in his fiction and in his letters, probably influenced by the great scene in chapter 17 of Hawthorne's *The Marble Faun* (1860): 'That black cross marks one of the special blood-spots of the earth where, thousands of times over, the dying gladiator fell, and more of human agony has been endured for the mere pastime of the multitude than on the breadth of many battlefields.' It is used by the protagonist in *Daisy Miller* ('he looks at us as one of the old lions or tigers may have looked at the Christian martyrs' (Ch. 4)), and returns in later works, such as 'The Two Faces' (1903) and *The Wings of the Dove*, where Milly Theale appears as 'a Christian maiden, in the arena, mildly, caressingly, martyred' (Book VI, Ch. 3). The image also appeared in the short story 'Yvette' by Guy de Maupassant: 'Et elle descendit d'un pas ferme, avec quelque chose de la résolution des martyres chrétiennes entrant dans le cirque où les lions les attendaient' ('And she went down with a firm step, with something of the resolution of the Christian martyrs entering the circus where the lions were awaiting them'), published in the *Figaro* (29 August – 9 September 1884). 'The Path of Duty' was published a few months later in the *English Illustrated Magazine*. The eponymous collection *Yvette* (1884) is mentioned by James in his 1888 essay on the French writer (*LC2* 540).

286 **the whispering-gallery of St. Paul's:** Designed in the late seventeenth century by Sir Christopher Wren (1632–1723), St Paul's Cathedral in London features, under its dome, a circular wall which allows whispered communication to travel around the internal side of the circumference. This particular effect, produced by the so-called 'whispering-gallery waves' moving over concave surfaces, was discovered by English physicist Lord

Rayleigh (1842–1919) in this very cathedral around 1878. In 'A London Life' (1888) Laura Wing accompanies an American, Mr Wendover, on a visit to this famous cathedral.

287 **Norfolk:** A low-lying county in the east of England, particularly well stocked with the birds that provided 'sport' for the late Victorian and Edwardian upper classes.

288 **a comedian:** In the French sense of a theatrical performer, not necessarily a 'comic' one. Compare 'The Aspern Papers', note 442.

289 **Upper Brook Street:** One of the principal streets on the Grosvenor estate in the exclusive central district of Mayfair. It was developed in the first half of the eighteenth century and runs between Grosvenor Square and Hyde Park.

290 **December fog:** See note 256.

291 **the Park:** Hyde Park, where fashionable society aired and displayed itself, in carriages and on horseback (see note 283).

292 **under the influence of "suppressed exaltation":** The phrase was used in an anonymous story called 'Consule Julio: An Episode under the Commune de Paris', which appeared in *Cornhill Magazine*, edited by James's friend Leslie Stephen, in August 1871, about a passionate martyr for democracy: '"I am but a soldier in a great cause", said he, shortly. There was something of the suppressed exaltation of the fanatic in his tone.'

293 **without being made aesthetic:** At the time of the tale's writing in the mid-1880s, the term 'aesthetic' suggested a taste for the controversially avant-garde such as Lady Vandeleur might wish to avoid, a taste mocked for example by Gilbert and Sullivan's *Patience* in 1881. See also notes 168, 206 to 'A New England Winter'.

294 **She protested too much, perhaps:** See note 270.

295 **He was going to be beheaded:** The association of marriage with beheading draws on the legendary fate of Saint Valentine, the third-century Roman priest martyred for marrying young Christian couples.

'Mrs. Temperly'

296 **the tall gas-lamp [...] the Fifth Avenue:** The first crude gasworks were set up in New York near City Hall in 1816. By 1823 the city had organized street lighting in prosperous districts and better-off neighbourhoods

through the New York Gas Company. Fifth Avenue runs south to north from Washington Square; rich mansions were built along it in the latter part of the nineteenth century.

297 **an immense hotel:** The Fifth Avenue Hotel was opened by Amos Eno on Fifth Avenue at Twenty-third Street in 1859, with a 2 million-dollar investment, 400 servants, rooms with private bathrooms, and elevators. It still existed in the 1890s and lasted until 1908. James may also have been inspired by the lavish Astor House, nearby on Broadway, which opened as the Park Hotel in 1836 (it was demolished in 1913). According to Henry, William James was born there in 1842, but Collister suggests this may be unlikely, quoting Alfred Habegger, as on 3 March (two months after WJ's birth on 11 January) the family was still living at 5 Washington Place. In his autobiography James 'makes out' his parents 'to have betaken themselves for the winter following their marriage to the ancient Astor House—not indeed at that time ancient, but the great and appointed modern hotel of New York' (*SBOC* 10–11). The Waldorf Astoria, built on the site of one of the Astor houses on Fifth Avenue and Thirty-second Street, was built only in 1893 (it was demolished in 1930). In an earlier story, 'An International Episode' (1879), the two English protagonists see a luxurious hotel on the Fifth Avenue; it looks like 'a huge transparent cage, flinging a wide glare of gaslight into the street' (*S1874–1884* 329).

298 *premiers* [...] **the Champs Elysées:** This French term refers to first-floor apartments (that is, second-floor, American style) in the elegant houses along the famous avenue in Paris, which stretches from the place de la Concorde to the Arc de Triomphe in the place de l'Étoile (now place de Gaulle). Baedeker's *Paris and its Environs* (1878) states that 'The name "Champs Elysées" was given to the avenue in the reign of Louis XIV on account of the refreshing verdure of its trees' (156).

299 **Susan Winkle:** Charles Dickens's Mr Winkle in *The Pickwick Papers* (1837) is the obvious precedent for this name.

300 **a sound, productive Alderney cow:** A breed of dairy cattle, originating on Alderney, one of the British Channel Islands. Alderney cows are known to be very docile.

301 **perpetual gaslight:** See note 296.

302 **the steamer:** Robert Fulton developed the first steamship or steamer in New York, that travelled on the Hudson River from New York to Albany

and back again, in 1807. Steamers were first used on rivers. Regular steamer services across the Atlantic began in 1838 with voyages by the British-built *Sirius* and *The Great Western*, followed by the establishment of the Cunard Line in 1840, and the rival American Collins Line in 1846. By the 1850s the voyage took on average ten to twelve days, but by the 1880s it was down to eight or nine (see note 182 to 'A New England Winter'). The transatlantic migrations of the James family in the 1840s and 1850s made such voyages a well-known experience for Henry James junior and his siblings. James's first known description of a passage from New York to Southampton seems to be in a letter of 18 November 1859 to Thomas Sergeant Perry: 'Our passage was of eleven days in length and of scarcely more than eleven hour[s] in fine weather. The Demon of <u>the</u> sea was not behind hand in paying me a visit, and a very long and tedious one he made' (*CLHJ 1855–1872* 1:17). There are no full descriptions of these Atlantic crossings in James's memoirs, even if there are several passages in his novels and stories relating to the Atlantic crossing and to characters embarking and disembarking from steamers crossing the ocean, mostly from New York to Liverpool and vice versa. The story 'The Patagonia' (1888) takes place almost totally on board a steamer, ending with the suicide by drowning of the main female character, before arriving in England.

303 **California:** James only went to California in 1905, but he had 'intensely' wished to visit it, as he wrote to his brother William in a letter dated 24 May 1903 from Rye (*HJL* 4:273). However, some of his characters either come from or have been to California: Christopher Newman in *The American*, Bernard Longueville in *Confidence* (1879), Mrs Headway in 'The Siege of London' (1883), Lady Agatha in 'Lady Barberina' (1884), among others. See also Philip Horne, 'Sense of the West', *Times Literary Supplement*, 19 September 2018.

304 **Effie and Tishy:** Short for Euphemia and Letitia (or Patricia) respectively, these names recur as those of characters in two of James's later novels, Effie (Bream) in *The Other House* (1896) and Tishy (Grendon) in *The Awkward Age* (1899).

305 **long pull:** *Brewer's* says that '[i]n the USA the term is applied to long and diligent effort'; it seems related to the phrase '[a]long pull, a strong pull and a pull all together', dating back to at least 1800, which Brewer defines as '[a] steady, energetic and systematic cooperation. The reference may be to the oarsmen in a boat, to a tug of war or to the act of hauling with

a rope, for all of which a simultaneous strong pull is required' (*Brewer's Dictionary of Phrase and Fable*, 19th edn, ed. Susie Dent (London: Chambers Harrap, 2012).

306 **Philistines**: Persons perceived as 'hostile to art or culture' (*OED*). A derogatory term popularized in *Culture and Anarchy* (1869) by Matthew Arnold, who used the word to scorn those whose chief mental character-istic was an 'inveterate inaccessibility to ideas' ('Heinrich Heine', in *Essays in Criticism*, first series, 1865). It indicates a bourgeois, rather than an aes-thetic or artistic, view.

307 **angular**: A favourite adjective of James's that he used to describe charac-ters, situations, paintings, and furniture. Catherine Sloper, for example, stands before her father 'in her rather angular earnestness' (*Washington Square*, Ch. 11); Lady Aurora Langrish is described as 'a figure angular and slim' (*Princess Casamassima*, CFHJ 9, p. 73); Milly Theale is seen by Mrs Stringham as 'agreeably angular' (*Wings of the Dove*, Book III, Ch. 1) and described later as 'the angular pale princess' (Book VII, Ch. 3). In *A Small Boy and Others* (1913, Ch. 19) James described a childhood visit to Bryan's Gallery of Christian art: 'It cast a chill, this collection, of worm-eaten dip-tychs and triptychs, of angular saints and seraphs, of black Madonnas and obscure Bambinos, of such marked and approved "primitives" as had never yet been shipped to our shores' (*SBOC* 208). This description is sim-ilar to one in 'The Madonna of the Future' (1873): 'little worm-eaten dip-tychs covered with angular saints on gilded backgrounds' (*S1864–1874* 743).

308 **the Crusades**: The series of wars waged by the Western powers between 1095 and 1291 to conquer the Holy Sepulchre and other Christian sacred places in Jerusalem and Asia Minor; the source of much mediaeval romance.

309 **marriage-fee**: Dowry.

310 **reticule**: A woman's small bag, made of net or other material, with a string to pull it open or closed. In *Washington Square* Aunt Penniman proposes a secret rendezvous to Morris Townsend, declaring that, as if in disguise, 'I would carry a little reticule, like a woman of the people' (Ch. 28). In act 1 of James's comedy *The Reprobate* (1894) much play is made in the stage direc-tions with Mrs Freshville's 'small smart reticule' (*The Complete Plays of Henry James*, ed. Leon Edel (Philadelphia: Lippincott, 1949), p. 407). In *What Maisie Knew* Mrs Wix is 'armed with a small fat rusty reticule which, almost in the manner of a battleaxe, she brandished in support of her words' (Ch. 31).

311   *Murray*: Popular British guidebooks started by the publisher John Murray in 1836. See notes 354, 356, 357 to 'Louisa Pallant', and note 428 to 'The Aspern Papers'.

312   **she introduced him, very definitely, to the whole group**: James underlines here the differences between American punctiliousness about introducing each guest to all the others and a relaxed, sophisticated, more fashionable European neglect of such introductions. The *Baltimore Sun* of 3 January 1882 records a reception at Chester Arthur's White House at which there was 'WHOLESALE HANDSHAKING', but makes a point of noting that 'Mr. Brown did not introduce each one, and frequently as many as four or five shook the hand of the President without the formality of an introduction. The ladies, however, were introduced by name' (1).

313   **Napoleonic plans**: James was extremely interested in the life and career of Napoleon Bonaparte (1769–1821), the French emperor from 1804, whose plans for world domination led to campaigns in Egypt, Austria, Italy, and Spain, among other countries. James mentions Napoleone (sic) and merges identities with the James family in his 'Deathbed Dictation' (*CN* 583–584).

314   **Saint-Saens**: Camille Saint-Saëns (1835–1921), recognized as France's leading composer at the time of this tale's writing. A famous performer himself, he wrote many single short piano pieces in established forms such as the song without words (*Romances sans paroles*) and the mazurka.

315   **Mr and Mrs Parminter**: W. S. Gilbert's 1878 play *The Ne'er-Do-Weel* includes a 'Miss Parminter', and Arthur Pinero's 1881 play *Imprudence* has characters called Mr and Mrs 'Parminter Blake'.

316   **Parc Monceau**: Elegant park in the Eighth Arrondissement, with beautiful houses fronting it after 1861, when it became public. It features at the end of *The American* when Christopher Newman visits the nearby Carmelite convent in which Claire de Cintré is immured. Gustave Flaubert's apartment was also close at hand; James had been taken there and introduced to the French novelist and his circle by Ivan Turgenev in December 1875.

317   **immensely valuable specimens of contemporary French art**: One may think of such French painters as Alexandre Cabanel (1823–89), William-Adolphe Bouguereau (1825–1905), and Carolus-Duran (1837–1917), popular at the time, on whom James had written, reviewing the Salon of 1876 in his letters to the *New York Tribune* (*CWAD1 179–96*).

318 **Bastien-Lepage**: French painter Jules Bastien-Lepage (1848–84), known in the last ten years of his life for his country scenes, but also for his portraits (see Introduction, p. lxvi).

319 **the Conservatoire**: The Paris music school founded in 1795, formerly the École Royale de Chant (1669), located in the Ninth Arrondissement, in the rue Bergère (now rue du Conservatoire), where it remained until 1911 when it was moved to rue Madrid. It is now in the Cité de la Musique, at La Villette. James does not state whether Dora is actually enrolled.

320 **this quiet, dimly-shining maiden**: The paradoxical phrase 'dimly-shining' anticipates a description of the virginal Pansy Osmond near the end of *The Portrait of a Lady* (Ch. 45), when her pretty dress, which was 'vaguely shining' in the early versions of 1881/2, becomes 'dimly shining' in the revised *NYE* of 1908. (*CFHJ 7*, p. 451 and p. 901).

321 **Madame de Brives**: A French marquise. James also used the name for a slightly disreputable character, about whose extramarital connections the heroine Francie innocently prattles to the devious journalist George Flack, in *The Reverberator* (1888): "Yes, he likes other ladies better. He flirts with Mme. de Brives." / Mr. Flack's hand closed over it. "Mme. de Brives?" / "Yes, she's lovely," said Francie. "She ain't very young, but she's fearfully attractive" (*CFHJ 10*, pp. 87–8).

322 **his hostess would give up introducing people**: See note 312.

323 **a woman of Plutarch**: Greek historian (*c.* 46–120 CE), best known now for his *Parallel Lives*. The reference however is to Plutarch's *Moralia* (vol. 3), where there is a chapter on 'The Bravery of Women.'

324 **a society tired of its own pessimism**: A note that James often struck in describing contemporary French society and its representation in literature, most notably in the fiction of Émile Zola (1840–1902), 'an extraordinary effort vitiated by a spirit of pessimism on a narrow basis' ('The Art of Fiction' (1884); *LC1* 65).

325 **a bust of Effie […] one of the sculptors who are the pride of contemporary French art**: One could think of Jean-Baptiste Carpeaux (1827–75), who became famous with his group *La Danse* (1865–9) commissioned for the Opéra Garnier, which shocked the most conservative Parisians: it is unlikely, however, that Effie's mother would have hired such an artist. He was also the sculptor of many busts.

326 ***bal blanc***: An all-female ball. 'There are *Bals-roses* and *Bals-blancs*; the former for young unmarried women, the latter for girls who have but

recently left the schoolroom. At both varieties of entertainments dancing is carried on, no longer in tame spiritless fashion, but in truly energetic style' (Violette Johnstone, 'February Fashions: Paris', *Woman's World* (London, Paris, New York, and Melbourne), 1.4 (February 1888)).

327 **New England, at old homesteads**: Indicating simple tastes, opposing country (New England) and city (Paris) manners, America and Europe.

328 **the Cinderella of the house**: The character from the fairy tale, the neglected stepsister, relegated to lowly services.

329 **Her sisters were neither ugly nor proud**: Further reference to the fairy tale, where Cinderella's two elder sisters are indeed ugly and proud. See Tintner, *Pop World of Henry James*, pp. 30–6.

330 **in the fairy-tale [...] *femme forte***: French, meaning a strong woman; in *Cinderella* the stepmother is relentlessly opposed to Cinderella's happiness.

331 **she would never put on the screw**: As in the title of James's well-known tale, 'The Turn of the Screw', this is figurative language for an intensification of some kind of action. Here, the mother would never force (or torture) the girl. In *The Bostonians*, Basil Ransom 'by nature, took things easy; if he had put on the screw of late, it was after reflexion, and because circumstances pressed him close' (*CFHJ* 8, pp. 11–12; Ch. 2).

332 **old Gobelins**: Famous and beautiful tapestries, made at the Manufacture des Gobelins, in avenue des Gobelins 42, in Paris, active from 1601. The factory took its name from a family of weavers.

333 ***sergents de ville***: After 1870 '*sergents de ville*' were called '*gardiens de la paix publique*', although they continued wearing the same uniforms. It is not clear whether James was aware that the term was outdated.

334 **stars of the first magnitude**: James may be recalling the musical evenings he experienced in Paris in 1876 at Pauline Viardot's. Viardot was an intimate friend of Turgenev, and although James found her evenings 'rigidly musical' and therefore, to him, 'rigidly boresome', when she herself sang it was 'superb' (*CLHJ 1872–1876* 3:97). James represents another socially elevated musical evening in Paris in 'The Velvet Glove' (1909), where the dazzled hero John Berridge hears at the artist Gloriani's studio 'an eminent tenor' sing something 'Wagnerian'.

335 **'faculty'**: The *OED* describes this as '[g]eneral executive ability, *esp.* in domestic matters', ascribing it chiefly to the United States, and citing a sentence from *Harper's Magazine* (1884): 'Lizzie had "faculty", and proved a notable housekeeper.'

336 **decorations and stars:** Medals and other signs of official recognition of services rendered to the state. Compare the account of the Bellegarde ball in Chapter 16 of *The American*, where among the guests Christopher Newman confronts some 'elderly gentlemen, of what Valentin de Bellegarde had designated as the high-nosed category; two or three of them wore cordons and stars'; in the *NYE* this becomes 'elderly gentlemen with faces as marked and featured and filled-in, for some science of social topography, as, to Newman's whimsical sense, any of the little towered and battered old towns, on high eminences, that his tour of several countries during the previous summer had shown him; they were adorned with strange insignia, cordons and ribbons and orders, as if the old cities were flying flags and streamers and hanging out shields for a celebration' (*NYE* II, 313).

337 **Americans with no badge:** Americans here bear no sign showing a specific rank or position, perhaps because, as James notoriously says in *Hawthorne*, there is in America '[n]o sovereign, no court, no personal loyalty, no aristocracy, no church, no clergy, no army, no diplomatic service' (Ch. 2).

338 **programmes, seats, ices, occasional murmured remarks and general support and protection:** Compare the proximity of 'ices' and 'remarks' in James's recent satirical account of items constituting a 'happy ending' in the Victorian novel of the kind approved by Walter Besant, as offered in 'The Art of Fiction' (1884): 'The "ending" of a novel is, for many persons, like that of a good dinner, a course of dessert and ices'; and 'it depends for a "happy ending" on a distribution at the last of prizes, pensions, husbands, wives, babies, millions, appended paragraphs and cheerful remarks' (*LC1* 48).

339 **the great Gregorini:** An apparently fictitious figure with an Italian name; popular opera singers were often Italian. James may have been recalling another Italian performer: *The Orchestra* of October 1875 records that at Crystal Palace 'On Sept. 23, Sig. Gregorini made his sensational descent as Jupiter Tonans, wielding an enormous thunderbolt, along a wire rope extending from the top of the North Tower (250 feet high), alighting at the centre basin, a distance of over 1600 feet, finishing amidst a volley of a hundred gigantic shells. The weather was very unpropitious' (77).

340 **to let the rest of the guests depart in peace:** Compare the Book of Common Prayer (1662): 'Lord, now lettest thou thy servant depart in peace according to thy word.' (Luke 2.29).

'Louisa Pallant'

341 **Kursaal at Homburg:** German, literally the 'hall of treatment' where people drank the spa water; more generally the building. Bad Homburg vor-der-Höhe, in Hesse, at the foot of the Taunus Hills, was one of the most famous spa towns in Germany in the nineteenth century, and as such was a meeting place for a strikingly cosmopolitan elite of American, British, French, German, Russian, and Italian visitors, among others. James spent about ten weeks there in the summer of 1873, publishing an essay, 'Homburg Reformed' (July 28, 1873), in which he spoke about the changes that took place after gambling was outlawed (1872), which resulted in the town becoming a mere watering place. Coming from Italy, he initially contrasted the beauty of Italy to Germany, but eventually was fascinated by the great woods, which resounded, to him, with legends and the tales of the brothers Grimm (*CTW2* 635–43). In his letters he writes about trying the water cure, with at first inconsequential but then some good results, as he conveyed to his parents on 14 August (*LL* 55). The castle of Homburg is also described at the beginning of the essay 'Darmstadt' (6 September 1873) (*CTW2* 644–5).

342 **Frankfort:** Frankfurt-am-Main, the German city about twelve miles south of Homburg. James may well be remembering Turgenev's novella 'Torrents of Spring' (1872), which he chose as 'the text of these remarks' in his long appreciative essay 'Ivan Turgénieff' (1874). Its Russian hero Sanin remembers, thirty years later, 'meet[ing], at Frankfort, a young girl of modest origin but extraordinary beauty', named Gemma Roselli; they fell in love, but, under the spell of another woman, he shamefully aban-doned her (*LC2* 987, 989). At the end of the story, back in Frankfort, he re-establishes contact by letter. Gemma is married and in America.

343 **excellent band:** Part of spa life was listening to the music, even at 6.30 a.m., while taking the cure. As mentioned in note 341 above, the gambling stopped in 1872, as James wrote in his essay 'Homburg Reformed' (*CTW2* 635–6), but in the story it is still going on.

344 **Louisa:** James used this name several times in his work, as for instance in 'The Point of View' (Louisa Whiteside, 1882), in 'The Visits' (Louisa Chantry, 1892), in 'Glasses' (Flora Louisa Saunt, 1896), in 'The Beldonald Holbein' (Louisa Brash, 1901) and in the play *Daisy Miller: A Comedy* (Winterbourne's aunt, Louisa Costello, 1883).

345 **the London season:** See note 277 to 'The Path of Duty'.

346 **for mere fleshpots**: Abundance, wealth, luxury. The word has scriptural associations: the people of Israel, out in the wilderness, yearn for the 'fleshpots' of Egypt that they have left behind (Exodus 16:3). See note 227 to 'A New England Winter'.

347 **Archer Pringle**: 'Archer' had of course been the surname of the protagonist in *The Portrait of a Lady*, though here he rapidly becomes 'Archie', and in the *NYE* he is named 'Archie Parker' from the outset.

348 **fall off an Alp**: Ironic as the statement might seem, James has the title character, whilst staying in the Alps, fall into a ravine at the end of *Roderick Hudson*.

349 **the Taunus**: See note 341.

350 *Wirthschaften*: Small inns or guest-houses (German). Now usually spelt *Wirtschaften*, without the 'h', which was used in James's time.

351 **I was not paid, as the French say**: An idiomatic expression in French, meaning that one refuses to make a comment on a person.

352 **Interlaken**: A Swiss town attracting 'numerous visitors in summer, chiefly German, English, and American, and noted for its mild and equable temperature' (*Baedeker's Switzerland: Handbook for Travellers* (1879), p. 139). Roderick Hudson in the eponymous novel falls to his death on the way to Interlaken to see Christina Light.

353 **Italian lakes**: Such as Lake Como and Lake Garda in northern Italy.

354 **Lago Maggiore at Baveno**: Baveno is 'in a lovely situation, opposite the Borromean Islands, from which it is about 3 m. distant. The steamers call at the Pier morning and afternoon for Arona and the upper parts of the lake', according to *Murray's 1877*, 112. The guidebook describes the itinerary from the Simplon, along the Simplon Road, passing by Isella, Domo d'Ossola, Vogogna, Gravellona, Fariolo, and Baveno, with an excursion to Monte Mottarone, Stresa, Arona. On 31 August 1869 James wrote his sister a long letter from Cadenabbia (on Lake Como) on his journey, following this itinerary from Switzerland to Baveno (and back into Switzerland and Italy); see *CLHJ 1855–1872* 2:81–5. He also described this itinerary in the story 'At Isella' (1871). See note 128.

355 **post-chaise**: A usually covered four-wheel carriage, drawn by horses, used to transport mail and people.

356 **Stresa**: 'A good-sized village in one of the most beautiful situations on Lago Maggiore, with a first-rate hotel, Hotel des Iles Borromées'; 'All the steamers call at Stresa' (*Murray's 1877*, 113). In July 1887 James stopped in Stresa

for several days, en route back to London from Venice and Florence, to meet his aged friend, the actress and writer Fanny Kemble, whom he found 'more & more an extinct volcano—the shadow of her former self' (*HJL* 3:197).

357 **Borromean Islands:** '4 islands in the West bay of the Lago Maggiore [...] the Isola Bella, the Isola Madre, the Isola di San Giovanni, near Pallanza, these three belonging to the Borromeo family, and the Isola Superiore, or dei Piscatori' (*Murray's 1877*, 115). Isola Bella is still famous for its gardens, 'this singular creation of art' (116), and for its palace.

358 **Archie proposed to her to take a turn with him in his boat:** In the opening chapter of 'Daisy Miller', which takes place at Vevey, on Lake Geneva, Switzerland, Winterbourne proposes to take Daisy to Chillon Castle by rowing boat. That outing does not take place (they go by steamer two days later).

359 *Votre siège est fait:* French, your siege is done. The declaration 'Mon siège est fait' is attributed to René Aubert, abbé de Vertot (1655–1735), author of *Histoire des Chevaliers Hospitaliers de Saint-Jean de Jérusalem* (1727), who refused to add some historical data to his description of the siege of Malta in 1565 by the Ottomans.

360 **She's cased in steel:** The phrase comes from Longfellow's poem of 1876–9, praising a French poet Olivier Basselin, known for his drinking songs, titled 'Vire: Oliver Basselin': 'In the castle, cased in steel, / Knights, who fought at Agincourt, / Watched and waited, spur on heel; / But the poet sang for sport / Songs that rang / Another clang, / Songs that lowlier hearts could feel' (ll. 50–6).

361 **she's the work of my hand!:** An expression owing resonance to its roots in Ecclesiastes 2:11: 'Then I looked on all the works that my hands had wrought, and on the labour that I had laboured to do: and, behold, all was vanity and vexation of spirit, and there was no profit under the sun' (KJV); see for example Mary Shelley's *Frankenstein* (1818), another work associated with Switzerland and lakes: 'But now I went to it in cold blood, and my heart often sickened at the work of my hands' (Ch. 19).

362 **honour among thieves:** The phrase is proverbial – as when Falstaff plays with it in *1 Henry IV*, 2.2.27–8: 'A plague upon it when thieves cannot be true one to another!'

363 **sinews of war:** 'The money and equipment needed to wage a war; the phrase is first used in English in the mid 16th century, and refers to the

Fifth Philippic of the Roman orator and statesman Cicero (106–43 BC)' (*The Oxford Dictionary of Phrase and Fable*, 2nd edn, online (2006): accessed 23 April 2020). In Shakespeare's *Henry V*, 'sinews' is used in the king's monologue in the sense of 'tendons', which can be enlarged to the other meaning: 'But when the blast of war blows in our ears, / Then imitate the action of the tiger; / Stiffen the sinews, conjure up the blood' (3.1.5–7): the image of the tiger may relate to Linda's mother's position.

364 **I think she has views upon London**: Compare 'The Siege of London' (1883), James's earlier story about an American woman, Mrs Headway (older and a divorcee), attempting to get into English society.

365 **gone off to Milan (to see the cathedral)**: The road from Stresa to Milan is about fifty miles. Murray describes Milan's cathedral and encourages the visitor to climb to the top in order to see the beautiful view (*Murray's 1877*, 162–4). James wrote at length on the interior of Milan Cathedral as a place of cool and picturesque refuge from the hot Italian summer in 'The Splügen' (1874, *CTW2* 653–5). If the cathedral is not an 'intellectual church', like St Peter's or the cathedral of Florence, 'its splendid solidity of form, its mysterious accumulations of shadow, the purple radiance of its painted windows, and the dark magnificence of the whole precinct of the high altar and choir, make it peculiarly gratifying to the sensuous side of one's imagination' (*CTW2* 654).

366 **a small portmanteau**: A case or bag for carrying clothes when travelling.

367 **Mrs. Gimingham's admired photographs [...] may be obtained from the principal stationers**: An article in the *Washington Post* about a doctored photograph – in which an American girl sees her photograph in a Regent Street shop window 'almost as undraped as the Venus de Milo', only the head being hers – declared that 'The matter has caused so much indignation and so much comment that it is not impossible it may check the mania now so prevalent among society beauties for having themselves photographed for sale at a shilling a *carte de visite*' ('Popular Beauties: How Ladies Get Themselves into Trouble by Having Their Pictures Taken'; 28 November 1878).

'The Aspern Papers'

368 **Mrs. Prest**: For the source of this character in James's American friend, Katharine de Kay Bronson (1834–1901), see Introduction, p. lxxvii. This name may have been inspired by the Italian adverb *presto* (speedily,

quickly), as Mrs Prest is the one who, according to the narrator, 'has invented the short cut'.

369   **the Gordian knot**: The intricate knot tied by Gordias, the king of Phrygia, which was said to have been cut through by Alexander the Great. An oracle had declared that the man who loosened the knot would conquer Asia. See also Shakespeare's *Henry V* 1.1.46 where the Archbishop of Canterbury praises the abilities of Henry V ('Turn him to any cause of policy, / The Gordian knot of it he will unloose') in spite of his 'unletter'd, rude, and shallow' youth. James used the phrase in an early tale, 'The Story of a Year' (1865): 'If that event would only come, whatever it was, and sever this Gordian knot of doubt!' (*S1864–1874*, p. 51)

370   **in a dilapidated old palace**: For the identification of the palace with the Palazzo Soranzo Capello in Rio Marin, see Introduction, p. lxxvii–lxxviii. Palazzo Capello was at the time inhabited by the painter Eugene Benson (1839–1908), Mrs Fletcher and her daughter Julia Constance Fletcher (1858–1938), author of the novel *Kismet* (1877), written under the pseudonym of George Fleming. Benson, formerly a tutor in the Fletcher family in New Jersey, had eloped with Mrs Fletcher, her daughter going with them. The palace is in a rather peripheral area of Venice (see p. 279); it is now a regional office for the Superintendence of Archaeology, the Fine Arts and Landscape, and still has a beautiful garden, less unkempt than in the story.

371   **as their name implied**: See Introduction, p. lxxviii. A *bordereau* in French is a register for the notation of expenses and for the recovery of invoices; *eau*, again in French, means water; the two women live on the 'border' of the water, i.e. both the canal over which their house looks and more generally the city of Venice, and on the border of society.

372   *sala*: Italian, hall. The typical plan of the two main floors (*piani nobili*) of Venetian palaces involves a central hall (*sala*) on to which the side rooms open.

373   **Jeffrey Aspern**: Aspern-Essling in May 1809 was a battle in the Napoleonic Wars, at which Napoleon was driven back from his attempt to cross the Danube by the Austrians under Archduke Charles – his first personal defeat for more than ten years. James may have been aware of an obsolete sense of the word: '*Obsolete. rare* To despise, spurn'. The *OED* cites from *Hall's Union* of 1548: 'Yt was prudente pollecie not to asperne and disdeyne the lytle small powre.' The one notable figure of the Romantic period with the

name Jeffrey was Francis Jeffrey, Lord Jeffrey (1773–1850), Scottish judge, literary critic, and editor of the *Edinburgh Review*.

374 **the sociable hood:** A moveable, black wooden cabin, called a *felze* (see p. 280), covering the passengers of a gondola in the winter or in bad weather; it has a door and a small window on either side with movable windowpanes. Such structures have not been in use since the mid-twentieth century, but an example can be seen on the gondola preserved on the ground floor of Ca' Rezzonico. In the summer the *felze* was replaced by a white fluttering awning (*tenda*) on four poles.

375 **the light by which we walk:** Following references to 'god' and 'heaven', this carries echoes of the New Testament, and the Gospel According to St John: 'In him was life; and the life was the light of men' (1:4 KJV), and the First Epistle General of John: 'if we walk in the light, as he is in the light, we have fellowship one with another' (1.7 KJV). The phrase was common in religious discourse, and occurs in an 1878 poem by the Scots cleric Horatius Bonar: 'It is but taper-light by which we walk / Here on this earth' (*My Old Letters*, ll. 736–7).

376 **Mrs. Siddons [...] Queen Caroline [...] Lady Hamilton:** Sarah Siddons (1755–1831), born into the Kemble acting dynasty and an aunt of James's friend Fanny Kemble, was a famous tragic actress and unusual in remaining untouched by sexual scandal; Queen Caroline (1768–1821), the very popular wife of George IV, who accused her of adultery in order to divorce her; Emma Hamilton (1765–1815), a model for George Romney, the fascinating wife of the British ambassador in Naples, Sir William Hamilton, and the mistress of Admiral Nelson. These are 'three female celebrities collectively signifying "the Byronic Age"' (Poole 240).

377 **John Cumnor:** See Introduction, p. lxxvii.

378 **"served" as the London populace says:** The *OED* notes that the sense of treating someone 'in a specified (usually unpleasant or unfair) manner' stretches back to the Middle Ages but is now chiefly colloquial. James is characteristically alert to such shifts of usage.

379 **"Orpheus and the Maenads!":** Legendary poet and musician, torn to pieces by the Thracian Maenads, also known as the Bacchae (as in the tragedy of 405 BCE by Euripides), devotees of the god Dionysus or Bacchus. According to the influential account of his death in 8 CE by the Roman poet Ovid (*Metamorphoses* Book XI), the Maenads were enraged

by Orpheus's rejection of women, after losing his beloved Eurydice in the underworld. See note 494 to 'The Liar'.

380 **the age of newspapers and telegrams and photographs and interviewers**: See Introduction, p. xliv.

381 **a city of exhibition**: Compare James's development of the image four years later in 'The Grand Canal' (1892) of Venice as a 'vast mausoleum' with 'a turnstile at the door': 'The shopkeepers and gondoliers, the beggars and the models, depend upon it for a living; they are the custodians and the ushers of the great museum—they are even themselves to a certain extent the objects of exhibition' (*CTW2* 315).

382 **to France, to Germany, to Italy**: James here brings together and mixes up the countries most associated with different major Romantic poets: Wordsworth with France; Coleridge with Germany; Shelley, Byron, and Keats with Italy. All these countries were in fact visited in 1826–9 by the American poet Henry Wadsworth Longfellow (1807–82), whom James knew.

383 **no brick gables [...] more Dutch than Italian, more like Amsterdam than like Venice**: Traditionally, Dutch architecture is characterized by rounded or stepped gables made of brick; but Amsterdam is almost as famous as Venice for its canals. The monumental tympanum (gable) in the upper part of the facade may remind Mrs Prest of Dutch architecture.

384 **a Protestant Sunday**: Certain public and private activities were restricted on Sundays in Protestant societies; theatres, for example, (and later cinemas) were closed.

385 *quartier perdu*: French, a district that is 'out of the way'.

386 **for five shillings a year**: In the second part of the nineteenth century Venetian 'palaces' could be rented or bought for very little money. See note 399 on the figure the narrator is required to pay.

387 **Her calling him 'Mr. Aspern'**: In this context, this mode of address implies a personal relation between Juliana and the poet, as she is reported to address him as any other person and not as a literary celebrity, as the sentence 'You don't say, "Mr." Shakespeare' shows.

388 **the gulf of time**: A phrase much used in nineteenth-century poetry, as for example in Wordsworth's early composition 'An Evening Walk. Addressed to a Young Lady': 'Even now she decks for me a distant scene, / (For dark

and broad the gulf of time between) / Gilding that cottage with her fondest ray' (ll. 345–7).

389   **the scagliola floor:** A *terrazzo* floor, made of pieces of coloured marble and stucco, then polished. See p. 284: 'the hard, shining floor', and note 140 to 'Georgina's Reasons'.

390   **clicking pattens:** These are 'little wooden shoes which have nothing but toes', as James has Hyacinth Robinson describe them on his visit to Venice in *The Princess Casamassima* (*CFHJ* 9, p. 305) – that is, wooden shoes open at the back, similar to clogs.

391   **the inevitable challenge:** '*Chi xe?*' [*sic*] ('Who is it?'), to which the answer is '*Amici!*' ('Friends!'), as Logan Pearsall Smith reports of his visit to the Bensons in Palazzo Capello in Rio Marin (*Saved from the Salvage: A Memoir* (Edinburgh: Tragara Press, 1982), p. 11). The expression is still in use. See note 437.

392   **escutcheons:** Shield-shaped ornaments bearing coats of arms.

393   **hair which was not "dressed":** The *OED* notes this specific use of the verb (sense 10), meaning 'to comb, brush, and do up (the hair)'.

394   **great capabilities:** Possibly a reference to Lancelot 'Capability' Brown (1716–83), the famous landscape designer and architect, so-called because he saw 'capabilities' in country estates.

395   **the name of this high tremulous spinster:** In the *NYE* James changed her name from Tita to Tina. See Introduction, p. lxxviii, and TV2, p. 686.

396   **my gondolier:** Families or individuals used to employ a gondolier, who was responsible for the family gondola and other house chores; the Misses Bordereau used to have a gondola (p. 290). Well-to-do visitors to Venice usually hired a gondolier and a gondola, often recommending the former to friends from abroad who were spending some time in Venice.

397   **a horrible green shade:** See Introduction, pp. lxxv–lxxvi for the different possible sources.

398   *terra firma*: Latin, indicating the mainland, as opposed to the city itself. In the *terraferma*, or hinterland of Venice, one can find gardens and Palladian villas.

399   **a thousand francs a month:** James uses the word *francs* as equivalent to *lire*. After the Napoleonic Wars the French *franc* gained wide circulation throughout Europe. The Latin Monetary Union, made by France, Belgium, Italy, and Switzerland, decreed the currencies of these countries equivalent in value in 1865, although each country kept the name of their

money (*lira* for Italy). A thousand francs would have been equivalent to about £40 (just under $200). Poole suggests an equivalent of £3,000 or $5,000 in present-day value (Poole 241). See note 386.

400 **chaffering:** The latest usage recorded for the verb by the *OED* is 1871, so this word meaning 'To treat about a bargain; to bargain, haggle about terms or price' is distinctly old-fashioned. James himself, however, uses it a dozen-odd times – including in 'The Grand Canal', when he declares that 'Venetian life is a matter of strolling and chaffering, of gossiping and gaping, of circulating without a purpose' (*CTW2* 314).

401 **the times when you receive:** Formal visiting hours when friends and acquaintances could expect the lady of the house to be 'at home'.

402 **wasted antiquity:** In *A Small Boy and Others* (1913) James refers to his great-aunt Wyckoff as 'an image of living antiquity' (*SBOC* 107).

403 **bring the money in gold:** Juliana mistrusts the promissory nature of the banknotes increasingly current in the later nineteenth century, preferring payment in the hardest possible cash (gold coin) to paper money.

404 **her annual migration:** Residents of Venice would leave the city in the hot summer months, often going north to the Dolomite mountains in the Belluno area.

405 **a dead wall:** A charged image for James. In Chapter 42 of *The Portrait of a Lady* Isabel 'had suddenly found the infinite vista of a multiplied life to be a dark, narrow alley, with a dead wall at the end' (*CFHJ 7*, p. 410); and in 'The Art of Fiction' (1884) the conventional view of fiction, James asserts, 'condemns the art to an eternal repetition of a few familiar *clichés*, cuts short its development, and leads us straight up to a dead wall' (*LC1* 58).

406 **such a violent *parti pris* of seclusion:** The *OED* explains 'parti pris' as 'A preconceived view; a bias or prejudice'; in the *NYE* James altered this to 'so stiff a policy of seclusion'.

407 **like hunted creatures feigning death:** Probably referring to the slang phrase (originally American) 'to play possum', meaning 'to feign, dissemble; esp. to pretend to be ill or dead (in allusion to the opossum's supposed habit of feigning death when threatened or attacked)'. The *OED* cites from William H. Simmons's *Notices of East Florida* (1822): 'After being severely wounded, they have been known to lie for several hours as if dead ... Hence, the expression of "playing possum" is common among the inhabitants, being applied to those who act with cunning and duplicity.'

408 **Pasquale's:** A name used by James to indicate a typical gondolier ('Venice', 1882) and again used for a servant/gondolier in *The Wings of the Dove*. *Don Pasquale* is an 1843 comic opera (*opera buffa*), a farce in which the ageing, foolish Don Pasquale nearly gets married, by Gaetano Donizetti.

409 **stringer of beads:** Pasquale's lady friend works occasionally as a bead stringer, a job common to many women in Venice at the time. Many photos document women threading beads sitting in front of their doors, in the street. The painting *Venetian Bead Stringers* (c. 1880–2) by John Singer Sargent shows women threading beads in a bare hall. For the representation of bead stringers see Rosella Mamoli Zorzi, '"Foresti" in Venice in the Second Half of the 19th Century: Their Passion for Paintings, Brocades, *and* Glass', in *Atti, Study Days on Venetian Glass*, 174.1 (Venice: Istituto Veneto di Scienze, Lettere ed Arti, 2015–16), 27–8. In his 1882 essay on 'Venice', James commented disparagingly on the way 'the young Venetians who sell bead bracelets and "panoramas" are perpetually thrusting their wares at you' (*PPL* 7).

410 **his bright ghost:** A phrase associated with Shelley, in whose poem *The Revolt of Islam* (1818) the name of 'Laon' acts as a rallying cry: 'Like a bright ghost from Heaven that shout did scare / The slaves' (Canto v, section vii).

411 **rosy air:** In the 1882 *Venice* essay, after describing the 'suffusion of rosiness' of the island of San Giorgio, James lingers on the pink colour of the city: 'If we were asked what is the leading colour at Venice, we should say pink' (*PPL* 15).

412 **went back, went back, as I used to phrase it:** Compare James on the English novelist James Payn (1830–98): 'Without the aid of years or other creaking machinery, he "went back"—went back as a link, in imagination and sympathy, to the taste and tone that I had supposed I should have come too late to catch' ('The Late James Payn', in *Autobiographies*, ed. Philip Horne (New York: Library of America, 2016), p. 688).

413 **the Adriatic:** The sea into and out of which the waters of the Venice Lagoon flow.

414 **an artist […] who had left the western world […] to study in the ancient schools:** James himself recalled the 'artist-fraternity in especial, the young Americans aspiring to paint, to build and to carve, and gasping at home for vital air', in *William Wetmore Story and His Friends* (Edinburgh and London: William Blackwood & Sons, 1903; Boston: Houghton, Mifflin & Co., 1903), 1:9. The sculptor William Wetmore Story (1819–95) can be

seen as the focus of these circles: he was in Rome in 1847 (and later lived
there all his life), a friend of Margaret Fuller (1810–50), who lived through
the events of the Roman Republic, reporting to the New York *Tribune* on
them. These artists had been preceded by such figures as John Singleton
Copley (1738–1815), who went to Italy in 1775, Benjamin West (1738–1820),
who was in Italy in the 1760s, Washington Allston (1779–1843), who went
to Italy in 1804, John Vanderlyn (1775–1852), who was in Rome in 1807,
and Thomas Cole (1801–48), who was in Italy in the 1830s. The generation
of W. W. Story was that of the 'precursors', as James called them in his
memoir, where he reconstructed the world of American artists who went
to Europe to look for culture while 'our native land was nude and crude
and provincial', as the narrator here puts it (p. 306). These artists' milieu
was portrayed by James in *Roderick Hudson*. See Van Wyck Brooks, *The
Dream of Arcadia: American Writers and Artists in Italy, 1760–1915* (New
York: E. P. Dutton, 1958); Regina Soria, *Dictionary of Nineteenth-Century
American Artists in Italy, 1760–1914* (Rutherford, NJ: Fairleigh Dickinson
University Press, 1982); Nathalia Wright, *American Novelists in Italy: The
Discoverers, Allston to James* (Philadelphia, PA: University of Pennsylvania
Press, 1965).

415 **not as ambiguous as the sonnets [...] of Shakespeare**: The 'ambiguity' of
Shakespeare's sonnets was a lively spur to discussion for nineteenth-century readers, scholars, and critics, particularly the nature and objects of
the desire they seem to express, even before Oscar Wilde's provocative
tale, 'The Portrait of Mr. W. H.' (1889). Adrian Poole summarizes these
debates in *Shakespeare and the Victorians* (London: Arden Shakespeare,
2004), pp. 160–71.

416 **the steep footway of renunciation**: In a sentence making explicit reference to Shakespeare, this sounds like a conscious variation on Ophelia's
'the steep and thorny way to heaven' (*Hamlet* 1.3.48).

417 **a queer old-fashioned, expatriated, artistic Bohemia, in the days when
the aesthetic was only the academic**: James is referring to the early
American expatriate artists of the first half of the nineteenth century
whose milieu he later reconstructed in *William Wetmore Story and His
Friends*: see note 414. Academic painting, with historical, mythical, and
genre scenes, was then the fashion. This 'old-fashioned' Bohemia had evidently not taken on the more emphatically 'aesthetic' style promoted by
Mürger in his Parisian *Scènes de la Vie de Bohème* (1851): see note 204 to 'A
New England Winter'.

418 *contadina* **and** *pifferaro:* Italian, a peasant woman and a piper, the traditional figures, beloved by painters, which symbolized the picturesque
nature of Italy. James had commented on them as stereotypes in the
essay 'Italy Revisited' (1878), referring to Thackeray's novel *The Newcomes*
(1855), which mentions a young painter sending to the Royal Academy a
painting full of these clichés: 'A Contadino dancing with a Trasteverina at
the door of a Locanda, to the music of a Pifferaro' (*PPL* 45).

419 **peaked hats and long hair:** Although the sentence refers to the Bohemian
painters of the time, this description also recalls the *pifferari*, mentioned
here, who were often represented with such hats and hair. James describes
a young Roman model 'in short-clothes, a sheepkin jacket and a peaked
hat' in his essay 'Very Modern Rome' (1878, *CTW2* 758). None of the portraits or photos of American painters or sculptors of the 1830s and 1840s
show any of them wearing 'peaked hats'.

420 *bric-à-brac:* It is of some historical interest that according to the *OED* this
expression for '[O]ld curiosities of artistic character, knick-knacks, antiquarian odds-and-ends, such as old furniture, plate, china, fans, statu-
ettes, and the like' only enters the English language from the French in the
mid to late nineteenth century (its earliest citations are from Thackeray).

421 **When Americans went abroad in 1820:** See note 414.

422 **tossing brig:** A two-masted vessel rigged with square sails. Brigs operated
throughout the period in which commercial sailing ships were in use,
as they were very efficient. Steamers started working on lakes and large
rivers as early as 1811, and the first regularly scheduled transatlantic crossing of a British steamer had begun as early as 1838, although crossing by
steamer became the rule only by the 1870s. See note 302.

423 **yellow diligences:** Stage-coaches

424 **inns where she dreamed of travellers' tales:** This might be an allusion to
the work of one of the 'precursors', Washington Irving (1783–1859), who
published his *Tales of a Traveller* in 1824. The stories in part three, 'The
Italian banditti', are those purporting to be frightening, told in Italian
inns. See note 414.

425 **when literature was lonely there and art and form almost impossible:**
A view to which James had himself given provocative and controversial
expression less than ten years previously in his book on Hawthorne.
Other writers before Hawthorne and James had lamented this condition: for example, James Fenimore Cooper (1789–1851), in his preface to

Home as Found (1838), had complained that 'it would be indeed a desperate undertaking to think of making anything interesting in the way of a *Roman de Société* in this country'.

426 **Saint Mark:** The basilica in the square, the origins of which go back to the ninth century, was rebuilt and decorated over the centuries. It is famous for its Eastern appearance and its Byzantine mosaics. It used to be the church of the ducal government, while San Pietro di Castello was the city's cathedral. James described his impressions of it in the essay *Venice* (1882); after dwelling on '[t]he strange figures in the mosaic pictures', and underlining the dusky character of its interior, he proceeded with a description that evokes the experience of the senses while being in the church: 'Beauty of surface, of tone, of detail, of things near enough to touch and kneel upon and lean against—it is from this the effect proceeds' (*PPL* 13). In the same essay James also contrasts 'the sacred dusk' inside the church with the 'bazaar' of the pedlars who follow one in from outside (*PPL* 9).

427 **Florian's *cafè*:** One of the historical cafés on St Mark's Square, on the side of the Procuratie Nuove. It was opened by a Floriano Francesconi, on 29 December 1720, with the name 'Alla Venezia Trionfante', but soon became known by the owner's name. James's characters often sit at Florian's, from Mr and Miss Evans and Mr Brooke in 'Travelling Companions' (1870) to the family of 'The Chaperon' taking ices (1891), to Lord Mark reading the *Figaro* there, in *The Wings of the Dove* (Book ix, Ch. 2), to Sir Luke Strett going there 'for rest and mild drinks' in the same novel (Book ix, Ch. 4). Sitting at Florian's is one of the 'superficial pastimes' that compose a Venetian day ('Venice', 1882; *PPL* 5).

428 **Bädeker:** The very popular guidebooks printed by Karl Baedeker (1801–59) in Koblenz from 1827, and then by his heirs in Leipzig from 1872. The first guidebook in English, *The Rhine*, appeared in 1861. James may have used the 1886 edition of Baedeker's *Guide to Northern Italy*. Baedeker guidebooks are still being printed. Characters with a Baedeker in their hands are often present, sometimes with an edge of criticism, in James's later works:'They were only people, as Mrs. Stringham had said, staying for the week or two at the inns, people who during the day had fingered their Baedekers, gaped at their frescoes and differed, over fractions of francs, with their gondoliers' (*WD*, Book iii, Ch. 3). Yet more ambiguous references may also be found, as for example in *The Golden Bowl*: 'So it was that in the house itself, where more of his waiting treasures than ever

were provisionally ranged, she [Charlotte] sometimes only looked at him
[Mr. Verver]—from end to end of the great gallery, the pride of the house,
for instance—as if, in one of the halls of a museum, she had been an earnest young woman with a Baedeker and he a vague gentleman to whom
even Baedekers were unknown' (Book 1, Ch. 38). In earlier works of the
1870s and 1880s it is the Murray guidebooks which are normally used
by James's characters, for instance in 'Travelling Companions' (1870), 'At
Isella' (1871), 'The Madonna of the Future' (1873), 'Madame de Mauves'
(1874), and *Roderick Hudson*. In 'At Isella' both guidebooks are mentioned,
to signify the narrator's impatience to arrive in Italy: 'In Switzerland [...]
Instead of dutifully conning my Swiss Bädeker, I had fretfully deflowered
my Murray's North Italy' (Corrected text from James's MS: see *The Tales
of Henry James*, vol. 2, ed. Maqbool Aziz (Oxford: Clarendon Press, 1978),
p. 102).

429   **Piazzetta**: Italian, small square, but the name specifically indicates the
space opening onto the Bacino or Basin of St Mark's, with its two distinctive columns carrying symbols of Saint Theodore (the crocodile) and
Saint Mark (the lion, sometimes identified as a chimera).

430   **the odour of the canal**: In his 'Venice' essay of 1882, James remarks, when
listing possible reactions against the city, that 'The canals have a horrible
smell' (*PPL* 7).

431   **Romeo's vows**: Romeo's declarations of love to Juliet, in Capulet's orchard
(in Verona) in *Romeo and Juliet*, 2.2.26, beginning 'But soft, what light
through yonder window breaks? / It is the east, and Juliet is the sun.'

432   **Carmelite nuns**: The order founded in Florence in 1452, following the
rules of the Mount Carmel friars, going back to the thirteenth century.
Nunneries as places of reclusion or isolation from the world appear in
The American, where the heroine at the end of the novel retreats to a
Carmelite convent, and *The Portrait of a Lady*, where Isabel's stepdaugh-
ter Pansy is schooled in such a convent.

433   **those clear bells of Venice**: The sound of bells seems linked in James's
imagination with Catholic countries such as France and Italy. In his
review of George Eliot's poem 'The Spanish Gypsy' (1868), James appreciatively quotes a line – 'And bells make Catholic the trembling air' (Book
1, l. 31) – that seems to confirm this connection (*LC1* 946).

434   **to the Lido**: The long and narrow island closing off the lagoon from the
Adriatic Sea, to which people used to go in a gondola, getting off at one

end in order to walk, and being picked up at the other end by the same gondola, as Daniel S. Curtis records doing with Robert Browning in 1889 (*Diary of Daniel S. Curtis*, quoted in *Robert Browning a Venezia*, ed. R. Mamoli Zorzi (Venice: Fondazione Querini Stampalia, 1989), p. 68).

435 **Cavaliere Bombicci [...] the Contessa Altemura [...] the Churtons and the Goldies and Mrs. Stock-Stock:** These names are meant to sound ridiculous. However, the Italian names do exist: Luigi Bombicci (1833–1903) was a mineralogist, and there is a Museum of Science with his name in Bologna. Altemura or Altamura is a name coming from the region of Puglia. 'Churton' would have had a certain resonance at the time of writing, in that the literary critic John Churton Collins (1848–1908) had perpetrated a violent attack in the *Quarterly Review* (October 1886) on James's friend Edmund Gosse for the sloppy scholarship in the latter's *From Shakespeare to Pope* (1885). Both 'the Goldies and Mrs. Stock-Stock' are imaginary names used ironically to evoke moneyed people.

436 *avvocato* **Pochintesta:** Italian, *avvocato* means lawyer, while the family name, which has the same farcical sound as the preceding ones, means 'with little in his head'. Again, the name does exist, and there was a painter called Ernesto Pochintesta (1840–91) who exhibited at the first Venice national exhibition in 1887 (*Esposizione Nazionale Artistica Illustrata 1887*, Venice, Sala XVII, no. 33: *Nei campi*) (Elizabeth Anne McCauley, Alan Chong, Rosella Mamoli Zorzi, and Richard Lingner, *Gondola Days: Isabella Stewart Gardner and the Palazzo Barbaro Circle* (Easthampton, MA: Antique Collectors' Club, 2004), p. 153). James mentions 'Poor Pochintesta!' in a letter of 'late June or early July 1876' from Paris to Lizzie Boott, in a context referring to the painter Thomas Couture (1815–79) (*CLHJ 1872–1876* 2:146). The reference seems to be to Ernesto Pochintesta, as he was a pupil of Couture at his atelier in Villiers-le-Bel, mentioned in the letter, and exhibited at the Paris Salons of 1876 and 1877. The Venice exhibition opened on 2 May 1887, and in spite of his ominous 'There is to be a senseless exhibition here a couple of months hence' (2 March 1887, *HJL* 3:175), James may have come upon Pochintesta's name in the catalogue or seen his work in the exhibition itself when he was in Venice from May 25 for several weeks. It also included two large paintings by Ralph Curtis, son of the Curtises with whom James was staying at the time, *Acquasanta* and *Scirocco*, in Sala IV (*Esposizione Nazionale Artistica Venezia*, Stabilimento dell'Emporio, 1887). See Rosella Mamoli Zorzi, *Ralph Curtis, un pittore americano a Venezia* (Venice: Supernova, 2019), 63.

437 **this invertebrate dialect**: In the essay 'Venice' (1882), James commented on the 'delightful garrulous language' of the Venetians, which helped to 'make Venetian life a long *conversazione*'. He also added specific comments on the qualities of the dialect: 'This language, with its soft elisions, its odd transpositions, its kindly contempt for consonants and other disagreeables, has in it something peculiarly human and accommodating. If your gondolier had no other merit, he would have the merit that he speaks Venetian' (*PPL* 20).

438 **The queer rococo Venice of Casanova**: Under the influence of John Ruskin (1819–1900), James did not appreciate eighteenth-century Venice, the Venice of Giacomo Casanova (1725–98), the famous lover and author of the *Mémoires*, written in French (1789–98) and described by James as 'cheap loose journalism' (*LC2* 913). In the *New York Edition* James added to Casanova's the name of the famous playwright Carlo Goldoni (1707–93), of whose *I Quattro Rusteghi* (*The Boors*, 1760) he had said in 1873 that 'with all its fun, it wasn't so good as Molière' (*TS* 205; in *Italian Hours* (1909) the first phrase is revised to 'for all its humanity of irony' (*CTW1* 481)).

439 **lift [...] the veil [...] temple**: Language drawing on poetic and scriptural sources, such as Shelley's sonnet 'Lift not the painted veil' (1818), and the 'veil of the temple', concealing the Holy of Holies, that is 'rent in twain' at the time of Christ's death (Matthew 27:51; Mark 15:38).

440 **the amusement of philosophers [...] great captains**: The title character famously declares at the end of Voltaire's 'conte philosophique', *Candide* (1795), that 'il faut cultiver notre jardin' ('we must cultivate our garden'). Of course, Candide's declaration is also metaphoric; in James's text the garden does exist, but it is used by the narrator to achieve his goal. *Candide* was one of the favourite works of Daniel S. Curtis, who would read aloud from its pages to his guests in the Palazzo Barbaro, and James refers to *Candide* in his essay 'The Grand Canal' (1892). The narrator is also vaguely invoking the ideal of 'rural retirement' established by the Roman poets Horace and Virgil, and eagerly embraced by seventeenth- and eighteenth-century English poets, statesmen, and 'great captains'. These last included Thomas Fairfax (1612–71), commander in chief of the Parliamentary forces, whose attempts to retire from public life prompted Andrew Marvell (1621–78), author of 'The Garden' (see Introduction, p. lxxvi), to write his poem 'Upon Appleton House' (*c.* 1651).

441 **the funny old church:** That is, St Mark's.

442 **a comedian:** Meaning simply actor, as in French, rather than comic actor, as in English. Compare note 288 to 'The Path of Duty'.

443 **the Grand Canal:** The main seawater thoroughfare of Venice, the S-shaped canal crossing the city, with many beautiful palaces along it. In his essay 'The Grand Canal' (1892), James describes this '*promenade historique* of which the lesson, however often we read it, gives, in the depth of its interest, an incomparable dignity to Venice' (*CTW2* 320), dwelling on some of its palaces and inhabitants. He starts from the Salute (the beginning of the Grand Canal) and finishes at the railway station (its end), following the example of the little nineteenth-century booklets that illustrated the buildings on each side of the waterway.

444 **Piazza:** Italian, *Piazza* (square) in Venice implicitly indicates Piazza S. Marco; all the other squares are called *campi* (fields).

445 **the Piazzetta:** The landing point for St Mark's: see note 429.

446 **the long arcades:** The reference is to the Procuratie, old (on the north side), built in the sixteenth century, and new (on the south side), finished in the seventeenth century. The name derives from the fact that they were the abode of the 'Procuratori di San Marco', the most important office after that of the doge in the Venetian Republic. Shops were and are located under these arcades.

447 **the unholy flame:** A poeticism of the early nineteenth century, as for instance in Ebenezer Elliott's 'Withered Wild-Flowers' (1834), 'But, oh, when Virtue flies what demons come; / Seize on her throne, convert her light to gloom, / Pollute her altar with unholy flame, / And of her *temple* make a den of shame!' (Bk 3, ll. 93–6).

448 **The present has such a rough way of treading it down:** Perhaps a reminiscence of Keats's 'Ode to a Nightingale' (1819): 'Thou wast not born for death, immortal Bird! / No hungry generations tread thee down'.

449 **a small oval portrait:** *The Oval Portrait* (1850) is a story by Edgar Allan Poe (1809–49), who has been seen as a possible source for the figure of the American poet Aspern. However, small oval portraits such as that held out by Juliana were quite usual in the nineteenth century. For the oval portrait as an element of Gothic fiction, see Poole 243. Oval portraits had a further association for James with a poem by Théophile Gautier (1811–72), 'J'aime à vous voir en vos cadres ovales, / Portraits jaunis

des belles du vieux temps' ('I like to look at you in your oval frames, / yellowing portraits of the beauties of old times'). On a visit to Flaubert in April 1876, James heard the great novelist recite this poem and others, 'in a way to make them seem the most beautiful things in the world' (*CHJL 1872–1876* 3:98). James was never able to find the poem again (*LC2* 320), but this was because he was looking for 'Les Portraits Ovales', when the poem is in fact entitled 'Pastel'. See Leon Edel, *Henry James: The Conquest of London, 1870–1883* (London: Rupert Hart-Davis, 1962), p. 225.

450 **a high-collared green coat and a buff waistcoat:** Men's attire fashionable in the 1810s and 1820s, as witnessed, as regards the high collar, by several portraits of Lord Byron, especially the sketch by G. Harlow (1815). A buff waistcoat is a beige- and cream-coloured waistcoat.

451 **a tall, old secretary [...] of the style of the Empire:** Empire was a furniture style that became popular after Napoleon's campaigns in Egypt (1798) and Italy (1799), and lasted through the nineteenth century. Mahogany was the wood used. See note 170.

452 **bandboxes:** Slight boxes made of cardboard, usually cylindrical in shape, to carry light articles of attire, so called for originally accommodating the 'bands' or ruffs of the seventeenth century (*OED*).

453 **the tall hat of his profession:** In some nineteenth-century portraits doctors wear tall hats, although they are indistinguishable from those worn by bankers, gentlemen, etc.

454 **your real name:** The names of James's first-person narrators are seldom given in the tales they narrate, such as 'The Turn of the Screw' (1898) and *The Sacred Fount* (1901).

455 **as if death had descended on her:** A moment which recalls a possible source for the story, Alexander Pushkin's tale 'The Queen of Spades' (1834), where the anti-hero Herman conceals himself in an old countess's room at night in the hope of forcing her to give him the supposed secret of winning at cards, which she is rumoured to have obtained through a pact with the devil: '"Will you tell me the names of the magic cards, or not?" asked Herman after a pause. / There was no reply. / The young man then drew a pistol from his pocket, exclaiming: "You old witch, I'll force you to tell me!" / At the sight of the weapon the Countess gave a second sign of life. She threw back her head and put out her hands as if to protect herself; then they dropped and she sat motionless. / Herman grasped her arm roughly, and was about to renew his threats, when he saw that she

was dead!' See Neil Cornwell, 'Pushkin and Henry James: Secrets, Papers and Figures', in Robert Read and Joe Andrews (eds.), *Two Hundred Years of Pushkin* (Amsterdam and New York: Rodopi, 2004), vol. 3, pp. 193–210.

456 **to Treviso, to Bassano, to Castelfranco**: Beautiful small historical cities in the Veneto region, visitable from Asolo, where Mrs Bronson would buy a house in 1889, 'to please Mr. Browning' (*LPB* 186), who had set his poem *Pippa Passes* in that small and lovely town. James visited Mrs Bronson in Asolo from Venice more than once in the early 1890s. In 'Casa Alvisi' (1902) he recalls various day trips from Asolo in Mrs Bronson's carriage: 'The rumbling carriage, the old-time, rattling, red-velveted carriage of provincial, rural Italy, delightful and quaint, did the office of the gondola; to Bassano, to Treviso, to high-walled Castelfranco, all pink and gold, the home of the great Giorgione' (*CTW2* 364).

457 *la vecchia*: Italian, the old woman. In the *New York Edition* it is changed to *quella vecchia* ('that old woman').

458 **the other yesterday... passeggio**: 'the other yesterday' is modelled on the Italian 'l'altro ieri.' Passeggio means tour (in this case in a gondola).

459 **the cemetery**: The island of San Michele. A decree of Napoleon instituted a 'general cemetery' for Venice on 7 December 1807. In order to make space for it, in 1836 the island of San Michele was joined to the contiguous island of San Cristoforo della Pace. As the narrator notes, it is on the way to Murano, in the northern part of the lagoon.

460 **the Giorgione at Castelfranco**: The famous altarpiece by the painter known as Giorgione (*c.*1477/8–1510), *Madonna col Bambino in trono e i santi Francesco e Liberale* (*Madonna with Child Enthroned, with Saints Francis and Liberal*) in the cathedral church of Castelfranco.

461 **to go to the station**: The Venice railway station of Santa Lucia was started in 1860. In order to make space for it the convent and the church of Santa Lucia were torn down in 1861. The railway had arrived in Venice in 1846. The present station is in the same place, but the plan dates to the 1930s.

462 **sewn, as the phrase is, with white thread**: Visible, blatant. An anglicization of the French phrase 'c'est cousu de fil blanc'.

463 **"*Dove commanda?*"** Meaning, 'Where do you order (me to go)?' James also uses the incorrect form '*Commanda, signorina!?*' (*commanda* rather than *comanda*) in a letter of 31 March 1880 to Charles Eliot Norton, referring to Norton's sister Grace (*CLHJ 1878–1880* 3:151). James's use of double

consonants in Italian is often shaky, as when he writes *piazetta* (*CLHJ 1855–1872* 2:121) for *piazzetta*, *Posilippo* for *Posillipo* (*CLHJ 1878–1880* 2:153, 159, 161, 173), the *Uffizzi* for the *Uffizi* (*CLHJ 1878–1880* 2:149). He is also guilty of spelling *Baeddeker* once with two 'ds' (*CLHJ 1855–1872* 2:95).

464 **with my hat pulled over my face**: In the *NYE* revision James makes this 'my hat pulled over my brow', a phrasing which more closely recalls, as Adrian Poole writes, 'Macduff's retreat into private grief at the news of his family's murder, the posture indicated by Malcolm's exhortation to him: "What, man, ne'er pull your hat upon your brows" (*Macbeth* 4.3.209)' (Poole 244).

465 **Malamocco**: A small village on the southern end of the Lido, giving the name to one of the port entrances to Venice.

466 **the church of Saints John and Paul**: The big Gothic church of the Dominicans, consecrated in 1430 but built over the two preceding centuries, north and not far from St Mark's and near the Fondamente Nuove. It was the pantheon where many doges were buried.

467 **the small square-jawed face of Bartolommeo Colleoni, the terrible *condottiere***: Correctly: Bartolomeo; the bronze monument to Bartolomeo Colleoni (*c.*1400–75) on a horse, a sculpture by Andrea Verrocchio (*c.* 1435–88), begun in 1481 and inaugurated in 1496. See Illustration 2. Colleoni, born in Bergamo, had been a famous *condottiere* (leader of mercenary troops) in the service of the Venetian Republic. He bequeathed substantial moneys to the state, on condition of having a monument erected in the Piazza San Marco. However, it was placed in front of the Scuola Grande di San Marco, as laws forbade any monument in the Piazza. For Walter Pater, in his essay on 'Leonardo Da Vinci' in *The Renaissance* (1873), it was a high point of the civilization of the time: 'What, in that age, such work was capable of being – of what nobility, amid what racy truthfulness to fact – we may judge from the bronze statue of Bartolomeo Colleoni on horseback, modelled by Leonardo's master, Verrocchio (he died of grief, it was said, because, the mould accidentally failing, he was unable to complete it), still standing in the piazza of Saint John and Saint Paul at Venice.' The narrator confronts the male power of Colleoni, considered the image of super-masculinity as having three testicles ('coglioni') reproduced also in his coat of arms. Andrew Hewish, 'Cryptic Relations in Henry James's "The Aspern Papers"', *Henry James Review*, 37.3 (2016), 259.

468 **Marcus Aurelius [...] the Roman Capitol**: The equestrian statue of the emperor Marcus Aurelius (161–80), which survived the destructions of

the Middle Ages, and was transported from the Piazza del Laterano to the Piazza del Campidoglio in 1538, according to the wish of Pope Paul III, and against the wish of Michelangelo, author of the plan of the Piazza del Campidoglio, or Capitol, one of the city's seven hills, and the centre of political and religious power in ancient Rome. The pedestal basement of the statue is the work of Michelangelo. The statue was praised by Hawthorne in *The Marble Faun* (1860) as 'the most majestic representation of the kingly character that ever the world has seen' (Ch. 18).

469 **fondamentas:** Italian, the quays or streets with a canal on one side in Venice, the plural for which would be *fondamente* (though if used in another sense, as the basis of a building, *fondamenta*).

470 **strike you as members of an endless dramatic troupe:** James's 1882 'Venice' essay proposes that in the Venetian June 'the life of its people and the strangeness of its constitution become a perpetual comedy, or, at least, a perpetual drama' (*PPL* 35). He was to develop this metaphor towards the end of *The Wings of the Dove*, where the men in the Piazza San Marco 'resemble melancholy maskers' (Book IX, Ch. 2).

471 **the unconscious cerebration of sleep:** James here borrows a phrase used (though not invented) by his psychologist brother William in *The Principles of Psychology* (1890), in the chapter 'The Mid-Stuff Theory' (Ch. 6). In Lecture 9, on 'Conversion', of *Varieties of Religious Experience* (1902), William said that 'Dr. [William] Carpenter first [...] introduced the term "unconscious cerebration"' (*William James: Writings 1902–1910*, ed. Bruce Kuklick (New York: Library of America, 1987), p. 192). In the Preface to *The American* (1907), William's novelist brother relates it to his own creative processes: 'precisely because it had so much to give, I think, must I have dropped it for the time into the deep well of unconscious cerebration: not without the hope, doubtless, that it might eventually emerge from that reservoir, as one had already known the buried treasure to come to light, with a firm iridescent surface and a notable increase of weight' (*LC2* 1055).

472 **force of soul:** Perhaps an allusion to Goethe's *Faust*, which in the 1834 translation by John Stuart Blackie has the brooding Faust tell himself, in the first scene, 'Thy innate force of soul upwells, / As speaks one spirit to another.' The phrase also occurs in George Meredith's *Evan Harrington* (1861), where 'he, gaining force of soul to join with hers, took her hands and related the contents of the letter fully' (Ch. 12).

'The Liar'

473 **Stayes:** According to the *OED*, this is one alternative spelling of the plural of *staithe*, a word for 'an embankment'. There is a seventeenth-century country property, more a grand farmhouse than a country house, called Stayes Wood, near Henley-on-Thames in Buckinghamshire, though it is not known whether James was familiar with it.

474 **the literature [...] mainly American and humorous:** Along with Mark Twain (1835–1910) and Ambrose Bierce (1842–1914), who became popular respectively in the 1860s and late 1880s, the best-known American humourists in Britain were Josh Billings (1818–85), Charles Leland (1824–1903), Artemus Ward (1834–67), and Bret Harte (1836–1902).

475 **'goody' engravings:** '[C]haracterized by or expressing weak and sentimental morality' (*OED*).

476 **Mr. Le Fanu:** The Irishman Joseph Sheridan Le Fanu (1814–73) was one of the leading ghost story and mystery writers of the nineteenth century. Among his works are *The House by the Churchyard* (1863), *Uncle Silas* (1864), and *Carmilla* (1872), the last of which has been suggested by William Veeder as a source for 'The Turn of the Screw' (1898).

477 **foggy London:** See note 256 to 'The Path of Duty'. James appreciated the aesthetic properties of the London fog, as in his essay 'London', first published in the same magazine as this tale, the *Century*, later in the same year (1888); he finds romantic 'the clubs in Pall Mall, which I positively like best when the fog loiters upon their monumental staircases' (*EL* 31).

478 **Hertfordshire:** A county just north of London, within easy reach by rail. Hertfordshire is also briefly mentioned in 'The Chaperon' (1891). As testified by his letters, James went more than once to Hatfield House (Hertfordshire), built in 1611 by Robert Cecil, 1st Earl of Salisbury. In James's time the owner was the 3rd Marquess of Salisbury (1830–1903), secretary of state for India and British prime minister in 1885, 1886–92, and 1895–1902 (*CLHJ 1876–1878* 1:133–4; *Letters to Isabella Stewart Gardner*, ed. Rosella Mamoli Zorzi (London: Pushkin Press, 2009), p. 56, note 2).

479 **withered ruddiness:** James would return to elderly faces as a favourite subject for a painter in the story 'The Beldonald Holbein' (1901).

480 **the human mask:** An image of abiding interest for James. In the 'London' essay (1888) he would describe the London Season as 'a fine, decorous, expensive, Protestant carnival, in which the masks are not of velvet or of

silk, but of wonderful deceptive flesh and blood, the material of the most beautiful complexions in the world' (*EL* 42). In *The Sacred Fount* (1901) the narrator describes an unsettling painting, an old portrait of a pale young man without eyebrows, whose stare is 'like that of some whitened old-world clown': 'In his hand he holds an object that strikes the spectator at first simply as some obscure, some ambiguous work of art, but that on a second view becomes a representation of a human face, modelled and coloured, in wax, in enamelled metal, in some substance not human. The object thus appears a complete mask, such as might have been fantastically fitted and worn' (*CFHJ* 16, p. 33). There is a record of James himself wearing a mask, from the diary of his later amanuensis, Theodora Bosanquet: 'He looked "real lovely" in a cracker mask after dinner – we all did – but he was the best! They were pleasant, benevolent sort of masks only down to the mouth & with a hole for the nose. Mr. James's most successful one was a fat old lady with side curls – which made us so hilarious that he had to send for a shaving-glass to see himself in. "Why," he propounded, "don't we all wear masks and change them as we do our clothes?"' (Theodora Bosanquet, Diary, 25 December 1909; Houghton Library, bMS Eng 1213.1 Box 1).

481 **Colonel Capadose**: See Introduction, p. lxxxiii.

482 **He has been a great deal in India**: James never visited India or indeed Africa, major parts of what he would call on 26 December 1898 in a letter to Charles Eliot Norton 'the great grabbed-up British Empire' (*LHJ* 4:309), but they figure recurrently in his fiction as an off-stage space, even just in 1888 alone. In 'A London Life', whose periodical publication overlapped with that of 'The Liar', Selina Berrington's previous lover Lord Deepmere 'has gone to India'; and in 'The Lesson of the Master', published a month after this tale, Marian Fancourt and her father, a General, have recently returned from India, and Paul Overt asks her, 'Haven't you administered provinces in India and had captive rajahs and tributary princes chained to your car?' When the aesthete Gabriel Nash mysteriously disappears in *The Tragic Muse* (1890), the hero Nick Dormer declares, 'I have a notion he has gone to India, and at the present moment is reclining on a bank of flowers in the vale of Cashmere' (Ch. 50). On 24 February 1909 James was to write to Caroline Fitzgerald, the wife of explorer Filippo De Filippi, who had both been in Cashmere: 'Isn't Kashmere of divine beauty—the loveliest vale of Earth—& won't you lie upon beds of asphodel surrounded by tame gazelles?' Henry James, '*Su letti di asfodelo*' *Lettere a Caroline Fitzgerald*, ed. Rosella Mamoli Zorzi and Gottardo Pallastrelli (Milan: Archinto, 2018),

p. 74. James borrowed the expression from Tennyson's *Lotos Eaters* (1833), inspired in its turn by book IX of the *Odyssey*. James's friends Ariana Curtis and Isabella Stewart Gardner told the writer of their trips to India and the Far East. Walter Roper Lawrence, an English Civil Servant, had published *The Valley of Kashmere* in 1895, a survey of the economy, history, and future perspectives of Kashmere, which had been a great success (*ibid.*, p. 60).

483 **he says that which is not:** This locution for lying derives from book four of Jonathan Swift's *Gulliver's Travels* (1726), in which Gulliver's hosts the Houyhnhnms, rational and articulate horses, are puzzled by his description of the human habit of warfare, of which they have no conception, and respond: 'I cannot but think you have said the thing which is not' (Ch. 5).

484 **an old mummy:** The image and phrase occur in Nathaniel Hawthorne's story about a false rumour of murder, 'Mr. Higginbotham's Catastrophe', collected in *Twice-Told Tales* (1837), where a character says about the supposedly dead Higginbotham, 'I never saw a man look so yellow and thin as the squire does [...] Says I to myself, to-night, he's more like a ghost or an old mummy than good flesh and blood.' 'Mummy' also occurs in a passage quoted by James in 1876 from Balzac's letters, about a visit to the Romantic writer Ludwig Tieck (1773–1853) *en famille* in Berlin: 'He had an old countess, his contemporary in spectacles, almost an octogenarian — a mummy with a green eye-shade, whom I supposed to be a domestic divinity' (*LC2* 86). (The 'green eye-shade' suggests this may be a possible source also for 'The Aspern Papers': see Introduction, pp. lxxv–lxxvi).

485 **as seriously as she might have played whist:** A card game associated with the trivialities of English social life (Mr Weston in Jane Austen's *Emma* (1815) plays five times a week); in 'Eugene Pickering' (1874) England is symbolized by 'whist with sixpenny stakes'. In Chapter 53 of *The Portrait of a Lady*, Isabel's sense of her own situation changes profoundly, 'now that she knew something that so much concerned her, and the eclipse of which had made life resemble an attempt to play whist with an imperfect pack of cards'. (*CFHJ* 7, p. 539). James repeats the image in the 'Charleston' chapter of *The American Scene* in 1907: 'the attempt to play whist with an imperfect pack of cards' (Ch. 13).

486 **art-student at Munich:** Lyon was evidently an art student at the Academy of Fine Arts of Munich (Akademie der Bildenden Künste München). Founded in 1808 by Maximilian I Joseph of Bavaria, this is one of the oldest and most significant art academies in Germany, and throughout the nineteenth century Munich was one of Europe's most important centres for the arts. The

American painter Frank Duveneck (1848–1919), praised by James as a very talented artist, and husband of James's close friend, the painter Elizabeth Boott (1846–88), had studied here under Wilhelm von Diez. In 1878 Duveneck opened his own school in Munich. His pupils, who were described as the 'Duveneck boys', included Otto Henry Bacher, Robert Frederick Blum, Theodore M. Wendel, George Edward Hopkins, John Alexander White, Julius Rolshoven, Charles Abel Corwin, and Harper Pennington.

487 **Roman type [...] glorified *contadina* [...] daggers into her head:** A *contadina* is an Italian peasant woman, regularly featured in English and American writings about Italy. Commenting on the phrase 'like a dagger in a contadina's hair' in *The Ambassadors* (Ch. 28), Nicola Bradbury notes a passage towards the end of Hawthorne's novel set in Rome, *The Marble Faun* (1860), in which Kenyon comes across 'many a contadina [...] [with] a silver comb or long stiletto among her glossy hair' (Ch. 49) (*CFHJ* 18, pp. 436–7, note 238). In the version of this tale for the *New York Edition*, 'contadina' is replaced by 'Trasteverina', a woman from Trastevere, a popular area of Rome, on the right bank of the Tiber. The Trasteverine, like the *contadine*, were perceived as very picturesque due to their particular costumes.

488 **Werther's Charlotte:** Reference to a scene in Goethe's novel *The Sorrows of Young Werther* (*Die Leiden des jungen Werthers*, 1774; translated by R. D. Boylan), where Werther, the protagonist, records 'the most charming spectacle I had ever witnessed. Six children, from eleven to two years old, were running about the hall, and surrounding a lady of middle height, with a lovely figure, dressed in a robe of simple white, trimmed with pink ribbons. She was holding a rye loaf in her hand, and was cutting slices for the little ones all around, in proportion to their age and appetite. She performed her task in a graceful and affectionate manner; each claimant awaiting his turn with outstretched hands, and boisterously shouting his thanks' (letter of 16 June). He falls in love with this beautiful young woman, Charlotte (Lotte), despite knowing beforehand that she is already engaged to a man named Albert, eleven years her senior. Werther finally kills himself. The analogies implied here seem to be between Albert and Capadose, Charlotte and Mrs Capadose, and Lyon and Werther. For Goethe in James's fiction, see note 29 to 'Pandora'.

489 **Thackeray's Ethel Newcome:** In William Makepeace Thackeray's novel *The Newcomes* (1853–5), the aspiring painter Clive (son of the protagonist Colonel Thomas) falls in love with his cousin Ethel, whose family are bankers. The narrator's friend the old Major Pendennis comments of Clive's

aspirations that he 'could no more get that girl than he could marry one of the royal princesses. Mark my words, they intend Miss Newcome for Lord Kew. Those banker fellows are wild after grand marriages' (Ch. 24). On the relation between the female protagonist of James's story and Ethel Newcome, see Bo Jeffares, *The Artist in Nineteenth Century English Fiction* (Atlantic Highlands, NJ: Humanities Press, 1979), p. 181, note 47. The first chapter of *Notes of a Son and Brother* (1914) ends with a fond memory of James's childhood sense of Thackeray in serial form: 'I witnessed, [...] with all my senses, young as I was, the never-to-be-equalled degree of difference made, for what may really be called the world-consciousness happily exposed to it, by the prolonged "coming-out" of The Newcomes, yellow number by number, and could take the general civilised partic-ipation in the process for a sort of basking in the light of distinction' (*NSBMY* 21–2). Other references to *The Newcomes* in James's fiction can be found in *Roderick Hudson*, 'Daniel Deronda: A Conversation' (1876), *Watch and Ward*, and *The Wings of the Dove*.

490 **he had come a cropper**: The phrase is here applied literally to denote 'a heavy fall' during a hunt, as first identified in the popular novelist of the hunting world, R. S. Surtees, in 1858 (*OED*); the 1874 revision of *Hotten's Slang Dictionary* offers, more metaphorically, '*Cropper*, "to go a cropper", or "to come a cropper", i.e., to fail badly.'

491 **touch and go**: The *OED* records this as in use already in the mid-sixteenth century: '*to touch and go*: to touch for an instant and immediately go away or pass on; (frequently figurative) to deal with briefly or cursorily'.

492 **jungle fever**: '[*J*]*ungle-fever* n. a form of remittent fever caused by the miasma of a jungle; the hill-fever of India' (*OED*).

493 **the ghouls**: First used in English literature in 1786, in the Orientalist Gothic novel *Vathek* by William Beckford (1760–1844), the word draws here on the literal sense of 'An evil spirit supposed (in Muslim countries) to rob graves and prey on human corpses' (*OED*). On 8 April 1895 the fall of Oscar Wilde would lead James to write to his friend Gosse of 'this gulf of obscenity over which the ghoulish public hangs and gloats' (*Selected Letters of Henry James to Edmund Gosse 1882–1915: A Literary Friendship*, edited by Rayburn S. Moore (Baton Rouge, LA: Louisiana State University Press, 1988), p. 126).

494 **vine-leaves and a leopard skin—a kind of Bacchante**: A follower of the Greek god Bacchus (or Dionysus), also known as a Maenad. Bacchus and

the Bacchantes were popular art subjects from ancient to modern times. In a letter to his painter friend, John La Farge (20 June 1869), James wrote of his appreciation of Titian's *Bacchus and Ariadne* (1520–3), exhibited at the National Gallery: 'Then they have the great Titian—the Bacchus & Ariadne—a thing to go barefoot to see' (*CLHJ 1855–1872* 2:35). In the short story 'Travelling Companions' (1870), the two protagonists Mr Brooke and Miss Evans, while on a visit to the Ducal Palace in Venice, discuss a painting with the same subject, this time by Tintoretto (*Bacchus, with Ariadne Crowned by Venus, c.* 1578). In Chapter 19 of *A Small Boy and Others* (1913) James recalls his early exposure to the figure of the Bacchante: 'the classic marble bust on a pedestal between the two back windows, the figure, a part of the figure, of a lady with her head crowned with vine-leaves and her hair disposed with a laxity that was emulated by the front of her dress, [...] This image was known and admired among us as the Bacchante; she had come to us straight from an American studio in Rome, and I see my horizon flush again with the first faint dawn of conscious appreciation, or in other words of the critical spirit, while two or three of the more restrictive friends of the house find our marble lady very "cold" for a Bacchante. Cold indeed she must have been—quite as of the tombstone temperament; but that objection would drop if she might only be called a Nymph, since nymphs were mild and moderate, and since discussion of a work of art mainly hung in those days on that issue of the producible *name*' (*SBOC* p. 210–1). In 1888 the *Magazine of Art* published a print of a painting called *A Priestess of Bacchus*, a portrait of a lady in vine leaves and tiger skin, by the English artist John Collier (1850–1934). Collier's *Maenads*, from the same period, depicts numerous underdressed Maenads hunting, in leopard skins and with leopards on leads. See also note 379 to 'The Aspern Papers'.

495 **the Grand Duke of Silberstadt-Schreckenstein:** The imaginary realm of Silberstadt-Schreckenstein features in James's earlier novel *The Europeans*, where Eugenia, the Baroness Münster, is married to Prince Adolf, younger brother of 'the Reigning Prince' (see *CFHJ* 4, note 33, pp. 165–6).

496 **pagan head:** See note 487.

497 **the principal thing that had happened to him was that he had never married:** This seems to anticipate the central idea of James's 1903 tale 'The Beast in the Jungle', where John Marcher 'had been the man of his time, the man, to whom nothing on earth was to have happened'.

498 **Two hundred pounds**: The approximately equivalent purchasing power in 2021 would be £25,000: see note 263 to 'The Path of Duty'.

499 **Everina Brant**: An uncommon name, to say the least, and one that James appears not to have used anywhere else in his fiction, "Everina" echoes the middle name of the Anton Capadose who wrote to James in inquiry about his use of the name "Capadose." His "Everdinus" inevitably recalls "Everina," a name that, in James's artist's economy, fits rather closely a wife whose constancy to her lying husband meets successfully every challenge put to it by James' scheming portrait-painter narrator. / The point of all this [...] is that the Capadoses, Sephardic Jews all, were originally Portuguese' (George Monteiro, 'New Christians and "The Liar"', in *Reading Henry James: A Critical Perspective on Selected Works* (Jefferson, NC: McFarland, 2016), pp. 79–92, 88–9. Brant is a kind of goose (also known as a 'brent goose'), Brant Broughton is a village in Lincolnshire, and Brant is a not uncommon last name: Isabella Brant (1591–1626) was the first wife of the painter Peter Paul Rubens.

500 **a suit of crimson foulard**: A spectacular and evidently fashionable outfit made out of '[a] thin flexible material of silk, or of silk mixed with cotton' (*OED*), more than a regulation 'smoking-jacket', into which gentleman could be expected to change after dinner.

501 **the period of colour [...] a Venetian of the sixteenth century**: A reference to the colourful clothes of Venetians in that century, as can be seen in the portraits by Titian (c. 1490–1576), Tintoretto (c. 1518–94), and Veronese (1528–88), renowned for their use of colour.

502 **the haunted room**: A predictable feature of a house in which the spirit of Sheridan Le Fanu is at home (see note 476). James exploited the Gothic theme of the haunted room in works such as 'The Ghostly Rental' (1876), 'Owen Wingrave' (1893), and 'The Jolly Corner' (1908).

503 **Charing Cross**: A junction named after the Eleanor Cross that was erected to commemorate Edward I's wife Eleanor of Castile, who died in 1290, and destroyed under Cromwell in 1647, in central London, off the Strand close to Trafalgar Square, cited by Lyon for its ordinariness or even banality. James particularly disliked the railway station at Charing Cross, opened in 1864. In 'London' (1888) he wrote: 'the Charing Cross railway-station, placed where it is, is a national crime' (*EL* 39).

504 **rather "creepy"**: The inverted commas indicate the comparative novelty of the adjective used in this sense; the *OED*'s first citation is from 1883. James

employs it again to describe Paramore, the 'impoverished Jacobean house' in 'Owen Wingrave', as 'shabby and remarkably "creepy"' (Ch. 2); and the hero's confidante in 'The Two Faces' (1901) says 'I feel creepy' (Ch. 3).

505   **Dean of Rockingham**: This title is fictitious. There is a small village called Rockingham in Northamptonshire, famous for the relics of a Norman castle built in the eleventh century (Rockingham Castle), and Lord Rockingham was a Whig prime minister twice in the eighteenth century, but the title died out with him in 1782.

506   **Eton**: The prestigious English school, founded in 1440 by King Henry VI and located in Eton, near Windsor. James provided a description of a visit to Eton in 'The Suburbs of London', published in the *Galaxy* (December 1877): 'I approached it with a certain sentimental agitation, for I had always had a theory that the great English schools are delightful places to have been to. [...] The courts of the old college, empty and silent in the eventide; the mellow light on the battered walls; the great green meadows, where the little clear-voiced boys made gigantic shadows; the neighborhood of the old cathedral city, with its admirable church, where early kings are buried—all this seemed to make a charming background for boyish lives, and to offer a provision of tender, picturesque memories to the grown man who has passed through it' (*CTW1* 283).

507   **put to grass**: Applied to persons retired from the world of work and regular commitments, on the analogy with horses.

508   **handle the long bow**: A colloquialism meaning 'to make exaggerated statements' (*OED*). See also 'to draw such a bow', note 515.

509   **the canker within the rose**: An image favoured by Shakespeare, as for example in Sonnet 95: 'How sweet and lovely dost thou make the shame, / Which like a canker in the fragrant rose'.

510   **by her quality's altering [...] the alteration**: A faint reminiscence of one of Shakespeare's most famous sonnets: 'Let me not to the marriage of true minds / Admit impediments; love is not love / Which alters when it alteration finds' (Sonnet 116).

511   **the liar platonic**: The phrasing draws on Shakespeare's *As You Like It* 5.4.85-7, where Touchstone explains his quarrel over 'a certain courtier's beard': 'I durst go no further than the Lie Circumstantial, nor he durst not give me the Lie Direct; and so we measur'd swords and parted.'

512   **art for art**: The slogan of the Aesthetic movement, based on Théophile Gautier's 'l'art pour l'art', often translated as 'art for art's sake', which took

resonant form in the 1870s in Walter Pater's *The Renaissance* (1873), especially its provocative 'Conclusion', and by the time of 'The Liar' was strongly influenced by Pater's paradoxical Oxford follower Oscar Wilde. In 'The Author of "Beltraffio"' (1884) the narrator recognizes the writer Mark Ambient's pioneering pursuit of beauty in the novel form: 'Nothing had been done in that line from the point of view of art for art' (Part I). See note 206.

513   **an author's order**: A complimentary ticket.

514   **six rows deep**: An odd metaphor to employ for the depth of meaning in a painting; in more common usage it draws on the sense of an organized mass formation, such as an audience in the theatre or troops on a battlefield.

515   **to draw such a bow**: See note 508.

516   **the season [...] the general dispersal**: See note 277 to 'The Path of Duty' and note 571 to 'The Modern Warning'.

517   **the Academy**: The Royal Academy of Painting, Sculpture, and Architecture, commonly referred to as the Academy, founded by King George III in 1768 and located from 1868 in Burlington House on Piccadilly in London. James often wrote on the Royal Academy exhibitions. See for example 'The Picture Season in London' (1877) and 'The London Exhibitions – the Royal Academy' (1878) (*CWAD1* 243–67 and 287–93 respectively). James progressively came to dislike the exhibitions at the Academy, praising other kinds of venue like the Grosvenor Gallery (see the series of reviews between 1877 and 1882 in *CWAD1* 234–42, 280–92, 304–18, 339–55).

518   **magnificent Moroni at the National Gallery**: James is here referring to *The Tailor* (*Il Tagliapanni*, 1565–70), a late work by the Italian portraitist Giovanni Battista Moroni (1520?–78). In 1877 James praised Joshua Reynolds's *Portrait of Two Gentlemen* in the National Gallery by saying that 'before this beautiful work the depressed Anglo Saxon, wandering from the presence of the Moronis, hard by [one of them *Il Tagliapanni*], may hold up his head' (*CWAD1* 218). In *The Tragic Muse* (1890) the painter Nick Dormer considers Moroni along with Van Dyck as an unsurpassable master.

519   **St. John's Wood**: An area of London at the north-west end of Regent's Park. In 1855–6 the James family resided in this quiet and leafy area, full of secluded villas, at 10 Marlborough Place. When he returned to London from the United States in 1883, James planned to move from Piccadilly to this district, which featured many artists' studios, particularly in the period of the St John's Wood Clique or Group (1869–90), of which James's friend George du Maurier (1834–96) was a member, along with

painters including William Frederick Yeames (1835–1918), David Wilkie Wynfield (1837–87), and Frederick Walker (1840–75). 'They were subject painters with a preference for domestic, pathetic or frivolous situations; most lived in and around St. John's Wood' (Caroline Dakers, *The Holland Park Circle: Artists and Victorian Society* (New Haven, CT: Yale University Press, 1999), p. 283, note 47). In a letter to his friend Elizabeth Boott dated 14 October 1883, James wrote: 'I am in treaty for a small house in St. John's Wood' (*CLHJ 1883–1884* I: 243). However, James abandoned the idea, as he wrote in another letter to Boott from 3 Bolton Street, dated 11 December: 'I am completely re-domiciled here—though not in St. John's Wood—having at the last moment changed my mind about that move and given up the house. It was a perfect little residence, with a pretty garden & a most commodious & agreeable interior—it had once belonged to a painter and the studio had become the dining room, a really noble apartment; but the place was too far from the centre of things & it was revealed to me in a dream that I shld. spend 1/2 the time on the roads. So that, *per ora* [for now], having resisted that temptation I shall remain in these after all very comfortable & central rooms' (*CLHJ 1883–1884* 1:276–277). In *The Tragic Muse* the actress Miriam Rooth resides at a fictitious address in this area ('Balaklava Place, St. John's Wood'). James chose a picture of a house in St John's Wood for the frontispiece of Volume VIII of the *New York Edition* (*The Tragic Muse*, Part Two). On painters' studios see Rosella Mamoli Zorzi, ' "A studio was a place to learn to see": Henry James, the London 'Picture Sundays' and the Artists' Studios", in *American Phantasmagoria. Modes of Representation in US Culture*, Rosella Mamoli Zorzi and Simone Francescato (eds.) (Venice, Supernova, 2017), 139–172.

520 **a dress with many bugles**: A bugle is 'A tube-shaped glass bead, usually black, used to ornament wearing apparel' (*OED*).

521 **unpractised in the *h***: The dropping of the 'h' is a recognized sign of lower-class or uneducated speech. One may think of Eliza Doolittle's way of speaking in George Bernard Shaw's play *Pygmalion* (1912).

522 **Mortimer Terrace Mews, Notting 'ill** : This place is fictitious. Mortimer Terrace is located in the London borough of Camden. A mews was originally a 'court, street, or yard with stables, coach-houses, and accommodation for servants, at the rear of London town-houses', though many have now been converted into homes. (See James Stevens Curl, *A Dictionary of Architecture and Landscape Architecture* (Oxford: Oxford University Press, 2007), p. 479.) Notting Hill is an area of London close to the north-western corner of Kensington Gardens, and figures as a setting in James's story

'Nona Vincent' (1892). Charles Warren Adams's *The Notting Hill Mystery*, thought to be the first detective story of novel length to have appeared in English, had appeared in 1862–3 and was illustrated by George Du Maurier.

523 **it's the Mews**: See note 522.

524 **picked up their form**: A colloquial use of 'form' to mean 'style' or 'appearance', as when Millicent Henning asks Hyacinth Robinson, in *The Princess Casamassima* (Ch. 5), 'is *that* your form?' (*CFHJ* 9, p. 46).

525 **bottle of vitriol**: Often used figuratively to mean '[v]irulence or acrimony of feeling or utterance' (*OED*), 'vitriol' is a sulphate of metal with fierce corrosive properties. It frequently featured as an instrument of violence in writing of the time, as for example in George Gissing's *The Nether World* (1889) and Robert Louis Stevenson's *The Ebb-Tide* (1894).

526 **Moorish rug**: Evidence of the Oriental taste in the decoration of interiors typically displayed by late nineteenth-century British artists and painters. A major example of this trend can be found in the Arab Hall (1877–9) in the London home of Frederic Leighton (1830–96), a room furnished with an impressive collection of Islamic art. Lyon has already noted that the St John's Wood streets 'looked slightly Oriental' (401). On painters' studios and houses see in particular Charlotte Gere, *Artistic Circles: Design and Decoration in the Aesthetic Movement* (London: V&A Publishing, 2010).

527 **a small Eastern dagger […] dragged the instrument down**: With this further Oriental object James seems to be consciously recalling his own early tale, 'The Story of a Masterpiece' (1868), in which a painting telling a painful truth about a person's character is also savaged: 'He looked about him with an angry despair, and his eye fell on a long, keen poinard, given him by a friend who had bought it in the East, and which lay as an ornament on his mantel shelf. He seized it and thrust it, with barbarous glee, straight into the lovely face of the image. He dragged it downward, and made a long fissure in the living canvas. Then, with half a dozen strokes, he wantonly hacked it across. The act afforded him an immense relief.' On 4 May 1914 a portrait of James by John Singer Sargent was itself savaged at the Royal Academy's summer exhibition, in the course of a spate of attacks on works of art by militant suffragettes who wanted to show that nothing was safe as long as women did not have the right to vote.

528 **Marlborough Road station**: Marlborough Road is a now disused London Underground Railway station, the first section of which was inaugurated in 1863. It was opened in 1868 on the Metropolitan & St John's Wood

Railway – the first northward branch extension from Baker Street to Swiss Cottage of the Metropolitan Railway (now the Metropolitan Line) – and remained in use until 1939. James was quick to experience London's new 'underground railway' on his first solo visit to Britain. In a letter to his sister from London (10 March 1869), he praised this 'marvellous phenomenon—ploughing along in a vast circle thro' the bowels of London, & giving you egress to the upper earth in magnificent stations, at a number of convenient points' (*CLHJ 1855–1872* 1:234).

'The Modern Warning'

529 **Macarthy Grice**: In 1880 James had met Justin McCarthy (1830–1912), an Irish nationalist writer and politician, recently elected as an MP. He may have in mind the sense of 'grice' as 'A pig, esp. a young pig, a sucking pig; †*occasionally* and *spec*. in *Heraldry*, a wild boar' (*OED*). In *The Times* of 21 September 1887 he might have read an item, 'The Railway Outrage', about the violent attempted rape of a young schoolteacher by a 'puddler' or iron-worker named George Grice (11).

530 **Liverpool**: Together with Southampton, the usual port for passenger ships to and from America in the nineteenth century, familiar both to James and to his fictional characters, including Lambert Strether at the start of *The Ambassadors*.

531 **Cadenabbia**: A village on the western bank of Lake Como, in northern Italy, quite well known in the nineteenth century, visited by royalty, poets, musicians, and tourists, including Queen Victoria, Longfellow, and Verdi. 'A shady avenue leads to the *Villa Carlotta* [...] belonging to the Duke of Saxe Meiningen, which contains groups of Cupid and Psyche [...] by Canova; and bas-reliefs [...] by Thorwaldsen', as Murray's 1877 guide specifies (*Murray's 1877*, 147). James stayed at the Hotel Belle-Vue in Cadenabbia at the end of August 1869, on his enchanted first visit to Italy: see note 545 and note 354 to 'Louisa Pallant'. James described Cadenabbia and its surrounding area in his essay 'From Chambéry to Milan' (1872): 'I wondered [...] where I had seen it all before—the pink-walled villas gleaming through their shrubberies of orange and oleander, the mountains shimmering in the hazy light like so many breasts of doves, the constant presence of the melodious Italian voice. Where, indeed, but at the Opera [...]?' (*TS* 83–4).

Cadenabbia, Bellagio, and Colico are also mentioned in the essay *The Splügen* (1874; *CTW2* 657–8).

532 **most of the people [...] being out of town, the middle of August was a bad time:** Because the London Season was over around the end of June, and 'the general dispersal', referred to in 'The Liar', would have taken place (see note 516). See notes 277 and 281 to 'The Path of Duty'.

533 **on the steamboat to the other end of the lake:** Probably to the north end of the lake, to the village of Colico, by way of Bellagio. Several steamers departed daily, calling at Cernobbio, Cadenabbia, and several other stops en route to Colico, according to the Murray handbooks.

534 **frockcoat:** Man's fitted coat with knee-length skirts.

535 **the three Graces:** The Charites in Greek mythology, represented as nude women. Euphrosyne, Thalia, Aglaia, as they are named, were the daughters of Zeus, and signified charm, beauty, and creativity. They were represented by such famous painters and sculptors as Raphael (1483–1520) and Antonio Canova (1757–1822), often embracing.

536 **panjandarum:** More usually spelt 'panjandrum'; '(A mock title for) a mysterious (freq. imaginary) personage of great power or authority; a pompous or pretentious official; a self-important person in authority' (*OED*).

537 **K.C.B. [...] M.P.:** Knight Commander of the Bath, a British order of chivalry created by George I in 1725. 'The Bath' refers to the purifying ritual used in mediaeval times to create a knight. M.P.: Member of Parliament.

538 **Philadelphia:** The largest city in Pennsylvania, founded by the Quaker William Penn in 1682, and the place where the First and Second Continental Congresses met, leading to the signing of the Declaration of Independence in 1776. For this reason, it is often considered the cradle of American democracy. James devoted a chapter to the city in *The American Scene* (Ch. 9), praising its historical past, which provided a contrast to the 'bristling' New York, Chicago, or even Boston. 'Philadelphia, manifestly, was beyond any other American city, a *society*, and was going to show as such, as a thoroughly confirmed and settled one—which fact became the key, precisely, to its extension on one plane, and to its having no pretext for bristling' (*CTW1* 582).

539 **it's not the custom, down here, for young girls to walk round—at night**: James often underlines the different social codes for young girls in America and Europe. 'Daisy Miller' is the most obvious example of an American girl ignoring this difference, carelessly walking with men both in broad daylight and at night, and being judged for this.

540 **something stippled and retouched**: Terms from painting. To 'stipple' is to 'produce gradations of shade or colour in a design by means of dots or small spots'; to 'retouch' is to 'improve or repair the appearance of (a painting, composition, photographic negative or print, etc.) by small alterations or fresh touches; to touch up' (*OED*), suggesting that Sir Rufus looks like a work of art.

541 **the ditch**: In this case the Atlantic Ocean. It is more often used to indicate the English Channel.

542 **some rocks ahead**: Maritime expression referring to difficult sailing; here it is used metaphorically of the American future, perhaps with reference to the Gilded Age and the growing power of corporations, the depression of 1882–5, the widespread strikes by organized labour, public unrest epitomized by the Haymarket Riot in Chicago of May 1886, the rise of political extremism or at least anxiety about it, issues of race and mass immigration, and the corruption of democratic politics, among other concerns.

543 **Lady Bolitho**: This is a Cornish name belonging to a family of bankers, but it was probably best known at the time of the tale through the sporting prowess of William Bolitho (1862–1919), a first-class cricketer who toured America with an English team in 1885.

544 **the Engadine**: The Engadine Valley, a beautiful mountainous region of Switzerland, famously cold even in summer, in which the well-known skiing resort of Saint Moritz is located. The Upper Engadine, called by Baedeker 'the most attractive part of the valley' (*Baedeker's Switzerland* (1879), p. 373), is where Ned Rosier first encounters Pansy Osmond in *The Portrait of a Lady*: 'He passed a month in the Upper Engadine and encountered at Saint Moritz a charming young girl' (Ch. 36 *CFHJ* 7, p. 345). James had planned to go to the Engadine with his Aunt Kate and sister Alice in 1872, but abandoned the plan ('we are letting the Engadine project die a natural death' (*CLHJ 1872–1876* 1:66)).

545 **go on to Venice**: As James himself had done on his first solo trip to Europe in the late summer of 1869, making his way from Switzerland to Venice,

'via Lake Maggiore and Lake Como, Milan, Pavia, Brescia, Verona and Vicenza' (*LL* 24).

546 **another winter in Rome**: James had known winters in Rome, on his visit to Europe in 1869–70 and more extensively in 1872–4, for part of which he was joined by his brother William, who had come to Europe to regain his health.

547 **the London *Times***: See note 284 to 'The Path of Duty'.

548 **'The situation in South Africa'**: Tension between English- and Dutch-born settlers in South Africa was severe between the first Anglo-Boer War (1880–81), in the Transvaal, and the second, more decisive war (1899–1902). On 21 December 1886 the anti-imperialist historian of the Zulus, Frances Ellen Colenso (1849–87), had published a powerful letter in *The Times* condemning British policy as tacitly condoning the seizing of Zulu lands by Boer settlers: 'For every step in this wanton destruction of a race, England, through her representatives, is directly responsible' (14).

549 **she had acquired them by force and fraud**: The phrase 'force and fraud' had a specific application at the time to England's treatment of Ireland in the existing Union, as denounced by the Liberal leader William Gladstone on 12 June 1886 in his 'manifesto' for the impending election: his Tory opponents falsely claimed the title of Unionists, he said, as 'the Union which they refuse to modify is in its present shape a paper union, obtained by force and fraud, and never sanctioned or accepted by the Irish nation'. Though feeling that 'Home Rule [for Ireland] must come', James told his brother William on 13 June 1886, he regarded Gladstone's conduct as 'high political egotism' (*CLHJ 1884–1886* 2:118).

550 **the lake of Como**: Beautiful lake in northern Italy, famous in Italian literature: 'Quel ramo del lago di Como' ('That branch of the Como lake') are the opening words of Alessandro Manzoni's novel, *I Promessi Sposi* (*The Betrothed*, first published in 1827). James figured it as the setting for 'novels of "immoral" tendency' (e.g. Stendhal's *La Chartreuse de Parme*), but realized that 'even the Lake of Como has been revised and improved; the fondest prejudices yield to time; it gives one somehow a sense of an aspiringly high tone' (*CTW2* 374). More reflections on Como are to be found in 'The Splügen' (*CTW2* 657–8).

551 **the courage of his prejudices**: Ironic perversion of the more common phrase, 'the courage of his convictions'.

552 **a thousand international marriages**: A leading feature of the closer ties between Britain and post-bellum America in the later decades of the nineteenth century, such as those between Jennie Jerome and the Tory politician Lord Randolph Churchill in 1874 and between Sara Sedgwick (1839–1902) and William Darwin (1839–1914), son of Charles, in 1877. See Kathleen Burk, 'Anglo-American Marital Relations: 1870–1945', in *Old World, New World: The Story of Britain and America* (London: Little, Brown, 2007), pp. 529–59, in which Burke states that 'By 1914, sixty peers, and forty younger sons of peers, had married American women' (p. 536).

553 **Tory**: Belonging to the Conservative Party, one of the two major parliamentary and political parties in Great Britain from 1689 onwards, originally opposed to the Whigs but by this date to the Liberals. James, associated with the Liberal Party by his membership of the Reform Club in London, wrote to Grace Norton on 16 July 1886 declaring 'I cannot weep for the downfall of the G.O.M. ['Grand Old Man' = Gladstone]' in the election, which the divided Liberals lost, but telling her, 'Don't think I am turning into a heartless Tory, for I am not—in the least. The Tories, as such, are terribly stupid company, & I could never long live with them' (*CLHJ 1884–1886* 2:133).

554 **salaamed and kowtowed**: Forms of salutation indicating respect and submission, associated with India and China respectively – and ironically invoked by a character associated with British imperialism.

555 **of Irish descent**: Presumably of Irish Catholic descent, such as to justify, historically, Macarthy Grice's hostility to the English. Henry James was himself of Presbyterian Irish descent; his paternal grandfather, William James of Albany (1771–1832), had emigrated to the United States from Bailieborough, County Cavan, in the 1790s. See notes 557 and 582.

556 **If the Yankee were to let me off the Paddy would come down!**: Originally derogatory colloquialisms for American ('Yankee') and Irish ('Paddy'), respectively.

557 **Lady Laura Fitzgibbon**: As Agatha notes, 'she wasn't of our kind!' Sir Rufus's connections are not with the impoverished Irish seeking a new life in America, but with the dominant landowning class, members of the so-called Protestant Ascendancy. For James's complex relations with Ireland and his Irish ancestry, see Colm Tóibín, 'Henry James in Ireland: A Footnote', *Henry James Review*, 30.3 (Fall 2009), 211–22; reprinted in *All a Novelist Needs: Colm*

Tóibín on Henry James, ed. Susan M. Griffin (Baltimore, MD: Johns Hopkins University Press, 2010). See notes 555 and 582.

558 **the south of England:** The south coast had several resorts attracting invalids in search of health, such as Bournemouth. In May 1885 James visited his sister Alice there and began a friendship with Robert Louis Stevenson and his American wife Fanny (see Introduction, pp. xxxvi–xxxvii).

559 **the house [...] in Thirty-seventh street:** Thirty-seventh Street runs west to east in what is now midtown Manhattan, south of Times Square and north of the Empire State Building. From the elegant area of Washington Place, west of Washington Square, where James lived as a child, at the foot of Fifth Avenue, just north of Fourth Street (see note 571), the city spread quickly upwards. By the time J. P. Morgan built his mansion on Madison Avenue at East Thirty-sixth Street in 1882 (now part of the Morgan Library and Museum), in the neighbourhood known as 'Murray Hill', the area had become populated by the wealthy and the upper-middle class.

560 **Bologna:** Mediaeval university city in central Italy. James spent 'three good days' there at the beginning of October 1869, en route from Venice to Florence, describing Bologna to his sister Alice as 'rich in all great gifts' (*CLHJ 1855–1872* 2:128). He was there again briefly in June 1874, to enjoy a clash of 'two festas', one civil and one religious – 'the first time an Italian festa had worn to my eyes that warmth of coloring, that pictorial confusion, which tradition promises' ('Ravenna' (1874); *TS* 328).

561 **the very midst of the Parliamentary session:** The length of a parliamentary session varied. In 1881 it lasted from 6 January to 25 August, while in 1882 it lasted longer, from 7 February to 2 December (with a break of two months from mid-August to mid-October). In 1883 and 1884 it only lasted from February to August, but in 1884 it reopened on 23 October to last until 14 August 1885. In 1886 it lasted from 12 January to 25 September, with an interval between 25 June and 5 August. See note 281 to 'The Path of Duty'.

562 **deserted him for the sake of an English title:** See Introduction, p. xliv.

563 **big blue-books:** 'Official reports of Parliament and the Privy Council [...] issued in a dark blue paper cover' (*OED*).

564 **conservatives had come into power:** The Conservatives under the Marquess of Salisbury had won electoral victories over Gladstone's Liberals and formed governments, briefly in 1885 and more durably a year

later in 1886 (until 1892). Lord Randolph Churchill (see note 552) became chancellor of the Exchequer.

565 **permanent official:** That is, a civil servant who continues in post irrespective of the party in power, and is therefore 'supposed to have no active political opinions', as the narrator will shortly comment.

566 **made a peer on his retirement:** Ennoblement and elevation to the House of Lords in the form of a life (as opposed to hereditary) peerage, a recognized reward for political service.

567 **married into a tremendous Tory 'set':** See Introduction, p. xliii.

568 **feelings that she was not prepared to publish on the housetops:** Cf. Luke 12:3: 'that which ye have spoken in the ear in closets shall be proclaimed upon the housetops' (KJV). Cf. 'The Birthplace' (1903): 'he was not to proclaim on the housetops any point at which he might be weak'.

569 **penitentiaries and chambers of commerce:** In the nineteenth century it was quite usual to visit penitentiaries, prisons, and hospitals, as for instance Charles Dickens did during his first American trip in 1842. Sir Rufus's enthusiasm for inspecting institutions is characteristic of the 1880s in Britain, when Charles Booth (1840–1916), Sidney Webb (1859–1947), his wife Beatrice (née Potter, 1858–1943), and others were developing new methods of social research based on statistical analysis, usually with a more liberal or even proto-socialist agenda than Sir Rufus and his Tory 'set' would approve of. However, Sir Rufus's plans for 'a book about America' (p. 453) smack more of Dickens's critical and controversial *American Notes* (1842). James was very aware of the work of his Irish friend, the eminent Liberal politician and author James Bryce (1838–1922), whose epoch-making three-volume study, *The American Commonwealth*, was a conscious revision of Alexis de Tocqueville's *Democracy in America* (1835, 1840) and was published in the same year as this story, 1888.

570 **Indian summer:** Name given to a period of warm weather during the early autumn/fall season, characterized by clear skies and beautiful light.

571 **Washington Square [...] Fifth Avenue:** The James family used to live in Washington Place, on the western side of Washington Square, as James remembers in *A Small Boy and Others* (1913, Ch. 4; see note 559); revisiting it in *The American Scene*, he finds the house of his birthplace 'ruthlessly suppressed', the effect of which was 'of having been amputated of half my history' (Ch. 2, 'New York Revisited'). The stretch of the Fifth Avenue

between Washington Square and Fourteenth Street was part of his child-hood memories and freedom.

572 **the American humour**: James's famous account of the bareness of American social life in his controversial study *Hawthorne* is qualified by the comment that 'The American knows that a good deal remains; what it is that remains—that is his secret, his joke, as one may say. It would be cruel, in this terrible denudation, to deny him the consolation of his national gift, that "American humour" of which of late years we have heard so much' (Ch. 2; *LC1* 352).

573 **up the Hudson [...] to West Point**: The river west of Manhattan, flowing through the Hudson Valley. West Point, the US military academy, founded in 1802, is located on the west bank of the Hudson, in Orange County, New York. Peter Collister comments on the nostalgia James felt for the Hudson steamboat (*SBOC* 146, note 318), pointing to his appreciation of American river-steamers that 'have had, from the earliest time, for the true *raffiné*, their peculiar note of romance' (*American Scene*, Ch. 3: 'New York and the Hudson: A Spring Impression'). Looking at the river from the train, James comments: 'Its face was veiled, for the most part, in a mist of premature spring heat, an atmosphere draping it indeed in luminous mystery, hanging it with sun-shot silver and minimizing any happy detail, any element of the definite, from which the romantic effect might here and there have gained an accent.' The picture becomes 'a constant combination of felicities', even without those 'accents' or details, blurred by the fast journey of the train (*CTW1* 479).

574 **Canada, the Mississippi, the Rocky Mountains and California [...] New York [...] Boston [...] Philadelphia and Washington**: Sir Rufus's trip takes in the northern American continent (Canada), the great Mississippi River (the mid-west and south), the majestic chain of mountains in the western US (the Rockies), and the most western state (California). James was to visit the south and the west in his trip to the United States in 1904–5, from which *The American Scene*, including some chapters devoted to the south, was generated. Sir Rufus also visits four of the cities on which James was to base chapters in this work.

575 **Mrs. Eugene [...] Mrs. Ripley [...] [...] Mrs. Redwood [...] Mrs. Long**: James had published the tale 'Eugene Pickering' in 1874; Ripley was the middle name of James's failed publisher James R. Osgood, whose financial collapse had made *The Bostonians* a disaster for him in 1886; the

Redwood Library was a place of resort for the young James in Newport (on 18 November [1859] he wrote to his friend T. S. Perry from Geneva, 'How is the Redwood getting along; I miss it very much for there is no place of the kind here' (*CLHJ 1855–1872* 1:19)); James would name a character Gilbert Long in *The Sacred Fount* (1901).

576 **write a book about America:** See Introduction, pp. lxxxv–xxxvi.

577 **reading lectures to other nations:** James may have been recalling his friend Matthew Arnold's controversial lecture tour to America in 1883–4, of which he wrote to Grace Norton on 14 November 1883, 'I take much interest in poor Matt. Arnold's career, & fear that it won't be brilliant. Have you seen, heard, heeded, scorned, evaded—& invited—him?—I am very fond of him, & if he is more or less ridiculous over there shall love him the more' (*LL* 149).

578 **Grosvenor Crescent:** The elegant eighteenth-century street in Belgravia, central London, joining Belgrave Square to Hyde Park Corner. Grosvenor Place, of which we hear a few pages later (p. 461), is the large street skirting Buckingham Palace Gardens and intersecting with Grosvenor Crescent at Hyde Park Corner. In James's novella 'A London Life', which began publication the same month as 'Two Countries' first appeared (June 1888), the young American Laura Wing's unbridled sister, Selina Berrington, and her boorish husband Lionel, reside in Grosvenor Place.

579 **on the stocks:** Figurative, a work being written. A ship on the stocks is a ship 'supported while in process of construction' (*OED*).

580 **"lobbying":** A relatively recent coinage at the time of writing, originating in the United States. To lobby is to 'influence (members of a house of legislature) in the exercise of their legislative functions by frequenting the lobby. Also, to procure the passing of (a measure) through Congress by means of such influence' (*OED*; first citation is from 1837).

581 **"shunted":** Another comparatively recent expression drawing on the movement of a train from a main line to a sidetrack; the *OED*'s first citation of its figurative use ('to push aside or out of the way; to side-track; also, to get rid of') is from 1858.

582 **her Celtic cousins [...] the blessed English dispensation:** Immigrants from Ireland to the United States in the colonial era were mainly Protestant Scots-Irish from Ulster, like Henry James's grandfather, but after the Great Famine of the 1840s (1845–52) the massive tide of

577

immigrants mainly consisted of impoverished Catholics. The English were accused of calling the potato blight that contributed to the famine 'a dispensation of Providence', but the consequences were clearly the result of deliberate actions, such as the Encumbered Estates Act (1849). This allowed the auctioning off of estates in debt, which were then bought by English land speculators. Irish tenant farmers were either evicted or charged enormous rent prices. See notes 549 and 557.

583 **Tennyson [...] the little rift within the lute**: An allusion to the lines in the 'Song' in Tennyson's long poem *Vivien*, in *Idylls of the King* (first published 1859), where 'wily' Vivien tries to seduce Merlin, following him to Broceliande: 'It is the little rift within the lute, / That by and by will make the music mute, / And ever widening slowly silence all.' The phrase is applied here to the change that Agatha's condemnation of Sir Rufus's book has caused in his love for her. Tennyson's phrase recurs in *The Wings of the Dove* (Book IV, Ch. 8), casting its shadow on the relation between Milly Theale and Kate Croy, and in *The Golden Bowl* (Ch. 22), in an exchange between Prince Amerigo and Charlotte Stant about the crack in the bowl of the title.

584 **in the watches of the night**: See note 189 to 'A New England Winter'.

585 **the hospital, round the corner**: St George's Hospital at Hyde Park Corner, first established in 1733, rebuilt in the middle of the nineteenth century, and active up until 1980, when it was relocated to Tooting. The building is now (from 2015) a luxury hotel, the Lanesborough.

586 **from Euston**: The railway station, founded in 1837, and then developed further, on the same site as the present Euston Station. Euston Station is located directly north of Bloomsbury, on the northern side of Euston Road, in central London. It was the capital's first intercity railway station, opening in 1837 as the terminus of the London and Birmingham Railway. The original station was designed by Philip Hardwick; his son, Philip Charles Hardwick, was responsible for its expansion and the creation of its impressive 'Great Hall', built in the Classical style. The station also featured a famous landmark, the imposing 'Euston Arch', a 72-foot-high Doric propylaeum, at its entrance. The station and its arch were demolished in 1961–2.

587 **it was not by mistake**: See Introduction, p. lxxxvii.

TEXTUAL VARIANTS I

Substantive Variants up to Copy Text

The abbreviation TV1 lists variants in the texts of the tales that precede the copy text; for the first four tales –'Pandora', 'Georgina's Reasons', 'A New England Winter', 'The Path of Duty' – we have also listed the differences between the American and British first book edition (see Textual Introduction, p. xcii).

There are differences in the presentation of these tales in their magazine and volume versions, mainly attributable to publishers' house style. Punctuation is frequently changed: commas disappear; dashes are substituted for commas, semicolons, brackets, and sometimes full stops, and vice versa; commas, semicolons, colons, and full stops are substituted for each other. These changes have not normally been recorded.

Typographical differences also attributable to publishers' house style – such as the capitalization, italicization, or spelling of certain proper names, titles, and words or phrases of foreign origin (such as *café*/café, *table d'hôte*/table d'hôte); differences regarding American and British spelling (honor/honour); abbreviations (haven't/have n't); dates (twentieth/20th); simple inverted commas changed into double inverted commas (or vice versa); indentations before the separation into parts in the magazine editions (Part I, Part II, etc.): these differences have not been recorded. We have however recorded italicizations (when used for emphasis), the change of full stops into exclamation or question marks (and vice versa), and the introduction or deletion of new paragraphs. The symbol § indicates a new paragraph.

Particularly significant excisions and/or additions are discussed in the notes to the tales.

Pandora

> **NYS** 'Pandora', *The New York Sun*, 1 June 1884, 1–2; 8 June 1884, 1–2. (US)
> **AB** *The Author of Beltraffio; Pandora; Georgina's Reasons; The Path of Duty; Four Meetings* (Boston, MA: James R. Osgood & Co., 1885), pp. 81–156.
> A1 (*SR1*) *Stories Revived*, vol. 1, 'The Author of Beltraffio', 'Pandora', 'The Path of Duty', 'A Day of Days', 'A Light Man' (London: Macmillan & Co., 1885), pp. 71–143.

For choice of copy text (A1), see Textual Introduction, pp. xcii–xcii.
When either **NYS** or **AB** is not cited, it is identical with A1.

3.29   for study. The process] **AB** for study. § The process

4.3   organs. § He was an excellent **NYS, AB** organs. He was an excellent

4.17   and that happiness was] **NYS, AB** and happiness was

4.24   demanded. § Count Vogelstein] **NYS** demanded. Count Vogelstein

5.8   this evidence] **NYS, AB** *this* evidence

5.27   so high. § At last] **NYS** so high. At last

5.34   be pretty—he hardly knew] **NYS** be pretty. He hardly knew

6.12   if they would. § It still wanted] **NYS** if they would. It still wanted

6.29   no doubt; it was modesty] **NYS** no doubt. It was modesty

7.4   this author. § In the great] **AB** this author. In the great

7.7   companion-way. In itself] **AB** companion-way. § In itself

7.10   rather pretty. Vogelstein] **AB** rather pretty; Vogelstein

7.36   acts so flagrant] **NYS, AB** arts so flagrant

8.13   his invader] **AB** his aggressor

8.19   That's all right] **NYS** That's all

8.30   we have such a small name] **NYS, AB** we have got such a small name

9.22   see a great deal of them?] **NYS** see plenty of them?; **AB** see at least enough of them?

9.23   did see a great deal] **NYS** did see plenty; **AB** saw a great deal of them

9.33   apprehended for himself. She] **NYS** apprehended for himself; she

10.17 Count Otto. § He could see] **NYS** Count Otto. He could see

10.22 her lips and cheeks moved] **NYS, AB** her lips moved

10.26 leaving among its convolutions] **NYS, AB** having among its convolutions

11.10 arrested. § Mrs. Dangerfield] **NYS** arrested. Mrs. Dangerfield

11.29 the interior. The voyage] **AB** the interior. § The voyage

12.8   almost familiar] **AB** almost fraternal

12.16 for the day. § Her brother] **NYS** for the day. Her brother

12.33 nineteen.] **NYS** 19.

13.25   exposed, lonely, thankful] *NYS, AB* exposed, and thankful

13.28   Vogelstein's imagination. She assured] *NYS* Vogelstein's imagination; she assured

14.1   like the rise in prices, the telephone, the discovery of dynamite] *NYS, AB* like the railway, the telegraph, the discovery of dynamite

14.2   modern life. § It would] *NYS* modern life. It would

14.18   scratched. One morning] *AB* scratched. § One morning

15.3   his attention. § It was] *NYS* his attention. It was

15.19   this prospect] *NYS, AB* this pretext

15.31   was her lover] *NYS, AB* were her lover

15.32   betrothed to him] *NYS, AB* engaged to him

16.15   this extraordinary odyssey] *NYS, AB* this extraordinary pilgrimage

16.35   is very neat] *NYS, AB* is very nice

17.1   Oh, social position!] *NYS, AB* Oh, social position,

17.4   small minority] *AB* small majority

17.6   should she have found it] *AB* should she have got it

17.11   Very what, Count Vogelstein?] *NYS* Very what? Count Vogelstein.

18.13   had had a good deal of sameness.] *NYS* had been "kind of dull."; *AB* had been "rather glassy."

18.21   like that. § He was] *NYS* like that. He was

19.1   Vogelstein's servant, an Englishman (he had taken him for practice in the language) had gone] *NYS, AB* Vogelstein's servant had gone

19.10   Count Vogelstein said] *NYS, AB* Mr. Vogelstein said

19.17   I presume he's] *NYS, AB* I guess he's

19.32   to our country, Count?] *NYS* to our country, sir?

20.11   say a word in] *AB* speak a word of

20.18   the customs-officer] *AB* the agent of the customs

21.2   to his throat. He thanked] *AB* to his throat; he thanked

21.13   I wouldn't do for you] *NYS, AB* I shouldn't do for you

21.18   as I like showing them] *NYS, AB* that I like showing them

21.27   his servant, with a face] *NYS* his English servant with a face] *AB* his English servant, who had a face

21.34	fatherland] *NYS* Fatherland
22.13	what he should do. That absence] *NYS*, *AB* what he should do; that absence
22.18	had become rather familiar] *AB* having become rather familiar
22.19	in Washington—there were] *NYS*, *AB* in Washington. There were
22.38	of newspapers might] *AB* of the newspapers might
23.2	necessary lapses] *NYS*, *AB* necessary errors
23.7	prejudices. Mrs. Bonnycastle] *AB* prejudices.§ Mrs. Bonnycastle
23.19	many of their acquaintance] *NYS*, *AB* many of their acquaintances
23.20	thought it expensive] *NYS*, *AB* thought it pleasant
24.2	invite the President!"] *NYS*, *AB* invite the President."
24.32	in the hall and on] *NYS*, *AB* in the halls and on
24.34	these functionaries] *AB* these latter functionaries
25.19	well in Europe] *NYS*, *AB* well for Europe
25.20	isn't any girl] *NYS*, *AB* isn't *any* girl
25.27	nor thought of her] *NYS*, *AB* or thought of her
25.32	and a great success] *NYS*, *AB* and a great belle
26.7	point the other way] *AB* point another way
26.11	belonging to the brilliant city] *NYS* belonged to the brilliant city
26.26	the daughter of the Days. But] *NYS*, *AB* the daughter of the Days, but
26.27	might see her again] *AB* might behold her again
26.36	account for. § He wandered] *NYS* account for. He wandered
27.4	showing much] *NYS*, *AB* and showed much
27.8	some of them] *NYS*, *AB* *some* of them
27.12	Spielhagen or not. On the] *AB* Spielhagen or not.§ On the
27.18	possessed the great] *AB* and possessed the great
27.36	bright Bostonian] *AB* judicious Bostonian
27.36	and contented himself] *AB* contenting himself
28.2	sceptical key. § At last] *NYS* skeptical key. At last
28.9	his hand, presidentially] *NYS* his hand. Presidentially

28.10   a mere constituent] *AB* a mere subject

28.24   approached—he heard her say] *NYS, AB* approached. He heard her
         say

29.11   took two ices] *NYS, AB* took some tea

29.21   had he recovered from] *NYS, AB* had he got over

29.32   isn't spoiled yet."] *NYS* isn't spoiled—*yet*."; *AB* isn't spoiled—yet."

30.8   the hostess accompany] *NYS, AB* the host and the hostess accompany

30.17   I find she is] *NYS* I find she *is*

30.20   you Europeans:] *AB* you Europeans!

31.24   to my country] *NYS, AB* to *my* country

33.3   very crude] *NYS* very reckless; *AB* very superfluous

33.6   young lady belongs.] *NYS, AB* young lady belongs?

33.25   *what* type it is!] *NYS, AB* what type it is!

33.27   by the newspapers] *NYS, AB* in the newspapers

35.11   open windows] *NYS, AB* open window

35.23   in innumerable ways] *NYS, AB* in different ways

35.25   personality. In this view] *NYS, AB* personality—in this view

36.6   fragrant wreath] *NYS, AB* fragrant breath

36.11   sudden quotations] *AB* familiar quotations

37.10   gives a tone] *NYS, AB* would give a tone

37.15   to judge really] *NYS, AB* to see really

37.30   too comical] *NYS* too critical

37.30   anything else. § But Pandora] *NYS, AB* anything else. But Pandora

38.4   chamber of the Senate] *NYS* Senate Chamber

38.7   old thing. Throughout] *AB* old thing.§ Throughout

38.11   yellow sheen] *NYS* yellow shine

38.19   again. § He did so] *NYS, AB* again. He did so

38.25   of love? Was he to be] *NYS* of love, was he to be

38.36   to relinquish relations] *NYS* to cease relations; *AB* to terminate
         relations

39.4   over these ideas] *NYS, AB* over these questions

39.6   disinterested. They haunted] *AB* disinterested.§ They haunted

39.7   established. § Mrs. Steuben] *NYS, AB* established. Mrs. Steuben

39.8   picknickers] *NYS* accessories; *AB* confederates

39.11   aware of a shore] *NYS, AB* conscious of a shore

39.15   a revelation of] *NYS, AB* a picture of

39.30   his villeggiatura] *NYS, AB* his country seat

40.2   noble and genial. § Vogelstein] *NYS* noble and genial. Vogelstein

40.19   would they, after all] *NYS, AB would* they, after all

40.25   humorous, edifying] *AB* whimsical, edifying

40.32   familiar. § "Oh, he] *AB* familiar. "Oh, he]

40.34   things. §Vogelstein] *AB* things. Vogelstein

41.20   fraternising voice] *NYS, AB* cheerful voice

42.12   lunch would be] *AB* luncheon would be

42.23   she had asked of] *AB* she had begged of

42.27   asked of her whether] *AB* inquired of her whether

42.33   them once more] *NYS, AB* them again

43.32   She lets him slide.] *NYS* She lets him slide?

44.5   returning revellers] *NYS, AB* returning picknickers

45.16   over the side] *NYS, AB* over its side

45.23   postures of inclination] *AB* slanting postures

45.25   How sweet of you] *NYS, AB* How good of you

46.5   his own nearness] *NYS, AB* his own proximity

46.12   an instant in silence] *NYS* for a moment in silence; *AB* briefly, in silence

Georgina's Reasons

NYS The New York Sun, 20 July 1884, 1–2; 27 July 1884, 1–2; 3 August 1884, 1–2. (US)

AB The Author of Beltraffio; Pandora; Georgina's Reasons; The Path of Duty; Four Meetings (Boston, MA: James R. Osgood & Co., 1885), pp. 159–257.

A2 (SR2) *Stories Revived*, vol. ii, 'Georgina's Reasons', 'A Passionate Pilgrim', 'A Landscape-Painter', 'Rose-Agathe' (London: Macmillan & Co., 1885), pp. 1–95.

For choice of copy text (A2), see Textual Introduction, pp. xcii–xciii. When either **NYS** or **AB** is not cited, it is identical with A2.

47.32	these opportunities] **NYS, AB** these advantages
47.32	being fond of] **NYS, AB** being very fond of
48.3	his speech. He was] **AB** his speech. § He was
48.10	as one could see] **NYS** as we could see
48.11	as a person accustomed] **NYS, AB** as one accustomed
48.19	the two. § He had] **NYS, AB** the two. He had
48.30	smitten with him] **AB** in love with him
48.31	seemed willing] **NYS, AB** appeared willing
48.32	was marked out] **NYS, AB** seemed marked out
49.6	laugh. This may] **AB** laugh. § This may
49.22	whether he had] **NYS, AB** whether *he* had
49.26	empress—that was] **NYS, AB** empress. That was
52.16	a polite young man] **NYS, AB** a young man
52.18	different. § They had] **NYS, AB** different. They had
53.1	on the spring afternoons] **AB** on the afternoon of spring
53.13	this rustling] **AB** this bridling
53.16	been still more simply packed off] **NYS, AB** been simply packed off
53.16	Europe. Benyon's] **AB** Europe. § Benyon's
53.23	martyr. § Benyon] **NYS, AB** martyr. Benyon
54.6	scarcely needed] **NYS, AB** scarcely needful
54.7	a few hundred a year] **AB** a few hundreds a year
55.18	with little hard, piercing eyes] **AB** with hard, screwing eyes
55.33	cynical modesty] **NYS, AB** natural modesty
56.20	the way she had] **AB** the manner in which she had
57.5	that the nature of women is a queer mosaic] **NYS, AB** that women are full of inconsistencies

57.7	It now appeared that] *NYS, AB* Now, too, it appeared

57.7   It now appeared that] **NYS, AB** Now, too, it appeared

57.8   to manage and temporise.] **NYS, AB** to manage, to cultivate opportunities and reap the fruits of a waiting game.

57.14   the finest girl] **NYS, AB** the loveliest girl

57.28   of her: this finally presented itself] **NYS** of her. This rather promptly presented itself; **AB** of her, — this rather promptly presented itself

57.28   to the young officer] **NYS, AB** to the young man

57.28   of a lover and a gentleman] **NYS, AB** of a person of spirit

58.15   that pleasant part] **NYS, AB** that charming part

59.10   of tension; they went] **AB** of tension. They went

60.5   to act out] **NYS, AB** to *show*

60.5   believed. She was] **AB** believed. § She was

60.27   wistful eyes] **NYS, AB** lustrous eyes

60.30   to give actuality to this vision] **NYS, AB** to gratify her in this way

61.6   familiar challenge] **NYS, AB** familiar bravado

61.24   to measure the truth] **NYS, AB** to challenge the truth

62.10   a dear old man] **NYS, AB** an old, old man

62.11   three times himself, and the first time in the same way] **NYS, AB** three times himself

62.20   She should like to go] **NYS, AB** She would like to go

62.22   was over. § Mrs. Portico's heart] **NYS** was over. Mrs. Portico's heart

62.24   domestic girl] **NYS, AB** familiar girl

62.25   her extraordinary tale] **NYS, AB** this extraordinary tale

62.28   she would remain] **NYS, AB** she was to remain

62.35   she *would* do something] **NYS** she would do something; **AB** she must do something

63.6   goodness knew where] **NYS** heaven knew where; **AB** Heaven knew where

63.9   for it was over] **NYS, AB** for it *was* over

64.3   she had so little] **NYS, AB** *she* had so little

64.7   sank back, and sprang] *NYS* sunk back, and sprang; *AB* sunk back, and sprung

64.16   paymaster; it was much] *NYS, AB* paymaster. It was much

65.16   they were dense] *NYS, AB* they *were* stupid

65.25   you don't remember!"] *NYS, AB* you don't remember,"

66.9   very odd effect] *AB* very peculiar effect

66.12   come immediately] *NYS, AB* come quickly

66.14   a living wonder!] *NYS* a strange creature; *AB* a wonderful creature!

66.18   I would stick to him] *NYS, AB* I should stick to him

66.20   what mine are,"] *NYS* what mine are!"

67.2   his baby] *NYS, AB* his infant

67.16   honour, and I know] *NYS, AB* honor. And I know

67.18   fairly bounced] *AB* fairly bounded

67.19   You do know what you are about!] *NYS* You *do* know what you are about.; *AB* You *do* know what you are about.

67.20   more demented] *NYS, AB* more fantastic

67.21   putting his head into such a noose] *NYS* taking such a vow; *AB* taking such an imbecile vow

68.2   what you wanted of 'em] *NYS, AB* what *you* wanted of 'em

68.10   implying, for Mrs. Portico, more subtlety:] *NYS, AB* uttered,—for Mrs. Portico,—with much solemnity

68.24   a precious mixture] *NYS, AB* a queer mixture

69.16   she was stylish] *AB* she was elegant

70.7   the successive phases of the girl's appeal] *NYS* the details of the girl's urgency; *AB* the details of the girl's hard pleading

70.15   transmuted the cynical confession] *NYS, AB* resolved the harsh confession

70.18   she absolutely couldn't] *NYS* she couldn't; *AB* how could she?

70.26   her own devices. So, from one] *AB* her own devices. § So, from one

70.30   that robust Miss Gressie] *NYS* that healthy Miss Gressie

71.6   done it openly] *NYS, AB* done it frankly

71.8	mercurial young men] *NYS*, *AB* agile young men
71.14	a few plain words] *NYS*, *AB* a few words
71.20	*He might choose*] *NYS*, *AB* He might choose
71.26	to be altered] *AB* to be changed
72.28	Her nerve] *NYS*, *AB* Her nerves
72.32	things. Georgina] *AB* things. § Georgina
73.5	her pocket handkerchief] *AB* her rude pocket-handkerchief
73.12	to the end. § The two ladies] *NYS*, *AB* to the end. The two ladies
74.11	already. This] *AB* already. § This
74.21	adopt the poor little mortal] *NYS*, *AB* adopt the child
74.23	in a wretched village in Italy] *NYS*, *AB* in a poor village in Italy
74.24	She could pretend—she could pretend] *NYS*, *AB* She would pretend—she could pretend
74.29	surrendered herself.] *NYS*, *AB* lent herself
74.30	dragged her into such an abyss] *NYS* drawn her into such a criminal way of life; *AB* drawn her into an atrocious current
75.4	her detestation of] *NYS*, *AB* aversion to
75.5	of clay and iron. She was] *NYS*, *AB* of brass, of iron; she
75.16	for years. Mrs. Portico] *AB* for years. § Mrs. Portico
75.21	if she should know] *NYS*, *AB* if *she* should know
77.10	couch on which] *NYS*, *AB* couch, where
77.11	don't be affected."] *AB* don't be affected!"
77.16	*poverina,*] *NYS* —poor darling—; *AB* poor darling!
77.19	then—" § But with this] *NYS*, *AB* then—" But
77.25	was just to remind her that] *NYS*, *AB* was simply to intimate that
78.1	how to arrange and how to rearrange] *NYS* how to arrange and to re-arrange everything; *AB* how to arrange and rearrange everything
78.5	till it was remodelled] *NYS*, *AB* rearranged]
78.30	Neapolitan winter] *NYS*, *AB* Neapolitan winters
79.15	been tried. § Meanwhile the latter] *NYS* been tried. Meanwhile the latter

79.24	meagre and dusky] *NYS, AB* small and dark
79.29	another lady] *NYS, AB* another soul
81.4	Mildred remarked] *AB* Mildred only remarked
81.19	not very well off] *AB* not enormously rich
82.3	glad you like] *NYS, AB* glad *you* like
82.18	with Mrs. Theory] *NYS, AB* with Mrs. Percival
82.24	with them. The sisters] *NYS, AB* with them; the sisters
82.33	the Miss Theorys] *NYS* the Miss Theories
83.6	it was in his line to call] *NYS* it was his line to call
83.7	the particular emotions] *NYS, AB* the soft emotions
83.9	strong grounds. And he] *NYS, AB* strong grounds; and he]
83.13	to the danger of becoming entangled with] *NYS, AB* the chance of seriously caring for
83.30	rather she was very attracting] *AB* rather very attracting
83.35	a sad face] *NYS, AB* a dull face
83.36	to a sick-bed. She spoke] *NYS* to a sick-bed. § She spoke
84.11	gentle, jocular friendliness] *NY, AB* gentle friendliness
84.11	their intercourse] *NYS, AB* of their greeting
85.2	for a decidedly youthful mariner] *NYS, AB* for a man scarcely out of his twenties
85.3	the talk of a man] *AB* the talk of one
85.7	who had kept] *AB* of the kind that had kept
86.14	had various things] *AB* had many things
86.22	than a twelvemonth] *NYS, AB* than ten months
86.24	on that head] *NYS, AB* on that point
87.9	"diligance"! Of course] *NYS* diligence! Of course; *AB* diligance! § Of course
87.13	to tell Kate] *AB* to reveal to Kate
87.21	wished she would.] *AB* wished she would!
87.23	a husband. § Miss Mildred] *NYS, AB* a husband. Miss Mildred
88.35	*cara*] *NYS, AB* darling

89.16	"Oh, my darling dear!"] *NYS, AB* "Oh, my dearest, my poorest!"
90.3	saying, in the first place, that she proved very vapid] *NYS, AB* saying that, in the first place, she proved very silly
90.10	would be mortally] *NYS, AB* was mortally
90.13	one would have had] *NYS, AB* she would have had
91.4	was the New Yorkers] *NYS, AB* were the New Yorkers
91.8	Mr. Henry Platt] *AB* Henry Platt
91.31	to look at the royal palace] *NYS, AB* to seek the royal palace
92.16	who flattered] *NYS, AB* who sometimes flattered
92.27	his not having come back] *NYS, AB* his not having been back
92.32	a picture or a tapestry] *NYS, AB* a picture on a tapestry
94.3	I would give up my ship] *NYS* I would give up any ship
94.22	he rejoined] *NYS, AB* he said
94.22	remembering this!] *NYS* remembering *this*!
95.16	like a lady who has a big bill at Tiffany's] *NYS* like the wife of a man who has come down handsomely; *AB* a woman who has run up a big bill at Tiffany's
95.22	Do you call her] *NYS, AB* Do you call *her*
96.1	she had lightly] *AB* she had airily]
96.10	my sister Cora][1] *NYS, AB* my sister Dora
97.19	tremendously striking] *NYS, AB* tremendously stylish
99.2	That officer] *NYS, AB* This officer
99.8	the change consisted] *AB* the diversity consisted
99.10	as he sat alone] *NYS, AB* as he sat there alone
99.13	William Roy] *NYS, AB* Mr. William Roy
99.16	had mentioned] *AB* had happened to mention
99.29	But neither would he have] *NYS, AB* But he would not have
100.4	mocked him] *NYS, AB* amazed him
100.17	the human vitals] *NYS* the conscience; *AB* the vitals

[1] From now on 'Dora' *NYS* and *AB* is consistently replaced by 'Cora' in A2/N.

100.18   both of them. § All his] *NYS* both of them. All his; *AB* both of them!
§ All his-

100.33   baffling mendacity and idiocy] *NYS* baffling idiocy; *AB* baffling baseness of

101.15   inscrutable candidates] *AB* impenetrable candidates

101.26   name of perversity] *AB* name of wantonness

101.30   such baseness] *NYS, AB* such conduct

101.36   must think herself] *NYS, AB* must think herself now

102.4   another affair] *NYS* another affair!

104.2   what I have hinted] *NYS, AB* what I have noted

104.4   and rang] *AB* and the next day rang

104.7   that he was nervous] *AB* that *he* was nervous

104.8   if she were not] *NYS, AB* if she was not

104.9   pulled himself vigorously together] *NYS, AB* addressed himself a very
stern reprimand

106.10   she continued] *NYS, AB* she went on

106.15   the promise I made you] *NYS, AB* the promise made you

106.18   down at the front] *NYS, AB* down to the front

106.24   your desertion. I will simplify our situation."] *NYS, AB* your
desertion."]

107.11   all these horrid years? But every one is dead."] *NYS, AB* all these miserable years?"

107.31   proposed to you. It's a perfectly possible proceeding.] *NYS, AB* proposed to you.

108.9   I admit it is, tremendously] *NYS* I admit it *is,* awfully; *AB* I admit it is,
awfully

108.11   put it as strongly as] *NYS* put it as strong as

109.7   who apparently was] *NYS, AB* who was apparently

110.2   each other—she spoke] *NYS, AB* each other. She spoke

110.24   at the vacuity] *NYS, AB* at the stolidity

111.8   making a protest] *AB* making a pretext]

111.13   if I had to live] *NYS, AB* if I *had* had to live

591

111.14   never flinched] **NYS, AB** never flushed

111.15   what's that to you?] **NYS** what's that to you.

111.17   considered a moment] **NYS, AB** reflected a moment

111.21   me—me!] **NYS, AB** me—*me!*

111.24   You—you!] **NYS, AB** You—*you!*

112.7   I admire you so much.] **NYS** I admire you.; **AB** I admire you, esteem
          you: I don't many people!

112.19   the stammer of his lips] **NYS** the stammer of his life

112.26   she might never learn] **NYS, AB** she might learn

A New England Winter

> **C** = *Century Magazine*, vol. 28, no. 4 (August 1884), 573–87; no. 5 (September
> 1884), 733–43. (US)
> **TTC2** = *Tales of Three Cities*: 'The Impressions of a Cousin', 'Lady Barberina',
> 'A New England Winter' (Boston, MA: James R. Osgood & Co., 1884),
> pp. 269–359.
> A3 = (*TTC*) *Tales of Three Cities*: 'Lady Barberina', 'A New England Winter',
> 'The Impressions of a Cousin' (London: Macmillan & Co., 1884),
> pp. 129–208.

For choice of copy text (A3), see Textual Introduction, p. xx.
When either **TTC2** or **C** is not cited, it is identical with A3.

115.7   she had had time to see] **C** she had time to see

116.8   free use of the Atheneum,] **C** free use of the "Atheneum,"

116.30   there were many others that were more denuded.] **C** there were many
          others' that were more denuded than hers.

119.8   somewhat ambiguous] **C** somewhat precarious

120.3   to the *Transcript*] **C** to the "Transcript"

120.33   a period when she ascended to] **C** a period when she mounted to

120.35   she mounted and talked] **C** she ascended and talked

139.3   whether she might climb,] **C** whether she might come up,

121.6   nor did she presume [...] nor whether] *C* or did she presume ... or whether ...

125.5   Familiar with rubbish] *C, TTC2* Familiar with humbug

126.33   amuse Florimond.] *C, TTC2* amuse Florimond?

127.22   delight in him!] *C, TTC2* delight in him,

133.8   *P.S.*] *C, TTC2* P.S.

133.26   This responsibility, even after her revulsion, as we know, she regarded as grave; she exhaled an almost voluptuous sigh] *C, TTC2* This responsibility she now already, after her revulsion, as we know, regarded as grave; she exhaled an almost luxurious sigh

134.25   odour of the cold—] *C* odor of the cold; *TTC2* odour of the cold,—

134.31   either she should be] *C, TTC2* either that she should be

137.12   interpretation were] *C* interpretation was

139.6   mist—a vaporous blur—] *C, TTC2* mist—a tinted exhalation,—

141.18   Nuremberg),] *C* Nuremburg),

143.7   said Florimond, abstractedly.] *C, TTC2* said Florimond, a little confusedly.

143.29   but she would have him glad to precipitate it,] *C* but she would have been glad to precipitate it,

144.34   into a pose.] *C, TTC2* into a *pose.*

151.32   pretended irritation, "is it] *TTC2* pretended irritation,—"is it; *C* pretended irritation. "Is it

152.5   Don't profane this innocent] *C, TTC2* Don't sully this innocent

152.23   privilege. "I am afraid] *C* privilege. § "I am afraid

154.7   that *he,* after all,] *TTC2* that he, after all,

157.29   where you want to come out.] *TTC2* where you want to come out?; *C* where you want to come out!

159.25   ebbing, dodged the avalanches,] *C* ebbing, dodging the avalanches,

159.27   the horse-cars, made himself, on their little platforms, where flatness was enforced, as perpendicular as possible.] *C* the horse-cars, on their little platforms, where flatness was enforced, and made himself as perpendicular as possible.

160.13   Behind the plates of glass] *C* Beyond the plates of glass,

160.25   *intérieurs*] *C interieurs*

161.13   At Harvard, the buildings were square and fresh;] *C* At Harvard the buildings were simple and fresh;

161.31   in Paris, and never] *C*, *TTC2* in Paris and who never

165.35   throbbed. But at the first] *C* throbbed, but at the first

166.17   had said? For Lucretia] *C* had said! For Lucretia

The Path of Duty

EIM *English Illustrated Magazine*, vol. 2, no. 15 (December 1884), 240–56. (UK)

AB *The Author of Beltraffio; Pandora; Georgina's Reasons; The Path of Duty; Four Meetings* (Boston, MA: James R. Osgood & Co., 1885), pp. 261–317.

A4 (*SR1*) *Stories Revived*, vol. 1, 'The Author of Beltraffio', 'Pandora', 'The Path of Duty', 'A Day of Days', 'A Light Man' (London: Macmillan & Co., 1885), pp. 71–198.

For choice of copy text (A4), see Textual Introduction, pp. xciii–xciv. When either EIM or AB is not cited, it is identical with A4.

171.2   they are; the] *EIM, AB* they are. The

172.17   a person to admire or imitate,] *EIM, AB* an exemplary or edifying character,

174.23   "Of Roland Tremayne?"] *EIM, AB* "Of Roland Tremayne!"

182.31   and heaven preserve] *AB* and Heaven preserve

186.27   little lady] *EIM, AB* little woman

194.4   Joscelind, except] *EIM, AB* Joscelind's name, except

197.22   What I have told you…] *AB* What I have told you—

199.26   her normal equilibrium.] *EIM, AB* her normal state of nerves.

199.35   taken to me] *AB* taken me

203.25   are not unsubstantial] *EIM, AB* are not insubstantial

205.19   jilting Miss Bernardstone; and] *EIM, AB* jilting Miss Bernardstone would be; and

Mrs Temperly

HW (as 'Cousin Maria') *Harper's Weekly*, vol. 31, 6 August 1887, 557–8; 13 August 1887, 577–8; 20 August 1887, 593–4. (US)

A5 (*LonL*) *A London Life; The Patagonia; The Liar; Mrs. Temperly.* Vol. 11 (London and New York: Macmillan & Co., 1889), pp. 279–361.

For choice of copy text (A5), see Textual Introduction, pp. xcii–xciv.

208.37 memoranda] *HW memoranda*

208.35 cosy, a rustic] *HW* cozy, a kind of rustic

209.2 with a musing] *HW* with a kind of musing

210.4 She used, in a superior, unprejudiced way, every convenience] *HW* She used every convenience that the civilization of her time offered her, in a superior, unprejudiced way,

210.13 as a sound, productive] *HW* as a sleek, sound, productive

210.26 New York. But] *HW* New York; but

210.32 example. § When Raymond] *HW* example. When Raymond

211.32 an old maid—she] *HW* an old maid—that

212.13 afresh. § As the young man] *HW* afresh. As the young man

213.3 Tishy. § She was] *HW* Tishy. She was

213.29 the results of her own superiority.] *HW* the results of superior educative processes.

215.23 of which he resumed:] *HW* of which he remarked:

215.24 it seems curious your] *HW* it seems curious that your

216.6 Mrs. Parminter: they wanted to] *HW* Mrs. Parminter; they wished to

218.22 with a little floating motion, which suggested that she was in a liquid element, she] *HW* with a little gliding, zephyr-like motion, she

218.26 More than once, while] *HW* And more than once, while

219.22 confirmed. § Raymond] *HW* confirmed. Raymond

219.28 of all present thoughts] *HW* of all thoughts

219.29 leaving home again and] *HW* leaving home again within years

220.30 maiden. § He saw] *HW* maiden. He saw

221.26   We have the *entrée* of so many] **HW** We have the entrée of so many

222.21   was her title to this exalted position.] **HW** was her titles to this exalted position.

222.22   can't you see it?] **HW** can't you see them?

223.6   degree sociable and] **HW** degree friendly and

223.35   being vapid or vague.] **HW** being weakly sentimental.

224.35   by old tapestries] **HW** by red tapestries

225.31   annoy you.] **HW** annoy you!

228.11   collected at tea round] **HW** collected at tea, and

229.3   attitudes. § It was] **HW** attitudes. It was

229.20   son-in-law formed according to one of the types] **HW** son-in-law of one of the types

229.30   was not always free] **HW** was not always there

230.6   she would never lend herself] **HW** she wouldn't lend herself

231.9   small gesture. § "May I] **HW** small movement. "May I

231.30   gratification of every sense,] **HW** gratification of every individual,

231.31   to enjoy such a privilege] **HW** to enjoy such a sensation

231.32   side. § "And] **HW** side. "And

232.7   a joyous chant of praise, a glorification of] **HW** a joyous chant of praise of

232.12   *perfection*—] **HW** perfection, […]

232.16   wandering far,] **HW** wandering about,

232.33   a precocious duenna.] **HW** a premature duenna.

233.3   The conception was high, inasmuch as Cousin.] **HW** The conception was lofty, because Cousin

233.12   escort. Her friends would wish to quit her but would not wish to appear to give way to each other;] **HW** escort. Doubtless each wished to quit her, but didn't wish to appear to give way to the other;

233.14   give him a few] **HW** give him, apart, a few

233.36   the conservatory as if to see] **HW** the conservatory to see

Louisa Pallant

> **HNM** (as 'Louisa Pallant: a story') *Harper's New Monthly Magazine*,
> vol. 76, no. 453 (February 1888), 336–55. (US)
>
> A6 *(AP) The Aspern Papers; Louisa Pallant; The Modern Warning*. Vol. 11
> (London and New York: Macmillan & Co., 1888), pp. 3–96.

For choice of copy-text (A6), see Textual Introduction, pp. xcii and xciv.

239.20 the others as if they had paid for the privilege and were rather disappointed.] **HNM** the others with a kind of solemn dumbness.

240.2 quiet and decorous,] **HNM** quiet and graceful,

240.7 altogether honourable, and] **HNM** altogether respectable, and

240.19 that I forbore to speak] **HNM** that I didn't speak

240.26 permanent settlement there.] **HNM** permanent settlement.

241.15 difficult after her husband's death—virtually [...] bankrupt—in]
HNM difficult (after her husband's death, which was virtually [...]
bankrupt), in

241.19 with society, as it might be called, would] **HNM** with society (as it
might be called) would

241.21 wordly" I thought immediately of the object] **HNM** wordly", I thought
immediately, somehow, of the object

241.30 seat next to her] **HNM** seat next her

242.9 Linda smiled very sweetly and indefinitely, and I saw she remembered
me not at all.] **HNM** Linda smiled very sweetly, but vaguely, and I saw
she didn't remember me at all.

242.10 she failed to take it up.] **HNM** she didn't take it up.

242.15 if she had no acquaintances, it was because she did not want to— [...]
there was nobody] **HNM** if he didn't know people, it was because she
didn't want to— [...] there were none

242.28 I know not what] **HNM** I don't know what [...]

242.32 somewhat mixed] **HNM** slightly mixed]

243.1 the girl never put in] **HNM** the girl didn't put in

243.7 I made this reflection not all at once] **HNM** I didn't make this reflection all at once

243.9   had time to clarify.] *HNM* had time to settle.

243.11 She attributed […] to no refined] *HNM* She didn't attribute […] to any refined

243.28 a selfish bachelor, little versed in the care of children,] *HNM* a childless bachelor, with little of such experience,

243.29 he did not smoke too much nor fall off] *HNM* he didn't smoke too much or fall off

244.9   man and had brothers and sisters and] *HNM* man, and if he had brothers and sisters, and

244.11 little of him; I] *HNM* little of him, but I

244.13 sister at home, a delicate, unsuccessful child, demanding all the mother's care.] *HNM* sister, a poor, delicate child, demanding all the mother's care, at home.

245.8   if it did not quite achieve it.] *HNM* if it didn't achieve it.

245.21 this was not necessary at Homburg] *HNM* this didn't appear necessary at Homburg

246.8   some waxen orchid] *HNM* some orchid,

246.14 of every other religion.] *HNM* of every other inspiration.

246.24 pattern.] *HNM* pattern. She was like some one's grounds when you say they are well kept up; but just such a place seems a kind of courtship of nature, so Linda's enthusiasm appeared to have gone all the way with her high culture; she had enjoyed it and made it her own, and was not merely passive and parrot-like.

246.26 in her *rôle* of educated angel.] *HNM* in her evidently complete amiability.

246.35 I knew not what his impending] *HNM* I didn't know what his impending

247.2   with a candid circular countenance] *HNM* with a candid, pleasant countenance

247.9   to me that his want of wit was] *HNM* to me that his plainness was

247.10 It was not the sort of density] *HNM* It was not of the sort

247.16 life (as well he might] *HNM* life (as he might

247.29 the sort of "figure"] *HNM* the sort of figure

248.1   for she held her peace.] *HNM* for she didn't speak.

248.23   turned out so nice a nature as] *HNM* turned out as conscientious as

248.28   Linda's nature] *HNM* Linda's conscientiousness

249.4   exempt from periods of repose] *HNM* exempt from pauses

249.4   wondered how their association] *HNM* wondered how their intercourse

249.18   at her those of Miss Pallant] *HNM* at her, her own

249.22   was not for long—that] *HNM* wasn't for long, or that

249.23   it was many a day since] *HNM* it was a long time since

249.27   I never provided [...] he did not.] *HNM* I didn't provide [...] he didn't.

250.18   you should find him] *HNM* you should procure him

251.17   to act on a false alarm.] *HNM* to obey a false alarm.

251.22   would do for you."] *HNM* would do for you," she declared.

251.30   lived together twenty years in such intimacy for nothing.] *HNM* lived together for nothing for twenty years in such intimacy.

251.32   the occasion was not great:] *HNM* the occasion wasn't great.

252.3   needn't discuss] *HNM* needn't to discuss

252.11   summary, unnecessarily] *HNM* summary and unnecessarily

252.12   had no wish to move.] *HNM* didn't wish to move.

252.14   I should duck] *HNM* I should jump

252.17   considerable bitterness.] *HNM* certain bitterness.

252.19   There was a vibration [...] so that I exclaimed,] *HNM* There was a hint [...] and I exclaimed,

252.34   come up, for me,] *HNM* come up (for me)

253.12   the first intensely agreeable impression] *HNM* the first sharp impression

253.30   see the logic of it?] *HNM* see the logic of it.

254.20   It did not matter: with] *HNM* It didn't matter. With

255.2   This piece of strategy left me] *HNM* This quick manœuvre left me

255.23   attentive and wished not] *HNM* attentive, and didn't wish

255.29   we did not pursue her [...] that we were ignorant of where] *HNM* we didn't pursue her, [...] that I didn't know where

256.19   without giving us notice. Linda did not say] *HNM* without the usual forms. She didn't say

258.5   as a charming, clever [...] was puzzled afresh] *HNM* as a nice, clever [...] was puzzled, afresh,

259.6   "Afraid, my dear friend with that girl?"] *HNM* "Afraid, my dear friend? with that girl!"

259.12   "I see; I'm glad] *HNM* "I'm—I'm glad

259.23   was disconcerting, [...] served if] *HNM* was perturbing, [...] served, it

260.5   struck me as unnatural.] *HNM* struck me as cold, even unnatural.

260.9   I responded—] *HNM* I remarked—

260.16   "Your reparation, your expiation? What on earth] *HNM* "Your reparation—your expiation—what on earth

260.19   I [...] it does me or] *HNM* I [...] it does for me,

262.5   in a certain way and you don't like the trouble of changing. *Votre siège est fait.* But you will have to change—if] *HNM* in a certain way, and you don't like to change. But you will have to—if

262.12   something else?—] *HNM* something else—

262.18   It's true—it's true. She appals me!"] *HNM* It's true! it's true! She appalls me!"

262.29   worldly, I have thought only of that, and] *HNM* worldly; I have thought only of that;

263.1   abominably true?] *HNM* hideously true?

263.3   repeat to him—?"] *HNM* repeat to him—"

263.13   with a bitter laugh.] *HNM* with a curious, bitter little laugh.

263.18   lady! To climb] *HNM* lady. To climb

263.27   from the ferment of] *HNM* from the fulness of

263.34   with religious perversity.] *HNM* with a kind of religious perversity.

264.16   after which I resumed:] *HNM* after which I questioned:

264.27   want that and that I am acting a part.] *HNM* want that, and that I am acting,

265.26   picture it would seem that a] *HNM* picture, it would seem, a

266.36   "Poor Linda—poor Linda!"] *HNM* "Poor Linda! Poor Linda!"

267.6   for you?" And] *HNM* for you!" And

268.28   I had expected.] *HNM* I had expected to.

269.2   I was afraid] *HNM* I was almost afraid

269.3   She had spoken of these things as we parted there] *HNM* She had spoken of them, as we parted there,

269.13   loss of a great chance, if loss it was to be;] *HNM* loss, if loss it was to be, of a great chance;

269.21   showed few symptoms when] *HNM* showed very little, when

269.24   only to take away from us. One of these simply (in the given case) to do] *HNM* only to deprive us of. One of these is simply to do

269.26   My young man looked not] *HNM* My young man didn't look

270.9   as I observed him,] *HNM* as I watched him,

270.14   to whom I spoke at Baveno told me that my friends were] *HNM* of whom I asked for my friends at Baveno told me that they were

270.33   like Archie she was young enough to carry it off.] *HNM* like Archie, she had her youthfulness to relieve her from embarrassment.

271.29   a somewhat shabby pocket book and] *HNM* a rather shabby pocket-book, and

272.1   intention, the elder lady] *HNM* intention, she

272.20   uttered gracefully] *HNM* expressed gracefully

272.28   "No, and he never] *HNM* "No; and never

273.36   a large fortune, a fortune acquired] *HNM* a large fortune, acquired

274.2   from the principal stationers.] *HNM* at the principal stationers'.

The Aspern Papers

> *AM The Atlantic Monthly*, vol. 61 (March 1888), 296–315; (April 1888), 461–82; (May 1888), 577–94. (US)
>
> A7 (AP) *The Aspern Papers; Louisa Pallant; The Modern Warning*. Vol. 1 (London and New York: Macmillan & Co., 1888), pp. 1–239.

For choice of copy text (A7), see Textual Introduction, pp. xcii and xciv–xcv.

276.13   I had besieged it with my eyes] *AM* I had revolved about it

276.16   a faint reverberation] *AM* an attenuated reverberation

276.36   it seemed to me that she belonged to a generation as extinct.] *AM* it seemed to me that it was to that generation she belonged.

277.17   ourselves as the ministers.] *AM* ourselves as the priests.

277.25   several other ladies] *AM* several other women

277.27   acquit him conscientiously of shabby behaviour] *AM* acquit him, conscientiously, of disloyalty

277.29   no man could have walked straighter] *AM* no man could have behaved better

279.3   The gondola stopped, the old palace was there:] *AM* The gondola stopped, and the old palace was there:

279.20   of witches." § I forget] *AM* of witches." I forget

283.7   by some neighbouring water-steps] *AM* at some neighboring water-steps

283.23   my arrival was a great affair] *AM* my arrival was an event

283.31   at the place with my heart beating as I had known it to do in the dentist's parlour.] *AM* at the place in a sort of suspense

285.8   And I walked toward] *AM* And I walked, myself, toward

286.6   close to the window but looking at my shoes.] *AM* close to the window, and looking at my shoes.

286.17   the whole of the tune I played.] *AM* the whole of the tune I played on this occasion.

286.32   that it never heard of them.] *AM* that it did n't hear of them.

287.1   The rooms are very bare] *AM* The rooms are bare

287.13   They were bad economists—I had never heard] *AM* They were bad economists. I had never heard

288.5   most exquisite and most renowned lyrics.] *AM* most exquisite lyrics.

288.25   she would die to-morrow—then] *AM* she would die to-morrow, and then

289.19   not wholly out in my calculation?] *AM* not wholly out of my calculation?

289.28   her bleached and shrivelled face] *AM* her shriveled white face

289.31   then she inquired] *AM* then she remarked

290.15   the old woman remained impenetrable] *AM* the old woman remained inscrutable

290.25   another of her whimsical speeches] *AM* another of her incongruities

292.25   feel easier, for I foresaw] *AM* feel easier, and I foresaw

293.8   she asked with her shrunken grimness.] *AM* she asked with a sort of shrunken grimness.

293.22   if she would offer to show] *AM* if she would n't offer

294.6   it would not form a part of my *quartiere*] *AM* it would n't form a part of my *quartière*

294.19   which constantly marked her manner.] § "Perhaps you can't. *AM* which constantly marked her manner—"Perhaps you can't.

295.6   had no *locus standi* as a critic.] *AM* had no authority as a critic.

295.23   as if she failed to understand] *AM* as if she did n't understand

295.32   she had lived so very, very long.] *AM* she had lived so long.

296.10   with the glimmer of an illumination in her face.] *AM* with something like an illumination in her face.

296.31   I desired to ask her] *AM* I wanted to ask her

298.18   my derisive friend] *AM* my incisive friend

298.19   She had expected to gather amusement] *AM* She had expected to have amusement

298.20   of my intercourse with] *AM* of my relations with

298.20   with the Misses Bordereau] *AM* with my queer hostesses

298.21   disappointed that the intercourse] *AM* disappointed that the relations

298.30   she apparently thought nothing] *AM* she thought nothing, apparently,

299.6   the day before, murmuring] *AM* the day before, and murmured

299.18   it was like hunted creatures feigning death.] *AM* it was like holding their breath.

300.17   after which I relinquished] *AM* and then I relinquished

300.26   liberally bestowed] *AM* unmistakably bestowed

302.5   passed their days] *AM* passed their life

303.6   that I should not have grown] *AM* that I did n't grow

303.20   the local accent and fashion.] *AM* the accent and fashion

303.35   the daughter of an artist, painter or a sculptor,] *AM* the daughter of an artist, painter or sculptor,

303.36   when the century was fresh,] *AM* when the century was young,

304.17   a perfume of reckless passion,] *AM* a perfume of passion,

304.28   a *contadina* and *pifferaro*] *AM* a *contadina* and a *pifferaro*

304.33   *bric-à-brac*] *AM* bricabrac

305.3   of the present hour,] *AM* of the present day,

305.8   of Roman pearls and scarfs.] *AM* of Roman scarfs.

308.24   There was an unmistakable reference] *AM* There was a melancholy reference

309.4   The oddest mixture of the shrinking and the direct] *AM* the oddest mixture of the sensitive and the direct

309.10   respectable intelligent people] *AM* respectable people

309.12   at least some of] *AM* some, at least, of

309.13   I am intensely fond of Venice.] *AM* I am very fond of Venice.

309.28   less secluded, less confidential,] *AM* less secluded, less intimate,

310.1   the flight of time—never worried] *AM* the flight of time—did n't worry

310.6   and intended to] *AM* and she wished to

310.8   less well for a good many days and in a way that was rather new.] *AM* less well for a good many days, or at any rate had fallen into a condition without precedents.

310.9   no strength at all] *AM* no strength to speak of

310.12   her niece irritated her,] *AM* her niece disturbed her,

310.13   she had always done that, musing and dozing;] *AM* she had always done that, to a certain extent,

310.14   liking her companion to] *AM* she liked her companion to

310.17   moreover she took hardly] *AM* and she took hardly

310.17   she lived on] *AM* she lived upon

310.30   Poor woman,] *AM* Poor woman!

310.31   as to *her* capacity for] *AM* as to any capacity on her part for

311.3   there was scarcely a week] *AM* there was n't a week

311.24   her interest and never suggested.] *AM* her interest and didn't suggest.

311.31   something of the trick of] *AM* something of the manner of

312.4   world altogether. If she had not been so decent her references would have seemed to carry one back to the queer rococo Venice of Casanova.] *AM* world altogether.

312.15   the poet. I held it probable [...] had not read] *AM* the poet. I did n't believe [...] had read

312.26   she was far from doing everything] *AM* she did n't do everything

312.28   she murmured, at this] *AM* she declared, at this

312.34   for I had no wish to have it] *AM* for I did n't want seriously to have it

313.21   wait longer] *AM* wait any longer

313.26   Why should I indeed—was not] *AM* Why should I, indeed; and was n't

314.7   she still talked] *AM* she talked

314.27   shouldn't you, if she had] *AM* would n't you, if she had

314.34   I wished not to frighten her] *AM* I did n't wish to frighten her

315.5   a shake in her voice—] *AM* a tremor in her voice;

316.5   angular, diffident] *AM* nude, diffident

316.16   that she wouldn't suffer me near her.] *AM* that she would n't look at me.

316.16   was not embarrassed *AM* was not at all embarrassed

317.4   bandage over her eyes.] *AM* bandage, as it seemed to me, over her eyes.]

317.6   I made no motion to shake] *AM* I did n't advance to shake

317.13   I did not [...] suspect that Miss Tita had not just spoken] *AM* I did n't [...] doubt that Miss Tita had just spoken

319.11   some interesting talk,] *AM* some remarkable talk,

319.14   in a light more favourable,] *AM* in a more favorable light,

319.31   of being there and wondering] *AM* of my domestication and wondering

319.36   effect of something like cruelty in her implacable power of retort] *AM* effect of mockery in her quiet, sweet-voiced readiness

320.7   I shall never miss you;] *AM* I sha'n't miss you;

320.27 It diverts me more] *AM* It entertains me more

320.28 Don't you know it almost kills *me?*"] *AM* Don't you know it almost kills me?"

321.11 try to escape, but came closer, as it were, with a deprecating, clinging appeal to be spared, to be protected.] *AM* try to escape, if it was in some degree your fault; but came closer, as it were, as if to rest on you, almost to cling, to beg you to desist, to support and protect her.

321.14 dropped from her] *AM* dropped from her quickly,

321.27 We swept [...] into the Grand Canal; whereupon she] *AM* As we swept [...] into the Grand Canal, she

322.6 keeping the conversation] *AM* but kept the conversation

322.16 and then we sat] *AM* after which we sat

323.2 answer to this, but after a moment she broke out] *AM* answer to this; after a moment she remarked

323.9 I demanded, quickly] *AM* I asked, quickly

323.32 its smile of appreciation,] *AM* its smile,

324.6 simply. "You told her you found it so." "So I did;] *AM* simply. "So it is;

324.10 doing as others do, in spite of the interest she offers—for not leaving] *AM* doing as others do (in spite of the interest she offers), for not leaving

324.11 as if she failed to grasp] *AM* as if she failed to understand

324.25 if she had been less ingenuous.] *AM* if she had been less genuine.

324.30 I have never had them] *AM* I have n't had them

324.35 as if she was ignorant of] *AM* as if she did n't know

325.14 in the worst possible taste if anything less vital] *AM* in the worst possible taste, if anything less

326.27 So I simply inquired if that faithful domestic] *AM* So I simply asked if that faithful domestic

326.29 go home. § I laid] *AM* go home. I laid

326.30 moment. "What I] *AM* moment, and pursued— "What I

326.33 was half surprised, half frightened [...] play an active part.] *AM* was partly surprised, partly frightened [...] play a part.

327.11 to obtain more of that balm] *AM* to obtain more

606

327.15   she made a will] *AM* she made one

327.31   Miss Tita responded [...] while the movement] *AM* Miss Tita declared [...] and this movement

327.35   an injunction so solemn.] *AM* so solemn an injunction.

328.2   I said; and she uttered nothing to] *AM* I replied; and she said nothing to

328.4   place almost in silence] *AM* place, in a gondola, almost in silence

329.10   was sitting by the window] *AM* was sitting there by the window

329.19   —she could see the yellow] *AM* —the yellow

329.23   coarse in her cupidity] *AM* coarse in her avidity

330.18   Juliana responded] *AM* Juliana remarked

330.23   not so much as] *AM* not as much as

331.28   she pursued, like an auctioneer, moving] *AM* she pursued, moving

332.13   Miss Tita's graciousness] *AM* Miss Tita's kindness

332.16   to be obliging,] *AM* to be civil,

332.22   a fancy price] *AM* a "fancy" price

333.6   one could never tell] *AM* one could n't tell

333.33   entertainment—the humour to test me] *AM* entertainment to test me

333.34   I could not believe] *AM* I did n't believe

334.1   price on it] *AM* price upon it

334.3   not a supreme work] *AM* not a brilliant work

334.9   seen other likenesses] *AM* seen other pictures

334.12   my finger on him—I can't give him a label.] *AM* my finger upon him.

334.21   the precious thing] *AM* the precious object

334.23   I retained it.] *AM* I continued to retain it.

334.25   I shall be able] *AM* I should be able

334.27   a spasm of dread at having lost her treasure,] *AM* a spasm of terror at having lost the picture,

334.33   had had a strain or an escape.] *AM* had been strained or had an escape.

334.33   prevent her saying] *AM* prevent her from saying

335.6   entrust me with her property] *AM* entrust me with the picture

335.10 during her lifetime] *AM* during her own lifetime

335.21 a still greater scruple] *AM* greater scruples

336.3 as if there were no knowing what service] *AM* as if she did n't know what service

336.7 the gray ashes] *AM* the ashes

336.15 cried Miss Tita.] *AM* remarked Miss Tita.

336.16 this clever gentleman.] *AM* this gentleman.

337.22 from the goal of my hopes;] *AM* from the documents of my desire;

338.2 the precaution had not been] *AM* the provision had not been

338.12 I answered, bitterly.] *AM* I answered, with a certain bitterness.

338.24 an attack of "oppression,"] *AM* an attack of pain in her chest,

338.30 of any weird manœuvre.] *AM* of such a manœuvre.

339.2 me—a scene that] *AM* me, and the scene

339.4 I couldn't think what she was] *AM* I did n't know what she was

339.7 was passing out of] *AM* was getting out of

339.13 Do you think she can *see*?"] *AM* Do you think she can see"?

339.14 but forbore to say it?"] *AM* but did n't say it

339.21 which, wound round her head, descended] *AM* which had been wound round her head and descended

339.33 in whom the appearance of respiration was so slight as to] *AM* who was so motionless as to

339.35 with them the closets, the chests of drawers, the tables.] *AM* the closets, the chests of drawers, the tables, with them.

340.1 so that I felt rebuked, with reason,] *AM* so that I felt rebuked, deservedly,

340.6 a dire confusion; it looked like the room of an old actress. There] *AM* a confusion. It was not, it seemed to me, particularly well ordered. There

340.11 (forgetting I had no business to] *AM* (as if I had any business to

340.17 a queer, superannuated coffer,] *AM* a queer, superannuated receptacle,

340.26 met her with her companion in tow,] *AM* met her near the house, guiding her companion,

340.35   He was a short, fat, brisk gentleman who wore the tall hat and seemed to look at everything but his patient. He looked particularly at me, as if it struck him that I should be better for a dose, so that I bowed] *AM* He was a short, dusky gentleman, with a quick, clever eye and the tall hat of his profession; and he gave me at first more attention than he gave the patient. I bowed

341.19   a proof my anxieties] *AM* a proof that my anxieties

341.23   to me; he knew] *AM* to me, and he knew

341.25   so much time as that to enunciate] *AM* so much time as that to establish

341.27   *He* had been] *AM* He had been

342.3   no immediate danger." "No immediate danger?] *AM* no danger." "No danger?

342.4   That affects] *AM* It affects

342.23   hesitated a moment; though] *AM* hesitated a moment, and

343.10   balcony. The air] *AM* balcony, where the air

344.20   She hesitated; I thought] *AM* She hesitated, and I thought

345.11   moralised mournfully; and her tone ministered little to my patience] *AM* observed, with a sigh, and her tone did n't minister to my patience

345.23   I know not whether] *AM* I don't know whether

345.35   where my restlessness declined to quit me. I was unable to sit down] *AM* where my restlessness did n't diminish: I could n't sit down

346.1   round, and I did so half] *AM* round, which I did half

346.12   she would never go] *AM* she would n't go

346.16   room; this] *AM* room, and this

346.17   but it had no such effect. If] *AM* but it did n't. If]

346.18   the importunities, the indelicacies, of which] *AM* the indiscretions, the indelicacies, the brutalities, of which

346.20   this last indiscretion.] *AM* this last act of violence.

346.23   Miss Tita had accepted from me] *AM* Miss Tita had given me

346.26   I desired not to be released] *AM* I did n't want to be released

346.28   no sound—my] *AM* no sound, and my

346.31　to call her; I only waited] *AM* to call her, but I waited

348.2　is embarrassing for me to] *AM* is very awkward for me to

348.15　retreating before me in horror] *AM* retreating before me with horror

349.5　I failed to see] *AM* I did n't see

349.12　I scantily enjoyed] *AM* I did n't enjoy

349.15　the attachment of her bureau] *AM* the fastening of her bureau

350.1　for the sake of my dollars.] *AM* for the sake of my money.

350.6　he was unable to manage] *AM* he could n't manage

350.24　a dull little passeggio] *AM* a little passeggio

350.27　Miss Tita. His conception of funerals was apparently that they were mainly to amuse the living. I wanted] *AM* Miss Tita. I wanted

350.29　I took a bad view of it, especially of the idea] *AM* I did n't like it; especially I did n't like the idea

351.4　I had never made] *AM* I had n't made

351.18　of primitive, retarded sense of loneliness and violence.] *AM* of youthful, retarded sense of loneliness and fear of change.

351.28　have professed things!"] *AM* have professed"—

351.34　us; I did not ask] *AM* us, and I did n't ask

352.6　in a visible air] *AM* in a sort of air

352.9　I forbore to touch] *AM* I did n't touch

352.12　in her unsophisticated vision] *AM* in her simple vision

352.29　I was not on pins and needles to know] *AM* I did n't tremendously want to know

352.31　but she never glanced that way, and I thought this] *AM* but she did n't, and I thought that

353.16　destined, as it happened] *AM* destined, however, as it happened

353.20　I preferred not to be] *AM* I did n't want to be

353.29　but to go to the station;] *AM* but to depart;

353.32　should I be indebted?] *AM* should I be obliged?

353.33　if she *had* saved] *AM* if she had saved

353.34　to reward such a courtesy.] *AM* to repay such a courtesy.

354.28 to see them, to take them?] *AM* to see them?

355.4 if she had no greater hindrance] *AM* if she had no greater impediment

355.7 I would rather] *AM* I had rather

355.26 said Miss Tita, reddening again.] *AM* said Miss Tita, coloring again.

356.2 announced, taking] *AM* announced, and took

356.5 I questioned, staring] *AM* I asked, staring

356.25 had begun to trouble me,] *AM* had begun to give me pain,

356.27 declaration; I only privately] *AM* declaration, but I privately

356.34 I demanded in a moment] *AM* I asked in a moment

357.7 full of her dolefulness.] *AM* with all her dolefulness.

358.13 I failed to follow] *AM* I did n't follow

358.30 Mercy on us, what must] *AM* Good heaven, what must

358.31 Miss Tita cried with sudden] *AM* cried Miss Tita, with sudden

359.6 inspired, transparent astuteness as it was and sewn, as the phrase is, with white thread.] *AM* inspired, halting, illogical and, I may add, transparent astuteness as it was.

360.24 I am far from remembering clearly] *AM* I don't remember clearly

360.30 the case, however it might have struck others, seemed to me so little amusing. It would have been better perhaps for me to feel the comic side] *AM* the case did n't seem to me amusing. It would have been better perhaps if it had.

360.32 bundle of tattered papers,] *AM* bundle of old papers,

361.4 Aspern's relics,] *AM* Aspern's papers,

361.10 I got clear] *AM* I had got clear

361.18 crumpled scraps;] *AM* tattered scraps;

361.33 at that hour] *AM* at that hour of the day

362.1 and if he were thinking] *AM* and if he was thinking

362.11 I would touch no meat.] *AM* I meant to eat no dinner.

362.29 dramatic troupe.] *AM* dramatic company.

362.30 very tired, without] *AM* very tired, and without

362.35 I found myself aware of] *AM* I became aware of

363.13   I had invented no alternative,] **AM** I had n't invented an alternative,

363.23   full of my literary concupiscence] **AM** full of the grossness of my desire

363.24   She stood in the middle] **AM** She stood there, in the middle

364.5   strangely, with] **AM** strangely, but with

364.30   she never sent it] **AM** she did n't send it

364.33   my chagrin at the loss] **AM** my distress at the loss

The Liar

> **C** *The Century Magazine*, vol. 36 (May 1888), 123–35; (June 1888), 213–23. (US)
> A8 = (*LonL*) *A London Life; The Patagonia; The Liar; Mrs. Temperly.* Vol. 11
> (London and New York: Macmillan & Co., 1889), pp. 147–275.

For choice of copy-text (A8), see Textual Introduction, pp. xcii and xcv.

365.19   the art consisted neither of the water-colour] **C** the art didn't consist either of the water-color

365.25   while he buttoned his shirt.] **C** while he buttoned his collar.

366.19   an enhancement of his subject.] **C** a sort of addition to his subject.

366.26   But he went into his neighbours little as yet;] **C** But he didn't go into his neighbors much as yet;

367.6   and of the other being seated] **C** and the other being seated

367.7   Arthur Ashmore was a fresh-coloured] **C** Arthur Ashmore was a good, fresh-colored

367.10   a banker: you could scarcely paint him in characters. His wife did not make up the amount;] **C** a banker—he failed of homogeneity. Mrs. Ashmore didn't make up the deficiency;

367.12   Lyon could scarcely tell whether] **C** Lyon couldn't tell whether

367.21   and that it was not less vivid than] **C** or that it was not less successful than

367.31   you would know him by? § This face] **C** you would know him by? This face

368.3   even human affection] **C** even human affections

368.15   a good cook lifts the cover of the next] *C* a good cook looks into the next

369.29   and this movement led to his observing a handsome creature who] *C* and this movement, after some minutes, led to his observing a lady who

370.9   with a kind of habitual, visible complacency.] *C* with a certain serene complacency.

371.26   like a glorified *contadina*.] *C* like a kind of glorified *contadina*.

372.36   weeks—for months, almost for years. He] *C* weeks—for months. He

373.19   very striking, but he wanted to ask him whether he had not shammed a little—not in relating it, but in keeping so quiet. He hesitated however, in time, to imply a doubt—he was so impressed with the tone in which Colonel Capadose said that] *C* very striking; such a prodigy of suspended animation reminded him of the sleeping beauty in the wood. He hesitated, however, to make this comparison—it seemed to savor the irreverence, especially when Colonel Capadose said that

374.10   he would do anything for me […] said Lyon, much startled.] *C* he'd do anything for me […] said Lyon, much impressed.

375.19   a friendly propulsion.] *C* a friendly push.

375.34   unalloyed pleasure.] *C* indubitable pleasure.

376.14   she dropped something that had] *C* she said something that had

376.16   her feelings, some of her reflections, about life. Lyon talked] *C* feelings. Lyon talked

377.11   something so distressing."] *C* something so disagreeable."

379.7   "She thinks I swagger about the child"] *C* "She thinks I brag about the child"

379.27   twinkle sociably.] *C* twinkle most sociably.

380.9   failed to make it cheerful.] *C* didn't make it cheerful.

381.4   I will invent a pretext] *C* I will invent a pretense

381.35   not a gusher.] *C* not a sentimentalist.

383.15   the most mystifying figure] *C* the most incalculable figure

384.8   as if portraiture in oils had] *C* as if portraiture had

384.9   giving an explanation] *C* and gave an explanation

384.31   The general was rather a smart soldier] *C* He was rather a smart soldier

384.32   to put his money into some rotten thing.] *C* to throw his money away.

385.26   of a series of the stiffest statements. They stuck, when I tried to swallow them, but] *C* of a series of crams! They stuck in my gizzard at the time, but

386.15   Mercy on us] *C* Good Heaven

386.19   with an interest deeply quickened] *C* with a deeply quickened interest

386.20   he had had his own troubles in life] *C* he had had his own trouble in life

387.1   that she took his false pieces at his own valuation. A little reflection rendered] *C* that she took his fiction at his own valuation. A little reflection, however, rendered

387.5   the profit they had made off his early picture.] *C* the disposal they had made of his early picture.

387.18   It was probable also that light] *C* It was probable, too, that light

388.21   Had she not seen—had she not felt—the smile go round when her husband executed some especially characteristic conversational caper?] *C* Good God! Hadn't she seen—hadn't she felt—the smile go round when her husband threw off some especially characteristic improvisation?

388.29   an inscrutable mask.] *C* an impenetrable mask.

389.12   singular futility] *C* singular uselessness.

389.16   But the supererogatory lie] *C* But the uninvoked lie

389.29   flat veracity.] *C* dull veracity.

389.32   keep the truce of God for a month at a time.] *C* keep the beaten path for a month at a time.

390.26   if some faint shade or spasm never passed over it.] *C* if a faint shade or spasm didn't pass over it.

390.36   no nefarious plan, no conscious wish to practice upon her shame or her loyalty;] *C* no nefarious plan—he didn't consciously wish to practice upon her sensibility;

392.13   so long as she failed to suppose (as she must)] *C* so long as she didn't suppose (and she couldn't)

392.23 but she neglected to say it was because] *C* but she didn't say it was because

393.26 a tacit confidence,] *C* a kind of confidence,

395.31 to this small exemplary group that he aspired to annex the canvas] *C* to this small, everlasting group that he aspired to attach the canvas

396.4 very fortunate,] *C* most fortunate,

396.11 The higher his companion soared, the more gyrations he executed, in the blue, the better he painted; he couldn't make his flights long enough.] *C* The more flights his companion indulged in the better he painted; he couldn't make him soar high enough.

396.13 became great at moments] *C* became very real at moments,

396.14 But he never did, apparently;] *C* But he didn't, apparently;

396.17 it was pretty well finished:] *C* it was nearly finished—

397.10 the side-door had been found] *C* this ingress had been found

397.14 She belonged, in fact, to a] *C* She proved to belong to a

397.18 turned her off and wouldn't] *C* turned her away, and wouldn't

397.24 lighted on her] *C* turn to her

397.27 evidently rounded] *C* evidently turned

397.28 failed to suggest] *C* did n't suggest

398.29 looking at the Colonel. § "If *you* should require me, sir—" § "You put] *C* looking at the colonel. § "You put

398.35 diffused a fragrance. "Perhaps *you* send postcards, eh?" she went on to the Colonel; and then she retreated with a wavering step.] *C* diffused a fragrance. The poor woman retreated, with an uncertain step.]

399.35 a bad one!] *C* a bad un!

400.21 to go that length.] *C* to go that.

401.7 he was unable to face the delay.] *C* he couldn't brook the delay.

401.29 I think it's military.] *C* I think he's a colonel.

401.36 wished her to forbear;] *C* wished her to wait;

402.25 very few and very short] *C* very few and very quick

404.14 this malediction] *C* this invocation

404.16 Lyon was unable for the instant] *C* Lyon couldn't, for the instant

615

404.26   the face of the likeness,] *C* the face of the figure,

404.28   figurative suicide.] *C* constructive suicide.

405.4   where it was, never touched it,] *C* where it was, didn't touch it,

405.24   on his mystification?] *C* on his bewilderment?

406.15   though little further enlightened,] *C* though much further mystified,

406.34   who appeared but little in public.] *C* who didn't come to luncheon.

407.25   the love of sitting to you?] *C* the love of sitting?

407.28   as if a highly suggestive idea] *C* as if a most suggestive idea

408.24   was not a carriage nor a cab] *C* wasn't a carriage or a cab

410.26   and then had been borne] *C* and then been borne

411.16   She neither sat down] *C* She didn't sit down

411.34   He had no desire to frighten her; only wanted to] *C* He did not wish to frighten her, he only wished to

The Modern Warning

> **HNM**   (as 'Two Countries') *Harper's New Monthly Magazine*, vol. 77 (June 1888), 83–116. (US)
>
> A9 = (*AP*) *The Aspern Papers; Louisa Pallant; The Modern Warning.* Vol. 11 (London and New York: Macmillan & Co., 1888), pp. 99–258.

For choice of copy text (A9), see Textual Introduction, pp. xcii and xcv.

413.8   were ignorant of them.] **HNM** didn't know them.

413.12   Liverpool, had] **HNM** Liverpool had

413.17   he *should* be] **HNM** he should be

414.26   when it came had no appetite for it.] **HNM** when it came didn't care to eat it.

415.29   nothing—she only] **HNM** nothing, but only

416.16   table d'hôte,] **HNM** *table d'hôte,*

418.36   wished not to have] **HNM** didn't wish to have

421.35   pointed and he wished not to] **HNM** pointed, and he didn't wish to

422.5   he never turned up, so that] **HNM** he didn't turn up, and

423.9   She had had a long] **HNM** She had a long

423.22   like thunder, I feel like hell!"] *HNM* like—well, I feel like thunder!"

424.25   effort at] *HNM* effort of

426.7   gracious, my son, don't,] *HNM* gracious! my son! don't!

426.31   what words she had had with Agatha,] *HNM* what had passed between her and the girl,

426.32   effect that the girl had declared with infinite feeling] *HNM* to the effect that Agatha had declared, with infinite feeling,

427.5   horizon. § No allusion] *HNM* horizon. No allusion

427.21   conscientious; he was capable] *HNM* conscientious, and capable

427.33   selfish; but the essence of his thought was that] *HNM* selfish: but the bottom of his thought, as the French say, was that

428.18   views. § Sir Rufus] *HNM* views. Sir Rufus

428.29   he cared little to] *HNM* he didn't desire to

430.3   that probably his own] *HNM* that very likely his own

430.10   each other three months was] *HNM* each other for three months, was

430.15   arrogant doctrines. Not] *HNM* arrogant theories; not

430.16   mattered;] *HNM* mattered, but

430.22   put him out not at all,] *HNM* didn't put him out at all,

431.22   projected over the place long shafts of lamplight which] *HNM* projected long shafts of lamp-light over the place, which

432.15   sad—touched too with] *HNM* sad, and touched, too,

432.23   even gratified her] *HNM* even entertained her

432.34   If she were not careful she] *HNM* If she didn't look out, she

432.34   away: in the] *HNM* away; and in the

433.10   it signified little how] *HNM* he didn't care how

434.3   me—no more] *HNM* me! No more

434.20   an hostility] *HNM* a hostility

435.28   I hate it!"] *HNM* I hate it."

435.34   exclaim in a voice which] *HNM* exclaim, in a tone which

436.20   like *her*—most] *HNM* like her—most

436.22   an hesitation.] *HNM* a hesitation.

438.20   She believed him not a bit and] *HNM* She didn't believe him, and

438.32   Good Lord, what] *HNM* Good Lord ! what

440.8   she forbore to express] *HNM* she didn't express

440.20   I say—a very simple one—had] *HNM* I say (it was a very quiet one), had

441.10   He had not the art of keeping house] *HNM* He didn't know how to keep house

441.11   unless one were a good deal richer than he,] *HNM* unless one had a larger fortune than his,

441.12   made no further allusion] *HNM* made to her husband no further allusion

441.17   came Macarthy] *HNM* came. Macarthy

441.26   Briton—that was necessarily the end] *HNM* Briton, and that was the end

442.11   the most frivolous and feather-headed] *HNM* the most frivolous and rattle-brained

442.19   prejudice—it was a] *HNM* prejudice, but a

442.26   at such moments] *HNM* at those moments

443.20   social and political, had practically the same large but fixed line as his.] *HNM* social and political, because for the time exclusively English.

444.8   bullying her not half so much] *HNM* and he didn't bully her half so much

444.24   Even if she had done so it] *HNM* Even if she had, it

444.30   How little] *HNM* Of how little

444.31   in due time to discover.] *HNM* gradually to discover.

445.5   acres. § All the same] *HNM* acres. All the same

445.8   things that failed to catch her sympathy.] *HNM* things that displeased and distressed her.

445.9   intended to mention them.] *HNM* intended to.

445.22   sitting-room and looked] *HNM* sitting-room, looking

446.6   magnanimity keenly] *HNM* magnanimity even, keenly

448.5   Macarthy's own demeanour] *HNM* Macarthy's own behavior

448.24 everything he never asked about] *HNM* everything he didn't ask about

449.10 'Sir'!"] *HNM* 'Sir.' "

449.11 The English visitor was prodigiously] *HNM* The English visitor was immensely

449.19 in spite of Sir Rufus's now comporting] *HNM* in spite of Sir Rufus's now demeaning

449.32 very appreciative] *HNM* most appreciative

450.8 an homage?] *HNM* a homage?

450.17 he cared too little] *HNM* he didn't care

451.20 relapsing interest] *HNM* personal interest

451.24 forgotten, incidents that it] *HNM* forgotten, which it

451.27 a great deal of the American humour.] *HNM* an immense deal of American humor.

452.3 neglected even to] *HNM* he didn't even

452.13 protested, eliciting from him the declaration that to] *HNM* protested, and elicited the declaration that, to

453.13 reassuring, so that] *HNM* reassuring, and

453.15 Congressman whom] *HNM* Representative, whom

453.20 Democratic Congressman.] *HNM* Democratic Representative.

454.3 prove, both [...] Macarthy, that] *HNM* prove (both [...] Macarthy) that

454.17 extremely vain. He could have no more affinity with Sir Rufus's print-ed ideas than with his spoken ones.] *HNM* positively vain. Sir Rufus's printed ideas could have no more value for him than his spoken ones.

454.26 she took this vow, but] *HNM* she made this declaration, but

454.31 colossal, imperturbable. Therefore, with] *HNM* colossal and imper-turbable. Still, with

455.15 pity them?"] *HNM* pity them!"

455.26 was far from her desire.] *HNM* she didn't wish to be.

455.30 nothing—she did not deny] *HNM* nothing, and she didn't deny

456.12 she identified the name as] *HNM* she recognized the name as

457.31 speak of this as] *HNM* speak of that as

619

457.33 she should also be much interested] *HNM* she should also be made interested

458.14 favourable [...] many things it would have occurred to him to commend, and] *HNM* favorable [...] many things of which he had thought well, and

458.14 were not most] *HNM* were the most

458.17 vivid warning,] *HNM* colossal warning,

458.20 ascendant and] *HNM* ascendant, and

458.22 over and master the subject.] *HNM* over and study it.

458.31 vulgar little legislator] *HNM* common little Congressman

459.2 representative had] *HNM* Congressman had

459.4 absorb so] *HNM* master so

459.13 as well as in the generals, she] *HNM* as well as in the generals. She

459.16 to worry the opposite party in England.] *HNM* to worry in England the opposite party.

459.32 vulgar, importunate one, would] *HNM* vulgar, superfluous one, would

460.25 assent. § As at last] *HNM* assent. As at last

461.5 Sir Rufus's asking] *HNM* Sir Rufus asking

461.7 seemed not quite right and *HNM* seemed rather poorly, and

461.19 a parcel of papers which] *HNM* some papers, which

461.26 he failed to recognise] *HNM* he didn't recognise

461.30 his prose "set up."] *HNM* his prose, and still more his verse, "set up."

462.12 perfect temper.] *HNM* lovely temper.

462.32 another? It was morbid—it was mad. When he accused her of this extravagance it was very simple for her to meet his surprise with a greater astonishment—astonishment at his being able] *HNM* another? With the simplest form of the national consciousness a woman had more than the tenor of the feminine existence and the scope of her responsibilities demanded: what, therefore, was the morbid fancy of his wife's to give it in her own case an indefinite extension? When he accused her of being morbid, it was very simple for her to deny it utterly, and to express her astonishment at his being able

463.8   her participation] *HNM* the participation

463.10   renewed association,] *HNM* renewed tenderness,

463.11   kindness, in the midst of memories] *HNM* kindness and memories

463.20   determined not to fall into that vice on his own side.] *HNM* determined not, on his own side, to fall into that vice.

464.29   drop the subject that night] *HNM* did not part that night

465.9   was unable to conceive] *HNM* couldn't conceive

465.19   he never made her] *HNM* he didn't make her

465.20   He neither sighed nor scowled nor took on] *HNM* He didn't sigh or scowl, or take on

465.22   smile, remaining to] *HNM* smile, and remained to

466.13   of air and were an offence to] *HNM* of air, and were an injury to

466.18   to an injurious strain.] *HNM* to a most unnatural strain.

466.27   interest. § It is] *HNM* interest. It is

467.1   round) he had let her know] *HNM* round), he let her know

467.23   him—the love that had had the] *HNM* him, the love that had the

467.34   unless he very soon broke off] *HNM* if he didn't very soon break off

468.19   had violated his express command),] *HNM* had violated his solemn injunction),

468.32   all pretensions of censorship;] *HNM* all pretensions of censureship;

469.2   might hammer away at it.] *HNM* might throw his weight upon it.

469.3   would not the morbidness be quite on *his* side?] *HNM* the morbidness would be on *his* side.

469.9   was now valid for earthly purposes.] *HNM* was now substantial and complete.

469.15   when valuable ideas are laid by to ripen,] *HNM* when a work is laid by to ripen,

471.6   "Your damned fantastic] *HNM* "your d—d fantastic

471.11   waiting-maid] *HNM* lady's maid

471.16   sniffed it—then] *HNM* sniffed it, and

471.19   on the bed] *HNM* in the bed

621

TEXTUAL VARIANTS II

Substantive Variants after Copy Text

Textual Variants II lists the differences between the copy-text and the text of the *New York Edition*. Of the nine stories presented in this volume, only four were selected and revised by James for the *New York Edition*: 'Pandora' (vol. XVIII, 1909), 'Louisa Pallant' (vol. XIII, 1908), and 'The Aspern Papers' and 'The Liar' (vol. XII, 1908). Both 'The Path of Duty' and 'A New England Winter' had been included in the original plan, but were later excised for various reasons (see Introduction, pp. xcv–xcvi).

In the record that follows the first entry is keyed to the page and line number in this Cambridge Edition; it is then followed by the corresponding text from the relevant *New York Edition* (1908, 1909). As might be expected, the *New York Edition* texts offer much more extensive changes than those between the magazine and first volume editions, as these revisions were made towards the end of James's writing career. The final revised texts of the four stories were sent to Scribner's between February and October 1908.

In the *New York Edition* one can observe the constant elimination of commas, and of 'that' to introduce a clause; also the extensive substitution of dashes for parentheses. James tends to amplify sentences, adding clauses:

> 4.4 he had not a high sense of humour.] whose only fault was that his sense of comedy, or of humour of things, had never been specifically disengaged from his several other senses. ('Pandora')

Or adding specifications:

> 368.33 more colour. And now] more colour. Don't you suppose Vandyke's things tell a lot about him ('The Liar')
> 5.3 hidden in their shawls.] hidden in remarkably ugly shawls. ('Pandora')
> 363.5 Miss Bordereau's papers.] Juliana's treasure. ('The Aspern Papers')

He often expands the text conveying an effect of abstraction:

> 243.6 putting their ideas into words] communicating by sound ('Louisa Pallant')

366.7 He was something of a celebrity and he was apparently in a society of celebrities] He was appreciably "known" and was now apparently in a society of the known if not of the knowing ('The Liar')

Sentences are sometimes shortened, to enhance dramatic effect:

346.30 with my lamp in my hand.] lamp in hand. ('The Aspern Papers')
375.34 with an expression of unalloyed pleasure] with frank delight ('The Liar')

Allusions tend to multiply:

363.23 full of my literary concupiscence] full of stratagems and spoils [Shakespeare, *The Merchant of Venice*] ('The Aspern Papers')

Proper names are often replaced with common nouns (and vice versa):

244.20 Mrs Pallant] my friend ('Louisa Pallant')
360.21 to Tita Bordereau.] to my victim. ('The Aspern Papers')
336.25 the old lady went on.] Miss Bordereau went on. ('The Aspern Papers')

Family names are often replaced with first names, indicating a greater familiarity of the narrator with the other characters.

352.28 Miss Bordereau's death.] Juliana's death. ('The Aspern Papers')

As in TV1, the following differences have not been recorded: typographical differences attributable to publishers' house style – such as the capitalization, italicization, and spelling of certain proper names and titles; differences regarding American and British spelling (honor/honour); abbreviations (haven't/have n't); dates (twentieth/20th); simple inverted commas changed into double inverted commas (or vice versa). We have however recorded variants between roman and italic type, the change of full stops into exclamation or question marks (and vice versa), and the introduction or deletion of new paragraphs.

Particularly significant excisions and/or additions are also discussed in the notes to the tales.

Pandora

3.13   later comers] those less fortunate than ourselves

3.14   the unprovided, the bewildered] the unprovided, the belated, the bewildered

3.22   concealment of thought] active concealment of thought

3.24   he was going to take] he was about

3.26   ceremonious, stiff, inquisitive, stuffed] ceremonious, curious, stiff, stuffed

3.27   that at present the German Empire is the country in the world most highly evolved.] that, as lately rearranged, the German Empire places in the most striking light the highest of all the possibilities of the greatest of all the peoples.

3.29   of the claims of the United States, and that this portion of the globe presented an enormous field for study.] of the claims to economic and other consideration of the United States, and that this quarter of the globe offered a vast field for study.

3.29   for study. The process] for study. § The process

3.30   had already begun,] had already begun for him,

4.1   for Vogelstein inquired not only with his tongue,—he inquired with his eyes (that is, with his spectacles), with his ears,] the case being that Vogelstein enquired not only with his tongue, but with his eyes —that is with his spectacles—with his ears,

4.6   organs. § He was an excellent young man and his only fault was that he had not a high sense of humour. He had enough, however, to suspect this deficiency, and he was aware that he was about to visit a highly humorous people. This suspicion gave him] organs. He was a highly upright young man, whose only fault was that his sense of comedy, or of humour of things, had never been specifically disengaged from his several other senses. He vaguely felt that something should be done about this, and in a general manner proposed to do it, for he was on his way to explore a society abounding in comic aspects. This consciousness of a missing measure gave him

4.13   But, on the other hand, the day] On the other hand the day

4.15   And he was by no means] Moreover he was by no means

4.18   which he was ashamed to use] such a man of his education should be ashamed to use

4.19   But lost in the inconsiderate crowd] Lost none the less in the inconsiderate crowd

4.22   so that, for the moment, to fill himself out, he tried to have an opinion on the subject of this delay] so that during the hour, to save his importance, he cultivated such ground as lay in sight for a judgement of his delay

4.24   It appeared to him that it might be proved to be considerably greater than the occasion demanded.] Mightn't it be proved, facts, figures and documents—or at least watch—in hand, considerably greater than the occasion demanded?

4.29   and he would have admitted it—] and under the pressure, being candid, he would have admitted it

4.32   in the United States.] in the great Republic.

5.1   with their shoulders on a level] their shoulders kept on a level

5.3   hidden in their shawls.] hidden in remarkably ugly shawls.

5.5   to swell the current of western democracy,] to swell still further the huge current of the Western democracy;

5.8   this evidence.] this particular evidence.

5.14   wrapped in striped shawls and crowned] wrapped also in striped shawls, though in prettier ones that the nursing mothers of the steerage, and crowned

5.17   occupants of the steerage,] occupants of the forward quarter,]

5.19   over the tarred sides of the ship.] over the latter's great tarred sides.

5.20   He observed that] He noticed that

5.22   a country of girls] the country of the Mädchen.

5.23   a question to study] an aspect to study

5.26   seemed to him of that same habit] struck him as of that same habit

5.30   evolutions which were] evolutions that were

5.36   were half the charm of travel. As yet] were notoriously half the charm of travel, and perhaps even most when they couldn't be expressed in figures, numbers, diagrams or the other merely useful symbols. As yet

5.36   very few on the steamer.] very few among the objects presented to sight on the steamer.

6.1   of the same persuasion,] of one and the same persuasion,

6.7   which is to be perceived] always to be noted

6.9   perceive that he is the victim] perceive himself the victim

6.10   a general objection] a sweeping objection

6.11   in these circumstances] in the general plight

6.17   to prepare him.] to prepare him for some of the oddities.

6.21   had even said that in his place he would have his coronet painted.] had even hinted at the correct reproduction of his coronet.

6.22   The cynical adviser] This marked man of the world

6.24   omitted this ensign of his rank; the precious piece] omitted every pictured plea for his rank; there were others of which he might have made use. The precious piece

6.26   is depended upon to remain steady among general concussions] is trusted never to flinch among universal concussions

6.32   outermost point] uttermost point

6.34   a kind of human expression,] a human expression

6.35   the ship was turned;] the prow was turned;

7.3   where the sky and sea, between them, managed to make so poor an opposition.] where the elements of air and water managed to make between them so comparatively poor an opposition.

7.4   author. § In the great curve] author. In the great curve

7.7   companion-way. In itself this was not] companionway. § This was not in itself

7.10   dressed, and rather pretty.] dressed, rather pretty;

7.12   She very soon saw that he was looking at her;] She was soon aware he had observed her;

7.14   which seemed to indicate that she was coming straight towards him.] that seemed to indicate a purpose of approaching him.

7.16   much older than this.] much older than that

7.18   they came straight towards one, like that. This young lady, however, was no longer looking at him, and, though she] they were apt to advance, like this one, straight upon their victim. Yet the present specimen was no longer looking at him, and though she

7.18   she had come upstairs] she had come above

7.20   she wished to see] she simply wanted to see

7.23   as if she were in search] as if in keen search

7.25   presently saw this was what she really had come up for.] finally arrived at a conviction of her real motive.

7.26   with her eyes bent] her eyes bent

7.27   after he had perceived] after he had gathered

7.30   about the people, especially the ladies,] about the tendency of the
        people, especially of the ladies,

7.30   taking to themselves] to take to themselves

7.33   without meeting her eye.] systematically avoiding her eye.

7.34   was conscious that she] was conscious she

8.1   by acts so flagrant to attract the attention of] by arts so flagrant to
        work upon the quiet dignity of

8.2   it became evident to him] it stood out that

8.13   That young man ended by speaking to his invader] That young man—
        though with more, in such connexions in general, to go upon—ended
        by addressing himself to his aggressor,

8.17   but she smiled] but smiled

8.21   It seemed to him indeed] It affected him indeed as

8.22   even a rather flippant mode] even rather a flippant mode

8.23   if she desired his seat.] if she desired of him the surrender of his
        seat.

8.30   went on, with a frank smile.] went on with a smile of which the seren-
        ity matched her other abundance.

8.32   "Our name is Day. If you see that on anything. I should be so obliged
        if you would tell me] "Our name's just Day—you mightn't think it *was*
        a name, might you? if we didn't make the most of it. If you see that on
        anything. I'd be so obliged if you'd tell me

8.36   I am much obliged to you."] I wouldn't disturb you."

9.20   a considerable waste of time;] but the loosest economy of
        consciousness;

9.22   be doubted that he should see] be doubted he should see

9.23   It may as well be said without delay that he did see] It may as well be
        written without delay that he saw

9.24   I have depicted with some precision the circumstances under which]
        I have sketched in some detail the conditions in which

9.26   this candid Teuton] this fair square Teuton

9.28   to do with regard to her,] to do in relation to her,

9.30   But in a very short time he perceived that] But he satisfied himself in a very short time that

9.32   save a certain local quality and the fact] save certain signs of habitat and climate—and save, further, the fact

9.36   Her local quality indeed, he took rather on trust than apprehended for himself. She was native to a small town in the interior of the American continent, and a lady from New York, who was on the ship, and with whom he had a good deal of conversation, assured him Miss Day was exceedingly provincial.] The local stamp sharply, as he gathered, impressed upon her he estimated indeed rather in a borrowed than in a natural light, for if she was native to a small town in the interior of the American continent one of their fellow passengers, a lady from New York with whom he had a good deal of conversation, pronounced her "atrociously" provincial.

10.1   ascertained the fact] arrived at this certitude

10.3   It is true that she threw some light on her processes by remarking to him that] It was true she gave it the support of her laying down that

10.5   to the discriminating class.] to the critical or only to the criticised half of the nation.

10.7   She was a Mrs. Dangerfield, a handsome, confidential, insinuating woman, and Vogelstein's talk with her took a turn that was almost philosophic.] Mrs. Dangerfield was a handsome confidential insinuating woman, with whom Vogelstein felt his talk take a very wide range indeed.

10.10   are often too stupid to perceive] often lack the intelligence to perceive

10.13   as in the most monarchical communities?] as in the most monarchical and most exclusive societies?

10.13   She laughed these ideas] She laughed such delusions

10.19   not her peculiar stamp.] not at all her grand air

10.20   looking straight before them.] and looked straight before them.

10.22   black curls, and her lips and cheeks moved] black curls; her lips moved

10.25   which covered her coiffure and encircled her neck, leaving] concealing her hair, encircling her neck and having

10.30   a kind of hard glaze.] a hard glaze

10.34   and truculent, if it had not been] and truculent, hadn't it been for

11.2   He liked to look at you, but he would not have pretended to under-
        stand you much nor] He liked to have you in sight, but wouldn't have
        pretended to understand you much or

11.3   sorry that it should put you] sorry it should put you

11.4   but they seldom talked] but seldom talked

11.5   something passive] something vague

11.6   they were victims of a spell.] they had become victims of a wrought
        spell.

11.6   evidently pleasant;] of no sinister cast;

11.9   upon this simple, satisfied pair, in which further development] on this
        simple satisfied pair, in whom further development

11.11   told Count Vogelstein] made it known to Count Otto

11.25   elaborate French clothes,] elegant French clothes

11.26   could see that for himself] could see this for himself

11.28   and settled most of the questions] settling on the spot most of the
        questions

11.29   interior. The voyage] interior. § The voyage

12.4   more serious and preoccupied,] more serious and strenuous

12.14   alone, not, apparently having made] alone, apparently not having
        made

12.31   these were the most transcendent flights of American humour.] these
        must be choice specimens of that American humour admired and
        practised by a whole continent and yet to be rendered accessible to
        a trained diplomatist, clearly, but by some special and incalculable
        revelation.

12.34   the tale I have so often mentioned,] the tale already mentioned,

13.1   who, in the Tauchnitz volume, was] who was, in the Tauchnitz volume

13.5   Count Vogelstein yielded] Count Otto yielded

13.7   in spite of Mrs. Dangerfield's warnings, sought an opportunity for] in
        spite of Mrs. Dangerfield's emphatic warning, sought occasion for

13.9   To mention this sentiment without mentioning other impressions of
        his voyage, with which] To mention that this impulse took effect with-
        out mentioning sundry other of his current impressions with which

13.12   a vague fascination] an irresistible appeal

13.13   a sort of originality] a rare originality

13.15   in absent-minded attitudes,] in musing attitudes,

13.19   Vogelstein's conception] his conception

13.20   Repeatedly warned] Repeatedly admonished

13.23   Mrs. Dangerfield reminded him, and he had made the observation himself] The lady reminded him, and he had himself made the observation

13.25   One is ignorant of proportions and values; one is exposed, lonely, thankful for attention] One was ignorant of proportions and values; one was exposed to mistakes and thankful for attention

13.27   prove a great encumbrance.] be as a millstone round one's neck:

13.28   struck a note which resounded in Vogelstein's imagination.] struck and sustained that note, which resounded in the young man's imagination.

13.29   falling in love with some American girl] committing himself to some American girl

13.31   when one fell in love with a girl, there was nothing to be done but marry her,] when one committed one's self there was nothing to do but march to the altar,

13.32   P. W. Day? (These were the initials] P.W. Day?—since such were the initials

13.33   Vogelstein felt the peril,] Count Otto felt the peril,

13.36   like the rise in prices, the telephone] like the railway, the telegraph

14.4   that Vogelstein was afraid of falling in love with Pandora Day; a young woman who] that he feared being carried away by a passion for a young woman who

14.5   as I say] as we recognise

14.6   a girl whose independence] a person whose high spirit

14.8   whose nose was so very well bred,] whose mouth had charming lines

14.10   There was something almost comical in her attitude toward these belongings; she appeared to regard them as a care,] There was an effect of drollery in her behaviour to these subjects of her zeal, whom she seemed to regard as a care,

14.13   inadvertent; then, suddenly, she remembered] inadvertent, and then suddenly remembered

14.14   to tuck her parents] to tuck them

14.17   came near] drew near

14.18   placidly, like a pair] after the fashion of a pair

14.19   brought up the captain] brought up the Captain of the ship

14.21   a sudden inspiration.] a sudden happy thought.

14.24   queer little people?] queer and rather dear little people?

14.26   looked up at the captain with] looked up at the high functionary who thus unbent to them with

14.27   and bent towards them] he inclined himself

14.29   as if she were explaining to the captain] as if in explanation to the good Captain

14.30   that they wouldn't speak.] that he needn't expect them to speak.

14.32   with the commander of the ship,] with the important friend,

14.34   in spite of his austere position, when, presently after, they separated.] for all his importance, when the two presently after separated.

14.35   moral of our episode] moral of our little matter

15.1   in spite of the meagreness of the conversation that had passed between them,] in spite of the limits of such acquaintance as he had momentarily made with her,

15.4   It was the evening after] It was in the course of the evening after

15.6   the evening being mild and brilliant] the hour being auspiciously mild

15.9   under the stars, with its swaying] under the low stars, its swaying

15.11   Vogelstein had come up] Count Otto had come up

15.13   under the veil that seemed intended to protect] under the veil worn to protect

15.15   cigar, and asked] cigar—then asked

15.16   he walked with her] he allowed her to enjoy it

15.18   he remembered afterwards some of the things she said.] he was to remember afterwards some of the things she had said.

15.21   as he knew] as he was aware

15.31   Vogelstein wondered whether] Count Otto wondered if

15.32   was her lover and if she were betrothed to him,] were her lover and if they had plighted their troth,

15.33   that is coming down."] who's coming down.

15.35   she told him that] she put it to him that

16.2   were fond of culture.] were rich in culture.

16.7   Pheidias] Phidias

16.9   while she was young;] while she was comparatively unformed ("comparatively!" he mutely gasped);

16.11   something of that sort in Goethe, somewhere.] something of that sort somewhere in Goethe.

16.13   Vogelstein thought] The young man thought

16.15   extraordinary odyssey of her parents, and wondered] extraordinary pilgrimage of her parents; he wondered

16.17   pleasant place,] important or typical place,

16.19   that it was horrid,] that this was a big question,

16.22   "Ah! You are going to live elsewhere?"] "Ah you're going to live elsewhere?" Vogelstein asked as if that fact too would be typical.

16.24   been away. They won't find Utica the same;] been away," the girl went on. "They won't find in Utica the same charm;

16.26   Utica—!" And the girl broke off with a little sigh.] Utica—!" She broke off as before a complex statement.

16.27   Utica is small?" Vogelstein suggested.] Utica is inferior?" Vogelstein seemed to see his way to suggest.

16.28   "Well, no, it's middle-sized. I hate anything middling,"] "Well no, I guess I can't have you call Utica inferior. It isn't supreme—that's what's the matter with it, and I hate anything middling,"

16.31   he thought there was] he recognised

16.32   that carried out such a spirit.] that matched such a pronouncement.

16.36   little burghers.] complete little burghers.

17.2   exclaimed, nodding two or three times, rather portentously.] nodded two or three times, portentously.

17.6   hasn't got any; where should she have found it?] hasn't got one; where, if you please, should she have got it?

17.7   to ask such questions as that.] to make her the subject of such questions as that.

17.8   that seems] it seems

17.11   Count Vogelstein?"] dear Count?"

17.14   murmured, helplessly.] returned with an irritated sense of wasted wisdom. She liked to explain her country, but that somehow always required two persons.

17.17   such people, it's a new type.] such people—it *is* a new type.

17.18   Count Vogelstein, smiling] Count Otto smiled.

17.19   with an explanation] with a demonstration

17.21   of wharf] of the wharf

17.29   Vogelstein's first impression] Our young man's first impression

17.31   under the feet, palisaded with rough-hewn, slanting piles,] under the feet, an expanse palisaded with rough-hewn piles that leaned this way and that,

17.34   brandishing their whips and awaiting] who brandished their whips and awaited

17.36   strange sound, at once] strange sound, a challenge at once

18.1   Vogelstein said to himself] Count Otto said to himself

18.2   a sense that he ought to] a sense that he should have to

18.8   had been intimate] had been fondly intimate

18.13   at them, imploring] at them, eloquent, imploring

18.13   a good deal of sameness.] "rather glassy."

18.14   performing their office,] discharging their duty

18.21   to see, would be like that.] to see—to *have* to see—a good deal of, would be like that.

18.23   Mr. and Mrs. Day, who were seated] Mr. and Mrs. Day seated

18.25   hitherto perceived,] hitherto recognised,

18.28   Mr. and Mrs. Day, as they would have said, were glad to] Mr. and Mrs. Day were, as they would have said, real glad to

18.29   Vogelstein remarked] our observer remarked

19.1   servant, an Englishman (he had taken home for practice in the language), had gone in pursuit of] servant was off in search of

19.2   he had got his things] Count Otto himself had got his things

19.4   taking off his hat] raising his hat

19.7   She was not much "formed" yet, but she was] She was indeed still unformed, but was

19.10   Count Vogelstein said.] Count Otto said.

19.11   The young man answered] The young American answered

19.12   "As soon as we begin we shall go straight.] "As soon as we're started we'll go all right.

19.20   I'll tell on you,"] I'll tell on you, sis,"

19.21   to his announcement;] to his menace;

19.22   she addressed herself to] she addressed herself only, though with all freedom, to

19.23   Vogelstein had no time] He had no time

19.24   the emissaries of the customs;] the dispensers of fortune;

19.26   very well treated.] naturally exempt from the common doom.

19.28   the formal declarations of the Count,] the Count's formal declarations

19.31   and he distributed freely a dozen chalk-marks. The servant had unlocked and unbuckled various pieces, and while he was closing them the officer] distributing chalk-marks as if they had been so many love-pats. The servant had done some superfluous unlocking and unbuckling, and while he closed the pieces the officer

19.33   we are after."] we're most after."

19.36   But Vogelstein's visitor left him] But this representative of order left our friend

20.1   very quietly uttered,] quite paternally uttered,

20.3   offer him a tip.] offer a tip

20.4   and it was very amicable, after all.] which had a finish of its own after all.

20.8   and he cast his eyes over it, deliberately, stroking] and over which he cast his eyes, thoughtfully stroking

20.9   upon their luggage.] on their luggage.

20.10   Vogelstein sent off] Count Otto sent off

20.16   if Utica was not—he had her sharp little sister's word for it—as agree-
         able as what was about him there,] if Utica—he had her sharp little
         sister's word for it—was worse than what was about him there,

20.18   the customs-officer] the representative of order

20.19   the captain of the steamer.] the Captain of the ship.

20.25   were not unversed in certain social arts.] rejoiced to extravagance in
         the social graces.

21.2   stars that he had not] stars he had n't

21.4   had been described by a member of Pandora's family as her lover.]
         had also been described by a member of Pandora's family as Pandora's
         lover.

21.5   remarked to Vogelstein,] remarked to him

21.12   a movement which sent] a movement that sent

21.14   returning the smile of the girl.] with an equal geniality.

21.17   over the coffer instantly, with] over the coffer with

21.18   murmured, modestly.] modestly murmured.

21.23   said Mr. Lansing, laughing.] said Mr. Lansing, good-humouredly.

21.27   his servant,] his English valet

21.28   ask whether] ask if

21.33   Count Vogelstein began] Count Otto began

22.2   Vogelstein went] He went

22.5   Of course, at the end of two winters] At the end of two winters

22.6   various kinds, and his study] various kinds—his study

22.12   become rather familiar to him in Washington.] become familiar to
         him by waters of the Potomac.

22.24   the little squares and circles] the Squares and Circles

22.26   benches—at this period of expansion] benches—under this magic of
         expansion

22.29   humorously inconsistent,] whimsically wilful,

22.31   show to be a mistake.] prove a mistake.

23.1   to Vogelstein's apprehension,] to Count Otto's apprehension,

23.2 himself to be in a society which was founded on necessary lapses.] himself in a society founded on fundamental fallacies and triumphant blunders.

23.4 to enjoy the United States] to enjoy the great Republic

23.7 prejudices. Mrs. Bonnycastle] prejudices. § Mrs. Bonnycastle

23.10 She perceived differences where he only saw] American promiscuity, goodness knew, had been strange to him, but it was nothing to the queerness of American criticism. This lady would discourse to him à *perte de vue* on differences where he only saw

23.11 the merits and defects] the merits and the defects

23.12 that society] this society

23.19 from a great many] from many

23.20 who only thought it expensive.] who only, with some grimness, thought it inevitable.

23.21 are saddled;] were saddled;

23.22 and you knew they had] and one knew they had

23.28 for persons of leisure.] for that body which Vogelstein was to hear invoked, again and again, with the mixture of desire and of deprecation that might have attended the mention of a secret service, under the name of a leisure-class.

23.29 the wings of their door,] the wings of their house-door,

23.33 he thought that, for Washington] it struck him that for Washington

24.2 let us have some fun—let us invite the President!"] let us be vulgar and have some fun—let us invite the President."

24.4 my little chapter] my chapter

24.6 the same functionary] the same august ruler

24.8 (the old one, then, was just] —the old one was then just

24.8 and Otto Vogelstein] and Count Otto

24.12 in the national capital, in the houses that he] at the national capital, in the houses he

24.14 whimsical proposal to invite him,] whimsical suggestion of their inviting him,

24.18 could not be said to] could scarce be said to

24.22   if they were not carefully watched.] if not carefully watched.

24.23   Vogelstein had grown to have] Our young man had come to entertain

24.28   lonesome glances] frequent lonesome glances

24.31   new to Vogelstein] new to the enquiring secretary

24.33   engaged for the evening to] engaged, under stress, to

24.36   these functionaries were almost always impressive, and had a com-
         plexion which served as a livery.] these latter public characters almost
         always to be impressive and of that rich racial hue which of itself
         served as a livery.

24.36   misleading figures] confounding figures

25.1   much less to be encountered] much less to be met

25.2   they never were to be encountered] they were never frequent

25.11   essence became] essence really became

25.15   reversing in his imagination a position which was not unknown]
         reversing in his fancy a position not at all unknown

25.16   He had often, in Washington, been discoursed to at the same moment
         by several virginal voices.] He has so repeatedly heard himself ad-
         dressed in even more than triple simultaneity.

25.19   well in Europe] well for Europe

25.20   any girl] *any* girl

25.21   a remarkable individual in a remarkable genus.] a remarkable speci-
         men in a remarkable species.

25.23   Vogelstein exclaimed, staring.] —and Vogelstein had a stare of
         intelligence.

25.24   stared a moment in return, then laughed very hard.] broke on her side
         into free amusement.

25.32   a great success] a great belle

25.34   said Vogelstein, reflecting] said Count Otto, considering

26.7   point the other way] point another way

26.11   and as belonging] and belonging

26.13   to ask in a moment, as he meditated.] to ask while he meditated.

26.13   way of uttering] way of putting

26.15   broke into mocking laughter.] met it, however, but with mocking laughter.

26.20   he ought not to have made such an inquiry.] he oughtn't so to have expressed himself.

26.25   a great many things which] innumerable things that

26.26   the daughter of the Days,] the heroine of the *Donau*,

26.27   see her again] see her and hear her again

26.28   parted but the day before;] parted the day before

26.30   he would judge America] he might judge America

26.31   Had he judged it correctly?] *Had* he judged America correctly?

26.33   terrible to Otto Vogelstein;] terrible to Count Otto;

26.35   take upon myself] take on myself

27.4   showing much acquaintance] and showed much acquaintance

27.8   some of them, but] *some* of them *very* much, but

27.12   could not have told you whether] could not have told us whether

27.12   or not. On the next] or not. § On the next

27.16   Vogelstein had been] Our young man had been

27.18   possessed the great advantage] and enjoyed the great advantage

27.21   to escape that boisterous interlude.] to escape, after a long winter, that final affront.

27.26   the discussion which could] the discussion that could

27.36   his bright Bostonian] his judicious Bostonian

27.36   and contented himself] contenting himself

28.2   in a lower and more sceptical key.] in a lower and easier key.

28.4   some half-an-hour] some half-hour

28.5   was not indicated] was never indicated

28.10   to see you] to meet you

28.10   Vogelstein felt himself taken for a mere constituent] Count Otto felt himself taken for a mere loyal subject

28.15   Here Vogelstein] Here our young man

28.16   on a sofa, in conversation] on a sofa and in conversation

28.18	in a kind of recess] in a shallow recess
28.23	was making him laugh,] ministered freely and without scruple, it was clear, to this effect of his comfortably unbending.
28.25	prettily dressed] beautifully dressed
28.26	and her eyes were attached] and her eyes attached
28.30	Vogelstein checked himself] Count Otto checked himself
28.31	It was not customary] It wasn't usual
28.33	Vogelstein felt it in this case to be less] the young secretary felt it in this case less
28.35	even in his momentary look he had perceived] even with half an eye, as they said, had taken
29.1	looked brilliant] shone, to intensity,
29.3	Vogelstein thought,] her old shipmate thought,
29.4	He didn't wish to speak to her yet; he wished] He didn't want to speak to her yet; he wanted
29.6	attractive in the thought] attractive in the fact
29.7	It was she whom Mrs. Bonnycastle] It was she Mrs. Bonnycastle
29.9	yet Vogelstein had seen] yet he had made out
29.10	suggested ambition] suggested a fine ambition
29.11	took two ices, which he did not want] took some tea, which he hadn't desired
29.12	the silent burghers] the silent senseless burghers
29.18	pretty sure that she] pretty sure she
29.20	that had been the purpose, of course, of Mr. Bellamy's letter.] this would naturally have been the purpose of Mr. Bellamy's letter.
29.20	with this gentleman,] with that gentleman,
29.21	he recovered from his sickness?] he got over the sickness interfering with the reunion?
29.21	All this passed through Vogelstein's mind,] These images and these questions coursed through Count Otto's mind,
29.22	saw that it was quite in] saw it must be quite in
29.23	there was nothing, evidently] there was evidently nothing
29.24	his cup he heard] his cup heard

29.27   Pandora asked.] Pandora benevolently asked.

29.31   Pandora remarked, sympathetically.] —and there was a high mature competence in the way the girl sounded the note of approval.

29.35   the President responded.] the great man responded.

30.2   these kind folks."] these bright folks."

30.3   companion, and he gave] companion; after which he gave

30.4   before him, which they did with] before him. They did it with

30.7   When, after a few moments, Vogelstein] When a little later he

30.8   he saw the hostess] he saw the host and hostess

30.11   if he spoke to her at all, he wished to speak to her alone.] if he should speak to her at all he would somehow wish it to be in more privacy.

30.14   opposite, in pink] opposite and in pink

30.17   I find she is] I find she *is*

30.18   make it out."] make it out," said Count Otto.

30.19   which provoked Mrs. Bonnycastle] that again moved Mrs. Bonnycastle

30.22   a simple question] a simple earnest childlike question

30.24   of a girl—in rose-colour—whose parents were in society?] of the parents of a triumphant girl in rose-colour, with a nose all her own, in society?

30.25   Count Vogelstein inquired, with a strain] he went on with a strain

30.27   stared at him a moment, with her laughter in her face] launched at him all her laughter.

30.33   What new type,] *What* new type,

30.34   said Vogelstein, pleadingly, and conscious that] he returned pleadingly—so conscious was he that

30.35   reply for a moment] reply a moment

31.3   Vogelstein waited] Count Otto waited

31.5   reinforced] re-enforced

31.5   a gentleman that] a gentleman who

31.6   Vogelstein had asked] He had asked

31.8   in Pandora's present situation that suggested isolation.] in her present situation to show her for solitary.

31.9   Vogelstein's taste;] our friend's taste

31.11   that matched the tone in which] matching to a shade the tone in which

31.12   I wondered whether you were] I wondered if you were

31.14   all with us!"] all with us."

31.16   At this the gentlemen] At which the gentlemen

31.16   and one of them remarked that that] one of them remarking that this

31.18   another said that he] another put on record that he

31.24   to my country] to *my* country

31.27   the girl returned] the ex-heroine of the *Donau* returned

31.28   which with her was evidently but] which evidently ranked with her but

31.30   any one here.] any right here.

31.32   on the ocean," said the young man smiling.] on the great ocean," the young man smiled.

32.1   Vogelstein exclaimed,] her associated in the other memories sighed

32.4   our home.] our natural home.

32.6   "And I hope they are happy," said Vogelstein.] Count Otto clung to his interest. "And I hope they're happy."

32.11   "Oh, no; there are some things I can't find out."] "Oh, no—there are some things I *can't* find out."

32.13   what I was on the ship.] what I was in that phase.

32.14   on the ship?] in that phase?

32.14   asked the cabinet minister] asked a cabinet minister

32.16   said Vogelstein.] Count Otto said.

32.22   signified to Pandora] signified to her young friend

32.24   an answer for each of them,] a vivid answer for each,

32.25   as he listened, that, as she said, she had advanced a great deal.] while he listened that this would be indeed, in her development, as she said, another phase.

32.26   as she was,] as she might be,

32.27   Vogelstein turned away] He turned away

32.28   asked her a question.] put her a question.

32.31   because he had not some direct acquaintance with Mrs. Steuben, as well as a] because he failed of all direct acquaintance with the amiable woman or of any

32.32   and he had been at her house.] and had been at her house.

32.33   a handsome, mild, soft, swaying woman,] was a handsome mild soft swaying person,

32.35   the Queen in *Hamlet*.] the *vieux jeu* idea of the queen in "Hamlet."

33.2   positive odour] positive strong odour

33.3   crude in Vogelstein] superfluous in our young man

33.6   young lady belongs.] young lady belongs?

33.7   upon the secretary] on the secretary

33.10   she asked.] she then began to flute.

33.18   he scarcely observed] he scarce heeded

33.20   so unsatisfactory.] so uninforming.

33.26   *what* type it is! It seems impossible to find out."] what type it *is*. It seems impossible," he gasped, "to find out."

33.32   Mrs. Steuben asked.] the elder lady asked.

33.35   demanded, smiling, of the young German.] demanded of the young German with untempered brightness.

33.35   the thing that you said] the thing you said

34.2   for a Southerner] for we of the Sooth.

34.5   hand to Count Vogelstein] hand to Count Otto

34.7   always meeting, and] always meeting again and

34.7   to come and see her.] to fail to wait upon her.

34.9   if Count Vogelstein and] if the Count and

34.10   the picnic that she] the picnic she

34.13   Vogelstein answered that] The Count answered that

34.27   Vogelstein gazed] Count Otto gazed

34.29   the explosion of Mrs. Bonnycastle's mirth.] a renewed explosion of Mrs. Bonnycastle's sense of the ridiculous.

34.30   continued his interrogation,] pushed his advantage, such as it was,

35.4   Vogelstein explained] The visitor explained

35.12   smell,—the smell of growing things.] smell, the smell of growing things and in particular, as he thought, of Mrs. Steuben's Sooth.

35.14   that almost inspired him.] that strongly impressed him.

35.21   that told the story;] who told the story;

35.22   saw that her parents] saw how little her parents

35.23   in innumerable ways;] in different ways.

35.23   the great fact on her own side being] As a great fact on her own side was

35.26   In this view, of course, it was to be] it was naturally to be

35.26   that she should leave the authors of her being] that she would leave the authors of her mere material being

35.29   let them slide;] let them slide altogether

35.29   confinement; sometimes] confinement, resorting to them under cover of night and with every precaution; sometimes

35.34   that she was much better than they.] that, though in some of her manifestations a bore, she was at her worst less of a bore than they.

36.1   on the contrary, she took] she took on the contrary

36.3   certain competitions] whole ranges of competition and comparison

36.5   exhibited to Vogelstein,] laid bare to the earnest stranger,

36.7   in the United States is much more] in the great Republic was more yearningly, not to say gropingly,

36.9   too obvious.] too restless and obvious.

36.11   with sudden quotations.] with familiar quotations.

36.12   in a developed form] as a developed form

36.13   Bonnycastle said that] Bonnycastle hinted that

36.15   the first thing they did.] the first place they got to.

36.16   By this means they sometimes got into society in foreign lands] By such arts they sometimes entered society on the other side

36.17   on the other hand,] at the same time,

36.18   in the United States,] in the American world,

36.19   in the latter country] in the Western hemisphere

36.20   All this applied perfectly to] All of which quite applied to

36.21   ship), the effacement,] ship), the relegation, the effacement,

36.23   with which she had advanced;] of her march;

36.25   of American society,] of the American mass,

36.26   account for it.] account for such things.

36.27   When she moved her family from Utica,] When she "moved" from Utica—mobilised her commissariat—

36.28   Vogelstein called on her] Count Otto called

36.31   and the young man] and our young man

36.34   for me to attempt to conceal it,] for us to fail of catching it

36.36   and took his way] and that he therefore took his way

37.1   which unfolds] that unfolds

37.4   and wondering why he had come.] even wondering why he had come there.

37.5   which seemed to Vogelstein] that struck him as

37.10   light gives] light would give

37.14   a relief to see the young lady] a relief to have the creature

37.15   to judge really to the end how well a girl] to see really to the end how well, in other words how completely and artistically, a girl

37.18   national history,] national annals,

37.18   its panels] its lower spaces

37.20   he had hoped for] he had been counting on

37.22   for his own.] for his very own.

37.24   white, bare passages,] bleak bare development,

37.26   and he asked himself what he was doing *dans cette galère*.] and asked himself what senseless game he was playing.

37.27   In the lower House there were] In the lower House were

37.28   there was a lobby] not to speak of a lobby

37.30   of eminent congressmen, which was too serious for a joke and too
        comical for anything else. § But] of eminent defunct Congressmen,
        that was all too serious for a joke and too comic for a Valhalla.
        But

37.33   was very good company;] proved a charming fellow tourist;

37.34   never insisted too much;] never said it too much;

37.35   to be less heavy, to drag less, in the business of walking behind a cicero-
        ne.] to drag in the wake of a *cicerone* less of a lengthening or an irritating
        chain.

38.3   the conductor] the guide

38.7   thing. Throughout the hour that he] thing. § Throughout the hour he

38.9   the magnificent terrace] the splendid terrace

38.15   asked Vogelstein if] asked Count Otto if

38.16   on his replying in the affirmative, inquired] on his admitting so much,
        sought to know

38.18   the answer to this question] the satisfaction of this appeal

38.18   (in spite of the question)] —in spite of the appeal—

38.21   and he met her every evening] also met her each evening

38.27   and at which he had declared himself that] and he had himself taken
        oath that

38.29   danger, that he had taken his precautions too well.] that he had rather
        clinched his precautions.

38.31   but Vogelstein, on the whole, preferred] but this diplomatic aspirant
        preferred on the whole

38.31   it would not be agreeable to him] it wouldn't please him

38.36   to relinquish relations] to discontinue relations

39.4   would have been] would be

39.4   Vogelstein turned over] He turned over

39.6   disinterested. They] disinterested. § They

39.7   established. § Mrs. Steuben's picnickers] established. Mrs. Steuben's
        confederates

39.9   seemed to Vogelstein] seemed to our special traveller

39.10   he became aware] he became conscious

39.12   even though he was conscious] even though conscious

39.13   of idyllic talk in not sitting beside Pandora Day] of an idyllic cast in not having managed to be more "thrown with" a certain young lady

39.14   to contemplate] to hang over

39.15   was a revelation of] was a picture of

39.17   years before.] ages before.

39.19   a certain picturesqueness of decay] a touch of the romance of rich decay

39.21   bordered with old brick] lined with poor brick

39.24   of the rotting] of rotting

39.30   She declared that it had the finest situation in the world, and that it was a shame they didn't give it to the President for his villeggiatura.] She "claimed for it," as she said—some of her turns were so characteristic both of her nationality and her own style—the finest situation in the world, and was distinct as to the shame of their not giving it to the President for his country-seat.

39.34   Vogelstein wandered about with Pandora.] the young man roamed with his first and fairest acquaintance.

40.3   Vogelstein could joke] Count Otto could joke

40.5   looked like a false house, a "fly," a structure] resembled a false house, a "wing" or structure

40.9   admit the home of Washington was] allow the home of Washington to be

40.12   a charm which made him feel that he was] a charm that made him feel he was

40.19   And would they] And *would* they

40.20   some lessons. In] several thorough lessons. § In

40.21   Vogelstein and his] our young friend and his

40.26   familiar man, with a large beard and a humorous, edifying, patronising tone, which had] vulgar, heavily-bearded man, with a whimsical edifying, patronizing tone, a tone that had

40.29   cheerful thing even of] cheerful thing, an echo of the platform before the booth of a country fair, even of

40.32   but that he was too familiar. § "Oh,] but was too familiar. "Oh,

40.34   things.§ Vogelstein] things. Vogelstein

41.3   occurred to Vogelstein] occurred to her critic

41.5   ideal cicerone for] ideal minister to

41.6   he played upon] he played on

41.7   and drew them away] drawing them at the right moment away

41.8   the belief that it was] the belief it was

41.9   Vogelstein and Pandora] our interesting couple

41.11   upon which certain] where certain

41.13   view—the immense sweep] view; the immense sweep

41.15   in this spot] in this retirement

41.16   that fate had in store for him with] appointed for him, as was to appear, with

41.18   not interested.] not absorbed.

41.23   the ocean.] the Atlantic.

41.24   talked if you] talked quick enough if you

41.26   Vogelstein replied, rather] —and it affected him

41.28   "To Mrs. Dangerfield?"] He feigned a vagueness. "To Mrs. Dangerfield?"

41.33   the young man murmured, blushing very red.] Count Otto cried with a very becoming blush.

42.3   any girl I have ever seen;] any Mädchen I've ever seen—

42.5   never will understand] never *will* understand

42.8   Vogelstein attempted to tell her what difference it made, but I have not space] He attempted to tell her what difference, but I have no space

42.10   her companion's] the Count's

42.13   He walked] Her companion walked

42.14   had a vague feeling] knew the pang of a vague sense

42.15   he asked her] he appealed

42.17   some news] important news

42.19   expecting news made him] expecting news—and important!—made him

42.23   she had asked of] she had begged of

42.27   he asked of] he enquired of

42.28   he might not come and see her.] he mightn't pay her certain respectful attentions.

42.30   "You may come as often as you like," she answered; "but you won't care for it long."] "As many as you like—and as respectful ones; but you won't keep them up for ever!"

42.31   said Vogelstein.] said Count Otto.

42.32   She hesitated a moment.] She waited to explain.

42.33   see them once more."] see them again."

42.34   She hesitated again.] Again she just hung fire.

42.36   Count Vogelstein received] Vogelstein received

43.1   occasion on which] juncture at which

43.2   on the deck of a vessel] while sociably afloat with him

43.5   Mrs. Bonnycastle said.] said the lady of infinite mirth.

43.6   affections upon her] affections on her

43.6   has almost always got an impediment.] has almost an impediment

43.8   Vogelstein looked at her] He looked at her

43.8   but he smiled and] but smiled and

43.14   lived at home.] lived unconscious of her powers.

43.17   "Do you mean a betrothal—to be married?"] Count Otto somehow preferred to understand as little as possible. ""Do you mean a betrothal—to take effect?"

43.18   and transcendental.] and moonstruck.

43.19   that peculiarly American institution, a precocious engagement; to be married, of course."] that piece of peculiarly American enterprise a premature engagement—to take effect, but too complacently, at the end of time."

43.24   she would not have taken up the subject so casually if she had suspected that she] she wouldn't have approached the question with such levity if she had supposed she

43.26   The whole thing was one of her jokes, and the notification, moreover, was really friendly.] The whole thing was, like everything else, but for her to laugh at, and the betrayal moreover of a good intention.

43.26   "I see, I see," he said in a moment. "The self-made girl] "I see, I see— the self-made girl

43.31   with her present, with her future, I suppose it's all over.] with her present, with her future, when they change like this young lady's, I suppose everything else changes.

43.35   what we expect her to do."] what we *expect* her to do."

43.35   Mrs. Bonnycastle added, more thoughtfully.] she added with less assurance.

43.36   the type is new.] the type's new and the case under consideration.

43.36   complete observations.] complete study.

44.2   more apparent,] more audible,

44.5   returning revellers.] returning picnickers.

44.10   by a little friendly talk.] by a proper deference.

44.11   the only thing he could think of to say to her was] the only act of homage that occurred to him was

44.17   Vogelstein stared] Count Otto gazed

44.19   "Oh, I am so glad] "I'm so very glad

44.21   get engaged for?] fall in love with each other *for*?

44.22   before long."] when she gets round to it. Ah if she had only been from the Sooth—!"

44.23   "But why have they never done so, in] At this he broke quickly in: "But why have they never brought it off, as you say, in

44.25   better with her] better *with* her]

44.28   I presume he feels] I presume feels]

44.30   said Mrs. Steuben, who had a little flute-like way of sounding the adjective.] said Mrs. Steuben, whose sound of the adjective was that of a feeble flute.

44.31   Vogelstein asked] the Count asked

44.32   F. Bellamy, eh?] F. Bellamy, so?

45.1   a very fine man.] a very fine man—I presume a college man.

45.5   struck him as all the more credible as it seemed to him eminently strange.] was probably the more credible for seeming to him eminently strange.

45.8   was to fumble in] was about to fumble in

45.9   seemed to Vogelstein] seemed to Count Otto

45.17   and extracting] and extracted

45.19   also individuals with tufts] also vague individuals, the loosest and blankest he had ever seen anywhere, with tufts

45.23   various postures of inclination in] various slanting postures in

45.26   Vogelstein's shoulder] Count Otto's shoulder

45.27   and the young secretary of legation had] and he had

45.33   Vogelstein's observing] our young man's observing

46.2   with her friendly laugh; and for some moments she] with the laugh that seemed always to invite the whole of any company to partake in it; though for some moments after this she

46.4   at Pandora's visitor] at her visitor

46.5   of his own nearness.] of his own proximity.

46.9   and a business-like eye.] and he seemed to look at the world over some counter-like expanse on which he invited it all warily and pleasantly to put down first its idea of the terms of a transaction.

46.11   for a minute] several seconds

46.12   an instant in silence,] briefly, in silence,

46.13   an official seal] an official-looking seal

46.15   No one appeared to observe the little interview but Vogelstein.] No one but our young man appeared aware of how much was taking place—and poor Count Otto mainly felt it in the air.

46.16   pair was inconsiderable.] pair inconsiderable.

46.17   asked, dropping her voice.] very prettily and soundlessly mouthed across at him.

46.20   for an answer.] for answer.

46.23   Vogelstein turned away] Our silent sufferer turned away

46.24   with Pandora] with Miss Day

46.31   Pandora's long engagement had terminated at the nuptial altar.]
         Pandora, a thousand other duties performed, had finally "got round"
         to the altar of her own nuptials.

46.32   with the remark that] but who, shrieking at the queer face he showed
         her, met it with the remark that

Louisa Pallant

239.7   myself that I had] myself I had

239.9   one lovely night] one beautiful night

239.14   abstruse, and] abstruse, while

239.23   I scarcely know] I scarce know

239.23   I had sat there when] I had sat when

239.29   who passed her turned round to look at her.] who passed appeared
         extremely to admire.

239.30   to look at the] to notice the

240.2   The couple walked and walked, slowly, but] The couple slowly walked
         and walked, but

240.4   Everyone looked at them but no one spoke; they appeared even to
         talk very little to each other.] Every one observed them but no one
         addressed them; they appeared even themselves to exchange very few
         words.

240.5   with extreme composure] with marked composure

240.9   they were not altogether honourable [...] lady would have covered
         the younger up a little more from the public stare and not have been
         so ashamed to exhibit her] they were of an artful intention [...] lady
         would have handed the younger over a little less to public valuation
         and not have sought to conceal her

240.15   him of knowing very little of life and I was rather uneasy about my
         responsibilities.] him of great innocence and was uneasy about about
         my office.

240.15   when I perceived] when I became aware

240.17   grown up into a regular beauty?] grown up to charming beauty?

240.19　speak to the ladies immediately.] speak to my pair at once.

240.22　Homburg is [...] takes up] Homburg was then [...] took up

240.28　in which a handsome person is more appreciated. You will see that I took time,] in which such attractions are more appreciated. You will see what time I took,

240.34　Pallant after all turned out no] Pallant proved finally no

240.35　I had not felt that it was anything] I had n't felt if anything

241.4　pitifully proved, of flesh-pots; moreover [...] then, on the [...] Europe; we had looked [...] eyes, we had pretended to be free friends and] pitifully turned out, of flesh-pots. Moreover [...] then—on the [...] Europe; had looked [...] eyes, had pretended to be easy friends and

241.5　I knew then what] I knew by that time what

241.8　This had not been then and it could not] This had n't been before and could n't

241.10　It is my belief that it does not often minister to friendship that your friend] It seldom ministers to friendship, I believe, that your friend

241.12　the case when (if [...] may pass) he is a] the case if—let the solecism pass!—he be a

241.13　years elapsed, for me,] years went by for me

241.24　anything else, at this time] anything else, however, at this time

241.27　expressing great surprise] expressing as we stood face to face great surprise

241.31　I went [...] She looked up at me a moment, staring, as if] I had gone [...] She had then looked up at me a moment, staring as if

241.33　then, smiling [...] she broke out,] after which, smiling [...] she had broken out:

241.35　her own line, she at least carried] her own line she thus at least carried

242.1　immediately, however, that she] immediately, none the less, that she

242.3　of a disposition to borrow money. She had none too much—that I learned—but for the moment she seemed able to] of a desire to contract a loan. She had scant means—that I learned—yet seemed for the moment able to

242.4　we remained talking] we remained in talk

242.9   very sweetly and indefinitely, and I saw [...] not at all.] all sweetly and blankly, and I saw [...] not a whit.

242.9   mother intimated that] mother threw out that

242.15   there was nobody there who struck her as attractive:] because nobody there struck her as attractive:

242.20   to settle upon her. She was simpler than [...] and was evidently not] to besprinke her. She was of thinner consistency than [...] and clearly not

242.23   bright, pure, intelligent smile. A girl who [...] showing her teeth could never pass for heartless.] bright pure candid smile. No girl who [...] parting her lips could pass for designing.

242.28   I know not what Mrs. Pallant kept back, [...] I was frank enough.] I might n't judge of what Mrs. Pallant kept back, [...] I quite overflowed.

242.31   She confessed that they had drifted and that they were] She confessed they had drifted, she and her daughter, and were

242.33   got what is vulgarly called somewhat mixed, as I thought Linda perceived] took a wrong turn, a false flight, or two, as I thought Linda noted

242.36   made me feel like a cross-questioner, which I had no] made me rather feel a cross-questioner, which I had had no

243.2   her mother's ability] her parent's ability

243.6   of putting their ideas into words.] of communicationg by sound.

243.12   did not say that she was there because she always came] did n't put it that she was there from force of habit

243.14   admitted that the reason of her visit had been] admitted the reason of her visit to have been

243.18   which I used to value.] which I had ever made much of.

243.22   I told her that I had gone to Homburg because it was as good a place as another to wait for my nephew] I mentioned that I had arrived because the place was as good as another for awaiting my nephew

243.24   he was a youth named Archie Pringle and very modern indeed; he was coming of age in] his name was Archie Parker and that he was modern indeed; he was to attain legal manhood in

243.29   smoke too much nor fall off an Alp.] smoke nor flirt too much, nor yet tumble off an Alp.

243.32   she had seen her but once or twice.] she had scarce seen her.

243.32   which of the Pringles] which of the Parkers

243.34   rich lot."] rich set."

243.36   nice for him. She declared that she meant for me—I] nice for the boy. She pronounced the advantage rather mine—I

244.7   If I was a maundering old bachelor to-day it was no one's fault but hers.] If I had remained so single and so sterile the fault was nobody's but hers.

244.8   my nephew and I said it] my nephew—to which I replied

244.9   She inquired whether he] She wished to know if he

244.10   I told her that I had] I assured her I had

244.13   delicate, unsuccessful child, demanding] delicate, rather blighted child, demanding

244.19   that," I rejoined.] that," I returned.

244.20   Mrs. Pallant went on, with] my friend went on with

244.22   said the girl, smiling.] smiled the girl.

245.5   I asked them to] I took them to

245.9   if it did not quite achieve it. I liked it, for] if not quite achieving it I was pleased, as

245.12   a kind of sociable sense] a vague sociable sense

245.15   who, with regard to each other, still had discoveries] who still had in regard to each other discoveries

245.16   but we did not know] but did n't not know

245.21   sort of refreshment in finding] relief in my finding

245.22   She seemed to me, in the oddest way, both] She struck me, in the oddest way, as both

245.24   degenerate, as if in her nature the two processes had gone on together.] degenerate; the two processes, in her nature, might have gone on together.

245.27   something very stale] something rather stale

245.27   On the other hand she] At the same time she

245.28   becoming, as it] becoming, for it

245.31   prime, which had taken a form so unfortunate for me. [...] weary and indifferent, and as she struck me as having seen more of the evil of the world than of the good, that] prime, the mercenary principle I had suffered from. [...] weary and detached, and since she affected me as more impressed with the evil of the world than with the good, this

246.2   the cynicism that had formed itself in her nature had a softer surface than some of her old ambitions. And then [...] daughter had been a kind of] her accretion of indifference, if not of cynicism, showed a softer surface than that of her old ambitions. Furthermore—daughter was a kind of

246.4   better (charming as she was), but I have] better—charming as this one might be—but have

246.4   for the time I was] for the hour you were

246.6   impression passed, somehow, when [...] me more.] impression passed somehow when [...] you so completely.

246.8   the sort of attention she excited [...] she struck one [...] as a final product—just as some plant or fruit does,] the attention she provoked [...] she struck you [...] as a felicitous final product—after the fashion of some plant or some fruit,

246.9   More than any girl I ever saw she was the result of] She was clearly the result of

246.10   educative; a pressure exerted in order that she] educative, a pressure exerted, and all artfully, so that she

246.12   heaven (it hung [...] so definitely), and had been the source of the only light] heaven—it hung [...] so unquenchably—and had shed the only light

246.13   that shone upon] that was to shine on

246.14   other religion.] other ideal.

246.16   I mean, of course (for no [...] wrought), the most [...] that she] I mean of course, since no [...] wrought, the most [...] she

246.18   as it would have been possible for her] as could have been conceived for her

246.20   her manner, and everything] her manner, everything

246.23   as a kind of standard.] as the very measure of young grace.

246.23   her as a model, and yet] her thus as a model, yet

246.26 because one wondered [...] she never did [...] in her *rôle*] because you wondered [...] she never broke down [...] in her role

246.27 a great resource to him,] his greatest resource,

246.28 the world knows that] the world knows why

246.30 with a placidity all his own; but this same placidity was an element of success in our personal relations—] with a serenity all his own; but this very coolness was a help to harmony—

246.32 unsurprised acceptance] unperturbed acceptance

246.34 I knew not what] I wondered what

246.36 him (he did not look himself in the least as if the wind were rising), and] him—he did n't at all carry himself as if the wind of his fortune were rising—and

247.1 solicitude which] solicitude that

247.3 more transcendent studies.] more strenuous studies.

247.4 He was refreshingly natural,] He was reassuringly natural,

247.5 was a certain simplified serenity.] was in the clearing of the inward scene by his so preordained lack of imagination.

247.7 line which [...] the inane and simplification from death. Archie was not clever—] line that [...] inane, the simple from the silly. He was n't clever;

247.8 that theory it was not possible to maintain,] the fonder theory quite defied our cultivation,

247.9 it seemed to me that his want of wit was] it struck me his want of wit might be

247.12 suspicions, but on the contrary that imagination] suspicions, but that on the contrary imagination

247.14 In short he was a well-grown, well-washed, muscular] He was in short a well-grown well-washed muscular

247.14 whose extreme good-nature] whose extreme salubrity

247.17 life (as [...] money he was on the point of stepping into), and] life—as [...] fortune that awaited the stroke of his twenty-first year—and

247.19 His own habits] His habits

247.20 noteworthy sacrifices for the sake of my] numerous and generous sacrifices for my

247.21 for the sake of mine I must of course remember] for mine I must duly remember

247.23 regulating his long legs] adapting his long legs

247.28 she talked a great deal about him and thought him] she made him, with his easy uncle, a subject of discourse; she pronounced him

247.30 expressed the most hungry envy] professed a rage of envy

247.31 While we talked together] While we were so occupied Archie

247.32 the truth did he manifest] the truth did he betray

247.36 waltz that made me remember.] waltz that stirred my memory.

248.1 I know not, for she] I know not: she

248.5 the subject of […] kinsman this] the article of […] charge, that

248.6 frequent admiration that I] frequent admiration I

248.9 to which I noticed that she was apt to give but a small direct response. I was struck with something anomalous in her way of taking my remarks about her daughter—they] that drew from her, I noticed, but scant direct response. I was struck thus with her reserve when I spoke of her daughter—my remarks

248.11 prejudice seemed […] to amount to an affectation.] prejudice, seemed […] to savour of affectation.

248.12 vague, slightly impatient] vague and impatient

248.17 perceived that I am fond of looking at the explanations of things, and in regard to this I had my theory that she was disappointed in the girl. What had been her particular disappointment?] noted my fondness, in all cases, for the explanations of things; as an example of which I had my theory that she was disappointed in the girl. Where then had her calculations failed?

248.19 pleasing it could only be that Linda had not made] pleasing, the pang must have been for her not having made

248.20 to capture a prince the day after she left the] to "land" a prince the day after leaving the

248.21 After all there was plenty of time for this, as Linda was only two and twenty.] There was after all plenty of time for this, with Linda but two-and-twenty.

248.22 to wonder whether the source] to wonder if the source

248.26   innocent and in the second I was not paid, as the French say, for thinking that Louisa would much mind whether she were or not.] innocent,
and because in the second I was n't paid, in the French phrase, for
supposing Louisa […] much concerned on that score.

248.27   I should have resorted to] I should have invoked

248.30   be, without the smallest indication of a] be without betrayal of a

248.36   stupidity for wisdom.] stupidity for her law.

249.4   being not exempt from periods of repose;] abounding in comfortable
lapses;

249.5   pitch of friendliness of which it certainly bore the stamp.] pitch of
continuity of which it gave the impression.

249.5   the stamp.§ It was] the stamp. It was

249.7   if they had risen] had such risen

249.8   eyes and with liberty] eyes and with freedom

249.12   She was always doing something—finishing a flower in a piece of tapestry, cutting the leaves of a magazine, sewing a button on her glove
[…], or plying her pencil in] She had always something in hand—a
flower in her tapestry to finish, the leaves of a magazine to cut, a button to sew on her glove […], a pencil to ply ever so neatly in

249.13   indoors, at her mother's house, she] indoors—mainly then at her
mother's modest rooms—she

249.16   avocations enabled her to bear such close inspection with composure (I ended by […] for it—I told him he stared at the poor girl too
much),] pursuits supported her, they helped her to an assurance under such narrow inspection—I ended […] for it; I told him he stared
the poor girl out of countenance—

249.21   embarrassed, happy, pointless laugh.] embarrassed happy pointless
laugh.

249.21   wandered away from us] wandered off with him

249.22   in a manner which said that it was not for too long—that] in a manner that promised it was n't for long and that

249.23   If I was pleased with her it was for a good reason:] I liked her I had
therefore my good reason:

249.24   since any pretty girl] since a pretty girl

249.27 and I daresay he went to sleep.] and I fear he often dozed.

250.7 "What consequences?" She repeated. "Why, the consequences] "What consequences? Why the very same consequences

250.10 I hesitated a moment and then, […] eyes, I said, "Do you mean that she] I hesitated, but then, […] eyes, said: "Do you mean she'd

250.11 colouring quickly.] with a quick colour.

250.13 in love with her?"] in love with your girl?"

250.15 warning comes […] I said, smiling.] warning is […] I significantly smiled.

250.17 sense of responsibility?"] sense of the rigour of your office?"

250.19 for—that you should find him a wife—let him put his head into a noose] for: that you shall find him the first wife you can pick up, that you shall let him put his head into the noose

250.23 She thinks it's a mistake and that […] lived awhile—] She holds it the worst of mistakes, she feels that […] lived a while,

250.26 I consider that love itself, however young, is a sufficient choice. But my being a bachelor] I regard the fact of falling in love, at whatever age, as in itself an act of selection. But my being as I am

250.29 Archie tumble in?"] Archie fall—?"

250.31 now and take him with you." "Do you think he is in very far?" I inquired.] now—from where he *has* fallen—and take him straight away." I wondered a little. "Do you think he's in very far?"

251.2 —I am not narrow—I] —I am not narrow-minded.

251.4 "And don't you know that] "And don't you know," I returned, "that

251.7 was silent a moment, as if I partly mystified and partly vexed her.] had a pause—as if I mystified or vexed her.

251.10 warning me," I exclaimed,] warning me," I cried,

251.11 It seems to me that my] It seems to me my

251.12 when it should appear that your daughter herself was in danger."] at the moment your daughter herself should seem in danger."

251.15 "Oh, you […] that; I'll […] of her." "If you think … I'll take him away to-morrow," I went on.] "Oh you […] that—I'll […] of Linda." But I went on. "If you think […] I'll carry him off to-morrow."

659

251.17 "I don't know. I should] "I don't know—I should

251.19 there is anything."] there's any real symptom."

251.23 what I would do for you." What she would do for me] what I'd fain do for you." What she'd fain do for me

251.24 I said to her that I did not really see] I remarked that I failed to see

251.26 would fall into] would fall so very easily into

251.27 Might I inquire whether […] from her—whether she] Might I enquire if […] from her, if she

251.28 Mrs. Pallant answered that they did not need] Mrs. Pallant made me, on this, the point that they had no need

251.30 To this I rejoined […] much but] To which I returned […] much, but

251.31 for her the occasion] for *her* the occasion

251.34 Archie had not once spoken to me of the young lady, save to remark] Archie had spoken to me of the young lady only to remark

252.3 primitive; and then […] the matter] primitive; after which […] the case

252.4 Mr. Pringle] Mr. Parker

252.6 to you." § "Very good.] to you."§ I sought to defer then to her judgment. "Very good.

252.9 everything!' she murmured, in a peculiar tone of discouragement. 'Take him off— that's] everything!" She spoke as if with some finer view. "Remove him quickly—that's

252.10 the idea of taking him off; […] too summary, unnecessarily violent,] the idea of removing him quickly; […] too summary, too extravagant,

252.13 and, moreover, […] no wish to move. I did not consider it part of my bargain with] and moreover, […] no wish to change my scene. It was no part of my promise to

252.14 Europe. So I said:] Europe. So I temporized.

252.17 you are too superficial—too frivolous," Mrs. Pallant rejoined, with considerable bitterness.] you're incredibly superficial!" she made answer with an assurance that struck me.

252.20 There was a vibration of contempt in this which nettled me, so that […] from you.] The contempt in it so nettled me in fact that […] from *you*!"

252.22   from her; but at last she said, quietly: "I think [...] had better go away. We have [...] month—that's enough."] from her on this, rather to my surprise, and when she spoke again it was all quietly. "I think [...] had best withdraw. We've [...] month—it will have served our purpose."

252.23   "Dear me, [...] I ejaculated;] "Mercy on us, [...] I protested;

252.25   until we separated (our [...] dinner, at the Kursaal), she remained almost silent, with a subdued, injured air.] till we separated—our [...] dinner at the Kursaal—she said little, preserving a subdued and almost injured air.

252.26   This, somehow, did not soothe me, as it ought to have done, for it was too absurd] This somehow didn't appeal to me, since it was absurd

252.28   herself—! Archie and I usually] herself—! Archie and I, at all events, usually

252.30   from the Rooms—and we parted] from the Rooms—where we parted

252.35   English farewells sounded gay. On this occasion however they were not gay, for the difficulty that [...] for me, with [...] appeared to have extended by a mysterious sympathy to the young couple. They too were rather] English partings resounded. On this occasion indeed they rather languished; the question that [...] for me with [...] appeared—and by no intention of mine—to have brushed the young couple with its chill. Archie and Linda too struck me as [...]

253.3   asked him, by no roundabout approach to the question, whether he were] put to him, by no roundabout approach, the question of whether he were

253.4   know!"—this was all] know!" was, however, all

253.7   inn (we [...] subject), it [...] that I did.] inn—we [...] subject—it [...] that *I* did.

253.9   was not made to contain many objects at once, but Linda Pallant for the moment certainly constituted] was n't formed to accommodate at one time many subjects of thought, but Linda Pallant certainly constituted for the moment

253.11   as yet undefined and unformulated,] as yet informal and undefined,

253.12   she was the first intensely agreeable impression of his life. [...] how much I saw, and I slept not particularly well, for thinking that [...] intensely agreeable impressions.] she held, that she beguiled him as no one had ever done. [...] that perception, and I spent the night a prey to the consciousness that [...] the sense of being captivated.

253.17　To find him a wife [...] a judge of wives.] To put him in relation with a young enchantress [...] a judge of enchantresses

253.18　I had been strangely superficial in] I had given high proof of levity in

253.20　resources and one of them would be [...] to go away.] resources—one of which *would* be [...] to clear out.

253.26　strange that her conscience [...] before my own did and that she was more anxious on my nephew's behalf than I was. The ways of women were mysterious and it was not a novelty to me [...] one would find them.] strange her conscience [...] in advance of my own. It was strange she should so soon have felt Archie's peril, and even stranger that she should have then wished to "save" him. The ways of women were infinitely subtle, and it was no novelty to me [...] they would turn up.

253.27　in this narrative to reveal] in this report to expose

253.28　nature I will confess [...] whether Mrs. Pallant's solicitude] nature I shall confess [...] if my old friend's solicitude

253.30　him, as she might] him, which she

253.34　that I should carry the boy away to visit other cities.] that I should win my companion to curiosity about some other places.

253.35　many assuredly [...] worthy of his attention] many of course [...] worth his attention

254.1　morning (it [...] luncheon) I [...] Mrs. Pallant, to let her know that this truth had come over me with force; and while I did so] morning—it [...] luncheon—I [...] Mrs. Pallant's to let her know I was ready to take action; but even while I went

254.3　own, if they were real, to Linda.] own, so far as they had been roused, to Linda.

254.6　of such a subject,] of such a performer,

254.7　A young American who could give] A young American, the fruit of scant "modeling," who could give

254.8　if she were prepared] if she had been prepared

254.10　would be at least an English duke.] would be inevitably a "personage" *quelconque.*

254.11　Mrs. Pallant's lodgings] my friend's lodging

254.16　Sudden? Oh yes, tremendously sudden.] Sudden, their decision to move? Oh yes, the matter of a moment.

254.18 maid all the morning had scarcely had] maid, all the morning, had scarce had

254.19 But they evidently were] But they clearly were

254.21 matter; [...] there [...] at three o'clock.] matter— [...] at three.

255.3 and I confess it made me rather angry.] and made me, I confess, quite furious.

255.5 I was not in love] I was not now in love

255.9 he knew (through [...] Linda) what had become of our friends] he knew what had been on foot—through [...] Linda—lasted

255.11 by the facility] by the ease

255.12 shown that she] shown she

255.12 was not angry,] professed no sense of grievance,

255.13 was good-natured and in the second it was] was shy about it and because in the second it was

255.15 encouraged, having, I think, no very particular idea] encouraged— equipped as he was, I think, with no very particular

255.17 in which between the ingenuous young there may be so little question] in which there may between the ingenuous young be so little question

255.19 and would have had no opinion as to whether he had been provoked or jilted. I had no wish] and could by no means have told me whether he had been challenged or been jilted. I did n't want

255.21 I remarked [...] simple; it was plain they were just hiding] I observed [...] simple; they must have been just hiding

255.25 air (so at least I judged [...] questions) of thinking that the matter] air—so at least I inferred [...] questions—of judging the matter

255.29 pursue her [...] where she was.] pursue our fugitives [...] where they were.

255.31 the reflection [...] her own reasoning.] the reflexion [...] Louisa's reasoning.

255.32 She was dishonest and her departure was a provocation—I am afraid that it was] She was a dreadful humbug and her departure had been a provocation—I fear it was

256.1 I even said to myself that we] I even believed we

256.5   he told me that] he reported to me that

256.6   His manner of telling me was to inquire whether there were any particular] The form of his confidence was inquiring if there were particular

256.9   lakes; was not the fear of […] moreover in summer our native temperature, at an end, as it was already the middle of September?] lakes. Might n't the fear of […] moreover at that season our native temperature, cease to operate, the middle of September having arrived?

256.12   showed me the letter] showed me his letter

256.17   casually (the mention […] in the date) that they] causally—the mention […] in the words at the head of the paper—that the

256.19   they had to leave us without giving notice. Linda did not say] they had had so abruptly to leave us. Linda failed to say

256.21   accept "these few hasty words" as a] accept "this hasty line" as a

256.23   hoped we were passing our time in an intersting manner and having the same] hoped our days were passing pleasantly and with the same

256.25   remembrances to me.] remembrances—!

256.27   as I should judge,] as I should prefer,

256.30   on very familiar terms. It was however as] on easy terms. It was, however, for

256.33   at least so I was warranted in inferring from the very distinct nature of his determination […] I saw it was useless to] so at least I gathered from the touching candour of his determination […] I judged it idle to

256.36   asked him if he […] Linda Pallant ever since they] asked him to what tune he […] Linda since they

256.36   he replied, "Oh dear no; why should I?"] he replied: "Oh I have n't been thinking at all! Why should I?"

257.2   he must obey the young lady's call I must also go and see where] he was to obey his young woman's signal I must equally make out where

257.8   this would be indiscreet, considering our peculiar relations] this might be awkward in view of a strained relation

257.13   seriously and I could see that he immediately began to [...] for being
          afloat with] seriously, and I could see that he had at once begun to
          [...] for navigation with

257.21   in the midst of them.] set as great jewels in a crystal globe.

257.25   conscious Mrs. Pallant [...] were sitting there—on the terrace—
          quietly watching us.] conscious of Mrs. Pallant [...] seated on the ter-
          race and quiely watching us.

257.26   air of expecting us and I think we looked for it in them.] air of expec-
          tation, which I think we had counted on.

257.27   note; that was] note; this was

257.31   there was something very odd in our meeting with our friends—at
          least between Louisa and me. I was too much taken up with that part
          of it to notice very much which was the manner] our present address,
          all round, lacked a little the easiest grace—or at least Louisa's and
          mine did. I felt too much the appeal of her exhibition to notice closely
          the style

257.33   I have suffficiently indicated that I could not get it out of my head
          that] I could n't get it out of my head, as I have sufficiently indicated,
          that

257.33   was "up to" something,] was playing a game,

258.2   why I say we met in strange conditions. However, on this occasion
          we observed all forms and the admirable scene gave us plenty] why I
          speak of our meeting constrainedly. We observed none the less all the
          forms, and the admirable scene left us plenty

258.3   She looked even prettier] This young woman looked even prettier

258.5   She struck me so, afresh, as a charming, clever girl that I was puzzled
          afresh to] She again so struck me as a charming clever girl that I was
          freshly puzzled to

258.9   was admirable. So she was, and why should not the consequences be
          equally so?] was in every way beautiful. This was the clear fact: so why
          should n't the presumptions be in favour of every result of it?

258.9   One of them, on the spot] One of the effects of that cause, on the spot

258.15   I burst out laughing; it seemd so droll to me somehow that timidity
          should be imputed to this competent young lady. She gave me a quick,
          slightly sharp] I sought the relief of laughter: it must have affected me

as comic that this girl's general competence should suffer the imputation of that particular flaw. She gave me a quick slightly sharp

258.16   a little—to say, "Pray] a little—"Pray

258.18   Mrs. Pallant's eyes, […], were not turned to mine;] Mrs. Pallant's attention […], rather strayed from me;

258.20   crests which wore the flush] crests crowned with the flush

258.21   not even to watch] not even to follow

258.22   I respected her reverie;] I respected her mood;

258.26   I noticed that she had an expression of weariness which I had never
seen before; her delicate, agreeable face […] I made out there were
new lines of fatigue, almost of age, in it.] I found in her, it was true,
rather a new air of weariness; her fine cold well-bred face […] I noted
in it new lines of fatigue, almost of age.

258.27   of her and asked her, since she looked so sad, if she had any bad news.]
of her and—since she looked so sad—asked if she had been having
bad news.

258.30   "Ah, then he wrote?" I exclaimed.] "Ah then he wrote?"

258.32   I remarked, sitting down] I returned as I sat down

258.35   She slowly turned her face to me and rested her eyes on mine. "Take
care […] you'll insult me," she said, with] Slowly at last, and more directly, she faced me. "Take care […] you'll have been more brutal than
you'll afterwards like," she said with

259.1   you think I do so if I ask you if] you think me brutal if I ask you
whether

259.3   She hesitated a moment. "Yes; she] She had an hesitation. "Yes, she

259.5   what it was best to do.] what course was best.

259.8   follow that you would come—I didn't think it need follow."] follow
you'd come—I did n't take it for granted."

259.9   "I am afraid] "I too am afraid

259.11   do under the circumstances was] do—once he wished it—was

259.12   "I see; I'm glad you have done it," said Mrs. Pallant, thoughtfully.] "I
see. Well, there are grounds, after all, on which I'm glad," she rather
inscrutably added.

259.14   "Oh, I was […] I can't order him nor forbid him—I can use no force. Look] "Oh I was […] I can neither drive him nor stay him—I can use no force," I explained. "Look

259.18   she's a bad, hard girl, who […] my companion suddenly broke out, with a kind of passion. "Dear Mrs. Pallant, what] she's a bad hard girl—one who […] my companion broke out with a passion that startled me. At first I could only gape. "Dear lady, what

259.20   remained so for a minute; then she went on, in a different manner, as if] and so remained a minute; then she continued a little differently, though as if

259.26   I said, laughing. But my laughter was hollow, for I had been exceedingly impressed with her little explosion of a moment before. […] she is bad?"] I gaily professed. But my gaiety was thin, for I was still amazed at her violence a moment before. […] she won't do?"

259.28   Mrs. Pallant made no immediate answer to this; […] matter after all whether] She made no direct answer; […] matter whether

259.29   at the first opening.] at the first chance, the favouring moment.

259.32   with him?" I demanded, incredulous.] with him?"

259.33   makes him think she is—though] makes him think so—though

260.1   "If she makes him think so? Dearest lady, what do you mean? […] and after all what has she done? […] nice to him,] Still I was at sea. "If she makes him think so? Dear old friend, what's your idea? […] and when all's said w hat has she done? […] civil and pleasant to him,

260.3   shown him nothing but the common friendliness of a bright, good-natured girl. […] he showed it to me."] shown him, with her youth and her natural charm, nothing more than common friendliness. […] he let me see it."

260.5   word that she has said […] rejoined, with a persistence that struck me as unnatural.] word she has said […] returned with an emphasis that still struck me as perverse.

260.6   I exclaimed. She evidently] I promptly cried. She evidently

260.7   said, and this impression chilled me, made me really unconfortable.] said; but if this excited my curiosity it also moved, in a different connexion, my indulgence.

260.8   a very rare young woman.] a most remarkable young woman.

260.9   "You have a singular tone [...] I responded] "You have an extraordi-
         nary tone [...] I declared

260.11   I have observed it before but never so accentuated."] I've had the same
         impression from you—that of a disposition to 'give her away'. But nev-
         er yet so strong."

260.12   she stood there an instant, looking] she stood there looking

260.14   me rather startled, she began to move along the terrace.] still more
         astonished she moved along the terrace.

260.16   What on earth do you mean by that?"] What on earth are you talking
         about?"

260.19   at any rate I don't] at any rate," I said, "I don't

260.22   "Oh, I don't [...] she exclaimed, as we went, with a kind of perverse
         cheerfulness.] "Oh, I don't [...] she cried as we went, and with an ex-
         travagance, as I felt, of sincerity.

260.26   transition (it seemd to me to show such years of social practice), by
         which] transition, the fruit of such years of social practice, by which

260.27   us, she exchanged her excited, almost fevered expression for an air
         of recognition] us, her tension and her impatience dropped to
         recognition

260.28   asked with eagerness whether their mother were better.] enquired
         with sweet propriety as to the continued improvement" of their sister.

260.29   after which she said impatiently,] after which she had a peremptory
         note.

260.31   descended into the garden, strolled] descended to that blander scene,
         strolled

261.6   lake, at such] lake and at such

261.7   of ordinary sensibility] of common sensibility

261.8   each other. To this observation] each other. § To this observation

261.10   my dear sir,] my dear man,

261.14   much, when you are living at an expensive hotel?" "They take us]
         much—living as you are at an expensive hotel?" Well, she promptly
         met this. "They take us

261.16   to learn there are certain ways of doing things.] to learn all sorts of
         horrid arts.

261.20   She thinks that [...] it's the least that she should find a villa] She feels
          that [...] she ought, if things were decently right, to find a villa

261.21   "Well, her companion] "Then her companion

261.22   each other arms; I] each other's arms—I

261.27   facing me there in the twilight, and to let me know that she was more]
          facing me in the rich short twilight, and to describe herself as immeas-
          urably more

261.28   at me awhile without] at me without

261.30   she want, more than] she wants—more 'on the make' than

261.31   to tell me that it is my fault,] to tell me it's my own fault,

262.2   you are most extraordinary," I stammered, infinitely surprised and not
          a little pained.] you're wonderful, you're terrible," I could only stam-
          mer, lost in the desert of my thoughts.

262.5   and you don't like [...] you will have to change] and don't like [...]
          you'll *have* to change

262.6   and she looked remarkably handsome.] and the beauty of her youth
          came back to her.

262.7   expiation?" I inquired.] expiation?" I demanded.

262.10   I do it; it's for myself," she went on.] I do it—it's for myself," she
          strangely went on.

262.12   reasons, which I [...] else?—must you] reasons—which I [...] else?
          Must you

262.14   "She's my punishment and she's my stigma!" cried Louisa Pallant,
          with veritable exaltation.] "My only child's my punishment, my only
          child's my stigma!" she cried in her exaltation.

262.18   true. She appals] true," said Louisa Pallant, "She appals

262.19   upon the poor lady's;] on my poor friend's;

262.21   a bench which I perceived a few yards away.] a bench a few steps away.

262.23   what she was saying.] what she said.

262.27   for I have one, little as you think I] for I *have* one, little as you may
          think I

262.31   that now that I see it printed there in all her nature I am] that now I
         see it stamped there in all her nature, on all her spirit and on all her
         form, I'm

262.34   She has learned it so well that she has gone far beyond me. I say I am
         horrified, because] She has profited so well by my beautiful influence
         that she has gone far beyond the great original. I say I'm horrified,"
         Mrs. Pallant dreadfully wound up, "because

263.3   I say, if I save him." § "Do you expect] I say if I save him." § I could only
         gape again at this least expected of all my adventures. "Do you expect

263.5   protest, and she went on with a sort of simplicity:] protest, but she
         went on with the grimmest simplicity:

263.7   you interest me immensely."] you interest me," I rather ruefully pro-
         fessed, "immensely."

263.8   care for that—if I can interest him."] care if I do—so I interest *him*."

263.11   "You must remember then that your charges are strangely vague, con-
         sidering how violent they are. Never had a girl a more innocent ap-
         pearance. You know how I have admired it."] "You must reflect then
         that your denunciation can only strike me as, for all its violence, vague
         and unconvincing. Never had a girl less the appearance of bearing
         such charges out. You know how I've admired her."

263.13   of my hand!" Mrs. Pallant declared, with a bitter laugh.] of my hand!"
         And Mrs. Pallant laughed for bitterness.

263.20   lady! To climb up to the top [...] there—to do it at any cost [...] cru-
         elty, is] lady!" Her lucidity chilled me to the soul—it seemed to shine
         so flawless. "To climb up to the top [...] there," she went on—"to do
         that at any cost [...] cruelty is

263.23   with a tremendous low distinctness and an air of sincerity that was
         really solemn. I watched] with a cold confidence that had evidently
         behind it some occult past process of growth. I watched

263.26   she held me in a kind of stupor, but her strange, almost vindictive ear-
         nestness imposed itself. I found myself believing her, pitying her more
         than I pitied the girl. It was as if she had been bottled up] she held me
         breathless and frowning, but her strange vindictive, or at least retribu-
         tive, passion irresistibly imposed itself. I found myself at last believing
         her, pitying her more than I pitied the subject of her dreadful analysis.
         It was as if she had held her tongue for longer

263.29 suffering more and more from the ferment of her knowledge. It relieved her to warn and denounce and expose. "God has let me see it in time, in his mercy," [...] are strange, that he has] suffering more and more the importunity of truth. It relieved her thus to drag that to the light, and still she kept up the high and most unholy sacrifice. "God in his mercy has let me see it in time, [...] are strange that he has

263.31 he has let me see, myself [...] she is, I assure you [...] than I ever intended] he has let me see—myself [...] she *is*, I assure you [...] than I intended

263.34 at the faint stars with religious perversity.] at the southern stars as if *they* would understand.

264.2   I asked. "Have you ever admonished her, reproached her?" "Reproached her? How can I? when all she would have to say would be, "You—*you*—you base one you—...who made me!'"] I finally asked. "Have you ever put before her this terrible arraignment?" "Put it before her? How can I put put it before her when all she would have to say would be: 'You, *you*, you base one, who made nme—?'"

264.6   you and you wouldn't understand [...] a worse trick if I were to hold my tongue. "If he] you, and you would n't see my point [...] a far worse one if I were to stay my hand. Oh I had my view of this. "If he

264.8   to him simply] to him," I asked, "simply

264.10 perhaps affect him, if I lose no time.] perhaps helpfully affect him. Only," she added with her proud decision, "I must lose no time."

264.17 "That's a part of all the comedy!" We were silent a moment, after which I resumed: "Then she doesn't know you hate her?"] "Ah that," she cried, "is all a part of all the comedy!" It fairly hushed me to silence, and for a moment more she said nothing. "Then she does n't know you hate her?" I resumed.

264.19 I pity her simply, for what] I just pity her for what

264.21 person, at the rate] person," I wailed, "at the rate

264.23 "Oh, perfectly; she'll marry some one. She'll marry a title] "I beg your pardon—there's a perfect possibility," said my companion. "She'll marry—she'll marry 'well.' She'll marry a title

264.25 I murmured, smiling.] I attempted the grimace of suggesting.

264.26 She hesitated a moment.] She seemed to wonder.

264.28 natural: how can any one tell, with] natural. How can any one tell, asked Louisa Pallant—"with

264.29 The way she uttered these last words] Her utterance of these words

264.31 if he were my son," I said at last.] if he were my son."

264.33 'Oh, if he had been [...] himself; he's simple and honest] "Oh if he had been [...] himself: He's simple and sane and honest

264.34 an admirable, a devoted, mother-in-law," I went on.] quite the most remarkable of mothers-in-law!" I commented.

265.1 a little impatient sigh and replied that she was not joking [...]. We sat there some time longer, while [...] and she apparently did the same.] a small dry laugh—she was n't joking. We lingered by the lake while [...] and while she herself apparently thought.

265.3 side, with the echo of her passionate, broken voice still in the air, some queer ideas] side and under the strong impression of her sincerity, her indifference to the conventional graces, my imagination, my constitutional skepticism began to range. Queer ideas

265.9 brought forth these cruel imputations to help her to her end?] invented at once the boldest and the sublest of games in order to keep the game in her hands?

265.10 to denounce the girl to Archie] to address herself to Archie

265.11 overcome the suspicion [...] at so unnatural a proceeding.] overcome the mistrust [...] at a proceeding superficially so sinister?

265.16 The effect of them was poignant. She made herself humble indeed [...] ashamed, on my own side, that I saw her in the dust.] Their effect was to wring my heart. She seemed to kneel in the dust, [...] ashamed that I had let her sink to it.

265.17 staying very long, too long;] staying long, too long;

265.18 reason that she should deal with Archie that evening.] reason then she should deal with my nephew that night.

265.20 —for a man.] —for an an active man.

265.21 the terrace of the hotel she] the terrace above she

265.22 fine hands, quivering a little, on] fine consecrated hands fairly quiver on

265.24 do what she liked: [...] painfully and I wanted to] do as she prescribed; [...] painfully, she had given me a "turn," and I wanted to

265.27   By that picture it would seem that a reigning prince was the least she would look at.] By that account these favour to one so graceless were a woeful waste of time-

265.28   "Oh, she has reflected well;] "Oh she has worked it all out;

265.32   with you?" § "Lord!] with you?" My friend's wonderful face pitied my simplicity. § "Lord!]

265.34   talk over things [...] and we only have to act. We can take reasons] talk things over [...] and only have to act. We observe the highest proprieties of speech. We never for a moment name anything ugly—we only just go at it. We can take definitions

265.35   case she certainly doesn't know your point] case," I nevertheless urged, "the poor thing can't possibly be aware of your point

266.1   "No—that's] "No," she conceded—"that's

266.4   "How do you mean, to do the same?"] "What do you mean by the same?"

266.6   I should have been done.] I should have been 'done.'

266.8   with conviction. § "So you would] with conviction. § At this she appeared to have, in the oddest way, a momentary revulsion. "So you'd

266.12   hard, monotonous pinch] hard eternal pinch

266.15   beyond all others, and it's] beyond all others; which it's

266.15   should. That is] should! And it's

266.21   She will make him live here; she has not the least intention of settling in America. I think] She'll of course make him live in these countries; she has n't the slightest intention of casting her pearls—but basta!" said my friend. "I think

266.22   make him let her alone." "It strikes me that he would like that very much," I interposed; "that's not] make him leave her more or less to herself." "I don't know about his leaving her to herself, but it strikes me that he would like the rest of that matter very much," I returned. "That's not

266.26   princes," Mrs. Pallant pursued, as if [...] me. "Yes, they are] princes," she pursued as if [...] me. "They're

266.27   Therefore a title is out of the question, and we recognized] Therefore 'greatness' is out of the question—we really recognized

266.29   man we had constructed in advance—he was made on purpose.]
man we always built upon—if he was n't, so impossibly, your nephew.
From head to foot made on purpose.

266.31   spot! It's enough of a title to-day to be an American—with the way
they have come up. It does] spot! One's enough of a prince to-day
when one's the right American: such a wonderful price is set on one's
not being in the wrong! It does

266.35   in the complete evening.] in the sweet dark warmth.

266.36   good-night, I exclaimed,] good-night, I could n't but exhale a
compassion.

267.2   since you have described this as perfection?"] since you've described
all she finds Archie as perfection?"

267.3   She hesitated a moment. "I mean better for Mr. Pringle."] She knew
quite what she meant. "Ah better for *him!*"

267.4   hand—I remained looking at her.] hand—I still sought her eyes.

267.4   "How came it that you] "How came it you

267.8   "Ah, my friend, […] over I couldn't do this for you? And disengaging
herself she turned away quickly and went back to the hotel.] "Well, my
friend, […] over how could I do this for you?" On which, disengaging
herself, she turned quickly away.

268.2   whether she blushed as she made this avowal,] how deeply she flushed
as she made, in the form of her question, this avowal,

268.5   but I did, while I took my way to Stresa—it is a walk of half an hour—
in the darkness.] but was aware of the colour of my own cheeks while
I took my way to Stresa—a walk of half an hour—in the attenuating
night.

268.7   produced an effect of excitement which would have made it impossible for me to sit still in a carriage.] produced in me an emotion that
would have made sitting still in a carriage impossible.

268.8   This same agitation kept me up late after] This same stress kept me up
after

268.8   I knew that I should] I knew I should

268.10 ceremony Archie had not turned up when the lights in the hotel began
to be put out.] ceremony, Archie had not reappeared when the inn-
lights began here and there to be dispensed with.

268.13   nervous about him and wondered whether he had had an accident on the lake. I reflected that in this case—[...] sent after me.] anxious for him, wondering at possible mischances. Then I reflected that in case of an accident on the lake, that is of his continued absence from Baveno—[...] dispatched me a messenger.

268.14   suppose that anything] suppose anything

268.18   in circumstances much more difficult.] in a much tighter place.

268.20   season—to place us together.] season—to make us contiguous.

268.23   to his own apartment.] to his own quarters.

268.27   then—I had such a curiosity as to how [...] he had not wished to see me.] now—I was so anxious as to how [...] he had wanted to dodge me.

268.30   His dodging me that way (for [...] room) was] His so markedly shirking our encounter—for [...] room—was

268.31   had really come off.] would really have come off.

269.2   The impression of almost morbid eagerness of purpose that she had given me suggested possibilities that I was afraid to think of.] That almost morbid resolution I still seemed to hear the ring of pointed to conceivable extremities that I shrank from considering.

269.4   comment, as I walked away from her, that] comment in walking away from her that

269.5   It would not really be done till Archie had backed out.] It would n't truly be done till Archie had truly backed out.

269.8   at the sleeping mountains.] to the couchant Alps.

269.9   he backed out?—was [...] to back out?] he thought better of it?—was to think better of it?

269.10   contradiction in it;] contradiction in the matter;

269.11   I believed what Mrs. Pallant had told me about Linda,] I had taken from Louisa what she told me of Linda,

269.16   that the manner in which her mother had betrayed her (there was no other word) to her lover had been thoroughgoing. It would need very radical measures on Mrs. Pallant's part to excuse Archie.] her mother's grand treachery—I did n't know what to call it—had been at least, to her lover, thoroughgoing. It would need strong action in that lady to justify his retreat.

269.17   sorry, if she had made an impression on him—the impression she desired.] sorry—if she had made on him the impression she desired.

269.19   going in to condole with him, in my dressing gown;] of getting into my dressing gown and going forth to condole with him.

269.21   I am bound] But I am bound

269.22   he showed few symptoms when we met in the morning and break-fasted together.] when we met in the morning for breakfast he showed few traces of ravage.

269.23   that experience seems only to take away from us.] that later experience seems only to undermine.

269.24   is simply (in the given case) to do nothing—to say nothing.] is the masterly resource of beautiful blankness.

269.25   we think that is too] we think that too

269.30   departure (I explained […] for him—I was weary with my journey and wanted to go to bed), he replied:] departure—I explained […] for him; fagged with my journey I had wanted to go to bed—he replied:

269.31   "Oh, nothing […] than this.] "Oh nothing […] than this one.

269.32   in the least tired."] in the least fagged."

269.33   it seemed to me indelicate to try] it struck me as gross to try

269.36   granted that he would be glad to accompany me. Then he remarked] granted he would be glad to come too. Then he let fall

270.1   also he had some letters to write.] also that he had arrears of letters.

270.5   But he satisfied my curiosity […] this sentiment] But he soothed my anxiety […] this yearning

270.6   in the porch of the hotel] from the porch of the hotel

270.8   in this young man's face] in the poor youth's face

270.11   as if he wished to escape from my call.] as to escape my call.

270.12   that Mrs. Pallant had warned him off but] he had been indeed warned off, but

270.15   told me that my friends were in a certain summer-house] described my friends as in a summer-house

270.16   The place had] The place at large had

270.20   On finding this to be [...] awkwardly, for I had a sudden sense of being an unmasked hypocrite—a conspirator] On finding this the case [...] awkwardly—I might have been, from the way I suddenly felt, an ummasked hypocrite, a proved conspirator

270.22   about Linda Pallant, she looked up with a little cry] in lovely Linda; she looked up with a cry

270.25   with the most engaging frankness. I felt as if I had no right to touch her hand and I pretended not to see it. But this gave no chill to] with engaging frankness. I felt again as if I had no right to that favour which I pretended not to have noticed. This gave no chill, however, to

270.26   bench, so that [...] down, and praised] bench so that [...] down; she praised

270.28   mother's damning talk about her seem a hideous dream.] mother's awful talk about her a hideous dream.

270.28   She told me Mrs. Pallant] She told me her mother

270.31   the table was too rickety.] the table refused to stand firm.

270.32   pretexts between them in the way of letters: I judged this to be a token] pretexts of letters between them—I judged this a token

270.33   the only one however that] the only one nevertheless that

270.34   always together and] always together, yet

271.1   to say something about it; this] to speak of this—it

271.1   natural—it was almost unfriendly to omit it.] natural; her omission could n't but have a sense.

271.2   At last I observed] At last I remarked

271.3   he had left me to come alone.] he had n't seemed to see the attraction.

271.5   glad," she answered. "You [...] like." "If I tell him that he will come immediately,"] glad. You [...] like," said Linda Pallant. I wondered at her. "If I tell him he'll come at once."

271.8   night," Linda went on, "and [...] till the most dreadful hours.] night," she went on, "and [...] till I don't know what o'clock.

271.8   That isn't done] That sort of thing isn't done

271.9   or rather when we didn't come back.] or rather, you see, when we didn't!

271.12   It was very embarrassing."] It was awfully awkward."

271.13   made an impression upon me;] much impressed me;

271.17   maiden—had conceived the fine idea of] maiden—entertained the graceful thought of

271.20   evening!" I exclaimed.] evening!" I made answer.

271.22   face." § "Mamma was] face." § But my young lady was not to be ruffled. "Mamma was

271.23   scolding," the girl went on. "And to punish me] scolding. And to punish me

271.26   I forget what answer Mrs. Pallant made to Linda's appeal; she] I forget how her mother met Linda's appeal; Louisa

271.28   if she had any postage-stamps.] if she were possessed of postage-stamps.

271.29   a somewhat shabby pocket-book] a well-worn little pocket book

271.30   confessed that she was destitute;] confessed herself destitute;

271.30   gave her the letters, with] gave her the letter with

271.35   and I was on the point of] and was on the point of

272.2   told her she had no money and she fumbled in her pocket for] announced without reserve that she had n't money and Louisa then fumbled for

272.3   and the girl had taken it Linda kissed her] and bestowed it the girl kissed her

272.11   is—or she will […] hours, if] is. She'll satisfy herself […] hours—if

272.17   between you?" § "Don't you] between you?" § My question found my friend quite ready. "Don't you

272.20   gracefully between] conveniently between

272.22   so that if we understood each other it was enough.] so that, always, if we've understood each other it has been enough.

272.23   changed, because there has] changed. There has

272.29   she said, simply.] she answered simply.

272.32   said Mrs. Pallant, decisively.] my companion said with her fine authority.

273.6   "The truth?" I repeated.] "The truth?"

273.9   it's you that must] it's you who must

273.12   We will leave [...] myself." I took [...] farewell, and while I held it I
         said,] We'll break camp [...] myself," I added. I took [...] farewell, but
         spoke again while I held it.

273.15   I wanted to leave the neighbourhood.] I could n't stay.

273.19   morning in the summer-house with her, looking at] morning there
         with her, spend it before

273.20   I found that Archie] I found my young man

273.23   a small portmanteau with him.] a few clothes.

273.24   I got a telegram from him notifying me that he] I received telegram-
         notice that he

273.25   and requesting me to forward] and begged I would forward

273.28   leave the poor boy] leave him

273.30   we met in Paris, in November, I saw] we met that November in Paris I
         saw

273.32   from me, except [...] of what that lady had told him.] save [...] of
         what our extraordinary friend had said to him.

273.34   Christmas and then [...] had passed.] Christmas—when [...] over.

273.34   my old friend since.] the wronger of my youth.

273.36   after the time to which my story refers, Linda married [...] the posses-
         sor of] after our more recent adventure her daughter Linda married
         [...] the heir to

274.1   some useful industry.] some prosaic but flourishing industry.

274.1   photographs (such is her present name)] admired photographs—
         such is Linda's present name—

274.5   has not changed his state yet, and now even my sister is beginning,
         for the first time, to desire it. I related to her as soon as I saw her the
         substance of the story I have written here] has not even yet changed
         his state, my sister at last thinks it high time. I put before her as soon
         as I next saw her the incidents here recorded

The Aspern Papers

275.3   in truth without her I should] without her in truth I

275.6   It was she who invented the short cut, who severed the Gordian knot.]
         It was she who found the short cut and loosed the Gordian knot.

275.9   It is not supposed to be the nature of women to rise as a general thing
         to the largest and most liberal view—I mean of a practical scheme; but
         it has struck me that they sometimes throw off a bold conception—]
         It is not supposed easy for women to rise to the large free view of
         anything, anything to be done; but they sometimes throw off a bold
         conception—

275.10   Simply ask them to take you in] Simply make them take you in

275.14   to become an inmate.] to become an intimate.

275.16   facts which were] facts that were

275.19   and they lived now in Venice in obscurity, on very small means,] and
         they now lived obscurely in Venice, lived on very small means,

275.20   in a dilapidated old palace on an out-of-the-way canal:] in a seques-
         tered and dilapidated old palace:

275.21   for fifteen years] some fifteeen years

275.23   did not include the two] had never embraced the two

275.23   as it was somehow supposed,] as was somehow supposed,

275.26   (they were believed […], besides having had, as their name implied,
         some French strain in their origin), who] —they were believed,
         […] besides being as their name implied of some remoter French
         affiliation—who

275.30   though in reality as I afterwards learned she was considerably the big-
         ger of the two.] though in fact I afterwards found her the bigger of the
         two in inches.

276.1   had a suspicion that she was in want; and she had gone to the house
         to offer assistance, so that if they were suffering (and American suffer-
         ing), she should at least not have it on her conscience.] had a suspicion
         she was in want, and had gone to the house to offer aid, so that if they
         were suffering, American suffering in particular, she should n't have it
         on her conscience.

276.3   The "little one" received her in the great cold, tarnished Venetian
         sala... and did not even ask her to sit down.] The "little one" had
         received her in the great cold tarnished Venetian sala... and had n't
         even asked her to sit down.

276.5   She however replied with profundity] She replied however with profundity

276.13   (it had been [...] papers),] —it had been [...] papers—

276.13   and I had besieged it with my eyes] —laying siege to it with my eyes

276.16   implication, a faint reverberation.] implication and in a "dying fall."

276.18   curiosity, as she was always interested in the joys] curiosity, as always in the joys

276.22   movable window, I could see that she was amused by my infatuation, the way my interest in the papers had become a fixed idea.] moveable window, I saw how my eagerness amused her and that she found my interest in the possible spoil a fine case of monomania.

276.23   you expected to find in them the answer] you expected from it the answer

277.2   I saw that it was not strictly necessary that she should have exceeded by very much the common span.] I saw it not strictly involved that she should have far exceeded the common span.

277.3   she was very far advanced in life] she was of venerable age

277.12   was not so old, and she risked the conjecture that] was of minor antiquity, and the conjecture was risked that

277.17   the ministers.] the appointed ministers.

277.22   His early death had been the only dark spot in his life,] His early death had been the only dark spot, as it were, on his fame

277.26   in the same way.] in the same masterful way.

277.27   of shabby behaviour.] of any grossness.

277.30   These were almost always awkward.] These had been almost always difficult and dangerous.

277.33   head, and out of this pernicious fashion many complications, some of them grave, had not failed to arise.] head, and while the fury raged— the more that it was very catching—accidents, some of them grave, had not failed to occur.

277.36   the sweetest ever] the most charming ever

278.1   was the exclamation that rose to my lips] had been of course my foreseen judgement

278.3   insupportable] unbearable

278.5   it struck me in short that he was kinder, more considerate than, in his
         place (if I could imagine me in such a place!) I should have been.] it
         struck me that he had been kinder and more considerate than in his
         place—if I could imagine myself in such a box—I should have found
         the trick of.

278.8   lines of research] directions of research

278.18   a revelation to us that it was possible to keep so quiet as that in] a
         revelation to us that self-effacement on such a scale had been possible

278.21   And she had not taken great trouble about it either; she had not hid-
         den herself [...] she had boldly] She had taken no great trouble for it
         either—had n't hidden herself [...] had boldly

278.23   The only secret [...] that we could perceive was that [...] curiosities
         that were greater than she.] The one apparent secret [...] had been
         that [...] much greater curiosities.

278.28   Mrs. Prest had not mentioned this much to anyone; she appeared [...]
         she was there.] My friend indeed had not named her much to anyone;
         she appeared [...] the fact of her continuance.

278.29   she had not the responsibilities of an editor. It was no explanation]
         Mrs. Prest had n't the nerves of an editor. It was meanwhile no
         explanation

278.33   were spent.] had been spent.

278.35   all our publishings (some people consider [...])] all our promulga-
         tions—some people now consider [...]—

279.1   (and [...] what had become [...])] —and [...] what could have be-
         come [...]—

279.13   a clean, melancholy, unfrequented canal,] a clean melancholy rather
         lonely canal,

279.16   perversely clean,] eccentrically neat,

279.17   you can pass] you may pass

279.18   It has the air of a Protestant Sunday.] It's as negative—considering
         where it is—as a Protestant Sunday.

279.23   big, imposing] big and imposing

279.25   logical reply.] straight answer.

279.27   not amply lodged herself] not amply lodged

279.29   perfectly compatible] perfectly consistent

280.5   it belonged to the house. It suddenly occurred to me that if it did belong to the house I had my pretext.] attached to the house. I suddenly felt that so attached it gave me my pretext.

280.10   and I was afraid] and was afraid

280.16   I might obtain the documents] I might get what I wanted

280.19   which pushed me to throw myself upon your] which threw me on your

280.20   won't have the documents spoken of;] won't have her relics and tokens so much as spoken of;

280.21   hasn't modern notions,] has n't the feelings of the day,

280.22   I can arrive at the papers] I can arrive at my spoils

280.24   diplomatic practices.] diplomatic arts.

280.25   I am sorry for it, but for Jeffrey Aspern's sake I would do worse still.] I'm sorry for it, but there's no baseness I would n't commit for Jeffrey Aspern's sake.

280.27   when he wrote to her.] on his respectfully writing to her.

280.31   Mr. Aspern's papers, and if they had should never think of showing them] Mr. Aspern's 'literary remains,' and if they had had would n't have dreamed of showing them

280.32   She didn't know] She could n't imagine

280.35   a moment, provokingly] a moment and all provokingly

280.36   perhaps after all they haven't any of his things.] perhaps they really have n't anything.

281.9   of mementoes, of relics.] of mementoes, of tangible objects.

281.9   "Mr." touches me] "Mr." affects me

281.16   Venice on the business] Venice on the undertaking

281.17   were it not that for him there was the obstacle that it would be difficult to] were it not for the obstacle of his having, for any confidence, to

281.20   their correspondent] their snubbed correspondent

281.21   could say no without lying.] could protest without lying.

281.22   to change your name,] to take a false name,

281.24   but none the less she has probably heard of] but she has none the less probably heard of

281.26   a visiting-card, neatly engraved with a name that was not my own.] a visiting-card neatly engraved with a well-chosen nom de guerre.

281.27   "You are very extravagant; you might have written it,"] "You're very extravagant—it adds to your immorality. You might have done it in pencil or ink,"

281.29   you are prepared to go far! But] you've the courage of your curiosity. But

281.31   every day to fetch] every day to get

281.33   "Shall you only depend upon that?"] "Shall you depend all on that?"

281.36   as well as hereafter] as well as through the long hereafter

282.2   to the care of the *padrona*,"] to the care of the padrona."

283.3   later, as I waited] later and while I waited

283.5   impressive but it looked cold] impressive, yet looked somehow cold

283.8   by a little red-headed, white-faced] by a small red-headed and white-faced

283.13   inevitable challenge which in Italy precedes the hospitable act.] cautious challenge that in Italy precedes the act of admission.

283.14   As a general thing I was irritated by] I was irritated as a general thing by

283.15   though as I liked the old I suppose I should have] though as so fond, if yet so special, an antiquarian I suppose I ought to have

283.16   but I was so determined to be genial that I took my] but, with my resolve to be genial from the threshold at any price, I took my

283.20   an American,] a travelling American,

283.21   hostile, and I reflected that even that was perhaps] hostile—even that was perhaps

283.23   that visits were rare in that house,] that visits in such a house were rare

283.24   a sociable place.] a bustling place.

283.25   I felt that I had a foot in the citadel.] I felt my foot in the citadel and promised myself ever so firmly to keep it there.

283.31   in the dentist's parlour.] in dentists' parlours.

284.1   It was gloomy and stately—but it owed its character almost entirely to its […] doors—as high as the doors of houses—which] It had a gloomy grandeur, but owed its character almost all to its […] doors, as high as those of grand frontages, which

284.5   brown pictures, which I perceived to be bad, in battered frames, were suspended.] hung brown pictures, which I noted as speciously bad, in battered and tarnished frames that were yet more desirable than the canvases themselves.

284.6   chairs with their backs] chairs that kept their backs

284.7   and little even as] and scantly even as

284.9   by the time the door opened again through which the maid-servant had escaped] by the time the door through which the maid-servant had escaped opened again

284.10   I had not meant] I had n't meanwhile meant

284.18   I remarked, ingenuously.] I ingenuously cried.

284.22   she spoke with a kind of mild literalness.] she spoke very simply and mildly.

284.26   odiously intrusive,] horribly intrusive,

284.28   but it was simple; it was not fresh, but it was mild.] but it was candid; it was not fresh, but it was clear.

284.34   she gave a shy, melancholy smile.] she gave a wan vague smile.

285.2   I have felt that a garden is] I've felt a garden to be

285.3   I went on, smiling.] I went on with as sociable a smile as I could risk.

285.6   letting her embarrassed eyes wander over all my strangeness.] letting her weak wonder deal—helplessly enough, as I felt—with my strangeness.

285.10   and waited, as if I took for granted that she would] and waited as in the belief she would

285.12   I have been looking at furnished] I've looked at furnished

285.16   She came nearer to me] She came nearer, as if

285.23   She protested at this, with a queer little sigh which might also have been a gush of rapture at the picture I presented. Then she observed] She protested against this with a small quaver of sound that might have been at the same time a gush of rapture for my free sketch. Then she gasped

285.25 that is much more,] or rather much more,

285.27 helplessly while] in practical submission while

285.30 certainly shabby; but I perceived] in truth shabby, yet I felt

285.32 so lost in staring at me,] so lost in her blankness and gentleness,

285.36 ago—we are nothing.] ago. We don't seem to be anything now.

286.9 only one other; she] only one other than me. She

286.9 other; she is very old—she never goes down."] other than me. She's very old. She never goes down." § I feel again my thrill at this close identification of Juliana; in spite of which, however, I kept my head.

286.12 she repeated, in the same dazed way.] she repeated—almost as for the rich unwonted joy to her of spoken words.

286.14 I demanded:] I put the question straight.

286.15 you let me two or three? That] you for a good rent let me two or three? That

286.18 my interlocutress believe that I was an honourable person,] making my entertainer believe me an undesigning person,

286.25 Miss Tita[1] (for […] be) had] Miss Tina—for […] be—had

286.26 she had promised that she] she had promised me she

286.27 I inquired who] I invited information as to who

286.30 in Tita Bordereau […] an odd and affecting person.] in Miss Tina […] rather pleasingly incalculable and interesting.

286.31 the world should not touch them,] the world should n't talk of then or touch them,

286.32 that it never heard of] that it did n't hear of

286.32 In Tita at any rate] In Miss Tina at any rate

287.2 live very badly. The rooms are very bare—that you might take; they have nothing in] live very badly—almost on nothing. The rooms are very bare—those you might take; they've nothing at all in

[1] The name Tita is changed throughout to Tina in the *New York Edition*, see Introduction, p. lxxviii.

287.7 I can hire what I should want for a few months, for a trifle, and my] I can hire for a trifle what I should so briefly want, what I should use; my

287.10 fellow" (this [...] moment),] fellow"—this [...] moment—

287.16 spoken to in that way, with a kind of humorous firmness which [...] sympathy but was on the contrary founded on] spoken to in any such fashion—with a humorous firmness that [...] sympathy, that was quite founded on

287.19 consider the matter with] submit the question to

287.25 presentiment that I should succeed.] prevision of success.

287.27 in a quarter of an hour] in five minutes

287.30 for the editor ([...] analysis),] for the commentator – [...] analysis—

287.34 (it [...] in perfect perspective [...] omen)] —it [...] in large perspective [...] omen—

287.36 It was a large] It was a spacious

288.3 the successive feelings that accompanied my consciousness] the successive states marking my consciousness

288.8 to contain his,] to contain and express his own,

288.11 the niece was not there.] the niece not to be there.

288.13 alone with such a terrible] alone with so terrible a

288.15 with the perception] from the perception

288.16 which, for her, served almost] which served for her almost

288.19 she might scrutinise me without being scrutinised herself.] she might take me all in without my getting at herself.

288.19 it increased the presumption that there was a ghastly] it created the presumption of some ghastly

288.23 I had time to get what I wanted from her.] I should have time to compass my end.

288.25 I could seize her papers.] I could pounce on her possessions and ransack her drawers.

289.9 as if perhaps I had been shouting at her; and the chair] as if perhaps I had been shouting; and the chair

289.12   telling her that I was [...] that I had intruded, that I had not been prop-
          erly introduced and could only throw myself upon] assuring her I was
          [...] of my intrusion and of my not having been properly introduced
          and that I could but throw myself on

289.17   (she [...] stranger), and I had felt it was really a case] —she [...]
          stranger—and I had felt really a case

289.19   It would render me] It would make me

289.21   as an inmate they] as a co-tenant of the palace, so to speak, they

289.27   with great attention] with great penetration

289.31   then she began:] then she inquired,

290.3   "It's not in the middle [...] you can't see] "This is not the middle [...]
          you can't so much as see

290.4   wondering whether she wished] wondering if she wished

290.9   in one of the gondolas.] in one of the gondole.

290.10   as if the gondolas were a curious far-away craft which she knew only
          by] as if they designed a curious far-away craft known to her only by

290.12   I exclaimed. I had scarcely] I returned. I had scarcely

290.15   her attitude bothered me] her attitude worried me

290.20   purpose, because she herself wished to see me at first alone.] pur-
          pose—had had her reasons for seeing me first alone.

290.21   and I asked myself why she had judged this necessary and what was
          coming yet;] and I turned over the fact of these unmentioned reasons
          and the question of what might come yet;

290.23   delighted to see her] delighted to see our absent friend

290.23   so very courteous to me,] so very patient with me,

290.34   she added, with her soft, venerable quaver] she added in her soft ven-
          erable quaver

291.1   for a single instant, long enough to ask myself what she] but an in-
          stant, long enough to measure what she

291.8   she rejoined instantly] she said instantly

291.13   have enjoyed by the year] have enjoyed the whole of by the year

291.14   my small means allowed] my resources allowed

291.17   I would give myself the compensation of extracting the papers from her for nothing.] I would make it up by getting hold of my "spoils" for nothing.

291.18   occasion; so odious would it have appeared to me] occasion, so odious would it have seemed to me

291.23   with serenity and with no apparent sense] with apparent complacency and with no discoverable sense

291.23   would be becoming of her] would become her to

291.25   Our little bargain] Our little agreement

291.30   then she inquired,] then she brought out,

291.33   I answered, smiling.] I sturdily smiled.

291.35   as if she had become conscious that her own question might have looked far reaching.] as if she had felt how overreaching her own question might have looked.

292.6   the discussion of the rent.] the discussion of dollars and francs.

292.11   of making an epigram.] of an epigram.

292.12   "Yes, but for that!"] "Yes, for that—!"

292.23   be punctual; and I added,] be punctual. To which I added:

292.35   while she replied,] while she assented

293.9   said I, laughing,] I laughed,

293.12   signified that I might depart.] signified my dismissal.

293.17   But she made no such suggestion;] But she made no such overture;

293.19   competent youth which was almost] competent youth almost

293.21   as still more helpless, because her inefficiency was spiritual] as more deeply futile, because her inefficiency was inward

293.25   I only observed at the end of a minute.] A minute indeed elapsed before I committed myself.

293.30   give a good deal."] pay largely."

294.4   was not really foolishly] was n't foolishly

294.6   I said to her that I was] I observed that I was

294.7   if you go above, on] if you go above—to]

294.13   up above I was] above I should be

294.15   to pass from it to the garden-story] to pass from it to the garden-level

294.19   marked her manner. § "Perhaps] marked her manner: § "Perhaps

294.24   had a view of the blue lagoon, above the opposite rough-tiled house-
         tops.] had above the opposite rough-tiled house-tops a view of the
         blue lagoon.

294.27   to convert [...] into a convenient habitation.] to make [...] habitable
         enough.

294.32   no overt interest in my] none but the most veiled interest in my

295.1   those the old lady] those the old woman

295.2   in no explanations nor] neither in explanations nor

295.3   a sign that Juliana] a sign Juliana

295.20   with these women [...] the pecuniary question should constantly
         come back.] these women [...] should so constantly bring the pecuni-
         ary question back.

295.21   she replied, smiling.] she answered almost gaily.

295.25   I exclaimed, with genuine feeling] I cried, with genuine feeling

295.27   the possibility that she would destroy her papers [...] her end really
         approach.] the possibility of her destroying her documents [...] her
         end at hand.

295.29   I think I had an idea that she read [...] or at least pressed them] I was
         convinced of her reading [...] or at least pressing them

295.30   to have a glimpse of the latter spectacle.] for some view of those
         solemnities.

295.31   if the old lady were] if her venerable relative were

295.32   so very, very long.] so extraordinarily long.

295.33   were dead long ago;] had been dead for ages;

295.35   not at all content.] not at all resigned—resigned, that is, to life.

296.4   a moment and then she said,] a moment and then said:

296.10   with the glimmer of an illumination in her face.] with a dimness of
         glad surprise.

296.18   Oh, so easily!] You call it easily?

296.18   where is it that one could] where is it one could

296.25   She looked at me, at this,] She looked at me hereupon

296.33   such an inquiry would be premature.] such probings premature.

297.4   I remained a while longer] I stayed a while longer

297.5   bright desert (the sun was pouring in)] bright desert—the sun was pouring in—

298.8   I reminded Mrs. Prest,] I reminded my good friend,

298.9   wanting boldness] lacking boldness

298.11   She answered that the breach] She returned that the breach

298.15   very often, on the theory that it would console me] very often—all on the theory that it would console me

298.16   I began to perceive] I began to feel

298.17   especially when I was] especially since I was

298.18   when my derisive friend] when my ironic friend

298.20   to gather amusement [...] and she was] to draw amusement [...] and was

298.24   after she had gone away.] after her departure.

298.28   Miss Tita waiting for me] Miss Tina awaiting me

298.29   from my hand so that I did not see her aunt.] from my hand with a promptitude that prevented my seeing her aunt.

298.30   but she apparently thought] yet apparently thought

299.3   it was with simplicity] it was with a clearness akin to brightness

299.4   I replied that that would] I replied that this would

299.9   After this, for a long time] After that, for a long time,

299.10   I wondered that the common] I wondered the common

299.17   encountered such a violent parti pris of seclusion;] met so stiff a policy of seclusion;

299.21   without my having some observation] without my catching some view

299.22   for doing (reflecting [...] way):] for doing—considering [...] way:

299.23   let him divine] let him infer

299.24   he could pick up. But he picked up] he might glean. But he gleaned

299.27   His cleverness [...], it was not quite all I] His ability [...], if not quite
          all I

299.32   with such promptitude as was consistent with the fact that it was com-
          posed] with such dignity as answered to its being composed

300.9   an eye on the maiden] an eye on the possible rival

300.12   It seemed to me a [...] old lady's determination] It struck me as a [...]
          old woman's resolve

300.15   when I had given it up, I wasted] when I had given it up, wasted

300.18   reminder, after which I relinquished the idea ([...] case),] reminder;
          after which I put by the idea—[...] case—

300.21   I consented not to be so.] I consented not to be.

300.25   perceived [...] the poor old woman's desire] gathered [...] the poor
          lady's desire

300.28   she would not give me even a morsel of] she would n't add to that so
          much as a morsel of

300.30   the whole episode was essentially delightful to me.] the whole situa-
          tion had the charm of its oddity.

300.32   of holding my opportunity was much greater than the sense of losing
          it.] of playing with my opportunity was much greater after all than
          any sense of being played with.

301.3   fraternally, cheerfully] fraternally and fondly

301.19   praying it would open] praying it might open

301.22   to feel a certain joy at being under] to know the joy of being beneath

301.26   also went back, went back,] also went back, and still went back,

301.30   handled the papers and (even [...] stupid)] handled all mementoes
          and—even [...] stupid—

301.36   her survival more palpable.] her survival more vivid.

302.2   a certain sort of reciprocity, during the hours that I] a certain shade of
          reciprocity, during the hours I

302.6   proved to me that they had something [...] demonstrate.] empha-
          sized they had matters [...] prove.

302.9   in thinking that at all events though invisible [...] they saw me] in the
          probability that, though invisible [...] they kept me in view

302.13   give the proper thought to the matter] give the question proper thought

302.16   wild, rough tangle,] wild, rich tangle,

302.19   I formed this gracious project that [...] I would [...]—I would] I clung to the fond fancy that [...] I should [...]—I should

302.22   a mountain of carnations should be piled up] a mound of fragrance should be heaped up

302.26   for my bouquets to the] for my "results" to the

302.28   I reflected that the ladies would see [...] that they must have been bought] I felt sure my friends would see [...] where such tribute couldn't have been gathered

302.29   make up their minds from this that I was a humbug. So I composed myself and] might so make up their minds against my veracity. I possessed my soul and

303.3   began to flush in it and] began to recover and flush, and

303.6   it is remarkable that I should] it is wonderful that I should

303.6   tired of wondering] tired of trying to guess

303.10   It was clear that they must have had other habits and other circumstances;] It was supposable they had had then other habits, forms and resources,

303.16   it was plain that the American name] it was clear the American name

303.20   dropped the local accent and fashion. There was nothing in them that one recognized, and putting] shed and unlearned all native marks and notes. There was nothing in them one recognized or fitted, and, putting

303.27   There was an implication in the poem (I hope [...] phrase)] There was a profession in the poem—I hope [...] phrase—

303.28   We had no real light upon] We had no real light on

303.33   something positively clandestine] something quite clandestine

304.8   and adventurous, [...] and that she had passed through some singular vicissitudes.] and reckless, [...] and that she had braved some wondrous chances.

304.9   by what sufferings] by what adventures and sufferings

304.17   perfume of reckless passion] perfume of impenitent passion

304.21   suffered an imputation.] suffered injury.

304.26   Bohemia, in the days] Bohemia of the days

304.31   less furnished […] to-day (in […] strewn), with] less awake […] to-day—in […] strewn—to

305.3   the present hour, when] the present hour at which

305.4   Miss Bordereau sailed with her family] Miss Bordereau had sailed with her family

305.7   and was struck] and was most struck

305.8   pearls and scarfs.] pearls and scarfs and mosaic brooches.

305.11   done so a great deal more.] done so with greater force.

305.16   had ordered otherwise] had ruled otherwise

305.17   how the old world] how the general old order

305.18   however, that I watched him;] however, I watched him;

305.18   had entertained with the new] had entertained with the special new

305.21   what I had loved him for] what I had prized him for

306.7   the strange old basilica] the strange old church

306.12   (the only […] it), is like an open-air] —the only […] it—is an open-air

306.14   degustation—that of the exquisite] degustation, that of the splendid

306.18   The wonderful church with its] The great basilica with its

306.21   as if a rich curtain were swaying] as if a rich curtain swayed

306.24   did not prevent from being stuffy.] could n't relieve of some stuffiness.

307.5   that solicited me was the vague reflection that it would be pleasant to […] on a garden bench.] that occupied me was that it would be good to […] on a garden-bench.

307.9   stood among the flowers] stood among the thick flowers

307.12   on summer nights in her youth, might] might on the summer nights of her youth

307.16   Miss Tita was seated in my little bower.] my younger padrona was seated in one of the bowers.

307.17   At first I only made out] At first I made out but

307.19   some sentimental maidservant [...] with her sweetheart.] some en-
          amoured maid-servant [...] with her sweet-heart.

307.25   and adding to that eccentricity by creeping into the garden.] and by
          adding to that oddity my invasion of the garden.

307.29   I took for granted that the words she uttered expressed discomfiture
          at my arrival;] I took the words she uttered for an impatience of my
          arrival;

307.33   almost as if she were going to] almost as if to

307.34   to add that she did nothing of the kind; she did not even shake] to add
          that I escaped this ordeal and that she did n't even then shake

307.35   It was a gratification to her to] It was an ease to her to

307.36   nervous when she was out-of-doors] nervous when out-of-doors

308.1   The plants and bushes] The plants and shrubs

308.5   I guessed that nocturnal prowlings were not in the least her habit,] I
          felt how little her nocturnal prowlings could have been her habit,

308.7   (I had been struck with the circumstance [...] possession)] —I had
          been afflicted by the same [...] possession—

308.8   to overestimate her simplicity.] to allow too much for her simplicity.

308.9   backwoods," I said, laughing.] backwoods," I cheeringly laughed.

308.13   mighty well [...] but I had a hope that you] amazingly so long [...]
          but I had a hope you

308.17   as if I were talking some strange tongue] as if I had spoken some
          strange tongue

308.18   was so little of an answer that I was considerably irritated.] was so
          little of one that I felt it make for irritation.

308.20   mystery when she gave] mystery, but she gave

308.21   But I never have been out at night] But I've never been out at night

308.24   There was an unmistakeable reference] There was a finer sense

308.26   a small advantage. As it would help me to follow it to establish a sort
          of grievance.] some advantage. As I might follow that further by es-
          tablishing a good grievance.

309.4   mixture of the shrinking and the direct.] mixture of shyness and
          straightness.

309.12   and we have at least some] and have at least some

309.15   My interlocutress appeared incapable [...] and she declared quickly]
          My friend seemed incapable [...] and she now spoke quickly

309.22   is she failing?" I demanded] is she really failing?" I demanded

309.23   than I intended to show. I judged this] than I meant to betray. I meas-
          ured this

309.26   somewhere and you will tell me] somewhere—while you tell me

309.35   I might have inferred] I might have gathered

310.4   with which they inevitably alternated] by which they were naturally
          broken

310.7   that her aunt had been less well for] how much less well her aunt had
          been for

310.9   She was weaker; at moments it seemed as if she had no strength] She
          was markedly weaker; at moments she showed no strength

310.12   she said her niece irritated her, made her nervous.] she pronounced
          poor Miss Tina "a worry, a bore and a source of aggravation."

310.12   together, as if she were asleep;] together, as if for long sleep;

310.14   she gave at intervals some small] she gave, in breaks, some small

310.16   Miss Tita [...] that she sometimes feared she was dead,] This sad per-
          sonage [...] as to create the fear she was dead;

310.17   moreover she took hardly any food] moreover she scarce ate or drank

310.20   and she had always, little company] and had always, little company

310.21   sitting in the parlour.] sitting in the great parlour.

310.24   of the strange circumstance that [...] the old lady [...] toward her
          end] of the strange fact that [...] the old woman [...] to her end

310.26   The story did not hang together [...] whether it were not a trap] The
          story hung indifferently together [...] if it might n't be a trap

310.29   At any rate, I kept] But at any hazard, I kept

310.30   to ask me if I had an *arrière-pensée*.] to ask me what I might really be
          "up to"

310.32   as to her capacity for entertaining one.] as to what she might be. She
          was up to nothing at nothing at all.

310.35   to feel that I listened, that I cared.] to feel me listen and care.

310.35   wondering why I cared [...] as she spoke of] wondering why I should [...] while describing

311.3   before (I saw that her mind was essentially vague [...] occurred), there was scarcely a] back—I found her essentially vague [...] occurred—there was never a

311.5   *passeggio* in the city.] *passeggio* in the town.

311.13   pleasant circle (this [...] own),] kind circle—this [...] own;

311.16   who was so kind] who was so attentive

311.21   made herself, like paper lamp-shades] turned out with her own hands, paper lamp-shades,

311.25   if the Venetians liked you] if the good Venetians liked you

311.26   There was something affecting] There was affecting matter enough

311.29   she had had a brilliant youth.] she had had a dashing youth.

311.31   I observed [...] that she had [...] something of the trick] I noted [...] how nearly she had — the trick

311.32   almost infantile speech] almost infantile prattle

311.33   I judged that she had] I judged her to have

311.36   her failing interest in] the failure of interest in

312.2   so that the matter of her reminiscences] so that her range of her reminiscence

312.4   If she had not been so decent her references would have seemed to carry one back to] Her tone, had n't it been so decent, would have seemed to carry one back to

312.5   I found myself falling into the error of thinking her] I found myself mistakenly think of her

312.7   I said to myself,] I indeed reasoned,

312.9   had not cared to lift even for her the veil that covered the temple of her youth.] had foreborn to lift for innocent eyes the veil that covered the temple of her glory.

312.11   until I remembered that we] till I remembered we

312.14   yet after all the effect of it was] though the effect of it withal was

312.17   escaped the interviewer there was] escaped invasion and research, there was

312.19   inasmuch as they had not heard of them; and Cumnor's] for people had n't heard of them. Cumnor's

312.27   things that I like," I said with a sigh.] things I like," I quite sincerely sighed.

312.29   at this, looking at me with] at this, facing me with

312.33   I saw that I only mystified] I saw I only mystified

313.2   I perceived that she felt that she should not [...] and wished] I made out in her the conviction that she should n't [...] and the wish

313.5   to a completely innocent woman.] to a perfectly artless and a considerably witless woman.

313.6   I know they are also meant for] I know them also meant for

313.9   a double lot of them.] a double lot.

313.19   at variance with the prudence [...] associated itself with her plain] at odds with all the prudence [...] glimmered at me in her plain

313.23   I go to sleep—very often in bed (it's a bad habit] I go to sleep (very often in bed; it's a bad habit

313.31   she murmured, smiling.] and, though dimly, she quite lighted.

313.34   I repeated, staring.] I guarded my tone.

314.1   she said, mirthfully,] she said amusingly,

314.4   Miss Tita replied.] Miss Tina returned.

314.15   it seemed such a direct testimony.] their sound might have been the light rustle of an old unfolded love-letter.

314.21   which on the ground floor corresponded with our grand sala.] that corresponded on the ground floor with our great sala.

315.3   two or three stairs.] two or three degrees.

315.6   bring out what she wanted to ask.] bring it out.

315.23   I never beheld her.] I kept missing her.

315.25   to stop the flowers.] to stop the "floral tributes."

316.2   One afternoon, as I came down] One afternoon, at last, however, as I came down

316.3   I found Miss Tita] I found her

316.5   in her angular, diffident directness.] in her honest angular diffidence.

316.7   she informed me of the fact and told me that] she mentioned it at once, but telling me with it that

316.10   upon the old lady.] on my benefactress.

316.15   so markedly and suddenly change. It had been only] change so suddenly. It was only

316.17   unexpected serenities as if] unexpected serenities, plausibilities almost, as if

316.19   my aunt changes,"] my aunt varies,"

316.22   found me overinsistent.] found me too pushing.

317.7   I felt too well on this occasion that that was out of place] I now felt too well that this was out of place

317.9   enjoined upon me that she was too sacred for that sort of reciprocity] enjoined on me that she was too sacred for trivial modernisms

317.13   to feel any doubt as to her knowing my secret, though I did not in the least suspect] to doubt her suspecting me, though I did n't in the least myself suspect

317.16   and she had guessed.] and had guessed.

317.17   would burn her papers.] would, even like Sardanapalus, burn her papers.

317.21   She replied that it was good enough] She answered that it was good enough

317.23   I exclaimed, laughing.] I returned with a laugh.

317.26   I liked to think that this was] I liked to take this for

317.29   a more delightful social gift] a happier social gift

317.31   But one did not!] But one did n't pretend!

317.33   some very remarkable conversation] some wonderful talk

317.36   I receive only at] I receive company but

318.11   as if it were an immense circumstance.] as if it were a great affair.

318.21   as you ought to know.] as you ought pretty well to have gathered.

318.24   and it was the first time I had heard her laugh.] and it was so I first heard the strange sound of her laugh, which was as if the faint "walking" ghost of her old-time tone had suddenly cut a caper.

318.25   was what drew out the divine Juliana most.] was most what drew out the divine Juliana.

318.27   They are all for you] The flowers are all for you

318.32   said the old woman, to my stupefaction.] the old woman said to my stupefaction.

318.33   would be a capital place for her to sit in.] will do very well for her to sit in.

318.34   The allusion to my arbour was] The allusion to the most elaborate of my shady coverts, a sketchy "summer-house," was

319.1   talk, a strange mocking lambency which must have been a part of her adventurous youth and which had outlived passions] talk, a vague echo of the boldness or the archness of her adventurous youth and which had somehow automatically outlived passions

319.8   this courageous allusion to the last receptacle] this free glance at the last receptacle

319.13   expected some interesting talk, but perhaps she found it less genial [...] (considering [...] intention)] expected, as I felt, rare conversation, but perhaps she found it less gracious [...]—considering intention—

319.13   to give the conversation] to give the position

319.19   I had when I was her age."] I had at her age."

319.20   must remember that it has] must remember it has

319.23   Juliana declared.] Juliana went on.

319.24   that I know of] that *I* know of

319.25   she pursued, and I well] she said, and I well

319.26   she gave to the speech.] she gave the speech.

319.26   "You have made me talk, talk!] "You make me talk, talk, talk!

319.28   detained me to ask.] detained me to put a question.

319.31   of being there [...] she broke out,] of my being there [...] she produced:

320.1   go with him as a cicerone!" said Miss Bordereau with an effect of something like cruelty in her implacable power of retort—an incongruous suggestion that she was a] go with him and explain!" said Miss Bordereau, who gave an effect of cruelty to her implacable power of retort. This showed her as a

320.14   it would [...] have seemed to a spectator [...] the old woman was
         amusing herself at our expense.] it would [...] have struck a spectator
         [...] our venerable friend was making a rare sport of us.

320.17   that she should not be] she really should n't be

320.21   from me, out of the window, as if she were going to cry; and] from me
         and out of the window, quite as if about to weep, and

320.25   then she inquired,] then she said:

320.35   you have never seen an agreeable woman. Don't try] you've never seen
         an agreeable woman. What do you people know about good society?"
         she cried; but before I could tell her, "Don't try

321.3   downstairs I waited] downstairs waited

321.4   after a minute Miss Tita] after a minute my conductress

321.9   not (as [...] would have done) turn] did n't—as [...] would have in
         like case—turn

321.10   from you and try to escape, [...] a deprecating, clinging appeal] floun-
         dering an hedging, [...] a deprecating, a clinging appeal

321.12   perpetually a sort of prayer for assistance, for explanation;] a constant
         prayer for aid and explanation,

321.14   dropped from her and] dropped and

321.16   which was the only thing she could conceive,] that was all she could
         conceive,

321.17   She told me she did not know what had got into her aunt; she had [...]
         she had] She did n't know, she now declared, what possessed her aunt,
         who had [...] who had

321.19   she must find out what the idea was and then let me know; we would
         [...] have an ice [...] and she should tell me] she must catch the idea
         and let me have it; we would [...] take an ice [...] and she should
         report

321.21   long time to find out!"] long time to be able to 'report'!"

321.29   how splendid the great water-way looked on a clear, hot summer] the
         splendour of the great water-way on a clear summer

321.30   the mind to sympathetic talk.] the mind to freedom and ease.

321.32   Miss Tita [...] to her satisfaction I felt that she surrendered herself.]
         my friend [...] to her glee I was sure of her full surrender.

322.1   since she had been in a boat] since had thus floated

322.3   the only example she gave me of her extreme vagueness] the only show of her extreme vagueness

322.4   which marked off the period when Miss Bordereau flourished.] marking off the period of Miss Bordereau's eminence.

322.5   keep her out too long,] keep her out long.

322.7   keeping the conversation on purpose away from her domestic situation] holding off by design from her life at home

322.8   I poured treasure] I poured, rather, treasures

322.9   about Venice [...] described [...] discoursed] about the objects before and around us [...] describing also [...] discoursing

322.11   everything I pointed out to her,] everything I noted

322.13   with Miss Bordereau.] with her kinswoman.

322.14   At last she asked, with] At last she said with

322.16   straight; and then] straight, after which

322.17   however, she said suddenly, of] however, she broke out of

322.19   go!" "What] go!" I quite gasped. "What

322.25   candour showed itself a match for my own.] candour but profited.

322.27   I asked, laughing.] I asked with all the gaiety I now felt.

322.36   to give them up!"] to give up my reasons!"

323.2   after a moment she broke out] after a moment broke out

323.6   mean, being] mean by being

323.8   It made her fearfully] It makes her fearfully

323.9   she has got papers] she has papers

323.9   value?" I demanded, quickly.] value?" I precipitately cried.

323.13   For some minutes I was too agitated to speak,] I felt them too deeply to speak,

323.16   whether she would [...] at the door of the café;] if she would [...] before the great café;

323.22   she has got everything!"] she has everything!"

323.28   I saw that she enjoyed it [...] she was agitated with the multitude of her impressions.] I saw she felt it all [...] but her impressions were well-nigh too many for her.

323.29   She had forgotten what an attractive thing the world is, and it was coming over to her that somehow she had] She had forgotten the attraction of the world and was learning that she had

323.32   but as she looked all over [...] the flush of a sort of wounded] but as she took in [...] the flush of a wounded

323.34   She became silent, as if she were thinking with secret sadness of opportunities, for ever lost, which ought to] She did n't speak, sunk in the sense of opportunities, for ever lost, that ought to

324.4   she thinks it's interesting,"] it must be interesting,"

324.17   a somewhat troubled face.] a troubled face.

324.19   thing?" I asked, as if I myself could] thing?"—and I asked as if I could

324.22   she was speaking the truth] my friend spoke the truth

324.36   as if she was ignorant of the meaning of the word.] as if vague as to what that meant.

325.1   "I mean their containing] "I allude to their containing

325.2   I don't think they are painful.'] I don't think anything's painful."

325.3   you don't think they affect] there's nothing to affect

325.5   At this a singular look came into [...]—a kind of confession of] An odder look even than usual came at this into [...]—a confession, it seemed, of

325.8   I seemed to let her perceive that all this had been a bribe] I appeared to show it all as a bribe

325.10   a person who was kind to her;] a person markedly kind to her;

325.16   "Do you mean that she did something] "Do you mean she ever did something

325.18   I added, laughing, "it was] I agreeably put it, "it was

325.28   This put the case very crudely, though I am sure there was no irony in her intention.] This put the case, superficially, with sharp irony, but I was sure of her not intending that.

325.29   myself; there is no personal avidity in my desire.] myself, or that I should want them at any cost to any one else.

325.33   her usual manner, as if my speech were full of references to things she] her usual way, as if I abounded in matters she

325.33   I felt particularly like the reporter] I felt almost as base as the reporter

325.35   This was especially the case when after a moment she said,] This was marked when she presently said:

326.2   ashamed of myself for not having her rectitude.] ashamed of not having my friend's rectitude.

326.5   Miss Tita replied, simply.] Miss Tina replied categorically.

326.10   poor gentleman!" I exclaimed.] poor gentleman!" I groaned.

326.14   for you," said Miss Tita, smiling.] for you," my companion smiled.

326.16   you can't fib,] you *can't* fib,

326.23   asked," my companion rejoined.] asked," my poor friend pleaded.

326.27   inquired if that faithful domestic could not be managed.] put it that this frail creature might perhaps be managed.

326.29   And then she observed that] And then she remembered that

326.33   She was half surprised, half frightened at my wishing to make her play an active part.] She was half-surprised, half-frightened at my attaching that importance to her, at my calling on her for action.

326.35   horrible sacrilege."] dreadful sacrilege."

327.7   I felt this inquiry] I felt this question

327.16   "Why, she has so little to leave.] "Ah she has so little to leave.

327.19   America, from a lawyer.] America, from a gentleman—I think a lawyer—in New York.

327.25   she added, "But she had a lawyer once,] she added: "But she had an *avvocato* here once,

327.29   legatee; she has left] legatee. She must have left

327.31   a little character] a small character

327.33   accompanied with a command] accompanied with a proviso

327.35   an injunction so solemn.] an injunction so absolute.

328.2   to mitigate the severity of] to mitigate the rigour of

328.3   later, just before […] on our return, which] later on, just before […] after a return which

328.8   the old woman was very cunning.] the old woman was full of craft.

329.4   I almost figured to myself that it was her duty] I almost read it as her duty

329.7   determined to judge so far as was possible with my own senses.] determined to put the case to the very touch of my own senses.

329.27   I recognized after all that it behoved me to make a large allowance for her.] I after all recognized large allowance to be made for her.

330.6   of view when they are old] of view late in life,

330.19   dear," I said.] dear, much too dear," I said.

330.21   at me in her barricaded way,] at me as from the mouth of her cave.

330.23   A little—not] A little, a very little—not

330.25   made by literature.] made by good letters.

330.26   choose good subjects.] choose nice subjects.

330.27   Miss Bordereau inquired.] Miss Bordereau implacably pursued.

330.28   a critic, an historian,] a critic, a commentator, an historian,

330.32   and can't speak] and can't, poor darlings, speak

330.36   women!" I answered, laughing.] women!" I replied as for pleasantness.

331.1   I spoke with great deliberation, but as my words [...] they struck me as] I had measured, as I thought, my risk, but as my words [...] they were to strike me as

331.2   However, I risked them and I was not sorry,] However, I had launched them and I wasn't sorry,

331.3   It seemed to be tolerably obvious] It seemed tolerably obvious

331.4   drag the matter out?] drag the process out?

331.7   I don't know that I know what [...] raking it up; but how] I don't feel that I know what [...] raking it up. How

331.11   the old woman declared, with her fine tranquillity.] my hostess declared with her hard complacency,

331.24   to look at this place] to look at this part

331.31   will you give for] will you give me for

332.11   corner, to be] corner and having to be

332.15   a very nice girl."] a very fine girl."

332.25   to pay the venerable woman] to pay the precious personage

333.2   she had annihilated the papers.] she had sacrificed her treasure.

333.10   moment and then she asked,] moment and then resumed:

333.20   with a hand of which I could only hope she did not perceive the trem-
          or,] with fingers of which I could only hope they did n't betray the
          intensity of their clutch,

333.22   and I was well aware] and was well aware

333.24   tell me who it is."] tell me who he is."

333.25   "It's an old friend] "he's an old friend

333.26   He gave it to me] He gave it me

333.32   to sport with me that way] to sport to that tune

333.33   practise on me.] practise on me and befool me.

333.34   production of the portrait.] production of the relic.

334.6   I judged the picture to have a valuable quality of resemblance and to
          have been] I felt in the little work a virtue of likeness and judged it to
          have been

334.7   twenty-five years old.] twenty-five.

334.9   but none of them is of so early a date as this elegant production.] but
          none of so early a date as this elegant image.

334.9   the original but I have seen other likenesses,"] the original, clearly a
          man of a past age, but I've seen other reproductions of this face,"

334.18   with a gesture which though ineffectual] using a gesture which though
          ineffectual

334.21   the precious thing;] the charming thing;

334.28   her treasure, she were going to attempt the immense effort of rising]
          her prize, she had been impelled to the immense effort of rising

334.30   with your ideas I could never afford it."] with your ideas it would be
          quite beyond my mark."

334.32   I thought I saw her catch her breath a little, as if she had had a strain]
          I heard her catch her breath as after a strain

335.4   I exclaimed, laughing; [...] part of my laughter came from my satis-
          faction in finding that I had been right] I returned with gaiety; [...]
          part of my cheer came from this proof I had been right

335.5 when he went to her father's] on his going to her father's

335.7 advice upon it;] advice on it:

335.8 she made no answer to this save to] she made no other reply than to

335.13 "Remember that I am] "Remember me as

335.16 I had just cause to complain of such an insinuation] I might well complain of such a tone

335.18 in the evening.] of an evening.

335.20 become a habit.] become our pleasant custom.

335.22 Has she got confidence?"] Has my niece confidence?"

335.31 she stood looking down at her immemorial companion with a sort of helpless wonder, as if all their years of familiarity had not made her perversities] she looked down at her yoke-fellow of long years with a vacancy of wonder, as if all their contact and custom had n't made her perversities

335.34 with a cynical little sigh.] with a crudity of cynicism.

335.36 with a pacifying intention.] for conciliation.

336.1 she insisted that we should] she insisted we should

336.7 out of the gray ashes of her vanity] out of the white ashes of her vanity

336.8 "I suppose—that they have] I took it pleasantly up. "I suppose [...] they've

336.9 it is, when they like you."] it is—when they like one."

336.16 "Nonsense, my dear;] "Nonsense, dear;

336.19 sitting-room?" I inquired.] sitting-room?" I asked.

336.22 but I don't see you."] but don't see you."

336.23 "You excite her dreadfully] "you agitate her dreadfully

336.24 reproachful, appealing look.] reproachful deterrent headshake.

336.25 the old lady went on.] Miss Bordereau went on.

336.27 I don't care where—and] I don't care where. That

336.29 her aunt's chair] the wheeled chair

336.31 Miss Bordereau exclaimed, as she felt] the old woman cried as she felt

336.33 commanded me to stop,] bade me stop,

336.34   a magnificent house!"] a prodigious house!"

336.36   told me that she should] let me know she should

337.5   to think that I was nearer the documents I coveted—that they were
          probably] to feel myself so close to the objects I coveted—which would
          be probably

337.7   which did not suggest hidden treasure; there were no dusky nooks nor
          [...] no massive] that suggested no hidden values; there were neither
          dusky nooks nor [...] neither massive

337.8   perhaps even probable that] perhaps even likely, that

337.12   I scrutinised [...] furniture, every] I turned an eye on [...] furniture,
          on every

337.16   somewhat rickety [...] a great many secrets.] somewhat infirm [...]
          rare secrets.

337.17   fascinated me so, inasmuch as I certainly had no definitive purpose of
          breaking into] so engaged me, small purpose as I had of breaking into

337.21   hard to remove my eyes from] hard to turn my attention from

337.22   a simple panel] a plain panel

337.23   but I remembered my prudence and [...] of Miss Bordereau.] but I
          gathered up my slightly scattered prudence [...] of my hostess.

337.26   Miss Tita asked, surprised.] Miss Tina asked in surprise.

337.33   to separate from Miss Tita] to separate from my younger friend

338.3   Miss Bordereau's niece appeared] Miss Tina appeared

338.6   a proof that I did not believe] a proof of my not believing

338.8   up to my rooms.] up to my floor.

338.26   all gone.] all spent and gone.

338.28   she had ever directed at me] she had ever favoured me withal

338.30   but I grant that in my heart] but I fear that in my heart

338.32   had told her that I had made her] had told her I had made her

338.32   I had done nothing—I] I had done nothing whatever—I

339.2   Miss Bordereau had assured] our friend had assured

339.3   that it was a scene of her own making] that the scene had been of her
          making

339.8 who appeared to feel that the situation was passing [...] were thickening] who seemed to feel the situation pass out [...] thicken

339.9 I said that [...] I had not a thousand pounds;] I answered her [...] I had no thousand pounds;

339.31 imagine that she had not wished to allow people a reason to say that the great poet] imagine her not having wished to allow any supposition that the great poet

339.32 in considering Miss Bordereau, in whom] in considering Juliana, in whom

339.34 I turned my eyes all over the room] I turned my eyes once more all over the room

339.35 Miss Tita met them quickly] Miss Tina at once noted their direction

340.2 for a preoccupation that was almost profane] for an appetite wellnigh indecent

340.3 I took another look] I took another view

340.4 the place to try first] the receptacle to try first

340.6 like the room of an old actress.] like the dressing-room of an old actress.

340.11 I judged the air of the place (forgetting [...] all),] I judged such appearance—forgetting [...] all—

340.12 of complicity in such untidiness: § "She likes] of complicity in the disorder: § "She likes

340.16 a sofa where there was] a sofa that just allowed

340.17 It appeared to be a queer] It struck me as a queer

340.27 Miss Bordereau's room,] the padrona's room,

340.28 I saw him peeping over] I saw him peep over

340.30 that I myself had almost as little to do there] how little I myself had to do there

340.31 looked at me, appearing to take me] eyed me, his air of taking me

340.34 He looked particularly at me, as if it struck him that I should] He kept me still in range, as if it struck him I too should

341.2 but it seemed to me important] but I felt it important

341.4 and looking at the light] and studying the light

341.8   pass away;] pass away?

341.11   moving about to perform the offices that] just going and coming over
          the offices that

341.13   as it came over me again that] while it assailed me again that

341.15   for an hour—for an hour and a half.] about an hour and more.

341.18   my cigar moving about in the dark] my cigar in the dark

341.18   and feel that I wanted eminently to know] and feel sure I was hanging
          on to know

341.19   a proof my anxieties had made me gross] a proof of the grossness of
          my anxieties

341.22   that could take place in her life, they were uppermost also in poor
          Miss Tita's mind.] that could fall on her, poor Miss Tina's having also
          a free mind for them.

341.25   taken so much time as that to enunciate the contrary.] taken so long
          to attest her decease.

341.31   which I, had I known them,] which, had I more exactly known them,

341.32   but I ascended no higher] but I mounted no higher

342.3   condition strange!"] condition serious."

342.5   because she excites herself.] because she works herself up.

342.8   a deeper placidity.] a deeper detachment.

342.9   as that, if you begin to] as that," I permitted myself to ask, "if you be-
          gin to

342.15   if you are frightened."] if you're scared and upset."

342.16   Well, I am not frightened now," […] Miss Tita, cheerfully.] Well, I'm
          not upset now," […] Miss Tina, placidly enough.

342.20   "Yes," I rejoined,] "Yes," I returned,

342.23   Miss Tita hesitated a moment;] Miss Tina waited a little;

342.27   tiptoe, as inaudibly as possible."] tiptoe, as soundlessly as possible."

342.30   ; Olimpia is sitting there."] —Olimpia sits there."

342.31   On my side I hesitated.] On my side I debated.

342.31   Shall we then step in there?"] Shall we then pass in there?"

342.35   but I was too conscious that] but I felt too much this

343.1   So I proposed that we should walk] Thus I hinted we might walk

343.2   disturb the old lady.] disturb our friend.

343.8   I suggested that we should remain there] I submitted that we had best remain there

343.9   arrive still better.] arrive the sooner.

343.13 singing, with his jacket] singing, his jacket

343.22 seemed to imply that she had] seemed to mean she had

343.27 found them?" I asked, almost trembling.] found them?" I fairly trembled with the question.

344.3   I did drive her on or at last did insist too much:] I did push her, or at least harp on the chord, too much:

344.7   felt now as if I must tell her] felt now I must make a clean breast of it, must tell her

344.9   and would refuse to] and so refuse to

344.10 and also that I had] as well as that I had

344.12 looking at me with parted lips,] almost in fact gaping for wonder,

344.16 "So do I," I said, laughing.] "So do I"—and I felt my laugh rueful.

344.19 leaving out Mrs. Prest of course.] leaving out of course Mrs. Prest.

344.20 She hesitated; I thought] She considered; I thought

344.21 to say that we had been vary base.] to pronounce us very base.

344.21 But she remarked […] in a candid, wondering way,] But this was not her way, and she remarked […] as in a candid impartial contemplation:

344.23 I conceded, smiling.] I grinned, I fear, to admit.

345.3   "I feel as if you were a new person, now that] "I rather feel you a new person, you know, now that

345.8   again, but for all answer to this inquiry I said,] again, but I returned for all answer:

345.10 moralised mournfully;] mournfully moralised :

345.18 I thought you said] I thought you promised

345.21 I replied, rather foolishly] I answered rather foolishly

345.22 submission to delay] acceptance of delay

345.23 more than] more for me than

345.23 whether she guessed this] if she guessed this

345.24 she appeared to become aware of the necessity for being a little more rigid.] she seemed to bethink herself of some propriety of showing me more rigour.

345.27 I don't think Miss Tita would have contested] Nothing is more possible than that she would n't have contested

345.30 believed that Miss Bordereau] believed that our proprietress

345.34 out of the house and took a long walk,] out of the house and walked far,

346.1 down (it was [...] but there were [...] cafés); I could only walk round and round,] down; it was [...] though there were [...] cafés; I could but uneasily revolve,

346.2 I was uncomfortable, but it gave me a certain pleasure to have told Miss Tita] The only comfort, none the less, was in my having told Miss Tina

346.4 slowly getting all but inextricably lost,] getting gradually and all but inextricably lost,

346.10 an intimation [...] to bed, tired of waiting for me.] a hint [...] to bed in impatience of waiting for me

346.17 prevented me from going in,] prevented my entrance,

346.18 If I have candidly narrated] If I have frankly stated

346.19 had rendered me capable] had made me capable

346.20 shrink from confessing] shrink, it seems to me, from confessing

346.20 I think it was the worst thing I did;] I regard it as the worst thing I did,

346.22 news of the old lady] news of Juliana

346.24 It may be said that] It may be objected that

346.26 I desired not to be] I wished not to be

346.30 with my lamp in my hand.] lamp in hand.

346.31 to me if she were with her aunt, as she must be.] to me if, as I could n't doubt, she were still with her aunt.

346.36 thinking of something else.] given up to something else.

347.1 but I felt myself held] but felt myself held

347.2   For what I could not have said,] Opportunity for what I could n't have said

347.4   I might commit a theft. Even if it had been] I might proceed to thievery. Even had this tempted me

347.8   the hour of temptation and secrecy, nearer to the tormenting treasure] the hour of freedom and safety, nearer to the source of my hopes

347.14   But what could I do, when it came] Yet might I, when it came

347.16   looking at it very idiotically;] gaping at it vainly and no doubt grotesquely;

347.20   they had not been destroyed the old woman] they had n't the keen old woman

347.22   if she had the idea of their safety] with the idea of their safety

347.23   conspicuous, more accessible] conspicuous, more exposed

347.26   something more than this at that moment;] something more, for the climax of my crisis;

347.28   if she did not wish me to understand,] if she did n't so wish me,

347.32   indicated by the quick, fantastic idea] indicated by the super-subtle inference

347.34   This theory fascinated me and I bent over very close to judge.] This possibility pressed me hard and I bent very close to judge.

348.3   for I had not heard anything.] for I had really heard nothing.

348.5   Miss Bordereau stood there in her night-dress, in the doorway] Juliana stood there in her night-dress, by the doorway

348.8   They glared at me, they made me horribly ashamed.] They glared at me; they were like the sudden drench, for a caught burglar, of a flood of gaslight; they made me horribly ashamed.

349.2   the next morning, as soon as I learnt that the old lady] the next morning, directly on learning that my hostess

349.10   pictures and spent] pictures; I spent

349.13   I scantily enjoyed my journey: there was too strong a taste of the disagreeable in my life.] I scantly enjoyed my travels: I had had to gulp down a bitter draught and could n't get rid of the taste.

349.15   to be found by Miss Bordereau] to be found by Juliana

713

349.19 I had killed her. In writing to Miss Tita I attempted to minimise these irregularities; but as she gave me no word of answer] I had killed her. My humiliation galled me, but I had to make the best of it, had, in writing to Miss Tina, to minimise it, as well as account for the posture in which I had been discovered. As she gave me no word of answer

349.21 It rankled in my mind that I had been called a publishing scoundrel, for certainly I did publish and certainly I had not been very delicate.] It rankled for me that I had been called a publishing scoundrel, since certainly I did publish and no less certainly had n't been very delicate.

349.23 the only way to make up for this latter fault was to take myself away altogether on the instant;] the only way to purge my dishonour was to take myself straight away on the instant;

349.27 my own hopes that I] my own hopes I

349.29 It would perhaps be sufficient if I stayed away long enough to give the elder lady time to think she was rid of me.] It would perhaps answer if I kept dark long enough to give the elder lady time to believe herself rid of me.

349.31 that nocturnal scene would have cured] that midnight monstrosity would have cured

350.5 while I observed that she quite failed to comply with my earnest request (I had given [...] *restante*) that she would let me know how she was getting on.] while I noted that she quite ignored my earnest request—I had given [...] *restante*—for some sign of her actual state.

350.9 It struck me there was a kind of scorn in Miss Tita's silence (little [...] been), so that I was uncomfortable and sore. I had scruples about going back and yet I had [...] so, for I wanted] Could n't I measure the scorn of Miss Tina's silence—little [...] been? Really the soreness pressed; yet if I had scruples about going back I had others [...] so, for I wanted

350.13 against Miss Bordereau's steps a certain palpitation of suspense told me that I had done myself a violence in holding off so long.] against our palace steps a fine palpitation of suspense showed me the violence my absence had done me.

350.14 I had not telegraphed] I had n't even telegraphed

350.17 the earth, *la vecchia*,] the earth, *quella vecchia*,

350.20 "She's dead!" I exclaimed,] "She's dead!" I cried,

350.22 "It's all over?] "it's all over then?

350.24   it was a dull little passeggio of two gondolas.] *roba da niente—un piccolo passeggio brutto* of two gondolas.

350.26   of funerals was apparently that] of funerals was that

350.27   Miss Tita—how she was and where she was—but] Miss Tina, how she might be and generally where; but

350.32   I could only hope that the doctor had given her assistance and] I could only hope the doctor had given her support and

351.3   it appeared from these circumstances] it appeared from these signs

351.9   five words written on a card, to ask Miss Tita if she would] five words on a card to ask if Miss Tina would

351.11   and gathering flowers.] and picking flowers quite as if they belonged to her.

351.16   mourning (as if […] end), and in this respect there was no appreciable change in her appearance. But she evidently] mourning, as if […] end; and in this particular she made no different show. But she clearly

351.18   with a sort of primitive, retarded sense of loneliness and violence.] with a primitive retarded sense of solitude and violence.

351.19   none of the formalism or self-consciousness of grief,] none of the airs or graces of grief,

351.21   to see her standing there […] of flowers, smiling at me with her reddened eyes.] to see her stand there […] of admirable roses and smile at me with reddened eyes.

351.23   I had had an idea that she would be a good deal disgusted with me— would consider that I ought] I had n't doubted her being irreconcileably disgusted with me, her considering I ought

351.24   though I was sure there was no] though I believed there was no

351.26   for a difference in her manner] for a change in in her manner

351.27   for some little injured look, half familiar, half estranged,] for some air of injury and estrangement,

351.30   Tita Bordereau's countenance expressed unqualified pleasure in seeing her] this poor lady's dull face ceased to be dull, almost ceased to be plain, as she turned it gladly to her

351.33   with her for half an hour.] with her as long as seemed good.

351.36   suppose that she had] suppose she had

351.36   Miss Bordereau surprised me] Miss Bordereau had surprised me

352.4   strolled and really] strolled, though really

352.6   manner and in a visible air that she had] manner and in the expression she had

352.7   I took an interest in her.] I still took an interest in her.

352.8   Miss Tita had none of the pride that makes a person wish to preserve the look of independence;] Miss Tina's was no breast for the pride or the pretence of independence;

352.8   she did not in the least pretend] she did n't in the least suggest

352.10   forbore to touch particularly on that] forbore to press on that question,

352.12   I felt that her knowledge of life was] I felt her knowledge of life to be

352.13   should not look after] should n't somehow look after

352.17   friends (fortunately [...] house; and she [...] the Italians [...] life);] friends—fortunately [...] house. She [...] the "nice" Italians [...] life,

352.19   impressions, the places] impressions, my adventures, the places

352.20   in my depression I had not seen much;] in my disconcerted state I had taken little in;

352.22   a little journey!"] an amusing little journey!"

352.25   some tour, say I would take her [...] some excursion] some enterprise, say I would accompany her [...] a pleasant excursion

352.27   a word to her about the Aspern documents; asked no questions] a word of the Aspern documents, asked no question

352.28   Miss Bordereau's death.] Juliana's death.

352.30   to betray my anxiety so soon] to show greed again so soon

352.32   Later, however] Later on, however

352.33   her silence was somewhat strange; for] her silence was matter for suspicion; since

353.4   possibly mean simply that nothing had been found.] possibly just mean that no relics survived.

353.5   alone in the rooms] alone on the piano nobile

353.7   in regard to visiting her there.] in regard to the invasion of it.

353.8   I asked her if she had any general plan—had [...] better do.] I asked if
         she had some general plan, had [...] best do.

353.12   practical questions, for this] practical questions, as this

353.13   question to be touched upon] question now to be touched upon

353.16   destined, as it happened, to] destined, as it befell, to

353.19   she would very soon discover I was there.] she would promptly see me
         accessible.

353.33   as it were, to reward] as it were, reward

353.34   Might not that circumstance] Might not that service

354.3   pounced upon me [...] afterwards.] pounced on me [...] the next day.

354.5   expected to guess that I was there;] expected to act on my calculation;

354.6   I said to her that I had been waiting] I mentioned I had been waiting

354.7   I was glad the next day] I was glad a few hours later

354.9   that I wished to see if a friendly intuition would not tell her: it became
         a satisfaction to me that I had not indulged in that rather tender joke.]
         that a friendly intuition might have told her: it turned to comfort for
         me that I had n't played even to that mild extent on her sensibility.

354.14   She was different from what she had been the evening before—less
         natural, less quiet.] Yes, she was other than she had been the evening
         before—less natural and less easy.

354.15   and she was not crying now, and yet] and was not crying now, yet

354.18   and complicated.] and more complicated.

354.19   Had she simply perceived that] Had she simply begun to feel that

354.29   My delight at learning] My joy at learning

354.32   she added.] she lamentably added.

354.33   I groaned with a voice of infinite] I broke into a tone of infinite

355.1   I saw that it cost her a kind of anguish to take such a stand but that
         a dreadful sense of duty had descended upon her.] I measured the
         anguish it cost her to take such a stand, which a dreadful sense of duty
         had imposed on her.

355.4   it appeared to me I had been extremely encouraged [...] I almost con-
         sidered that Miss Tita had assured me] it seemed to me I had been
         distinctly encouraged [...] I quite held Miss Tina to have assured me

355.8	outright than that!"] outright than to have to reckon with such a treachery as that."
355.11	She hesitated and then she said] She hung fire, but finally she said
355.13	"In her bed?"] "In her bed—?"
355.17	she shouldn't touch the bed—] she shouldn't undo the bed—
355.32	I know that."] I know that," she dismally sounded.
356.2	Miss Tita announced,] the poor woman announced,
356.6	I questioned, staring, as it passed] I gasped as it passed
356.11	spoke as if she wished to make] spoke as if for making
356.13	according to the ideas] according the idea
356.15	sell it?" asked Miss Tita.] sell it?" my friend threw off.
356.20	think so," I replied;] think so," I returned;
356.22	and this was a truthful speech, for the singular creature [...] to have some very fine reference in her mind, which] and this was true enough, for the good creature [...] to have in her mind some rich reference that
356.23	for me," said Miss Tita.] for me," she said.
356.25	look at that of my interlocutress,] look at that of my companion,
356.27	—it was so self-conscious, so unnatural. [...] I only privately] —it had taken so very odd, so strained and unnatural a cast. [...] I but privately
356.29	own (they [...] so wise, so full of vision); I] own—they [...] wise and so deep: I
356.30	friendly mockery, as if he were amused] mild mockery; he might have been amused
356.35	the papers?" I demanded in a moment, perversely.] the papers?" I presently and all perversely asked.
356.35	"Much as I value it, if I were] "Much as I value this, you know, if I were
357.2	Miss Tita asked, slowly, lamentably.] Miss Tina returned slowly and woefully.
357.4	the interdiction that rests upon you] the interdiction that rests on you
357.7	Miss Tita [...] full of her dolefulness,] She [...], only lost in the queerness of her case.

357.13 "You are nervous,] "You've grown nervous

357.18 Miss Tita, at this, looking at me, [...] to heaven] My friend, at this, with her eyes on me, [...] to goodness

357.23 I answered, smiling.] I returned not quite so desperately.

357.24 tempt you to do anything] tempt you to anything

357.24 you will understand] you understand,

357.26 were still rather] were still there rather

357.31 the words was tragical—] the words was tragic—

358.4 "No, I have thought—] "No, I 've tried to think—

358.5 "And for instance?"] "As for instance?"

358.7 "If I were] I wondered. "If I were

358.9 mine—would be] mine would be

358.10 I couldn't prevent you] I should n't be able to prevent you

358.12 with a little nervous rush, as if she were speaking words she had got by heart.] with a nervous laugh and as if speaking words got by heart.

358.13 an impression of subtlety and at first] the impression of a subtlety which at first

358.14 a light came into my mind.] the queerest of lights came to me.

358.19 with tears in her eyes, but she seemed] through pitiful tears, but seemed

358.21 then I went on,] then I went on:

358.25 to consider [...] for a moment; after which she declared,] to weigh [...]; after which she answered

358.29 And she paused blushing.] And she paused, very red.

358.31 Miss Tita cried] my companion cried

358.33 a moment before increased.] a moment before spread further.

359.2 Miss Tita added, incongruously.] Miss Tina added with an effect of extreme inconsequence.

359.5 as it was and sewn,] as it was and stitching,

359.7 be agreeable to me."] be agreeable to *me*."

359.8 but to me.] but quite to me.

359.11 "You could see them—] "You could see the things—

719

359.12   She stopped, seeing that I perceived the sense] She stopped, seeing I grasped the sense

359.13   some sign which] some sign that

359.15   that was ever painted] ever painted

359.21   whether I did any better.] whether I knew better.

359.23   she was facing me] she was up at me again

359.29   it wouldn't do—it wouldn't do!" pensively,] it would n't do, it would n't do!"—saying it pensively,

359.31   as if there were a beautiful view there.] as at something very interesting.

359.34   "*Dove commanda?*" I replied, in a tone] "*Dove commanda?*" replied, in a tone

360.2   with my hat pulled over my face.] my hat pulled over my brow.

360.6   sitting there under the fluttering] motionless there under the fluttering

360.12   where my gondolier […] on the lagoon, with slow, rare strokes.] on the lagoon, my gondolier took me; we floated aimlessly and with slow, rare strokes.

360.21   never said it to Tita Bordereau.] never said it to my victim.

360.30   It would have been better perhaps for me to feel the comic side] I should have been better employed perhaps in taking in the comic side

360.31   or not it went without saying that] or not there was no doubt whatever that

360.35   that she did not think the idea would come to me, her having determined to suggest it] of how little she supposed the idea would come to me that she should have decided to suggest it herself

360.36   heroic way, in which the timidity] heroic way—with the timidity

361.10   writing a note to Miss Tita, to be placed] addressing Miss Tina a note which should be placed

361.13   a strong sign that I was embarrassed that […] in my mind in advance (I […] bed), I] strong proof of my quandary that […] to my taste in advance—I […] bed—I

361.16   I might go away without writing a word,] I might get off without writing at all,

361.18   attached to Miss Bordereau's] attached to Juliana's

362.11 I told him that that day, for a change, I would touch] I told him that till the morrow, for reasons, I should

362.25 with actors tripping] with its actors tripping

362.30 tired, without [...] a letter] tired and without [...] an address

362.34 a very odd revulsion] the oddest revulsion

363.6 Miss Bordereau's papers. They were now more precious [...] a kind of ferocity had come into my desire to possess them.] Juliana's treasure. The pieces composing it were now more precious [...] a positive ferocity had come into my need to acquire them.

363.7 attached to the possession of them no longer] attached to that act no longer

363.9 It was absurd that I should] It was absurd I should

363.11 the only way to get hold of the papers] the only way to become possessed

363.12 I would not unite myself and yet I would have them.] I might n't unite myself, yet I might still have what she had.

363.12 though to do so I had had all the time that I was dressing.] though in fact I drew out my dressing in the interest of my wit.

363.14 would not think my errand was to tell her I accepted her hand] would not think my announcement was to be "favourable."

363.18 She certainly would have made the day before the reflection that I declined it.] She certainly would have understood my recoil of the day before.

363.19 she had drawn this inference,] she had done so,

363.20 full of my literary concupiscence.] full of stratagems and spoils

363.23 Now I perceived it;] Now I took it in;

363.28 This optical trick gave her a sort of phantasmagoric brightness, and while I was still the victim] This trick of her expression, this magic of her spirit, transfigured her, and while I still noted it

363.28 seemed to me I was ready to pay] seemed to me I could pay

363.33 effect she made upon me] effect she made on me

363.32 then I perceived] then I recognised

364.6 doubted that I had left her] doubted my having left her

364.6   How could she,] How *could* she,

364.7   form, such an idea?] form, even as an act of common humanity, such
         an idea?

364.9   at me in her humiliation.] at me in her abjection.

364.13   them?" I faltered.] them?" I wailed.

364.16   by one?" I repeated, mechanically.] by one?" I coldly echoed it.

364.18   for a moment descended upon] for a moment descended on

364.22   in this character that she] in this character she

364.28   sent her in exchange for] sent her, as the price of

364.30   I wrote to her that I had] I wrote her that I had

364.32   (I met her in London, in the autumn), that] —I met this other friend
         in London that autumn—that

364.33   When I look at it my chagrin at the loss of the letters becomes almost
         intolerable.] When I look at it I can scarcely bear my loss—I mean of
         the precious papers.

The Liar

365.8   became suggestive] might have been one of the minor instruments in
         a big orchestra

365.10   pay many country visits] pay country visits

365.14   at a country house he always] in some occasions he always

365.16   these things gave a sort of measure of the culture and even of the char-
         acter of his hosts] these things would give in a sort the social, the con-
         versational value of his hosts

365.20   principally portraits] mainly portraits

365.27   but perceived from the way] but saw from the way

365.30   went out in a group of unmatched men, without this appendage]
         went out unimportant and in a group of unmated men

366.1   made him think that he was in] made him suppose himself in a]

366.5   himself as very young] himself as notably young

366.7   He was something of a celebrity and he was apparently in a society of
         celebrities] He was appreciably "known" and was now apparently in a
         society of the known if not of the knowing

366.13   to see the spectacle of human life before him in the intervals] to feel
         the human scene enclose it as in a ring

366.19   in which things in general contribute to the particular idea and fall in
         with it, help it on and justify it, so that he feels for the hour as if noth-
         ing in the world can happen to him, even if it come in the guise of dis-
         aster or suffering, that will not be an enhancement of his subject.] in
         which things in general interweave with his particular web and make
         it thicker and stronger and more many-coloured.

366.26   he went into his neighbours] he appraised his neighbours

366.26   busy looking out for Sir David] busy with question of Sir David

366.29   circumstance which constituted] circumstance forming

366.32   with great pleasure to the chance of painting a nonagenarian, and
         though] with pleasure to painting a picked nonagenarian, so that

366.36   bloom of his cheek] bloom of such a cheek

367.2   if the eye were still alive] if the eye should be still alive

367.5   glad his commission had been to delineate the father rather than the
         son] glad his call had been for the great rather than the small bearer of
         the name

367.6   and of the other being seated there before him now in the happy ex-
         pansion of liberal hospitality.] and of the other's being seated there
         before him now in the very highest relief of impersonal hospitality.

367.9   paint him in characters] paint him in character

367.12   a sort of appearance of] an appearance as of

367.14   a gilt frame, suggesting reference to] a gilt frame and be dealt with by
         reference to

367.17   her neighbour and the gentleman] her neighbour, while the gentleman

367.18   looked shrinking and scared] looked detached and desperate

367.22   and that it was not less vivid than it was (sometimes it ran its success
         in this line very close), since he was] and that it had such a need, fre-
         quently even in spite of itself, to testify, since he was

367.24   lest if he should make] in him, lest should he make

367.26   worthy to *aborder*] worthy to handle

367.31   decent that you would know him by?] decent you might know him by?

368.15   with a methodical air, as a good cook] with the promptness of a good cook who

368.22   that he says that which is not?] if he thinks he has done things he hasn't?

368.23   no—because I never know.] no; because I never really know the difference between what people say—!

368.33   more colour. And now] more colour. Don't you suppose Vandyke's things tell a lot about him? And now

369.2   eight o'clock or something of that sort] eight o'clock after porridge and milk

369.4   waistcoats, and that sort of thing] waistcoats and sits by the fire

369.9   it was a kind of superstition] it was his pet superstition

369.21   still the title] still the "title"

369.26   observation, and they had some fragmentary talk] observation, as if it had been a move at the chess, exciting in Lyon however a comparative wantonness

370.1   often in relation to a person one has not seen for twelve years] often, even for fidelity, when it has been kept up a dozen years

370.4   she who could look like that: of the most charming head in the world (and this lady had it) there could never be a replica] she who could carry that head, the most charming head in the world and of which there could never be a replica

370.5   in profile, apparently listening to some one on the other side of her] in profile, slightly turned to some further neighbour.

370.6   listening, but she was also looking] listening, but her eyes moved

370.9   rested, as it appeared to him, with a kind of habitual, visible complacency] rested, he made out, as with an habitual visible complacency

370.11   but Lyon was slightly disappointed that] but Lyon felt it as the source of an ache that

370.15   without hearing of it] without some echo of it

370.18   a queer accident] an odd business

370.19   her husband liked it or didn't notice it:] her husband was satisfied

370.21   (as he had not heard that she had become a widow)] —as he had not heard—

370.22   she had refused *to him*, the poor] she had refused to a poor

370.23   Capadose appeared to be] Capadose seemed aware

370.24   this circumstance] this fact

370.25   rather irritated Lyon than gratified him] rather annoyed Lyon than pleased him

370.27   she gave him no response] she made no response

370.31   the fifth person behind him] the fourth person behind him

370.35   who appeared very vague] to whom it appeared to mean little

370.36   his vagueness] his ignorance of these values

371.1   only the day before] but the day before

371.2   definite to Lyon] definite to our friend

371.3   he had married her] he might have married her

371.4   very faithful] very fond and true

371.5   three minutes later to the lady] three minutes later, with a small ironic ring, to the lady

371.13   glancing forward] with a crook that took him in

371.15   she is faithful] she's—what do you call it?—tender and true?

371.23   a sort of Roman type] a sort of nobleness of the Roman type

371.26   like a glorified *contadina*] like a transfigured Trasteverina

371.28   increase that effect] bring out that effect

371.28   he is so clever] he *gives* so much

372.5   she was simple and frank and kind about it] only perfectly simple and frank about it

372.10   he added.] he added. "I mean that it's no mistake."

372.15   most of the gentlemen communicated their adventures and opinions] most of the men had a comment or an anecdote, several had many

372.18   from his remarks] from his allusions

372.20   for his allusions] for his points

372.21   close shaves] close shave

372.21   Lyon perceived after a little] Lyon noted after a little

372.23   relation to the interest] proportion to the interest

372.27   —Colonel Capadose appeared to take so much sympathy and assent for granted] —the narrator building on the tribute so rendered

373.3   He leaned forward; Lyon leaned forward to listen, and Colonel Capadose mentioned that he knew from personal experience that there was really no limit to the time one might lie unconscious without being any the worse for it.] He leaned forward (Lyon leaned forward to listen) and mentioned that he knew from personal experience how little limit there really was to the time a fellah might lie like a stone without being the worse for it.

373.10   it was touch] it had been touch

373.12   they couldn't feed him] couldn't feed him

373.15   He appeared to intimate that] He conveyed, though without excessive emphasis, that

373.17   Lyon thought his story very striking, but he wanted to ask him whether he] Lyon was struck by his story, but wanted to ask if he

373.18   to imply a doubt] to betray a doubt

373.19   Colonel Capadose said that it was] Colonel Capadose pronounced it

373.22   died of jungle fever—they clapped him into a coffin] died of jungle fever and whom they clapped into a coffin

373.24   Ashmore made a move and everyone got up to adjourn to the drawing room] Ashmore said a word and every one rose for the move to the drawing room

373.25   heeding what his new friend said to him] heeding his new friend's prodigies

373.26   They came round] These two came round

373.27   while the gentlemen dawdled before going out] while their companions hung back for each other

373.28   your friend was literally] your comrade was literally

373.30   Colonel Capadose] The Colonel

373.31   looked at him a moment, as if he had already lost the thread of the conversation] looked at him as with the thread of the conversation already lost

373.33   chucked into the ground] shoved into the ground

373.34   "And was he left there?" § "He was left there] "And left there?" § "Left there

374.8   brought him to] brought him round

374.9   anything for me."] anything for me," the narrator added.

374.13   something or other] some confounded brain-wave or other

374.16   and Colonel Capadose, who went among the first, was separated from Lyon] and this master of anecdote, who went among the first, was separated from his newest victim

374.17   he joined him again] he had come back

374.19   acquaintance; my wife used] acquaintance. My wife used

374.23   with indulgent humour] with genial ease

374.29   with her. § "Do you mean that one with the children] with her. § Our friend lived over again for a few seconds a lost felicity. "Do you mean one with the children

374.32   leopard skin—a kind of Bacchante] leopard skin. A regular Bacchante

374.35   she'll be mortified] she'll feel it awkward

375.1   "Mortified?"] "Awkward?"—our artist wondered.

375.12   "Oh, he has got it] "Oh he keeps it

375.15   Lyon remarked] Lyon modestly urged

375.17   he seemed to be thinking of something] his thoughts now seemed elsewhere

375.19   he gave the artist] he gave his fellow visitor

375.30   her failure to respond to his recognition at table contradicted that, but he felt an extreme desire to go and occupy it] her failure to take up his shy signal at table contradicted this, but his desire to join her was too strong

375.33   before his old friend. § "I hope you don't mean to repudiate me," he said.] before her with his appeal. "I hope you don't mean to repudiate me."

375.34   with an expression of unalloyed pleasure] with frank delight

375.35   I was delighted] I was charmed

375.36   but I couldn't."] but I couldn't," Lyon returned.

376.6   that he enjoyed, while the reason for which he used to like her so came back to him, as well as a good deal of the very same old liking] that smote old chords in him; the sense of what he had loved her for came back to him, as well as not a little of the actual effect of that cause

376.7   absence of coquetry or any] absence of the "wanton" or of any

376.9   there were moments when she struck her interlocutor as] she affected him at moments as

376.12   whether there were a good fire in her bedroom] if there were a good fire in her bedroom, or at the very most in theirs

376.15   something that had a sifted, selected air—the sound of an impression at first hand] something, some small fruit of discrimination, that might have come from a mind, have been an impression at first hand

376.16   but she had added up her feelings, some of her reflections, about life] and only the simpler feelings, but several of these had grown up to full size

376.18   and she told him in return that she was] and she spoke in return of her being

376.20   he would speak to her or that his little sign at table] he would notice her or that his mute appeal at table

376.28   his own personal history and he said that the principal thing that had happened to him was that he had never married] his own story, and he described it mainly as his not having married

376.30   "I like that—from you!" he returned.] "I like that—from you!"

376.32   "That's just why I can't be.] "That's just why I can't be," he returned

377.3   her good gray eyes on Lyon] her good grey eyes on this recovered "backer"

377.7   "Yes, we have been in so many places] "Ah we've been in so many situations

377.9   "You must bring her] Lyon rose fully to the occasion. "You must bring her

377.16   I mean about that beautiful picture you gave me] I mean on the subject of the lovely picture you gave me

377.19   And she paused a moment] It fairly pulled her up

377.26   said Lyon, smiling] the artist smiled

378.5   and Lyon saw that she coloured a little] and Lyon now saw her change colour

378.15   it was not in her eyes to-day] there was not such subterfuge in her eyes to-day

378.18   and thought—perhaps it was only a fancy—that she was rather absent] and imagined—perhaps too freely—her equilibrium slightly impaired

378.21   gather themselves together to go to bed] gather themselves for bed

378.26   "Well, I didn't."] "*I* didn't then!"

378.30   he's so nice] he's so awfully nice

378.30   Lyon knew she thought it] Lyon knew this was her faith

378.31   to hear her say it] to hear her proclaim it

379.9   in a brilliant equipment, a suit of] brilliantly equipped in a suit of

379.15   while he emitted great smoke-puffs] and emitting great smoke-puffs

379.16   wonder that Everina] wonder Everina

379.17   All the gentlemen] All the men

379.21   it was devilish stupid] it was a great sell

379.22   for women were so extraordinary] women being so tough that

379.25   —not all of them—] —not all—

379.31   he perceived that this wonderful man had but little loss of vital tissue to repair] he felt how little loss of vital tissue this wonderful man had to repair

380.1   The modern portion] The modern piece

380.8   essentially gloomy] deadly depressing

380.10   about a skeleton having been found] of how a skeleton had been found

380.21   exclaimed the Colonel, smiling] the Colonel warningly smiled

380.26   dangerous house] spooky house

381.3   and you'll take the 10.20] and take the 10.20

381.4   do you mean I will invent] do you mean I shall invent

381.15   I must paint my picture] I must do my job

381.19   this inquiry] this query

381.20   three or four gentlemen] three or four of their fellow guests

381.22   This however] This on the other hand

381.26   at having had so little direct conversation with him as yet] for the delay of his pleasure

381.28   Lyon remarked] The latter observed

381.34   as well as very eulogistic, and Lyon could see that he was a very nice old man] as well as a little extravagant, and Lyon felt sure he was a fine old boy

382.2   I don't keep my servants up] past this hour I don't keep my servants up

382.9   in houses conspicuously haunted] at places of markedly evil repute

382.10   (having the artistic temperament)] —having too much imagination—

382.11   to his imagination] for his nerves

382.19   with a certain sense of the risk, was the impression that the Colonel told queer stories] despite the risk was a need that had suddenly come to him to measure the Colonel's accuracy

382.19   he said to Arthur Ashmore] he said to his host

382.23   but *que voulez-vous?*] but they're difficult to raise,

382.30   "Perhaps I had better wait till I have done my work."] "Perhaps I had better wait," Lyon smiled, "till I have done my work." But he was to have presently the slightly humiliated sense of having been "arch" about nothing.

383.3   "I don't know what you're talking about. There was no] "I don't know what you're talking about"—the son of Stayes was sturdy and blank. "There was no

383.15   the last door—to look into the room of evil fame; but he reflected that this would be indiscreet, since Colonel Capadose handled the brush— as a raconteur—with such freedom. There might be a ghost and there might not; but the Colonel himself, he inclined to think, was the most mystifying figure in the house.] the last door, to look into the room his friend had incriminated; but he felt this would be indiscreet, that gentleman's warrant was somehow a document of too many flourishes. There might be apparitions or other uncanny things and there mightn't; but there was surely nothing in the house so odd as Colonel Capadose.

384.3   a capital subject and a very comfortable sitter into the bargain] a beautiful subject as well as the serenest and blandest of sitters

384.3   a very agreeable old man] a very informing old man

384.5   that Lyon would have chosen] that his portrayer would have chosen

384.8   from sitting there as submissive as if portraiture in oils had been a branch of surgery] his submitting to the brush as bravely as he might have to the salutary surgical knife. He sat there with the firm eyes and set smile of "Well, do your worst!"

384.15   the totality of his experience] the sum of his experience

384.16   that that period was not a real compendium] as he would have done in many a case, that this was not a real synthesis

384.17   for there had been no crack] since there had been no crack

384.21   the people in the house] the company at Stayes

384.24   the visitors at Stayes: people came and went whom he knew nothing about, and he liked to hear Lyon describe them] the people in his house—processions that came and went, that he knew nothing about and that he liked to hear Lyon describe

384.27   gentlemen who are repository of] persons who keep the book of

385.4   had some military talent] had apparently some gift for arms

385.6   at Eton with his son] at Eton with Arthur

385.7   Lately, coming back to England] Lately, back to England

385.21   "A monstrous foible?" said Lyon. "He's a thumping liar." Lyon's brush stopped short, while he repeated, for somehow the formula startled him, "A thumping liar?" "You are very lucky not to have found it out." "Well, I confess I have noticed a romantic tinge—" "Oh, it isn't always romantic. He'll lie about the time of day, about the name of his hatter. It appears there are people like that." "Well, they are precious scoundrels," Lyon declared, his voice trembling a little with the thought of what Everina Brant had done with herself. "Oh, not always," said the old man. "This fellow isn't in the least a scoundrel.] "A monstrous foible?" Lyon echoed. "He pulls the long bow—the longest that ever was." Lyon's brush stopped short, while he repeated, for somehow the words both startled him and brought light: "'The longest that ever was'?" "You're very lucky not to have had to catch him." Lyon debated. "Well, I think I have rather caught him. He revels in the miraculous." "Oh it is n't always the miraculous. He'll lie about the time of day, about the name of his hatter. It's quite disinterested." "Well, it's very base," Lyon declared, feeling rather sick for what Everina Brant had done with herself. "Oh it's an extraordinary trouble to take," said the old man, "but this fellow is n't in himself at all base."

385.24 I suppose, was mendacious] I now see, was tarred with that brush]

385.25 stiffest statements] steepest statements

385.29 like intermittent fever] with changes of the wind

385.30 usually understand it and don't haul him up—for the sake of his wife."] quite allow for it and don't pin him down—for the sake of his wife, whom every one likes."

385.35 the long bow] that instrument

386.1 They are connoisseurs—they have sympathy for a fellow-performer." § Lyon was silent a moment] "They are connoisseurs in the business," Sir David cackled with a harmless old-time cynicism. "They've a sympathy for a fellow performer." § Lyon wondered;

386.6 considered Sir David] considered his host

386.6 in the light of a model] in the light of a sitter

386.9 The old man hesitated; then he answered, smiling, "You're in love with her."] The old man grinned and brought out: "My dear sir, you're in love with her."

386.12 Lyon remarked] Lyon returned

386.19 such a predicament] such a position

386.21 as he was now to see what the loyalty] as about this question of what the loyalty

386.25 an absolutely truthful mind. Oh, he held it as immutably established that whatever other women might be prone to do she, of old, had been perfectly incapable of a deviation.] a perfectly candid mind. Oh he would answer for it that whatever other women might be prone to do she, of old, had stuck to the truth as a bather who can't swim sticks to shallow water.

386.25   simple to deceive] simple for deviation

386.27   It was the last thing] The lie was the last thing

386.29   turned his somersaults] gave the rein

386.31   at the expense of one's honour?] at the expense—Lyon would have been ready to say—of one's decency?

386.33   these two alternatives] these alternatives

386.33   suffered tortures] suffered misery

386.34   her husband's humiliating idiosyncrasy] her husband's exorbitance

386.34   only an added] but an added

386.36   his false pieces] his coinage

387.5   made off his early picture] made of his early picture

387.7   contemplate the case.] stare at the misery!

387.9   tenderness for Mrs. Capadose] interest in Mrs. Capadose

387.10   still have presented itself to him as a very curious problem, for] still have been attaching and worrying; since, truly

387.12   something of a psychologist] curious of queer cases

387.12   His inquiry] His attention

387.15   this gentleman was such a rare anomaly] the fellow was *so* queer a case

387.17   Lyon was too scrupulous to ask other people what they thought of the business] Lyon was at once too discreet and too fond of his own intimate inductions to ask other people how they answered his conundrum

387.18   probable also] probable indeed

387.19   the rest of the company] their companions

387.19   the Colonel's queer habit] the Colonel's idiosyncrasy

387.27   He took a couple of longish walks with her (she was fond of that)] He took a couple of good walks with her—she was fond of good walks—

387.34   he looked into her eyes (deeply, as he occasionally permitted himself
to do)] he sounded her eyes—with the long plummet he occasionally
permitted himself to use

387.36   the least idea that he remembered] any sense of himself remembering

388.3   and asked (with an inward audacity at which he trembled a little)] and
asked, with an amount of "cheek" for which he almost blushed,

388.6   told me that already] insisted on that already

388.7   exclaimed, with exaggerated ruefulness] growled to exaggeration

388.10   good and kind] good and true and kind

388.11   as having great ability] as having great, great ability

388.18   looking, it seemed to him, as she smiled, handsomer than he had ever
seen her. She was either deeply cynical or still more deeply impenetrable, and he had little prospect of winning from her the intimation
that he longed for—some hint that it had come over her that after all
she had better have married] looking still handsomer in the act than
he had ever seen her. She was either utterly brazen or of a contrition
quite impenetrable, and he had little prospect of extorting from her
what he somehow so longed for—some avowal that she had after all
better have married

388.21   Had she not seen—had she not felt—the smile go round when her
husband executed some especially characteristic conversational ca-
per] Hadn't she seen, hadn't she felt, the smile, the cold faded smile of
complete depreciation, go round when her husband perjured himself
to some particularly characteristic blackness?

388.22   her quality endure that] her quality live with that

388.24   fascinated by his problem and yet half exasperated] held by his riddle
and yet impatient of it

388.26   let his falsehoods pass without a protest?] let *his* lies pass without
turning a hair?

388.32   the day's hideous performance, she made him the most scorching
scene.] the day's low exhibition, she had things out with him in a manner known only to the pair themselves.

389.2   he could have taken the diverting view of the Colonel's delinquencies; but as it was they turned to the tragical in his mind, even while
he had a sense that his solitude might also have been laughed at.] he
would surely have taken the Colonel's delinquencies less to heart. As

734

the case stood they fairly turned to the tragical for him, even while he was sharply aware of how merely "his funny way" they were to others—and of how funny his, Oliver Lyon's, own way of regarding them would have seemed to every one.

389.6   he is disinterested, he doesn't operate] he's disinterested, as Sir David said, he doesn't operate

389.8   by the love of beauty] by some love of beauty

389.11   by the simple substitution of a *nuance*. He paints, as it were, and so do I!' His manifestations had a considerable variety, but a family likeness ran through them,] by the simple substitution of a shade. He lays on colour, as it were, and what less do I do myself?" His disorder had a wide range, but a family likeness ran through all its forms,

389.12   made them offensive;] made them an affliction;

389.15   converted it into a sort of brilliant sun-shot fog. For a fib told under pressure a convenient place] turned it into the desert of a perpetual shimmering mirage. For the falsehood uttered under stress a convenient place

389.16   the supererogatory lie] the mere luxurious lie

389.19   In one particular Lyon acquitted] Of one possible charge Lyon acquitted

389.23   But he perceived that he respected the service—that august institution was sacred from his depredations. Moreover though there was a great deal of swagger in his talk it was, oddly enough, rarely swagger] But it was to be made out that he drew the line at the Service—over that august institution he never flapped his wings. Moreover, for all the personal pretension in his talk it rarely came, oddly enough, to swagger

389.28   reminiscences of lonely danger and escape. The more solitary the scene the bigger of course the flower. A new acquaintance, with the Colonel, always received the tribute of a bouquet: that generalisation] reminiscences of what he had prodigiously done and miraculously escaped when off by himself. The more by himself he had been of course the bigger the commemorative nosegay bloomed. A new acquaintance always received from him, in honour of their meeting, one of the most striking of these tributes— that generalisation

389.29   lapses into flat veracity.] lapses into the very commonplace of the credible.

389.31 that his aberrations came in fits or periods—that he would] that he flourished and drooped by an incalculable law and would

389.32 The muse breathed] The muse of improvisation breathed

389.32 at her pleasure; she often left him alone.] at her pleasure and appeared sometimes quite to avert her face.

389.34 in the teeth of the breeze.] with everything against him.

389.34 the false [...] the true,] the impossible [...] the certain,

390.1 yet this proportion was sometimes strikingly reversed. Very often he joined in the laugh against himself—he admitted that he was trying it on and that a good many of his anecdotes had an experimental character.] though this too had lively exceptions. Very often, when it was loud enough—for he liked a noise about him—he joined in the reprobation that cast him out, he allowed he was trying it on and that one didn't know what had happened to one till one *had* tried.

390.3 Lyon divined that he was capable at intervals] Lyon guessed him capable on occasion

390.4 but only when it was a very bad one.] though only when it was very bad.

390.5 become calumnious.] not care whom he touched.

390.5 Such occasions] Such moments as those

390.6 his wife's equanimity] his wife's philosophy

390.9 his rich tone] his big brush

390.11 to elicit the judgment of those who might have shared his own surprise.] to bring to a point those impatiences that might have resembled his own.

390.13 his largest drafts on a sceptical attention] his largest appeals even to proved satiety

390.14 life and gaiety] life and high spirits

390.14 almost of good looks.] almost of simple good looks.

390.16 He was fond of portraying his bravery and used a very big brush, and yet he was unmistakably brave.] If he was fond of treating his gallantry with a flourish he was none the less unmistakeably gallant.

390.16 capital rider] first-rate rider

390.17 as clever and] as clever and brave

390.18   his career] his adventures and observations

390.18   as wonderful as he pretended.] as numerous and wonderful, as the list
          he unrolled.

390.20   interest and credulity] interest and favour

390.24   not only lied but made one feel one's self a bit of a liar, even (or
          especially) if one contradicted him.] not only was mendacious but
          made any charmed converser feel as much so by the very action of
          the charm—of a certain guilty submission of which no intention of
          ridicule could yet purge you.

390.25   our friend watched] our friend, better placed for observation than the
          first night, watched

390.26   she showed nothing] she continued to show nothing

390.32   from their pilferings.] from their depredations.

390.35   no nefarious plan] no harsh design

390.36   her shame or her loyalty] her sensibility or her loyalty

391.2   he should like to bring her round to feel that there would have been
          more dignity in a union with a certain other person.] he should have
          liked to bring her round, liked to see her *show* him that a vision of the
          dignity of not being married to a mountebank sometimes haunted
          her dreams.

391.2   He even dreamed of the hour] He even imagined the hour

391.3   she would ask *him* not to take it up.] she might ask *him* not to take the
          question up.

391.5   Lyon finished his picture] He finished his picture

391.10   that his separation from the lady] that his parting with Everina

391.15   Lyon's curiosity on this point may strike the reader as fatuous, but
          something must be allowed to a disappointed man.] The point he
          made of some visible contrition in her on this head may strike the
          reader as extravagant, but something must be allowed so disappointed
          a man.

391.18   some sign she was sorry.] some sign she didn't feel her choice as *all*
          again.

391.21   wondering whether she told] wondering if she told

391.21   This idea gave him much entertainment] This idea much occupied
          and rather darkly amused him

391.23 symptoms of heredity.] symptoms of paternal strain.

391.23 That was a nice occupation for Everina Brant!] That was a pleasant care for such a woman as Everina Brant!

391.27 other than he said? Lyon doubted this:] other than his account of them? Lyon scarcely thought that probable:

391.29 the only safety for the child would be in her being too stupid to analyse.] the only guard for Amy would be in her being too simple for criticism.

391.29 she was too young.] she was too young to show.

392.4   masterpiece of subtle characterisation] masterpiece of fine characterisation

392.6   of producing something which should bear the stamp of the psychologist as well as of the painter,] of some work that should show the master of the deeper vision as well as the mere reporter of the items,

392.8   no one drew the Colonel out more than he,] no one "drew" the Colonel in the social sense more effectively than he,

392.9   he was almost frightened] he almost winced

392.11 look at Lyon between the eyes] look at his critic between the eyes

392.13 (as she must)] —and she couldn't divine it—

392.17 at other people's expense.] at the expense of others.

392.19 that this sort of life was particularly little to her taste, for he had an idea that it was in] the general gregarious life, the constant presence of a gaping "gallery," particularly little to her taste, for it was naturally in

392.22 and a luxury to her. She told Lyon in fact] and her nearest approach to luxury. She mentioned to her friend in fact

392.23 she neglected to say it] she didn't say it

392.25 to draw such a bow, but it was vulgar:] to deal in such "whoppers," but it was damned vulgar;

392.28 he would become a noxious animal. Yes, in the meantime he was vulgar, in spite of his talents, his fine person, his impunity.] he would practise the fraud to which his talked "rot" had the same relation as the experiments of the forger have to the signed cheque. And in the meantime, yes, he was vulgar, in spite of his facility, his impunity, his so remarkably fine person.

392.32 whether the desire not to miss two of his visits had something to do with her immobility.] if the wish not to miss two of his visits might have had something to do with this course.

392.33 he began to paint the child and she always came with her.] he began to paint her daughter and she made a rule of coming with her.

392.34 to pretend] to affect motives

393.4 but the portrait of the simple-faced child bade fair to stretch over into the following year.] but the simple face of the child held him and worried him and gave him endless work.

393.5 it would have struck any one who might have witnessed the affair] it might have struck a solicitous spectator

393.10 Then her mother and Mr. Lyon sat and talked;] Then her mother and their so patient friend—much more patient than her piano-mistress—sat and talked;

393.12 What Mrs. Capadose did not know was the way that] What Mrs. Capadose couldn't suspect was the rate at which

393.15 In fact Lyon put off everything and made several celebrities wait.] Lyon in fact put off everything and made high celebrities wait.

393.18 nor bored by it.] nor bored by any lapse of communication.

393.21 every stroke that represented her daughter.] every stroke that was to contribute to his result.

393.24 more embarrassed than she was, but he was agitated;] more embarrassed than she, but was more agitated;

393.25 beautifully quiet] admirably quiet

393.25 something was growing between them] something had beautifully settled between them

393.27 He felt it that way; but after all he could not be sure that she did.] He at least felt it that way; but he after all couldn't be sure she did.

393.28 it was not even to confess] it wasn't even to allow

393.32 He would be superabundantly gratified if she should simply let him know, even by a silent sign, that she recognised that with him her life would have been finer. Sometimes he guessed—his presumption went so far—that he might see this sign in her contentedly sitting there.] She wouldn't satisfy him by letting him know even by some quite silent sign that she could imagine her happiness with him—well, more unqualified. Perhaps indeed—his presumption went so far—that was what she did mean by contentedly sitting there.

394.3   the general dispersal] the common dispersal

394.7   Lyon had given her] Lyon had sacrificed to her

394.8   and he had seen what] —he knew what

394.10 this beautiful memorial of the child—beautiful it would evidently be when it was finished, if he could ever satisfy himself;] this wondrous memorial of the child—wondrous it would evidently be when he should be able to bring it to a finish

394.11 possession which they] possession that, this time, they

394.11 his generosity] their generosity and their indiscretion

394.13 the picture—of course he would] the picture, which of course

394.14 for they knew] since they knew

394.19 at last he said:] at last returned:

394.20 I ask of him. It will] I ask of him. All the generosity and charity will so be on your side. It will

394.27 Why, of his nature] Why, of his inner man.

394.28 his nature] his inner man

394.29 a great portrait gives you, and I shall make] a great portrait gives you, and with a splendid comment on it thrown in for the money. I shall make

395.2   I'm insatiable! Do consent,] I'm an insatiable climber. So don't stand in my way,

395.3   Well, his nature is very noble," Mrs. Capadose remarked.] Well, everything in him is very noble," Mrs. Capadose gravely contended.

395.4   "Ah, trust me, I shall bring it out!" Lyon exclaimed,] "Ah trust me to bring everything out!" Lyon returned,

395.6   Mrs. Capadose said before she went away that] Mrs. Capadose, before she went, humoured him to the point of saying that

395.14 confident that he should produce a fine thing. He was in the humour; he was charmed with his *motif*] confident of producing what he had conceived. He was in the spirit of it, charmed with his motive

395.20 able to give the title, for the catalogue, simply as "The Liar." However, it little mattered, for he had now determined that this character should be perceptible even to the meanest intelligence—as overtopping as it had become to his own sense in the living man.] able to inscribe it in the catalogue under the simple rubric to which all propriety pointed. He couldn't in short send in the title as "The Liar"—more was the pity. However, this little mattered, for he had now determined to stamp that sense on it as legibly—and to the meanest intelligence—as it was stamped for his own vision on the living face.

395.21   painting nothing else.] "rendering" nothing else.

395.23   but it seemed to him that the mystery of how to do it was revealed to him afresh] but he felt a miracle of method freshly revealed to him

395.29   he regarded them as immortal,] he thought of them always as immortal things,

395.31   to annex the canvas] to attach the canvas

396.2   but as regards the masterly clearness with which the individual should be rendered his work would be on the same line as that. He had to a degree in which he had rarely had it before the satisfaction of feeling life grow and grow under his brush.] the very man, body and soul, should bloom into life under his hand with just that assurance of no loss of a drop of the liquor.

396.3   while he was sitting:] while sitting:

396.4   largely constituted Lyon's inspiration.] was half the inspiration of the artist.

396.6   Lyon put into practice that idea of drawing him out which he had been nursing for so many weeks:] Lyon applied without mercy his own gift of provocation;

396.9   his only interruptions were when the Colonel did not respond to it.] his own sole lapses were when the Colonel failed, as he called it, to "act."

396.10   Lyon felt that the picture also languished.] Lyon knew that the picture also drooped.

396.14   the more gyrations he executed, in the blue, the better he painted; he couldn't make his flights long enough. He lashed him on when he flagged; his apprehension became great at moments that the Colonel would discover his game. But he never did apparently;] the more he circled and sang in the blue, the better he felt himself paint; he only couldn't make the flights and the evolutions last. He lashed his victim on when he flagged; his one difficulty was his fear again that his game might be suspected. The Colonel, however, was easily beguiled;

396.17 it was astonishing what a short business it was, compared with the little girl's.] astonishingly faster, in spite of its so much greater "importance," than the simple-faced little girl's.

396.19 as he was leaving town] —he was leaving town

396.21 what remained, with or without his friend's attendance. At any rate, as there] the little that remained, in respect to which his friend's attendance would be a minor matter. As there

396.23 he would come back] he should come back

396.24 come and see it the next day, if she should find] have a sight of it next day, should she find

396.25 —this was so greatly her desire—] —this being so greatly her desire—

396.26 he was so far from satisfied as yet.] what he had yet to do was small in amount, but it would make all the difference.

396.29 he had then asked for a delay—declared that he was by no means content. He was really delighted, and he was again a little ashamed of himself.] he had then recommended her not coming till he should be himself better pleased. He had really never been, at a corresponding stage, better pleased; and he blushed a little for his subtlety.

396.31 sat straight and gossiped] sat at his usual free practice

397.2 a crooked picturesque staircase enabled you to descend to] a winding staircase, happily disposed, dropped to

397.9 you smelt something sweet and you heard the birds.] there was a sweetness in the air and you heard the birds.

397.12 perceived her and whom he perceived before she was noticed by his friend.] was aware of her, but whom he was then the first to see.

397.15 importunate class—the model] importunate class of the model

397.23 Lyon went on with his painting;] Lyon continued to paint;

397.24 his eyes lighted on her no more.] his eyes were only for his work.

397.27 evidently rounded several corners of life and had a face] clearly rounded several corners of life; she had a face

397.28 but that somehow failed] yet that failed

397.28   Nevertheless she was pretty] She was nevertheless rather pretty

397.34   an interrupted profession or even of a blighted career.] a precarious
         profession, perhaps even of a blighted career.

397.34   rather soiled] perceptibly soiled

398.4   Lyon answered.] Lyon protested.

398.18   wouldn't look like me," said the Colonel, laughing.] wouldn't look like
         a gentleman," the Colonel sociably laughed.

398.23   suggested, comfortingly.] suggested for comfort.

398.26   Lyon was beginning to be bored and] Lyon's amusement had turned
         to impatience and

399.5   Lyon's declaration. And then she disappeared.] Lyon's charge. On
         which she disappeared.

399.10   The Colonel was silent a moment;] The Colonel just waited;

399.12   drop too much] 'drop too much'

399.18   he began to wonder what was coming now.] he wondered what now
         would come.

399.23   he didn't believe a word of this.] without a single grain of faith.

399.24   delighted with it] delighted with what he heard

399.25   The story had bloomed, fragrant] The story had shot up and bloomed,
         from the dropped seed

399.27   I was annoyed] I was vexed

399.27   but I wasn't startled] but I wasn't upset

399.31   I have seen] I've noticed

399.33   with such a *toupet*?] with such charming 'cheek'?

399.34   "Yes, she has that,"] "Yes, she has plenty of cheek,"

399.35   Still, there was a cheek, as they say, in her coming in.] Still, she carried
         it off as a cool hand.

399.35   she's a bad one!] she's a bad 'un!

400.2   a stupid young gander] a young jackanapes

400.5   I cut in and made him get rid of her—I sent her] I was able to make a
         diversion and let him get off—after which I sent her

400.11   Lyon asked, most attentive. The details always began to multiply, to
         abound, when once his companion was well launched—they flowed
         forth in battalions.] Lyon was all participation. He had always noted
         that when once his friend was launched there was no danger in asking;
         the more you asked the more abundantly you were served.

400.13   a rum appellation?] a rum notion?

400.14   the promptitude of this response] this flow of facility

400.20   Lyon asked, laughing.] Lyon asked with amusement.

400.23   on the men who have deceived them, and I never deceived her] on the
         fellows who have 'undone' them, and I never undid her

400.27   He felt that this was little to pay for his entertainment.] He felt this
         little to pay for what he was getting.

400.30   for a letter recounting the fictive sequel; but apparently his brilliant
         sitter did not] for some sequel to match—a report, by note, of the next
         scene in the drama as his friend had met it, but this genius apparently
         did not

400.31   they had taken a rendezvous] they had taken a tryst

401.2   as he ever felt with the translation of the idea by the hand—always,
         as it seemed to him, a pitiful compromise.] as decency permitted, the
         translation of the idea by the hand appearing always to him at the best
         a pitiful compromise.

401.3   as he was smoking] as he smoked

401.8   he was seized with the desire to see it again and do two or three things
         more to it: he had thought of it so often while he lounged there. The
         impulse was too strong to be dismissed, and though he expected to
         return to town in the course of another week he was unable to face
         the delay. To look at the picture for five minutes would be enough]
         he was taken with a fancy for another look at what he had lately done,
         and with that in particular of doing two or three things more to it: he
         had been much haunted with this unrest while he lounged there. The
         provocation was not to be resisted, and though he was at any rate so
         soon to be back in London he was unable to brook delay. Five minutes
         with his view of the Colonel would be enough

401.9   questions which hummed] questions that hummed

401.10   train for London.] train for town.

401.13   Lyon found unmitigated emptiness] Lyon found mere desolation

744

401.15 slightly Oriental.] feebly Oriental.

401.17 having a theory that it was well sometimes to take servants unprepared.] it being a matter of conscience with him sometimes to take his servants.

401.18 was mainly in charge] set in authority over them

401.20 (he cultivated] —as he cultivated

401.22 He told her that she needn't mind the place being not quite straight,] He reassured her as to any other effect of unpreparedness—

401.23 —he should be busy] and should be busy

401.23 To this she replied that] She announced that

401.25 he was away from home] he was absent

401.28 the housekeeper concluded.] this informant concluded.

401.31 Lyon said, the identity of his visitors being clear.] Lyon read the identity of his visitors.

401.32 for she usually had little to do] having when he was at home so little to do

401.36 at Mrs. Capadose's having come to see her husband's portrait when she knew that the artist himself wished her to forbear;] at the advent of Mrs. Capadose, who knew how little he wished her to see the portrait unfinished,

402.3 who wanted a portrait] who perhaps wanted a portrait

402.13 He pushed aside the curtain that hung in the door of communication the door opening upon the gallery which it had been found convenient to construct at the time the studio was added to the house. When I say he pushed it aside I should amend my phrase; he laid his hand upon it, but at that moment he was arrested by a very singular sound. It came from the floor of the room beneath him and it startled him extremely, consisting apparently as it did of a passionate wail a sort of smothered shriek accompanied by a violent burst of tears.] He laid his hand upon the curtain draping the door of communication, the door opening upon the gallery constructed for relief at the time the studio was added to the house; but with his motion to slide the tapestry on its rings arrested in the act. A singular startling sound reached him from the room beneath; it had the appearance of a passionate wail, or perhaps rather a smothered shriek, accompanied by a violent burst of tears.

402.13   listened intently a moment, and] listened intently and

402.14   he passed out upon the balcony] passed in to the balcony

402.15   though he had not endeavoured to make it so] without his trying to keep it so

402.18   In truth they were] They were in truth

402.21   one of the most extraordinary they had ever rested upon.] more extraordinary than any he had ever felt free to overlook.

402.21   failure to comprehend] failure to understand

402.22   from interrupting it—for what he saw] from interfering—what he saw

402.27   and these influences were succeeded after a minute (the minutes were very few and very short) by a definite motive which presently had the force to make him step back behind the curtain. I may add that it also had the force to make him avail himself for further contemplation of a crevice] after which surprise and discretion gave way to a force that made him step back behind the curtain. This same force, further—the force of a *need* to know—caused him to avail himself for better observation of a crevice

402.28   the two halves of the *portière*.] the two halves of his swinging tapestry.

402.32   that a very odd business, in which his confidence had been trifled with, was going forward, and that if in a measure it didn't concern him, in a measure it very definitely did] that something irregular, as to which his confidence had been trifled with, was on foot, and that he was as much concerned with the reasons of it as he might be little concerned with the taken form.

402.35   weeping, sobbing] weeping; she sobbed

403.1   by the words, vehemently uttered,] by the vehement imprecation

403.5   rummaged out his unfinished portrait] rummaged out the canvas before which he had been sitting

403.6   out of the way, with its face to the wall] out of the way and its face to the wall

403.6   set it up before his wife] set it up for his wife

403.9   She was too busy sobbing] She was too overcome

403.10   reiterating his objurgation] re-expressing his wrath

403.11   that he could not take it, on the spot, as a proof] that all impulse failed him on the spot for a proof

403.13   came a little later.] was yet to come.

403.14   Yet he could see the portrait] He could see his projected figure, however,

403.15   he had not thought it so masterly.] he hadn't supposed the force of the thing could so prevail.

403.17   dropped into the nearest chair, buried her face in her arms, leaning on a table.] dropped into the nearest chair, leaned against a table, buried her face in her arms.

403.17   Her weeping suddenly ceased to be audible,] The sound of her woe diminished,

403.19   Her husband remained a moment staring] Her husband stood a moment glaring

403.22   Lyon heard her answer.] Lyon fairly drank in her answer.

403.29   He has made me rather handsome."] I'll be bound to say he has made me handsome."

403.36   it needn't go."] it needn't go," the poor branded man declared.

404.1   "Oh, he'll send it] "Ah he'll send it

404.3   the poor man cried.] the victim cried.

404.12   again, and again he stood looking at it.] again—again he covered it with his baffled glare.

404.13   It was not clear to Lyon] Yet it was not clear to Lyon

404.14   the original or the painter of the portrait.] the guilty original or the guilty painter.

404.17   and moved rapidly about the room, as if he were looking for something; Lyon was unable for the instant to guess his intention. Then the artist said] and moved about as if looking for something; Lyon for the moment wondered at his intention; saying to himself

404.18   rush down and stop him;] raise a preventive cry,

404.21   rushed back with] strode back with

404.22   Lyon perceived that the object he had seized was] Lyon recognized the object seized as

404.23   and that he had plunged] and saw that he had plunged

404.24   He seemed animated by a sudden fury, for with extreme vigour of hand] Animated as with a sudden fury and exercising a rare vigour of hand,

404.28   the oddest effect—that of a sort of figurative suicide.] the most portentous effect—that of some act of prefigured or rehearsed suicide.

404.30   as he did so, as if he expected it to reek with blood] in this motion as for the sight of blood

404.30   closing the door after him.] with a bang of the door.

404.32   made no movement] lifted neither voice nor hand

404.32   But he did not feel] The point is that he didn't feel

404.34   did he feel that he was gaining] was he conscious of gaining

404.36   even though the picture had been reduced to rags.] even at the sacrifice of his precious labour.

404.36   The revelation excited him so] The revelation so excited him

405.4   hacked it to death.] hacked himself to death.

405.4   where it was,] there where it grimaced,

405.6   still excited, for an hour.] with a sense of such achieved success as nothing finished and framed, varnished and delivered and paid for had ever given him.

405.7   to recommend that he should have some luncheon]; to offer him luncheon;

405.17   Lyon said.] Lyon magnificently said.

405.24   During the two months that he was absent from England he expected something—he could hardly have said what; a manifestation of some sort on the Colonel's part. Wouldn't he write, wouldn't he explain, wouldn't he take for granted Lyon had discovered the way he had, as the cook said, served him and deem it only decent to take pity in some fashion or other on his mystification?] There was something he found himself looking for during these two months on the Continent; he had an expectation—he could hardly have said of what; of some characteristic sign or other on the Colonel's part. Wouldn't he write, would n't he explain, would n't he take for granted Lyon had discovered the way he had indeed been "served" and hold it only decent to show some form of pity for his mystification?

405.26   and make a considerable draft upon his genius, in view of the certain
         testimony of Lyon's housekeeper,] would really put his genius to the
         test, in view of the ready and responsible witness

405.28   the violence wrought.] that perpetration.

405.30   expression of that destructive petulance] expression of that exasperat-
         ed wonder.

405.31   so potently] so fatally

405.32   either to declare] either to take oath

405.33   he would have to tell a fine story.] would be at costs for a difficult
         version.

405.34   for the story and, as no letter came, disappointed that it was not pro-
         duced.] for this probably remarkable story, and as no letter came was
         disappointed at the failure of the exhibition.

405.36   Mrs. Capadose's version, if version there was] Mrs. Capadose's inevi-
         table share in the report, if report there was

406.2   or for him, Oliver Lyon, on the other.] or for himself on the other.

406.4   He wanted to draw her out] It would have met his impatience most to
         draw her out

406.7   narrating his wanderings, hoping they should soon meet in town] tell-
         ing her of his movements, hoping for their reunion in London

406.8   upon which he reflected] on which he reflected

406.10   was still too much under the influence of the emotion produced by
         his "betrayal."] was still too deeply ruffled, too disconcerted, by his
         "betrayal."

406.10   that emotion] that resentment

406.12   and it was a complete rupture and everything was at an end.] the rup-
         ture was therefore complete and everything at an end.

406.13   Lyon considered this prospect rather ruefully,] Lyon was frankly rue-
         ful over this prospect,

406.17   part of it to Lyon] part of it to him

406.18   which consisted of these words:] which ran as follows:

406.26   Lyon's return to London was] Lyon's return was

406.29   he had availed himself of it several times.] he had several times profit-
         ed by it.

406.29 the occasions (before he sat to him)] the occasions, before his sittings,

406.31 (he went out] (went out

407.10 the Colonel's next words didn't confirm this interpretation.] his friend's next words made this impossible.

407.11 it gives such a chance to my *bavardise*.] you want me animated, and it leaves me so to wag my tongue.

407.12 I had almost finished," Lyon remarked.] how near I had to go to the end," Lyon returned.

407.15 said Oliver Lyon with a laugh, looking at] laughed the painter with his eyes on

407.15 meet his eyes] meet them

407.17 Mrs. Capadose asked,] cried Everina,

407.21 cried the Colonel.] cried the Colonel—"what a jolly shame!"

407.22 Lyon turned his eyes to him, smiling.] Lyon took him in with a wide smile.

407.22 didn't do it?"] didn't go for it?"

407.23 "Is it ruined?" the Colonel inquired.] "Is it done for?" the Colonel earnestly asked.

407.28 if a highly suggestive idea] if a lurid light

408.1 with a sigh.] with a vague recovery.

408.3 little brute] horrid little brute

408.7 Lyon had reminded] He had reminded

408.8 when the Colonel] when her husband

408.10 immediately made his achievement plain to her.] at once mentioned his misdeed.

408.11 if he had not mentioned] if he hadn't reported

408.15 deceived him in the slightest degree.] affected him as in the least convincing.

408.18 London female model in all her varieties] London model in all her feminine varieties

408.24 not a carriage nor a cab] neither carriage nor cab

408.26 close to the Marlborough Road station] near the Marlborough Road station

408.27   coming to his sittings, more than once had availed himself of] repeating his pilgrimage so often, habitually made use of

409.2   a very determined hand—a perfect wild-cat."] a very determined
hand that did the deed—in the spirit of a perfect wild-cat."

409.6   off her head] practically off her head

409.7   Lyon said, laughing.] Lyon amusedly urged.

409.9   The more portraits there are the less employment] The more portraits, the less employment

409.12   The inquiry baffled] The question baffled

409.13   in a vicious muddle! As I say, she's off her head."] so bad she goes it
blind. She doesn't know where she is."

409.14   They went into] They passed into

409.15   too bad] too low

409.16   painting masterpieces] throwing off masterpieces

409.18   Lyon demanded] Lyon put to her

409.20   Mrs. Capadose appeared not to perceive it] She seemed not to feel it

409.27   a false statement, for he had] a false pleas for the truth: he had

409.29   to himself, but he had no desire to expose them to any one else,] to his
own view, but without wish to expose them to others,

409.31   You're safe!" the Colonel exclaimed.] You're all right *now!*" the Colonel
guaranteed.

409.34   what a deceiver!] what a practised deceiver!

409.35   the Colonel went on.] his host went on.

410.4   our conferences.] our interviews.

410.7   said the Colonel.] said the subject of Geraldine's pursuit.

410.11   "My dear fellow, don't curse me!] "Ah my dear fellow," the Colonel
groaned, "don't utterly curse me!

410.12   Lyon asked tragically.] Lyon tragically cried.

410.14   exclaimed in a tone of exquisite reproach.] reproachfully wailed.

410.15   groaned, dramatically;] almost howled for compunction;

410.19   that he looked very strange.] how strange he must have looked.

410.20   He murmured something about it being useless to cry over spilled milk] He attempted some platitude about spilled milk and the folly of crying over it

410.20   turn the conversation] turn the talk

410.21   whether they felt it as much as he.] how it pressed upon *them.*

410.36   had really vanished] must have vanished

411.1   to quit the subject] to cut loose, in his disgust,

411.4   he only replied] he only made answer

411.8   "Oh, I loved it!"] "Oh *cher grand maître,* I loved it!"

411.17   denoted that she intended to go out.] betrayed some purpose of going out.

411.27   tacit confession, in a word, if she] tacit confession if she

411.33   It's a clew] It's a clue

411.34   He had no desire to frighten her;] He didn't want to scare or to shake her;

412.1   Mrs. Capadose replied,] Everina replied:

412.10   For you, I am very sorry.] For you, *cher maître,* I'm very sorry.

412.11   Lyon turned away.] he turned away.

412.14   the way he had seen] of how he had seen

412.15   Lyon stopped] He stopped

412.17   She was still in love with the Colonel—he had trained her too well.] Nor should he ever sound her abyss. He believed in her absolute straightness where she and her affairs alone might be concerned, but she was still in love with the man of her choice, and since she couldn't redeem him she would adopt and protect him. So he had trained her.

EMENDATIONS

121.25   'of the Daintry's' emended to 'of the Daintrys'

131.18   'to momentary intermission' emended to 'to a momentary intermission'

143.29   'But she would have him glad to' emended to 'But she would have been glad to'

160.36   'He stretched away' emended to 'It stretched away'

304.13   'Aspern's poem's' emended to 'Aspern's poems'

APPENDICES

A

Extracts from James's *Notebooks*

Henry James's notebooks are collected in Volume XXXIV of The Complete Fiction of Henry James. *The editor of that volume, Philip Horne, has excerpted and prepared the text for this Appendix, and has supplied essential annotations; more extensive notes can be found in* The Notebooks.

'Pandora'

London, January 29th, 1884

I don't see why I shouldn't do the "self-made girl," whom I noted here last winter, in a way to make her a rival to D[aisy]. M[iller]. I must put her into action, which I am afraid will be difficult in the small compass (16 magazine pages, which I now contemplate.) But I don't see why I shouldn't make the thing as concise as *Four Meetings*. The concision of *Four Meetings*, with the success of *Daisy M.*—that is what I must aim at! But I must first invent the action! It must take place in New York. Perhaps indeed Washington would do. This would give me a chance to *do* Washington, so far as I know it, & work in my few notes, & my very lovely memories, of last winter. I might even *do* Henry Adams & his wife. The hero might be a foreign Secretary of Legation—German—inquiring & conscientious. New York *and* Washington, say. The point of the story would naturally be to show the contrast between the humble social background of the heroine, & the position which she has made—or is making—for herself—&, indirectly, for her family. He must meet her first, in New York, then in Washington, where she has come to stay[,] (with Mrs. Adams,) & is seeing the president, cabinet &c; then again in New York; then finally in the country, in summer. Her people—her impossible father & mother—the way she carries them &c. The picture admiring & appreciative. It must be a case of "four meetings," each with its little chapter &c., each a picture. The thing must have the name of the girl, (like D. M.) for its title—carefully selected. Each chapter (if there are 4) 20 pp. of MS.—I may make the thing a "little gem"—if I try hard enough.

'Georgina's Reasons'

London, March 26th, 1884

Mrs. Kemble repeated to me the other night a story told her by Edward Sartoris, & told him by his daughter in law, Mrs. Algie,[1] in which it seemed to me that there was a "situation." The story has only the *tort*[2] to be very incredible, and almost silly: it sounds "made up." Mrs. A. relates at any rate that she knows of a young girl, in one of the far Western cities of America, who formed an attachment to a young U.S. officer quartered in the town and of whose attentions to her her family wholly disapproved. They declared that under no circumstances would they consent to her marrying him, and forbade her to think of doing so, or to hope for a moment for this contingency. Her passion, however, was stronger, and she was secretly married to the officer. But she returned to her father's house, and it was determined to keep the marriage absolutely secret. Both parties appeared to have repented, to a considerable degree, of what they had done. In the course of time however, the girl discovers that secrecy is becoming difficult; she has the prospect of being confined. She is in despair, doesn't know what to do, &c; and takes a friend, a married woman, into her confidence. This lady, pitying her, offers to take her to Europe and see that in some out-of-the-way place, the child is brought secretly into the world. The girl's parents consent to her making the journey, she goes to Europe with her friend, and in some small Italian town the young lady is delivered. The child is made over, with a sum of money, to a woman of the place, and the others go their way. In due time the young lady returns to her native town and her family, and is reinstated as a daughter of the house. The officer has been ordered to a distant post, and relations between them have ceased. After a while another prétendant presents himself, who is agreeable to the family and who ends by becoming agreeable to the girl. (I should mention—for it is the most important point of the whole!—that before she married the officer she extracted from him a promise that he would never demand of her to recognise their union, would never claim her publicly as his wife &c. He has given this promise in the most solemn form.) She marries the new suitor, the officer makes no sign, and she lives for several years with her new husband, in great happiness,

---

[1] Fanny Kemble (1809–1893), a famous actress and author, had been a close friend of Henry James since 1872. Adelaide Kemble Sartoris, Fanny's sister, was an opera singer before marrying Edward Sartoris; Algernon, son of Edward and Adelaide, married Nellie Grant, daughter of General Ulysses S. Grant, who thus became 'Mrs. Algie'.

[2] *tort* (French): fault.

and has several children. At the end of this time the officer turns up. He tells her that it is all very well for *her* to be a bigamist, but that he doesn't choose to, and that she must allow him to institute a divorce suit against her, on the ground of desertion, in order that *he* too may marry a second time, being much in love with another woman & desiring to do so. That he may institute this suit she must release him from his old promise not to claim her as his wife &c. It was not made clear to me, in Mrs. K.'s story, what the heroine did; but I was arrested by the situation I have just indicated: that of two persons secretly married, and one of whom (the husband, naturally) is tied by a promise to be silent, yet wishes to break the marriage in order to recover his freedom—to marry again, to beget legitimate children. The interest of the other is that this marriage never be known—her honour, her safety concerned, &c. The husband pleads that after the vow she has broken, he may surely break his promise, &c. Her entreaties, in opposition, her distress at the prospect of exposure &c. The only endurable dénouement that I can see is in the officer's agreeing to let her off—giving up his own marriage—making the sacrifice to his word. It will add to the tragic impression of this[,] &c, that he is unable to account to his new *fiancée*, or, at any rate, his new *inammorata* [*sic*] for his backing-out. He can't tell her why he gives her up—can't explain to her his extraordinary conduct. His only alternatives are to commit bigamy and to wait for the death of his bigamous wife. The situation, as presented in the foregoing anecdote (which is singularly crude & incoherent) might be variously modified. The dropping of the child in Europe would be an impossible incident. It isn't necessary that she shld. have had a child—though, of course, if she has none at first it is almost necessary that she shld. have none afterwards.

'A New England Winter'

[London], January 18th, 1881

Mrs. T., living in America, (say at Newport,) has a son, young, unmarried, clever and selfish, who persists in living in Europe, and whom she therefore sees only at long intervals. He prefers European life, & takes his filial duties very lightly. She goes out to see him from time to time, but dares not fix herself permanently near him, for fear of boring him. At last however he comes home, to pay a short visit, and all her desire is to induce him to remain with her for some months. She has reason to believe that he will grow very tired of her quiet house; & in order to enhance its attraction she invites a young girl—a distant relative, from another part of the country, to stay with her. She has not the least desire that her son shall fall in love, seriously, with the girl; and does not believe that he will—being of a cold and volatile disposition and having a connection with some woman abroad. She simply thinks that the girl will make the house pleasant, and her son will stay the longer. That *she* may be sacrificed—that is, that *she* may become too much interested in the son, is an idea which she does not allow to stand in her way. The son arrives, is very pleasant for a week—then very much bored and disposed to depart. He stays awhile longer, however, at the mother's urgency, and then does become interested in the girl. The latter, who is very intelligent and observant, has become aware of the part that she has been intended to play, and, after little, has enough of it and departs. The son meanwhile is seriously in love; he follows the girl, leaves his mother alone, and spends the rest of the time that he is in America in vainly besieging the affections of the young lady—so that the mother, as a just retribution, loses his society almost altogether. The girl refuses him, and he returns in disgust and dudgeon to Europe, where he marries the other person, before-mentioned, while the mother is left lamenting!—The subject is rather trivial, but I think that something might be made of it. If the dénouement just suggested appears too harsh, it may be supposed that the girl at last accedes to the son's passion and that he marries her—the separation from his mother—being none the less complete. The story may be told as a journal of the mother.

'The Path of Duty'

London, January 29th, 1884

I heard the other day at Mrs. Tennant's[3] of a situation which struck me as dramatic, & a pretty subject. The story was told of young Lord Stafford,[4] son of the Duke of Sutherland. It appears he has been for years in love with Lady Grosvenor[5] whom he knew before her marriage to Lord G. He had no expectation of being able to marry her, however, her husband being a young, robust man of his own age, &c. Yielding to family pressure on the subject of

---

[3] Gertrude Collier Tennant (1819–1918), a London society hostess with an important literary salon. She had been a close friend of Gustave Flaubert's, whom she had originally met in France in 1842. In the 1870s she helped edit his correspondence.

[4] Cromartie Sutherland-Leveson-Gower (1851–1913) became Duke of Sutherland in 1892.

[5] Sibell Mary Lumley, (1855–1929) married Victor Alexander, Earl Grosvenor (1853–84) in 1874; three years after her husband's premature death, she married the Right Hon. George Wyndham.

taking a wife, he offered his hand to a young, charming, innocent girl, the daughter of Lord Rosslyn.[6] He was gratefully accepted, & the engagement was announced. Suddenly, a very short time after this, & without any one's expecting it, Lord Grosvenor dies & his wife becomes free. The question came up—"What was Lord S. to do?"—to stick to the girl—or to get rid of her in the best way he could &—after a decent interval—present himself to Lady G? The question, as a matter of ethics, seems to me to have but one answer; if he had offered marriage to Miss Rosslyn (or whatever her name) by that offer he should abide. But the situation might make, as I say, a story, capable of several different turns, according to the character of the actors. The young man may give up Miss R. & betake himself to Lady G., who may then refuse him, on account of his having done an act she deems dishonourable. Or Miss R., guessing or learning the truth, may sacrifice herself, & liberate him of her own free will. Or she may still[,] knowing the truth, cling to him because she loves him, because she cannot give him up, & because she knows that Lady G. has refused to marry him. (I use these initials simply as convenient signs—knowing nothing of the people.) This attitude Miss R. may maintain until she meets Lady G., when a revulsion may take place, born simply of her fears. She may feel, as the impression of the older more brilliant woman is stamped upon her, that though the latter refuses to marry him at the cost of his tergiversation, she *must* be queen of his thoughts & will finally end by becoming his mistress. A conviction of this—a real presentiment of it may take possession of her; so that she renounces her brilliant marriage, her noble suitor, rather than face this danger. There is another line which one may imagine another sort of girl taking: a girl, ambitious, tenacious, *volontière*,[7] unscrupulous, even slightly cynical. The state of things becomes apparent to her—she *has* to recognize that that her suitor would give millions to break off his engagement. But she says, ["]No, I won't give you up, I can't, it would kill me, for I have set my heart on everything that a marriage with you would bring me. But I don't ask for your affection—if I hold you to our betrothal, I leave you free in conduct. Let me be your wife, bear your name, your coronet, enjoy your wealth & splendour, but devote yourself to Lady G. as much as you like—make her your mistress, if you will. I will shut my eyes—I will make no

---

6 Lady Millicent Fanny St Claire Erskine (1867–1955), daughter of the fourth Earl of Rosslyn, married Earl Stafford at a very young age in 1884, later becoming Duchess of Sutherland. She later became an author and a friend of James.

7 This seems to be a slip of the pen for *volontaire*, meaning headstrong in French.

scandal.["]—If I were a Frenchman & a naturalist, this is probably the treatment I shld. adopt.—These things all deal with the matter from the point of view of the girl. As I began by saying, the quandary of the man is dramatically interesting; & one may imagine more than one issue, though only one is rigidly honourable. Lord S. may determine to stick to the girl—he may resist the temptation—he may have a frank understanding with Lady G. about it; in which she (in love with him) rises also to the height of his own lofty view of the matter, agrees that they must give each other up, that he *must* marry Miss R. & that he & she (Lady G.) must see eachother [*sic*] in future as little as possible. The girl, in this, remains innocent & unconscious, but the light of the pathetic is projected upon her by the narrator of the story. It might be told by a friend & confidant of Lord S., who is in the secret throughout. *He* knows the force of Lord S.'s passion for Lady G., he knows that his engagement to Miss R. was merely perfunctory, because a man in his position *must* marry & have an heir, & his father has badgered him till he has done so. *He* knows also a good deal about Lady G., & what she is capable of. Therefore when they plan together this noble renunciation, he doubts & fears—he thinks it is of bad omen for the poor little bride, & is sure that it is only a question of time that Lord S. shall become the other woman's lover. "Ah, they have agreed to give each other up!—Poor little woman!" That is the note on which this particular story would close. This arrangement would be congenial to the characteristic manner of H. J.—I shall probably try it. In this case the whole story might be told by Lord S.'s friend, who has observed it while it went on. He may relate it to an American visitor. The point de départ of this might be the sight of Lord S. & Lady G. together, somewhere, in public; which is an intimation that what the friend has foreseen has happened.

'Louisa Pallant'

Florence, January 21st, 1887

The idea of a worldly mother & a worldly daughter—the latter of whom has been trained up so perfectly by the former that she excels & surpasses her, & the mother, who has some principle of goodness still left in her composition, is appalled at her own work. She sees the daughter, so hard, so cruelly ambitious, so bent on making a great marriage & a great success at any price, that she is almost afraid of her. She repents of what she has done—she is ashamed. The daughter fixes a rich, soft & amiable young man as an object of conquest—& the mother finds herself pitying the lad. She is tempted to go to him & warn him. They may all be Americans—in Europe: since Howells[8] writes to me that I do the "international" far better than anything else. The story may be told by an elderly American—the uncle, or cousin, of the very rich lad whom the girl considers a *parti* worth her efforts. He has known the 2 ladies of old—he has seen the mother's great worldliness, & he observes the change. The mother shall have been an old flame of his & shall have thrown him over. After that their relations shall have become frank—intensely candid. She knows he knows her views & efforts—& they have openly talked of them. He doesn't like the daughter—he is responsible for his rich young nephew—he warns the mother off—says the boy is not to be their game. The mother takes the warning—or perhaps it's not definitely given, for that after all might be too brutal. However, that's a point to be settled. She may see for herself that her old sweetheart fears their bagging the boy (for the girl is superficially charming,) & determines to retrieve herself in the uncle's eyes by preventing the capture. She has always been ashamed of the way she has treated her old admirer. She sees that her daughter is determined to collar the young man. So she goes to the latter clandestinely, denounces the girl (after a fashion,) & recommends him to go away. He consents—he is affected by what she says—and escapes. The mother is in a kind of exaltation—she feels as if she had purified herself. She goes to the uncle & says—"Ah, well, you must respect me now." He admires her, and he must describe this in a good tone. But he feels even a little sorry for the girl—& after a little he even expresses this. Then the mother may reply, as a last word—"Oh, after all, I don't know that it matters! She will still get a prince!"* The narrator says—"She *is* now the Countess So-and-So."

[The next page continues:] The narrator must begin this story—"Never say you know the last word about any human heart! I once was treated to a revelation which startled and touched me in the nature of a person whom I knew well, whom I had been well acquainted with for years, whose character I had had good reason, heaven knows, to appreciate, and in regard to whom I flattered myself I had nothing more to learn. It was on the terrace of the Kursaal at

---

* This business might begin & indeed take place wholly at some watering place—say Homburg—or perhaps better in Switzerland. No room for description. Perhaps Florence might do. At any rate the narrator meets the ladies after a long interval. The nephew arrives—joins him—later.

8 William Dean Howells (1837–1920), American novelist, poet, critic, and editor of the *Atlantic Monthly* (1871–81), a long-time ally of James in promoting a non-scandalous realism in America.

Homburg, nearly ten years ago, one lovely summer night. I was there alone, but I was waiting for my nephew &c, &c. The band played—the people passed & repassed in front of me; I smoked my cigar & watched them. Suddenly I recognized Mrs. Grift & her daughter. I hadn't seen Linda since she was fifteen—but I had then seen how she was going. She had become exceedingly pretty—& wonderfully like what her mother was twenty years before." They walk (the mother & daughter up & down together) & he watches them, unseen, for some time before he speaks to them. No one else does so, it is almost as if they were not respectable. (I don't know that that is very important.) I must give his little retrospect while he regards them. Then he gets up & goes to them—and the rest comes on. I don't see why this shouldn't be a little masterpiece of *concision*, all narrative—not too much attempt to *fouiller*,[9] with every word telling. If M. Schuyler[10] doesn't find *Cousin Maria* possible for his "holiday number" of *Harper*, this might very well serve.

'The Aspern Papers'

Florence, January 12th, 1887

Hamilton[11] (V. L.'s brother) told me a curious thing of Capt. Silsbee[12]—the Boston art-critic & Shelley-worshipper; that is of a curious adventure of his. Miss Claremont,[13] Byron's ci-devant mistress (the mother of Allegra) was living, until lately, here in Florence, at a great age, 80 or thereabouts, & with her lived her niece, a younger Miss Claremont—of about 50. Silsbee knew that they had interesting papers—letters of Shelley's & Byron's—he had known it for a long time & cherished the idea of getting hold of them. To this end he laid the plan of going to lodge with the Miss Claremonts' [*sic*]—hoping that

---

[9]   *fouiller* (French): excavate; go deeply into [a problem].

[10] Montgomery Schuyler (1843–1914) was managing editor of the New York journal *Harper's Weekly* from 1885 to 1887.

[11] Eugene Jacob Lee-Hamilton (1845–1907) was an English diplomat and poet, the half-brother of the novelist and critic Violet Paget ('Vernon Lee'), with whom James had an uneasy relationship. He became bed-ridden in 1875 and lived in Florence until the death of his mother in 1896, around which time he made a recovery.

[12] Edward Augustus Silsbee (1826–1900), a retired American merchant seaman and a Shelley devotee who wanted to get hold of the Shelley papers, as James relates. John Singer Sargent made a charcoal portrait of him in 1899.

[13] Claire Clairmont (1798–1879), Mary Shelley's stepsister, was the mother of the poet Lord Byron's daughter Allegra (1817–22). In later life she converted to Catholicism, and lived in Florence from 1870 with her niece Paulina.

the old lady[,] in view of her great age & failing condition, would die while he was there, so that he might then put his hand upon the documents, which she hugged close in life. He carried out this scheme—& things *se passèrent*[14] as he had expected. The old woman *did* die—& then he approached the younger one—the old maid of 50—on the subject of his desires. Her answer was—"I will give you all the letters if you marry me!" H. says that Silsbee *court encore.*[15] Certainly there is a little subject there: the picture of the two faded, queer, poor & discredited old Englishwomen—living on into a strange generation, in their musty corner of a foreign town—with these illustrious letters their most precious possession. Then the plot of the Shelley-fanatic—his watchings & waitings—the way he *couvers*[16] the treasure. The dénoument needn't be the one related of poor Silsbee; & at any rate the general situation is in itself a subject & a picture. It strikes me much. The interest would be in some price that the man has to pay—that the old women—or the survivor—sets upon the papers. His hesitations—his struggle—for he really would give almost anything.

— The Countess Gamba came in while I was there: her husband is a nephew of the Guiccioli[17]—& it was àpropos of their having a lot of Byron's letters of which they are rather illiberal & dangerous guardians, that H. told me the above. They won't show them or publish any of them—& the Countess was very angry once on H.'s representing to her that it was her duty—especially to the English public!—to let them at least be seen. Elle se fiche bien[18] of the English public. She says the letters—addressed in Italian to the Guiccioli—are discreditable to Byron; & H. elicited from her that she had *burned* one of them!

'The Liar'

London, *June 19*[th], *1884*
One might write a tale (very short) about a woman married to a man of the most amiable character who is a tremendous, though harmless, liar. She is very intelligent, a fine, quiet, high, pure nature, and she has to sit by and hear him

---

[14] *se passèrent* (French): took place, happened.
[15] *court encore* (French): is still running.
[16] *couvers* (French verb with English ending): *couver* (the infinitive) means 'to brood over'.
[17] Contessa Teresa Guiccioli (1800–73) was the married lover of Byron, whom she met in 1818, for his last years; according to Edel and Powers in *Complete Notebooks*, 'The Countess Gamba, reputed to be the natural daughter of the Tuscan satirist-poet Giuseppe Giusti, married a nephew of Lord Byron's last mistress, Teresa Guiccioli' (34n.).
[18] Elle se fiche bien (French): She doesn't care a rap [for].

romance—mainly out of vanity, the desire to be interesting, and a peculiar, irresistible impulse. He is good, kind, personally very attractive, very handsome, &c: it is almost his only fault though of course he is necessarily very *light*. What she suffers—what she goes through. Generally she tries to rectify, to remove any bad effect by toning down a little, &c. But there comes a day when he tells a very big lie which she has—for reasons to be related—to adopt, to reinforce. To save him from exposure, in a word, she has to lie herself. The struggle &c. She lies—but after that she hates him. (Numa Roumestan)[19]

'The Modern Warning'

London, July 9th, 1884

This idea has been suggested to me by reading Sir Lepel Griffin's[20] work about America. Type of the conservative, fastidious, exclusive Englishman (in public life, clever &c,) who hates the U.S.A.—thinks them a contamination to England, a source of *funeste* warning &c, & an odious country socially. He falls in love with an American girl & she with him—this of course to be made natural if possible. He lets her know, frankly[,] that he loathes her country as much as he adores her personally, and he begs her to marry him. She is patriotic in a high degree—a genuine little American—she has the sentiment of her native land. But she is in love with the Englishman, and though she resists on patriotic grounds she yields at last, accepts him and marries him. She must have a near relation—a brother, say—who is violently American, an Anglophobist, (in public life in the U.S.A;) and of whom she is very fond. He deplores her marriage, entreats her to keep out of it, &c. He and the Englishman *loathe* each other. After the marriage the Englishman's hostility to the U.S. increases, fostered by the invasion of Americans &c. State of mind of the wife. Depression, melancholy, remorse and shame at having married an enemy of her country. Suicide? There is a certain interest in the situation—the difficulty of choice & resignation on her part—the resentment of a rupture with the brother, &c. Of course internationalism &c, may be found overdone, threadbare. That is to a certain extent a reason against the subject; but a weak, not a strong one. It is always enough if the *author* sees substance in it.

[19] *Numa Roumestan*, novel of 1880 by James's friend Alphonse Daudet (1840–97).
[20] Sir Lepel Henry Griffin (1840–1908), British administrator in India, then travel writer and historian, was the author of *The Great Republic* (1884). He was in favour of an Anglo-American union. See Introduction, pp. lxxxv–lxxxvi.

B

Extracts from the Prefaces to the *New York Edition*

Henry James's New York Edition Prefaces are collected in Volume XXXIII of The Complete Fiction of Henry James. The editor of that volume, Oliver Herford, has excerpted and prepared the text for this Appendix, and has supplied essential annotations; more extensive notes can be found in The Prefaces.

'Pandora': *NYE* XVIII, viii–xi

A good deal of the same element has doubtless sneaked into "*Pandora*", which I also reprint here for congruity's sake, and even while the circumstances attending the birth of this anecdote, given to the light in a New York newspaper (1884), pretty well lose themselves for me in the mists of time. I do nevertheless connect "*Pandora*" with one of the scantest of memoranda, twenty words jotted down in New York during a few weeks spent there a year or two before. I had put a question to a friend about a young lady present at a certain pleasure-party, but present in rather perceptibly unsupported and unguaranteed fashion, as without other connexions, without more operative "backers", than a proposer possibly half-hearted and a slightly sceptical seconder; and had been answered to the effect that she was an interesting representative of a new social and local variety, the "self-made", or at least self-making, girl, whose sign was that—given some measurably amusing appeal in her to more or less ironic curiosity or to a certain complacency of patronage—she was anywhere made welcome enough if she only came, like one of the dismembered charges of Little Bo-Peep,[1] leaving her "tail" behind her. Docked of all natural appendages and having enjoyed, as was supposed, no natural advantages; with the "line drawn," that is, at her father and her mother, her sisters and her brothers, at everything that was hers, and with the presumption crushing as against these adjuncts, she was yet held free to prove her case and sail her boat herself; even quite quaintly or quite touchingly free, as might be–working

---

[1] The reference is to a popular nursery rhyme whose first stanza reads: 'Little Bo Peep has lost her sheep / and doesn't know where to find them; / leave them alone, And they'll come home, / wagging their tails behind them.'

out thus on her own lines her social salvation. This was but five-and-twenty years ago; yet what to-day most strikes me in the connexion, and quite with surprise, is that at a period so recent there should have been novelty for me in a situation so little formed by more contemporary lights to startle or way-lay. The evolution of varieties moves fast; the Pandora Days can no longer, I fear, pass for quaint or fresh or for exclusively native to any one tract of Anglo-Saxon soil. Little Bo-Peep's charges may, as manners have developed, leave their tails behind them for the season, but quite knowing what they have done with them and where they shall find them again—as is proved for the most part by the promptest disavowal of any apparent ground for ruefulness. To "dramatise" the hint thus gathered was of course, rudimentarily, to see the self-made girl apply her very first independent measure to the renovation of her house, founding its fortunes, introducing her parents, placing her broth-ers, marrying her sisters (this care on her own behalf being—a high note of superiority—quite secondary), in fine floating the heavy mass on the flood she had learned to breast. Something of that sort must have proposed itself to me at that time as the latent "drama" of the case; very little of which, however, I am obliged to recognise, was to struggle to the surface. What is more to the point is the moral I at present find myself drawing from the fact that, then turning over my American impressions, those proceeding from a brief but profusely peopled stay in New York, I should have fished up that none so very precious particle as one of the pearls of the collection. (*LC*2 1271–3)

'Louisa Pallant': *NYE* XIII, xx–xxi

Madame de Mauves[2] and *Louisa Pallant* are another matter; the latter, in espe-cial, belongs to recent years. The former is of the small group of my produc-tions yielding to present research no dimmest responsive ghost of a traceable origin. These remarks have constituted to excess perhaps the record of what may have put this, that and the other treated idea into my head; but I am quite unable to say what, in the summer of 1873, may have put *Madame de Mauves*. Save for a single pleasant image, and for the fact that, dispatched to New York, the tale appeared, early in the following year, in *The Galaxy*, a periodical to which I find, with this, twenty other remembrances gratefully attached, not a glimmer of attendant reference survives. I recall the tolerably wide court of an old inn at Bad-Homburg in the Taunus hills—a dejected and forlorn little

---

[2] A story by James published in 1874.

place (its seconde jeunesse not yet in sight) during the years immediately following the Franco-Prussian war, which had overturned, with that of Baden-Baden, its altar, the well-appointed worship of the great goddess Chance—a homely enclosure on the ground-level of which I occupied a dampish, dusky, unsunned room, cool, however, to the relief of the fevered muse, during some very hot weather. The place was so dark that I could see my way to and from my inkstand, I remember, but by keeping the door to the court open—thanks to which also the muse, witness of many mild domestic incidents, was distracted and beguiled. In this retreat I was visited by the gentle Euphemia; I sat in crepuscular comfort pouring forth again, and, no doubt, artfully editing, the confidences with which she honoured me. She again, after her fashion, was what I might have called experimentally international; she muffled her charming head in the lightest, finest, vaguest tissue of romance and put twenty questions by. *Louisa Pallant*, with still subtler art, I find, completely covers her tracks—her repudiation of every ray of legend being the more marked by the later date (1888) of her appearance. Charitably affected to her and thus disposed, if the term be not arrogant, to hand her down, I yet win from her no shadow of an intelligible account of herself. I had taken possession, at Florence, during the previous year, of a couple of sunny rooms on the Arno just at the point where the Borg' Ognissanti begins to bore duskily westward; and in those cheerful chambers (where the pitch of brightness differed so from that of the others just commemorated) I seem to have found my subject seated in extreme assurance. I did my best for it one February while the light and the colour and the sound of old Italy played in again through my open windows and about my patient table after the bold loud fashion that I had had, from so much before, to teach myself to think directly auspicious when it might be, and indirectly when it might n't.

'The Aspern Papers': *NYE* XII, v–xii

I not only recover with ease, but I delight to recall, the first impulse given to the idea of The Aspern papers. It is at the same time true that my present mention of it may perhaps too effectually dispose of any complacent claim to my having "found" the situation. Not that I quite know indeed what situations the seeking fabulist does "find"; he seeks them enough assuredly, but his discoveries are, like those of the navigator, the chemist, the biologist, scarce more than alert recognitions. He *comes upon* the interesting thing as Columbus came upon the isle of San Salvador, because he had moved in the right direction for it—also because he knew, with the encounter, what "making land" then and there represented. Nature had so placed it, to profit—if as profit we may measure the matter!—by his fine unrest, just as history, "literary history" we in this connexion call it, had in an out-of-the-way corner of the great garden of life thrown off a curious flower that I was to feel worth gathering as soon as I saw it. I got wind of my positive fact, I followed the scent. It was in Florence years ago; which is precisely, of the whole matter, what I like most to remember. The air of the old-time Italy invests it, a mixture that on the faintest invitation I rejoice again to inhale—and this in spite of the mere cold renewal, ever, of the infirm side of that felicity, the sense, in the whole element, of things too numerous, too deep, too obscure, too strange, or even simply too beautiful, for any ease of intellectual relation. One must pay one's self largely with words, I think, one must induce almost any "Italian subject" to *make believe* it gives up its secret, in order to keep at all on working—or call them perhaps rather playing—terms with the general impression. We entertain it thus, the impression, by the aid of a merciful convention which resembles the fashion of our intercourse with Iberians or Orientals whose form of courtesy places everything they have at our disposal. We thank them and call upon them, but without acting on their professions. The offer has been too large and our assurance is too small; we peep at most into two or three of the chambers of their hospitality, with the rest of the case stretching beyond our ken and escaping our penetration. The pious fiction suffices; we have entered, we have seen, we are charmed. So, right and left, in Italy—before the great historic complexity at least—penetration fails; we scratch at the extensive surface, we meet the perfunctory smile, we hang about in the golden air. But we exaggerate our gathered values only if we are eminently witless. It is fortunately the exhibition in all the world before which, as admirers, we can most remain superficial without feeling silly.

All of which I note, however, perhaps with too scant relevance to the inexhaustible charm of Roman and Florentine memories. Off the ground, at a distance, our fond indifference to being "silly" grows fonder still; the working convention, as I have called it—the convention of the real revelations and surrenders on one side and the real immersions and appreciations on the other—has not only nothing to keep it down, but every glimpse of contrast, every pang of exile and every nostalgic twinge to keep it up. These latter haunting presences in fact, let me note, almost reduce at first to a mere blurred, sad, scarcely consolable vision this present revisiting, re-appropriating impulse. There are parts of one's past, evidently, that bask consentingly and serenely enough in the light of other days—which is but the intensity of thought; and there are other parts that take it as with agitation and pain, a troubled consciousness that heaves as with the disorder of drinking it deeply in. So it is at any rate, fairly in too thick and rich a retrospect, that I see my old Venice of *The Aspern Papers* that I see the still earlier one of Jeffrey Aspern himself, and that I see even the comparatively recent Florence that was to drop into my ear the solicitation of these things. I would fain 'lay it on' thick for the very love of them—that at least I may profess; and, with the ground of this desire frankly admitted, something that somehow makes, in the whole story, for a romantic harmony. I have had occasion in the course of these remarks to define my sense of the romantic, and am glad to encounter again here an instance of that virtue as I understand it. I shall presently say why this small case so ranges itself, but must first refer more exactly to the thrill of appreciation it was immediately to excite in me. I saw it somehow at the very first blush as romantic—for the use, of course I mean, I should certainly have had to make of it—that Jane Clairmont, the half-sister of Mary Godwin, Shelley's second wife and for a while the intimate friend of Byron and the mother of his daughter Allegra, should have been living on in Florence, where she had long lived, up to our own day, and that in fact, had I happened to hear of her but a little sooner, I might have seen her in the flesh. The question of whether I should have wished to do so was another matter—the question of whether I should n't have preferred to keep her preciously unseen, to run no risk, in other words, by too rude a choice, of depreciating that romance-value which, as I say, it was instantly inevitable to attach (through association above all, with another signal circumstance) to her long survival.

I had luckily not had to deal with the difficult option; difficult in such a case by reason of that odd law which somehow always makes the minimum of valid suggestion serve the man of imagination better than the maximum. The historian, essentially, wants more documents than he can really use; the dramatist only wants more liberties than he can really take. Nothing, fortunately, however, had, as the case stood, depended on my delicacy; I might have "looked up" Miss Clairmont in previous years had I been earlier informed— the silence about her seemed full of the "irony of fate"; but I felt myself more concerned with the mere strong fact of her having testified for the reality and the closeness of our relation to the past than with any question of the particular sort of person I might have flattered myself I "found". I had certainly at the very least been saved the undue simplicity of pretending to read meanings into things absolutely sealed and beyond test or proof—to tap a fount of waters that could n't possibly not have run dry. The thrill of learning that she had "overlapped", and by so much, and the wonder of my having doubtless at several earlier seasons passed again and again, all unknowing, the door of her house, where she sat above, within call and in her habit as she lived, these things gave me all I wanted; I seem to remember in fact that my more or less immediately recognising that I positively ought n't—"for anything to come of it"—to have wanted more. I saw, quickly, how something might come of it *thus*; whereas a fine instinct told me that the effect of a nearer view of the case (the case of the overlapping) would probably have had to be quite differently calculable. It was really with another item of knowledge, however, that I measured the mistake I should have made in waking up sooner to the question of opportunity. That item consisted of the action taken on the premises by a person who *had* waked up in time, and the legend of whose consequent adventure, as a few spoken words put it before me, at once kindled a flame. This gentleman,[3] an American of long ago, an ardent Shelleyite, a singularly marked figure and himself in the highest degree a subject for a free sketch—I had known him a little, but there is not a reflected glint of him in *The Aspern Papers*—was named to me as having made interest with Miss Clairmont to be accepted as a lodger on the calculation that she would have Shelley documents for which, in the possibly not remote event of her death, he would thus enjoy priority of chance to treat with her representatives. He had at any rate, according to the legend, become, on earnest Shelley grounds, her yearning, though also her highly diplomatic, pensionnaire—but without gathering, as was to befall, the fruit of his design.

Legend here dropped to another key; it remained in a manner interesting, but became to my ear a trifle coarse, or at least rather vague and obscure. It mentioned a younger female relative of the ancient woman as a person who, for a queer climax, had had to be dealt with; it flickered so for a moment and then, as a light, to my great relief, quite went out. It had flickered indeed but at the best—yet had flickered enough to give me my "facts", bare facts of intimation; which, scant handful though they were, were more distinct and more numerous than I mostly *like* facts: like them, that is, as we say of an etcher's progressive subject, in an early "state". Nine tenths of the artist's interest in them is that of what he shall add to them and how he shall turn them. Mine, however, in the connexion I speak of, had fortunately got away from me, and quite of their own

---

[3] Captain Silsbee, see Appendix A.

movement, in time not to crush me. So it was, at all events, that my imagination preserved power to react under the mere essential charm—that, I mean, of a final scene of the rich dim Shelley drama played out in the very theatre of our own "modernity". This was the beauty that appealed to me; there had been, so to speak, a forward continuity, from the actual man, the divine poet, on; and the curious, the ingenious, the admirable thing would be to throw it backward again, to compress—squeezing it hard!—the connexion that had drawn itself out, and convert so the stretched relation into a value of nearness on our own part. In short I saw my chance as admirable, and one reason, when the direction is right, may serve as well as fifty; but if I "took over", as I say, everything that was of the essence, I stayed my hand for the rest. The Italian side of the legend closely clung; if only because the so possible terms of my Juliana's life in the Italy of other days could make conceivable for her the fortunate privacy, the long uninvaded and uninterviewed state on which I represent her situation as founded. Yes, a surviving unexploited unparagraphed Juliana was up to a quarter of a century since still supposeable—as much so as any such buried treasure, any such grave unprofaned, would defy probability now. And then the case had the air of the past just in the degree in which that air, I confess, most appeals to me—when the region over which it hangs is far enough away without being too far.

I delight in a palpable imaginable *visitable* past—in the nearer distances and the clearer mysteries, the marks and signs of a world we may reach over to as by making a long arm we grasp an object at the other end of our own table. The table is the one, the common expanse, and where we lean, so stretching, we find it firm and continuous. That, to my imagination, is the past fragrant of all, or of almost all, the poetry of the thing outlived and lost and gone, and yet in which the precious element of closeness, telling so of connexions but tasting so of differences, remains appreciable. With more moves back the element of the appreciable shrinks—just as the charm of looking over a garden-wall into another garden breaks down when successions of walls appear. The other gardens, those still beyond, may be there, but even by use of our longest ladder we are baffled and bewildered—the view is mainly a view of barriers. The one partition makes the place we have wondered about *other*, both richly and recogniseably so; but who shall pretend to impute an effect of composition to the twenty? We are divided of course between liking to feel the past strange and liking to feel it familiar; the difficulty is, for intensity, to catch it at the moment when the scales of the balance hang with the right evenness. I say for intensity, for we may profit by them in other aspects enough if we are content to measure or to feel loosely. It would take me too far, however, to tell why the particular afternoon light that I thus call intense rests clearer to my sense on the Byronic age, as I conveniently name it, than on periods more protected by the "dignity" of history. With the times beyond, intrinsically more "strange", the tender grace, for the backward vision, has faded, the afternoon darkened; for any time nearer to us the special effect has n't begun. So there, to put the matter crudely, is the appeal I fondly recognise, an appeal residing doubtless more in the "special effect", in some deep associational force, than in a virtue more intrinsic. I am afraid I must add, since I allow myself so much to fantasticate, that the impulse had more than once taken me to project the Byronic age and the afternoon light across the great sea, to see in short whether association would carry so far and what the young century might pass for on that side of the modern world where it was not only itself so irremediably youngest, but was bound up with youth in everything else. There was a refinement of curiosity in this imputation of a golden strangeness to American social facts—though I cannot pretend, I fear, that there was any greater wisdom.

Since what it had come to then was, harmlessly enough, cultivating a sense of the past under that close protection, it was natural, it was fond and filial, to wonder if a few of the distilled drops might n't be gathered from some vision of, say, "old" New York. Would that human congeries, to aid obligingly in the production of a fable, be conceivable as "taking" the afternoon light with the right happy slant?—or could a recogniseable reflexion of the Byronic age, in other words, be picked up on the banks of the Hudson? (Only just there, beyond the great sea, if anywhere: in no other connexion would the question so much as raise its head. I admit that Jeffrey Aspern is n't even feebly localised, but I *thought* New York as I projected him.) It was "amusing", in any case, always, to try experiments; and the experiment for the right *transposition* of my Juliana would be to fit her out with an immortalising poet as transposed as herself. Delicacy had demanded, I felt, that my appropriation of the Florentine legend should purge it, first of all, of references too obvious; so that, to begin with, I shifted the scene of the adventure. Juliana, as I saw her, was thinkable only in Byronic and more or less immediately post-Byronic Italy; but there were conditions in which she was ideally arrangeable, as happened, especially in respect to the later time and the long undetected survival; there being absolutely no refinement of the mouldy rococo, in human or whatever other form, that you may not disembark at the dislocated water-steps of almost any decayed monument of Venetian greatness in auspicious quest of. It was a question, in fine, of covering one's tracks—though with no great elaboration I am bound to admit; and I felt I could n't cover mine more than in postulating a comparative American Byron to match an American Miss Clairmont—she as absolute as she would. I scarce know whether best to say for this device to-day that it cost me little or that it cost me much; it was "cheap" or expensive according to the degree of verisimilitude artfully obtained. If that degree appears *nil* the "art", such as it was, is wasted, and my remembrance of the contention, on the part of a highly critical friend who at that time and later on often had my ear, that it had been simply foredoomed to be wasted, puts before me the passage in the private history of *The Aspern papers* that I now find, I confess, most interesting. I comfort myself for the needful brevity of a present glance at it by the sense that the general question involved, under criticism, can't but come up for us again at higher pressure. (*LC2* 1177).

'The Liar': *NYE* XII, xxiii–xxiv

Little else perhaps meanwhile is more relevant as to "The Liar" than the small fact of its having, when its hour came, quite especially conformed to that custom of shooting straight from the planted seed, of responding at once to the touched spring, of which my fond appeal here to "origins" and evolutions so depicts the sway. When it shall come to fitting, historically, anything like *all* my small children of fancy with their pair of progenitors, and all my reproductive unions with their inevitable fruit, I shall seem to offer my backward consciousness in the image of a shell charged and recharged by the Fates with some patent and infallible explosive. Never would there seem to have been a pretence to such economy of ammunition!

However this may be, I come back, for "The Liar," as for so many of its fellows, to holding my personal experience, poor thing though it may have been, immediately accountable. For by what else in the world but by fatal design had I been placed at dinner one autumn evening of old London days face to face with a gentleman, met for the first time, though favourably known to me by name and fame, in whom I recognised the most unbridled colloquial romancer the "joy of life" had ever found occasion to envy? Under what other conceivable coercion had I been invited to reckon, through the evening, with the type, with the character, with the countenance, of this magnificent master's wife, who, veracious, serene and charming, yet not once meeting straight the eyes of one of us, did her duty by each, and by her husband most of all, without so much as, in the vulgar phrase, turning a hair? It was long ago, but I have never, to this hour, forgotten the evening itself—embalmed for me now in an old-time sweetness beyond any aspect of my reproduction. I made but a fifth person, the other couple our host and hostess; between whom and one of the company, while we listened to the woven wonders of a summer holiday, the exploits of a salamander, among Mediterranean isles, were exchanged, dimly and discreetly, ever so guardedly, but all expressively, imperceptible lingering looks. It was exquisite, it *could* but become, inevitably, some "short story" or other, which it clearly pre-fitted as the hand the glove. (*LC2* 1189–90)